C

Radicalism in American Silent Films,
1909–1929

BY MICHAEL S. SHULL AND DAVID EDWARD WILT

Hollywood War Films, 1937–1945:
An Exhaustive Filmography of American
Feature-Length Motion Pictures
Relating to World War II
(McFarland, 1996)

Doing Their Bit:
Wartime American Animated
Short Films, 1939–1945
(McFarland, 1987)

Radicalism in American Silent Films, 1909–1929

A Filmography and History

by
MICHAEL SLADE SHULL

McFarland & Company, Inc., Publishers
Jefferson, North Carolina, and London

Library of Congress Cataloguing-in-Publication Data

Shull, Michael Slade, 1949–
Radicalism in American silent films, 1909–1929 :
a filmography and history /
by Michael Slade Shull
p.   cm.
Filmography: p.
Includes bibliographical references and index.
ISBN 0-7864-0692-5 (library binding : 50# alkaline paper) ∞
1. Silent films—United States—History and criticism.   2. Politics
in motion pictures.   3. Working class in motion pictures.
I. Title.
PN1995.75.S54   2000   791.43'65821—dc21   99-43011

British Library Cataloguing-in-Publication data are available

Manufactured in the United States of America

*McFarland & Company, Inc., Publishers
Box 611, Jefferson, North Carolina 28640
www.mcfarlandpub.com*

To the struggle
and
in memory of
Beatrice (1913–1997)
and
Jack (1929–1999)

Acknowledgments

Intense research in the arts inevitably leads to the realization that some answers must forever remain elusive. Arriving at this realization is both an enlightening and a profoundly humbling experience. Quixotic intellectual journeys, I have learned, cannot be made without the hard labor, indulgence and love of others. I want to thank the late Professor Emeritus "Dr. Tom" Alyward for his unaffected humaneness, his sense of humor and his inimitable ability to bloodlessly slay the dragons of academia; Professor David Grimsted for suffering through numerous early drafts, his amusingly catty, yet informative reprimands, and for always maintaining an equanimous demeanor, even when a certain alter ego resembling Donald Duck had stormed into his office; Dr. David Wilt for his unstinting help in countless ways; Dr. Joseph Marusiak for his last minute grammatical surgery, made relatively painless by his vintage wit.

I would also like to thank Regents Professor Peter Rollins of Oklahoma State and editor of *Film & History* for his helpful comments on the manuscript. Bob Reynolds, editor of *Labor's Heritage*, likewise deserves mention for his work with me on an article based upon material from this book. I would further add that my understanding of labor's point of view was greatly enhanced by the late Professor Stu Kaufmann, distinguished head of the George Meany Center and a true mensch. Finally, I could not have completed the research and photographic work for this project without the assistance of James Plumer, Richard Schellenberg of FCC, Mary Corliss of MOMA and Russell P. Kennedy.

I would like to offer my gratitude for the professional assistance extended to me over the years by the staff of the Motion Picture Division of the Library of Congress. And I specifically wish to thank David Parker, Pat Loughney, Madaleine Matz and Rosemary Hanes.

I proffer my sincerest love and respect to B and B for their aid, and most especially for their faith and patience—and the occasional kick in the pants.

Michael S. Shull
Gaithersburg, Md.

Contents

Preface

Radicalism in American Silent Films, 1909–1929 is the first book to systematically identify, quantify, and compile a statistical data bank based upon content analysis of virtually all commercially produced fictional American films (both shorts and feature length works through 1917) whose plots centered upon, or in any way contained references to, the radical left or militant labor activities.

This book is not some idle academic exercise with the sole purpose of gathering arcane data, but rather a determined effort to create an informed case study of early mass media propagandistic methods as they evolved in American silent film—and as they were specifically directed at assorted demons of the left, including anarchists, socialists, communists, Bolsheviks and politically motivated labor activists who espoused violence or some other form of "direct action" by America's workers against their so-called capitalist oppressors.

This combination monograph and reference represents a unique methodological approach to the study of motion pictures that incorporates under one cover a huge chronologically arranged filmography with extensive content analysis data and a separate historical-critical analytic text whose conclusions have been based upon a fully integrated application of those data. This combination is significant on a number of counts, including enabling a reader to trace, with considerable accuracy, the public's varying attitudes towards the political left during a critical period in United States history. In addition, the text shows how the American film industry responded to or even helped mold these attitudes and, over a relatively short period of time, developed more or less standardized cinematic means, both in form and content, by which to stereotype and demonize the left—and by extension, any future designated "Others." While some of these silent means, such as theme-oriented tinting of scenes (including the not uncommon use of red tinting during scenes of social mayhem), were largely abandoned with the introduction of synchronous sound films at the end of the twenties, most of the demonological panoply deployed against the left prior to 1930 would be repeatedly used on American movie screens throughout the remainder of the century. A few examples should suffice: the routine use or advocacy of violence, sexual deviance, violation of the family; attacks upon religion, substance abuse, physical repulsiveness and/or pejorative alien attributes, anti-Americanism, ideological hypocrisy.

Many studies of silent film are flawed by their concentration on surviving or critically acclaimed films—a particularly serious problem for those works when one is reminded that relatively few of these silent era motion pictures still exist, and that of these few, many are incomplete, damaged or only available in difficult to access archives or private collections. In this study, every effort has been made to provide *complete* coverage of the period 1909–1929.

Because high-quality images from most of these films do not exist, several of the photographs that appear herein are of a low grade. Every effort was made to locate the best available images and reproduce them at highest possible quality. Ultimately the author and publisher both believed that the documentary value of these rare photographs justified their inclusion.

Research and writing of this book involved two steps. The first was data collection. Films were screened when available, in as complete a form as possible, or were reconstructed from printed documents. The topically relevant references were then coded and recorded under sixty-four coding terms in separate charts created for each of the three thematic and chronological chapters (1909–17; 1918–20; 1921–29). A glossary of the coding terms used may be found at the beginning of the Filmography.

Coding films in this manner often requires interpretation of film content. For instance, the code "Bolshevik" does not necessarily signify that the film contains a specific mention of the term in an inter-title, or a character identified as a Bolshevik. Any reference to Russian communism or "Red" revolutionaries in a Ruritania was considered a valid reference. Similarly, the mere appearance of the hammer and sickle symbol was considered a sufficient reference point for coding under "Bolshevism." On the other hand, the presence of an individual who is specifically designated in the film's text as a Russian was *not* automatically coded as "Russian" if there was no political connotation attached to the ethnicity. In the case of nationality, the primary concern was to code ethnic stereotypes linked to political biases. Therefore, both a striking Russian worker and an Irish girl who delivers an Americanism-laden speech before a mob that has been incited by political or labor agitators would be coded.

Some of the coding fields are highly specific to this study and are thereby subjectively applied. An example is the Liquor Linkage coding in the Filmography of *Radicalism in American Silent Films*. The teens volume of the AFI catalogue has extensive related listings under the subject codings—Alcohol, Alcoholics, Alcoholism. In comparison, this study is not concerned with alcohol abuse, per se, but it is very much concerned with film scenes like the one in which workers are incited to become a strike mob while gathered at a bar or, in another, where Bolsheviks are portrayed committing atrocities while under the influence of alcohol. Liquor, like other topics, becomes important to this study when tied to a film's presentation of political or economic radicalism.

Because gaps in the data are many, there are numerous coded references marked with a "?" in the Filmography. These refer sometimes to ambiguous meanings: Is a labor agitator named Israel Heimstone deliberately meant to be a German Jew and to have negative connotations? The "?" may also signify the inherent plot uncertainties related to motion pictures which were not screened, but for which the information revealed in the reconstruction would suggest that a coding designation is appropriate.

Although the majority of coding references are clearly identifiable within the descriptive analysis provided for each film, it is not the case for all codings. It would sometimes become awkward to include specific references to every coding field in the plot description of a film, particularly with regard to secondary plots and minor characters. For example, workers of various ethnic backgrounds at a factory influenced by a Russian anarchist may be coded for their ethnic identities, but the plot summary does not always list them.

Each entry in the Filmography has also been classified according to its predominant discernible biases (PDB). The purpose is to provide the reader with an overview of the dominating *political* biases expressed within the plots of this topically specific subset of fictional American motion pictures. There are ambiguities in such classifications, but with the potential use of up to three categories, such typing is usually self-evident. For example, a typical "Capital vs. Labor" film from the teens, when the viewpoint tended to greatest complexity, might show that loyal workers, their families starving, request a wage hike; they are callously dismissed by their capitalist stereotyped employer; an agitator exploits class differences to incite a violent strike; the daughter of the capitalist intercedes; labor peace is restored and wages are increased. Both negative capitalist and labor images are presented, followed by harmonious reconciliation, so this film's PDB would be: anti-capital (ANTI-CAP); anti-labor (ANTI-LAB); capital-labor cooperation (CAP-LAB COOP). But if the capitalist locks out his employees after their legitimate request, hires scabs and sends in the militia or private police when the workers begin picketing the factory, the labeling would be only ANTI-CAP. If the primary factor behind the labor dispute and subsequent acts of violence results from the actions of an agitator, the film is coded anti-revolution (ANTI-REV) and ANTI-LAB. If the workers expel radical agitators from their midst, refusing to carry out acts of sabotage during their legitimate peaceful strike, the film is coded as PRO-LAB, ANTI-REV.

There is also what this author refers to as the CM factor, or "contraband message." This refers to casually expressed political biases in an otherwise non-political film. For example, in one Douglas Fairbanks film the hero has an unexpected encounter with a bearded nihilist stereotype, and in another his capitalist father calls his madcap son an "anarchist," thus the coding CM/ANTI-REV. Or, again, in a Capital vs. Labor film where the workers are non-violently striking against an evil capitalist, but at one point a belligerent worker begins spouting communist slogans and is put down by his co-workers as an "I Won't Work" (pejorative code for a member of the I.W.W.), the coding is PRO-LAB; ANTI-CAP; CM/ANTI-REV. Finally,

motion pictures displaying no direct or indirect political bias have been listed as NDB (no discernible bias).

In the case of many comedies, such as *The Painted Anarchist*, some may question why the PDB for this obvious and literal parody has been listed as ANTI-REV. It is true that this 1915 short film, centering on an artist placing a live anarchist in a frame and passing off the so-called painting as a masterpiece of realism, would not have been taken seriously in a political context by its contemporary audience. However, the portrayal of the standard anarchist stereotype would still tend to subliminally reaffirm the negative image associated with radicalism.

The coding references, once assembled, were then collated and analyzed in pursuit of coherent patterns. These statistics are utilized in the context of the chronological and thematic chapters as shaping and supporting evidence. Each of these chapters deals with the dominant thematic patterns in relevant films during a particular period. In the context of history, how did the motion picture industry portray labor radicals, capitalists and Bolsheviks? How did film fiction shape, distort, and give meaning to events and realities that concerned the audiences attending America's movie theaters? All these matters are carefully explained.

This book will not only shed new light on American society and its reactions to the radical left in the two decades preceding the Depression, but will also show the merits of using fictional films as historical documents. In addition to the textual examination of the material, the Filmography will provide a valuable reference for future researchers—one that should stimulate the debate surrounding so-called "contested" histories and memories related to events that took place in the United States during the period. Furthermore, it is hoped that *Radicalism in American Silent Films* will encourage other scholars, particularly those who commute through the dynamic intersection of social history and cultural studies, to examine more closely the socio-political context of all motion pictures.

Introduction
Red Tinted Flickers of History

"The moving image media would not have attained their enormous presence and influence in modern societies unless they spoke directly to society's needs and wants and changed in tune with other facets of their culture."[1]

The first third of the twentieth century, particularly the period leading up to and immediately following World War I, represents a time of tremendous social upheaval in the United States. Throughout these years, an incipient film industry quickly became a vibrant new factor in American culture—one that would totally dominate all other popular entertainment media by 1929. Initially borrowing heavily from the conventions of nineteenth century theater and vaudeville, the movies rapidly created a hybrid artistic style that has also become an ideal transmitter and perpetuator of the nation's political-cultural symbols.

To varying degrees, all societies have needed to project their animosities upon a negative "Other" or set of Others. The Others may change in the dynamics of any society's shifting fears, joys, prejudices and circumstances. Throughout twentieth-century America, and despite two world wars fought against coalitions of right-wing regimes, there was a persistent interest and substantial fear in this country of militant labor or

of those radical individuals and organizations associated with anarchism, socialism or communism. The complex film response to capitalism and its critics and rivals before World War I became, by war's end, a strongly antagonistic picture of both foreign and domestic radical Others, a position modulated and largely depoliticized during the 1920s. Yet the rhetoric, symbols and stereotypes representing hostility to radical Others in the motion pictures of the "Red Scare era" (1918–1920) were deployed in such a compelling manner that they would not disappear in the twentieth century, though they were subject to a steady change of emphasis.

When addressing the topic of the portrayal of radicalism in the United States, there has been a tendency to dwell on left-wing organizations, regimes or ideologies. Marxist historians who have imbibed Althusser are particularly fond of pointing a finger at an amorphous "dominant ideology" that manipulated the "cultural imaginary" of the American masses in a systematic calumniation of class consciousness and political

5

Dangerous Hours (Paramount-Artcraft, 1920): One page from a six-page trade journal ad (*Moving Picture World* 5/19/19), under the film's working title. This segment emphasized the threat to America posed by Bolshevism. Note how the visualized concept of anarchism has been blurred with communism.

movements of the left. Rather than the motion picture industry sinisterly managing an ideological consensus, the producers of American films were prisoners of their own interpretations of what was *perceived* as socially and politically acceptable at various times by the country's ever expanding middle-class.[2]

Any class-oriented theory tends to oversimplify the inherent complexities of human interactions. With regard to the motion pictures and their impact upon society, all one can be sure of is a significant and intricate degree of mutual influence. In part, the situation in these early years, especially in the developmental period before 1920, is complicated because the American film industry was not the monolith that it later became.

Unlike the Hollywood-based motion picture industry, dominated by fewer than a dozen studios, that would evolve by the mid-1930s, the number of American companies producing commercial entertainment films in the period between 1909 and 1920 exceeded one hundred.[3] Although primarily situated in New York, Florida and California, several studios were located in other regions of the country. The volume of their production by the latter half of the teens was staggering— a yearly average of 750 feature-length films and over a thousand shorts. To illustrate this point, one need only consider that the famous silent film comedian Harold Lloyd appeared on screen between late 1915 and early 1917 in over fifty shorts as the series character Lonesome Luke.[4]

By the early 1920s a so-called "classical" Hollywood style of film presentation had been fully developed. Its essence centered around an unambiguous linear narrative plot whose development and ineluctable socially positive resolution is speeded along by means of a film editing format that highlights interactions between individuals through fluid camera movements and the rapid cutting of shots within scenes. In pre–1920s (or "pre-classical") films, plot continuity was less certain and minimally edited static scenes were quite common.[5] Dialogue was restricted

to inter-titles, sometimes more descriptively referred to as "spoken" titles.[6] Furthermore, controversial topics were repeatedly addressed head-on and were not always neatly resolved.[7] A number of distinct film genres based specifically upon socially controversial issues existed throughout the pre–1921 period. For example, in addition to the "Nihilist" and "Capital vs. Labor" genres discussed in Chapter 1 of this book, there were well over fifty motion pictures released during the period devoted to the Italian Black Hand, and another fifty or more concerning women's suffrage.[8]

Particularly noteworthy is the highly variable nature of political ideology applied to these social issues in the texts of motion pictures up to 1917—obviously, in large degree, a reflection of the class diversity of the film audience. This is especially true with regard to films that addressed the "labor question" before the United States entered World War I. For instance, although labor violence was never shown to directly succeed, sympathy for the plight of workers was frequently portrayed, thereby justifying their militant actions within the context of the film. Both evil capitalists and labor agitators regularly received negative treatment upon the nation's movie screens. A hint at the ideological complexities related to what this book calls "Capital vs. Labor" films during the 1909–1917 period can be gleaned from statistics relating to their predominant discernible biases, as compiled by this author: 54 were Anti-Capital and 39 Anti-Labor; 49 urged some form of Capital-Labor Cooperation; 5 were Pro-Capital and 26 Pro-Labor.[9]

With the advent of the international turmoil associated with the first World War and the Bolshevik Revolution, attitudes changed. Both the United States government and the American public rapidly developed a remarkably consistent unfriendliness to the political left. Ever since that time, these attitudes have been clearly reflected, refined, and at times, deliberately manipulated for reasons of *commercial* much more than political exploitation in the fictional films produced by

"COME UNTO ME, YE OPPREST!"

—Alley in the Memphis *Commercial Appeal.*

This late 1919 print cartoon, appearing at the Red Scare's zenith, attacked postwar immigration into the United States. The stereotyped image of the foreign born, bearded anarchist, holding a bomb with burning fuse, is portrayed as creeping up from behind to menace the icon of America, Miss Liberty.

the American motion picture industry. Because the radical left challenged the validity of a supposed cross-class consensus aspiring to a consumerist (pro-capitalist) society, labor militancy and the various political movements identified with socialism became linked in the public mind with an ever-present threat to American ideals.

Throughout the early years of the twentieth century, culminating in the Red Scare of 1918–20, a concern over preserving the values associated with a mythologized

American past grew increasingly urgent in the face of industrialization, urbanization, massive new waves of immigration from non–Anglo Saxon areas of Europe, and, finally, a world war and communist revolutions. Many of the native-born, as well as major interest groups like some conservative Protestant religious denominations and the Roman Catholic Church, sought simplistic explanations and solutions to assuage their fears of the resulting transformation of American society.

At about the same time, technological innovations were introduced that allowed for the evolution of the motion picture industry. From its beginnings the movie-making *business* was motivated by profits from a ticket-buying public. The industry assiduously courted the widest audience and attempted to minimize any offense to the socio-political sensitivities of the American citizenry. And since the film industry was highly successful at responding to the public's moods, the narrative and visual content of American motion pictures yields a great deal of information about popular attitudes toward particular topics.

This information can be highly informative, not only about acceptable political attitudes but also about the means by which the negative left Other was visualized and often demonologized. For example, a careful examination of motion pictures can help us to better understand the factors contributing to the mass hysteria associated with the post–World War Red Scare. With the exception of the loved ones of a small American expeditionary force in Russia and a few investors in Tsarist bonds, who among America's 110,000,000 citizens in mid–1919 had any legitimate reason to believe themselves to be in imminent physical, economic or ideological peril from the fledgling Bolshevik regime? For a society seemingly hell-bent upon isolating itself from international affairs, this could only make sense if the ideological virus (violent anti-capitalism) of Bolshevism was perceived to be germinating within United States borders—menacing

America's Americanism. The actual number of militant domestic radicals was minuscule and their influence upon events nominal.[10] But disturbances throughout the nation, particularly over 3000 strikes in the year following the Armistice, were oftentimes linked by the mass media to social revolution and therefore became palpably threatening to many Americans.[11]

This is where the power of the media in the United States (including the supposedly more responsible print journalism), having indulged in a chauvinistic paroxysm during the war years, comes significantly into play—by indiscriminately stigmatizing liberal intellectuals, strike leaders, socialists, "free love" advocates, and so on, together with the bloody red spectre of Bolshevism. And, in a largely successful attempt to capitalize upon the public's hunger for news topicality to spice their entertainment fare, the motion picture industry created movies reflecting its perceptions of the evolving political biases of the public. As a result, fictional films wound up in the forefront of the frenzied media exercise that erupted during the Red Scare. For on a weekly basis in America during 1918–1920, tens of millions of movie patrons from across the class spectrum were regularly entertained while watching lurid images (supplemented by inflammatory buzzwords and catchphrases in the titles and inter-titles) of dirty bearded wild-eyed men and sexually promiscuous short-haired women. These stock "heavies," often foreign born, waved bombs while fulminating against democracy and inciting facile intellectuals and impressionable laborers to violently overthrow American capitalism in the name of working-class solidarity and revolutionary Bolshevism.

To what extent did film manipulate predominant American attitudes towards the left Other? To what extent did it exploit pre-existing opinion and images (the stereotype of the bomb thrower borrowed from print cartoons, for example) or help to create and perpetuate them through its stylistic imagery or narrative content? Can these socio-political manifestations upon America's movie

Dangerous Hours (Paramount-Artcraft, 1920): **During the first labor dispute portrayed in this film, a group of stereotypical radical agitators, including women, harass police officers outside the factory gates. (Academy of Motion Picture Arts and Sciences.)**

screens be quantified? And can previously obscure or even unrecognized patterns or absences (biases through omission, such as the failure to portray affirmative union rituals) thereby be revealed?

With the above questions in mind, this author has identified the majority of those fictional motion pictures produced and released in the United States between 1909 and 1929 (both "shorts" and four-reel or longer "features" from 1909 to 1917) that in any way reflected anxieties about politicized labor militancy or the socialist-communist movements. *Radicalism in American Silent Films* offers a historical-critical analysis based upon contextual readings of the socio-political content of these films—content that suggests

the changing concerns and values they reflected.

Methodology

Over the past four decades, silent film scholarship has accumulated an inventory of assumptions regarding both form and content of fictional motion pictures. Yet, few scholars have spent time examining either low-budget or inaccessible films—a decision based largely upon their own aesthetic biases. Thus they have effectively removed from serious consideration thousands of films that were watched by tens of millions of viewers, across socio-economic lines, on a weekly basis.[12] This makes suspect some of their conclusions concerning the silent period, since less than 20 percent of the films remain extant.

Recent important feminist and minority cinema studies frequently employ a highly selective and qualitative form of content analysis. Scholars in these disciplines accept the proposition that women or minorities have been presented a certain way in the media. More often than not, they wind up emulating the currently much maligned, but venerable, Siegfried Kracauer and his claim that Weimar era films demonstrated a predilection for fascism in German society. The tendency, then, even when dealing with a large number of motion pictures produced over an extended period of time, is for these scholars to "round up the list of usual suspects" (sometimes referred to as the "masterpiece tradition") and then closely scrutinize them to expose the films' offending content—thereby substantiating their particular set of claims.[13]

In contrast, this study identifies and examines *all* commercially produced fictional films released from 1909 to 1929 whose content in any way engages the issues of militant labor or revolutionary radicalism—thereby interweaving historical context and film intertextuality. Four hundred and thirty-six films were eventually so classified and included in this book's Filmography. The plot of every one of these motion pictures has been outlined and fully annotated, with an emphasis upon historical contextualization.

Because of the paucity of American silent films known to still exist—less than 15 percent are available through commercial channels or in publicly accessible archives in the United States—the researcher is forced either to make do with the examination of a very limited number of films or to resort to the laborious process of "reconstructing" (creating the most accurate and detailed synopsis possible of a film's content as viewed by its original audience). The problem of recovering such information becomes evident when one examines print availability for a

single year. Of the nearly 850 feature-length fictional films produced in the United States in 1918, barely thirty titles survive in complete form in the public archives of America; about an equal number are known to exist only in foreign archives.[14]

Even when a silent era film is available for screening, there frequently remain a myriad of impediments to access. Most extant pre-dialogue films, originally shot on 35mm nitrate stock (extremely flammable; it later also proved to be explosively unstable), have been physically damaged or remain only as almost monochromatic 16mm safety prints.[15] In addition, many are missing significant sections (including entire reels) and rarely retain their original color tinting and art-painted titles. The matter of tinting and art-titles, though seldom discussed, is highly significant. This introduction's title, "Red Tinted Flickers of History," was chosen to spotlight the fact that many filmed scenes of social violence would have been tinted red or in sepia. At least four motion pictures viewed for this work actually retain this colorization for such scenes: *Intolerance* (Biograph, 1916) *Hawthorne of the U.S.A.* (Paramount-Artcraft, 1919), *Orphans of the Storm* (United Artists, 1921) and *The Volga Boatman* (Producers Distributing Corp, 1926).[16] Both colored (sometimes hand-painted) and black and white art-decorated titles were even more common. For instance, as early as 1909, D. W. Griffith's *Voice of the Violin* (Biograph) had art titles liberally augmented with images of the American eagle—presumably to emphasize its patriotic, anti-radical message. And *Dangerous Hours* (Paramount-Artcraft, 1920) contains lurid painted titles of a blood-dripping cleaver, bomb with burning fuse, and similar images introducing scenes featuring the film's Bolshevik heavy. Attempts to recreate an original viewing experience are further complicated by the fact that there was no standard speed of projection during the silent days.[17] Finally, viewable motion picture prints from the pre-Depression years are usually presented either with no sound or with a monotonous

musical soundtrack added sometime after 1927. These soundtracks are quite unlike the original scores—selected incidental music cued with scenes—provided for feature films after the mid-teens in many studio press-books and in the musical sections of the leading trade journals as a guide for the movie theater's rinky-tink piano accompanist, organist or house orchestra.[18]

To illustrate the problem of textual integrity, take, for example, a nine- to ten-reel 1918 film available for screening at the Library of Congress, *My Four Years in Germany* (First National). What the scholar may actually access is the following: reels 3–6 and reel 9 on 35mm, and reel 2 on 16mm (no soundtracks of any kind; most of the art-titles remain, but their original coloring has not been preserved).[19]

Further complicating matters, it was not uncommon for motion pictures to be rereleased within a couple of years of their initial exhibition. In addition to the frequent removal or reediting of entire sequences or reels in these reissued versions, dialogue inter-titles and expository titles could also be rewritten. Often such changes were minor, but sometimes they ideologically rescripted the film, significantly altering its plot—especially in response to the motion picture industry's perceptions regarding changing socio-political sensitivities of its audiences. For instance, D. W. Griffith toned down the stronger anti-capitalist aspects of *Intolerance*'s modern sequence when during the Red Scare he rereleased his 1916 classic as a separate film titled *The Mother and the Law* (World, 1919). Similarly, motion pictures could be updated to reflect more recent historically germane events. In the print this author viewed of the *1916* film *The Cossack Whip* (Edison), a titled prologue has been

added that endorses "the overthrow of the Czar and the establishment of a new, free and representative government." Obviously, this title had to have been inserted for a rerelease print sometime after the February-March 1917 Republican revolution and before the October-November 1917 Bolshevik revolution.[20]

Substitutions of expository titles or dialogue inter-titles were sometimes made to placate local censors or accommodate regional preferences. The change of a title or a few inter-titles could transform a pregnant character from fallen woman to proud mother simply by indicating that she and the father were secretly married. Viewer sympathy could likewise be increased or decreased, depending upon the ethnic or sectional biases of the audience, by switching the heroine's name from Ruth Rothstein to Mary Walker. Hence, the trick for the researcher is not only to acquire a general sense of the plot outline of the motion picture, but also to look closely for either conformity or inconsistencies in topically-similar releases. Only then can the scholar begin to concentrate on details relevant to a specific subject.

For example, an evil anarchist in a film takes on changing significance if his name has an explicitly ethnic origin, such as the Slavic-sounding Martoff, or a generic evil name such as "The Fiend," or some sort of suggestive combination such as Odoroskavitch or Bombsky. Can one identify the actor? If so, is he someone who regularly played heavies, of a specific physical description? (Actor Louis Wolheim, a well-known Broadway and moving picture star, was frequently cast as a radical villain because his physical appearance was dark and stocky and his face had a prominently distorted nose.) Do the print sources provide other pertinent information

Opposite, top: The Volga Boatman (PDC, 1926): **The stern commissar at a Red Tribunal, the entire sequence tinted red, decides the fate of the peasant hero and his aristocratic lover. Note the prominent Red Star on the breast of his tunic.**

Opposite, bottom: The Volga Boatman (PDC, 1926): **In the melodramatic prose typical of silent era inter-titles, the boatman hero pleads for his aristocratic lover's life before the Red Tribunal, reminding them of his contributions to the Bolshevik Revolution.**

about a designated anarchist in a particular film? For example, does he wear a beard, in keeping with the common negative radical stereotype? Can one assume pejorative associations are intended with regards to the character if he is listed in the credits as "The Anarchist"? And what differs significantly if the stereotype was used as an object of laughter rather than threat, such as in the 1915 Kriterion release entitled *The Painted Anarchist*?

If descriptions of our hypothetical anarchist do not appear to conform to the negative stereotype, perhaps there is a problem. Or, it may simply indicate that the film is a comedy. For instance, one can imagine a scenario in which a physically diminutive, henpecked husband, with an obviously fake beard that does not even match the color of his hair, is portrayed attempting to frighten his formidable spouse by pretending to be an anarchist waving a bomb-laden hatbox — one that housed the hat she is wearing.

Motion picture copyright deposits at the Library of Congress were not begun until 1912, and the original requirements for information on the films' contents were ill defined. Thus the material available for scholarly scrutiny can range from a one-sentence notification of a work's existence, to single paragraph or multi-paged plot synopses, to a cut-out copy of a trade review, to studio promotional materials, and to scripts of varying descriptions. Occasionally, production or publicity stills are available for examination. In fact, when they do exist, these stills are usually the only photographic evidence remaining of the motion picture. For instance, the set of photoprints on deposit at the Library of Congress for *The Blacklist* (Lasky/Paramount), a 1916 feature recreating the infamous Ludlow Massacre of nineteen striking Colorado miners and family members, was a major source of material for the researcher on this important Capital vs. Labor film.[21] Often the material submitted for deposit with the Library of Congress was put together before or during production, rather than based upon a screening of the final

product. As a result, particularly with regard to the short comedies of the early teens (often highly improvisational), the actual film released might be substantially different from the description provided in the copyright deposits.

The various trade reviews from the period, particularly *The Moving Picture World* and *Motion Picture News*, available in crumbling folio format at the Library of Congress and on microfilm, are invaluable resources for the film scholar. Along with rich information on the industry, these two journals provided detailed information for exhibitors on nearly all films released, ranging from straightforward and rather detailed plot descriptions to idiosyncratic observations upon the style, reception and even political content of the film. These are especially valuable since, after 1914, they usually represent reactions to a screening of the film. However, sometimes the plot descriptions were based solely upon print material supplied to the journal from the motion picture producers, often in the purple prose associated with melodramas.

Nothing can be taken for granted when carrying out silent film research, not even the names of characters and of the actors playing the roles. Prior to 1913 actors frequently went uncredited. Many leads of the day are virtual unpersons today, with no basic biographical information available in standard reference sources such as Katz's *The Film Encyclopedia*.[22] For secondary characters, so-called "types," the problem is more acute, even when they have received credit.

Even if detailed plot information is unavailable, one can be reasonably sure about the nature of a character called "The Menace," played by Raymond Hatton (who often portrayed heavies during the earlier years of his long film career) in *Ace of Hearts*, a 1921 Goldwyn release featuring a band of anarchists. But what about a character called Danglo in a virulently anti–Bolshevik Red Scare era film that centers around labor discontent in a factory town? Since Danglo was

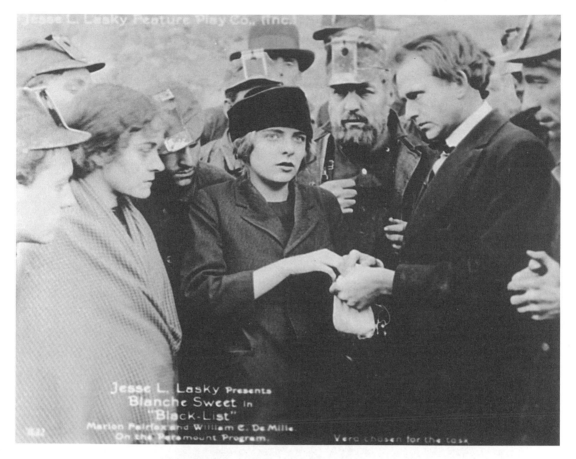

The Blacklist (Lasky/Paramount, 1916): "Vera chosen for the task." Vera, her miner father (bearded; a Slavic designator) at her side, draws for the honor of being chosen to kill the mine owner. Substantial biographical information is easily accessible for Blanche Sweet, the popular actress playing the female lead. However, it is difficult to acquire career details on regular teens heavy Horace B. Carpenter, the actor who plays her father.

played by a well-known Italian-born character actor named Henry Armetta, one could deduce the name Danglo is a play on the pejorative "Dago," but without further information such conclusions are highly speculative.

The most daunting challenge facing American film scholars venturing back into the pre-thirties history of motion pictures is to coax those "photo-plays," or their reconstructions, to communicate with the contemporary reader or spectator. The only hope is to immerse oneself in the world of the audience to whom these silent dramas were originally addressed. Therefore, in addition to reconstructing most of the films, one is

also attempting to "reconstruct earlier acts of comprehension."[23] More often than not, this experience is rather like placing oneself in Plato's dimly lit allegorical cave and attempting to make sense out of the flickering shadows on the opposite wall.

What did film patrons buy a ticket to see? What did they find most entertaining? What would most likely have left a lasting impression upon the viewers: a haggard agitator haranguing a group of disgruntled workers, or that same agitator placing a bomb beneath the home of the factory owner? And would the targeted movie audience(s) be more likely to identify with the threatened capitalist or with the individual driven to

The Blacklist (Lasky/Paramount, 1916): An out-of-costume publicity still of Blanche Sweet that indicates her star status.

class-motivated violence by social injustice or political conviction?

Thus, depending upon circumstances, particularly one's class orientation, in the mind's eye of the historically specific viewer the mob projected upon a screen by a "picture machine" could be figuratively running in quite opposite directions—Umberto Eco's concept of "open texts."[24] For example, I.W.W. (the well-known identifying initials of the radical union called the Industrial Workers of the World) could pejoratively stand for "I Won't Work" or, alternately, positively suggest "I Want Work."

Study of silent films constitutes a series of encounters with a mass of overlapping vestigial texts in languages in which we can never be fully assured of achieving fluency. What was obvious to the cinematically literate individual in 1910 is often largely incomprehensible to a contemporary specialist (let alone the uninitiated), simply through the film's language codes and stylistic conventions.[25] For in order to conduct a meaningful dialogue with the primary film texts, they must be "properly questioned" by the historian.[26] But how does one gauge the degree of aggressiveness projected to a typical teens WASP spectator (with lingering Victorian sensibilities) in a scene of a mob of gesticulating, East European or Slavic appearing, working-class men?[27]

A detailed examination of the political content of a large number of motion pictures addressing a specific topic reveals not only intertextual clashes but also screen absences, such as the absence of ideological explications or discourse. At least through 1916, a sympathetic counter-narrative for militant labor was often projected in the cinema. For example, the texts of numerous Capital vs. Labor films exploited the negative stereotype of the evil capitalist, thereby providing moral justification for radical actions by workers.[28] However, the political ideologies associated with the Bolshevik regime that were so feared and attacked in film beginning in early 1918 are virtually never given an articulate voice. Instead, their demonic representatives are almost universally depicted as cut-out stereotypes spouting polemical buzzwords, such as "comrade," and performing assorted heinous acts. Thus, from the Red Scare period through the late twenties, ideological conflict between mainstream society and challengers from the left is almost always cinematically presented in the form of choreographed shadow boxing with a phantom Other.[29]

Fleeting or even seemingly dispassionate topical references in films that deal less directly with militant labor or radical politics are also significant. A rabidly anti–Bolshevik film released in early 1920 such as *Dangerous Hours* tells much about the attitudes the cinema caught and perpetuated, but there may be an even stronger cumulative impact created by works that contain casual pejorative references to the negative Other.

While there is currently no annotated subject catalogue for *short* films for the period of primary concern to this study, 1909–1917, there are, as of this writing, the American Film Institute (AFI) comprehensive subject catalogues of feature-length fictional films for the two decades under consideration.[30] In theory, their subject indexes should reveal the majority of pertinent films, but that is not always the case. The extended footnotes accompanying many of the descriptive annotations in the teens volume provide a wealth of information on production background, but rarely do they give historical contextualization. Random topical references, such as jokes or politically specific slogans, posters, pictures or reading materials that might appear in a scene or scenes, are seldom acknowledged in the AFI catalogue or in any other standard reference sources. As an example, take the brief entry in the 1920s AFI Catalogue for *The Adventurer*, a 1928 MGM production whose story centers around a Moscow-directed communist-led revolution in a Caribbean Ruritania. The subject indexes list the film under revolution, but there is no indication in the short plot analysis of a Soviet connection; the single clue of *possible* Soviet involvement is the Russian-sounding name of Samaroff in the cast credits.

The only way to identify the maximum number of topically relevant motion pictures for a base set is to read *every* review in the trade journals and AFI catalogues, including the cast lists. The task is immense. The number of American-produced fictional films released in the United States between 1909 and 1929 (including shorts of less than four reels) is conservatively estimated to be in excess of 30,000 titles. Although this academic venture began with a set of topically specific interests, the profile defining the subject's parameters shifted as research progressed. For example, the frequent intentional cinematic linkage of the radicalization of workers with alcohol abuse was not originally deemed significant. After this connection was observed to manifest itself in numerous films, the content of many reviews had to be reassessed—

an exercise involving repeating the original process with the primary documents.

Today's film scholars labor in the face of problems that sometimes seem overwhelming. The study of silent film is often an attempt to decipher a series of faded, sometimes discontinuous, multi-layered images that may have been altered in any number of ways. Yet the scholar is motivated by the promise of insight into years gone by. In the present study, it has proved valuable, in this age of changing attitudes toward America's economy and its international competitors, to explore early twentieth century American films that engaged the themes of left radicalism and capital-labor problems. These silent dramas, numbering in the hundreds, both reflected and helped to shape the American public's attitudes about these important social issues.

1. A Red Blur

The Mixed Message on Class and Radicalism in Progressive Era Films, 1909–1917

So many [Capital vs. Labor films] ... have been displayed on the screen there is hardly a new angle left. —Variety *review of* The Bigger Man *(1915)*

The picture will go great in the cosmopolitan neighborhoods where the wives of prospective Reds are hoping that bomb throwing will be wiped out for all time to come. —Variety *review of* The Bomb Throwers *(1915)*

[T]he fiend [Tsarist secret police official] tortured her, until she died. —The Cossack Whip *(1916)*

In March 1909 William Howard Taft assumed the presidency of the United States. Despite being the designated heir of Teddy Roosevelt, an avid promoter of progressive measures, Taft was socially conservative. For instance, during the 1908 campaign he had only grudgingly conceded labor's right to strike. In essence, unlike his pugnacious predecessor, Taft preferred a laissez faire approach to social issues. Thus, the corpulent top-hatted Taft riding to his inauguration in a horse-drawn carriage on a bitter wintry day very much symbolized a curtailment of governmental social activism. And the subsequent restoration of a more favorable environment for big business interests thereby was bound to contribute to a resurgence in the war between capital and labor.[1]

As a mammoth wave of new immigration peaked in the early twentieth century and the ethnic make-up of the United States was unalterably changed, there arose a deep concern among established Americans regarding a perceived threat to American democracy, particularly an increasingly rancorous relationship between capital and labor resulting both from capitalism's injustices as well as radicalism's militancy.

Progressivism represented the awakening of America's wealthy elite and educated middle-class to the need of addressing these overlapping concerns and reestablishing social justice by both reforming the abuses of predatory capitalists and taming the aggressive impulses of radicalized workers. But this required a commitment to social compromise and a reconstituted sense of national identity—intimately linked with lofty republican values. One means of achieving this was through a revival of the iconic imagery of American democracy.

Through cross-class accommodation based upon mutual respect, older, white, small town Protestant America presented itself as having a duty to perpetuate the American ideal. In the process, they became crusading missionaries in their own land. The physical frontier of the continental United States had been conquered, and now the new social frontier created by urban industrialization and the stresses of immigration must also be subdued.

Progressives both wanted to curb the obvious abuses of capitalism by the new industrial elite and socially control and politically democratize the unruly immigrant masses into embracing an idealized vision of America. The exploitative "robber barons," "Simon Legrees," "fat cats," and "plutes" must be exposed, reformed and then hopefully restored to grace. But there should be no suggestion that capitalism was inherently flawed.[2] Competing "isms" must therefore either be ignored or ridiculed. The preferred method of dealing with the outside challenge was through a form of secular improvement and Christian example whereby the Others were converted into accepting the temporal God of Americanism. For the privileged classes this was not viewed as an altruistic exercise, but rather as an act of self-preservation, forestalling what might otherwise result in violent revolution.[3]

Because the early development of motion pictures coincided with the Progressive Era in the United States, there should be little surprise that the problems of society commonly appeared on movie screens. Contrary to some popularly held misconceptions of today, the myriad of small pre-corporate, geographically dispersed film companies, in existence until America's entrance into the first World War, regularly fictionally addressed, often with considerable candidness and passion, an "astonishing range" of the social issues that concerned their contemporaries.[4] The degree to which this occurred is quite startling, for over the ensuing decades, the social content of early silent cinema has largely been forgotten. One central reason for the continuing historical neglect of the social significance of teens motion pictures is the lack of accessibility. Comparatively few of these films survive, and those that do are often damaged, incomplete and/or altered. Additionally, the films that have been preserved and repeatedly revived are heavily biased toward those works that display the talents of the critically recognized pantheon of directors and stars ("picture personalities"), including D. W. Griffith, Cecil B. DeMille, Charlie Chaplin, Lillian Gish, Douglas Fairbanks and Mary Pickford.

Film historians Kevin Brownlow and Steven J. Ross have both written books in the 1990s that discuss class issues in America during the silent era, but neither has attempted to systematically identify and quantitatively analyze the political content of these motion pictures. Ross, in *Working-Class Hollywood*, liberally defines labor oriented films to embrace any commercial motion picture that he designates to have broached the topic of class.[5] Yet, when discussing the societal impact of these works, Ross proceeds to spend a significant portion of his well-researched and compelling study on non-commercial films produced by labor organizations and by the manufacturing industry. Brownlow, on the other hand, in *Behind the Mask of Innocence*, has engaged the broader area of social problem films, including depictions of prison conditions and "white slavery" as well as the labor question. Brownlow's seminal work also concentrates upon examining extant film examples, while devoting many pages to genre aesthetics and background material on the industry and its personalities. Neither Ross nor Brownlow devote much space to Red Scare era motion pictures, their intimate relationship with earlier militant labor films and their significance in establishing the anti-radical demonology that would routinely be exploited in American cinema throughout much the rest of the twentieth century.[6]

This study, in contrast, examines the textual narrative paradigms of American motion pictures that dealt explicitly with political radicalism and capital versus labor violence. By attempting to identify the totality of these films, the number of such films that actually appeared can be stated with accuracy, while also helping to develop a much clearer image regarding the socio-political content and presentational style of these motion pictures.

Debate among film historians continues as to the social make-up of the pre–World War I movie audience who was presumably receiving the medium's social messages.[7] We may assume that at a relatively early date, no later than 1911, there existed an essentially dual class movie spectatorship—the primarily urban working-class concentrated in ethnic neighborhoods, along with ever increasing numbers of the middle-class, a majority of whom resided in small towns. In fact, by 1910 just over 25 percent of the audience was comprised of the middle-class and the so-called "leisure" class.[8] In early 1911 an editorial in the *New York Dramatic Mirror* asserted that "attendance at the better picture theaters does not wholly include people in search of cheap amusements. In the audience at these theaters will be seen persons of the class that also patronizes the regular [stage] theater."[9]

Kay Sloan makes an astute observation upon this situation in her book on America's social problem films of the teens, *The Loud Silents*: "The early cinema vilified those in power in a way that both justified and softened a harsh reality for working-class audiences. Anger at the elites, the leisure class, and the institutions they represented was validated but transformed into something to be endured or cautiously channeled into reform, thus giving an appeasing message to the new middle-class moviegoers."[10] Due to an increasing social mobility within the society,

many among the toiling classes were also beginning to identify with middle-class values. The frequent employment of comedy in films that engaged these divisive issues probably helped to further defuse social tensions.

Beginning in the mid–1890s, the earliest motion pictures produced in the United States were predominantly short vignettes of life, both staged and unstaged. But as the viewing public expanded and appetites waned for quotidian banalities, filmmakers began to seek out the more exotic or topical events as subjects to record. For instance, President William McKinley (1843–1901) was shot by a probably insane, self-proclaimed anarchist, named Leon Czolgasz on September 6, 1901. McKinley died eight days later. Before the end of the year, an American motion picture entitled *Execution of Czolgasz* (Edison) simply recreated the electrocution of a *bearded* anarchist convicted of the assassination. What is particularly interesting here is that this film dramatization of a real event not only represents a very early example of the cinematic appropriation of history, but also of its reconfiguration, since contemporary police "mug shots" of the 28 year old Polish-American Czolgasz show the president's murderer to have been clean shaven.[11]

Purely fictional films, with discernible dramatic plots, rapidly evolved as well. After 1908, hour or longer programs made up primarily of fictional one-half reel and one reel (6–12 minutes) "flickers" were the standard fare shown at thousands of small makeshift places of exhibition, usually referred to as nickelodeons—everyone paid a nickel and could sit where they pleased. Weekly attendance at these theaters exceeded 25 million by 1910.[12] Multi-reel productions (frequently released to exhibitors in separate reels, referred to as "parts") became increasingly popular over the next few years. By 1915 four or more reel length "feature" films were the dominant form, exhibited in larger purpose-built movie houses and even in luxurious theaters known as "picture palaces."[13]

Although the fledgling American moving picture industry borrowed heavily from the theater, this new mass entertainment business quickly perceived the public's interest in topicality and therefore incorporated current events and adversarial sociopolitical issues into some of their earliest fictional works. A few thematically-relevant examples released before 1909 include: *The Nihilists* (Biograph, 1905); *The Anarchists* (Lubin, 1907); *The Girl Nihilist* (Manhattan, 1908); *The Molly Maguires* (Kalem, 1908).

The patterns that reveal themselves within American motion pictures released during the decade preceding 1918 suggest a complex intermingling of screen images within related genres and subgenres, such as films dealing with strike violence and those that portray revolutionary terrorism in Russia. Paralleling the social turmoil of the Progressive era, these images and the messages they imparted were highly ambivalent. Yet, by the end of 1918, the growing monopolization of the American film industry, along with the culmination of a decades-long shift in the demographics and social mores of the nation, and the profound effects of World War I and the Bolshevik Revolution, all combined to more or less eliminate controversial ideological discourse from appearing in typical commercial releases. The silent screen's language of description was thus increasingly in the hands of a few, and the new medium's ability to redescribe history created a novel and unusual power over the nation's mass culture. One industry could now channel political thought and behavior towards predetermined socially acceptable ends.

As movies became a story-telling medium, a distinct *set* of genres evolved whose plots involved the central characters interacting with melodramatic and/or comically pejorative images of indigenous anarchists/socialists/labor activists or foreign revolutionaries.[14] Radicalism was increasingly viewed as a threat to America as well as the institutions associated with a capitalist-oriented democratic nation. Most of the basic overlapping components of these genres were firmly established *prior* to the 1917 Bolshevik Revolution. Film radicals were invariably portrayed as physically unattractive, their negative attributes including swarthiness, beards and vulgar gesticulating (symbolizing the linguistic cacophony associated with new immigrants). Furthermore, they were heavily represented in groups that were viewed as alien, especially Russians and Jews. Politically, they disdained traditional American values and wanted a new order. Their labor agitation, socialism or communism was accompanied by acts of iniquitous violence (particularly the use of bombs—sometimes referred to as "infernal machines"), sexual depravity, substance abuse and criminality to underline that their professed class-motivated politics was but a cover for indulgence and destructiveness.

Another *group* of films, or genre, that can be related to anti-radicalism in the United States were the "Black Hand" motion pictures. The Black Hand, sometimes referred to as the Camorra, was used to designate the Mafia. These films featured dark ethnic stereotypes representing Italians (frequently identified as "wops," "dagos," and "garlic eaters") who were portrayed as being engaged in such "impassioned" crimes as kidnapping, blackmailing, murder or bombings. Although the format was often comedic and the on-screen motivation of Black Hand members was usually either financial or personal revenge, their violent cinematic methods reinforced negative images that overlapped with the sinister trappings of radical political stereotypes.[15] Two examples of this genre intermingling are *A Bum and a Bomb* (Champion, 1912) and *Giovanni's Gratitude* (Mutual, 1913).[16] The former film's title is self-explanatory, while the latter release portrays Black Hand stereotypes with a militant labor agenda. Many of these motion pictures incorporate the comedic element of misconceptions concerning an individual's relationship with a real or supposed bomb, playing upon the audience's associations with images of anarchist bombers. Black Hand films largely disappeared following Italy's entrance into the World War on the side of the Western powers in May 1915.[17]

While any politics deemed radical, including women's suffrage, could be attacked in motion pictures by such stereotyping, four intersecting topical genres were primary: *Capital versus Labor* films, emphasizing those in which members of the struggling working-class, frequently influenced by a labor agitator, contemplate and/or carry out acts of militancy against their real or supposed capitalist oppressors; *Soapboxer* films, involving propagandists of the word, rather than the deed, such as loquacious anarchists and socialist idealists; *Bomb Thrower* films, featuring domestic radicals plotting and/or carrying-out acts of terrorism, with a Bomb Parody subgenre, which included comic anarchists or domestic radicals engaging in acts of social violence or individuals impersonating or misidentified as bomb throwers; *Nihilist* films that specifically addressed revolutionary terrorism and/or organized active resistance to the autocratic Tsarist regime in Russia. Themes, images and arguments in these seemingly often colliding genres evolved into the fully developed cinematic communist demon of the Red Scare that closely followed the Bolshevik Revolution.

From the over 20,000 short and feature-length fictional films produced and released in the United States between 1909 and 1917, 250 have been identified as topically relevant to this book. Only a few of these motion pictures are known to be extant; less than forty complete or partial prints have been screened of those works listed in the Filmography through 1917. The remaining films have been reconstructed from studio synopses, trade journal reviews, photo stills and assorted copyright materials on deposit at the Library of Congress.

When examining this selected group of pre-Bolshevik Revolution motion pictures that deal with various aspects of radicalism, two fundamental paradoxes quickly become apparent. First, although labor-initiated violence in Capital vs. Labor films is uniformly condemned, it is frequently *justified*, and, even more surprisingly, a majority of these films do not flinch from directly challenging the abuses of the employing class. Secondly, a seemingly incompatible dichotomy arises between anti-Tsarist American motion pictures, the Nihilist film genre, that positively portrays violent opponents of the Imperial Russian regime (sometimes female Jewish victims of depraved Tsarist officials) and films that either condemn or poke fun at domestic radical revolutionaries or anarchists. In fact, the stereotyped cinematic conventions and images that evolved within these parallel genres and subgenres more or less continuously intermingled before 1918. Thus it would take the combined impact of the consolidation of the motion picture industry, massive government-sponsored wartime propaganda and anti-Bolshevik hysteria following the success of the October Revolution, to force these cinematic elements to coalesce into a distinct anti-radical genre operating within customary melodramatic and comedic forms.

Silent Agitators: Workers versus Capitalists, or, the Class Struggle as Competing Stereotypes

It is rather ironic that while the professional agitators from the I.W.W. (Industrial Workers of the World) were routinely using "silent agitators," a slang term for paste-up sticker slogans, urging the working-class to organize and resist assorted abuses of capital-*ism*, another form of silent agitation quickly acquired the potential to visually address and simultaneously entertain millions, across class lines. Motion pictures gave labor a voice and provided an elementary textual explanation to its audiences concerning concepts of class consciousness and labor activism. Yet paradoxically, the movies were also "silent" (non-dialogue), due to technological constraints. Nevertheless, the many fictional films that exploited the capital versus labor problem during the pre-World War I years created a unique as well as lively venue in which these socio-political issues were frankly vetted. In the years between 1909 and 1917 roughly two films a month, more than 150 movies, portrayed workers taking some form of "direct action" against their capita*list* employers.

The strike was the action most commonly associated with the bitter struggle between capital and labor in the United States during the teens, a period dubbed by Graham Adams as the "age of industrial violence."[18] The American film industry did not shy away from this social phenomenon; at least 107 motion pictures released between 1909 and 1917 highlighted labor turmoil resulting from work stoppages.[19]

Strike is a harsh-sounding word in the English language that resonates of violence.[20] In the context of militant direct actions by labor it implies a blow against unfettered capitalism. And, although labor-oriented motion pictures were often benignly referred to as "Capital vs. Labor" films, they virtually always gave prominence to a strike or threatened walk-out by the industrial workforce directed against real or perceived injustices of the representatives of capitalism—usually a prototypical capitalist skinflint, his extravagant family and/or abusive underlings.

During an era in which American cinema was dominated by the melodramatic and comedic forms, Capital vs. Labor films were most often climaxed by scenes that featured an angry throng of striking laborers. The militant strike mobs were usually composed of immigrants who were either uneasily aligned with native-born workers or at cross purposes with them.[21] These motion pictures constantly presented graphic visualizations of mortal combat on American soil between armies of the working-class and mercenaries hired to defend the capitalist system. Some form of resolution almost always occurred by the film's conclusion, usually facilitated by a cross-class romance or a generically ritualized blood-letting.

In numerous early American films labor, excepting those individuals or organizations who advocated and/or conducted class-motivated violence, was presented more sympathetically than capital. Even alternatives to

capitalism, such as socialism, received positive treatment in a few motion pictures. Thus, while 26 Pro-Labor films have been identified between 1909 and 1917, only five films produced throughout the period are unambiguously Pro-Capitalist.[22]

The dominating cinematic clashes of a class nature, when examined from a broad perspective, represent the dread of a radicalized working-class. One of the primary indicators in pre–1918 motion pictures became the negatively affective imagery and language associated with the nomadic "paid" labor agitator—such as the unnamed, pistol-packing, black-suited agitator in *Toil and Tyranny* (Balboa, 1915; #12 of the 12-part "Who Pays?" series). This agitator, once trouble erupts at a lumberyard, appears out of nowhere and immediately begins to violently gesticulate before a crowd of disgruntled workers. Yet the particular union affiliation of these individuals, such as the Brotherhood of Locomotive Engineers, usually remains non-specified in films dealing with capital versus labor issues. Significantly, it is only popular locally recognized leaders from the workers' rank-and-file who received positive treatment on America's movie screens; for example, Joe, the "union" representative of railroaders admired by his peers in a typical labor oriented short, *The Strike of Coaldale* (Eclair, 1914).[23]

In fact, there are only a few motion pictures in which the anarcho-syndicalist Industrial Workers of the World, founded in 1905, was directly identified or where membership in that militant labor organization can be textually inferred, and none of these appear before 1911.[24] Members of the I.W.W. (often referred to as "Wobblies" or "Wobs") are either overtly or implicitly portrayed in eleven, or 4 percent, of the topically relevant 1909–1917 films—all released between 1911 and 1917. Without specifically mentioning the I.W.W., it can be deduced that in a number of pertinent films, the so-called "agitator" or "walking delegate" was intended by the producers and/or understood by the contemporary audience as a euphemism for

The Wage Earners (Atlas, 1912): An ad for a typical capital vs. labor film, employing a tie-in with the 1912 presidential election.

The Girl at the Cupola (Selig, 1912): **An angry mob of foundry workers, some of whom have been laid off by an "efficiency expert," declare a strike outside the plant office. The eldest worker's daughter, played by Kathlyn Williams, urges restraint. The burly man on the left is the primary troublemaker.**

the peripatetic I.W.W. union representatives. Two short release examples of these probable cinematically coded "footloose" members of the I.W.W. would be the "professional agitators" in *Greater Wealth* (Selig, 1913), at least one of whom disparages the American flag, and the out-of-town "troublemaker," ominously named Black, in *The Strike* (Thanhouser, 1914). *The Strike*'s Black (mis)leads workers in a demonstration outside factory offices, hurling rocks and shouting such radical-tinged slogans as: "Down with factory tyranny!" "Down with Boss rule!"[25]

Although no plot information has been found that labels any individual in *The Song of the Wage Slave* (Metro, 1915) as a member of the I.W.W., at the very least, this highly sympathetic feature-length portrayal of the working-class (directed by Herbert Blaché;

based upon a popular Robert W. Service poem) must have created associative linkages with the Wobblies. As a term for underpaid manual laborers, "wage slave" was widely recognized in the American vernacular at the time of the film's release. In addition, "wage slave" and being paid "slave wages" were well known catchphrases in the rhetorical arsenal of the I.W.W. The concept of a wage slave's song may also have reminded many moviegoers of the Wobbly's *Little Red Song Book*, which contained such provocative pieces as Joe Hill's "The Preacher and the Slave." Ned Lane, a burly proletariat hero played by stage and screen star Edmund Breese, achieves class consciousness while wandering the countryside as a "bindle stiff"—such itinerant laborers carrying their meager possessions in a bag slung over their

Toil and Tyranny (Balboa, 1915): A black-suited outside agitator harangues lumberyard workers who have gathered to protest a management decree that increased their hours without offering a corresponding adjustment in their wages.

shoulders symbolizing that segment of the toiling classes most attracted to the I.W.W. And, it is while "ceaselessly working and creating wealth for others" that the crumpled cap–wearing Ned becomes a dedicated activist, who engineers a number of confrontations with capital at a large paper mill in order to advance the rightful cause of labor.

Consider also, the "wild-eyed" agitator from Denver in *The Plunderer* (Fox, 1915) and the "sleek delegate from Denver" named Trimble, who uses dynamite for nefarious purposes, in *By Right of Possession* (Vitagraph, 1917). Although these two full length films may allude to the I.W.W., in all likelihood they were actually meant to refer to the United Mine Workers (UMW; founded 1890). The UMW, with regional headquarters in Denver, had been a major organizer and supporter of striking miners during the Colorado coalfield wars of 1913–14. No other commercial motion picture is known to directly identify any particular organized labor union, such as the craft-oriented American Federation of Labor (A.F.L.).[26] Perhaps this is because many of the real-life I.W.W. leadership actually held dual membership in the Socialist Party or encouraged dual membership in local unions—popularly known as "mixed locals."[27]

As alluded to above, a larger number of Capital vs. Labor films from the 1909 to 1917 period contained a distinct Anti-Capital rather than a clear Anti-Labor bias—22 percent and 16 percent, respectively. A few motion pictures actually strongly expressed both biases or advocated Capital-Labor Cooperation. Two examples of multi-biased films would be the feature-length *Facing the Gattling Guns* (Mittenthal Film, 1914) and *The Man with the*

The Song of the Wage Slave (Metro, 1915): An early full-length feature with a pro-labor theme—
the film may have created associations with the I.W.W. Note the traveling bag carried by the actor
(Edmund Breese), indicating he is an itinerant worker. (*MPN* 10/2/15:36)

Iron Heart (Selig, 1915), a three-reeler made by actor-director George Nichols. The primary target of animus in anti-capital films is the non-cooperative, selfish capitalist, whereas the labor agitator, appearing in 22 percent of the motion pictures, is the usual negative focus in those works classified as anti-labor.[28]

Virtually all anti-labor films show acts of violence by so-called "outside" agitators and/or those workers duped by an agitator's class-shaped proselytizing. Two of the more extreme examples would include *The Strike* (Thanhouser, 1914) and *The Unsigned Agreement* (Gold Seal, 1914). In both of these motion picture shorts, strikebound manufacturing plants are destroyed by the sabotage of agitators.[29] And, following this ruinous conclusion of these cinematic strikes, the soon-to-be destitute workers are abandoned by the unscrupulous agitators. The idled men are also left with scant hope of future employment in their respective communities, since the embittered capitalists have refused to rebuild the factories.

On the other hand, almost every motion picture with a strong anti-capitalist slant portrays wealthy industrialists economically exploiting their employees. Thus, the dominant message repeatedly appearing in Capital vs. Labor films is that the working-class is inherently good, but that they can be easily led astray by militant labor agitators. Consequently, it is in the best interest of the nation for labor to abstain from violence and to seek a harmoniously symbiotic relationship with capital. Likewise, capitalists are reminded that they must not mistreat faithful wage earners, and that they often share the guilt with "agitators" when trouble develops and must change their ways or deserve the hateful opposition they foment.

Capitalists are occasionally shown aiding their workers, sometimes secretly and even during periods of labor strife, like the capitalist's handsome son, Jack, in *Destruction* (Fox, 1915), who persuades a baker not to prosecute the starving laborer's son who had stolen bread while his father was out on strike. So the print cartoon cliché of the silk top-hatted, bloated capitalist with a large cigar clenched between his teeth, while certainly exploited in some films, such as Eclair's 1913 three-reeler, *Why?*, never became a universal stereotype on America's movie screens.[30] Caricaturing of capitalists in American films was as likely to be established through showing attitudinal class-based biases that were disrespectful of or detrimental to the well-being of the working-class. This is commonly projected on screen as wanton neglect of the basic needs of laborers, the hypocritical rationalizing by capitalists of their hegemonic exploitation of the working-class in the guise of social altruism and/or mean-spirited patronizing of the proletariat. For example, in *Why?* a young man of the privileged classes has a nightmare about capitalist abuses of unorganized labor that includes, in addition to the cigar-puffing stereotype, vivid images of barefoot child laborers walking a treadmill, railroad ties made from worker's skeletons and a seamstress at home with piecework who is forced to dye the thread of the embroidery she sews with blood obtained from a self-inflicted wound.

Anti-capitalist representations often center upon extravagant lifestyles and a refusal to listen to the "kicks" (complaints) of their workers, or to even attempt to understand the nature of labor problems.[31] This is particularly so as related to dangerous work site conditions and the needs associated with basic human survival of the laborers and their families. For instance, the wan capitalist Jenkins of *Intolerance* (Biograph, 1916), played by Sam De Grasse, in no way conforms to the fleshy, top-hatted, cigar-smoking caricature associated with print cartoons, but neither is he ever portrayed communicating in any way with his workers.

Wages, invariably at or near subsistence levels, are arbitrarily reduced in several motion pictures in order to make up expenses incurred through the irresponsible or profligate activities of the capitalist-owners' or managers' families. The anti-capitalist message in

The Cry of the Children (Thanhouser, 1912): Mill workers, outside the factory gates, are forced by low wages to contemplate a strike. Note the traditional lunch pail carried by Alice's father.

these films is especially effective since it is textually demonstrated that class conflict has occurred because of the selfishness of insensitive individuals rather than because of failures of the capitalist system, such as business losses resulting from a period of economic downturn. A strike that leads to the disintegration of an immigrant Lithuanian family is directly attributable to a drastic wage cut in *The Jungle* (All Star, 1914), whose lurid feature-length exposé about the meatpacking industry closely adheres to the eponymous Upton Sinclair source novel. In fact, the directorial team for this film adaptation of "the *Uncle Tom's Cabin* of wage slavery" was headed by the distinguished playwright, Augustus Thomas. The allegorical prologue of *The Absentee* (Majestic, 1915), whose screenplay was co-written by director William Christy Cabanne, in which the power-hungry general manager's wife and daughter are descriptively named "Extravagance" and "Vanity," clearly foreshadows the underlying causes of the future hatters' strike that will take place in the main body of the motion picture. In a similar vein, *Destruction*,

Opposite, top: The Cry of the Children (Thanhouser, 1912): a family of mill workers outside their company-owned home discuss whether or not to allow the owner's wife to adopt their youngest— the "joyous" little Alice. After a failed strike, the only choice remaining to the family will be to send Alice to the mills. Note the rich woman's fine hat and furs as compared to the simple shawl worn by the child's mother.

Opposite, bottom: The Cry of the Children (Thanhouser, 1912): In stark contrast to the worker's wretched housing, at the owner's fine home his pampered wife is attended by a servant wearing gaudy livery—visualizing the concept of an "industrial aristocracy."

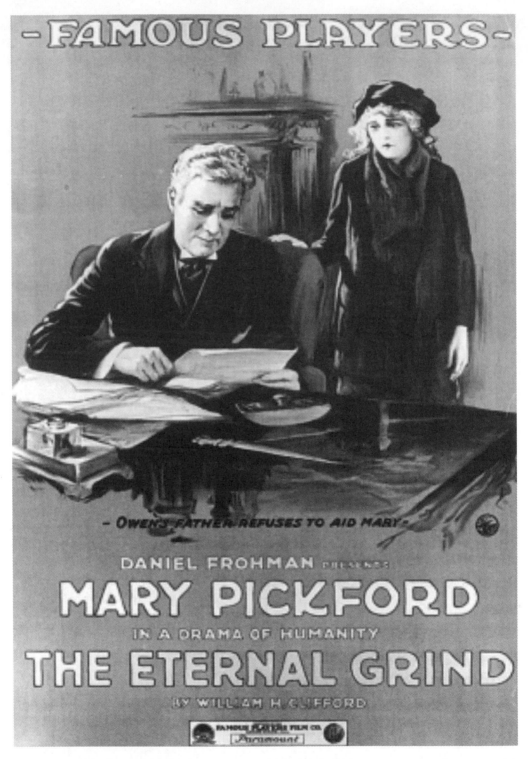

The Eternal Grind (Famous Players/Paramount, 1916): Mary Pickford unsuccessfully pleads with the factory owner to help pay for TB treatment for her younger sister, who has contracted the deadly disease while working in his sweatshop.

Jesse L. Lasky Feature Play Co., (Inc.)

Jesse L. Lasky present
Blanche Sweet
"Black List"
Marion Fairfax and William C. DeMille
On the Paramount Program.

The spenders.

The Blacklist (Lasky/Paramount, 1916): "The Spenders." While labor trouble brews at his mines, the absentee owner enjoys the wealth created by the toil of his oppressed workers.

a five-reel project directed by Will S. Davis, portrays the moral turpitude and business machinations of a capitalist's greedy younger wife, salaciously played by screen femme fatale Theda Bara, as the primary factors responsible for inciting labor strife.

The cryptic title of *Money* (United Keanograph/World, 1915), a multi-reel spectacular written and directed by James Keane, suggests a reprimand of monopolistic capitalism. In fact, the heart of the film's condemnation of capitalist abuses features an opulent "Million Dollar Dinner" whose centerpiece is a skimpily-clad showgirl emerging from a large papier-mâché oyster shell.[32] While the rich hosts' guests, dressed in the finest evening attire, fill their bellies with delicacies and revel in decadent display, his threadbare workers, who have gone on strike

after he reduced their wages, are starving outside.

In nearly a third of all films in which a strike is called, a labor committee or an appointed delegate is first portrayed attempting to rationally present the workers' case before the capitalist owner or his superintendent. These employees, in spite of usually assuming a deferential stance, are invariably harshly rebuffed; sometimes they are even fired on the spot. The iron works owner in *The Rich and the Poor* (American, 1911), named Howard Armstrong, browbeats a labor committee that has audaciously delivered an ultimatum to him, and a vicious superintendent tears up a miner's petition for a "living wage" in *The Strike at the 'Little Jonny' Mine* (Essanay, 1911). The hat-in-hand delegations of millhands in both *The Cry of the Children*

(Thanhouser, 1912) and *The Royal Pauper* (Edison, 1917) are verbally abused before being thrown out of their employers' offices—the young owner in the former film manages to do this between taking puffs off his cigar.

Rather surprisingly, the pattern that begins to emerge in many motion pictures addressing labor strife is one in which capitalists or managerial surrogates are frequently responsible for violence taking place through their employment of scabs and/or their unrestrained use of armed guards. In the most extreme cases labor conflict is attributable to the capitalists calling out the militia while attempting to either intimidate or subdue their more hostile workers.[33] Several films clearly demonstrate this capitalist culpability for labor disturbances—at least five in 1913 and another ten over the next three years. Examples include: *Locked Out* (Reliance, 1911), *The High Road* (Metro, 1915), *The Man With the Iron Heart* (Selig, 1915) and *Intolerance*. The owner of a streetcar company who calls out the militia to guard strikebreakers in *The Better Man* (Famous Players, 1914) is suggestively named *General* Wharton. An evil mine operator actually levels a gun at his protesting workers in *The Riot* (Nestor, 1913). *Locked Out*'s mill owner Johnson, after refusing to even listen to the entreaties of the replaced strikers' hunger-crazed families, orders his private guards to disperse them with rifle fire! And in *By Man's Law* (Biograph, 1913), another directorial effort by William Christy Cabanne, a capitalist calls in the police to quell protesting strikers, while hypocritically supporting the Civic League and Society for the Prevention of Vice. These films strongly attack, if not the system, those "autocratic" owners who are "oppressor[s] of the laboring classes."[34]

This negative portrayal of America's wealthy elite is particularly vigorous in the "modern" portion of D. W. Griffith's *Intolerance*, a multi-reel epic about injustice over the ages, that was released in September of 1916. An extravagant but sterile party held at the cavernous mansion of mill owner Jenkins, the scenes tinted a deep red, graphically suggests the wealthy are living off the blood of their workers, while devoutly worshipping at a cathedral dedicated to Andrew Carnegie's "Gospel of Wealth."[35] When the stone-faced Jenkins is privately approached by his spinster sister to financially support her newly-sponsored moral "Uplifters Society" (the footage now in stark black and white), the capitalist agrees, coldly noting the funds will be raised by cutting his workers' wages ten percent. His communication of this decision to the mills' manager over the phone further accentuates Jenkins' remoteness from his workers.

By creating, supporting and staffing their Uplifters Society, the capitalist upper class seeks paternalistically to impose a moral order upon their workers' non-laboring hours, in addition to exercising dictatorial control over the working-class within the factory gates. The day after the Uplifters' formation, two male members exit from a chauffeur-driven car in front of a hall where their workers are holding the annual employees' dance. A series of interior scenes have established a joyous and wholesome family atmosphere, in which only a few men are observed in the background moderately consuming alcohol (craft and union badges, or regalia, are noticably absent). But, without entering the hall themselves, the two capitalists quickly confirm in their minds a set of prejudicial preconceptions regarding the lack of working-class discipline. One of the Uplifters almost immediately bends over, picks up and then fingers a nickel he finds on the pavement. This simultaneously implies the tight-fistedness of capitalism, while suggesting these two patricians have prejudged the working-class' monetary irresponsibility.[36] Put another way, Griffith's skillful editing makes it appear to the movie audience that the capitalists have surmised that, if the modestly well-dressed workers can afford to hold a dance and literally throw their money away, they can easily absorb a wage cut. The capitalist representatives complacently conclude that the workers would even be better off if denied the disposable

The Jungle (All Star, 1914): A movie poster for the 1914 adaptation of Upton Sinclair's classic muckraking novel. The smaller illustration portrays the infamous scene in which a meatpacker tumbles into a vat of boiling lard. The main illustration shows the hero and another co-worker preparing to recover the body.

income that allows them to indulge in morally questionable behavior. But the true motivations lying behind the Uplifters' altruistic facade are revealed when one of the men comments that at 10 o'clock *they* [author's emphasis] should be in bed so they can work tomorrow"—a twelve hour work day, six day week, was typical—also common, the dreaded "Blue Mondays." Both of these pious hypocrites also react with contemptuous glances to the innocent flirting of an unescorted young girl preparing to enter the hall—as if they had been crudely propositioned by a prostitute.

Behind the benevolent guise of bettering their laborers' conditions and creating a so-called morally sound workplace, these capitalists seek to dominate their employees' lives in order to maximize labor efficiency. In a desperate attempt to preserve their dignity, Jenkins' workers are propelled by events and maneuvered by agitators into taking an ill-advised antagonistic stance: "They squeeze the money out of us and use it to advertise themselves by reforming us."

Although the factories of Jenkins are featured in *Intolerance*, it is significant that on several occasions, it is made clear that he is the leading member of a consortium called Allied Manufacturers. The name imparts the concept of a monopolistic group that is joined for a common purpose, united in an alliance directed against the interests of labor.[37]

Dust, a feature-length American/Mutual production under the journeyman direction of Edward Sloman, was yet another film released during 1916 with a strong anti-capitalist slant. This time the greedy capitalist, *John D.* Moore (as in John D. Rockefeller; a magnate who craves more; played by Harry Von Meter) lords it over his lint-covered workforce (including child labor) in the woolen mills. What makes this motion picture particularly interesting is how a less than subtle linkage is made between the mistreatment of American workers and the suffering of civilians from the war in Europe. A "reformist" author named Frank Kenyon (Franklin Ritchie), who has lobbied for improved conditions in the mills, is also in love with the capitalist's daughter, Marion. At a benefit for Belgium War Victims where Marion is appearing in a tableau vivant as "Humanity," the young writer makes a dramatic gesture by leaping up on stage and rebuking the onlookers for being more concerned about foreign victims of German militarism in the World War than about domestic victims of capitalist oppression in the ongoing war between the classes.

But this capital-versus-labor friction is usually mitigated by some form of reconciliation.[38] A cross-class romance frequently terminates labor violence and usually results in the granting of concessions to the employees. On several occasions, the films culminate with a pledge by the capitalist to his/her working-class sweetheart, symbolizing a form of class-based pre-nuptial agreement, to honor the rights of the workers. This is particularly poignant in *The Blacklist* (Lasky/Paramount, 1916). In this film, the mine owner, shot in the name of the working-class by a miner's daughter, who is actually in love with him, solemnly pledges to her from his sickbed that in the future they will strive together to resolve the issues that have separated capital and labor.

Unlike the majority of the few motion pictures to address labor issues after 1920, many teens Capital vs. Labor films actually take place on or near work sites as "the point of production." Some of these films, including *The Cry of the Children*, *The Struggle* (Kalem, 1913), *The Jungle* and *The Eternal Grind* (Famous Players/Paramount, 1916), contain extended scenes of stained-clothed laborers surrounded by churning machinery, performing their backbreaking tasks in ways that create sympathy for and sometimes even heroize the workers' skill or hard labor—further accentuated in these films by their apparent lack of union organization. *The Eternal Grind*, for example, a major full length film directed by John B. O'Brien, spotlights one of the teens' most popular screen stars, "Little Mary" Pickford, toiling with a sewing machine in a dangerous sweatshop; as

The Blacklist (Lasky/Paramount, 1916): "A dangerous woman." The mine owner, played by Charles Clary (left), is informed by his manager that the Russian-born teacher to whom he is attracted is a dangerous labor sympathizer. Note that the owner is *not* portrayed as a capitalist stereotype.

well as being sexually harassed by one of the owner's sons. *The Eternal Grind* is also one of four 1916 releases to portray workers disabled by their jobs. However, such exploitative policies ("economic whips") rife on shop floors as production "speed-ups," pay deductions for mistakes and fines for petty infractions of arbitrary rules, appear to be absent from these labor oriented movies. Nevertheless, the pre–1918 period is the only time when significant fictional film footage is actually spent at the workplace.[39]

In a related vein, Capital vs. Labor films regularly depicted the deprivations suffered by the families of laborers. In fact, a recurrent motif to engender sympathy for the working-class is juxtaposing scenes of their struggles to overcome squalid living environments with the extravagances of the capitalist elite. In the most extreme cases, the industrialists display a haughty callousness to the problems of those human beings whose labor has significantly contributed to the creation of their wealth. One of *The Jungle*'s reviewers was moved to make an unusually emotive comment: "The vivid distinction shown between the employer and the employed and the wide and bridgeless chasm that yawns between the selfish and arrogant rich and the dependent poor contains much that is of heart interest."[40] D. W. Griffith's *A Corner in Wheat* (Biograph, 1909) is a classic early example of this type of film, in which a capitalist's greed is shown to inflate artificially the price of bread. Both *The Jungle* and *Destruction* dramatically demonstrate a

The Eternal Grind **(Famous Players/Paramount, 1916): Mary Pickford (foreground), "America's Sweetheart," plays a long-suffering seamstress in an unsafe sweatshop. (AMPAS)**

direct correlation between the financial excesses of members of a factory owner's family and the lowering of his laborers' wages in order to cover their expenses. And in *Intolerance*, the early scenes of the happy domestic life of workers are ambiguous; bucolic backyard scenes of company-owned housing with gardens and fowl could also be interpreted as depicting the precariousness of the workers' lives, in that in order to have enough nutritional food to eat they are required to grow vegetables and raise poultry.[41]

In a number of these motion pictures, striking labor is portrayed as being compelled to return to work due to the extreme privation of their families. A walk-out of female garment workers is broken by starvation in *The Girl Strike Leader* (Thanhouser, 1910), the recalcitrant heroine of this one-reeler saved only by marriage to the owner's sympathetic son. At one point in *Locked Out* (Reliance, 1911) the destitute families of the locked-out workforce are reduced to begging the company president to reinstate their menfolk. In another film short from 1911, Vitagraph's *Tim Mahoney, the Scab*, an Irish-American union firebrand becomes a rotten blackleg scab, betraying his fellow strikers, after his wife is forced to pawn her wedding ring in order to feed the starving "little ones." Such suffering of immediate relatives during labor strife is a key element in eliciting movie audience sympathy.

Indeed, strikes can be viewed as anti-family activities, with the women as natural defenders of family and, thus, the primary peacemakers. Therefore, female-initiated radical labor action in motion pictures is comparatively rare—only appearing in about a half dozen films, including *The Girl Strike*

STARVATION WILL SOON FORCE MILL WORKERS TO ABANDON STRIKE

Large Families Endure Many Hardships--Children Cry for Bread

Starvation impends for their fight against the mill

The Cry of the Children (Thanhouser, 1912): The rich owner of the mill, indifferent to the suffering of his striking workers and their families, celebrates this news headline with some guests being entertained at his home.

Leader and *The High Road* (Rolfe Photoplays/Metro, 1915). In the latter film, a feature-length work directed by John W. Noble, actress Valli Valli played Mary, the young heroine who returns to small town America, abandoning the futility of labor activism, after surviving a tragic fire in the shirtwaist factory where she had been employed—the manager had locked Mary and the other girls in his unsafe sweatshop so as to force them to work overtime. Most female labor activists on screen, clothed in the ankle-length skirts and long-sleeved blouses of their day, are single women, with no apparent family obligations. But, they are almost never portrayed promoting or carrying-out acts of violence.[42] And the capital-labor reconciliation that usually concludes these films most often takes place through a romance with a capitalist Prince Charming. This is precisely what happens in *The Girl Strikers* (Kalem, 1912), when Kotton, Jr., having come to admire her personal virtues, marries an organizer of mill girls at his father's plant.[43]

Significantly, despite the sometimes dire results of their machinations, many domestic labor radicals appearing in motion pictures agitate more or less in the open rather than conspiratorially. Frequently, they are actually shown addressing workers during breaks on the job. In fact, on a few occasions, the withdrawal of their labor is formally *voted* upon by the closely packed workers at a turbulent "mass meeting" (Meeting coded $^{10}/_{11}$ percent), as in *The Strike* (Solax, 1912), *How the Cause Was Won* (Selig, 1912) and *The Valley of the Moon* (W.W. Hodkinson, 1914). Such public labor agitation, inherently democratic, while still relatively prevalent in pre–1919 films, became largely non-existent afterwards.

Another common social space where workers and labor militants interact on movie screens is the saloon—symbol of the evils of intemperance and lack of restraint, which ultimately discredits labor more often than not, as it can lead to a strike declaration. The venue of the strike committee in *The Strike at the 'Little Jonny' Mine*, an Essanay one-reeler, is a saloon.

The foreign-born or foreign-looking strike mob incited by an anarchist/agitator while under the "demon drink's" influence would have been particularly disturbing to many moviegoers. The iniquitous saloon, often owned or operated by immigrants in class-segregated neighborhoods, thus became a recurrent film locale for the plotting of labor unrest. The heavy use of dark, smoke-filled interiors as opposed to the traditional outdoor political meeting reinforced this and may also have created a subliminal link with underground meeting places. In this context, affirmative daylight scenes of workers participating in company-sponsored sports activities, such as playing on baseball teams, are noticeable by their absence from the screen. Alcohol, in essence, represented a socially irresponsible and inflammable agent when added to the equation in capital versus labor situations.[44]

Released by Thanhouser in 1914, *The Strike*, as an example, shows workers, congregated at a bar, deciding to throw in their lot with an agitator. But in *The Girl at the Cupola* (Selig, 1912), a one-reeler directed by Oscar Eagle, there is no need to even depict the strikers wetting their whistles in the saloon, let alone soberly gathered to rationally discuss the issues. Instead, a number of them are simply portrayed as a surly group exiting a drinking establishment and joining their work mates outside to form a strike mob that attacks some imported scabs. The mixed message in many of these films is made clear in *The Rich and the Poor* (American, 1911) where labor violence at a sooty iron works begins because of "weak minds influenced by weeks of starvation and liquor."[45] In such ways, the motion pictures illustrate Paul Boyer's point of how, "drained of much of their concrete meaning and specificity [by Progressive reformers], terms like 'the saloon' ... became, at times, simply code words for the larger menace of urban social change."[46]

Equally large doses of liquor and rabble-rousing are demonstrated to be responsible for the outbreak of labor strife that takes place on a ranch in *The Agitator* (American, 1912). Dave Walker (J. Herbert Frank), the primary troublemaking workman in Fox's *Destruction*, is introduced to the movie audience swilling alcohol in one of these so-called "workingman's clubs!" Walker hates capitalists and beats his wife. This bar bred villain, who has teamed-up with a rhetorically self-intoxicated agitator named Lang, later rapes the capitalist's immoral wife—the full-bodied Theda Bara in one of her earliest wicked "vamp" roles. Near the film's conclusion she and Walker die together in a symbolically hell-like conflagration.

In *The Dynamiters* (IMP, 1911) foreign worker types drinking beer are shown in attendance at an anarchist meeting. With their glasses filled from a large metal pail presumably brought from some local "bucket house," this film lends credence to the concept of the worker's minds being confused, muddled by the dizzying rhetoric of anarchists, agitators, etc. It also implicitly contravenes the positive concept of the contented, well-paid workingman returning home with a "full dinner pail."

Apart from saloons, some significant Capital vs. Labor film scenes take place either in a designated local union hall or at strategy meetings between national labor leaders, as in *The Right To Labor* (Lubin, 1909) and *How the Cause Was Won*.[47] On those few occasions, where capital and labor reach a formal accommodation, the capitalist is shown entering the crowded meeting hall and communicating with his employees. But rarely is any form of "collective bargaining"

The Valley of the Moon (Bosworth/W.W. Hodkinson, 1914): **Based on a Jack London story, this scene shows San Francisco teamsters cheering their decision to declare a strike. Positive portrayals of workers voting to take action at a mass meeting were not uncommon prior to 1918. (AMPAS)**

depicted, as if that would be too cinematically staid.[48] Still, this meeting place device is a preferable contrast to secret gatherings to plot sabotage against the factory or destruction of the capitalist's home, as in *The Strike* (Solax, 1912), where the workers assemble and vote to blow up the plant they are striking.

Capitalism itself is seldom attacked head-on in anti-capital motion pictures. But a comeuppance for egregiously greedy capitalists does occur in a number of films, such as 1915's *Money*, in which a Rockefeller surrogate named John D. Maximillian is killed in a climactic storm, along with his evil associate, and his grandiose home destroyed.[49] Less cataclysmically, in *The Price of Power* (Triangle, 1916), a humble millhand abandons his origins, changes his name to John Roberts and becomes an unfeeling businessman, but is driven insane by the conse-

quences of labor conflict for which *he* was responsible. The self-made and maddened Roberts eventually winds up as a "wage slave" in the factory he once owned.

A few other venal capitalists do pay the ultimate price, or close to it. In the 1913 Rex short, *Rags to Riches*, for example, the factory superintendent is beaten senseless by strikers. And a decadent capitalist named Linsay, played by Lionel Barrymore, is physically attacked by his mill operatives in *A Modern Magdalen* (Life Photo, 1915), a five reel feature directed by Will S. Davis. In the 1916 Kay-Bee/Triangle release, *The Corner*, the heartless capitalist Waltham (George Fawcett), who has cornered the food supply in a large city, is imprisoned and left to die in one of his warehouses by Willard Mack's workingman, whose life his monopolistic actions had ruined. A tragic divergence within

Toil and Tyranny (Balboa, 1915): An in-your-face professional agitator and two members of a strike committee (background) confront the owner of a lumberyard—interrupting the birthday party for the capitalist's "spoiled" daughter. Note the formally attired butler on the left, who is about to be ordered to eject these audacious members of the working-class.

this theme occurs at the conclusion of the Balboa three-reeler starring Ruth Roland, *Toil and Tyranny*. In this 1915 series production, released in the fall, the popular heroine plays the "spoiled" daughter of a rich lumberyard owner, who is mistakenly shot to death by a distraught worker whose family was destroyed as a direct result of her father's ruthless policies.

Several motion pictures released during the period depict an insensitive capitalist undergoing a change of heart after witnessing the suffering of the proletariat, often enough so that a *Variety* review noted "so many of this type have been displayed on the screen there is hardly a new angle left."[50] A good example of such a film would be *The Riot*, a 1913 short released by Nestor, in which a brief visit by the mine owner to the suffocating hovel of one of his locked-out workers is sufficient to induce him to accede to their demands and renew operations.

A variation on this theme is to show the capitalist as having a less happy life than one of his humble employees. The commonality of human suffering becomes a social equalizer demonstrating that a satisfying domestic life is ultimately more important than material riches. Steel manufacturer John Sharon in *Greater Wealth*, played by the multi-talented Hobart Bosworth, for example, is tormented by a drunken son and his daughter's fatal illness. So in the end, he is left with a "palatial home and empty heart," while a downtrodden worker in his mills survives adversity and overcomes the influence of anarchists to embrace the opportunities facilitating upward social mobility offered only in America. Likewise, in the D. W. Griffith short, *The Iconoclast* (Biograph, 1910), a disgruntled printing shop laborer, performed histrionically by Henry B. Walthall, has made his family suffer through a debilitating combination of insobriety and radicalism. But the fires of the worker's discontent are stanched when he discovers that his capitalist employer has silently endured the pain of raising a crippled child. The degree of family interaction and humanization in these films, used to stress individuation over ethnic stereotyping and deprecatory characterizations, is directly related to the wholesomeness of the particular cause.

Similar to the mythic American family, the belief in an idyllic democratic republic was also particularly strong at this time because of the large number of rural Americans of Anglo-Saxon origin who had recently emigrated to the cities. *The Valley of the Moon*, directed by Hobart Bosworth, highlights the struggles of a teamster named Billy Roberts (Jack Conway) and *Saxon*, the laundress whom he marries, amid an atmosphere of labor tension in San Francisco. In this adaptation from a Jack London story, the troubles of the youthful protagonists are lessened when they leave the city and join a rustic "artists' commune."

Motion pictures like *The Valley of the Moon* played upon or depicted (according to a viewer's particular perception) the fear within the middle-class of "social dynamite" existing among the urban proletariat—a class-peril anxiety created by the combustible cultural-political-ethnic mixture resulting from a huge influx of newcomers over the past several decades coinciding with an internal exodus from America's farms. Nevertheless, *The Valley of the Moon* clearly concludes with redemptive catharsis for its working-class couple. Other films were more ambiguous, like *Capital vs. Labor* (Vitagraph, 1910), in which factory workers forced their way into the capitalist's house and began demolishing its furnishings, as

well as physically threatening their employer and his daughter. One of the daughter's suitors, a young minister, restores order and secures future cross-class cooperation by persuading the capitalist to respect his workers' rights. Fortunately, such a "labor action" remained something of an exception and not the rule, presumably dampening the fear of "social dynamite."

Another dampening factor was religion or perhaps "moral thinking," as in *The Better Man* (Famous Players, 1914), where the "better man" of the title, a politically reformist Episcopal minister named Mark Stebbing (William Courtleigh, Jr.), nullifies class antagonisms by addressing social issues head-on and acting constructively upon his humanitarian principles.

The middle-class, on rare occasions, could also be portrayed engaging in or energetically supporting labor activism. But striking white collar wage earners were distinguished by their near total absence from the silver screen. In fact, only two examples have been identified—*Lazy Bill and the Strikers* (Eclipse, 1912) and *Bill Organizes a Union* (Komic/Mutual, 1914). And, both of these film shorts were of the comedy genre, as if cinematic challenges to capitalism from within the middle-class (or those people aspiring to achieve middle-class status) would be considered dangerously subversive. To emphasize this point, both of the films clearly present the protagonist's militancy as acts of folly. In the former motion picture, the office clerical force, having determined that they are overworked, walkout and hold the "usual indignation meeting" at a local hall. Pumped-up by *Lazy* Bill's sloganeering, the strikers engage the police in a series of skirmishes. Exhausted, the strikers seek refuge in their homes. However, after hastily fleeing unsympathetic wives, they individually slink back to the office and plead for their old jobs—so much for solidarity. At the end of *Bill Organizes a Union* the parading teenaged strikers, who had impulsively formed a union to protest stringent new office rules, are hosed down by the fire department and then unceremoniously dragged back to work! What is particularly noteworthy about this latter film is its unique, albeit mocking, portrayal of union organizational procedures and rituals, such as the collecting of dues and the wearing of membership badges.

At other times, an "honest" laborer is portrayed as being manipulated by an agitator into committing or preparing to carry out an act of violence in order to avenge a real or perceived social injustice. *The Strike* (Solax, 1912), a one-reeler directed by Alice Guy Blaché (president of Solax), presents a moral parable on this theme by showing that a cigarette butt tossed irresponsibly by an incendiary agitator sets fire to the home of a worker who had agreed to bomb his capitalist employer's factory. Only with the timely aid of that capitalist is the worker able to save his loved ones from the resulting conflagration. The cooperation with his employer in effecting the rescue also conveniently snuffs out the smoldering flames of labor discontent. The obvious message presented upon the screen is of labor agitators as malicious incendiaries who not only disrupt capital-labor peace, but whose conduct threatens the lives of workers' families.[51] They are not "progressive" forces. Consider the other film titled *The Strike* (Thanhouser, 1914), where an impressionable younger worker, mechanic Jim Price, listens to the radical union representative and later pays a heavy *price*—namely, loss of employment and of his home for following the dark path of the labor agitator.

Some films further segregate the labor agitator and/or anarchist from the other workers by giving him a foreign-sounding name, thus establishing pejorative ethnic designators—so-called "types" being the term usually applied by the trade at the time. Among those instances: Schmidt in *The Right To Labor* (Yankee, 1910); Tony Gazeco in *The District Attorney's Conscience* (Lubin, 1913); Lavinsky in *The Bigger Man, or, The Bridge* (Metro, 1915); Bloom in *The Strike at the Centipede Mine* (Domino, 1915); Israel Heimstone in *The Car of Chance* (Bluebird, 1917).

In a Darwinian variation on dampening the "social dynamite," retributive labor against labor violence is not unusual. Sometimes this is the direct result of a member of the working-class taking sides with his capitalist employer, as does the "rugged individual" named John in *The Right To Labor* (Lubin, 1909). This film short was described in a trade review as a "sermon on strikes which deserves the consideration of every thoughtful man who may someday be called upon to decide whether he shall go with a crowd of agitators or shall choose the conservative course and stand by his firm."[52] There is also *The High Cost of Living* (Solax, 1912), where a laborer becomes disillusioned with the apparent insincerity of his fellow workers' militancy. The protagonist of this one-reeler, directed by Edward Warren, is an elderly iron worker on trial for accidentally killing a drunken, younger and more radically inclined co-worker. The story of Old Joel's legally and morally justifiable act of self-defense may have assumed wider implications for the spectator by suggesting society's right to take extreme measures to curb uncontrolled passions such as the disruptive social influences of militant labor.

Naturally, the most intense labor versus labor encounters usually take place when scabs from the "floating army" of itinerant laborers, oftentimes portrayed as foreign-born, arrive at a workplace to replace native-born strikers.[53] Antagonistic reactions to the imposition of cheaper scab labor are in both *The Girl at the Cupola* and *The Valley of the Moon*, each of which feature riotous confrontations between opposing mobs of workers that begin as the imported scabs debark at the train station. *The Girl at the Cupola* shows running skirmishes from the station platform to inside the foundry, and *The Valley of the Moon* includes graphic scenes of a pitched street battle between striking teamsters and scab replacements, with the police entering the fray (a thousand extras were purportedly used).[54] In neither motion picture, however, is violence portrayed as resolving the labor dispute. *The Girl at the*

Cupola even concludes with an older, native-born worker subduing a knife-wielding striker and then helping to restore order by using stern but rational language.[55]

The importation of black strike breakers, such as occurs in *Locked Out* (Reliance, 1911), would have been considered inflammatory by many white northern laborers since newly arrived black workers from the South were viewed as a cynical capitalist challenge to labor solidarity. Taking into account a societal reluctance at the time of the film's release to in any way seriously engage the topic of contemporary racial antagonisms, the plot of *Locked Out* is unusual. But, without making it clear how this subject is dealt with in the motion picture short, the *New York Dramatic Mirror* review seems deliberately to minimize its potential social implications by noting that only two "negro" workers appear on screen.[56] This could have been a "dampening" element that society chose not to view that directly.

In this context of the often violent struggle of the labor movement, two films actually use as their title the single word "struggle" to clearly signify labor conflict as their themes. *The Struggle*, a short released by Kalem in 1913, features a gritty confrontation over factory workers' basic human rights being violated by a brutish Irish foreman named Mooney (Paul C. Hurst)— whose ill-tempered, hard-fisted supervision epitomizes the worst aspects of the so-called "driving" method of workplace motivation.[57] Rex's *The Struggle*, released two years later, frankly addresses the issues of the "war" between capital and labor that have led to a nationwide strike of railroad engineers and firemen.

Labor militancy, particularly acts of sabotage, were usually shown to be incited by cynical individuals—anarchist fanatics or professional labor agitators.[58] Significantly, these characters are most often portrayed as having no family and as being outsiders. The agitator appearing in *The Strike* (Solax, 1912), who has manipulated the workers into walking off the job and is planning to blow-up their factory, is an Italian stereotype. Aside from the related negative Black Hand linkage, many Italian laborers were associated with participation in organizations, such as the I.W.W., that advocated anarcho-syndicalism.[59] As Richard Hofstadter has noted, the more remote the villains, the more plausible are the exaggerations of their villainies.[60] This is in contrast to the suffering of workers' families through starvation or horror at direct acts of violence, which constrains workers to return to their jobs, often at the original wage rates, as in *The Strike at the Mines* (Edison, 1911), *Tim Mahoney, The Scab* (Vitagraph, 1911), *The Cry of the Children* (Thanhouser, 1912) and *The Strike Leader* (Reliance, 1913). The ostensible lesson for the working-class is that unchecked social passions can lead to the elimination of their livelihoods and ultimately to the dissolution of their families.

The enraged armed throng of workers bent on committing socially disruptive activities was probably particularly disturbing to the middle-class cinema audience. The labor mob appearing on teens' movie screens, usually comprised of numerous non-Anglo-Saxon types in ragged trousers, symbolized the dreaded power of the "unwashed masses," if not the potential social destructiveness created by unchecked immigration from non-northern European areas.[61] Some of the most compelling scenes in Capital vs. Labor films, in fact, take place when a seething club-waving mob of drunken (often "no-nameovich" foreign-born) strikers confronts the authorized might of the police or militia. Wearing uniforms as distinct as those encountered between armies on the battlefield, the two sides in the class war are graphically portrayed fighting for opposing visions of social justice in a democratic America. In both *The Man with the Iron Heart* (Selig, 1915) and *The Royal Pauper* angry strike mobs attack scabs escorted by armed police. After bombarding a column of scabs with stones, striking mill workers in *The Royal Pauper*, a five reel production released by Edison in 1917, are repeatedly

The Struggle (Kalem, 1913): The worksite victim of an abusive Irish foreman (Paul C. Hurst) is comforted by his sister, played by Marin Sais. Other workers angrily stare at the man who had beaten their young comrade.

fired upon and dispersed by shotgun-wielding guards.

The militia is called out in response to labor disputes in twelve films released between 1914 and 1916. In *The Bigger Man*, a 1915 Metro feature directed by John W. Noble, workers are confronted by a line of militia with rifles pointed at them (possibly meant to replicate the widely circulated still photo of millhands facing the fixed bayonets of National Guard troops, dubbed the "grey wolves," during the 1912 Lawrence strike). In *Facing the Gattling Guns* (Mittenthal, 1914), strikers at a dam construction site are mowed down by machine gun fire as a result of a vicious secret switch of live ammunition issued to the militia.

Most notably, during the climactic strike scene of D. W. Griffith's *Intolerance*, successive waves of formerly loyal and docile workers, driven to despair by the intransigence of their capitalist employer, make a series of desperate, futile, frontal assaults upon the Gatling guns of the militia that have provocatively taken up position across the street leading to the factory—assaults reminiscent of Pickett's regiments before the entrenched forces of the Union Army at Gettysburg. But instead of fighting beneath the American flag, the militia men stand before a symbolic banner emblazoned with "Allied Manufacturers"—the name of the consortium that controls the factory under strike, starkly painted in huge letters across a brick wall that looms prominently in the background.

The entire strike sequence of Griffith's film is tinted sepia—the reddish brown symbolizing the khaki uniforms of the militia or the dirtiness of the dust-laden mills mixed with the blood of the martyred workers. To further emphasize the utter futility of the strikers' actions, between the scenes of carnage that take place with the militia and capitalist Jenkins' private guards, a brief shot is shown of a mass of gaunt, stoic-faced laborers watching the event from a distance—the permanent underclass made up of countless potential scabs. The accompanying title reads: "Hungry ones who wait to take their places."

Regrouping, egged on by a few armed individuals (an unidentified mustachioed man with a pistol shouts at the swirling mob), the strikers storm the factory gates. Notified of this development over the phone by an excited manager, Jenkins ruthlessly orders his property "cleared." Leveling their rifles and indiscriminately firing into the mass of humanity clawing at the entrance gates, the armed guards of the factory then advance in military-like formation. The strikers' ranks shattered, their cause lost, the survivors carry off their casualties (including the mortally wounded father of "the Boy" hero) and begin the retreat into an exile that will lead to self-imposed imprisonment in the vice-ridden tenement district of the propinquitous city. A crowd of scabs are subsequently shown passively shuffling through the factory gates, literally walking over the battleground where their working-class brothers recently shed blood for the cause, under the watchful eye of militia troops, who carry rifles with fixed bayonets over their shoulders—giving the appearance of an army of occupation guarding the native inhabitants of newly conquered territory.

The apotheosis of militia-labor confrontations in this period would be the Ludlow massacre, which had a noticable influence upon several significant films.[62] *The Lily of the Valley* (Selig, 1914), directed by Colin Campbell, was most likely the first to show the impact of Ludlow, which had happened only a few months before the film's release, although the motion picture was set in the textile industry rather the western coalfields. In fact, the *New York Dramatic Mirror* review of the three-reeler commented, in its lead paragraph, that the film's action "strongly reminds one of the very tragic conditions in Colorado recently."[63] Certainly, the portrayal of an extended period of violent industrial conflict and of a slaughter of strikers would suggest a linkage to the notorious Ludlow incident that occurred at the height of the great 1913–14 Coalfield War in Colorado.[64]

In *The Lily of the Valley* the workers of Commercial Valley shut down the mills in a walk-out, driven to hopelessness by the cold-hearted policies of the town's mill owner, descriptively named Old Man Winter (Frank Clark). The striking mill operatives are led by foreman Bill Hanks, a bearded stereotype played by R. H. Kelly, who is "blindly enraged by the capitalist class." Further prodded by his fiery daughter Anna, the strikers riot. At one point an angry mob of workers, many of whom are armed with rifles, beset the top-hatted patriarch in his chauffeur-driven limousine. The National Guard is summoned by the governor. Amid the ensuing labor warfare, the virginal daughter of a wealthy family, Lily Vale (a diminutive Olive Drake in the role), selflessly administers to the needs of the working-class. Symbolically dressed in white and adorned with her favorite lilies-of-the-valley, she attempts to restore peace to the troubled community. But while Miss Vale is presenting an equitable labor agreement to Winter, a stone is hurled through his window, providing him with an excuse for refusing to sign.

When Lily is later killed by a striker's stray bullet while commiserating with her brother, a militia lieutenant played by Wheeler Oakman, the officer goes berserk and butchers many of the demonstrating workers with his machine gun. The victims of this vivid demonstration of the negative repercussions of capitalism's willingness to use the forces of the state to stifle the working-class, include

The Lily of the Valley (Selig, 1914): **A young settlement worker, played by Olive Drake, is killed by a striker's stray bullet while trying to stop labor violence in a mill town. Her brother, a lieutenant in the militia (Wheeler Oakman; background), and the owner, dressed in stereotypical formal attire, pay their respects—note her blood-spattered face.**

Hanks and his son. Near the film's conclusion, the repentant lieutenant-turned-mill-hand, during a renewed outbreak of labor violence, also dies from a bullet fired by a rioting laborer. And the woman whom he had married, the doubly bereaved Anna, has assumed the habiliments of Lily and become an evangelist among the suffering toilers of Commercial Valley. The conclusive effect of this motion picture obviously can be related to the later-released *Intolerance*, but at a much different stylistic level.

The *Sons of Toil*, released by Domino a year after Ludlow, would also appear to have recycled that bloody historical event. *The Sons of Toil* was directed and probably also written by the talented as well as prolific silent filmmaker, Thomas H. Ince. Significantly, the miners' leader in this motion pic-

ture, a "natural orator" named Marsden, is positively portrayed. Trouble begins to brew at the western coal mine when its owner, John Wesley, refuses to sign a new wage scale proposed by the trade union—conspicuously unnamed. The situation is exacerbated by the machinations of a management-hired spy who frames the miners' foreman as the "secret spy" of Wesley.[65] But with the subsequent abandonment of the pits depicted as a localized disturbance, the strikers' behavior is made to appear more justified than those of the real life UMW sponsored actions in the south of Colorado at Ludlow. And the strikers do not initiate violence until the introduction of out-of-town scabs by the proprietor. In one scene, Federal troops, not the militia, fire upon the workers. But a major turning point of this

THE PINKERTON LABOR SPY

BY
MORRIS FRIEDMAN

"The Pinkerton Labor Spy" (1907): The title page of this pro-labor work emphasized the disdain for management's worksite spies, by exploiting the well known image of the wolf in sheep's clothing.

tightly-packed two-reeler's plot is when the miners' ex-foreman, who had rejoined the army after being driven away from the colleries, refuses to shoot at his former comrades.

The mine operator's name, John Wesley, would probably have created an associative linkage among contemporary viewers with the same named 18th century English clergyman who had founded Methodism. Furthermore, awareness of the Methodist church's strong connections with the temperance movement may have been considered manipulatively anti-labor by many immigrant workers and, conversely, as sober pro-American valorizing by substantial numbers among the middle-class.

1916's *The Blacklist*, a major Lasky/Paramount production directed and co-written by William C. DeMille, brought many of the domestic radical genre themes together in a thinly veiled dramatization of the Ludlow incident.[66] But, instead of primarily southern European workmen as in Colorado in 1914, the film miners were portrayed as mostly Russian-born. The motion picture's heroine is a young Russian girl named Vera Maroff (the assertive, popular actress Blanche Sweet), a miner's daughter and the schoolteacher for the miners' children.

The mine guards are shown to abuse the workers and to evict those who resist from company housing. The vicious head mine guard, named King (played by a thick-mustached Billy Elmer, who swaggers about with a holstered pistol strapped to his waist), has also accosted the heroine as if exercising feudal rights. In desperation, the miners lay down their picks and summon a professional anarchist named Frederick Holtz, suggesting the character is meant to be of German origin. This German-Russian link was significant as the United States moved toward an active role in the current European war. Holtz and mine owner Warren Harcourt arrive at the scene on the same train—two different kinds of outsiders with two responses to the labor problem, both steeped in violence. Led by manager Norton, a stocky man who smokes cigars, the mine guards and additional private police forces man the hill above the strikers' tent city. (Many of these men are wearing the suit jackets with vests and fedoras associated with the well-known Pinkerton detectives, sometimes referred to as "special detectives." Mine guards from the notoriously violent Baldwin Feltz Detective Agency were actually sent to Colorado.) After one of the miner's sharpshooters fires upon them, the outraged guards unleash a deadly fusillade with rifles and a machine gun.[67]

The Blacklist is one of the last American films to project a heroic image of striking foreign-born workers. Vera's father, however, is in league with an anarchist society called "The Red Brotherhood." Following the cinematic recreation of the massacre at the strikers' tent city, Vera is shamed by her dying father to avenge the martryed working-class by killing Harcourt (whom she has come to love).

After a melodramatic face-off in the mine offices, Vera and the handsome middle-aged owner are romantically reconciled. In the end, the wounded capitalist tears up the infamous blacklist banning the hiring of labor activists (figuratively "sacking" them in a black economic shroud) and asks Vera, who stands at his bedside, to teach him to love her people. This patently sentimental solution to the capital versus labor problem once again shows an American film resorting to a cross-class love affair to ameliorate disaffection between the classes—a situation that may have called for the use of the "Internationale" as musical accompaniment being replaced by one in which "Hearts and Flowers" would be more suitable.[68]

Although these foreign workers were just as likely to be depicted as victims as culprits, the mere presentation or recognition in motion pictures of the reality of massive waves of immigration was a visual affront upon the idyllic conception of America. Tenements and smoke-shrouded factory complexes teeming with alien workers were classic symbols of progress and power, but they also represented

The Blacklist (Lasky/Paramount, 1916): "The Threat": The head mine guard threatens Big John, who had defended the honor of Vera Moroff, the company-hired school teacher played by Blanche Sweet *(right)*.

ineluctable demographic changes taking place in the United States—the dreaded death of America's idealized rural past.

The opposite of this unruly, red-driven rabble is repeatedly portrayed as the strong, stable family. A primary scenario in pro-labor films is to show labor militancy as resulting from the suffering of families; from their sacrifices in support of legitimate working-class grievances. Concerns over the welfare of workers' loved ones often inspire labor compromise or even capitulation—in essence, the primary melodramatic way of proving the class argument.

In *The Strike* (Solax, 1912), labor's action collapses after the boss helps save the family of the worker who had been selected by the union, under the sway of an agitator, to bomb the factory. Indeed, the young daughter of this

worker's family delivers the conciliatory message that ends the labor strife. Such a narrative ploy could be construed as affirming the traditional role of women as caretakers of family and nurturers of the moral order, but it might also be a grudging acknowledgment of the growing power of women in society. There are several strong female characters in these films, such as the humbly-born immigrant heroine in *Arms and the Woman* (Pathé, 1916), played by Mary Nash, who attempts to save her husband's munitions plant from (in this case) justified sabotage.

During the early teens, the growing strength and reputation of combative unions, such as the Industrial Workers of the World, were increasingly reflected in motion pictures. Beginning in 1912, the I.W.W. was at the forefront of such major strikes as the

The Blacklist (Lasky/Paramount, 1916): "Big John is killed." The wife of the popular miner is informed that her husband has been murdered by the mine guards. The head mine guard holsters his weapon.

Lawrence textile strike in Massachusetts and the 1913 Paterson Silk Strike in New Jersey. Many of the workers involved were East European immigrants.[69] Interestingly, of the numerous Capital vs. Labor films that were made, many included union agitators who instigate strikes and encourage acts of violence by the otherwise peaceful and loyal workforce. Frequently, the militant lusts as well for the starring young girl in the cast. Thus, the predatory union agitator both manipulates the lowly workers and menaces the nurturing figurehead, the woman. Lust in this way becomes metaphorical for radical activists "violating" sacred America.

The Spirit of the Conqueror (Phoenix, 1914) blends the motif of growing union strength with that of the archetypal Ameri-can family. In this feature-length motion picture the fantasized/literalized spirit of Napoleon visits from the other world and enters the body of a capitalist's son who, after graduating from college and falling out with his father, organizes an international labor association and calls a general strike. So there are allusions to the I.W.W. and militant labor, but the instigator is now a capitalist's son. It would not have been unusual for marginalized foreign workers in the teens to identify with the radical aspects of the French Revolution and the militarism of Napoleon, as well as with the premise of upcoming power as the young—even the capitalist young—become radicalized.[70] In a crucial strike scene, the militia and army both refuse to fire on their brother workers, signaling the

The Blacklist (Lasky/Paramount, 1916): "They shot him—like a dog." Big John's widow and children are comforted by the families of other miners.

familial solidarity of the working-class and a possible preventative to any future Ludlow-type incidents. It cannot be unintentional on the part of the film's creators to have named the idealistic capitalist's son James Morgan and the father, Peter Morgan, as in the recently deceased king of financiers, *J. P.* Morgan (1837–1913).

Several months later, *The Spirit of the Conqueror*, concludes triumphantly for the workers when the desperate representatives of capital in America accede to their demands. But the strain of leading the soldiers of labor against the forces of capital mortally wounds the film's Labor Napoleon: "when his father comes to call on him and acknowledge the son a better general, James passes away—the spirit of the Conqueror goes again to Paradise, where his soul is wel-comed back by the other shades, while millions of men on earth have their joy in the great labor victory dimmed by the loss of their beloved leader."[71] In this unusually provocative social film document, the romanticized workers are actually seen to have forced capital to deal with them as equals. Napoleon's late eighteenth century-early nineteenth century proletarian armies, that had defeated the military forces of several reactionary coalitions, are symbolically transformed to represent the potential for both social violence and power of a unified twentieth century working-class in the United States rising up and taking arms.

The mythic working-class family is decisively Americanized in *The Dawn of Freedom*, a Vitagraph production released in the summer of 1916. In this decidedly bizarre

The Blacklist (Lasky/Paramount, 1916): "The attack on the miners." Company guards and private police fire upon the striking miners' tent city, in a cinematic recreation of the infamous 1914 Ludlow Massacre. Note the machine gun in the right foreground.

film a Revolutionary War hero, revived from a century-old trance by a mine explosion, assumes the mantle of defending labor's rights against his greedy capitalist descendants and incipient domestic radicals. In place of Napoleon and images of European-centered militancy, *The Dawn of Freedom* provides instead the ultimate conjuration of pure American icons as weapons or antidotes in the war between capital and labor. The spirit of "The Patriot," after sacrificing himself to calm a rampaging mob of coal miners, is transferred to the socially conscious son of the evil capitalist. Thus the righteousness of labor's cause is not only acknowledged, but also legitimized, by invoking the founding fathers of the United States—and America's social harmony is thereby restored through a symbolic union of the classes.

Soapboxers

Speaking to American-nationalistic responses to foreign forms of radicalism, there are nine motion pictures released between 1909 and 1917 listed in the Filmography whose predominant discernible bias has been classified as Pro-Socialist—primarily dealing with homegrown socialists. Quite amazingly, there were only three commercial films released during this period that contained a distinct Anti-Socialist bias. All nine motion pictures displaying a strong support of socialism were released between 1912 and 1915, roughly paralleling the period in which the political power of the Socialist Party in the United States peaked.[72] The pro-socialist slant is unequivocal in several of these films, particularly Occidental's *From Dusk*

The Blacklist (Lasky/Paramount, 1916): "The Fatal Lot." Vera is sworn to carry out the deadly deed. The man with eyes averted at her side, not dressed in miner's garb, is an anarchist from the "Red Brotherhood"—versatile character actor Lucien Littlefield.

to Dawn (1913), All Star's *The Jungle* (1914), the independent Joseph Leon Weiss production *What Is To Be Done?* (1914) and two W. W. Hodkinson 1914 releases based upon Jack London novels, both produced and directed by Hobart Bosworth: *Martin Eden* and *The Valley of the Moon*. Yet, with the possible exception of *What Is To Be Done?*, none of these movies attempted a serious explication of the ideological tenets of socialism.

From Dusk to Dawn, an extreme example of a pro-Socialist, pro-Labor film, was a four reel work directed by an avowed socialist, Frank E. Wolfe, and released late in 1913.[73] Mixing in actuality shots of affirmative Party events with acted scenes, it featured a working-class couple who meet as a result of their common commitment to the labor struggle. He later runs for governor and wins on the Socialist ticket. Dan Grayson and Carlena, who face additional challenges together while fighting for the rights of their class, were possibly meant to be an allusion to the career of the famous progressive politician, one-time governor of Wisconsin (1901–06) and U.S. Senator (1906–25) Robert M. "Battling Bob" La Follette and his journalist/suffragette wife Belle. The most well-known social-activist lawyer of the time, Clarence Darrow, also had a prominent role, in which the "great defender" played himself.

From Dusk to Dawn's title evokes a "new dawn" with a reddish hue for working people. And its real-life images as well as its explicitly radical political message apparently struck a chord with the contemporary urban audience. Demand for the film was so great in New York City that exhibition magnate Marcus Loew booked it into his entire theater chain, where it was viewed by an estimated half-million moviegoers.[74]

Released the following year, *What Is To Be Done?* was a six reel melodrama made in New York by Brooklyn socialist Joseph Leon Weiss, that used the setting of a bitter factory strike to dramatize the history of the capital-labor struggle in America, including a vivid flashback depicting the recent massacre of miners and their families at Ludlow. Unlike most other related films, the text of *What Is To Be Done?* provides both a wider historical context for the class conflicts of its time and an explanation of the socialist response to the "capitalistic problem."[75] This is achieved via another cross-class romance, in which a factory-employed stenographer named Louise Lafayette, who is also a passionate labor activist, teaches the capitalist owner's son, through socialist literature and socialist-inspired deeds, to appreciate the cause of the hard-working wage earners of the world.

On the other side of the spectrum would be *The Dynamiters*, a semi-comic half-reeler released by the Independent Motion Picture Company (IMP) in early 1911. This film gives prominence to the I.W.W. "free speech" campaign, or "fights," of 1908–1917, but without ever specifically mentioning that militant labor organization.[76] The thin, top-hatted Jenkins is in a drunken stupor when he stumbles upon a radical street corner rally. Jenkins' fatuous extemporaneous "free speech" advocacy is well-received and wins the special attention of a disheveled agitator (with a presumably inflammatory leaflet sticking out of one of his coat pockets). The agitator hustles Jenkins off to a secret assembly of anarchists being held in the basement of a ramshackle building. Those individuals in attendance include shoddily-dressed stereotypes with beer glasses filled from a large metal jug (usually referred to in working-class slang as a "growler"). They

are listening to the harangue of a bearded radical, who was probably intended to be a Jewish caricature.

As Jenkins is ushered into the room, the anarchists exit and then reappear wearing masks. Their accessories include a human thigh bone and skull. Still in an alcoholic daze, Jenkins is sworn in and given a time bomb (a small black box with a handle, giving it the appearance of a satchel) with which to blow up a factory the next day. When the hungover Jenkins awakens in the morning with the ticking bomb at his bedside, he becomes hysterical. Having calmed his nerves with a shot of liquor at a bar, Jenkins' predicament is solved when a dog takes his explosive laden box and returns it to the anarchists' meeting place.

Its comedic Bomb Parody elements aside, *The Dynamiters* represents a crude assault both upon those members of the middle-class who would dabble with radicalism and upon workers who may have favorably imbibed I.W.W. rhetoric. It presents Jenkins' encounter with radicalism as a form of drunken nightmare and points out to the working-class that the consequences of enacting the anarcho-syndicalism of the I.W.W. may directly threaten their livelihoods and could even lead to self-destruction.

In a lighter film comedy short, *Bill Joins the W.W.W's* (Komic/Mutual, 1914), the "W.W.W." (as in I.W.W.) street agitators are not emphasized nor heavily stereotyped, but a simplified and misleading version of the I.W.W.'s socialistic discourse is presented— signs proclaiming "We Won't Work" and leaflets reading "We are becoming wise at last; Not Work But Money We Want...." Series character Bill (Tammany Young) is a mischievous adolescent office boy from Brooklyn, who still wears knickers. On his way to his job, Bill comes upon the "W.W.W." meeting and loiters in the street while taking in their radical message. The childish concept of not working, but still getting paid, is so appealing to Bill that he can't wait to tell his employer about it. Not surprisingly, "the Boss" (Tod Browning) is unimpressed.

Besides, the man has more important matters to address, specifically a motor outing during working hours with a pretty young lady.

Left to attend to the office on his own, a miffed Bill decides to abandon his post and return to the "W.W.W." meeting. Somewhat larger now, the animated crowd includes a smiling man with Hebrew lettering on his cap. But soon after Bill rejoins the street corner gathering, nightstick-swinging police break it up—in spite of the fact that no overt acts of social disobedience (reflecting the real-life passive resistance policy of the Wobbly's Free Speech fights) have taken place. Apparently, any public open-air meeting of radicals is sufficient provocation to produce a violent response from the forces of law and order—suggesting a less than positive image of the police.

It is noteworthy that *Bill Joins the W.W.W's*, directed by Edward Dillon, is portrayed in the context of a white collar office worker, not with the itinerant, semi-skilled laborers frequently associated with the activities of the I.W.W. The incendiary nature of I.W.W. propaganda is innovatively suggested when one of the juvenile title character's new W.W.W. comrades later uses a folded "We Won't Work" leaflet to funnel nitro into the company safe, even though the blasting of the safe has nothing directly to do with either labor militancy or criminality. Instead, it is a crude expedient to obtain bail money for the Boss, jailed for a traffic violation, necessitated by Bill's inability to remember the safe's combination.

Between 1911 and 1914 the Socialist Party reached its apex of power in the United States—particularly in the southwest where the 1912 socialist candidate for President, the spirited Eugene V. Debs, received his largest number of votes. A well-organized movement of grass roots workers, spearheaded by the activist salesmen of socialist literature immortalized by Upton Sinclair as "Jimmie Higgins," were largely responsible for Debs' strong showing at the polls.[77] Several motion pictures were produced that reflected

this phenomenon. One with a ranch setting, directed for American by Allan Dwan in 1912, was *The Agitator*, pointedly alternatively titled *The Cowboy Socialist*. This one-reel drama portrays a ranch foreman, who has been exposed to radical (I.W.W.?) propaganda while in the city to deliver some cattle. He incites his fellow cow punchers back on the ranch to demand an equal share of their employer's profits. The principal weapon in this saddle tramp's radical arsenal is a bottle of whiskey. Again, radicalism is fueled by alcohol, not a realistic projection (with a possibly positive spin) of socialist or I.W.W. tactics. Once the militant foreman is shot and wounded during an onslaught upon the rancher's home, the other cowboys, whom he had politically misguided, immediately give up their armed struggle and thereby disavow the cause.

A more mixed message is delivered in *The Benefactor* (Lubin, 1913), wherein a dignified socialist character, a young man named Boris Kreshnef, passionately advocates the redistribution of wealth, but later casually abandons those beliefs to work for the very capitalist whom he has repeatedly disparaged. Could this short drama be a counter-suggestion, however veiled, to the I.W.W.'s core constituency, namely, itinerant workers? Perhaps the largely foreign-born industrial or agricultural workers ("harvest stiffs") wanted—like any good Americans would—to be more than a perambulating "temp." After all, even "radicals" can be socially assimilated (refer to *The Dawn of Freedom*).

One final motion picture should be noted. *The Mayor's Crusade*, released by Kalem in late 1912, was probably a response to local socialist electoral successes in the southwest, particularly in Oklahoma.[78] This one-reeler features a "reform" (a euphemism for socialists and/or progressives at the time) party mayor of a western town going undercover to observe the deplorable situation in a local "sweatshop." The mayor then convinces the sweatshop's seedy owner to sign an agreement to improve his workers' conditions.

Progressivism could be a positive agent of reform and not all of the "labor types," apparently, were wantonly destructive or degenerate.

Bombs and Beards—the Bloody Spectre of Anarchism

By the early twentieth century, the image of a hand-held bomb had become the quintessential emblem of social warfare. And it would also quickly become American cinema's most prevalent caricature of radicalism. The bomb was an instantly recognizable signifier of violent anarchism. This use of the "proletariat's artillery" was perceived as particularly threatening to mainstream society when the (mad/maddened) bomber acted as a member of an ideologically motivated organization.[79] Who could tell how many more there were, or what they could do? But, when portrayed as taking place in the United States, the specific party affiliation of the groups to which these individuals may belong was usually left unspecified. Significantly, in virtually all pertinent pre-Bolshevik Revolution films, members of radical groups carried out their violent acts alone or with only a couple of compatriots. Furthermore, in most of the motion pictures where the bomb is actually exploded, it has been pre-emptively defused by being delivered in a comedic format—unlike the Gatling guns of the olive-clad militia in Capital versus Labor films that served only one purpose—naked intimidation.

The organizational affiliation of these cinematic bomb throwers remains noticably sketchy. It is mainly in post–1918 films that one begins to see, on screen, an armed revolutionary of a specific ideological persuasion at the head of a mob, such as the crazed Bolsheviks in *The Right to Happiness*, a 1919 Universal-Jewel production, and the notorious *Dangerous Hours* (Lasky/Paramount-Artcraft), released early in 1920.

The introduction of a bomb into the plot of the motion picture helps to further simplify the moral dichotomy. The bomb, or some other explosive device, such as a stick of dynamite, is a potential obliterator of class enemies. But on America's movie screens, its presence usually served as a convenient eliminator of ideological discourse. Continually appearing in fictional Capital vs. Labor films released during the teens, the bomb represented the unrelieved social tensions created by the implacable struggle between the interests of capital and the needs of labor. Symbolizing a distillation of class rage, the discharge of cinematic explosives by militant workers tended to dissipate pent-up frustrations while also demonstrating that, ultimately, such actions were the wrong way to handle class based grievances. Evidence for this derives from the fact that attacks directed at members of the capitalist establishment *not* directly linked to labor issues are extremely rare.

The cinematically projected bomb of the teens possessed immense social power, in that its selective use in a constrained melodramatic setting curtailed the need for armies of the poor or mobs of malcontented workers to be portrayed participating in acts of uncontrolled collective violence.

The relatively few random acts of class-motivated terrorism portrayed in American motion pictures, such as take place in *The Infernal Machine* (Vitagraph, 1909), are largely limited to the 1909–11 period. An early cinematic depiction of home-grown (and potentially bomb-bearing) radicals appears in D. W. Griffith's 1909 melodrama, *The Voice of the Violin*. In this Biograph film, a handsome young violinist with Bohemian leanings, named Schmitt, played by Arthur Johnson, joins a secretive anarchist band (including bearded stereotypes and masculine-looking women) to compensate for feelings of social ostracism. Schmitt is selected by his intemperate new comrades to assist in the delivery of a bomb to the New York brownstone of a capitalist—a portly cigar smoker (George O. Nichols) who flies an American flag from his first floor window.

But, when the violinist discovers the woman whom he loves in the home's parlor, he turns against his anarchist companion and wins the lady's hand. Ideologically, the film intimates that anarchists were not above attempting to desecrate the icon of the American flag and were quite willing to kill an innocent woman in order to strike a blow at capitalism.

The anarchist attack scene in *The Voice of the Violin* is particularly interesting since it portrays the hard core bomb thrower, with a prominent mustache, entering the capitalist's house through the coal chute and subsequently being trapped with his smoking device and subdued in the basement. This suggests the smoldering underworld of hell, the last refuge for malcontented anarchists.

With the exception of two scenes in which the American flag is insulted by "professional agitators" in *Greater Wealth*, a Selig one-reeler directed by Colin Campbell in 1913, traditional symbols of Americana were almost never accosted on film until the advent of the cinematic Hun and Bolshevik during World War I and the Red Scare. Since there are alternating references to the agitators as "anarchists" in this particular motion picture, their unpatriotic "direct action" may have implied a linkage to the foreign-bred anarcho-syndicalism of the I.W.W. In fact, a Washington state newspaper editor and Congressional candidate, Albert Johnson, received nationwide attention during 1912 for his "holy war against radicalism … raging at the I.W.W. as a flag-hating foreign conspiracy out to wreck the country."[80]

The use of Jewish or German-Jewish surnames in the identification of agitators/anarchists *hints* not only at a xenophobic streak but also at an underlying anti-Semitism that would unambiguously manifest itself during the Red Scare era with the appearance of the so-called "Jew-Bolshevik."[81] The "foreign" anarchist Max Veltman in *The Clarion* (Equitable/World, 1916) would be a pre-Red Scare example of a radicalized individual of Jewish descent. The Lavinsky character in *The Bigger Man* (Metro, 1915) is further stereotyped/dehumanized by not being given a first or "Christian" name and by wearing what was described in a trade journal as a "flousy" beard.[82]

Aside from ascribing to Jews such physical traits as a beard and a long nose, the evolving image of the itinerant Jew peddling foreign ideologies/carrying the virus of labor discontent, could be subtly visually reinforced in motion pictures through showing the agitator traveling with a satchel. By identifying the individual as living out of his "grip" (small traveling bag with a handle), the message is conveyed that he is an outsider with no roots in the community (shadows of xenophobia). Furthermore, it had been established in the popular media of the time that the grip was the preferred bomb carrier. Just big enough for concealing the archetypal spherical device, the grip could be easily opened with one hand and the bomb removed and thrown with the other hand. The very title of a non-labor oriented Bomb Parody film released by Lubin in 1910, *The Anarchist's Grip*, proves that this stereotype was firmly embedded in the popular culture at an early date.

Significantly, unlike what takes place repeatedly in Russian-set Nihilist films, public institutions and those individuals who represented them, such as the courts and police stations, were rarely targeted by domestic radicals. For instance, the familiar castellated armories that housed many state militias are never shown being assaulted by working-class mobs. In fact, the militia itself was considered a middle-class social institution and defender—its fortress-like armories highly symbolic.[83]

And on the few occasions when a police station does come under attack, such as in the satiric short *Rastus Knew It Wasn't* (Lubin, 1914), political motivations are clearly subsumed by attempts to achieve revenge for some personal affront. Domestic radicals appear to be conducting class warfare against the court system in *The Bomb Throwers*, a somber three reel 1915 Pathé release, but their enlistment of an Italian with a personal grudge against the judge they have targeted for extermination blurs the issue.

Two 1914 comedy shorts, *After Her Dough* (Komic) and *Worms Will Turn* (Lubin), do actually conclude with assaults upon police headquarters. A 1917 one-reeler released by Cub, *The Flying Target*, goes a step further. In this farcical short, a series character named Jerry is duped by some I.W.W.s into delivering a package containing a bomb to the local police station—a comic form of radical behavior that is used as an introduction to the film's frantic action, not as its thematic focus. Mostly, the bastions of the American system were sacrosanct to "our" radicals.

One could not always depend on the civilities of "outside agitators," however, and so they usually had to be clearly designated in motion pictures as untrustworthy or, simply, as Others. Although there was no coding in this book's Filmography under beard or unshaven, over twenty-five films between 1909 and 1917 portray a bearded domestic radical, bomb thrower or labor agitator. The actual number of such characterizations was probably much higher—an example of the inherent problems related to silent film research in which one is forced to depend heavily upon reconstructions. In any event, anarchist stereotypes became folk devils as visually amplified via the film media. They appear on screen as moral monsters, corrupting workers and reveling in class-motivated acts of violence. Physically, they traditionally sport shaggy black beards, an appendage associated with recently arrived Slavs. The attendant connotations are clear: a lack of cleanliness; hiding one's face, if not one's true intentions, behind a face full of whiskers. Beards are hairy masks used to conceal their wearer's nefarious plans, thereby lending credence to the concept of being conspiratorial. Increasingly, the film presentation of violence-prone bearded men is molded into a grotesque stigmata that both pictorially isolates and symbolically estranges the radical Other.

As visualized by these motion pictures, the exaggerated physical movements of grimacing foreign-born radicals that seemingly roiled the movie screen were often juxtaposed with the more controlled emotions, emphasized through restrained facial expressions, of true blue Americans. Silent film agitators were intended to be visually disconcerting to the mainstream movie audience; their histrionic tirades offensively grating (possibly accentuated by the musical accompanist with a few discordant chords) to genteel sensibilities and concepts of civility. The waving hand and thrusting fist of the envenomed, spittle-spraying (a coded form of swearing) agitator rips across the screen and visually flails the middle-class, accosting its sense of social decorum. The mob, led by a bomb carrying agitator/anarchist, becomes a sentient cinematic punctuation mark to the stereotyped agitator's own beast-like physical presentation, exacerbating the establishment's fear of potential social chaos!

With the increasing militancy of unions like the I.W.W., combined with a continued public fascination and/or fear of the perceptual image of the anarchist, came the production and release in the United States of a large number of films depicting domestic bomb-throwing radicals. The majority of such motion pictures incorporating relevant generic components were released after 1911. Typical is this contemporary description of *Fanatics* (Triangle, 1917), wherein "...labor is misled by a wild-eyed anarchist whose one object is to destroy property and annihilate the owners of wealth...."[84]

Some of these melodramas with radical stereotypes linked the heavies more closely with criminal behavior than with any discernible politics. In Pathé's 1915 work, *The Bomb Throwers*, the violence-prone compatriots of "Red Mike" Davis are mainly interested in blowing up the prosecutor responsible for Davis' execution. On other occasions, anarchists are destroyed by their own explosive devices, symbolic of their message being self destructive. Blown back into the social hell from whence they came, such scenes literally portray the backfiring of their revolutionary theories. This is exactly what occurs in the semi-comic *After Her Dough* (Komic, 1914), that concludes on a deadly as well as destructive note.

Bomb Parodies

Clearly, cinematic bombs can be simultaneously both destroyers and amusers, with the film industry addressing radicalism by creating one milieu in which the middle-class can be portrayed as being either frightened or fooled (or both) by members of the working-class, especially those of the radical persuasion. Such bomb parodies, centered around characters mistakenly believed to be anarchists, are a form of politicized burlesque— the fears of the destructive repercussions of radicalism being neutralized in the process of entertaining the ticket-buying public.[85]

Motion pictures with individuals pretending to be anarchists or mistaken as dastardly bomb throwers were common in the teens. A few examples would include *Lulu's Anarchist* (Vitagraph, 1912), *Boarders and Bombs* (Biograph, 1913), *The Funny Side of Jealousy* (Big "U," 1915), *Gus and the Anarchists* (Lubin, 1915) and *Fatty's New Role* (Keystone, 1915). *Gus and the Anarchists* features some waiters posing as bearded radicals with violent intentions in order to so alarm a co-worker that he will stop his sexual advances upon an unreceptive waitress. Similarly, in *Fatty's New Role*, havoc ensues when Keystone's rotund actor-director comedy star (Roscoe "Fatty" Arbuckle) saunters into a bar dressed as a tramp and carrying a large round cheese, the saloon's proprietor having confused his shabby patron with a notorious bomb thrower.

Anarchists motivated by romantic jealousy were another source of comedy in the Bomb Parody films. For instance, in *Cupid in a Hospital* (L-KO, 1915), a convalescent anarchist (possibly injured by his baneful activities) tries to blow up a fellow patient in the ward after the anarchist discovers the tipsy Chaplinesque tramp flirting with his favorite nurse. In a typical example of the prevailing slapstick style of film comedy, known at the time as "knockabout," both the anarchist and his intended victim are knocked-out of the building, becoming human projectiles who splash-down in a nearby pond.

Thus, by 1915, anarchists were more apt to be laughed at than dreaded. In Kriterion's *The Painted Anarchist*, Syd, a less than honest artist, mounts a real-life anarchist in a frame and passes him off as a brilliant new composition. But then the recalcitrant "painted" Red decides to light the fuse of his bomb and break up the studio party celebrating Syd's artistry. With predictably explosive comedic results, the painter and his mad out-of-frame subject end up in the street entangled upon some telephone wires. Besides twitting the radical left, this comedy short could also be construed as a satire upon the "cultural insurgency" of the Ash Can school, a new artistic movement that accentuated raw urban realism. In the bourgeois public's mind, this modernist form of expression typified a perverted trend in art that could be attributed to the collusion between fatuous artists and "philosophical" anarchists, such as those associated at the time with Greenwich Village and the Bohemian habitués of Mabel Dodge's famous 5th Avenue salon.

Though not really a Bomb Parody, per se, *The Red Widow*, a full-length comedy directed by James Durkin and released by Famous Players-Paramount in 1916, is an interesting film with which to conclude this section. Based upon a popular stage play, this film combines elements of the subgenre with those of the Nihilist genre.

Cicero Hannibal Butts, a dapper young American corset salesman played by John Barrymore, winds up on a business trip in Russia accompanied by a charming lady dancer, played by Flora Zabelle, who had persuaded him to allow her to pose as his wife. But soon after getting past the Russian border guards, Hannibal discovers that instead of being on a pleasant foreign tryst he is in the clutches of the notorious "Red Widow"—a nihilist who is more interested in tossing bombs than in making love.[86] As noted in a trade review, the scene in which "the salesman is forced to draw lots for a killing, makes comedy of seemingly stern moments."[87] A nervous bomb-carrying Hannibal is later caught "red-handed" by the Tsarist secret police during a raid upon a nihilist "seance." Hannibal is relieved to be escorted by officials to the frontier. Yet, although he has avoided Siberian exile or being blown up, Hannibal cannot escape being the butt of his angry new wife, who had been detained at the Russian border when it was mistakenly believed by the secret police that she was the "Red Widow."

Virtuous Terrorism: The Nihilist Films

By the beginning of the twentieth century, American filmmakers, and apparently the American public, visualized Tsarist Russia as an ethnically polyglot empire of over 135 million people that retained a semblance of order through the callous exercise of authority by decadent representatives of the Romanoff dynasty. As a result, the title Tsar had become a synonym in the United States for the unlimited powers of autocracy. And by extension, Russia under the rule of the Tsar became synonymous with oppression.[88] Since the Tsarist autocracy was identified as the primary impediment to achieving democracy in Russia, the elimination of the abusive apparatus supporting the monarchy became morally justifiable to many Americans.

A myriad of political parties and/or terrorist organizations on the left, collectively referred to in the West as nihilists (a label coined for the revolutionary figure named Bazarov in Ivan Turgenev's 1862 novel, *Fathers and Sons*), arose in Russia in the latter part of the nineteenth century and the early twentieth in opposition to Tsarist despotism. As state-sponsored repression intensified, the attraction of terror as a weapon

against the ruling state likewise increased.[89]

In the collective mind of American popular culture, Russian politics had thereby become inextricably linked with violence. In response to this, there briefly arose, from immediately following the failed 1905 Russian Revolution until the Bolshevik Revolution, the Nihilist film genre.[90] Motion pictures concentrating upon a nihilist theme show a curious American affinity with Russian terrorism. Russian nihilists, in effect, were transformed on the movie screens of this era into valiant freedom fighters for democracy.

The Nihilist genre is generally accepted as embracing all films in which some form of opposition to the autocratic government of Imperial Russia is expressed. However, use of the genre in this study is confined to those motion pictures in which the person seeking revenge has demonstrated some direct connection with a revolutionary band whose extremism leads to a violent confrontation; i.e., active membership in or unequivocal association with a nihilist group—35 films released between 1909 and 1917 have been coded under Nihilist. A few examples of so-called Nihilist films in which apparently *no* anti–Tsarist revolutionary terrorist activities take place include: *The Hebrew Fugitive* (Lubin, 1908); *A Russian Heroine* (Pathé, 1910); *The Russian Black 107* (Ruby, 1913); *The Kiss of Hate* (Columbia/Metro, 1916).[91]

The Nihilist films, numbering about fifty by 1917 when broadly defined, were obviously a popular draw at movie houses.[92] They apparently appealed to a genuine American resentment of the blatant abuses of Tsarist Russia, including numerous anti-Semitic excesses.[93] For the more prurient viewers, the genre also provided a relatively safe environment in which to participate vicariously in acts of sadism. There seemed to be a public fascination with women who turned into bomb throwers as a result of being sexually assaulted by Tsarist officials. The irony is that Slavic-looking *men* who threw bombs in America were so universally condemned—those previously mentioned anarchists or "outside agitators." The appeal of the violent fanatic stereotype then had its distinct geographical and gender parameters. And chronological ones as well. Kevin Brownlow notes how "[t]he early nihilist pictures would have horrified audiences had they been shown ten years later at the height of the Red Scare, for their sympathies lay firmly with the revolutionists, whatever ghastly crimes they may have committed."[94]

The homemade bomb became the nihilist weapon of choice—a fetishism of the elegant bomb which became associated in the western mind with a "cult of negation."[95] Bombs were portable and easily concealed, did not require much skill to manufacture or to deliver, and yet the "magic" effects of "the deed" could be quite spectacular. A great deal of attention for the cause could be achieved because these "infernal machines" could quite literally obliterate their human targets. Ironically, when one considers the negative associations with bomb carrying domestic radicals in fictional American films, these "good-intentioned" *nihilist* bombs were frequently depicted as working efficiently in effecting the symbolic annihilation of the nefarious representatives of a non-democratic Russian government.

Outbursts of revolutionary violence in Nihilist films were *only* directed at the autocratic injustices of the Tsarist regime. No pre-Bolshevik Revolution films specifically advocate the overthrow of Tsar Nicholas II (1894–1917) until early 1917, when the abdication of Russia's monarch had become a fait accompli. Nor do *any* Nihilist films ever openly develop the underlying theme of a social revolution in which the wealth of the elite would be redistributed among the peasants and the urban working-class. Only one motion picture, *Lost in Siberia* (Selig, 1909), is known to make a direct linkage between socialism and nihilism. Until 1917 the ideological locus of Nihilist films would thus appear to have been the introduction of western-style democracy as a means of reforming, rather than totally eradicating, the Russian monarchical state.

Virtually all the Nihilist films take place in Russia.[96] Their plots usually center around individuals who seek violent revenge after being cruelly oppressed by agents of the Tsarist regime. Most often, the victims are idealistic young Russians (sometimes Jewish, or "Hebrew" and/or "maidens"). Banishment to the Siberian wastes, followed by a lovers' escape to the West, particularly to the United States, usually occur. If the heroine has been violated and participates in attempts at killing the wanton Tsarist official, her escape is as likely to be in the form of her own death, a classical Pyrrhic victory. As an example, there is *Rachel* (Kalem, 1910), where the beautiful protagonist shoots herself after failing to kill the insensitive aristocrat who had abused her family.

The Nihilist genre in American motion pictures seems to have been initially stimulated by the 1905 Russian Revolution and the furious destructiveness of political radicals and ruthless state repression that constituted the uprising's gory aftermath. Terrorists, many of them women, actually claimed several thousand victims in Russia during 1906 and 1907.[97] One of the earliest examples of this anti-Tsarist film genre is a 1905 Biograph tear-jerker entitled *The Nihilists*. Released only two months after the notorious "Bloody Sunday" massacre in Moscow in January 1905, it shows pitiless Tsarist officials oppressing an ethnic Polish family linked with a ritual-performing revolutionary sect. In the end, a vengeful daughter blows up the hated Chief of Police.[98] Later motion pictures with similar plots include *The Girl Nihilist* (Manhattan, 1908) and *Queen of the Nihilists* (Yankee, 1910).

With torture appearing as a regular motif, the Nihilist genre became in the teens a form of cinematic Grand Guignol. Approximately one half of the pre-Bolshevik revolution Nihilist films portray some act of state-sponsored cruelty and therefore contain the Atrocity coding in the Filmography—19/8 percent—particularly floggings, using the infamous knout.[99] The heroine in *Queen of the Nihilists*, for example, becomes a nihilist leader following the traumatic childhood experience of witnessing the death of her father under the knout. Another Tsarist victim, in *The Cossack Whip* (Edison, 1916), is radicalized after surviving a wintertime raid upon her village by horse-mounted Cossacks uttering "bloodcurdling yells." The invaders' butchery, which had been ordered by the evil Prefect of the Imperial Police in retaliation for the peasants harboring revolutionaries, includes a graphic scene of a Cossack grabbing an old woman (probably the girl's grandmother) by the hair and beating her with his knout.

The willingness of nihilists to sacrifice themselves for the cause implied a suicidal fanaticism that often bordered on madness. In the earlier motion pictures, this is less strident, but in the teens it becomes more pronounced, and with a negative edge. *The Scarlet Oath* (Peerless/World, 1916) features a female nihilist, played by Gail Kane, who is killed by Tsarist agents after avenging her father, a victim of torture at the hands of the Chief of Police (Montague Love). And in *The Rose of Blood* (Fox, 1917), Theda Bara plays a common-born revolutionary who murders her bemedaled aristocratic Tsarist official husband and then kills herself by detonating an explosive device in the family villa. Though these women are hardly fellow travellers to the redemptive women characters in America-based labor films, they are positive tragic heroines willing to risk their sanity or even sacrifice their lives for principle.

Social revolution is largely an abstraction in the Nihilist films; neither material gain nor political power is ever directly sought. In the classic form of personalization associated with melodrama, the nihilists simply desire to weed out those individuals and institutions serving the Tsarist regime that tyrannize the people, most particularly the secret police, officially known as the Okrana.

In fact, many film nihilists in pre–1913 motion pictures are not initially portrayed as dedicated democrats, but solely as victims of

Tsarist atrocities committed against themselves or members of their families—who, only then, become nihilists in order to achieve revenge by joining a conspiratorial organization primarily dedicated to terrorism. The more routine human rights abuses of Russia's vast peasantry, such as the required carrying of internal passports, never appear in these Nihilist films. And a future form of government is seldom explicated, except in a few of the later motion pictures released immediately preceding and following the revolutions of 1917, when American democracy is invoked—*The Sowers* (Lasky/Paramount, 1916); *Darkest Russia* (Peerless/World, 1917).

The carnage created by film nihilists is textually justified as the means by which to eliminate those individuals abusing Tsarist power. The revolutionaries seek to restore moral responsibility to those who govern, not to destroy the institution of the monarchy. Hence, nihilists are usually portrayed as middle-class liberals or as enlightened democratically inclined members of the aristocracy. In fact, *The Sowers'* Russian League of Freedom is described in an introductory title as "a vast organization headed by a powerful young noble who determined to free the peasants from the terrible conditions of the present system." Yet at the climactic point of a conspiratorial meeting (shot in deep-focus) in which its members proclaim that "within a year we will sweep Russia [with] Our Revolution," the diverse group collectively gazes up at a portrait of Peter the Great (1672–1725)—an apparent paradox that only begins to make sense if one is familiar with the protean imagery of the "enlightened despot" and, most particularly, with the phenomenon beginning in the late nineteenth century of the emerging Russian intelligentsia embracing the Petrine myth as a symbol of western reform.[100]

Jews, sometimes peasants, but more often members of the radicalized intelligentsia, are the preferred martyrs of the regime, but not the engines of reform, which largely remains the purview of urbane patricians who know what is in the best interest

The Rose of Blood (Fox, 1917): A Revolutionary vamp, played by Theda Bara, places a red rose on the corpse of her aristocratic husband—she murdered him after discovering he had betrayed Mother Russia in the service of Germany. Note the vamp's heavily mascaraed eyes.

of the masses, or saintly Tolstoy-type characters such as Simeon Novotsky in *Lost in Siberia* (Selig, 1909). Obviously, such high-minded figures would be more apt to elicit empathy with American audiences than dirty, loutish Russian peasant stereotypes.

The ultimate negative symbols in Nihilist films were the omnipresent and corrupted Russian Secret Police representatives and vicious Cossacks (the Tsar's Imperial Guard)—menacing enough in their cartridge-festooned tunics, shako military caps and knee-high boots, their evil connotations were frequently compounded by their wearing thick black beards.[101] In a more sophisticated variation on this theme, anti–Tsarist sentiments were

most likely reinforced in 1917 by *Darkest Russia* which portrayed the wicked Minister of Police, Count Kalnoky, with a Van Dyke beard, thereby creating a visual linkage with the real-life image of Nicholas II.

Escape from the clutches of the Tsarist secret police in Nihilist films involves outwitting the captors or overcoming them by force of will. Cinematic nihilists are daring, righteously motivated individuals joining together to oppose despots who are inherently venal and hypocritical. On the other side, Tsarist officials represent a negative form of nationalism—demanding unquestioning submission to the dictates of the monarchy. Secret nihilist meetings become de facto democratic expressions of the "peoples' will" to resist oppression, and by logical extension, escape by nihilists, usually to America, is a form of cinematic referendum endorsing democracy, and in turn justifying the open immigration policies of the United States.

An example of this flight pattern is *The Sorrows of Israel* (Victor, 1913), directed by Sidney Goldin, in which a student and Jewish convert to the Russian Orthodox church marries a sympathetic young noblewoman, played by black-haired beauty Irene Wallace—the couple must later flee their homeland for America to escape the vengeful and anti-Semitic actions of his wife's aristocratic ex-suitor. It can be presumed that these motion pictures communicate strong admiration for those who are portrayed fighting for their rights over there, concurrent with respect over here for the peaceful democratic ideals of America. These cinematic Russian revolutionaries resisting the Tsar's moribund regime (the Romanoff dynasty had ruled for three centuries as of 1913) are invariably youthful and pure of heart, while those they oppose are usually older and morally depraved. Attractive female advocates of the nihilist cause are Lady Libertys with Russian-sounding names.

Siberian exile was another facet of Russian brutalism. American motion pictures portrayed Siberia as a frozen world of forced labor, torture—madness—a physically and spiritually barren place from which to escape. An inter-title in *The Cossack Whip* perfectly captures this conceptualization in its laconic thematic introduction of Siberia as the "dreaded word." This Russian frontier was an implicit perversion of America's frontier myth, embodying the concepts of spiritual liberation and of economic advancement.

No acts of "expropriations" are depicted in pre-Bolshevik Revolution Nihilist films, which as previously stated remained somewhat contextually abstract. Verbal assaults or physical violence aimed specifically at the Tsar, the "Little Father" to many of the "muzhiks," are very rare—even in 1916–17 films.[102] Only implied or indirect blame can be attributed to the Tsar for allowing the situation to continue, and this is seldom enunciated in these motion pictures.

An exception would be the scene in which a revolutionary Jewess, who is studying to be a violinist, refuses to lead the playing of "God Save the Tsar" in *Darkest Russia* and is publicly humiliated with a lashing while bound to a post for her act of defiance. Starring the popular Alice Brady, the film was distributed by World in April 1917, *after* the March abdication of the Tsar. In *Rasputin, The Black Monk*, released later in October with Montague Love in the title role, it is clear that the Romanoff dynasty, although the immediate members of the Royal Family are given fictitious names, had become fair game in American motion pictures. More importantly, the Romanoffs' legitimacy was seriously undermined by their intimate real-life association with Grigori Rasputin, a debauched charlatan cleric.

Attacks upon the Tsar's German-born wife and Rasputin were quite vitriolic after America's entrance into World War I. Though no nihilists appear in the film, a First National release from early 1918, *The Fall of the Romanoffs*, actually portrays the two collaborating with the German enemies of their nation. Rasputin (Edward Connelly), whose filthy appearance "with knotted hair and tangled beard" is mimicked in this high-budgeted Herbert Brenon production, conveniently conforms to the negative anarchist stereotype and thus was a perfect villain. The Tsarina's treachery could also serve to link related Nihilist films to the anti-militarism motif in certain Capital vs. Labor films. For example, *Arms and the Woman*, a late 1916 Astra/Pathé feature release, suggested capitalist exploitation of the World War was exacerbating domestic social conflict.[103]

By mostly romanticizing revolution, Nihilist films avoid the trouble of trying to identify specific groups and political parties, or even making ideological definitions. Youthful, attractive bomb throwers blowing

The Fall of the Romanoffs (Iliodor Picts/First National, 1917): An ad for a high-budget film that actually centered upon the story of the notorious Rasputin, and his evil influence upon the Tsar's family.

up the subordinates of an odious autocratic regime were heroic, and female activists were exotically titillating. These people were saving Russia from corrupted Tsarism. Because they were Russians, not Americans, they could be more comfortably sacrificed, for dramatic effect, in the name (usually to be inferred) of democracy. Like the famous bare-breasted French revolutionary waving the tricolor with one hand and holding a musket in the other, atop the corpses of her fallen comrades on the Paris barricades of 1830, immortalized by Delacroix's "Liberty on the Barricades (Le 28 Juillet)," these liberated women, sometimes sexually sullied Jewesses, were waving bombs as well as other weapons. Figuratively baring their breasts for the cause and only implicitly the blood-red flag of revolution, these radicalized ladies frequently exploited their sexual attractions to lure the repugnant enemy of the people to his well-deserved destruction.

The very title of another film, *Beneath the Czar* (Solax, 1914), a four-reel directorial effort by Alice Guy Blaché, implies physical suffering under the Tsar. It also invites associations with Christian martyrs meeting in the Catacombs of Rome, since the nihilists (coyly labeled "Reformers" in this film's titles) literally conspire to undermine the regime in subterranean headquarters. Anna Pavlova, a beautiful young woman of the liberal propertied classes played by Claire Whitney, eventually exacts revenge upon the aristocratic Tsarist secret police chief who had tortured her father before her eyes, reminiscent of *Queen of the Nihilists* and *The Cossack Whip*. After tricking the villainous Tsarist official into placing himself under her control, Anna binds him with an explosive device to the same pillar upon which her father was brutally killed. Following the secret police chief being blown to smithereens, she flees to the United States, thus uniting the escape and familial revenge motifs.

Another example of Tsarist atrocities—which also links the Russian ruling family and the royal family of Germany—occurs in *The Silent Man* (Lubin, 1915). Falsely accused of being a nihilist, the red, black and orange Romanoff double-headed eagle, similar to that of the Hohenzollerns, had been branded on the chest of a Russian prince. Years later, having survived being cast adrift upon the sea, the now-insane "silent man" is a gruesome visual reminder of the barbarism carried-out in the name of the Romanoff dynasty.

The Cossack Whip, one of the best surviving examples of the Nihilist genre, incorporating many innovative screen crossing wipes, was directed by John Collins. An Edison Studio "Super Feature," with tinted scenes, released in the fall of 1916, it balanced righteous revolutionaries with a stereotypical degenerate middle-aged official (aided by a sinister "oriental" lackey) who rapes and then whips the heroine's sister to death. The audience appeal of the revolutionary Darya is maximized by having her portrayed by Viola Dana, an alluring, dark-haired, teenaged screen star. In the final reel, the wronged young woman exacts revenge by killing the lascivious "fiend" with his "oppressor's scourge"! Darya and her lover then flee to America in the escape tradition—the film concluding with an iris out upon the two embracing on the ship's bridge as they sail past the Statue of Liberty.

As noted earlier, this flight to freedom across the ocean is a recurring motif in the Nihilist genre, i.e., *The Girl Nihilist* (Manhattan, 1908), *Waiter No. 5* (Biograph, 1910); *The Dancer's Ruse* (Biograph, 1915). Nihilist films repeatedly reinforce the theme of people coming to the United States to flee tyranny; to be free of the social limitations imposed by a class-dominated society. The cinematic nihilists make their declarations of personal freedom by proclaiming their opposition to the stifling climate of Tsarist autocracy. After having proven their commitment to political reform, they have earned the right of refuge in the best of all democratic countries, the promised land of America—but only if their violent activities are abandoned at the point of embarkation. If not, they could become the despised "foreign-seeming anarchists" discussed earlier. Films like *Waiter No. 5* and *In Exile* (Selig, 1912) pointedly highlight aristocratic families affected by nihilism fleeing to America and becoming humble, hard-working citizens, paragons of assimilation.

In another manifestation of the American "family of man" myth, *The Sowers* portrays members of the Russian nobility actively conspiring with revolutionaries from other social classes to help end the Tsarist oppression of their people—as stated in its forward: "the first step toward a Republic." *The Sowers*, a spring 1916 feature directed by William C. DeMille and produced by Lasky-Paramount, represents a significant *shift* in American motion pictures, suggesting an endorsement of the termination of Tsarism. The Tsar orders a marriage of state for the protagonist Prince Paul Alexis, played by popular leading man Thomas Meighan—a forced marriage between an aristocratic advocate of a democratic Russia, who loves a commoner (portrayed by Blanche Sweet), and a degenerate female member of the nobility who symbolizes both the moral and political bankruptcy of the regime.[104] Princess Tanya is induced to spy on her new democracy-loving husband, but pays for this perfidy with her life. Cross-class solidarity in opposition to the regime is created by showing a Jewish peddler and a middle-class/radical intellectual book seller as being major co-conspirators with the revolutionary aristocrats. Additionally, the internal spy network of the Russian chief of police in the film may have created an associative linkage with the growing concern in America after August 1914 about German espionage agents operating within the United States. The cinematic characterization of the secret police and domestic spies is virtually identical.

The final negative component in the Nihilist film genre is the wartime introduction of the theme of collusion between representatives of the Kaiser and the Tsar, such as takes place in *Anton the Terrible*, another 1916 Lasky-Paramount production directed by William C. DeMille. In fact, Anton, a diabolical member of the Tsarist government traitorously spying for the Germans, is played by veteran stage and screen actor Theodore Roberts, renowned for his roles as patriarchs and dominant heavies.

The employment by the Okrana of informers or spies, the carrying out of pogroms/massacres of innocent civilians, and their extensive use of the notorious flesh-peeling knout bear distinct similarities to the cinematic portrayal of German "frightfulness" in occupied Belgium. The Teutonic demon wartime American audiences would later "love to hate," Erich von Stroheim, actually played a Russian secret police lieutenant in *Panthea*, a Selznick production released in January 1917.

There evolved during 1916–17 a theme of the menace of all autocracies to democracy. The royal familial bridges between Russia and Germany were too suspicious to many Americans. In fact, one impediment to U.S. entrance into the World War was an unwillingness of many Americans to ally themselves with Tsarist Russia—a problem only eliminated by the February 1917 Republican Revolution and the abdication of Nicholas II the following month.

After late 1916 only a few American films would appear, most notably World studio's April 1917 release *Darkest Russia*, that still positively depicted Russian revolutionaries who violently opposed the Tsarist government. This should not appear surprising, since on April 6, 1917 the United States formally declared war on Germany, thereby joining the recently formed "Provisional Government" of Russia in her World War alliance with France and Britain.

The various generic components of radicalism that had evolved in American films throughout the decade preceding the October 1917 Soviet Revolution were now largely in place. All that was needed to fully establish the new anti-communist genre was the amalgamation of additional elements and stereotypes introduced during the war propaganda paroxysm of 1917–18 and the subsequent hysteria directed at Bolshevism while the infamous Red Scare of 1918–20 ran its course.

However, what is truly remarkable is the intricacy of the genre intermingling that took place in the years between 1909 and 1917 and the high profile cinematic attention directed toward the struggle against the abuses of ruling elites. For an ephemeral historical moment upon America's movie screens, the working-class and assorted politically marginalized Others were given a "voice" with which to address the nation.

2. The Red Scourge on Film

From Wartime Xenophobia to Being in the Vanguard of Anti-Bolshevik Hysteria, 1918–1920

To be a red in the summer of 1919 was worse than being a Hun in the summer of 1917.—John Dos Passos, 1919 (1930)

[A] great city purged itself of the Red Scourge.—studio promo for The World Aflame *(1919)*

During the 1918–20 Red Scare, the cinematic "reality" of Bolshevism was largely established through images and stories. Motion pictures, with considerable help from the popular press, rapidly infused life into Bolshevism for the public—personifying and mythologizing abstract political concepts and ideologies in intense melodramatic conflicts and stereotypes. The characteristics of the Bolshevik Other became a prototype of demonic vileness, drowning actualities in a tidal wave of anti-Communist invective.[1] And whenever fears of radicalism resurfaced in the nation, most notably during the Cold War period following the conclusion of World War II, these prefabricated negative images and stories of the Red Scare era reemerged.

Certainly the movies never made any attempt "to understand what the word 'bolshevism' actually meant or what its relationship was to other isms...."[2] In fact, by 1920, "Bolshevik," "Bolsheviki," "Bolshevism," "Bolshevist," "Bolshie," had become simply terms of derision in the popular vernacular. Note, for example, Sinclair Lewis' repeated satirical usage of Bolshevik in his classic 1922 novel, *Babbitt*, and its casual pejorative appearance as late as 1937 in a scene with a smalltime gangster from the Warner Brothers B-film *Midnight Court*.

From the spring of 1918 through the fall of 1920, the American motion picture industry was in the forefront of the popular media helping to shape, channel and sustain the nation's collective loathing toward foreign "enemies" and domestic radicals. The frequent portrayal of collusion between the two intensified these antagonistic sentiments. Variations on the preestablished radical stereotype mingled and hardened; the Bolshevik was often a crazed, bearded bomb thrower who was exploiting liquor abuse by immigrants or workers to encourage radicalism. At the same time, elements of earlier Nihilist films, like the Russian predilection for conspiratorial organizations and political violence and the decadence of representatives of the Russian state, were reconfigured into a new ideological guise. In addition, the negative alien Others tied to Bolshevism came to include the radical "new woman," spineless intellectuals, malevolent Jews and so-called "free lovers."

The zenith of Red Scare hysteria was reached between August 1919 and February 1920 — the public's emotional gamut stretching from abject fear to bitter scorn, to petty ridicule and cruel burlesque. Two films released at the beginning of 1920 suggest the range of emotive attack: a major feature-length work that drew together the melodramatic images, stereotypes, and stories that had developed in this genre, *Dangerous Hours* (Lasky/Paramount-Artcraft), and an unidentified animated cartoon depicting the actual shipboard deportation from the United States on December 19, 1919, of 249 "undesirable" radical aliens.

Crudely capturing the nation's emotions at the time, the cartoon concludes with New York's iconic statue of Miss Liberty bending over and sternly rebuking the squealing, insect-like deportees passing by below, as they stand crowded aboard the ex-Army transport USS *Buford*, labeled the "Soviet Ark" by the press. The cargo of "Reds" includes an unnamed bushy-mustached caricature of the notorious anarchist Alexander Berkman and an equally unflattering caricature of the likewise unnamed radical ideologue Emma Goldman.[3]

Dangerous Hours, a highly sophisticated propaganda film for its time, encapsulates anti-radical demonology in juxtaposition with American iconography to create the perfect on-screen Red Scare era political/moral dichotomy. The movie subjects the headstrong hero, handsome John King, to temptation. A recent college graduate, King's naiveté and Wilsonian desire to "save humanity" will lead

to his being politically manipulated by a sensuous dark-haired bohemian named Sophia Guerni (possibly foreign-born) and a bloodthirsty, licentious bearded Russian Bolshevik called Boris Blotchi.

Through saintly patience, democratic righteousness, capitalistic common sense and moral equanimity, John's sweetheart, the virginal Mary (who happens to own and run the shipyard the Bolshevik-led band attacks) wins back the romantic heart and political soul of her fallen man. Having scorned the promiscuous "new woman" for damning America, John proceeds to annihilate the rampaging radicals and then beg for and receive absolution from America-the-beautiful Mary.

How was it that in less than three years, the pre–1917 American cinematic representation of Russian revolutionaries and domestic labor militancy was transformed from one of profound ambivalence to one of almost total intolerance?

With the entrance of the United States into the World War in April 1917, Americans came to view any domestic opposition to participation as subversive. A Sedition Act was passed the following year that was primarily aimed at radical aliens, many of whom were politically suspect or linked with the new German enemy in the eyes of the general public. Animosity directed against the vicious "Huns," pacifists and Americans believed to be in sympathy with Germany reached hysterical levels by late 1917. One of the specific manifestations of such fears was a concern over sabotage and strikes in the strategic materials industries and in plants manufacturing military equipment. Beginning as early as the latter half of 1916, before the United States became formally involved in the World War, these fears began to be transferred to the movie screens of America.

From the outbreak of the "Great War" in August 1914, Germany was allied with Austria-Hungary, which incorporated within its borders millions of disaffected Slavs. Not surprisingly, then, as early as 1916 two films show European anarchists in league with German foreign agents plotting to blow up American munitions plants supplying arms to opposing belligerents. In both motion pictures, Astra's *Arms and the Woman* and Universal-IMP's two reel short, *The Circular Room*, the Americanized girl related to the alien evil-doers attempts to prevent the bombing. The heroine of the former film fails. Yet, *Arms and The Woman* is unique because its pacifist theme subsumes its inherent anti-radicalism.

During these war years, the Nihilist film genre began to undergo change, some of the films taking on a sinister new twist with the evil Tsarist official traitorously conspiring with the German enemies of Russia—and, by extension, of Russia's two most important wartime allies, Britain and France. This phenomenon is particularly pronounced in *Anton the Terrible* (Lasky/Paramount, 1916), *Rasputin, the Black Monk* (World, 1917) and *The Rose of Blood* (Fox, 1917). In the first motion picture the corrupt and brutal police official, Anton Kazoff, is compelled to commit suicide by accused revolutionaries after his spying for the Germans is discovered. A considerable portion of the second film's plot centers around the notorious Rasputin and the German-born Tsarina attempting to arrange a separate peace with the Kaiser. And in the third motion picture, a murderous radical female played by Theda Bara, in the tradition of the Nihilist genre, blows up a "Royal Council" of Tsarist government ministers, including her husband, for betraying Mother Russia to Germany.

Collusion between the Russians and the Germans is further dealt with in several transitional works released during the first half of 1918. All associate the Tsarist autocracy attacked in earlier Nihilist films with Russian officials treasonously conspiring with their German foes. A good "American agitator" in *The Firebrand* (Fox, 1918) is portrayed as the victim of Tsarist mistreatment, while imprisoned in the Slavic wastes of Siberia. Following the February revolution, forces of the new Kerensky regime save the

American from pro-German Tsarist agents. With the United States as the first country to extend diplomatic recognition to Alexander Kerensky's Provisional Government, this early melding of hatred of Russian with German autocracy was a natural tactic in motion pictures. Hence, a promo for *The Firebrand* appearing in a *Moving Picture World* review suggested placing a "crown" under a banner on which should be lettered: "This crown was once the Czar's. It now belongs to the people...."[4]

The Legion of Death, one of Metro's Special Deluxe Productions, directed by Tod Browning, also presents the shaky republican government of Russia as threatened by venal officials of the discredited Romanoff autocracy conspiring with the Hohenzollern autocracy. A patriotic women's "Battalion of Death" is saved from imminent military and sexual dishonor, and the potential German domination of the Russian motherland is prevented, only by the last minute intervention of Allied troops. By the time of the film's release, in late March 1918, British Royal Marines had actually landed in Murmansk to oppose the Bolsheviks, who had just formally removed Russia from the war as one of the major concessions to the Central Powers (Germany and Austria-Hungary) in the Treaty of Brest-Litovsk.[5]

In fact, just as Tsarist "autocracy" was repeatedly attacked in pre–1917 Nihilist films, the "autocracy" of the Kaiser's regime was likewise disparaged in wartime films. For example, the term is specifically used in a pejorative context about half a dozen times in *My Four Years in Germany* (First National).

As many as 10 percent of 1917 American feature-length films and about 15 percent of 1918 releases were explicitly war-related.[6] A number of these motion pictures contributed to war hysteria in the United States by portraying atrocities committed by beastly, militaristic "Kaiserites." Significantly, they frequently depicted forces of the German army (wearing the evocatively phallic spike-helmet/"pickelhaube") invading villages in Belgium and France and then killing, raping and otherwise brutalizing the civilian population. In *Private Pete* (Famous Players-Lasky, 1918), French villagers are shot by German troops and also used as human shields from Allied shellfire.[7] D. W. Griffith's *Hearts of the World* (1918) portrays his French heroine, "The Little Disturber" (Dorothy Gish), being flogged with a cat-o'-nine-tails while performing forced labor in the fields and, later, barely escaping rape at the hands of a vicious Hun officer. *To Hell With the Kaiser* (Screen Classics-Metro, 1918) contains scenes of German troops sacking Belgium, including sexually violating nuns.[8] And *The Kaiser, Beast of Berlin* (Renowned Pictures-Jewel, 1918), among numerous other unspeakable atrocities portrayed, shows the killing of Belgian babies by German occupiers.[9]

Wartime films also regularly featured German spies and/or their domestic associates operating in the United States, creating a fear of an "enemy within" and implicitly reinforcing the concept of the dangers of porous borders/open immigration into the country.[10] Two September 1918 releases with similarly suggestive titles, and which feature "Hun intrigue," strongly emphasize this point: *The Hun Within* (Paramount-Artcraft/Famous Players-Lasky) and *Huns Within Our Gates* (Arrow Film).[11] The latter film, re-edited and retitled *Commercial Pirates*, was rereleased in March 1919. This 1919 version probably de-emphasized the German connection to espionage activities, while foregrounding the "alien" aspects of the evil-doers.[12]

Many of the anti-radical generic components that would fully manifest themselves during the Red Scare appear in a single motion picture, *Draft 258*, released by Metro late in 1917, after the Bolshevik revolution. This seven "part," or reel, production was co-written and directed by top-ranking filmmaker William Christy Cabanne. *Draft 258* features a German spy conspiring with a Russian anarchist in the United States. Together with their compatriots, they

secretly plot to destroy a government factory building warplanes. Meanwhile, an American family is riven by the introduction of military conscription in July 1917.

Draft 258 opens with a revealing dichotomy: a shot of the socialist-influenced brother Matthew, idly reading during his work hours about the "repressive power" of the state, is juxtaposed with a shot of his salesgirl sister Mary, played by popular actress Mabel Tallaferro, on her break studying Woodrow Wilson's *History of the American People*. Matthew later takes his patriotic younger sister to a public meeting at which the new draft law is vociferously denounced.[13] Through the liberal dispersal of his German gold, foreign agent van Bierman has arranged the meeting. Bierman's surname also suggests a symbolic coffin in which the villains wish to bury the democratic institutions of the United States. By employing the loaded gambit of linking American socialists and Russian radicalism with German subvention/manipulation, *Draft 258* represents a prototypical format for the explicitly anti-Bolshevik films that would begin appearing in less than a year.

Mary, whose boyfriend has already joined the army, then disrupts the gathering by rousing most of the men to the defense of the Stars and Stripes, including brother Matthew—the symbolism is dramatically visualized through having a superimposed image of the German flag dissolve before the arch-iconic American flag. In a series of flashbacks, the "little woman" invokes America's most famous military encounters, including Bunker Hill, the Alamo and San Juan Hill.[14] Having meanwhile learned of the plot against the plane factory, Matthew tries to intercept the saboteurs. Mary's boyfriend, accompanied by his cavalry troop of "Rough Riders" and a lady Secret Service agent, come to Matthew's aid. A second mission is conducted to rescue Matthew's abducted sister, arriving just in time at the conspirators' wooded headquarters to prevent an infuriated van Bierman from violating "true-hearted" Mary. *Draft 258* concludes with the

The Little American (Fox, 1917): **In 1916 one of Mary Pickford's film roles featured her struggle for economic survival while working for a harsh capitalist and his womanizing son. But in this World War I propaganda classic golden-haired Mary was forced to fight for her honor with leering German soldiers.**

Mother, a San Juan Hill hero's widow, proudly gazing upon a masculinized Matthew and her new son-in-law, both of whom will now fight for the same cause for which her husband died.[15]

The events of 1918 certainly mark a historical watershed that would forever change America's place on the world stage. At the beginning of the year the United States was still the ungainly industrial behemoth across the sea. But by the end of 1918, the massive introduction of American arms and men on the Western Front proved decisive in the final defeat of Imperial Germany and her allies.

Nonetheless, the American people were not easily shaken loose from their traditional parochialism. For instance, although the United States had formally entered the World War in April 1917, conscription had not gotten fully underway until September. Mobilization could proceed at a leisurely pace because no belligerent power directly threatened the country's borders. But tangible enemies were still required by America's population in order to stoke the flames of their patriotism. German-Americans were an obvious target for chauvinistic abuse. Yet most of the nation's millions of citizens of German descent were highly assimilated. Thus, increasingly, *any* so-called "hyphenated Americans" (a term for recent immigrants attributed to Teddy Roosevelt, but also exploited by Woodrow Wilson and the

Democrats, particularly during the 1916 presidential campaign) were deemed unpatriotic by the public and became objects of suspicion and even of physical violence.[16] Attacks also were made on the major vocal opponents of America's war effort. Aside from those who were genuine pacifists, these were mainly socialists, active members of the militant I.W.W. and anarchists, such as the Russian-born Emma Goldman.[17]

Anyone who belonged to or sympathized with such radical organizations was also suspected of involvement with secret agents of the German government. For instance, it was commonly asserted in the wartime media that the Industrial Workers of the World's initials actually stood for "Imperial Wilhelm's Warriors."[18]

As was noted earlier, most Americans during the course of the war, came to demand a total commitment to the cause of victory against their new foreign enemies. No resistance to this effort was tolerated. With "100 percent Americans" necessary on the home front to insure that General Pershing's "Crusaders" on the Western Front would make the world safe for democracy, any opposition to this cause was considered tantamount to treason. The democratic concept of a "loyal opposition" was largely abandoned for the duration of the war and throughout the period of the ensuing Red Scare. For instance, such a real-life individual as anti-war Senator Robert M. La Follette from Wisconsin was caricatured in *The Prussian Cur* (Fox, 1918) and former Secretary of State, William Jennings Bryan, an avowed pacifist, was indirectly attacked in *My Four Years in Germany*.

During 1918, additional factors contributed to the xenophobia that by then had gripped the nation. First, the new Soviet government had signed in March at Brest-Litovsk a separate peace pact with Germany. This punitive treaty not only removed the Russian "Giant" from the war as an American ally, but also freed hundreds of thousands of battle-hardened German soldiers for transfer to the Western Front. As a direct result of these developments, by the spring-summer of 1918 the newly deployed American Expeditionary Force (AEF) was fighting and dying in significant numbers on the battlefields of France. Finally, in late summer, American troops began landing in Vladivostok and Archangel as part of a major Entente military operation directed at undermining the incipient Soviet state. Five films released in 1918–19 specifically refer to Allied intervention in Russia, including *For the Freedom of the East* (Betzwood Film/Goldwyn, 1918) and *Common Property* (Universal, 1919).[19]

The mass media in the United States significantly contributed to this growing anti-Bolshevik hysteria during 1918 by repeatedly questioning the patriotism of aliens with radical connections. Furthermore, the media regularly and interchangeably linked anarchists, the I.W.W. and American socialists with the Bolsheviks. There developed a general lack of distinction in society, as in film, between anarchism and Bolshevism; hence, the deportation of anarchists to Russia. As a matter of fact, Anarchism is coded in 15/17 percent of the Red Scare–oriented motion pictures released between 1918 and 1920; seven are matched in some way with Bolshevism—including two 1919 productions, *The Burning Question* (Catholic Art) and *The New Moon* (Select). By the spring of 1918 there had also begun to appear in the newspapers and other popular media many laudatory accounts of vigilante-style actions by self-proclaimed Yankee superpatriots, such as forced flag-kissings, imposed upon individuals whose loyalties were deemed suspect.[20]

An interesting film manifestation of this phenomenon appears in the lengthy 1918 release, *My Four Years in Germany*. After delivering a formal complaint to German Foreign Minister von Jagow, protesting the May 1915 U-Boat sinking of the passenger liner *Lusitania*, American Ambassador Gerard ominously intimates the fate awaiting an alleged 500,000 German "reservists"/sympathizers prepared to rise within the United

Newspaper cartoon—captioned: "The I.W.W. and the Other Features That Go with It." This 1917 political cartoon from the *New York Globe* clearly indicates the linkage in the public mind between the Wobblies' labor activism and advancing the cause of America's German enemy.

States: "We have five hundred and one thousand lamp-posts where they'll find themselves hanging by night!"

Throughout the 1918–20 period, the film industry in the United States produced at least ninety-one fictional feature-length works that dealt, often confrontationally, with domestic radicalism, including labor militancy and socialism, or with the new Bolshevik regime.[21] For example, six films released during 1918 attacked supposed collaboration between America's German enemies and crafty Bolsheviks, including *The Firebrand* and *For the Freedom of the East*.[22] By mid–1919 a satiric Metro production, entitled *The Uplifters*, would strongly disparage both domestic radicals and Bolshevism.

As this unrestrained xenophobia grew, the Hollywood-based studio system was beginning to solidify at this time as well. This had been dramatically accelerated by the World War, wartime propaganda, the rapid expansion of the domestic movie audience and, simultaneously, the significant reduction of foreign-made competition. The resulting emergence of large film companies run by entrepreneurial studio executives (dubbed "movie moguls" by the popular press) and their now highly paid contract directors and matinee idols probably contributed to a much more pro-capitalist stance in the cinema, with attacks on radicals used to discredit any questioning of the system.[23]

One form of such questioning, of course, would be labor militancy. Despite the fact that evidence of wartime sabotage was very limited, an unprecedented degree of labor unrest had occurred during 1917, with nearly 4500 work stoppages. Strike activity declined throughout most of 1918 but would then explode with renewed intensity in 1919.[24] Consequently, any accident at a war manufacturing plant quickly raised suspicions of treason. Those few domestic radicals who continued to advocate violent strike actions were stigmatized as deliberately aiding or being manipulated by the nation's enemies. To make this perfectly clear, the majority of films portraying such activities in

America specifically identified the responsible culprits as enemy agents or as individuals with foreign-sounding names in the pay of German spies. Eight of the twelve films released during 1918 and coded under Spy-Saboteur reveal the "Hun's Hand" behind their plots. Their titles include *The Girl of Today*, a Vitagraph "Blue Ribbon Feature," and Fox's *Mr. Logan, U.S.A.* Directly linked to German agents, the I.W.W. was also viciously attacked in the latter film. Not surprisingly, there was a very high incidence of thematic overlapping among the 1918 motion pictures coded Spy-Saboteur, the three coded I.W.W. and the sixteen coded German. The United States government further encouraged these and other xenophobic outbursts through its wartime propaganda, the so-called Creel Committee, formally known as the Committee of Public Information, or CPI, and by the passage of the Espionage and Sedition Acts—the extra-legal powers of which would be frequently abused in order to suppress domestic radicalism.[25]

The thirty-one germane motion pictures of 1918 fall mainly into two groups—those dealing with European enemy powers and/or Allied military intervention in Russia, and those centering around German agents or domestic radicals, frequently in league with each other, who instigate labor unrest or plot acts of sabotage against America's vital defense industries. In the foreign-set films, the authoritarianism of the Tsarist regime in pre–1917 movies was supplanted first by the Kaiser's Germany as a propaganda target and then by revolutionary Bolshevik autocracy, sometimes acting in tandem with imperialist Wilhelmine Germany.

In a number of pertinent films, "Germanized" indigenous radicals are patently portrayed as surrogates for the military forces of the Second Reich. Two examples from 1918 are *The Prussian Cur* and *The Road to France* (World). A major subplot of writer-director Raoul Walsh's *The Prussian Cur* deals with labor agitators and German agents, led by the descriptively named Wolff von Eidel, working together to incite a strike

The Yellow Dog **(Universal-Jewel, 1918): One example from an ad campaign promoting this film—** *Motion Picture News* **(9/7/18). It viciously condemned as German agents people who obstructed the war effort, singling-out socialist-influenced members of labor for particular abuse. The image makes a none-too-subtle suggestion regarding the desired fate for such individuals.**

at a military aircraft plant. In the latter motion picture, a German secret agent likewise attempts to disrupt production of transport ships, only to be thwarted by the movie's muscular star, Carlyle Blackwell.

America's bout of anti-foreign/radical hysteria did not dissipate with the formal conclusion of the World War on November 11, 1918. In fact, anti-radical alien sentiment was sustained as the collective vituperation and outrageous atrocity stories so recently directed towards the Kaiser and the forces of Imperial Germany ("Prussianism") were refocused upon the revolutionary Bolshevik regime in Russia and anyone who espoused their cause in the United States. Numerous films set out to illustrate the basic themes of a typical polemical tract published in 1919 by the American Protective League (APL), a self-described secret "volunteer army" organized with government approval to combat foreign espionage:

> The mischief makers of all classes make recruits for Bolsheviki—socialists, radical I.W.W.'s, anarchists, the red flag rabble of every country united in the general ignorant greed of the wolf pack.... It will grow out of the ... discontented foreigners unassimilated in this country. We must expect it naturally to come from these and from the pro-Germans in this country, because those people never have been satisfied with what we did in the war.[26]

Though the APL's amateur sleuths never found a single real spy, their cohorts in film had much better luck.[27] In many Red Scare movies, one often saw "home wrecking and incendiary scenes much like the Hunnish demonstrations shown in recent war dramas."[28] This fear of Bolshevism was further intensified in late 1918 and early 1919 because of additional communist outbreaks in Europe and the declaration in favor of world revolution made at the Moscow-dominated communist Third International in March 1919. In addition, as part of an Allied intervention force in Russia, some U. S. troops were actually engaging in limited combat with the Red Army.[29]

That an undeclared film war had been initiated against Bolshevism before the end of 1918 is intimated in the lead editorial of a December issue of the *Motion Picture News*, an industry trade journal: "This War and the Next." The writer suggested that in the postwar "class strife to come," the members of the film industry resolved to "never aid the production, distribution, or exhibition of a picture that directly or indirectly gives strength to the venom of the *bolshevik* or cripples the arm of Uncle Sam in his trying task of reconstruction."[30] In this new time of tensions, the increasingly more centralized film capitalism knew which side it was on.

As the end of 1918 approached, some Americans also saw the postwar peace as being potentially threatened by a defeated Germany secretly colluding with the Bolsheviks in order to manipulate events in Russia. The logic was that if the Germans could acquire a significant degree of influence over the vast country after its political collapse, Germany would be freed from the constraints imposed upon it by the Armistice and the formal peace treaty being negotiated at Versailles. This concern is addressed in several contemporary articles appearing in *The Literary Digest*. For instance, the use of so-called "German gold" to undermine Russia is discussed in a winter 1919 article entitled "Bolsheviki in the United States."[31] The plots of *For the Freedom of the East*, *The Legion of Death* and *Bonds of Honor* (Mutual, 1919) deal with this topic head-on.

In subsequent films, autocracy was also to be attributed to the Bolsheviks, now in active support of the Kaiser's Germany. This change and the fear of further defections from the Allies is cinematically expressed in Goldwyn's October 1918 release, *For the Freedom of the East*. This film justifies Allied intervention in Siberia by presenting a bizarre plot in which the Bolshevik "hordes" and evil Huns are prevented from raising a revolutionary army in a politically unstable China by the unified efforts of a patriotic Chinese princess with martial arts skills and an American Secret Service man! A corrupted

Chinese viceroy ("Who Loved German Gold") is promised he will be made ruler of China in exchange for helping the Bolsheviks complete their conquest of Russia. To emphasize the nefarious nature of the conspirators' agreement, the audience is shown a photograph of a "scrap of paper" that would "Belgiumize" Asia.[32] The German agent, Franz von Richtman, was intended to evoke audience associations with the real-life ambassador to Mexico, Heinrich von Eckhardt, thereby creating parallels with the notorious 1917 Zimmermann telegram affair.

As revolutionaries along with autocrats became the enemies in wartime foreign-placed motion pictures, indigenous radicals were increasingly the center of trouble in the United States. *Life's Greatest Problem*, a J. Stuart Blackton production which premiered in New York City right before the November 1918 Armistice, implied that loyal laborers on the home front are also soldiers—that they too are fighting, in this case against domestic radicalism, to make the world safe for democracy.[33] Labor agitators, some of whom are specifically identified as members of the I.W.W., were portrayed traitorously resisting the Selective Service's "Work-or-Fight" order of May 1918 and plotting to blow up a vital American shipyard.[34] Actual footage of Wilson Administration officials meeting with workers at a ship's launching, intercut with scenes showing members of *Life's Greatest Problem*'s cast, appears at the film's conclusion, apparently underlining the stalwart patriotism of all involved in the motion picture.

In *Mr. Logan, U.S.A.*, released by Fox in September 1918, Western movie star Tom Mix plays Jimmy Logan, a Secret Service agent in the guise of the quintessential Stetson-wearing American. The title, *Mr. Logan, U.S.A.*, implies that Jimmy is a *soldier* in the iconic uniform of America's mythic western hero. This clean-living cowboy crosses a No Man's Land in the southwest and enters Sunrise, a wide-open mining town occupied and dominated by the forces under vice kingpin J. Alexander Gage, whose real name is Adolph

Meier (German-Jew?; actor Val Paul). Headquartered at the town's "Opera House," a venue featuring gambling and "showgirls," Gage has used his alluring German gold to purchase the services of an army of local collaborators, including prostitutes, a cocaine-addicted rabble-rouser and his I.W.W. cohorts. In fact, after agitator Crosby assures Gage at a secret meeting that he can "arrange a strike any time," the scene concludes with the German paying Crosby in gold coins.[35] Their object is to disrupt government-contracted deliveries of strategic tungsten—a treasonous act in the context of wartime America.[36] During a meeting at the "White Elephant" bar (a place no longer desirable to American society, but highly valued by Gage), an "anarchist type" harangues the miners to declare a strike. Gage and some of his wildcatting associates meanwhile prepare to sabotage the mineshaft with a dynamite charge.[37] Entering the saloon, Logan rallies the "loyal Americans" among Sunrise's miners to defeat the German-led radicals, "hired enemies" whose cynical bravado is "breeding malice and discontent." At the end, the surviving I.W.W. members are literally corralled by whip-wielding patriots and then herded onto a freight train to be shipped out of town! (This sadistic conclusion of *Mr. Logan, U.S.A.* was based upon a well-publicized incident that had actually taken place in Bisbee, Arizona, in July 1917, during which hundreds of striking copper miners were forcibly transported in boxcars from whence they were later dumped off in the New Mexico desert.[38]) Meanwhile, Jimmy Logan, with Mix employing some of his famous "straight shooting" and "daredevil" horse-riding stunts, has saved the mine owner's fair-haired daughter from the lecherous German agent in addition to liberating the town.

Only a few motion pictures that directly dealt with communism were released during the winter of 1919, but this was little more than a brief respite from the anti-Bolshevik excesses that would appear on America's movie screens during the next year and a

Mr. Logan, U.S.A. (Fox, 1918): Cowboy star Tom Mix, playing a wartime federal agent in disguise, saves the heroine from a lecherous German agent, who has paid domestic labor agitators to stir up trouble in a western mining town.

half. By the early spring of 1919 the open hostility of the film establishment toward Bolshevism was made unequivocal in the weekly comment section of the *Exhibitor's Herald*, written by editor Martin J. Quigley: "In no way so effectively and graphically can the evils of this movement be impressed upon the masses as by the motion picture."[39] After catching its breath, the industry unleashed a springtime flood of anti-Bolshevik films.

There was a similar revulsion expressed toward the new Bolshevik regime in most of the other Western nations. For instance, in addition to British and French troops intervening alongside American Doughboys in Russia, the newly independent Polish state engaged in a full scale war with the Red Army during 1919–20.[40]

At least one 1919 American film, *Boots*, a top-of-the-line production released by Famous Players-Lasky in March, clearly reflects the international aspects of the Red Scare. Dorothy Gish's eponymous English "slavey" in *Boots* becomes a symbolic soldier of the king in the postwar struggle against the Bolsheviks.[41] While cleaning the shoes of guests at the dilapidated London inn where she is employed, Boots is responsible for removing the filth generated by the tunneling activities of the female Bolshevik, described as a sculptress, who keeps vermin in her studio. The female radical also creates "horrible" statues—like her revolutionary acts—in secret, away from the eyes of the public. Additionally, she is shown to be sexually loose with a mysterious student lodger played by Richard Barthelmess, really the hero working incognito. Heroine Boots later crashes through the basement floor exposing a subterranean Bolshevik bombing plot to assassinate Allied leaders gathered to discuss terms of the forthcoming Versailles Peace Treaty. After overcoming the "Amazonian" Red and disposing of her ticking "engine of death," the petite Boots is able to rescue Scotland Yard agent Everett White ("Whites" vs. "Reds"), the handsome man whom she has admired from afar.[42] Again, the humble, inherently loyal, worker undermines the strategies of the artistic intelligentsia *and* the Bolsheviks.

This reactionary atmosphere was sharpened in late April-early May by the anonymous mailing of a series of letter bombs to over thirty prominent Americans. Addressees on the "Bomb Honor List" included associate justice of the United States Supreme Court Oliver Wendell Holmes, Jr., and Attorney General A. Mitchell Palmer.[43] Then, there were the largest May Day demonstrations ever held in the United States.[44] Using these incidents as a pretext, the federal government and many states launched a nationwide anti-radical crackdown that blatantly and routinely ignored basic human rights. It was during the next fourteen to sixteen months that a massive wave of anti-communist/anti-militant labor hysteria swept through the country. This unique period of unrestrained public hostility and concomitant media vilification focused upon radicalism has become known as *the* Red Scare. Before these passions had begun to abate in mid–1920, the civil rights of thousands of individuals had been violated and hundreds of people had even been forcibly deported.[45]

Seventeen feature films exhibited between March and September of 1919 (an average of over two a month) contained a distinct anti-Soviet and/or anti-Revolutionary bias. Three of the more extreme of these motion pictures were: *Bolshevism on Trial* (Select), released in April; *The New Moon* (Select), released in May; *The Volcano* (W.W. Hodkinson), released in August. There was probably a direct correlation between the large number of August 1919 releases (nine) and the Independence Day/July 4th scare of a *nationwide* General Strike that some in organized labor proposed but which never materialized.[46]

American domestic problems also fueled the anti-radical themes of Red Scare films. Business and labor, both of whom had largely cooperated and prospered during the war, were determined after the Armistice to protect their respective gains.[47] The resulting power struggle, particularly as manifested by increasing

THE

GENERAL STRIKE

BY
WILLIAM D. HAYWOOD

ALSO
THE LAST WAR
BY
G.B.

I.W.W. PUBLISHING BUREAU
CHICAGO

A general strike conducted by a united working class was the dream of radicalized labor activists and one of the greatest nightmares of the capitalist establishment. This was the title page of the provocative pamphlet written by Wobbly leader William S. ("Big Bill") Haywood.

strike activity, created the actual "class strife" that popular (and filmic) anti-Bolshevism was intended to settle in favor of the wealthy.

More than a third of all topically relevant Red Scare era movie releases, are coded in the Filmography under Strike.[48] Some of the key negative buzzwords, usually linked and appearing repeatedly in the texts of these films or in explanatory literature, were "alien," "agitators," and/or "propagandists," e.g., *The Volcano*; *Virtuous Men* (S-L Picts/Ralph Ince Film, 1919); *The World Aflame* (Frank Keenan Prods/Pathé, 1919); *The Face at Your Window* (Fox, 1920). Commonly, the strike activity in these films was related to the appearance or interaction of agitators, German agents and/or Russian characters.[49]

Labor unrest in the United States had occurred throughout the war, but it had significantly accelerated by early 1919—exacerbated by the hasty termination of war contracts and the chaotically swift-paced demobilization of several million servicemen. To many Americans, events took an ominous turn in the direction of radical social revolution when on February 3rd workers declared a short-lived general strike in Seattle. Eleven of the germane films released in 1919 prominently feature strike activity, including one whose plot was directly based upon the labor disturbances in Seattle, Pathé's *The World Aflame*—produced and co-scripted by its star, the venerable Frank Keenan.[50]

One can compare the story of *The World Aflame*, purportedly depicting reality, with what actually took place during Seattle's general strike, that began as a shipyard workers' strike on January 21, 1919.[51] For instance, whereas real-life mayor Ole Hanson (1874–1940) more or less reacted to events as they evolved, hyperbolically branding the strike a "revolution," *The World Aflame* portrays millionaire manufacturer Carson Burr (played as a pure patrician type by the white-haired, crag-faced Frank Keenan) running for mayor specifically to neutralize the incipient radical influences upon labor which he has personally experienced—including the unsavory effects of a "propaganda" newspaper entitled the *Red Messenger* upon his cook and chauffeur.

The "alien" agitators are led by a dark bearded anarchist named Nicolai (as in Lenin) Poppoff, played by German-born actor Bert Sprotte. The dramatic highlight of *The World Aflame* takes place when Burr, aboard an American flag-draped streetcar accompanied by armed police, directly confronts a club-wielding mob of agitated workers and, through his convincing sloganeering, breaks the strike. To guarantee domestic tranquillity, thousands of former "Dough Boys" have also been "organized under efficient leadership" and placed on guard around the city's factories.[52]

Burr's son Theodore, named in honor

of Teddy Roosevelt, enticed by radical vamp Emma Reich, was kidnapped by the Reds in an attempt to intimidate the ultra patriotic mayor.[53] But soon after the general strike collapses, the cowed political agitators are rounded-up and compelled to hand over the injured son to his stalwart family. Arrangements are promptly made for the deportation of the so-called "Bolshevik" aliens.[54] Meanwhile, a cross-class romance has developed between daughter Roxy and Burr's chauffeur-cum-radical dupe-cum-secretary Knox.

The *general* strike as portrayed in *The World Aflame* is of one day's duration, contrary to the series of strikes that, in actuality, convulsed Seattle between January 21 and February 10, 1919. The motion picture's concentration on the more sensational transport aspects of the general strike not only distorts historical reality but accentuates a threat of paralyzing the city and thereby endangering the livelihoods of all. As uniformed civil servants, the actions of the streetcar workers proved a fortuitous link with the notorious Boston police strike—which began a month *after* the film's release. In addition to volunteer "special deputies," many of whom were Doughboy citizen-heroes, the National Guard and federal troops were called in to Seattle, yet the general strike was peacefully terminated.

The Boston police strike of September 1919 particularly disturbed the public, since the police were considered a bulwark against radicalism.[55] And many in the middle-class began to believe, further egged on by outrageous press coverage of the fall 1919 nationwide steel and coal strikes, that a radical American revolution was just around the corner.[56]

Films either never broached legitimate grievances of labor or gave them only a fleeting nod before invoking destructive agitators as the true cause of social discord—*The Road to France* and *Life's Greatest Problem* are two more prominent examples. In such films, workers, manipulated by assorted radicals and/or spy-saboteurs shaking their

POST-INTELLIGENCER, FEBRUARY 6, 1919

Newspaper cartoon—captioned: "Not in a Thousand Years!" Appearing at the height of the Seattle general strike, this political cartoon from a Seattle newspaper played upon the American concern over a Red-inspired revolution, while asserting the determination to never let it succeed in the United States. Note the stark dichotomy between the Red flag and the iconographic stars and stripes.

clenched fists against social injustices, are just as easily swayed to abandon labor interests by some vigorous flag-waving. These chauvinistic interludes are seldom delivered by fellow workers, but instead are usually presented by members of the middle-class. Labor's concerns and labor's voice, often heard in prewar films, now all but disappear.

Praise of the wealthy is accentuated by the wartime film motif of the rich man who, unable to join the army, dons overalls and temporarily enters the industrial labor force in order to do his bit for the war effort—*The Road to France*; *The Wasp* (World, 1918); *Life's Greatest Problem*; *Virtuous Men*.[57] These apprentice worker-protagonists (whose positive characterization camouflages the negative class-shaped image of hedonistic

This November 1919 print cartoon, released at the height of the Red Scare, reflected the xenophobic linkage with radicalism and its supposed threat to the forward progress of postwar American industry. Note the prominent exploitation of the stereotyped bearded, disheveled foreign anarchist/communist image. The leader of the agitators in *The World Aflame* (1919) matched the dark-bearded stereotype.

capitalists) are inevitably given the chance on screen to shine patriotically by engaging and defeating German spies and their labor agitator allies who have challenged America on the home front. This usually also involves, at an appropriately dramatic point, the physical beating of the villains.

In *The Girl from Bohemia* (Astra/Pathé), released during the summer of 1918, a liberated "shero" (played by dancing star Irene Castle), formerly of Greenwich Village, overcomes a strike mob by waving Old Glory from atop a building and fervently admonishing the workers for their misplaced loyalties. In that same year's *On the Jump* (Fox) and *The Road to France*, men deliver similarly passionate Americanism speeches to quell rebellious strikers—the musical accompanist most likely joining forces off screen with a few bars of Sousa's "Stars and Stripes," "Yankee Doodle," etc. Social class, though seldom dwelled upon, remains a prominent factor. In the latter film,

for example, hero Tom Whitney (he-man star Carlyle Blackwell) is finally moved to challenge the swarthy soapbox-mounted "spellbinder" Hector Winter, secretly in the pay of the Germans, who has been haranguing shipyard workers with "anarchy undiluted," after Winter points Tom out as "another of the damned rich men's spawn."[58] More importantly, clean-cut Tom's physical assertiveness exercised to visually reinforce his counter-arguments was particularly reassuring to a middle-class audience that tended, at the time, to associate brawn with morally healthy manhood—yet another foil to effete intellectualism and to those who harbored dangerously unclean political points of view.

Americanism speeches are, in essence, rhetorical lashings of Reds, wherein the persons delivering them constitute a cinematic version of the wartime "Four Minute Men," individuals organized by the government to give short patriotic addresses at public places, such as movie theatres—facetiously nicknamed by some contemporaries the "Stentorian Guard," they nonetheless evoked the valorism of the homespun-clad colonial Minutemen at Concord and Lexington. Feature films produced during 1919 that contained scenes of oppositional nationalistic imagery exuberantly counteracting radical gibberish would include *The Red Viper* (Tyrad Pictures), *The Undercurrent* (Select) and *Virtuous Men*. A comment in the *Motion Picture News* review for *The Red Viper* tells much of these stories: "This picture waves the flag at every opportunity and its titles preach an A–1 brand of Americanism."[59]

In sharp contrast to female stars like Irene Castle unfurling Old Glory to chauvinistically rouse the masses, politically radicalized "vamps" were frequently a primary focus of unfavorable attention in thematically relevant motion pictures. Nearly a score of the 1918–20 Red Scare films disapprovingly portray radical women. These vampiric feminine Others were dangerous, urban-bred creatures who could suck the life's blood of democracy out of their innocent male victims and convert them into zombie-like Red automatons.[60] Radicalized women become transmitters of the dreaded political virus called Bolshevism. Their unharnessed sexuality is viewed as a dramatic symbol of the new, but tainted, power of the Reds.[61] Yet once the vamp's erotic magnetism over these men is removed, the potency of American democracy can be fully restored.

Conversely, the male dupes of these radical she-devils, such as John King in *Dangerous Hours*, however ephemeral may be their unquestioning submission to the cause of Bolshevism, become Red slaves. An ironic gender reversal is thereby created on the silver screen that mimics the prewar female victims of enforced prostitution who had been featured in the sensationalistic "White Slave" genre.[62]

Motion pictures featuring female radicals might be best described as cinematic morality plays demonstrating the perils awaiting those wayward women who challenged the traditional male hierarchy. Isolation from family, madness and/or death awaits the promiscuous revolutionary woman, whereas a happy heterosexual life is the reward for the lady who spurns the much-vaunted freedoms of social rebellion. This dichotomy is especially stark in *The Right to Happiness* (Universal-Jewel, 1919) featuring twin American-born sisters who are separated during their infancy, one being raised by Russian radicals while the other grows up in the United States with her capitalist father. Death becomes the ultimate fate of the Bolshevik sister, while marriage is the final reward bestowed upon her capitalist-nurtured sibling.

Most female radicals are portrayed as foreign born/non-Anglo–Saxon named women who are provocatively lascivious. Openly disdainful of moral conventions, they are usually identified as bred on the East Side of New York City or as imported Jew-Bolsheviks from Russia with social, political and sexual radicalism conflated into a single Red menace. *The City of Purple Dreams* (Selig, 1918), produced and directed by Colin Campbell, is one of the earliest films to fully develop the character of a politically radicalized vamp. Esther, a black-haired "girl anarchist" whose name suggests a Jewish background, lures an innocent derelict, in fact the son of a wealthy family, into her bomb-throwing gang. The man's subsequent irrational involvement with the radicals leads to his being temporarily committed to an insane asylum! The *Variety* review notes that the actress in the role of Esther "plays the Anarchist with real Bolsheviki fervor."[63] Sexually sullied and driven totally mad by her failure to achieve her revolutionary aims, Esther eventually commits suicide. A rabid Bolshevik named Mariska in *The Undercurrent* will later choose an identical fate.

Revolutionary women represent dark and enigmatic Trotskys in shortened skirts, such as the sexually unconventional Sophia Guerni of *Dangerous Hours*, whose only family would appear to be a seedy group of Greenwich Village degenerates and whose political zealotry is manifested through an unnatural adulation of an even more depraved representative of godless Bolshevism from Russia. One of the other women with Sophia and her fellow "dangerous ... ghouls" creating a disturbance during the film's early labor demonstration verbally abuses a police officer and physically threatens him with her umbrella. She will also be prominent among those radicals who later attempt to disrupt a courtroom hearing. This unnamed woman, who is short and squat and wears a big floppy hat, strongly resembles the well-known German-Jewish communist ideologue, Rosa Luxemburg.[64]

The Bolshevik vamp named Emma Reich (possibly intended to be a German-born Jewess) in *The World Aflame* was played by the dark-haired actress named Claire DuBrey, who appeared only a few months later in a near-identical role as the wanton Sophia Guerni in *Dangerous Hours*—reinforcing an intertextual association with a particular female radical type. Since both these motion pictures were major productions, with prominently Anglo stars featured in the roles of the lead protagonists, obviously the film's creators deliberately attempted to present their audiences with politically contaminated gendered configurations as unsympathetic foils.

The erotica of radicalism is epitomized by the bomb-carrying Yolanda performing an exotic dance at a banquet in *The Red Viper*, a 1919 Tyrad release, the title suggestive of the serpent's menace in an edenic America. A two-page multi-chromatic ad in the *New York Dramatic Mirror* actually depicts the cringing working-class hero in the reptilian vamp's clutches, a huge viper with fangs bared curling up from behind her flowing low-cut gown, as if poised to strike.[65] Yolanda is a Red Mata Hari, but instead of finagling military information, Yolanda and her cohorts are meddling with America's ideals. The bomb is disguised in a floral bouquet to deceive the intended victim, a judge, as well as the other representatives of the social establishment in attendance at his home. Yolanda's associate, a revolutionary Goliath who goes by the name of "Smith," is destroyed by his own bomb when the youthful hero David—presumably a Jew of Russian descent: "born and raised in the foreign section of the city"—redeems himself by grabbing it out of the sensually undulating Yolanda's hands and tossing away the explosive device. At the film's conclusion, David is recuperating from his wounds and compares the darkness of the old country with the light from the star of freedom shining over America.

The Red Viper also makes it clear that the female radical is still redeemable as long as she has not been sexually promiscuous or successfully carried out some act of political violence. Virtually all female revolutionaries who do not fornicate or murder for the cause during the film, reverse their political orientation by the final reel. Conversely, their unrepentant radical sisters are invariably killed, or kill themselves. Sexual freedom is thus portrayed as ultimately leading to social anarchy. Only depravity can result when a woman, the traditional guardian of the nuclear family, abandons moral constraints to

live in "free union" with a man. Finally disdaining the "unshackled freedom" of Bolshevism, the lady ingenue of *The Uplifters* hastily agrees at the end of the film to submit to the "saner and safer 'shackles' of marriage" with her forgiving capitalist hero.[66]

Motion pictures that portray lusty Bolshevik vamps express an implicit fear of the potential political power these women have when they exercise sexual dominance over men. This may have also represented a subliminally misogynistic attack upon granting the vote/political equality to women.

There is an interesting variation on this theme in *The Face at Your Window*, a special Fox production released under government auspices during the waning months of the Red Scare in the fall of 1920. A Russian-born working girl, Ruth Kravo, receives unwanted attention from an agitator named Ivan Koyloff at a factory. He later viciously stabs the owner's son, Frank, who has shown her affection. Ruth is so repelled by Koyloff that she voluntarily works undercover with the Secret Service to terminate the Red influence upon her people. She and Frank are reunited at the film's conclusion. So impulsive behavior, like volunteering for espionage work, is acceptable if done for the right reason.

The ultimate ideological antidote in Red Scare–era motion pictures to the transgressive communist vamp is the introduction of a strong-willed but virtuous and patriotic American capitalist woman. Like their mythologized frontier sisters of a few generations earlier, these "true" women were simultaneously portrayed as both efficient, independent-minded capitalists and loving submissive mates or future mates. American women displaying these positive traits appear in a number of films, including: *The Girl from Bohemia* (Astra/Pathé, 1918), *The Girl of Today* (Vitagraph, 1918), *The Vamp* (Famous Players/Lasky-Paramount, 1918), *The Wasp* and *Woman, Woman!* (Fox, 1919). Mary Weston, the owner of a shipyard threatened by Bolshevik agitators in *Dangerous Hours*, exemplifies this "sweet type of clean American womanhood." Working-

The Red Viper (Tyrad, 1919): This multi-tone movie poster, which appeared as a two-page ad in a trade journal, the *New York Dramatic Mirror* (8/28/19), visualized the concept of the young working-class hero being caught in the blood red clutches of a reptilian Bolshevik-inspired vamp.

class counterparts to benign capitalist Mary also appear in several films—Red-slaying Lotta Nerve, who has put "Bolshevism off the map," of *Bullin' the Bullsheviki* (Eff & Eff, 1919); super-patriotic adolescent Mary Hogan of *The Red Viper*; immaculate housewife and devoted mother Lucy in *The Undercurrent*; feisty anti-radical shop girl Emily Ray of *Help Yourself* (Goldwyn, 1920).

Because several of the Bolshevik leaders and some American radicals were of Jewish descent, anti-Semitic sentiments in the United States surfaced and became exploited by the media. For instance, as early as December 1918, an issue of the widely-read national weekly, *The Literary Digest*, contained an article that addressed concerns regarding a Jewish-Bolshevik connection, "Are Bolsheviki Mainly Jewish?"[67] Furthermore, the sensationalized Overman Judiciary Subcommittee hearings in the U. S. Senate, beginning in February 1919, featured

a number of witnesses testifying about assorted Jew-Bolshevik atrocities in Russia and/or asserting that many members of the Soviet leadership were "apostate Jews" who had been raised in the ghettos on the East Side of New York City.[68] The Jew-Bolshevik was transmogrified on film into a conniving political ogre—an infanticide who in the name of the revolution slaughtered the less than year-old Republican Russia; a patricide of the Tsar; and a matricide, or ravisher, of the traditions of Holy Mother Russia.

Overt anti-Semitism in American motion pictures was largely confined to the Red Scare period. Jews frequently appear in this era's films, usually pejoratively stereotyped.[69] The deprecatory cognitive model of a Jewish-Bolshevik is distinct in nine motion pictures produced during the Red Scare—including *The City of Purple Dreams*; *The Burning Question* (Catholic Art, 1919); *The New Moon*; *The Right to Happiness*; *The World Aflame*; *The Face at*

Bolshevism on Trial (Select, 1919): One in a series of sensational ads for this film. It features the "Jew-Bolshevik" image and plays upon fears of a world-wide Bolshevik conspiracy spreading to America.

Your Window.[70] At least two of these films augment evil by creating a German-Bolshevik linkage. In *The New Moon* (Select, 1919), for example, an ethnically Jewish Bolshevik leader, Theo Kamenoff (Charles Gerard), is said to be in the pay of a foreign government—thereby lending credence to the concept of the Jew-Bolshevik who was born in Russia, but molded by Germany. The positive portrayal of the Simon family from New York's East Side in *The Other Man's Wife*, a June 1919 Film Clearing House release, is a rare unambiguous exception to this era's handling of Jews.

The hoary hooked-nose ethnic characterization of Jews, with its phallic associations, is used with particular effect in the closing scenes of *The Burning Question*, a 1919 film produced by the Roman Catholic Church. The star villain, an unnamed negative stereotype, is portrayed as a lustful comrade about to impale the innocent Mary with his facial protuberance when the square-jawed hero arrives and preserves her virginity.[71] That such type casting to impart threat was not uncommon, *Variety* made clear in its review of another 1919 release, *The Volcano* (W.W. Hodkinson): "[the Bolshevik] Alexis Minski (ovich) ... was probably cast for the role ... because of no other reason than his super-sized nose."[72]

The degree of anti-Semitism exhibited in the original version of *The Volcano*, directed by George Irving from a story written by Augustus Thomas, was so outrageous that it led to complaints.[73] As a result, the military intelligence officer who is the hero in *The Volcano* was converted in the general release prints from a gentile named Captain Garland to a man of Jewish descent named Captain Nathan Levison (Edward Langford). Furthermore, in the revised titles, to mitigate the unmistakable anti-Semitic physiognomy of the primary Bolshevik, "a gesticulating East Sider" named Minsky, his surname was awkwardly altered to Minskiovich.

Bolshevism as a diabolic anti-Christian aberration is made visually symbolic in *Dangerous Hours* by creating devil-like imagery in a smoldering dissolve upon a close-up of Boris Blotchi's demonic glare to introduce a flashback during which this Red Beelzebub's willful participation in revolutionary murder and rape is graphically portrayed. The film's climactic blowing up of Blotchi and a screaming throng of his maddened disciples thereby suggests a cinematic exorcism of Bolshevism. The Bolsheviks' bomb is in fact referred to as a "devil machine" in the studio synopsis of *The Red Viper*. One of the recommended promotional catchlines for *Uncharted Channels* (Hampton/Robertson-Cole, 1920) also clearly reflects this sentiment: "He Saved Her from Their [Bolshevik] Deviltry...."[74]

There are specific references to Leon Trotsky in three motion pictures, including a pejorative one to his lack of personal hygiene in Eff & Eff's 1919 slapstick production, *Bullin' the Bullsheviki*. Trotsky/Bronstein was probably better known to the American public than Lenin at the time. Also, his physical appearance and Jewish origins meant that Trotsky more closely conformed to the negative revolutionary stereotype and therefore was more prone to caricature.[75]

The erudite Trotsky, who was always pictured wearing a pince-nez, further reified the perception of the shifty Jew-Bolshevik as a mastermind of political revolution and thereby indirectly reinforced unfriendly attitudes towards the educated elite in America. Anti-intellectualism was central to the demonization and/or discrediting of the dirty alcoholic radical poet in *The Uplifters*; the glasses-wearing German socialist habitué of a beer garden in *The Undercurrent*; the probably coded homosexual at a Washington Square gathering named Andrew Felton, described as "a 'lecturer' in the cause of the downtrodden," in *Dangerous Hours*; the political charlatan, a so-called "parlor Bolshevik" called Professor Syle, in *Help Yourself*.[76] There is an additional failing related to the characters in the first two motion pictures, men who would have been of draft age the year before; their apparent avoidance of

Dangerous Hours (Paramount-Artcraft, 1920): In the climactic scene, the hero John (Lloyd Hughes) confronts a screaming mob of his erstwhile comrades in front of the besieged shipyard gates. Having seized their bomb, he is poised to wipe out the crazed enemies of American democracy.

either military service or volunteer work to aid in the war effort would have marked them in the minds of many of the contemporary audience as effete "slackers."

The avocation of an "alien" ideology becomes stigmatized as a substitute for honest capitalist enterprise—and idleness can easily nurture socially destructive thoughts. "Parlor Bolsheviks" talk sedition while using their hands only to make exclamatory gestures or to lift tea cups—not to perform honest labor—best exemplified by the fatuous caricaturizations and stereotypes that appear in two 1920 productions, *Help Yourself* and *Uncharted Channels*.[77]

Elsa Smolski, a self-proclaimed "intellectual" in the satiric *Uncharted Channels*, a mid–1920 Robertson-Cole release directed by Henry King, gleefully assists a radical compatriot named Nicholas Schonn in convincing an impressionable young heiress to part with a large sum of money. Ostensibly donated in the name of the laboring classes, it is actually earmarked for the personal use of the two hypocritical revolutionaries. Russian Elsa also spends time at the heiress' fashionable home with a shabby gathering of foreign-born factory workers, inciting them with her smoldering rhetoric to demand an exorbitant wage increase from their employer.

Where the "parlor Bolsheviks" were amusing and fortunately feckless, the cinematic importation of German spy-saboteurs,

"Trimmed with Red" is Trimmed with Laughs

"Comrade" Madge Kennedy, partially concealed behind a fake harem veil and flowing robe, effectually wrecks the plans of the Greenwich Village parlor radicals to paint society a bright red.

Meanwhile, her sweetheart has cornered the market in army mules, and this most delicious of farces ends in a burst of sunshine.

It is the sort of picture every audience loves—for the simple reason that every audience loves to laugh.

SAMUEL GOLDWYN PRESENTS

MADGE KENNEDY
TRIMMED WITH RED
BY WALLACE IRWIN
DIRECTED BY HUGO BALLIN

Help Yourself (Goldwyn, 1920): Under its more politically explicit working title, this movie ad features a feisty shopgirl who gets mixed-up with a fatuous group of Greenwich Village radicals. A spring release, the change of title and comedic format suggests that the Red Scare hysteria was abating and that so-called "parlor Bolsheviks" were increasingly viewed with amused contempt.

begun as early as 1916–17 in pre-war America, was the primary genesis of international communist conspiracy theories as portrayed on the nation's movie screens during the Red Scare. The literal image of a (cabalistic) web was actually used in promotional print ads for the 1918 wartime production, *My Four Years in Germany*, and the spring 1919 Select Pictures release, *Bolshevism on Trial*.[78]

The tyrannical Kaiser and his sycophantic military associates are shown plotting world domination on several occasions throughout the rather lengthy *My Four Years in Germany*. The German representative to China in *For the Freedom of the East* is introduced in the credits as the "Spider of Berlin." Likewise, Lenin and his scheming revolutionary comrades appear together in scenes in two 1920 releases, *Dangerous Hours* and *The Face at Your Window*. The suggestive phrase, "spinning the web," is actually used in an inter-title to describe the secretly planned activities of "a group of dark visaged plotters" in *The Undercurrent*. Although the film takes place entirely in an American city and primarily concerns the activities of U. S. citizens, the very title of *The World Aflame* lends credence to the concept of an international conspiracy.

In cinematic encounters with Bolshevism, the dominating self-image of Americans was a strange mix of exaggerated national innocence and zealous righteousness. This virtuous rage was usually vented by pitting candid altruistic democracy against hypocritical venal communism. An exceptional evocation of this perception of America's innocence appears in *The Undercurrent* when the politically misguided hero-veteran finally recognizes the real evil of Red terrorism and embarks upon an anti-Bolshevik rampage after envisioning his young son playing with ("showing") the American flag.

In response to perceived threats to the national identity, an apotheosis of Americanism occurs throughout the Red Scare years via a dramatic increase of American icons, such as flags and references to cultural heroes, appearing on movie screens: some 8 percent of the pertinent films released between 1909 and 1917 display secular relics, while at least 36 percent of the 1918–20 period films contain these symbols. Particularly striking is the virtual deification of the American flag, resulting in what amounts to a cult of "Old Glory."[79] In fact, the patriotic National Security League promoted the slogan: "One country, one language, one flag."[80]

American iconography, so heavily manipulated in the 1917–18 propaganda war against Germany, was rapidly remobilized during the Red Scare in an attempt to smother an inchoate Bolshevik monster. Yet some of the more obvious non-verbal communicated symbols associated with communism, such as the hammer and sickle, rarely appear on film during the Red Scare—as if it were considered unwise to dwell upon the communist's symbols. Nor are there any known instances of the reproduction in a 1918–20 American film of the highly-stylized pictorial posters that constituted the principal medium used by the Bolsheviks for agitational propaganda. What was more apt to be projected in movie theatres were variations upon the older demonology associated with anarchism, most particularly the dirty, bearded Slavic radical. Two examples from Red Scare era films would be the lampooned "Harvard Tramp" in *The Uplifters* and Odoroskavitch in *Help Yourself*.

Similarly visually exploited was the Red Star displayed upon Bolshevik uniforms and sometimes on the Red Flag.[81] But the emblematic Red banner, unless the scene is tinted red or hand painted (very rare) would, on black and white nitrate prints, more likely suggest a dark representation of deadly anarchism. Also, by not showing the hammer and sickle or red star on the red flag, the revolutionary banner retains a more universal, less nationalistic, even hollow symbolism. The older negative anarchist symbols were still regularly exploited, as in the use of familiar bomb thrower imagery for the art titles signifying the bearded Bolshevik leader in *Dangerous Hours*. Buzzwords, with pejorative connotations at the time, such as "comrade" or "brotherhood," would also regularly appear on titles and inter-titles.

An early scene in *The Volcano*, whose provocative title suggests an eruption of social discontent, incorporates newsreel footage of New York Governor Al Smith signing into law legislation banning the public exhibition of the Red Flag in that state.[82] This action is portrayed as directly inciting the Reds to plot violent reprisals, and then in turn, to be ruthlessly suppressed by a coalition of private citizens, the police forces of New York and members of military intelligence.

In contradiction to America-dwelling Bolsheviks, film representations of a radicalized industrial proletariat in the new Soviet Russia are notable by their absence. Instead, it is professional Bolshevik agitators and/or barbaric illiterate Russian peasant stereotypes—visually reinforcing on America's movie screens the concept of an opportunistic alliance between hypocritical intellectuals/political ideologues out of Dostoyevsky's *Possessed* and vodka-swilling, atavistic hairy Russian muzhiks. Variations on this theme are most clearly represented in *Common Property*, featuring ignorant peasants empowered by the Bolshevik revolution gleefully promoting the "nationalization" of women, and the extended flashback sequence of revolutionary Russia in *Dangerous Hours* that chillingly portrays peoples' militias, so-called "Red Guards," indiscriminately raping, pillaging and murdering in the name of the people— symbolizing a contagious lust of the foreign-born masses for the better life enjoyed and largely monopolized by the middle-classes.[83]

The use of revolutionary aliases by Bolshevik villains in Red Scare era motion pictures reinforce the concept of the inherent deviousness of radicals. It also reflected the actual use of revolutionary names by the Bolshevik leadership, including Vladimir I. Ulyanov, otherwise referred to as Lenin, and Lev Bronstein, better known to the world as Leon Trotsky. Furthermore, film examples of such aliases frequently tinkered with the English language or the preestablished popular culture to create negative associations. For instance, the name of the primary Red troublemaker in *Bolshevism on Trial*, Herman Wolff (Leslie Stowe), suggesting a stealthy, predatory, beast-like German, is in fact one Androvitch, as in Slavic man. And one of the leading Bolshevik agent provocateurs of *The Right to Happiness*, Sergius Kerkoff (Hector Sarno), is called "The Fox" by his comrades while operating in the United States. Fox not only is a synonym for

deceit, but *Kerk*off suggests a vicious Slav and/or a mongrel (cur) Slav.

The confrontational nature of earlier capital-labor films and the viciousness of World War I anti-German propaganda releases carried over into America's Red Scare era anti-Bolshevik motion pictures, where all political or social analysis was dissolved in stereotypes of gross villainy—Bolshevism was "a kind of social disease against which people could be vaccinated by large doses of 100 percent Americanism."[84] Militant laborers who espouse and/or emulate Red savagery are therefore punished or even sometimes killed without remorse. In the *Riders of the Dawn* (Hampton/W.W. Hodkinson, 1920), there is apparently little or no interference with vigilante activities from legally constituted authorities. Led by a World War veteran, these self-appointed watchdogs of Americanism become rabid para-militaries defending both the ideological and territorial integrity of the United States.

Nine percent of the germane Red Scare era films are coded Vigilante. Vigilante-style actions are actually portrayed in a number of motion pictures, including a forced flag-kissing in *The Prussian Cur*, the whipping of radicalized workers in *Mr. Logan, U.S.A.* and a tar-and-feathering of two ethnically Irish labor racketeers who had conspired with radicals that occurs near the conclusion of *Dangerous Hours*.[85]

Red Scare era films often link vigilante activities and veterans. Retired soldiers become primary defenders of traditional American values in peace as recently in war, their faded uniforms representing a license to hunt down Reds. Elderly Civil War veterans actually participate in the stifling of the radicals in *The Face at Your Window*. These spry vets are also a visual reminder of the horrendous price in blood and treasure the citizens of the United States once paid for allowing the nation to be divided into warring camps. And Bolshevism represents the potential class-oriented Balkanization of America, incited by outside forces. This is strongly reflected in the reactionary use of veterans in *The Spirit of '17* (Lasky/Paramount, 1918) and *The World Aflame*, as well as in *The Face At Your Window*.

Indicative of both an early and deliberate exploitation of anti-Bolshevik hysteria and a conscious association with/manipulation of veterans is this provocative tidbit from a full-page editorial promoting the commercial "play" of the Red card for *Bolshevism on Trial* that was printed in *The Moving Picture World*: "Bolshevik Play Has Big Points"—"Put up red flags about town and hire soldiers to tear them down if necessary and then come out with a flaming handbill, explaining that the play [film] is not an argument for anarchy."[86]

Red Scare films display a significant switch from private police forces as agents of labor suppression to elements of the Federal government. In fact, on several occasions the regular armed forces instantaneously respond to the cinematic summons of civilians announcing the presence of Bolshevik activities. Like modern day Minutemen, having answered the call to arms, they attack and ruthlessly destroy the "Red hordes" invading America in *Bolshevism on Trial*, *The Burning Question* and *The Undercurrent*. In *Bolshevism on Trial*, military action is initiated on a tip from a private citizen. It is only indicated at the very end of the film that *military* intelligence had been maintaining surveillance of the radical intrigues of the Bolshevik agent. The hero veteran of *The Undercurrent* seizes a train and arouses the men at the local Army barracks, reminiscent of a twentieth century industrialized midnight ride of Paul Revere rousing the soldiers of democracy to defeat their mortal Red enemies.[87]

The worldwide class warfare being promoted by a sovietized Russia in the wake of the just-ended horrific World War was truly a frightening prospect to America. Having regularly been portrayed on film sabotaging the war effort, postwar radicals were then excoriated as disturbers of the hard-won peace. As historian Burl Noggle argues: "Men who now sought to obstruct or overturn the soci-ety that war had preserved came under fire. The conformity of war became the conformity of peace."[88]

Nostalgia for a false vision of an idyllic past contributed to a postwar sense of disillusionment and fed the conditions for an endeavor like the Red Scare, with the Bolsheviks and their domestic radical advocates becoming convenient scapegoats for a variety of societal ailments. Historian Julian F. Jaffe has noted: "After the Armistice, the inflation, the great strikes, and the problems of demobilization provided further proof that 'un-American' elements were spreading confusion and preventing a return to 'normalcy.'" The Red Scare, thus, was "a massive act of political surgery which tried to cut out the disruptive elements."[89] Enforced conformity was the social scalpel; so-called "normalcy" was reassuring in a world that had forever changed. As Sinclair Lewis told us: "American Democracy did not imply any equality of wealth, but did demand a wholesome sameness of thought, dress, painting, morals, and vocabulary."[90] It was the prevalent secular faith.

The character David, *The Red Viper*'s newsboy protagonist played by Gareth Hughes, is touched by this Procrustean faith and has a religious-like patriotic epiphany, much like the John King character in *Dangerous Hours*. After witnessing frenzied mobs at night in the streets of New York, which the callow lad had helped to incite by working on a radical leaflet, David wanders in despair to Madison Square Park and falls asleep upon a bench. Awakened in the early morning by a fellow newspaper hawker telling him of the death of the little patriot Mary Hogan (Ruth Stonehouse) at the hands of the Reds, David walks over to The Victory Arch, and with the ascendant sun shining like a "benediction" upon him, he reads the inscribed names of America's famous battlefields—ending with the name of Mary's Irish neighborhood, "Finnegan's Alley," superimposed upon the site where she fell defending America against Bolshevism. David prays for her forgiveness and pledges to fight for his country.[91]

The presumption across the land was that the bombs tossed by Reds in the United States were primed in Russia—Bolshevik agents were Red torch-bearers whose acts of revolutionary radicalism in America could be traced back along a burnt trail strewn with destruction to Soviet Russia. This is graphically literalized in the art titles of bombs, pistols, etc., that introduce scenes with the odious Bolshevik leader in *Dangerous Hours*.

In *The Right to Happiness*, directed by Allen Holubar and aggressively distributed by Universal as a Deluxe production, the twin infant daughters of an American capitalist in pre–Bolshevik Russia are torn apart by a Cossack pogrom. Twenty years later, in 1919, the innocent gentile daughter left behind in Russia and weaned on Red bile by Jewish radicals, is sent to the United States as the rabid Bolshevik agent called "Comrade Sonia." The social havoc created by her revolutionary agitation of the workers at a factory, that just happens to be owned by her long-forgotten father, nearly completes the destruction of the family. It represents a perverse reversal of the escape from Tsarist Russia by the traumatized family motif associated with earlier Nihilist films. Near the motion picture's conclusion, Sonia achieves moral redemption by sacrificing herself to save the life of her twin sister during a radical-inspired labor riot.

The Right to Happiness is a cinematic parable regarding the different revolutionary paths—the American versus the Bolshevik. The title of the motion picture is an obvious variation on the first paragraph of "The Declaration of Independence," referring to man's "unalienable Rights," including "the Pursuit of Happiness." Implicitly, one cannot be content under Bolshevik rule and so a good capitalist must assure happiness for his workers by ameliorating the inevitable distresses of industrial labor, which the "purified" capitalist Hardcastle (his resistance to alien depredations as unyielding as the name) does after the sacrifice of his fallen Bolshevik daughter. At one point this dichotomy is further reinforced with a short

passage from the *Bible* and an insert of a Wilson speech, the latter musically accompanied by "Hail Columbia."

The Right to Happiness received an extended ad campaign in the *New York Dramatic Mirror* during September and October of 1919. In one of these numerous ads the film's dark-haired star, Dorothy Phillips, "America's Greatest Emotional Actress," is posed menacingly grasping a brick above her head, as if about to commit an act of social disobedience by throwing the object.[92]

Bolsheviks are repeatedly depicted on screen without families, estranged from their relatives, or as living in unnatural domestic situations. At that time, co-habitation of unmarried couples or groups of individuals who are *not* related sharing housing was considered by mainstream society to be particularly abhorrent. Communal living is presented as not only immoral, but also unsanitary, thereby posing a threat to the democratic health of the American family. *The Uplifters*, a semi-comic "All Star" Metro release of 1919, features an impressionable young white-collar working girl named Hortense Troutt (the blonde May Allison) who is easily lured by the seemingly attractive ideological red bait.[93] Having lost her stenographer job after impetuously renouncing capitalism and embracing communism, the political ingenue enthusiastically moves to a group house in Greenwich Village populated by an eccentric "bunch of parlor Bolshevists." But, instead of being treated equally as a sister comrade, the new convert "finds herself delegated to do all the work while everybody else takes it out in talking."[94] Hortense has also been romantically deceived by an unkempt university-educated poet who, she later learns, has three wives! This so-called "Harvard Tramp," named Larry Hoden, was probably intended to be a caricature of real-life radical John Reed.[95]

The hotel living quarters for the socialists on Paradise Island in *Bolshevism on Trial* is portrayed as a gigantic commune that almost immediately degenerates into a state of anarchy because its fatuous American members are ideologically undisciplined. This situation is exemplified by a short vignette portraying a prostitute named Blanche settling into a room with a smalltime hood—he quickly leaves her to find a card game! The predatory Bolshevik Wolff and his personal Red Guard cynically encourage these apolitical vices in order to facilitate their takeover of the island—simulating Lenin's revolutionary pragmatism as demonstrated by his Bolshevik Party's seizure of power in Russia from the fractious rival socialist-revolutionary parties.

Such characterizations were in line with the sexually rapacious stereotype of radicals in motion pictures of this time. One conspicuous example would be *Riders of the Dawn*, where the younger sister of the hero's girlfriend is mercilessly chased down and murdered by a fiendish radical tramp—reminding one of the scene in *The Birth of a Nation* (D.W. Griffith/Epoch Productions, 1915) in which a renegade black's attempted rape of the heroine's "pet sister" leads to her death. In fact, in *Riders of the Dawn* both the gorilla-looking henchman and his evil leader, Henry Neuman, appear to spend more screen time seeking sexual gratification than pursuing the cause of radicalism.[96] The thematic title of another film, *Common Property*, would make it seem that the primary objective of Bolshevism was the sexual domination of all women in Russia, rather than the political conquest of the Russian state.

Above and beyond their egotistic sexuality, the Russian Reds are even capable of destroying members of their own families. *The New Moon*'s Kamenoff becomes a fratricide after ordering the execution of his sister for refusing to obey a Bolshevik law decreeing that all women register themselves for sexual availability. This obviously was intended to highlight the allegedly perverse aspects of Bolshevism lurking behind its hypocritical ideological facade. Misinformed feminists and their male sympathizers are thereby graphically warned that women would be exchanging the chains of bourgeois morality for the right to be legally raped or

stood up before a firing squad and shot. Fratricide actually takes on a double meaning in the text of Select studio's *The New Moon*, since it occurs during the vicious ongoing civil war between the White and Red forces in Russia.

There is a silver lining to this creeping crimson menace, however. Because atheistic communists are beyond salvation, they may be killed with little or no remorse—like the demonic, church-burning mob of radicals destroyed with one of their own bombs in *Dangerous Hours*. Indeed, it becomes the duty of God-fearing Americans to combat the assorted heresies of anarchism, Bolshevism, etc.—the concept of going into ideological battle beneath the twin banners of the flag and the cross. Christianity itself could be directly challenged, as in *The One Woman* (Select, 1918), where a preacher comes under the influence of a vampish free love advocate and also confronts radical parishioners who attack conscription. The strategy to quell all this "red thinking" could be as simple as a reaffirmation of the family and Christianity during the wedding ceremonies with former radicals at the end of several films, including *The Volcano*, *The Uplifters* and *Help Yourself*. Even *Dangerous Hours* closes with a symbolic prayer for forgiveness by the repentant former Bolshevik sympathizer at a secular altar of Americanism, the bedside of his injured sweetheart, martyred by the violence of a crazed gang of radicals. There had been a nearly identical concluding sequence, with the genders reversed, in *The Red Viper*, a film released several months earlier, in the summer of 1919.

So reconversion was possible; you too can rediscover the American torch of liberty and be saved. This theme appeared in Red Scare era films, often as the well-meaning/idealistic individual being fooled by the Bolsheviks. Until they return to the bosom of American democracy, which they always do, these dupes are treated by their patriotically loyal friends and relatives with gestures of indulgent disgust. Examples include the upper-class man-turned-rootless hobo in

The City of Purple Dreams, the wealthy veteran and society girl protagonists of *Bolshevism on Trial*, the idealistic immigrant newsboy in *The Red Viper* and the emotionally/politically vulnerable, unemployed hero veteran of *The Undercurrent*.

Wealthy unmarried women seem to have been especially susceptible to radical manipulation, particularly regarding the laying-out of cash to support their activities. In *Bolshevism on Trial* the socially conscious debutante, Barbara, convinces her rich boyfriend to contribute the funds necessary to establish a socialist community on a tropical island. Rosamunde, a foolish dabbler in the occult, becomes the principal sponsor of a group of idle "parlor Bolsheviks" in *Help Yourself*. And in *Uncharted Channels* the beautiful young heiress named Sylvia Kingston is "ensnared by glib Russian tongues" into offering $50,000 for the "cause."[97]

Bolshevism on Trial was a premiere Mayflower production released by Select Pictures in April 1919, in the vanguard of the Red Scare, and was a particularly potent object lesson against utopian idealism gone astray. A number of sensational ads promoting this motion picture appeared in the trade journals over the next month, including a highly misleading one, vis-à-vis the film's content, that poses the provocative question: "Shall Bolshevism Spread Its Web Over Our Industrial Life?" The ad was dominated by a monstrous spider-like Bolshevik caricature looming out of a web with an American worker struggling within its grip. Its face, a grimacing, bearded, bushy-haired Jewish stereotype, wearing wirerimmed glasses, strongly resembles Trotsky, but in no way bears any likeness to the primary Bolshevik heavy portrayed in the film. Furthermore, despite the web clinging to a number of "Shut Down" factories, *Bolshevism on Trial* only obliquely addresses the industrial aspects of the capital versus labor issue.[98]

The timing of the theatrical release of *Bolshevism on Trial* fortuitously coincided with the revelation that letter bombs had been mailed to a number of prominent Americans. *Bolshevism on Trial* contains most elements of the culturally shared pre-Bolshevik Revolution anti-radical stereotype and establishes what would later become recognizable as the standard anti-Communist cinematic demonology, particularly sexual perversity, personal venality and the cynical betrayal of fellow ideologues in the name of the cause.

Captain Worth, played by Robert Frazer, is a man of material wealth and perhaps a wounded veteran of World War I (although the film is unclear on this, reflecting known title alterations). He loves Barbara, an attractive society girl with a social conscience who has embraced radicalized socialism. In her idealistic zeal to right social inequities, Barbara has fallen under the influence of a "professional agitator" named Herman Wolff.

At a mass meeting to raise funds for the cause, a white-bearded Marx look-alike and a glasses-wearing man resembling Trotsky are among those sharing the podium in the "Socialists Hall" with Barbara. These men are only two of the more prominent individuals amongst a deceptively amiable and innocuous group of revolutionary shills unctuously steering the impressionable debutante-cum-mark into the play with socialism. Her beau is moved to financially support their cause and accept a leading role in the establishment of an experimental socialist community on an island, dubbed "Paradise Island."

The balding middle-aged, Wolff, with an atavistic overhanging brow and dark receding eyes, has the look of the predator. In an early scene, he is pointedly introduced to the movie audience hunched over a table perusing radical literature, including *Das Kapital*, a copy of the leading socialist-sponsored newspaper, *The New York Call*, another book with the picture of Karl Marx on the front page and a pamphlet written by prominent American socialist John Spargo. As indicated in the accompanying inter-title, socialist sympathies are being exploited in the United States by emerging professional revolutionaries, such as Wolff.

Bolshevism on Trial (Select, 1919): This lurid segment from a promotional ad appearing in the *Moving Picture World* (5/17/19) features a spider-like Bolshevik caricature. Note its resemblance to the real-life Bolshevik leader Leon Trotsky, who was of Jewish descent.

Political agitator Wolff, who is really the Bolshevik Androvitch, begins plotting almost immediately to undermine "Chief Comrade" Worth's authority in order to "confiscate" the socialist paradise and to rule over it with his "Red Guard"—"Comrades, we can spread the Red brotherhood over the world, and come to power and riches." Unnamed and uncredited, two of Wolff's most intimate henchmen are bearded anarchist stereotypes. Wolff also wants to unilaterally divorce his plain wife and make the pretty

younger heroine his revolutionary "consort." Anticipating trouble, the hero's wealthy father, a capitalist "brain worker" whose inventions have "created work for thousands," Colonel Worth, sends his faithful Native-American retainer to secretly keep an eye on developments. Chief Saka, played by Chief Standing Bear, assures Colonel Worth: "Me Tame Indian—No Likum Red." The patently deliberate irony regarding this inter-title is further highlighted by showing the noble "Red" scout on the revolutionary frontier segregating himself from the Red savages at the hotel commune by setting-up his tepee on the nearby shore.

Underscoring the point further, political hypocrisy is visually delineated in *Bolshevism on Trial* by the sumptuous hotel quarters in which the radicals ensconce themselves—the encircling wide porch more suitable for aimless promenades by idle romantics than for anti-democratic tirades by dedicated revolutionaries.[99]

Social harmony in the commune of artistic dilettantes, misfits, women wearing masculine attire, and impotent parlor Bolsheviks, quickly degenerates when work assignments are made—political fantasizing is preferred over the pragmatic application of total social equality—representing a cinematic mockery of Marx's "workers' and peasants' paradise." In fact, the mass gathering of the Paradise Islanders to protest their job placements is reminiscent of the notorious scene depicting indolent Reconstruction era black legislators in D. W. Griffith's *The Birth of a Nation*—no idle linkage here, since the venomous pen of writer Thomas Dixon was responsible for both films' scripts.

So it becomes rather easy for Androvitch and his band of diehard radicals to discredit Worth and then place him under house arrest at night. Dutiful Saka rows back to the mainland and wires Colonel Worth about the "Heap trouble ... [caused by] Wolf Man." The next morning, U. S. "Naval Infantry" retake the island and arrest the Bolsheviks. Beneath a rising sun, young Worth

Bolshevism on Trial (Select, 1919): One of the more extreme examples of a Red Scare era film, this early scene portrays an idealistic young American couple from the privileged class succumbing to the foreign born ideology at a radical mass meeting. Note the Marx look-alike in the right background. (MOMA Filmstills Archive)

unceremoniously hauls down "that" Red Flag (thereby rendered visually lifeless) and then triumphantly hoists an enormous, vibrantly fluttering, symbolically regenerative Stars and Stripes—the musical cue sheet informing the accompanist to play the "Star Spangled Banner" until the end credits.

Bolshevism on Trial thus literally places the potential threat of social revolution right off America's shore, as opposed to thousands of miles away in an enigmatic Russia. In effect, the film's portrayal of American troops landing upon the Bolshevik-dominated island and overcoming its Red Guard becomes a cinematic device by which to positively allude to U.S. intervention forces still occupying Russian soil—but without confronting the real-life political complexities that had neutralized their military effectiveness.[100]

The reconquest of Paradise Island be-

comes a metaphoric assault upon a symbolic Red bastion. But the few Red Guards under Wolff's command offer no resistance—dramatically simulating/anticipating the raids upon the offices of "criminal aliens" in several American cities that would actually take place from May 1919 through early 1920, culminating in the notorious Palmer Raids of January 2, 1920.[101]

Several Red Scare era motion pictures are climaxed by raids upon Bolshevik headquarters, including *The Burning Question*, where the basement of the Reds' cavernous hall is used for conspiratorial meetings. *The Undercurrent* depicts revolutionary activities taking place during the evenings at a German beer garden and at the militant union's sardonically named Harmony Hall. The radicals are subsequently attacked, rounded up and prepared for deportation in the light of day. Milton's *Paradise Lost* refers to the consuming of the forbidden fruit as "Man's First Disobedience." Bolshevism, by promising a chimerical classless paradise, becomes the serpent in an edenic America. The dabbling with Bolshevism by political neophytes on the tropical Paradise Island in *Bolshevism on Trial* is the allegorical equivalent of nibbling upon a forbidden ideological apple which, if fully consumed, will cast one out of the Christian democratic paradise of the United States.

Bolshevism on Trial was the earliest unequivocal film manifestation of the genuine American fear of the Soviet desire to promulgate actively for a world-wide revolution of the proletariat. Its content was probably influenced by the February-March 1919 Overman Senate subcommittee investigation of Bolshevism that was the source of many specious documents, including those alleging the nationalization/sexual expropriation of Russian women.[102] Women are portrayed as being liberated only to become objects subject to sexual exploitation; a politicized variation upon the earlier white slavery (coercive prostitution) scare and resulting short-lived film genre.

Having just recently escaped the carnage of the World War, America's newest veterans (with discharge papers, a civilian suit and $60 in hand) turned their energies inwards, once home. There was a straightforward mission to defeat a specific enemy in the trenches, and the perceptual threat of Bolshevism would provide a clear enemy on the domestic economic and political fronts. Throughout the Red Scare period, veterans are coded as appearing in 16 percent topically relevant films.

One of the major interest groups that actively promoted the Red Scare was the newly founded (in May) veteran's organization, the American Legion.[103] During the latter half of 1919 and the first half of 1920, at least five anti-Red films depicted ex-soldiers targeting and engaging revolutionaries at home: *The Burning Question*, *The Volcano*, *The Undercurrent*, *The World Aflame* and *Riders of the Dawn*. The American Legion

is specifically identified and used as an anti-revolutionary para-military force in the October 1920 Fox release, *The Face at Your Window*.

The climax of *Riders of the Dawn*, released by W. W. Hodkinson in May 1920, features night riding vigilantes, commanded by AEF veteran Kurt Dorn (cowboy star Roy Stewart), rounding up (and possibly lynching, if true to the Zane Grey source novel) a group of I.W.W.s (led by a man with a Germanic surname) that have been disrupting the harvesting of heartland America's wheat crop. Indicative of the reactionary intensity of the Red Scare is the following comment appearing in a *Motion Picture News* review: "...*another* [my emphasis] indictment against the 'I Won't Works.'"[104]

The Undercurrent, a Select Pictures "Special Attraction," went into general exhibition in November 1919, at the height of the nationwide Great Steel Strike.[105] *The Undercurrent* featured a Doughboy tank driver named Jack Duncan (produced, written by and starring the barrel chested, square faced veteran and author of patriotic tracts, Sgt. Guy Empey) who returns home to his wife and child and takes up his old machine shop position at the Steel City mills. He quickly becomes the most popular man among the ex-soldiers working at the mills. Wishing to exploit his influence with the veterans, some Red agitators on the job secretly arrange it so that Jack is one of the first to be discharged when war contracts are canceled. The steel of Duncan's tank had protected him on French battlefields from the weapons of the opposing German army; now the former sergeant must steel himself against the pernicious propaganda of the new Bolshevik enemy who has collaborated with the Germans and who works to undermine confidence in American industry in order to render the country defenseless against a future radical onslaught.

As an embittered member of the recently unemployed, unable to make his house payments, Jack mingles with the malcontents and alien agents who congregate at the Beethoven Gardens, a German beer garden where under the corrosive influence of alcohol a socially disruptive "undercurrent flows."[106] A German immigrant socialist named Padris Thann, a dark curly-haired intellectual type wearing glasses, is a cafe strategist who uses alcohol, or "joy water," to fuel the flames of Duncan's discontent.[107]

The short plain-faced Jack in honest worker's clothes and cap is juxtaposed with/ dominated by the taller, black-swathed, heavily-rouged, hard liquor drinking Russian-born Mariska (Betty Blythe). Eventually, the duped veteran of *The Undercurrent*, mesmerized by a scarlet harlot and a German-born socialist, a Russian vamp (an implicit betrayer of traditional maternal duties) and her German stepbrother/pimp, becomes alienated from his wife and child. Is no one immune to this incestuous radical's snare, the film seems to wonder.[108]

The advocates of Bolshevism are foreign-born enemies preying upon gullible working-class Americans—enemies who gained power by exploiting the weaknesses of a war-ravaged regime in Russia. Thus the Reds are allegorical war profiteers, who likewise attempt to deceive and take unfair advantage of working-class vulnerabilities. Home front battles, then, must be fought in defense of an idealized traditional America. In the process, fragile wartime class unity dissipates and is threatened. Ironically, U.S. Army veterans portrayed in Red Scare era films engage in more combat against supposed Bolsheviks on the domestic front than they were ever shown on screen doing against the Huns on the Western Front during the World War. What is not directly addressed is the underlying middle-class fear of restless working-class combat veterans joining the Bolshevik cause.

But the paramount threat to Duncan's Americanism and to the moral integrity of his family emanates from the politically hypnotic siren song of a communist vamp who performs at the beer garden. Becoming enmeshed in a web of violence planned against the capitalist establishment, Jack's patriotic will is finally restored after confronting a Red accosting his wife and then having a vision of little Jack junior with the American flag, as the "Battle Hymn of the Republic" is played by the house musician/orchestra in the background. The popular patriotic lyrics suggesting to the audience how old truths can alert Americans to new dangers—a militant Messiah will "crush the serpent with his heel." The regenerated veteran then proceeds to a labor rally organized by the radicals, denounces them and destroys their Red flag.[109] Jack's assertive "Americanism" leads to rioting between loyal workers and the Reds. Thann, his "ideals shattered" by the brutal realities of class warfare, concludes he has been exploited by the Reds and helps Duncan escape. The former sergeant commandeers a train manned by a Red and proceeds to the local Army barracks. The troops pile into trucks and head over to the Harmony Hall to quell the discordant outbreak, effectively visualizing the concept of a flying squadron of rugged patriots putting out the flames of a radical workers' revolution menacing the house of democracy.[110] With the bestial Bolsheviks cornered in their filthy den, the fanatical Mariska, realizing the end is near, damns America, shoots her cringing comrades with a revolver and then commits a final mad act of self-destruction.

The musical scoring of *The Undercurrent* provides a good and further example of the more sophisticated means of manipulating the popular definition of Bolshevism. This aural coding, inherently variable in the context of "silent" films, is particularly effective when using (as suggested in the studio pressbook) for the film's "Plotting Theme," Gaston Borch's "The Crafty Spy."[111] Its near universal generic negative associations immediately discredits Bolshevism. Whereas the use of the more topically specific, well known and emotionally stirring "Internationale" to cue the key scenes with the communists would have potentially imparted an unwanted positive message to the movie audience.[112] Although the *Variety* review criticizes the poor "artistry" of the film, *The*

Undercurrent nonetheless hits upon virtually all of the pejorative themes that would
be tagged on the Red Other. It shows a veteran ultimately rejecting the socialist rhetoric
of intemperate German intellectuals and
physically resisting revolutionary actions incited by Russian-born Bolsheviks.[113]

Released by Paramount/Artcraft in February 1920, at the apex of the Red Scare, another filmic clarion call, *Dangerous Hours*,
employs the entire range of anti-Communist
demonology within the framework of a romantic melodrama—representing a lexicog-
raphy of the stereotypes that would, with the
singular exception of the World War II years,
periodically appear on America's movie
screens for the next seventy years. Furthermore, director Fred Niblo's use of cinematic
form to define opposing ideological symbols
is relatively refined—spatially and tempo-
rally complex.

A recent college graduate, John King
(Lloyd Hughes), who has "read" Russian liberals, falls for a black-haired radical new
woman, Sophia Guerni.[114] And, like the biblical disciple John, he must endure an ordeal
of faith.[115] Under Sophia's sway, young King
mixes with the decadent "intellectual" set
(including long-haired men and cigarette/
dope smoking short-haired lesbians) at her
Washington Square apartment—its darkness
suggesting a beast's lair. This collective of
social outcasts has come under the spell of
a bloodthirsty, bearded Bolshevik fanatic
from the "New Russia," Boris Blotchi (to be
covered with blotches; possibly meant to intimate cankers and thereby create a metaphor
for obscene corruption; actor Jack Richardson). Inspired by the headlined news of a
"National Strike" in a copy of *The New York
Times*, the group decides to exploit a sympathy strike in the small town of New Meadows at the shipyards owned by John's old
sweetheart, Mary Weston.[116]

Blotchi, with the aid of his new paramour, the now Bolshevik-possessed Sophia,
travel to the peaceful town and secretly
whip-up their radical followers into a revolutionary frenzy. To punctuate the agitation

of his fellow radicals, the devilish Blotchi
caresses and then waves an oversized
grenade/Mills Bomb that he has removed
from a grip.[117] This use of a grenade suggests a perverse love of violence, while simultaneously creating an associative linkage with the sanguinary warfare of the
World War trenches. And, in the revolutionary Russia flashback, Blotchi was pictured
in the uniform of the Red Guard. Having
thus been established as militaristically inclined, Blotchi also represents a symbolic
invader of the United States, leading an outcast army of the socially damned.

Blotchi and his gang of revolutionaries
then incite the "abandoned scum of the
seaboard underworld" to riot in New Meadows, leading to a destructive midnight (hour
of the Devil's dance) orgy against the symbols of American values; small businesses,
people's homes, the patriotic statue in the
town square (a Civil War soldier?) and culminating with the fiery razing of a church.
Blotchi is a Russian "Lord of the Flies"
reigning over assorted vermin who thrive in
the darkness of night. Thus Lenin's principle of a professional party elite being best
suited to recognize and seize the proper revolutionary moment is put to practice by his
odious pupil, Blotchi.

John recovers his senses after a glaze-
eyed Sophia maniacally damns America—
an art title featuring a winged eagle evokes
the nineteenth century concept of making
the American eagle scream.[118] His faith in
American democracy restored, John joins
the loyal union men now defending the shipyard and literally blows up the seething mob
of screaming Bolsheviks at its gates with one
of their own bombs—the bomb of retribution.[119] John then regains the estranged love
of Mary and the respect of his elderly father
(whose likeness resembles that of Uncle Sam,
sans the chin hair). For, having exterminated
the dangerous Reds who had desecrated small
town America, John can visit the bedside of
the injured virginal Mary and request absolution for having strayed from unquestioning
devotion to the spirit of Americanism. The

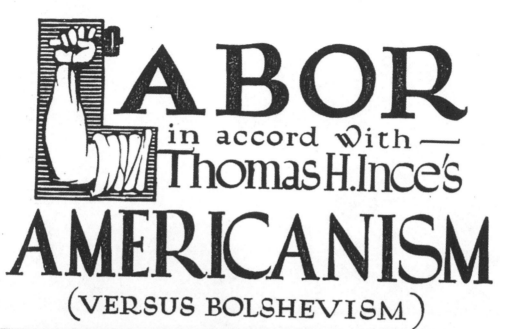

Dangerous Hours (Paramount-Artcraft, 1920): Under its original working title, this Spring 1919 ad featured an endorsement of the anti-radical film by AFL president Samuel Gompers.

Dangerous Hours (Paramount-Artcraft, 1920): True blue American girl Mary (Barbara Castleton), who happens to own a shipyard under strike, comforts the father of her sweetheart—whom they have just learned has fallen under the evil influence of Bolsheviks. Note the Uncle Sam look of the old man, played by Walt Whitman.

convalescing Mary, a symbol of America's resilience, signals forgiveness (in a tight closing shot) by gently stroking the forehead of her prodigal man.

In opposition to the open, daylight ceremonies legitimating the mythic American system, virtually all meetings of radicals take place at night and/or in dark smoky rooms and meeting halls. In *Dangerous Hours*, for example, the final gathering to plot out the details of the Red revolt takes place at night in an old barn. John, juxtaposed with painted art titles of the shining beacon beaming out from a lighthouse, wades through the muck of the barn to dramatically confront the shadowy evil conspirators. The light that guides John to moral righteousness also steers him away from a collision upon the dangerous rocks of Bolshevik-inspired anarchy. His patriotic speech before the scowling Bolshevik beasts in the barn is an affirmation of the secular religion of Americanism. John rises off the floor of the Stygian barn after being left unconscious by a blackjack blow to the back of his head, as if resurrected from moral death, to destroy the serpent that has violated the symbolic new world Eden of America.

The titles and inter-titles of *Dangerous Hours* are particularly effective in reinforcing American iconographic imagery and the demonization of the communist Other. For instance, when John allows himself to be duped by the Bolsheviks his scenes are introduced with painted art titles that feature a jester's cap. On the other hand, Blotchi, the devil's missionary from Russia, is juxtaposed with pictures of a blood-drenched butcher knife. And in scenes where the Bolsheviks plot disorder, the art titles contain the familiar image of the anarchist's smoking bomb, along with other arch symbols of

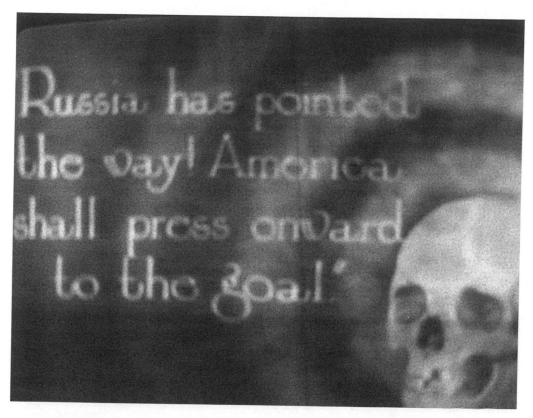

Dangerous Hours (Paramount-Artcraft, 1920): An art title whose image of the skull belies the Bolshevik rhetoric of progress—the film's painted backgrounds were by artist Irvin Martin.

violence like a pistol and a hangman's noose. In effect, such visual embodiments of the communist Other are the cinematic equivalent of illustrated anti-Communist leaflets scattered throughout the film's text.

American flags and eagles accompany John's rejoinders as he turns on the Bolsheviks, becoming the symbol-laden heraldry upon the armor of a patriotic knight. A classic evocation of an ideologically loaded image is the art title of a majestic American bald eagle in soaring flight that marks the moment when a morally reawakened John declaims before the frenzied mob of revolutionaries in the fetid barn where they have secretly gathered to plot social mayhem: "We in America do not fight that way...."[120]

Yet the competing ideologies of democratic capitalism and communism, per se, are *never* examined in the text of *Dangerous Hours*. John, while still under the spell of

the "Bull Shovers," never refers to Mary as a capitalist. Instead, at one point the amateur radical John politely and delicately admonishes her for being a "wealthy employer," albeit a fair and decent one, who is respectful to the workers even when they are striking.

An extended flashback in *Dangerous Hours*, designed to simultaneously horrify and voyeuristically titillate the spectator, portrays the Bolsheviks' brutal excesses during the Russian revolution. But throughout the entire sequence, the historical causalities of the revolution are never explained, nor is any tangible description provided of the ideology that imbued the Bolsheviks. Instead, the flashback begins with an ironic juxtaposition in which, after Blotchi has justified the violence of the revolution to his American admirers by explaining that "we killed to eat," the movie viewer is presented with a series of graphic scenes exposing the

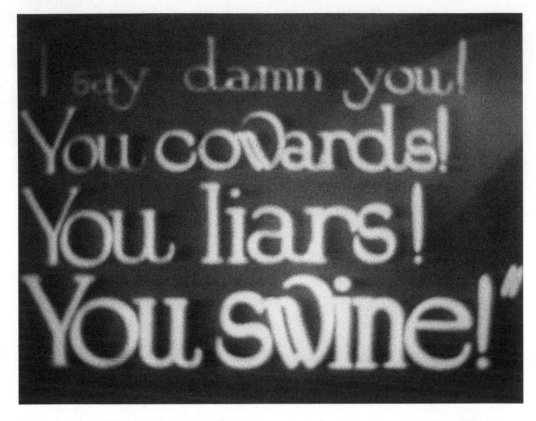

Dangerous Hours (Paramount-Artcraft, 1920): **An example of an inter-title—it is the hero's response to his former comrades, once he had learned of their brutal plan to destroy the town where his sweetheart's strikebound shipyard is located.**

Bolsheviks' hypocritical "curtain of lies." Following a smoke-shrouded dissolve, the opening shot of the flashback reveals the devilish-countenanced Blotchi holding an automatic gun in his right hand. Subsequent scenes within the flashback include atrocities committed by the Bolsheviks against the *people* of Russia, killing and abusing their equals for the sake of power and not for the betterment of Mother Russia.

Red Guard "Colonel" Blotchi is shown later during the flashback eagerly participating in the summary execution of the young sons of White Russian officers and the looting of private property. Soon afterwards, the morally depraved Blotchi literally tears a child away from its mother, rapes the woman and then apparently murders her—a brief shadowy shot portrays the victim's prostrate, naked corpse in one corner

of a darkened room while Blotchi admires his handiwork from the opposite doorway![121] The only hunger displayed, therefore, is that of the Bolshevik lust to sexually devour Russia's women. This scene is followed by one in which a man, who looks like Lenin, vociferously cheered by an assembled Soviet, decrees the "nationalization of women"—a near pornographic (for the time) *reductio ad absurdum* regarding the Marxist vision of a proletarian dictatorship. The flashback concludes with the triumphal Red Guard marching down a gutted Petrograd street trampling over the outstretched bodies of a peasant woman and her baby, side by side—graphically symbolizing the death of Mother Russia and her innocent offspring.

With such a cinematic demonology firmly established, it was easy for Hollywood in future decades to formulaically attack the

Dangerous Hours (Paramount-Artcraft, 1920): During an extended flashback of revolutionary Russia showing the "hypocritical curtain of lies" behind which the Bolsheviks hide, an art title graphically foreshadows the fate awaiting the captured young sons of White Russian officers—death by firing squad.

alleged madness of the various communist regimes and their domestic American advocates. During the first half of the 1920s, there were a number of films that employed the motif of White Russian refugees in the United States pursued for their royal baubles by crazed Red thugs. In the early thirties, American college students, including coed Barbara Stanwyck in *Red Salute* (UA, 1935), would often have to be protected from the insidious communist rhetoric of effete intellectuals and mad Russians. And then there were the "screwball" Reds of the late thirties, such as those brilliantly portrayed in the Lubitsch classic *Ninotchka* (MGM, 1939).[122] More and more, the ideology of communism is caricatured, the national consciousness is manipulated, and the actual issues fade into insignificance on America's romanticized movie screens.

3. From the East to the East Side
White Flight from the Red Hordes to America, 1921–1929

*You damn Romanoff! We've rid the world of you're [sic] kind—and we'll get you! —*The Face in the Fog *(1922)*

[T]he trail of tragedy, of crumbling thrones and blood-stained palace halls, finally led to America... —opening title of Drums of Jeopardy *(1924)*

In the decade following the Red Scare the American public displayed a dramatic decline of interest with matters related to radical politics, which was directly reflected in the content of the fictional motion pictures produced by Hollywood. Even in those few films that still touched on labor and/or communist issues, the former propensity for rhetorical shrillness and graphic violence was in most cases substantially toned-down. Increasingly, even when the old negative stereotypes were used, they functioned less in the political sphere than as shorthand for problems of a more personal nature. Pro-labor films were marginalized, while less sympathetic motion pictures related to the working-class' struggle with capitalism were largely de-politicized. Likewise, the Bolsheviks became progressively transformed into mere gangsters during the early twenties, while greater irony and evenhandedness in their cinematic portrayal came to prevail

in the decade's latter years. Yet new radical "trouble spots," such as Nicaragua, evoked older anti-communist themes, though usually in a quieter guise.

After 1920 the United States government rejected the newly founded League of Nations as well as many other manifestations of a great power's world responsibilities. At the same time, a majority of its citizens seemed to prefer largely to ignore those issues which might remind them of what they and their leaders had abandoned.[1] Two of the most salient international occurrences during the initial twenty years of the twentieth century were undoubtedly the 1914–18 Great War and the 1917 Bolshevik Revolution. The lingering implications of the former and the ongoing impact (both real and perceived) of the latter would continue to have a tremendous effect upon world events throughout the 1920s and beyond. In previous years, especially during the second

111

half of the teens, international issues had regularly been incorporated into the content of a significant number of fictional feature-length American motion pictures. Yet in the films produced and released in the United States during the decade following the Red Scare's conclusion in 1920, the communist revolution in Russia and its inter-relationship with the World War were seldom mentioned, let alone portrayed. The contemporary Soviet regime, which would not be formally recognized by the U.S. government until 1933, went similarly unrecognized, in any overt format, in American films.[2] As in the past, when the American motion picture industry handled so-called alien radical ideologies or their representatives, they presented them stereotypically, via the generic set of negative images or dialogue cues which had been fully codified into a demonology during the ephemeral Red Scare of 1918–20.

A simple recounting of the numbers tells much about this willful flight from political realities within the texts of American films of the 1920s. In the nine years prior to and including 1917 at least 250 motion pictures (both short and feature-length) dealt specifically with radical socio-political themes, while during the first three years following the Bolshevik Revolution 91 feature-length films concerned themselves with left-wing radicalism and/or the new Soviet regime. More than half of those works were released during the notorious period of reactionary hysteria between the spring of 1919 and the fall of 1920, almost all being virulently anti-Soviet/anti-revolutionary. Yet, throughout the next nine years, 1921–29, just 95 feature-length motion pictures dealt with domestic revolutionary radicalism (including violent labor disturbances), international communism and/or with the Soviet Union. More interestingly, only five of these films portrayed or even alluded to the contemporary revolutionary "utopia" being fashioned by the "one party dictatorship" under Lenin and his political disciples—*Fashion Row* (Tiffany/Metro, 1923); *Abie's Imported Bride*

(Temple/Trio, 1925); *Broken Hearts* (Jaffe, 1926); *Diplomacy* (Paramount, 1926); *The Adventurer* (Metro, 1928).[3]

What happened broadly was that the reactionary xenophobia in the United States associated with the Red Scare period was replaced by an era of relative political complacency vis-à-vis radicalism. During 1918–20, 36 films were released with a distinctly Anti-Soviet bias. Yet, over the next nine years, a total numbering only 35 of generally far less virulent ones came out. Normalcy's progeny lost interest in international intrigue, but occasionally White Russian refugees would be melodramatically juxtaposed with churlish Bolshevik intruders. The motion picture industry also increasingly imported its diminishing representatives of leftist terrorists. In fact, on screen indigenous radicals were essentially reduced to a few innocuous "parlor Bolsheviks," or the odd comic anarchist or two, such as can be found in Roscoe "Fatty" Arbuckle's *The Dollar-a-Year-Man* (Paramount, 1921). Ultimately, throughout the 1921–29 period less than 20 percent of all topically relevant films contain any reference to anarchism and/or domestic radicalism.[4]

The largest topically-linked unit among the relatively few germane films released concentrated on the travails of the displaced Russian nobility during the Bolshevik Revolution and the civil war that immediately followed; 43 percent of the 1921–29 films have a White Russian coding.[5] Thirty-one per cent of these motion pictures made reference to White Russian flight from the new "Red" Russia to a new "free world," and nearly a quarter showed struggling White Russian emigres living in America, frequently in the tenements of New York's East Side.[6]

The refugee phenomenon in American films was not new. In its various manifestations it provided a means by which to "exoticize" the otherwise commonplace immigrant story. The pre-Revolutionary Nihilist genre stressed the theme of resistance and eventual escape, occasionally to America, from the autocratic Tsarist regime. The physical flight from Russia usually followed an act of revenge for a violation by the state upon one's self (sometimes a Jewish heroine) or one's family. And as early as 1916 the problems of Belgium's victims of the World War's ravages were being thematically linked with domestic labor issues. For instance, the American/Mutual release entitled *Dust*, includes a scene in which the protagonist publicly condemns his fiancée at a war benefit for paying more attention to the plight of Belgian refugees than to the victims of the domestic war between capital and labor. In late 1917 Metro released *Draft 258*, featuring a German spy and his radical cohorts as the heavies, that includes a flashback depicting the atrocities suffered by a little Belgian refugee girl's family at the hands of the invading German army. By the end of the World War years the character of the innocent Belgian refugee fleeing from the wanton "Hun" had been outrageously exploited in such other "Hate-the-Hun" films as *The Kaiser, Beast of Berlin* (Renowned Picts-Jewel, 1918) and *To Hell with the Kaiser* (Metro, 1918).[7] With the advent of the Bolshevik revolution further thematic overlapping (paralleling Wilsonian foreign policy) inevitably appeared on the screen. In fact, the cinematic usage of fleeing White Russians in the 1920s would become the decade's favored adaptation of these earlier refugee dramas.

The 1920s East to East Side set of motion pictures was marked with an ironic ambience. In the older Nihilist films the heroes/martyrs were those who had violently resisted many of the very same people, the monarchy and their representatives, who on 1920s screens fled the successful destroyers of the Tsarist regime. Since at least three pre-revolution like Nihilist films appeared during the latter half of the 1920s, *The Midnight Sun* (Universal-Jewel, 1926), *My Official Wife* (WB, 1926) and *The Woman from Moscow* (Paramount, 1928), perhaps there existed an over-arching negative image with regards to an authoritarian Russian bureaucracy that transcended the more immediate pejorative associations with either "feudal" or "Red" Russia. Certainly, this negative image of the Russian royalists reasserts itself with some force in the waning years of the decade.[8] In a series of films that include flight from the Bolsheviks, e.g., *The Volga Boatman* (PDC, 1926), *The Last Command* (Paramount, 1928) and *Tempest* (UA, 1928), many of the Whites were portrayed as being as arrogant and cruel as their Red opponents. But positive, non-partisan political traits were also displayed in some of these later films. In *The Volga Boatman* the captured princess actually elects to remain in the "new Russia" with her handsome Bolshevik lover after he had arranged for her release from Soviet-controlled territory.

The not uncommon anti-Semitic Jewish-Bolshevik linkage in Red Scare era cinema, unequivocal in such films as *Bullin' the Bullsheviki* (Eff & Eff, 1919) and *The Burning Question* (Catholic Art, 1919), rarely manifested itself on American movie house screens after 1920.[9] Only two motion pictures released during the period appear to exploit the negative "Jew-Bolshevik" stereotype—the local Red leader named Egor Kaplan (Lou Tellegen) of *Siberia* (Fox, 1926) and the sinister Bolshevik proselytizing peddler, who is never addressed by name, portrayed two years later in United Artist's *Tempest*. In point of fact, in *The Rendezvous* (Goldwyn, 1923), an early precursor to the revisionist Russian refugee escape films, the fleeing nobles, in an ironic twist, are terrorized by rapacious White Russian Cossacks and aided in their escape to America by two ethnic vaudeville-style slapstick Jewish commissars.

These East to East Side films, usually in the guise of melodramas or comedies, also provided a low risk arena upon which to display the superiority of the idealized self-portrait of Americans in contrast to the negative image of the failed decadent ruling elites of Europe. In the relevant motion pictures produced through 1928, the White Russian nobility or aristocratic poseurs, fleeing the

The Last Command (Paramount, 1928): International screen star Emil Jannings plays a one-time
Tsarist general working as a Hollywood extra. The director (William Powell), a former Bolshevik, insists upon costume authenticity.

brutal Bolsheviks and defeating Red agents
in America, invariably experience an almost
mystical transformation into humble Americans. Their metamorphosis culminates in
their emergence as full-fledged bourgeois
capitalists, either through marriage or through
business enterprise that catapults them into
the American upper-middle classes. At the
same time, the enduring conception of the
decadent Russian nobility was so well entrenched that it was parodied in a number of
films. An early example of this is the gum
chewing shop girl in *Manhandled* (Paramount, 1924), played by silent screen idol
Gloria Swanson, who poses for awhile
among the New York bohemian set as a
Russian countess.

A new element introduced into twelve
per cent of the 1920s refugee films featured

White Russians who had or were purported
to have escaped with valuable jewels in their
possession, usually some part of the legendary crown jewels. The gems were most
often held altruistically, in trust, for the relief of fellow expatriates or to be sent back
to Russia to either finance a counter-revolution or to feed those left destitute by the ravages of the prolonged civil strife that had
afflicted revolutionary Russia. Audiences
most often encountered ruthless Red agents
in pursuit of these jewels, but with only
slight accompanying communist rhetoric or
displays of Soviet iconography.

The White Russian/crown jewel scenario
created the quintessential vehicle through
which obliquely to express the major points
of friction between the United States government and the Soviet Union, without in any

way reinforcing a positive image of the Bolsheviks or intellectually engaging the ideological issues. In actuality, a major objection raised by American officialdom against recognition of the USSR (Union of Soviet Socialist Republics; official name of the Russian state as of 1922) was the failure of the Soviets to renounce political subversion in foreign countries. What is most often portrayed in the relevant films are menacing Red agents, essentially exotic gangsters, attempting to seize the jewels from their White Russian owners or guardians. Regularly played by such 1920s' "heavies" as Louis Wolheim, Wallace Beery, Elmo Lincoln, Ivan Linow and Montague Love, these foreign gangsters represented an outlaw regime, creating some clear, if never especially stressed, political points. What better way to spotlight the very real financial distress of the politically and militarily successful revolution than by portraying the Bolsheviks as being forced to take violent extra-legal measures in a desperate attempt to acquire assets in order to prop up their faltering economy? Furthermore, how could the United States be expected to conduct normal relations with an ideologically anathema state that stole from others and refused to honor the debts of the ancient regime?[10] The seizure of crown jewels thus becomes a narratively economical and cinematically stimulating means by which Hollywood could represent the Bolsheviks' dependence on expropriation of vast amounts of the once privately-owned resources of Russia.

The flight of the White Russians from the Bolsheviks led to a diaspora during the early 1920s, comprising over a million people by 1923 (after 1922 Soviet authorities had virtually eliminated all emigration). Primarily from the middle-class, most of the refugees eventually wound up in Harbin and Shanghai in China, Poland, Constantinople, Paris, Berlin and in America (15-20,000)—particularly the East Side of New York City.[11] The earliest example of an American feature film to engage this phenomenon was the fall 1920 comedy release of Paramount's *Little Miss Rebellion*. Although technically occurring at the end of the Red Scare period, this film established the East to East Side precedent. The Grand Duchess Marie Louise, played by the coquettish Dorothy Gish, flees from the mythical kingdom of Bulgravia to America following a "Bolshevik uprising." On New York's East Side, Marie Louise and a faithful elderly servant live incognito in furnished rooms. But "Foreign Bolsheviki" track them down and attempt to seize the crown jewels held by the two. A former American Army sergeant, played by handsome leading man Ralph Graves, who had been stationed in Bulgravia and had recognized Marie Louise at her job in front of a pancake griddle, is able to save the Grand Duchess from the evil Reds. The theme of the aristocratic political refugee(s) living in humble circumstances, while holding on to the valuable crown jewels, would be used as late as 1937 in Warner Brothers' *Tovarich*.

A year later in 1921, variations on the East to East Side phenomenon began to appear in increasing numbers. In *Making the Grade* (Western Pictures), a comedy-drama, the carefree son of a wealthy American family, while serving with a private American relief expedition in Siberia, falls in love with a school teacher named Sophie Semenoff. Sophie is under pressure to submit sexually to the Red cause. Eddie Ramson, our wild young American, helps Sophie elude the lascivious Bolsheviks, marries her and then returns with his new Russian bride to the United States. Mother does not approve of her alien daughter-in-law. But father helps Eddie support his new wife by arranging a laboring job for his son. Mrs. Ramson becomes reconciled to her Eddie's marriage when she is later forced to confront local radicals who have abducted Sophie in the name of Soviet Russia. It turns out that Sophie is actually a former princess whose jewels are sought by the Bolshevik regime. Thus love in Russia and the jewels in America are employed as non-ideological means to allow for Americans to engage in surrogate combat with the communist government of Russia.

The filmmakers could easily have portrayed Eddie as part of the Allied Intervention forces in Russia during 1918–20, but apparently preferred to de-emphasize direct political conflict between the Soviets and the United States.

Such subjects continue in the composite portrait of several East to East Side films released between 1922 and 1924. In the fall of 1922, two major motion pictures came out that, together, contain all the key elements of the East to East Side theme. The first of these, distributed by Metro and starring actress Clara Kimball Young, is entitled *The Hands of Nara*. Nara Alexieff, the beautiful daughter of a wealthy Russian landowner, is swept away from the old life by the "Bolshevik catastrophe." She winds up being arrested through the connivance of a prototypical revolutionary who had sought to seduce her; this villain was so much the characteristic stereotyped ogre that it was not necessary to give him a name or to even credit the actor who played the part. Nara's release from prison and subsequent escape from Soviet Russia is arranged through the self-sacrifice of a "good" and less enthusiastic revolutionary who has come to admire her. This gambit of the simple Bolshevik mesmerized by the beauty of the White Russian female would occur a number of times throughout the decade, for example in *Bavu*, a 1923 Universal release.

After her arrival in America, Nara struggles to survive, living in a shabby room in the tenements of New York's East Side. But then she meets a wealthy widow who makes a habit of taking up "interesting" people. As a result, Nara winds up spending a great deal of her time in an "oriental" salon among the socially faddish bohemian set. The group includes a sculptor who falls for her and creates a majestic interpretation of Nara's exquisite hands. But jealousies lead to an attempted murder by a member of the household. The older association of bohemianism with immorality is forcefully reasserted.

Determined to get away from this new form of madness, Nara seeks out a man named Connor Lee, to whom she had brought a letter from her smitten revolutionary in Russia. Lee, a con man, convinces Nara that her hands have the power to restore health, with some suggested linkage to Russian Orthodox mysticism or the charlatanism of Rasputin. This leads to a number of healings among the people in the tenements, where Nara comes to be known as the "Angel." Since Connor Lee takes full financial advantage of this, a connection between Bolshevism and criminality is established. Simultaneously, his entrepreneurial capitalism implies ideological hypocrisy, which was a typical smear of so-called "parlor Bolsheviks."

Sometime later, Nara reluctantly agrees to try to help the dying mother of Emlen Claveloux, a skeptical young doctor who is in love with the enigmatic Russian. When Nara's ministrations appear to succeed, Emlen's belief in the power of faith over purely scientific methods of healing is established. It also provides the means by which he and Nara are able to begin to discover their love for one another. Thus, in the end, a form of Christian Science faith overcomes cosmopolitan and/or atheistic skepticism as well as criminal Bolshevism. Behind the romantic facade of this film's conclusion there exists an anti-intellectual, mystical subtext, to which more attention is given than to its political context.

Paramount's *The Face in the Fog*, directed by Alan Crosland, was also released in the fall of 1922, and put the components of the East to East Side phenomenon in their more common setting of action-oriented melodrama. As related in a flashback midway through the *The Face in the Fog*, the beautiful Grand Duchess Tatiana, played by Seena Owen, had barely escaped the Bolshevik terror visited upon her father's estate. Seconds after she and some other royalists slip out of the castle through a secret passageway, the drunken Bolshevik mob bursts through the main entrance of the building and tramples over the corpse of Tatiana's father. In a highly evocative (and very innovative for its time) overhead camera angle, the Grand Duke is portrayed as if crucified upon a floor mosaic of the Romanoff double-headed eagle. Tatiana is able to smuggle into "the land of the free" the lost Romanoff diamonds. Just before fleeing, she had sworn to her dying father eventually to return with the diamonds to Russia in order to finance an attempted restoration of the throne—paradoxically denying closure in a scene that amalgamates religious, political and violent imagery. Tatiana has been assisted and accompanied by her faithful servant Michael and her lover, Count Orloff. However, "Soviet savages" have relentlessly pursued the incipient revanchists and their jewels. These alien thugs are led by the "evil faced" Petrus (the crooked-nosed actor Louis Wolheim, whose character name also suggests a hard or thick head)[12] and by the lecherous Count Ivan, who has cynically joined forces with the Red agents.

Fortunately for our White Russian emigres, they are aided by the dapper reformed safe-cracker "Boston Blackie" Dawson, played by Lionel Barrymore, and an alert American Secret Service.[13] As a matter of fact, at the beginning of the film on a fog-shrouded night in front of a fashionable restaurant, Blackie is slipped a package containing the jewels by a mysterious blind beggar (Michael in disguise) just prior to the malevolent Petrus's brutally bludgeoning Michael to death with his beggar's crutch. Later that same evening, Petrus and his cohorts follow Blackie to his home, break in and threaten to torture Blackie's wife if he does not disclose to them the location of the diamonds. But Blackie is able to overcome his Red nemesis with the aid of an electrical device wired to the safe and the timely assistance of an old buddy, Huk, now a Secret Service agent.

As for the renegade Count Ivan, Boston Blackie and the good Count Orloff are able to intercept him in his fashionable apartment where he has kidnapped and is about to rape Tatiana. A brilliant piece of parallel editing precedes this rescue creating a beast-like

associative linkage between Petrus and Ivan, juxtaposed to the beauty of the tormented Grand Duchess. As Ivan corners the cowering Tatiana on a couch he is shown making an extended talon-like gesture (similar to the well-known shot of the vampire from F. W. Murnau's 1921 German horror film, *Nosferatu*) as he walks toward the camera in a shocking close-up of a demonic grimace. The scene is then cut to Count Orloff at Boston Blackie's residence, shouting at the captured Petrus that he is a vile "dog" and demanding to be informed of the whereabouts of Her Highness. A glowering Petrus raises his fist threateningly and then with a smirk retorts: "Ivan's got her!"

Learning of Tatiana's pledge to return to Russia with the Romanoff diamonds, of the good count's true love for the pretty lady, and of the United States government's determination to acquire the royal assets, Boston Blackie is able to satisfy all and simultaneously dispel any lingering doubts regarding his changed lifestyle by handing over the real jewels to the Secret Service and by providing a gorgeous set of paste replicas for the Grand Duchess. Apparently, the audience is to assume that the federal authorities may use the assets to support American relief efforts in the Soviet Union and that the aristocratic Russian couple will quickly and relatively painlessly (re)make their fortune in the capitalist paradise of America.

The text of *The Face in the Fog* depicts a multi-faceted series of images and linkages, though with little political stress, pertaining to the American public's negative perception of Bolshevism—including physical repulsiveness, degeneracy, decadence, cruelty, violence, and criminality. The motion picture also provides a contrast between the humbled aristocrats who will presumably settle down and prosper amidst capitalist America's social egalitarianism and the politically tainted lecherous anachronism, Ivan, epitomizing the mores that contributed to the destruction of the Romanoff dynasty as much as new Bolshevik treachery. Furthermore, *The Face in the Fog* portrays vigilant police authorities of the U.S. government directly intervening to neutralize the Bolshevik agents violating American soil and accepting the delivery of valuable assets belonging to the former Tsarist regime. It may be assumed that the taking of these jewels by American authorities was meant to imply a measure of moral ambiguity. This is clearly suggested in Paramount's Press Sheet in which exhibitors were encouraged to drum up trade by sending out announcements addressed to "all who are interested in the subject of Russian relief," at the time the staff of the American Relief Administration was directing wide scale famine aid operations in the Soviet Union.[14]

In November of 1923 Truart released the most biased anti-Soviet film from the 1922–24 group, *Drums of Jeopardy*. While largely taking place in contemporary New York City, the film, via a flashback, once again returns the audience to the turbulent days of the revolution in Russia. An armed group of Red Guards led by the bearded Gregor Karloff (Wallace Beery playing a similar role to the one he had performed earlier that year in *Bavu*) breaks into the home of the Grand Duke. They gleefully proceed to torture the hated aristocrat with a whip in an attempt to force him to disclose the hiding place of a gift from the Tsar—valuable twin emeralds in a setting known as the "Drums of Jeopardy." To spare the dying Grand Duke further agony at the hands of the Reds, his friend, Stephani, former imperial violinist, reveals to the Bolsheviks a secret panel located above the fireplace. The gloating Karloff fondles the Romanoff emeralds as his soldiers loot the room. The Grand Duke's American confidential secretary, Jerome Hawksley (Jack Mulhall), is accosted by the departing Reds on the walkway outside the villa and menacingly intimidated with a rifle butt.

In action that mimics American military intervention in Russia at the time set in the flashback, Hawksley and White Russian Stephani join forces and, in a bold nighttime operation, retake the crown jewels from a guarded Bolshevik compound.[15] Back in the present, the fall of 1923, Hawksley and Stephani have arrived in America with the emerald-encrusted statuette and have entrusted it to New York banker Barrows, the former financial representative of the "once powerful Russian monarchy." But Karloff and assorted stereotypical radical supernumeraries are also in New York City. Their headquarters is a speakeasy called "Little Russia," run by a communist vamp named Olga, that once again links liquor (contraband in Prohibition America) and radicalism.

One night Karloff murders Barrows in an attempt to retrieve the valuable emeralds. But Barrows had earlier handed them over to the Secret Service, who had already had their suspicions aroused by the aliens at the Little Russia. In order to expose the Bolsheviks, Hawksley, Stephani and Barrows' daughter Dorothy, wearing paste replicas of the emeralds as earrings, visit New York's East Side and watch the floor show at the Little Russia. The cafe's Red denizens take notice of their well-to-do guests and forcefully invite them to some back rooms. When Karloff discovers he has been tricked again, he becomes enraged and storms into the room in which Stephani has been imprisoned. In the climactic scene of the film, Karloff torments the frail Stephani, trying to make him reveal the whereabouts of the emeralds by threatening to smash the musician's beloved violin. Just as Karloff carries out his threat upon Stephani's prized instrument, the Secret Service agent bursts through the door. The audience soon learns that the Red "Bozo," in a bit of Hollywood poetic justice, was killed in the scuffle when he was thrown upon a shard of Stephani's shattered violin. The barbarous leader of the despoilers of the old culture is fatally impaled by a fragile remnant of that once great culture.

A politically modified version of the East to East Side phenomenon, that directly invokes American relief work in Russia, appears in the Tiffany production *Fashion Row*, released a month later in December. It features a blonde peasant girl named Olga who flees the revolution and comes to America, abandoning her illegitimate child and younger sister. In the States Olga becomes a celebrity by masquerading on Broadway as a member of the White Russian aristocracy. Despite strong objections from his family, Eric Van Corland, the son of a millionaire, marries Olga.

Meanwhile, Olga's look-alike sister, Zita (both parts are played by the glamorous Mae Murray), arrives by steerage in America and takes up residency in the home of a Jewish couple on the lower East Side. Olga refuses to acknowledge Zita. Also, Olga's brutish former lover, Kamineff (Elmo Lincoln), arrives on the same ship, his face bearing the scar of a fight with Olga. Though his actions conform to the anti-Bolshevik demonology, Kamineff is not explicitly tied to the Soviets. At a lawn party held for Russian Relief, Kamineff confronts Olga and shoots her. The mortally wounded woman confesses all to her husband.

The rich Van Corland family accepts Zita into their fold, while widower Eric finds solace by joining the relief expedition in the Soviet Union. Once again, the silver screen shows the superiority of the American system vis-à-vis the Soviets by stressing the willingness of the United States to both absorb and restore Russian refugees and to voluntarily send her capitalist sons to the revolutionary land to carry out humanitarian relief. The plot of *Fashion Row* also signals some American softening toward the Soviet regime, if not toward communism per se, in order to reach out to the Russian people. Helping the Soviets, which *The Face in the Fog* suggested directly only in its press book, is here subject to unambiguous praise.

Over the next two years, 1924–25, there was a significant decrease in motion pictures that in any way related to the Bolshevik revolution and/or the Soviet regime. In fact, just four of the twenty-one productions listed in the Filmography for those years are coded Anti-Soviet, all of which were released during the first quarter of 1924. Only *When a Girl Loves* (Halperin Prods.) spends significant

time in revolutionary Russia and has a fully developed evil Red — the dark-countenanced George Siegmann playing the role. A variation on the crown jewel scenario is used in a single film, First National's *Torment*.

Some motion pictures from the 1926 to 1928 period show other basic continuities while highlighting modest positive shifts in the American perspective with respect to communism and the Soviet regime that were timidly prefigured in *Fashion Row*. Changes, both subtle and not so subtle, toward friendlier handling of the Soviets begin taking place in 1926, epitomized by four works, *Into Her Kingdom* (First National, 1926), *The Volga Boatman* (PDC, 1926), *The Last Command*, and *Tempest*. Here, the Reds appearing in starring roles, if *not* most of those in secondary ones, are portrayed less stereotypically and as far more humane. On the other hand, the White Russians are increasingly presented as unwholesome — and sometimes as totally despicable. In the two films in which the lead characters, both former aristocrats, reach America, *Into Her Kingdom* and *The Last Command*, their transformation is from bad to good. Ultimately, love (patriotic as well as romantic) provides the vehicle by which most of the individuals are able to transcend the personal tragedies engendered both by their earlier aristocratic pretensions and by the Bolshevik revolution.[16]

Into Her Kingdom is a pivotal film in the East to East Side format. In the summer of 1918, the Romanoff family is herded into a dark cellar to be executed. But the second daughter of the Tsar, Tatiana (Corrine Griffith), has had her place taken by a faithful maid. Sometime later, the beautiful unidentified young lady is brought before a Soviet tribunal headed by Stephen Mammovitch. Stephen is a handsome peasant lad who has been hardened by seven years in a St. Petersburg prison. In fact, as an adolescent working on one of the royal estates, he had known and secretly loved Tatiana. It was there that an alleged insult upon her royal personage had led to his imprisonment and the exile of his parents to Siberia. Now, the orphaned Stephen is presented with an opportunity to exact swift revenge by simply denouncing the princess. Instead, Stephen decides to exercise his power by forcing her into marriage so that he may continually humiliate her. Tatiana initially disdains her Bolshevik husband. But her intrinsic kindness and delicate beauty (actress Griffith was known as the "Orchid Lady" because of her refined looks) begin to soften Stephen's heart. He surreptitiously arranges for their escape to America. In a New Jersey mill town the proud proletarian becomes a factory worker while his wife clerks at a little shop. Having grown to worship Tatiana and believing that she still yearns for the good old days, Stephen sails to Europe to arrange with imperial agents to confirm Tatiana as the only surviving child of the late Tsar Nicholas. However, when Stephen returns to their humble New Jersey home with the royalist representatives, Tatiana claims it is Stephen's delusion that she is a Romanoff princess and that her kingdom is that which she shares with her newborn daughter.

Into Her Kingdom suggests a major divergence from earlier Hollywood versions of the Russian situation. Stephen, although a Bolshevik believer in the beginning, is not only ultimately portrayed sympathetically, but also as a physically attractive clean shaven blond—a precursor of socialist realism's new Soviet man; such as the peasant "lad" hero who would later appear in the 1927 Soviet classic directed by Pudovkin, *The End of St. Petersburg*. In addition, having spent time in his youth with Tatiana's tutor Ivan, Stephen is placed above the ignorant peasant stereotype in such earlier cinematic Bolshevik caricatures like Petrus in *The Face in the Fog*. Instead, the completed film portrait of Stephen is that of an intelligent, hard-working immigrant and ennobled peasant who, with a little help from fate, eventually abandons the false love of Bolshevism to embrace a romantic love that has been nurtured in the democratic soil of America. To dramatically emphasize this

point, the film's director, Svend Gade, chose to periodically insert a Technicolor sequence of "The Weaver of Fate," much in the style of D. W. Griffith's "Cradle Endlessly Rocking" from *Intolerance*.

This altered cinematic image may also have borne some tie to the changing economic climate in the Soviet Union resulting from the relative success of the implementation of Lenin's New Economic Policy (NEP), which tried to attract Western capital. Although the United States would continue to deny diplomatic recognition, a significant amount of business was conducted between the two countries, particularly during the latter half of the twenties. One of the largest joint enterprises involved the construction of a Ford truck factory complex in Russia. There thus evolved the incipient notion of America as the patient midwife at the bedside of Bolshevik Russia waiting to help in the delivery of a reborn capitalist-oriented Russia—weaned away from its socialist mother, but rejecting its autocratic Tsarist father and willing to take lessons from its Uncle Sam.[17]

The cinematic manifestation of this rejection of the old Russia and embrace of doing business with the now-mellowing Soviet Union was most clearly portrayed in the 1926 Cecil B. DeMille color-tinted spectacular, *The Volga Boatman*. The title's traditional Russian song was used as the primary thematic melody in the musical accompaniment to the film, which evokes positive images of a pre-revolution bucolic non-threatening Russia. The hero is a peasant and a Bolshevik! And instead of the bearded, menacing, gesticulating stereotype, he is a young, fair-haired worker boatman named Feodor, played by the popular American film star William Boyd.

On the eve of the 1917 revolution, the proud boatman Feodor is publicly humiliated by the dark and haughty Prince Dimitri Orloff (Victor Varconi), an officer in the Tsar's Imperial Guard. When the Bolshevik takeover erupts, the castle of Dimitri's betrothed, Vera, is seized by Red Guards led by Feodor—whose Cyrillic lettered armband, "KOM POL," identifies him as a political commissar. This partially red-tinted scene is further highlighted by the playing of "The Internationale."[18] Vera (Elinor Fair; Boyd's real-life wife at the time) is captured and ordered to be executed in retaliation for the death of one of the attacking Bolsheviks. But when the boatman is left alone with her to carry out the deed, Feodor discovers that he does not have the will to shoot the beautiful young princess. The two are forced to flee for their lives from an angry mob when Feodor is discovered to have attempted to simulate Vera's death by sprinkling her with red wine and firing his pistol in the air. Feodor and Vera take refuge at an inn as man and wife.[19]

A White Army unit commanded by Dimitri reoccupies the area and captures the lovers. When Dimitri discovers their presence and the nature of their relationship, he orders that Feodor be executed at White headquarters. During a ball at headquarters the next evening Feodor, in his peasant's tunic (with a red star on the left breast—like a stylish fraternity monogram), is tied to the courtyard gate in front of an open grave. In an exquisite gown and tiara, Vera rushes up to the Red Leader and declares her eternal love. Just as Dimitri is about to command the firing squad to shoot the lovers, an artillery shell from the attacking Red Army wrecks headquarters. Soon afterwards, amid the taunts and beneath the whips of drunken revolutionaries, the surviving local aristocrats, including Vera, as well as the White officers, are forced to take up the towing harness of a Volga boat. Feodor joins Vera, and together the two sing the "Volga Boatman's Song."

Before a special Red Tribunal, the entire sequence tinted red, Feodor, invoking his work for the "Cause," passionately pleas for the lives of Vera *and* Dimitri. The Tribunal offers the two aristocrats a choice of either "joining us—or exile." Vera coldly turns away from Dimitri, grabs the hand of her more appealing young Bolshevik and then addresses the Tribunal: "You will need the blood of the old Russia to help you build the *new* Russia." Dimitri resigns himself to a life in exile. Quite graphically, the old and now enervated Russia having lost the will to resist, is frozen out of the new Russia—a reinvigorated soviet Russia resulting from the union of a paragon of the worker peasant with an alluring embodiment of the nobler traditions of mother Russia.[20]

Two years later, in early 1928, *The Last Command*, one of the final motion pictures that can be categorized as an East to East Side work was released by Paramount. Practically all of the aspects of the East to East Side mode, though still somewhat recognizable, have been altered. The vain and decadent aristocrat has become a White Russian exile in the United States, but now he lives in a cheap boarding house in East Los Angeles. Instead of being humbled and then establishing a new bourgeois life in America, he has become a member of the permanent underclass, made psychotic by his inability to escape the traumatic memories of the Red terror. This was an Academy Award-winning performance by actor Emil Jannings, in which he added a nervous tic to the mannerisms he adopted for the character of the demoted hotel doorman (stripped of his uniform, like the Tsarist general) in Murnau's 1924 German film classic, *The Last Laugh*.

The only Romanoff jewel the once supercilious General Dolgorucki, the Grand Duke Sergius Alexander, retains is the military Cross of St. George, presented to him by Nicholas II—of little material value and now an anachronistic symbol that he pathetically fondles. In fact, the Grand Duke's escape from the Reds was made possible by the use of the jewels returned to him by his Bolshevik paramour, who admired him for his unambiguous love for Russia and his unwillingness to uselessly sacrifice the lives of his soldiers at the front. Years later the ex–General is arbitrarily selected as a movie extra by an ex–Bolshevik agent, now a Hollywood director, from the glossies in the files of Central Casting! The former professional

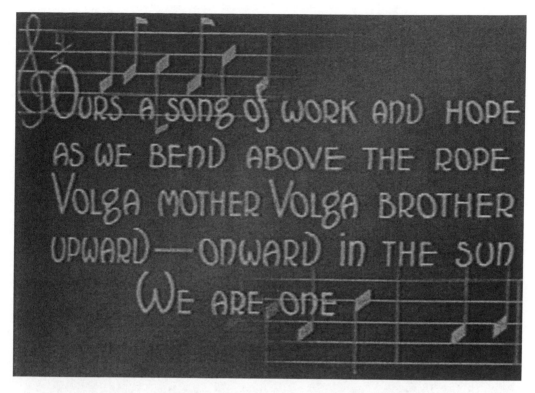

The Volga Boatman (PDC, 1926): The film audience had been first introduced to the worker hero Feodor pulling the towing harness with his fellow boatmen while singing the traditional "Volga Boatman Song." The musical accompaniment to the scene was augmented by titles with the song's lyrics.

director of conspiratorial revolutionaries who posed as a wartime Russian troop entertainer, played by William Powell, is now a suave professional director of actors accompanied by a swarm of sycophantic assistants, much like the military aides who had once attended the general. Instead of seeking crown jewels, or plotting to spread the revolution, this Bolshevik convert to capitalism wants to profit from producing another Hollywood spectacle portraying the downfall of imperial Russia.

Josef von Sternberg's *The Last Command*, unlike any other American motion picture from the 1920s dealing with the Bolshevik seizure of power, captures the inherent ambiguity of revolutionary violence by interchanging the roles of victim and victimizer. A brief sequence near the middle of the film helps illustrate this point. As pandemonium breaks out in the streets, a vicious Tsarist officer enters a jail cell containing a number of imprisoned Bolsheviks and harasses one of the "dirty revolutionary dogs" lying ill on a straw mat. A short time later an armed, banner-carrying mob of revolutionaries overwhelms a military unit on a nearby street, brutally seizes its officer and

Opposite top: The Volga Boatman (PDC, 1926): Red commissar Feodor, a former Volga boatman played by screen star William Boyd, is comforted by his aristocratic lover (Elinor Fair) just before he is to be executed by a White firing squad. Note the diaphanous gown and matching tiara, designed by Adrian.
Opposite bottom: The Volga Boatman (PDC, 1926): Aristocratic White Russian women, still wearing their ball gowns, are degraded by one of their Red captors.

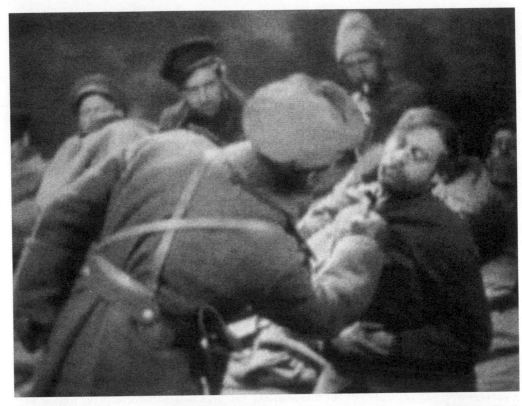

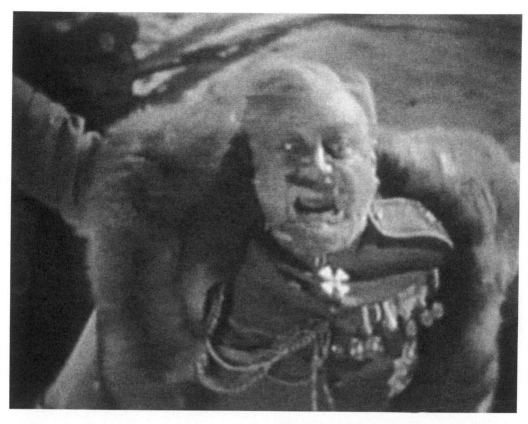

The Last Command (Paramount, 1928): In the film's final scene the former Tsarist general, now a pathetic man hired from Central Casting to *play* a general in a Hollywood movie about the Bolshevik revolution, succumbs to the cinematic illusion and begins maniacally screaming orders to his soldier extras.

then cheers vociferously around the tree from which his twitching body has been hanged. In the film's final scene, the exiled general dies in the arms of his former Bolshevik adversary after shouting his last command to soldier extras on the set. Here von Sternberg captured the growing ambivalence in the West toward the Soviet experiment in Russia—where perhaps the revolutionary excesses were necessary, or at least the product and producer of morally ambiguous circumstances. Tolerant irony prevails, as the one-time Bolshevik has be-

come a pillar of the capitalist system, while his tragic nemesis commands powers only in the filmic illusions created by the Hollywood director. The hate and fear of Soviet Russia portrayed in the Red Scare films gives way to a detached sense that the Bolshevik victory was lasting and could be accommodated.

Another major variation on the East to East Side theme was presented in the 1928 Pathé release, *A Ship Comes In*. It begins with the arrival in New York City of an East European *immigrant family* in pre-World War I America. "Papa" Pleznik (famous

Opposite top: The Last Command (Paramount, 1928): A vicious Tsarist officer has just entered a crowded cell and begun abusing a revolutionary prisoner.
Opposite bottom: The Last Command (Paramount, 1928): Soon afterwards, revolutionary mobs run amok in the streets. In this scene they cheer the lynching of a military officer.

German-born stage actor Rudolph Schild-kraut) immediately embraces his new country, shaving off his mustache and proudly going to work as a janitor in the Federal Building—the bronze seal of the United States receiving a special shining. Aside from his loving family, the only jewel Papa possesses is the American citizenship papers he is awarded several years later; the judge "making Uncle Sam a relation." But this jewel is stolen away from Papa the same day when he is accused of attempting to assassinate the judge with a bomb placed in a cakebox prepared by Mama Pleznik. Actually, an embittered anarchistic neighbor seeking to avenge the sentencing of a "comrade," Sokol (an overstated performance by Fritz Feld, who is made-up to look like *Lenin*), is responsible for the deed. Gripped by pervasive "war-time hysteria" the "grim jurors" convict "a bewildered patriot." Later, a now-crazed Sokol wanders into the street and is mortally injured when struck down by a truckload of Doughboys. The dramatic symbolism is further highlighted by the incident taking place exactly one year after the bombing, at 7 o'clock, July 4, 1918. A deathbed confession leads to Papa's release, but his joy is tempered by the knowledge that his beloved son was killed in action while fighting for his adoptive country in France.

A Ship Comes In, a democratized version of the East to East Side phenomenon, is unique, in that it is the only American film from the 1920s to evoke the excesses of the Red Scare, though without directly challenging the episode. Furthermore, since Sokol's likeness to Lenin is unambiguous, this film was a veiled attack upon the Bolshevik regime, as well as a hard-hitting condemnation of "undesirable aliens" attempting to promote communism while living in the United States.

The final American motion picture to be produced between 1921 and 1929 that in any way could be classified as an East to East Side film, *The Mating Call*, was released by Paramount in July 1928. With overall fears of Soviet communism continuing to abate,

this directorial effort by Hollywood workhorse James Cruze is a fitting example upon which to conclude. Leslie Hatton (Thomas Meighan), an American veteran of the World War, returns home to his Florida farm. Learning that his immoral wife had their marriage annulled while he was overseas, Leslie decides to travel up north in search of a new bride. At Ellis Island he meets an impoverished Russian girl, played by Renee Adoree, and induces her to agree to a marriage of convenience. It is much later that Leslie learns that she is a former princess. What is particularly ironic, though, is that the two must struggle to survive in Florida against "terrorists" of the local Klan, called the "Order" in the film, *not* against foreign Red agents. Furthermore, the most controversial aspect of the movie had nothing to do with politics, but instead concerned a scene in which Miss Adoree took a solitary swim in the nude. But it is only after Leslie and his Russian princess have overcome the Order that they may listen to the mating call.

Labor: The Silenced Twenties

The Red Scare of 1918–20 was largely successful in intimidating the labor movement. The number of violent strikes significantly decreased. Fleeing the social counter-revolution and hounded by the forces of capitalist reaction, militant labor, like the communists, was basically driven underground. In fact, labor would remain relatively quiescent throughout the 1921 to 1929 period.[21]

The classic Capital versus Labor films, a distinct genre in the teens, were significantly altered during the Red Scare with the ascendency of the ubiquitous foreign agitator. Prior to 1918 radical labor agitators were virtually always indigenous, albeit usually foreign-born, suggested in ethnic stereotyping and/or non-Anglo-Saxon surnames. For that matter, pro-labor films had sharply declined after 1916. Up to that year, twenty-four films displayed a distinct Pro-Labor bias, while between 1917 and 1929 there were only eight such films. Other related statistics show equally dramatic declines. For instance, coded references to the I.W.W. drop from 9 percent during the Red Scare years to only one per cent throughout the 1921 to 1929 period.[22]

The suffering heroine in a sweatshop of the teens, such as Mary Pickford's maudlin role in *The Eternal Grind* (Famous Players/Paramount, 1916), became virtually extinct in the 1920s. And the generally negative attitude of the public towards this type

Top: The Last Command (Paramount, 1928): A stunning close-up of Janning's Tsarist general, after his beating and humiliation by the Bolshevik-led mob. Note the white Cross of St. George.
Bottom: The Last Command (Paramount, 1928): Evelyn Brent's lady Bolshevik, with revolutionary banner in hand, persuades the bloodthirsty mob to send the general to a Red tribunal. Years later, traumatized by these events, the former general will labor as an underpaid Hollywood extra.

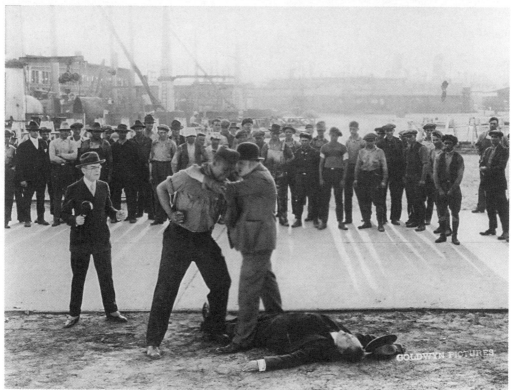

Triumph (Paramount, 1924): King (Rod La Rocque), the wastrel son of the Garnet Can Factory owner, visits the plant. Anna (Leatrice Joy), a forewoman with operatic aspirations, looks him over. The elder Garnet (George Fawcett) is not pleased. (MOMA Film Stills Archive)

of Capital vs. Labor motion picture is epitomized by the *Variety* reviewer's disparagement of a non-radical labor-oriented film released by Paramount in 1922, *Top of New York*, in which the critic acerbically compares it to the pre-Bolshevik "Bertha the Sewing Machine Girl" type films.[23]

Following the devastating impact of the Red Scare, sympathetic portraits of labor activism would not again appear in America's mainstream fictional films until the early 1930s. A growing conservative atmosphere in Hollywood and the rise of censorship legislation in over a score of states before the end of 1921, pertaining to the political as well as the sexual content of movies, further accelerated this trend.[24] But militant labor, in two independently produced motion pictures, briefly attempted a cinematic comeback during 1921-22—though largely transposed to non-revolutionary conformists.

In the spirit of Griffith's classic *A Corner in Wheat* of 1909, an outside-the-mainstream release, produced with union money by the Labor Film Service and employing an unknown cast, attempted to present the

Opposite top: The Stranger's Banquet (Goldwyn, 1922): Shipyard workers are passionately addressed during a union meeting. Subjected to a "siege of red flag propaganda," they will walk out on strike. (MOMA Film Stills Archive)
Opposite bottom: The Stranger's Banquet (Goldwyn, 1922): An anarchist labor agitator, who had decided to urge the shipyard workers to end their strike, has just been shot by one of his cohorts. An enraged foreign-born bomb thrower is forcefully restrained by stocky hero Rockcliffe Fellowes, prior to being arrested and deported. (MOMA Film Stills Archive)

Eve's Lover (Warner Bros., 1925): An unnamed labor agitator, played by Lew Harvey, confronts Eve Burnside, owner of a steel mill. Eve's aristocratic husband is by her side. Actor Harvey appears to represent a thickset Irish stereotype. Two "pugs," wearing fedoras, back him up. (MOMA Film Stills Archive)

worker's side of the capital-labor issue. Descriptively titled *The Contrast*, this spring 1921 release juxtaposes scenes of the lavish life-styles of vulgar mine owners with their virtuous miners struggling to earn a subsistence wage while enduring dangerous working conditions and the routine blacklisting of labor organizers. A walk-out is declared following an accident caused by safety violations. Forced to live with their families in a tent colony, the unionized workers persevere against vicious strike-busting tactics while fighting nobly for their basic civil rights and legal equality. The *Wid's Daily* reviewer's comments are instructive— the film was judged "Not Suitable for General Distribution," because although its "labor propaganda" might appeal to working-class and socialist organizations, "it

might also be *offensive* [emphasis added] to middle class audiences."[25]

The independent 1922 Federation Film production, *The New Disciple*, assumed a more compromising tone. In this motion picture John McPherson, a handsome World War veteran played by Pell Trenton, is the new disciple of a Wilsonian religion of capital-labor accommodation—with passages from Wilson's *The New Freedom* (1913) incorporated into its titles. A greedy capitalist named Fanning, who had excessively profited from wartime contracts, stirs up postwar trouble in the industrial town called Harmony. Following a ruinous strike and attempts at union-busting through the imposition of the open shop "American Plan," all is equitably resolved.[26] This is achieved when the bankrupted capitalist's holdings are purchased by the union-affiliated workers with an advance from the local farmers— the mills to be henceforth operated on a co-operative basis. A perceptive writer for the *New York Call*, in an otherwise positive review, did point out one problem concerning future capital-labor harmony in Harmony, by posing the following query: Since the farmers had raised the needed million dollars by mortgaging their farms, who remained ultimately in financial control?[27]

Even more typical of the 1920s labor-oriented film is a Paramount release entitled *The Whistle*. Shown at theatres in the spring of 1921, the venerable William S. Hart plays a factory worker in this film that he also produced. The worker's beloved son was fatally mangled in the mills' improperly protected machinery, yet Hart manages to create a nineteenth century-style melodrama that *never* clearly engages capitalism on even the obvious labor issues. In fact, in a rather perverse fashion, it is the factory owner and his family that are most sympathetically portrayed. The good worker suffers nobly and in silence.[28]

All in all, between 1921 and 1925, just over ten motion pictures released in the United States engaged head-on the topic of labor radicalism. Only four other films relevant to this topic would be produced by Hollywood throughout the remainder of the decade.[29] Ironically, even the by-now standard outside agitator is commonly motivated by some personal agenda rather than by solidarity with the working-class. This running away from politics is perhaps clearest in a couple of motion pictures from the latter half of the 1920s with plots that involve strike activity that never allude to labor militancy and/or politics. For example, *Seven Sinners* (WB, 1925) is a comedy that uses an apolitical, non-violent strike by private guards on Long Island as the catalyst for a plot centering around seven separate thieves converging upon a deserted mansion.[30]

One of only a few labor-oriented commercial features from the post–1920 decade to even remotely resemble earlier films of its genre was a star-studded Marshall Neilan production distributed by Goldwyn in late 1922, *The Stranger's Banquet*. When John Trevelyan is jilted at the altar because his bride-to-be is informed he is illegitimate, John leaves town in shame and goes to Europe. Some years later, Trevelyan, now a Bolshevik fanatic, returns to the United States and is living in an East Side tenement. He becomes friendly with a Russian bomb-making neighbor. Reading about labor unrest in the newspaper, the two decide that it is time to promote the cause of revolution in America. They hit the road and eventually wind up at a west coast shipyard owned by a young Irish-American woman named Derry Keogh (Claire Windsor). As a dedicated agitator Trevelyan joins up with the local Reds to incite a strike: "Down with your tools and off with your overalls ... you are not slaves .... And until she recognizes this, there shall be no peace under her, but Red rebellion!" One of the Reds, played by veteran character actor Jean Hersholt, is a drunk and known only as the "Fiend." When the strike turns ugly, Derry's Scot manager comes to her aid. They implore Trevelyan to curb the militants. Meanwhile, the militia has arrived. Fearing betrayal, the Fiend shoots Trevelyan. But before the mortally wounded man dies, he eloquently addresses the mob of workers, convincing them to end the strike. As usual, "outside" agitators including John (who has become politically tainted overseas), are mainly responsible for the violence. The inherently good native workers, presumably led by an individual named Uncle Sam (extant sources are vague), not the militia, restore labor peace. As he is led away to be deported, the bomb maker Krischenko completes his portrait of a despicable Other by vehemently damning America.

The plight of Derry Keogh, a woman shipyard owner whose business is threatened by communist agitation, is reminiscent of the situation confronting the virginal Mary Weston in the notorious 1920 anti-Bolshevik film entitled *Dangerous Hours* (Paramount-Artcraft). By violating her business, there is an implicit violation of American woman-hood, of the American motherland, by an insidious alien ideology. Even as a fallen American, Trevelyan can achieve final moral redemption by denouncing the other Reds before he dies, much like the repentance of John, the misguided idealist of *Dangerous Hours*, who redeems himself by his last minute change of sides.

A month later, in January 1923, *Bell Boy 13*, a comedy directed by William Seiter for First National, offhandedly but tellingly used a labor situation. Harry Elrod, a recent college graduate played by the thirty-plus Douglas MacLean, becomes a bellhop after he is disinherited by his broker uncle for attempting to elope with a pretty actress. Harry soon makes a mess of the new job. So, when Harry's uncle purchases the hotel and arranges to have his wayward nephew fired, Harry is relieved. To express his joy at leaving the proletarian ranks and, paradoxically, to gain his uncle's consent to marry actress Kitty, Harry glibly embraces "Bolshevism." Gesticulating wildly, Harry incites his former co-workers to come out from "under the heel of capital" by going out on strike. Uncle Elrod quickly capitulates to Harry's demands. Our erstwhile revolutionary just as swiftly abandons the cause of labor, triumphantly proclaiming to a lobby full of his "fellow agitators" that *all their* demands have been met. The hotel workers enthusiastically wave their raised hands and then melt away back to their jobs.

In *Bell Boy 13* the single word title, "Bolshevism!!," flashed across the screen when Harry begins to propagandize the workers, says volumes about rhetorical linkages at the time. It points out how by 1923 American popular culture comically dismissed the recently feared threat of labor militancy and now laughed at it as a real problem: a clever young capitalist (in an offbeat personification of the employee representation associated with "welfare capitalism") can jocularly exploit non-menacing labor demands to get both his girl and the gold. Second, the passive response of the

workers to the announcement that their unspecified demands have been satisfied provides a good metaphor for the pathetically real impotency of organized labor throughout the twenties decade.[31]

Eve's Lover (WB) came out in the summer of 1925 and was the last commercial feature film to be released in the United States during the decade to in any way deal seriously with domestic labor radicalism. Yet this film, directed by Roy Del Ruth, also avoids a strong political stance by portraying the militant actions of labor as directly resulting from the manipulations of a bad capitalist. The business rival of Eve Burnside (Irene Rich) desperately needs to buy out her steel mill in order for his company to survive. When Eve refuses to sell, he surreptitiously hires outside labor agitators to infiltrate her mills. From atop a soapbox the obnoxious leader (an unnamed stereotype) of the professional agitators incites the Burnside workers to make new and unreasonable contractual demands upon their employer. As the steel workers' spokesman, the agitator adamantly insists that Eve hand over control of management to her employees and grant them a fifty percent share in the profits. When Eve refuses these exactions, a mob of incensed workers, led by the agitators, physically push her aside and walk off the job. Eve's estranged aristocratic husband ("Count Leon Molnar"—a White Russian?—popular leading man Bert Lytell) comes to her aid, passionately addressing the striking workers at the mills' gates. Count Leon is treated with derision, given a collective "razz" (as in raspberry) by the men. But when the Count handily knocks down the labor troublemaker, who had lunged at him, Leon wins the respect of both the agitators and the men. The opportunistic professional labor militant then informs the steel workers that the man who hired him is watching them with binoculars from a nearby car. Without any further discussion of their former demands, the workers declare they will return to the mills, after a short visit to a certain parked automobile.

By 1925 cinematic labor agitators were no longer alien fanatics, but domestic entrepreneurs. With the single exception of Universal's January 1928 release, *Give and Take*, politically motivated labor violence as represented in commercial American motion pictures had all but vanished.[32] The unrelenting worldwide economic crisis that began in late 1929 and came to be known as The Great Depression finally prompted Hollywood in 1931 to begin again to (at least occasionally) frankly address the issues related to the problems of labor.

A Small World Revolution — Cinematically Contained

Although for the most part low-keyed throughout the 1920s decade, there persisted a concern in the United States over the Soviet Union's refusal to renounce world revolution. But as long as communist revolutionary outbreaks remained an overseas phenomenon, the United States government was loath to become involved. For its part, the American public refused to be distracted from the hedonistic excesses of the "roaring" twenties.[33] The assorted communist threats in Europe, such as the Spartacist rebellion in Germany and Bela Kun's Republic of Councils in Hungary, had quickly fallen before the end of 1919.[34] And, the indigenous Reds of Italy were routed by Mussolini's blackshirted Fascisti by the fall of 1922.[35] With the withdrawal of U.S. troops from their occupation zone of the Rhineland in 1923, the last vestige of an American military presence in Europe was removed.[36] In China, open warfare in 1927 between the communist Chinese and the newly declared Nationalist regime would evoke only mild American interest.[37]

Ironically, just as relations with and the image of the Soviet Union seemed to be improving in the latter twenties, anti-communist/anti-revolutionary sentiments again resurfaced in the United States. This was a direct result of fears of communism outside the Soviet Union, climaxed in the 1927 accusation by American Secretary of State, Frank B. Kellogg, that the new semi-socialist Mexican government of President Calles was operating in collusion with the Soviet Union to provide aid to the revolutionary forces in Nicaragua, thereby creating a Bolshevik foothold in the western hemisphere.[38]

Not surprisingly, these events were incorporated into the plots of a few 1920s Hollywood films. Although their numbers are statistically negligible, the new "Red menace" provided a bit of topicality with which to spice up some otherwise rather formulaic film scripts. Six films produced in the United States between 1924 and 1929 tie-in some reference to the concept of world revolution: *Isn't Life Wonderful?* (UA, 1924); *The Eternal City* (First National, 1924); *The Only Thing* (MGM, 1925); *Shanghai Bound* (Paramount, 1927); *Flight* (Columbia, 1929); *The Adventurer* (MGM, 1928).

D. W. Griffith's *Isn't Life Wonderful?* dealt with the post–war crisis in defeated Germany, but with little focus upon the military-political aspects of the situation.[39] Instead, Griffith concentrated on the daily struggles of a single displaced ethnic Polish family in its attempts to survive the harsh economic and social aspects of life during the first years of the Weimar Republic. Aside from a couple of brief scenes with a knife-carrying mad Russian stereotype identified as "Gloomy Russ," probably a play on the popular comic strip character, Gloomy Gus, the only allusion to the political unrest that afflicted Germany at this time is in the portrayal of the activities of a roving gang of unemployed workers. Their oafish evil-countenanced leader and their viciousness might suggest an associative link with communism. Yet they are identified simply as "workers," and their actions are explained in terms of their concern for their starving families.

The dramatic climax of *Isn't Life Wonderful?* occurs on a wooded path when the hero and heroine, pulling a cartload of valuable potatoes harvested from their own little plot, are brutally attacked by the unemployed mob. Even though wounded war veteran Paul's union card is shown, the men steal all of the couple's life-sustaining potatoes from the "profiteers." When Paul's fiancée, played by Carol Dempster, curses the men as "beasts," one of the workers responds: "Years of war and hell, beasts they have made us!" This last statement could be construed as an attack on capitalism or, more simply, on the horrors that follow as well as accompany war.[40] In a situation where it would be easy, and even logical, to make his villains communists, Griffith avoids making explicit political references. This is a strong contrast to his determination to directly link Bolshevism to the excesses of the French revolution in the opening titles of *Orphans of the Storm* (UA), released just three years earlier.

Reflecting the isolationism of 1920s America, only one motion picture produced in the country during the decade dealt specifically with the series of communist uprisings and reactionary counter-revolutionary responses that occurred in Europe between 1918 and 1922. *The Eternal City* was released by First National in January 1924, a "news-topical version" of a popular Hall Caine novel that had originally been published in 1901.[41] The "news" to which *The Eternal City* was adapted by first-rate director George Fitzmaurice was the violent struggle in Italy between militant workers and the fascists, the latter of whom justified their rise to power as revenging the abuses by the left of Italy's war veterans. The blackshirt-wearing fascist *squadristi* quickly gained the upper hand in the street fighting and in October 1922 Benito Mussolini embarked upon his triumphant March on Rome.[42]

The Eternal City resembles the American veteran/vigilante motion pictures released in the United States during the Red Scare, such as *The Riders of the Dawn* (W. W. Hodkinson, 1920). Conservative Americans, in fact, found the parallels compelling. The American Legion Commander publicly admired the Italian Blackshirts in 1923,

referring to them as the "Legionnaires of Italy,"[43] and Mussolini remained a popular figure in the United States until his invasion of Ethiopia in October 1935.

Released just over a year after Mussolini came to power, with the exterior scenes shot in Italy, the 1924 version of *The Eternal City* (a previous rendition had been released in 1915) grafted these recent historical events onto the 1901 love story. David Rossi (Bert Lytell) returns from military service in World War I to discover that his voluptuous girlfriend, Roma (Barbara La Marr), is living with the notorious Baron Bonelli, played by Lionel Barrymore—black caped and sometimes wearing a monocle. Even worse, David and his older peasant friend Bruno (Richard Bennett) find that their uniforms now target them in the streets for ridicule by communists. An incident in which Reds tear the veterans' war decorations from their tunics lead the two former soldiers to join the Blackshirts.

Baron Bonelli plots to become dictator of Italy by secretly financing the fanatic leader of Rome's Reds, played by one of Hollywood's leading silent movie villains, Montague Love. It is anticipated by Bonelli, who had become rich through war profiteering, that his behind-the-scenes manipulation will spur the Red into instigating an ill-conceived revolution. An increasingly impatient Baron also informs the still-innocent Roma, who believes David was killed at the front, that he would like her to share with him both his future power and his bed. But David, having just learned that Roma still loves him, rushes to Bonelli's villa to confront the evil cad. Meanwhile, Bruno, now one of Mussolini's lieutenants, gathers the Fascisti in the Colosseum for a massive rally to support David. At the same time hulking Bolshevik leader Minghelli has assembled his Reds in the Roman baths and condemned the duplicitous Baron. The two conflicting mobs surge towards each other and the Baron's palace for a climactic confrontation as David and Bonelli struggle over a gun inside. The Baron is killed when the weapon is discharged. Roma is denounced and accused of murder. Mussolini arrives on the scene and all is resolved! In essence, the film is a metaphorical recreation of the events that led up to and included the March on Rome. The heroic Fascisti overcome a decadent faction of the aristocracy seeking to exploit the communist sympathizers among Italian workers in a truly unique high budget American motion picture. *The Eternal City* concludes with actual footage of Mussolini sharing a balcony with King Victor Emmanuel as Blackshirts march beneath them in review.

Three years later Paramount released *Shanghai Bound*, a film that exploited recent communist-supported anti-foreign riots in China and the outbreak of civil war between the Chinese Communists and the new Nationalist government dominated by the Kuomintang Party (KMT) under Chiang Kai-shek. Soviet advisors, led by Michael Borodin, had previously worked for several years with the Chinese Republic coalition government, but were forced to flee when the KMT asserted control and embarked on a major military campaign to destroy the communists.[44] The studio press book shamelessly linked its timely attraction with these events:

> Modern China—mysterious with its age-old civilization, militant with its new western ideas, dangerous with its Bolshevism, revengeful with its hate of occidental interference, riotous with its famine—provides the background....
>
> [Richard] Dix' latest vehicle is laid right in the thick of the riots which have brought China into the consciousness of every newspaper reader.[45]

Jim Bucklin, played by the tall and rugged screen star Richard Dix, is the captain of a tramp steamer on the Yangtse. He rescues a group of the fatuous rich ostentatiously lunching at a little river town cafe when the rebellious locals go on a rampage over food shortages. Fighting off the yellow horde, they flee down the river aboard Jim's dirty freighter, which happens to be owned by an American named Louden, the most haughty member of the wealthy party. Having lost his mutinous Asian crew, Captain Bucklin is forced to recruit his ungrateful new passengers, including Louden's attractive daughter Sheila. Meanwhile, the "rebellious coolies"/"bandits," read communists, under the command of the maniacal Scarface (Tetsu Komai), follow the whites down the shore to intercept them in sampans at some narrows. Just as the little band of Americans is about to be overwhelmed by the attacking Chinese, a U.S. warship arrives. It turns out that Jim is actually a Lieutenant-Commander in the United States Asiatic Fleet who was on a secret reconnaissance mission.[46]

In response to the mildly socialistic regime of President Calles in Mexico, which had restricted American ownership in national industries, adopted anti-clerical legislation, and had begun to support the Sandino rebels in Nicaragua, the United States government, led by Secretary of State Kellogg, stigmatized the Mexicans as dupes of Moscow who were aiding the Russians in a Bolshevik conspiracy to dominate Central America. This was whipped-up into a war scare during 1927. Though animosities had abated by mid–1928, President-elect Hoover still felt compelled to make a series of courtesy calls in the area aboard a U.S. warship, including a stop in Nicaragua in the fall of 1928.[47]

Although a few motion pictures dealing with politically non-specific revolutionary bandits in mythical South American countries were released in the United States throughout the 1920s, including Paramount's 1922 adventure-comedy *The Dictator* and Harold Lloyd's hilarious *Why Worry?* (Roach, 1923), not a single American-produced feature film is known to explicitly discuss the Calles regime or the issues concerning the above mentioned war scare.[48] The closest thing to dealing with such new realities comes in *Flight*, an early directorial effort of Frank Capra. In its closing half, this 1929 "all-dialog" film portrays the U.S. Marines battling in Nicaragua with the rebel army of general

Lobo. The peasant rebels fight under a death's head-adorned black flag and wear black bandanas wrapped around their hats. Although their leader is called Lobo in the viewed print, he is listed as Sandino in the *Variety* review's cast credits and the studio press book specifically promotes the film as "an actual dramatization of the Sandino uprising."[49] However, the radical land reform politics of the Sandinos are never directly addressed. For instance, the major dramatic sequence concerns the efforts of two Marine aviators, one of whom is mortally injured when their plane is shot down, to survive in the jungle. But the Americans seem to have more trouble with an army of white ants than with the approaching Red bandits and their angry sombrero-wearing leader. Politics little intrudes, despite the setting, upon the adventure story.[50]

MGM's *The Adventurer*, released in the summer of 1928, alone pointed its cinematic finger at Soviet interference in the western hemisphere, albeit on an imaginary Caribbean island. Aside from audience apathy in the States, perhaps Hollywood, becoming more and more dependent upon foreign revenues, was simply reluctant to risk jeopardizing a lucrative market by alienating the Mexican government.[51]

An almost perfect allegorical representation of the actual crisis, as perceived by Washington, is created by director Viachetslav Tourjansky within the text of *The Adventurer*. On the peaceful mythical island republic of Santo Diego the people live in prosperity due to a large gold mine managed by benevolently capitalistic Americans. The island does not even have an army. But, like the White Russian crown jewels, the gold has attracted Bolshevik agents—suggesting once again that the Soviet regime can only survive

Mockery (MGM, 1927): After the obnoxious wife of a White Russian "war profiteer" labels him an "IDIOT," Sergei will impetuously join the revolutionaries and clumsily attempt to rape the heroine. Note: "IDIOT" appears in successively larger letters over Sergei's face.

financially as a parasite upon capitalism.

The Adventurer utilizes virtually every cinematic anti-communist cliche. Reviving American paranoia about a communist world revolution, the motion picture offers an international cast of "lawless men" descending upon Santo Diego. As stated in a title: "A Russian posing as a bullfighter and calling himself The Tornado, is the principal disturber."[52] By portraying a Russian assuming the role of a bullfighter there is an associative linkage created with Mexico from which it can also be implied that the Calles regime is being exploited as a revolutionary catspaw by the Bolsheviks.

The Tornado harangues the secretly assembled "riff-raff of all the world," insisting that the gold of Santo Diego should belong

Opposite top: The Eternal City (1st National, 1924): In this American made film, Italian Fascist Blackshirts (left center) and their sympathizers rally against the Reds at the Colosseum in Rome. Note that some are armed and that others are giving the fascist salute. (MOMA Film Stills Archive)

Opposite bottom: Mockery (MGM, 1927): An ignorant disfigured peasant named Sergei, played by Lon Chaney, listens to revolutionary talk from a fat cook. Note that this political message is being delivered while the two guzzle wine belonging to their White Russian employer.

to everyone. He tells the crowd of thugs that the next day, dressed as local citizens, they will incite a revolution and seize the gold mine. The Tornado then introduces their real leader, "our brave comrade from Russia—Samaroff"—played by an evilly grinning Michael Visaroff. The film text incorporates the classic fear of a communist-inspired rebellion: a Russian agent provocateur operating underground in a foreign country at the head of an international group of experienced troublemakers, directly receiving his commands from Moscow.

As in many so-called "Banana Republics" of Central America, the gold mine of Santo Diego is managed by an affable Yankee—Jim McClellan (western movie star Tim McCoy), an engineer from Texas who works closely with the local president. As the mine complex is overtaken, with the help of an American traitor, a bull (perhaps as in bull-sheviki?) is released into the streets during fiesta to signal the launching of the revolution. President de Silva and McClellan are taken prisoner separately.

Caressing a photo of the president's daughter Dolores, The Tornado, now identified as sexually decadent as well, sends his men to bring her to him. The Tornado promises his beautiful captive, played by Dorothy Sebastian, that he will not have her father shot if she will consent to become his wife. But as soon as Dolores agrees to the Tornado's demands, he secretly gives orders to one of his lieutenants that the execution of de Silva should take place immediately following the wedding.

With the help of his buddy Barney, Jim organizes the loyal local mine workers that night and they easily overcome their drunken revolutionary guards (reminiscent of the White Russian hero of *The Last Command* who escapes from captivity on a train because the Red soldiers guarding him are in a liquor-induced stupor). The usual climax involving the struggle to rescue the heroine ensues, with the virile Texan saving his little Latino brothers and sisters from the depredations of professional agitators receiving orders from Moscow. And once again, the threat as portrayed on American movie screens is less ideological than a physical one, directed at tangible images of capitalism and womanhood.[53]

Throughout the 1921–29 period the absence of socially oriented films in the United States is striking—the 95 germane motion pictures identified in the Filmography represent barely one per cent of the industry's total production. Most of the comparatively few films released whose texts touched upon social problems assiduously avoided confronting their ideological aspects. For instance, in *The Adventurer*, the fundamental issue of the redistribution of wealth derived from the gold mine is only briefly addressed and then seems largely to have been ignored throughout the remainder of the film. Instead, after seizing power, the revolutionaries are depicted as primarily concerned with the consumption of liquor and sexual gratification—which contributes to the rapid reassertion of capitalist control over the island kingdom. *Mockery* (MGM, 1927), showcasing the "Star Sinister" Lon Chaney as an ignorant, facially disfigured peasant caught-up in the post-Bolshevik revolution civil war in Russia, manages to graphically portray the violent vicissitudes between the warring sides without ever once specifically identifying the opponents or explicating their ideological positions.[54] Likewise, not a single fictional feature-length American motion picture released during the decade that dealt with labor issues precisely identifies a militant worker as a member of the I.W.W. or the Communist Party of the USA. Only the traumatic impact of the Depression would compel Hollywood to begin again in statistically significant numbers to seriously address social issues on the silver screen. However, the film industry's mode of discourse with the social problems of the 1930s would be far less candid than it had been during the years between 1909 and 1920.[55]

About the Filmography

How to Read the Filmography

Each entry contains, where available, the following information in the following order: title (alternate titles in parentheses), releasing company, director(s), number of reels (1909–1917), month of release, geographical setting (labor film subset: [u] urban; [r] rural; [s] suburban), genre.

There follows a plot synopsis, with emphasis on subject relevancy and historical-political context.

Following the plot synopsis are citations to the primary sources; this information appears in brackets, using the following abbreviations:

S . . . . .screened print
PE . . . . .print exists
BFI . . . . .British Film Institute, London
LC . . . . .Library of Congress, Motion Picture Division, Washington, D.C.
GEH . . . . .George Eastman House, NY
MOMA . . . . .Film Studies Center, Museum of Modern Art, NYC
NFM . . . . .Netherlands Film Museum, Amsterdam
Pvt Coll . . . . .Private Collection
UCLA . . . . .Film & TV Archive, UCLA
USC . . . . .Cinema-TV Library, USC
Vid . . . . .Video and/or Cable
(incomplete) . . . . .denotes missing footage
AFI,F1 . . . .*The American Film Institute Catalogue*, 1911–1920
AFI,F2 . . . .*The American Film Institute Catalogue*, 1921–1930
LC,LP;LU;MP . . . .The Library of Congress Catalogue Files—(s) script; (c) continuity
EH . . . .*Exhibitor's Herald*
ETR . . . .*Exhibitor's Trade Review*—(cs) a musical cue sheet
FD . . . .*The Film Daily*
MPG . . . .*The Motion Picture Guide*
MPH . . . .*The Motion Picture Herald*
MPN . . . .*Motion Picture News*

MPS . . . .*The Motion Picture Story Magazine*
MOT . . . .*Motography*
MPW . . . .*The Moving Picture World*—(cs)
NYDM . . . .*New York Dramatic Mirror*
NYT . . . .*The New York Times* (Film Reviews)
VAR . . . .*Variety*
Wid's . . . .*Wid's Daily*
(ad) . . . . .indicates a promotional ad rather than a review—for *all* the trade journals

After the source citations come the coding terms, 64 fields. These fields are not always evident in the plot synopsis. For information on these terms, see the "Glossary of Coding Terms" beginning below.

The final line of each entry (appearing in ALL-CAPITAL letters) lists the film's predominant discernible biases (1–3 per film). Abbreviations are as follows:

ANTI-CAP . . . . .anti-capitalism
ANTI-FASC . . . . .anti-fascism
ANTI-LAB . . . . .anti-labor
ANTI-REV . . . . .anti-revolution
ANTI-RS . . . . .anti–Russian state (pre-Bolshevik Revolution)
ANTI-SOC . . . . .anti-socialism
ANTI-SOV . . . .(anti–Soviet post-Bolshevik Revolution)
CAP-LAB COOP . . . . .capital-labor cooperation
PRO-CAP . . . . .pro-capitalism
PRO-LAB . . . . .pro-labor
PRO-SOC . . . . .pro-socialism
PAC . . . . .pacifism
NDB . . . . .no discernible bias
CM . . . . .contraband message (incidental references or references not relevant to plot, e.g., an anti-capitalist aside or joke in a conversation that is not essential to the advancement of the plot)

Glossary of Coding Terms

In identifying noteworthy features of each film, a total of 64 Fields, or coding terms of subject relevance, have been isolated and defined. Compounded codings, such as a Jewish Bolshevik, are coded separately. A "?" following a coding indicates ambiguity (e.g., an agitator addressing a crowd who is referred to as a "free speech" advocate—this could also be coded "IWW?"). A "*" in a coding definition signifies that topically nonrelevant ethnic characters are not coded.

Agit: Agitator. Explicit depiction of or reference to a political (communist/socialist) and/or labor agitator (particularly individuals who are identified as coming from outside the area and/or who advocate violence)—*not* peaceful union organizers or local labor leaders chosen by their peers.

Allied Interv: Allied Intervention. Explicit depiction of or reference to Allied military intervention in Russia, 1918–21.

Am Icons: American Icons. Visual and/or verbal evocations of patriotic symbols, including the U.S. flag, Declaration of Independence, the Statue of Liberty, Uncle Sam, historical Americans (Washington, Lincoln, etc.).

Anarch: Anarchism. Explicit depiction of or reference to anarchism and/or an anarchist (particularly the bearded bomb throwing stereotype).

Anti-Rel: Anti-Religion. Any reference to anti-religious activities instigated by the left and/or atheistic sentiments—*not* Tsarist pogroms directed at the Jews.

Artist: Depiction of or reference to an artist and/or to the bohemian life style, e.g., abstract art, communal living, etc.

Atroc: Atrocity. Politically motivated violence, of a cruel and unusual nature, that is sanctioned by a political organization and/or the state, i.e., pogroms, torture (particularly whippings), executions (including lynchings), public humiliations (including tar-and-feathering and so-called "flag kissings"), etc.

Bol: Bolshevism. Explicit depiction of or reference to Bolshevism and/or a member of the Bolshevik Party (founded in 1903)—including references to so-called "parlor Bolsheviks," "Bolshies" and pre-1930 references to "Reds."

Bol-Ger Link: Bolshevik-German Linkage. Depiction of or reference to collusion between representatives of Imperial Germany and members of the Bolshevik Party (particularly with regards to so-called "German gold" financing the Bolshevik Revolution).

Bomb: Explicit depiction of or reference to bomb making and/or politically motivated (terroristic) bomb throwing—including the use of dynamite for purposes of workplace sabotage. Also to parodies relating to individuals who supposedly possess an explosive device—sometimes referred to as infernal machines.

Breadline: Depiction of or reference to a breadline, soup kitchen, etc.

Camp Rad: Campus Radicalism. Explicit depiction of or reference to college radicals and/or radical activities that take place on or around American campuses. Also to recent college graduates whose education has led them to be receptive to radical manipulation—becoming so-called "dupes."

Cap: Capitalism. Explicit depiction of or reference to capitalism and/or a capitalist, e.g., a factory owner, a banker, a millionaire playboy, etc.—including the fat, cigar-smoking stereotype.

Chin Comm: Chinese Communism. Explicit depiction of or reference to Chinese communism and/or a member of the Chinese Communist Party—sometimes includes references in the mid–1920s through the mid–1930s to so-called "bandits" in China.

Decad: Decadence. Depiction of or reference to an individual (particularly a political radical or a Tsarist official) displaying sexual deviance and/or drug abuse, e.g., a womanizer; rapist; homosexual, "free love" advocate, etc.

Deport: Deportation. Depiction of or reference to the forced deportation of political radicals from *America*.

Dom Rad: Domestic Radical. Depiction of or reference to an American political radical, in which a specific political party or affiliation is *not* made.

Escape: Depiction of or reference to political activists fleeing Tsarist Russia or to non-communists, particularly White Russians, fleeing the Bolsheviks. Also refers to non-communist westerners fleeing the Chinese Communists.

Fasc: Fascism. Depiction of or reference to a fascist organization and/or a rightist ideologue, including Mussolini and his Italian fascists and the Ku Klux Klan (KKK)—but *not* including Russian reactionaries, such as the Black Hundreds.

Fem Rad: Female Radical. Depiction of or reference to a woman who espouses radical causes, e.g., "free love," socialism, pacifism. the suffragette movement, etc.—including women belonging to communist-affiliated military units or anti-fascist resistance movements (but *not* members of the Kerensky government's Womens' Battalion).

Ger: Appearance or explicit reference to German nationals or people of German descent*—including visual stereotypes (bar manager/owner, radical intellectual, etc.) and slang names, such as "fritz" and "kraut."

G Vill: Greenwich Village. Explicit depiction of or reference to the (in)famous bohemian section of New York City.

Note: Topically nonrelevant ethnic characters are not coded.

IWW: Industrial Workers of the World. Explicit depiction of or reference to the militant labor organization founded in 1905, or to its members ("Big Bill" Haywood, for instance)—including variations on IWW, such as "I Won't Works," "Won't Works," "Imperial Wilhelm's Warriors," etc., and/or itinerant labor organizers (sometimes referred to as "walking delegates") who advocate "free speech" and/or workplace "sabotage."

Irish: Appearance or explicit reference to Irish nationals or people of Irish descent*—including visual stereotypes (dipsomania, work shirkers; crooked labor leaders, etc.) and pejorative monikers, such as "mick."

Ital: Appearance or explicit reference to Italian nationals or people of Italian descent*—including visual stereotypes (fruit seller, garlic eater, thick mustache, etc.) and negative generic terms, such as "wop" and "dago." References to activities and/or members of the criminal Black Hand are *only* included when they can be linked to radical politics.

Jew: Appearance or explicit reference to character identified as a Jew*—including visual stereotypes (hooked-nose, bearded peddler, etc.), pejorative appellations such as "sheeny," "yid" and "Jew-Bolshevik," and given names and surnames that suggest Jewish origin, e.g., Sarah, Goldstein, etc.

Jewels: Depiction of or reference to valuable jewels, particularly so-called crown jewels, in the possession of White Russians (often held in trust, to be used to finance a counter-revolution)—and sought after by agents of the Bolshevik regime. Includes con artists claiming to possess and/or attempting to sell such items.

Lab: Labor. Depiction of or reference to workers (particularly unskilled and semi-skilled) and the working-class.

Lenin: V(ladimir) I(lyich), also called Nikolai, Lenin (1870-1924). Explicit depiction of or reference to the leader of the Bolshevik government, 1917–24.

Liq Link: Liquor Linkage. Depiction of or reference to alcohol consumption/abuse that is linked to radical labor and/or political activities, e.g., agitation taking place in a bar, class motivated violence attributable to insobriety, etc.

Mad Russ: Mad Russian. Depiction of or reference to a crazed Russian—either an ideological fanatic, criminally insane or acting (stereotypically) crazy in a comedic sense.

Marx: Karl Marx (1818-1883). Explicit depiction of or reference to Marxism and/or to the German–born communist theoretician who wrote *Das Kapital* in 1859.

Mtg: Meeting. Depiction of or reference to a publicly held radical political and/or labor meeting—*not* a secret conspiratorial gathering of anarchists, nihilists, etc.

Militia: Depiction of or reference to state controlled military organizations, such as the National Guard—particularly when called out to suppress labor demonstrations.

Mob: Depiction of or reference to a disorderly crowd, who have been incited by an agitator(s) to commit acts of violence (particularly against capitalists, their families and/or their property)—including rioting workers battling scabs, private police and/or armed representatives of the state.

Nih: Nihilist. Depiction of or reference to individuals or groups advocating and/or practicing revolutionary terrorism—particularly the violent opposition to the Tsarist regime through the assassination of its more brutal officials—often portrayed as Russian Jews resisting anti-Semitism.

Pac: Pacifist. Depiction of or reference to peace advocate and/or to the expression of anti-war/anti-militarism attitudes—including meetings of peace organizations and/or attacks upon conscription.

Pol: Police. Depiction of or reference to public police organizations and/or their members, such as sheriffs—also includes special sub organizations, such as riot squads, "vag" (as in vagrant) squads, so-called "Red" squads, etc.

Pvt Pol: Private Police. Depiction of or reference to private police organizations and/or their members—including the Pinkertons, factory guards and non-laborer strike breaking goons hired by business owners.

Rasputin: Grigori Rasputin (1871-1916). Explicit depiction of or reference to the mystical Russian monk/charlatan who gained extraordinary access to and influence upon the family of the Tsar between 1905 and 1916.

Reconcil: Reconciliation. Depiction of or reference to the peaceful resolution of capital-labor disputes—particularly those facilitated by a cross-class romance.

Note: Topically nonrelevant ethnic characters are not coded.

Rev: Revolution. Depiction of or reference to a radical political revolution, including the 1848 Revolutions and *communist* rebellions in ruritanias, but most particularly the 1917 Russian Revolution and/or the civil war that followed—*not* including right-wing revolutions and/or coups d'etat by would-be dictators, such as the numerous non–politically specific revolutions that are depicted taking place in Central and South America.

Rur Rad: Rural Radicalism. Depiction of or reference to farm and/or ranch radicalism, particularly during the 1912–14 period in the midwest and southwest.

Russ: Russian. Any appearance or explicit reference to Russian nationals or people of Russian descent*—including visual stereotypes (beard, peasant blouse, etc.) and names, such as Ivan and Olga.

Sab: Sabotage. Explicit depiction of or reference to labor agitators advocating and/or carrying out workplace sabotage (but *not* including politically inspired bombings of state institutions, such as police headquarters). Acts of sabotage, or attempted sabotage, that take place in war-related industries during 1917–1918 have the added onus of being linked to treason.

Sandino: Augustino Sandino (d.1934). Explicit depiction of or reference to the radical Nicaraguan revolutionary who led forces fighting American occupation troops in the late Twenties and early Thirties.

Scabs: Explicit depiction of or reference to workers hired to replace strikers. Also unorganized strikebreakers.

Sec Pol: Secret Police. Depiction of or reference to the state secret police organization of the Imperial Russian government (Okrana) or the Soviet Union (Cheka, OGPU and GPU).

Sec Ser: Secret Service. Depiction of or reference to the American Secret Service and/or to other government intelligence organizations of the U.S. or its allies.

Shp Flr Abu: Shop Floor Abuse. Explicit depiction of or reference to physical and/or verbal abuse of a worker by his/her employer or foreman—includes sexual harassment.

Siberia: Explicit depiction of or reference to being sent into political exile in Siberia.

Soc: Socialism. Explicit depiction of or reference to socialism and/or members of the So-cialist Party—sometimes includes references in the Teens to so-called social reformers.

Spy-Sab: Spy-Saboteur. Appearance of a character(s) depicted as an enemy national engaged in intelligence or sabotage operations in the United States or an allied country (*no* friendly agents included).

Strike: Explicit depiction of or reference to a work stoppage inspired by labor militancy and/or working-class animosities directed at capitalism—*not* strikes and/or violent labor episodes resulting solely from apolitical personal disputes.

Tramp: Explicit depiction of or reference to bums, hoboes and/or itinerant unskilled laborers.

Trotsky: Leon Trotsky (1879–1940). Depiction of or reference to this major Bolshevik leader and head of the Red Army during the Russian civil war.

Tsar: Tsar Nicholas II (1868–1918). Depiction of or reference to the autocratic leader of Russia, 1894–1917. Also, any reference to his immediate family and/or the Romanoff dynasty.

Unemployed: Explicit depiction of or reference to individuals who have been fired, or have lost their jobs in America due to a failing economy or in retaliation for labor militancy—including so-called employer lock-outs—particularly those who are subsequently driven to violence and/or are attracted to protest movements. Tramps and idled strikers are *not* included.

Vet: Veteran. Explicit depiction of or reference to former members of the armed forces—particularly to Doughboys who become involved in labor disputes and/or join reactionary veterans' organizations, such as the American Legion.

Vig: Vigilantes. Explicit depiction of or reference to quasi-organized reactionary groups/mobs who carry out extralegal, usually violent, actions—invariably in the name of patriotism—including private patriotic organizations.

Viol: Violence. Explicit depiction of or reference to acts of violence—particularly violence resulting from labor and/or class conflicts.

Visit/Wrk SU: Visit and/or Work in Soviet Union. Explicit depiction of or reference to Americans visiting or working in the Soviet Union. Also includes references to the American-sponsored food relief expedition in Russia, 1921–23.

Note: Topically nonrelevant ethnic characters are not coded.

White Russ: White Russian. Any explicit depiction of or reference to Russians who oppose and/or flee the Bolshevik revolution—including references to Alexander Kerensky and depictions of poseurs, people pretending to be former members of the Russian aristocracy.

Wrk Rel Dis/Inj: Work Related Disease/Injury. Explicit depiction of or reference to a worker who becomes ill or is injured as a result of worksite conditions—including fatalities—but *not* if a result of sabotage.

Yearly Film Totals, 1909–1929*

A tally, by year, of the number of radicalism films produced in the United States. Features and shorts are separated, reflecting as well the increasing or decreasing lengths of pictures by year. Shorts for 1909–17 are included in the total, as they are a part of the main Filmography. Short and feature films for 1909–17 represent 250 of the Filmography's entries. Shorts released between 1918 and 1920 are represented in brackets, as they can only be found in Appendix 2 and are not a part of the main Filmography. The total number of films in this study—features, 1913–29, and shorts, 1909–17—equals 436 radicalism pictures given full analysis within the main Filmography.

	Features	*Shorts*	*Totals*
1909		5	5
1910		13	13
1911		12	12
1912		28	28
1913	1	27	28
1914	17	22	39
1915	21	19	40
1916	33	18	51
1917	28	6	34
1918	32	[7; App]	32
1919	40	[10; App]	40
1920	19	[6; App]	19
1921	12		12
1922	7		7
1923	10		10
1924	10		10
1925	11		10
1926	15		15
1927	9		9
1928	11		11
1929	10		10
Totals	286	150	436

Coding Statistics, 1909–1917

The numbers reflect content of 250 short and feature films. Percentages represent the term's total divided by 250. See the "Glossary of Coding Terms" for definition of each of the 64 features listed alphabetically below.

	1909	*10*	*11*	*12*	*13*	*14*	*15*	*16*	*17*	*Totals*
AGIT	1	3	3	5	5	5	13	12	7	54 (22%)
ALLIED INTERV	0	0	0	0	0	0	0	0	1*	1 (.5%)

*The Bat *(UA, 1926) not included in any statistics.*

	1909	10	11	12	13	14	15	16	17	Totals
AM ICONS	1	2	0	2	3	3	3	2	3	19 (8%)
ANARCH	1	3	1	5	4	5	8	12	8	47 (19%)
ANTI-REL	0	0	0	0	1	0	0	1	0	2 (1%)
ARTIST	0	1	0	0	1	2	5	6	2	17 (7%)
ATROC	0	2	0	0	2	5	1	7	2	19 (8%)
BOMB	4	2	3	6	7	18	11	17	8	76 (31%)
BREADLINE	0	0	0	1	0	0	1	1	0	3 (1%)
CAMP RAD	0	0	0	0	0	0	1	0	0	1 (.5%)
CAP	4	7	8	17	20	22	28	33	19	158 (63%)
DECAD	1	2	0	2	1	5	12	10	8	41 (17%)
DOM RAD	2	1	0	1	0	0	3	1	1	9 (4%)
ESCAPE	1	3	0	1	2	4	5	7	4	27 (11%)
FEM RAD	2	2	1	2	1	12	6	12	5	43 (17%)
GER	1	2	1	1	0	4	3	10	6	28 (11%)
G VILL	0	0	0	0	0	0	0	1	0	1 (.5%)
IWW	0	0	1	2	1	3	1	2	1	11 (4%)
IRISH	0	1	1	1	3	3	2	4	3	18 (7%)
ITAL	0	0	1	3	4	3	2	3	4	20 (8%)
JEW	2	2	1	2	2	4	5	3	3	24 (10%)
LAB	2	7	11	22	19	21	24	33	19	158 (63%)
LIQ LINK	0	1	3	4	4	2	6	6	4	30 (12%)
MAD RUSS	0	0	0	0	0	0	1	0	0	1 (.5%)
MARX	1	0	0	0	0	0	0	0	0	1 (.5%)
MTG	0	1	2	5	3	8	8	0	2	29 (12%)
MILITIA	0	3	0	0	0	6	3	3	2	17 (7%)
MOB	0	3	4	3	5	10	15	8	4	52 (21%)
NIH	1	4	0	1	2	12	5	7	3	35 (14%)
PAC	0	0	0	0	0	1	1	2	1	5 (2%)
POL	1	2	3	9	11	14	16	14	6	76 (31%)
PVT POL	0	0	2	0	1	4	1	4	2	14 (6%)
RASPUTIN	0	0	0	0	0	0	0	0	1	1 (.5%)
RECONCIL	1	4	6	7	5	7	13	11	6	60 (24%)
REV	0	0	0	0	2	1	1	3	7	14 (6%)
RUR RAD	0	0	0	2	0	0	0	0	0	2 (1%)
RUSS	1	6	0	2	3	12	6	14	10	54 (22%)
SAB	0	1	5	3	1	7	5	10	7	39 (16%)
SCABS	1	0	4	3	2	6	4	7	4	31 (13%)
SEC POL	0	4	0	1	2	5	3	7	6	28 (11%)
SEC SER	0	0	0	1	0	1	0	2	3	7 (3%)
SHP FLR ABU	0	0	0	3	1	3	4	1	1	13 (5%)
SIBERIA	1	1	0	0	0	5	3	2	3	15 (6%)
SOC	1	1	0	3	5	6	5	6	4	31 (12%)
SPY-SAB	0	0	0	0	0	0	0	4	3	7 (3%)
STRIKE	1	4	9	14	14	16	18	20	11	107 (43%)
TRAMP	0	1	0	3	1	3	6	3	0	17 (7%)
TSAR	0	1	0	1	0	4	2	3	3	14 (6%)
UNEMPLOYED	0	1	2	3	8	2	6	5	1	28 (11%)
VET	0	0	0	1	0	0	1	0	0	2 (1%)
VIOL	5	8	6	14	18	30	32	38	22	173 (69%)
WRK RLT DIS/INJ	0	0	0	3	2	4	3	4	1	17 (7%)

*Note: Actual Allied intervention in Russia commences July 1918.

Coding Statistics, 1918–1920

The numbers reflect content of 91 feature films. Percentages represent the term's total divided by 91. See the "Glossary of Coding Terms" for definition of each of the 64 features listed alphabetically below.

	1918	1919	1920	Totals	
AGIT	11	10	6	27	(30%)
ALLIED INTERV	2	3	0	5	(5%)
AM ICONS	12	13	7	32	(35%)
ANARCH	5	8	2	15	(16%)
ANTI-REL	0	4	1	5	(5%)
ARTIST	0	5	2	7	(8%)
ATROC	8	4	2	14	(15%)
BOL	3	25	7	35	(38%)
BOL-GER LINK	6	4	1	11	(12%)
BOMB	8	7	5	20	(22%)
CAMP RAD	0	0	1	1	(1%)
CAP	18	22	15	55	(60%)
DECAD	12	12	6	30	(33%)
DEPORT	0	1	0	1	(1%)
DOM RAD	4	7	3	14	(15%)
ESCAPE	2	2	0	4	(4%)
FEM RAD	5	10	3	18	(20%)
GER	16	6	3	25	(27%)
G VILL	1	3	3	7	(8%)
IWW	3	4	1	8	(9%)
IRISH	4	4	3	11	(12%)
ITAL	4	1	3	8	(9%)
JEW	6	10	5	21	(23%)
JEWELS	0	1	2	3	(3%)
LAB	19	17	14	50	(55%)
LENIN	0	2	2	4	(4%)
LIQ LINK	6	8	5	19	(21%)
MAD RUSS	0	0	2	2	(2%)
MARX	0	1	0	1	(1%)
MTG	4	4	2	10	(11%)
MILITIA	1	1	1	3	(3%)
MOB	8	11	4	23	(25%)
NIH	1	0	1	2	(2%)
PAC	3	1	0	4	(4%)
POL	4	6	5	15	(16%)
PVT POL	1	1	0	2	(2%)
RASPUTIN	2	0	0	2	(2%)
RECONCIL	6	5	3	14	(15%)
REV	6	10	4	20	(22%)
RUR RAD	0	0	1	1	(1%)
RUSS	11	16	7	34	(37%)
SAB	10	3	4	17	(19%)
SCABS	0	1	2	3	(3%)
SEC POL	1	0	0	1	(1%)
SEC SER	5	6	2	13	(14%)

	1918	*1919*	*1920*	*Totals*	
SHP FLR ABU	2	1	0	3	(3%)
SIBERIA	3	0	0	3	(3%)
SOC	7	6	2	15	(16%)
SPY-SAB	12	8	1	21	(23%)
STRIKE	15	11	7	33	(36%)
TRAMP	3	4	2	9	(10%)
TROTSKY	0	3	1	4	(4%)
TSAR	2	1	1	4	(4%)
UNEMPLOYED	1	5	1	7	(8%)
VET	2	7	7	16	(18%)
VIG	4	2	2	8	(9%)
VIOL	24	24	12	60	(66%)
WHITE RUSS	3	5	3	11	(12%)
WRK REL DIS/INJ	1	1	0	2	(2%)

Coding Statistics, 1921–1929

The numbers reflect content of 95 feature films. Percentages represent the term's total divided by 95. See the "Glossary of Coding Terms" for definition of each of the 64 features listed alphabetically below.

	1921	*22*	*23*	*24*	*25*	*26*	*27*	*28*	*29*	*Totals*	
AGIT	2	2	2	0	1	3	1	1	1	13	(14%)
ALLIED INTERV	0	0	1	0	0	0	0	0	2	3	(3%)
AM ICONS	1	3	1	1	0	0	0	1	2	9	(10%)
ANARCH	3	2	1	1	1	1	0	1	0	10	(11%)
ANTI-REL	0	0	0	0	0	0	0	2	0	2	(2%)
ARTIST	2	1	1	1	4	1	1	2	0	13	(14%)
ATROC	2	0	1	0	2	4	1	5	1	16	(17%)
BOL	3	4	6	5	4	7	4	6	3	42	(45%)
BOL-GER LINK	0	0	0	0	0	0	0	1	1	2	(2%)
BOMB	1	2	1	0	1	1	0	1	0	7	(8%)
BREADLINE	0	0	0	1	0	0	0	0	0	1	(1%)
CAMP RAD	0	0	0	0	0	0	0	1	0	1	(1%)
CAP	8	4	7	3	6	5	3	2	5	43	(46%)
CHIN COMM	0	0	0	1	0	0	1	0	1	3	(3%)
DECAD	1	2	2	3	2	3	1	3	1	18	(19%)
DEPORT	0	1	1	0	1	0	1	0	0	4	(4%)
DOM RAD	1	2	0	1	0	2	0	0	0	6	(7%)
ESCAPE	2	2	5	3	2	8	1	5	1	29	(31%)
FASC	0	0	0	2	0	0	0	1	0	3	(3%)
FEM RAD	0	0	2	0	0	2	1	3	2	10	(11%)
GER	1	0	0	1	0	0	2	0	0	4	(4%)
G VILL	1	0	1	1	0	0	1	0	0	4	(4%)
IWW	1	0	0	0	0	0	0	0	0	1	(1%)
IRISH	1	1	1	0	0	2	3	0	0	8	(9%)
ITAL	0	0	0	2	0	0	2	0	0	4	(4%)
JEW	2	0	3	1	1	4	3	1	1	16	(17%)
JEWELS	1	1	2	1	0	3	2	1	0	11	(12%)
LAB	6	3	5	4	4	4	2	3	2	33	(35%)

	1921	22	23	24	25	26	27	28	29	Totals
LIQ LINK	1	2	1	1	2	2	1	3	0	13 (14%)
MAD RUSS	0	0	0	1	0	0	0	0	0	1 (1%)
MTG	0	0	1	0	0	0	0	0	0	2 (2%)
MILITIA	0	1	0	0	0	0	0	0	0	1 (1%)
MOB	2	0	4	1	1	3	2	4	1	18 (19%)
NIH	0	0	0	0	0	2	0	1	0	3 (3%)
PAC	1	0	0	0	0	2	0	0	1	4 (4%)
POL	1	2	2	3	1	1	1	1	1	13 (14%)
PVT POL	1	0	0	0	0	0	0	0	0	1 (1%)
RASPUTIN	0	0	0	0	0	0	0	1	0	1 (1%)
RECONCIL	1	0	2	0	1	0	0	1	0	5 (6%)
REV	2	2	5	3	4	8	5	7	5	41 (44%)
RUR RAD	0	0	1	0	0	0	0	0	0	1 (1%)
RUSS	2	2	6	6	3	8	5	8	3	43 (46%)
SAB	2	1	2	1	0	1	0	0	0	7 (7%)
SANDINO	0	0	0	0	0	0	0	0	3	3 (3%)
SCABS	0	1	0	0	0	0	0	0	0	1 (1%)
SEC SER	1	1	1	0	1	1	1	0	1	7 (7%)
SHOP FLR ABU	0	0	0	0	0	0	1	0	0	1 (1%)
SIBERIA	1	0	1	0	0	4	1	0	0	7 (7%)
SOC	2	1	1	0	0	1	1	0	0	6 (6%)
SPY-SAB	0	0	0	0	0	1	0	0	2	3 (3%)
STRIKE	3	3	3	2	3	1	1	1	0	17 (18%)
TRAMP	0	0	0	1	0	0	1	0	0	2 (2%)
TROTSKY	1	0	0	0	0	0	0	2	0	3 (3%)
TSAR	0	1	1	1	0	3	1	4	0	11 (12%)
UNEMPLOYED	0	0	0	2	0	0	0	0	0	2 (2%)
VET	0	1	0	4	0	0	0	1	0	6 (7%)
VIG	0	0	0	2	0	0	0	1	0	3 (3%)
VIOL	7	6	8	6	5	7	3	10	7	59 (63%)
VISIT/WRK SU	1	0	1	1	1	1	0	0	0	5 (5%)
WHITE RUSS	2	3	5	5	4	8	4	7	2	40 (43%)
WRK REL DIS/INJ	1	0	1	0	0	0	0	0	0	2 (2%)

Coding Totals, 1909–1929

(64 Fields/436 Films—an average of 7 codings per film)

AGIT	94 (22%)	CAP	254 (58%)
ALLIED INTERV	9 (2%)	CHIN COMM	3 (1%)
AM ICONS	60 (14%)	DECAD	90 (21%)
ANARCH	72 (17%)	DEPORT	5 (1%)
ANTI-REL	9 (2%)	DOM RAD	28 (6%)
ARTIST	37 (8%)	ESCAPE	60 (14%)
ATROC	49 (11%)	FASC	3 (1%)
BOL	77 (18%)	FEM RAD	72 (17%)
BOL-GER LINK	13 (3%)	GER	57 (13%)
BOMB	103 (24%)	G VILL	12 (3%)
BREADLINE	4 (1%)	IWW	20 (5%)
CAMP RAD	3 (1%)	IRISH	37 (8%)

ITAL	32 (7%)		SAB	63 (14%)
JEW	61 (14%)		SANDINO	3 (1%)
JEWELS	14 (3%)		SCABS	35 (8%)
LAB	242 (56%)		SEC POL	29 (7%)
LENIN	4 (1%)		SEC SER	27 (6%)
LIQ LINK	63 (14%)		SHP FLR ABU	17 (4%)
MAD RUSS	4 (1%)		SIBERIA	25 (6%)
MARX	2 (.5%)		SOC	54 (12%)
MTG	41 (9%)		SPY-SAB	31 (7%)
MILITIA	21 (5%)		STRIKE	157 (36%)
MOB	93 (21%)		TRAMP	28 (6%)
NIH	40 (9%)		TROTSKY	7 (2%)
PAC	13 (3%)		TSAR	30 (7%)
POL	104 (24%)		UNEMPLOYED	37 (8%)
PVT POL	17 (4%)		VET	24 (6%)
RASPUTIN	4 (1%)		VIG	11 (3%)
RECONCIL	79 (18%)		VIOL	291 (67%)
REV	76 (17%)		VISIT/WRK SU	5 (1%)
RUR RAD	4 (1%)		WHITE RUSS	51 (12%)
RUSS	132 (30%)		WRK REL DIS/INJ	21 (5%)

Predominant Discernible Biases, 1909–1917 (250 Films)

(1–3 per film)

	1909	*10*	*11*	*12*	*13*	*14*	*15*	*16*	*17*	*Totals*
ANTI-CAP	1	1	3	6	7	6	12	15	3	54 (22%)
ANTI-LAB	0	2	1	8	6	7	3	5	7	39 (16%)
ANTI-REV	2	3	2	8	8	12	11	16	12	74 (30%)
ANTI-RS	1	5	0	1	2	8	4	7	6	34 (14%)
ANTI-SOC	0	0	0	0	1	0	2	1	0	4 (2%)
CAP-LAB COOP	1	3	3	5	5	6	13	8	5	49 (20%)
PR0-CAP	0	0	0	0	2	0	0	0	3	5 (2%)
PRO-LAB	0	0	3	2	3	5	3	9	1	26 (10%)
PRO-SOC	0	0	0	1	2	4	2	0	0	9 (4%)
PAC	0	0	0	0	0	0	0	1	0	1 (.5%)
NDB	0	0	3	1	1	1	0	2	1	9 (4%)
CM	1	0	1	3	4	5	5	4	3	26

Predominant Discernible Biases, 1918–1920 (91 Films)

(1–3 per film)

	1918	*1919*	*1920*	*Totals*
ANTI-CAP	3	1	2	6 (7%)
ANTI-LAB	7	1	2	10 (11%)
ANTI-REV	9	8	6	23 (25%)

	1918	*1919*	*1920*	*Totals*
ANTI-RS	6	0	0	6 (7%)
ANTI-SOC	2	0	1	3 (3%)
ANTI-SOV	4	25	7	36 (40%)
CAP-LAB COOP	9	8	5	22 (24%)
PRO-CAP	0	0	0	0 (0%)
PRO-LAB	2	2	1	4 (4%)
PRO-SOC	1	0	0	1 (1%)
NDB	1	2	1	4 (4%)
CM	10	10	5	25

Predominant Discernible Biases, 1921–1929 (95 Films)

(1–3 per film)

	1921	*22*	*23*	*24*	*25*	*26*	*27*	*28*	*29*	*Totals*
ANTI-CAP	0	1	0	0	1	0	0	0	1	3 (3%)
ANTI-FASC	0	0	0	0	0	0	0	1	0	1 (1%)
ANTI-LAB	2	1	0	0	2	0	0	0	0	5 (5%)
ANTI-REV	3	2	1	5	3	3	1	3	6	27 (29%)
ANTI-RS	0	0	1	0	0	4	1	1	0	7 (7%)
ANTI-SOC	0	0	1	0	0	0	0	0	0	1 (1%)
ANTI-SOV	2	3	6	4	1	7	3	7	2	35 (37%)
CAP-LAB COOP	2	0	2	0	0	1	1	1	0	7 (7%)
PRO-CAP	0	0	0	0	0	0	0	0	0	0 (0%)
PRO-LAB	1	1	0	0	0	0	0	0	0	2 (2%)
PRO-SOC	0	0	0	0	0	0	0	0	0	0 (0%)
PAC	1	0	0	0	0	0	0	0	1	2 (2%)
NDB	1	0	0	1	3	1	3	0	2	11 (12%)
CM	0	2	2	1	1	2	2	1	2	13

Predominant Discernible Biases: Totals 1909–1929

(436 Films/1–3 Per Film)

ANTI-CAP	63 (14%)		CAP-LAB COOP	77 (18%)
ANTI-FASC	1 (.3%)		PRO-CAP	5 (1%)
ANTI-LAB	54 (12%)		PRO-LAB	33 (8%)
ANTI-REV	124 (28%)		PRO-SOC	10 (2%)
ANTI-RS	47 (11%)		PAC	3 (.7%)
ANTI-SOC	8 (2%)		NDB	24 (6%)
ANTI-SOV	70 (16%)		CM	64

The Filmography

1909

A Corner in Wheat, Biograph, D. W. Griffith, 1r, Jan, Am(u), Drama

This motion picture was inspired by the 1903 short story by Frank Norris, "A Deal in Wheat." But the death scene of the capitalist in a wheat silo was borrowed from the final chapter of Book Two of Norris' 1901 novel, *The Octopus*. As adapted by Griffith, the film portrays a straightforward contrast between a stereotypically greedy capitalist who speculates in wheat (the "Wheat King;" played by Frank Powell) and the working-class that suffers when prices are artificially inflated as a result of his actions. A cross cut juxtaposes a sumptuous banquet in which the capitalist wildly celebrates cornering the wheat market with a stark scene in a bakery showing the human "chaff of the wheat" cheerlessly waiting in a long line to buy bread. A poor woman with her hungry child is turned away at the counter when she cannot afford the latest increase in the price of a loaf of bread. And a bearded radical who responds to the price hike with threatening gestures is manhandled by the police. Moral justice is achieved when the capitalist, while showing off one of his grain silos to friends, is accidentally suffocated by a wheat pour (the scene tinted gold to create an exaggerated sense of irony). The motion picture is framed by two stark scenes of a solitary agricultural worker sowing grain in a vast field. Note: David Wark Griffith went by the stage name of Lawrence Griffith until 1910. Despite having personally directed over 100 films by the end of 1909, he was seldom given directorial credit before 1912.
[S (LC;Vid); *MPW* 12/18/09:878-879; *MPW* 12/25/09:921]
Cap; Dom Rad; Lab; Pol; Viol
ANTI-CAP

The Infernal Machine, Vitagraph, 1/2r, May?, Am, Drama

A "crank" leaves a package with a banker, then the banker reads in the paper about a mad bomber. On his way to dispose of the package two crooks notice the nervous capitalist and determine to rob him. While following the man, they steal a similar package that a woman was observed leaving on a doorstep and later substitute it for the banker's package. On the outskirts of the city, the banker places his unwanted parcel in an abandoned wooded area. But after walking away, he turns around to discover some children playing with it. The horrified man runs up to them only to see that the package contained fruitcake. Meanwhile, the nearby crooks open their stolen parcel and are blown up. The what-to-do-with-the-bomb (usually anarchist's bomb) routine would be repeated many times during the teens. It would remain a short film staple until the late 1930s, e.g. *Money on Your Life* (Educational, 1938).
[*MPW* 5/8/09:606; *NYDM* 5/22/09:17]
Bomb; Cap; Dom Rad?; Viol
CM/ANTI-REV

Lost in Siberia, Selig, 1r, Oct, Russ/Am, Drama

At a "socialist meeting" in St. Petersburg a young girl from the university, named Marie, is chosen to assassinate the hated aristocrat, Count Makaroff. She is joined in the plot by her sweetheart and Simeon Novotsky (Jewish given name), "the bitterest nihilist in Russia." On the day chosen for the deed, Marie loses her nerve as the Count's carriage approaches. But Simeon wrenches the bomb from her hands and tosses it at the vehicle. The revolutionaries are apprehended and then identified by the mortally wounded Makaroff. The three are sent in chains to Siberia where they are forced to work in the sulfur mines (since the mid 17th century exile to Siberia of political offenders and criminals was common). Escaping the "burly Czarian [sic] … [who] … has cast lecherous eyes on poor Marie," the trio make a dash for liberty. Simeon is shot down, but Marie and her lover find refuge with a visiting scientific expedition from America. Note: Minister of Internal Affairs Viacheslav Plehve (July 1904) and Grand Duke Sergei Aleksandrovich (February 1905) were blown to bits by bombs thrown into their carriages. Unwilling to believe that Christian Russians could perpetrate acts of violence against the government, the Tsarist regime routinely blamed so-called Jewish revolutionaries for the deeds.

[*MPW* 10/6/09:543&545; *NYDM* 10/23/09:16; *Var* 10/23/09:13]

Bomb; Decad?; Escape; Fem Rad; Jew; Nih; Russ; Siberia; Soc; Viol

ANTI-RS

The Right to Labor, Lubin, 1r, May, Am(u), Drama

John is a hard working family man at a steel plant. During lunch time an agitator harangues the men to demand higher wages. The workers then send a delegation to the general manager, who promises them that he will consider their request. But when he subsequently rejects granting them a wage increase, citing a depression in the business, the men declare a wildcat strike. John refuses to join his fellow steel workers and crosses their picket line, stating: "This is a free country. You have the right to strike. I have the right to labor." Some of the strike sympathizers are incensed by John's stand and attempt one night to blow up his home. Three months later the men have returned to work. John, the new superintendent, is told by the management that all is forgiven and that a ten percent wage hike has been approved. In the "Comments" section of *The*

Moving Picture World it was noted: "The closing scene, where Capital and Labor clasp hands and the angel of prosperity waves the olive branch above them, is well worth preserving as an inspiration to conservative action when any dispute of this character arises." This film was likely based upon muckraker Ray Stannard Baker's January 1903 *McClure's* expose of union abuses of scabs during a nationwide coal strike, "The Right to Work." Note: Organized union activity in the iron and steel industry had been crippled following the 1894 Homestead Strike.

[*MPW* 5/8/09:612; *MPW* 5/15/09:634,646]

Agit; Bomb; Cap; Lab; Reconcil; Scabs; Strike; Viol

CAP-LAB COOP

The Voice of the Violin, Biograph, D. W. Griffith, 1r, Mar, Am, Drama

A handsome German violinist, von Schmitt (Arthur Johnson), makes his living by giving music lessons. He falls in love with a pupil named Helen Walker (Marion Leonard), the daughter of a capitalist. When Helen's father insists the relationship be broken off, the enraged musician, who has read Karl Marx (many ethnic Germans were associated with the socialist movement in America), attends a secret meeting with some anarchist friends. The group consists of both women and men, including the usual bearded stereotypes—the man with a goatee may be intended to signify a Jew. In front of a sign that declares "Down With Wealth … All Will Be Equal," Schmitt swears an oath of loyalty. He then draws one of the lots to destroy a "monopolist" presented by a couple of caped and hooded men—their black outfits, adorned with skull and crossbones, resembling Klan robes. Schmitt and another "chosen" member of the group are respectively given an address and a bomb. The two are later shown sneaking into the basement of a luxurious townhouse (with American flags hanging prominently from two windows). But when Schmitt hears violin music and discovers it is Miss Walker playing, he attacks his anarchist companion. Schmitt, knocked unconscious and left bound near the lit device, revives and wriggles over to the bomb just in time to bite off its burning fuse! Members of the household staff rescue Schmitt, while Helen's father, played by George O. Nicholls, removes the smoldering bomb from his home.

[S (LC;MOMA); *MPW* 3/13/09:310]
Am Icons; Anarch; Bomb; Cap; Fem Rad;
Ger; Jew?; Marx; Viol
ANTI-REV

1910

The Anarchist's Grip (The Anarchistic Grip),
Lubin, 1/2r, Aug, Am, Comedy

A tramp steals a clock salesman's sample
bag, only to be so frightened by the ticking inside that he presents a local police officer with
the "infernal machine." The cop promptly "arrests" the grip and proceeds to the station
house. But at police headquarters, none of the
officers is willing to open the noisy bag to discover its contents. All are relieved when the
salesman calls to report the theft of his grip.
[*MPW* 8/27/10:479; *NYDM* 9/3/10:27]
Anarch; Bomb; Pol; Tramp
ANTI-REV

Capital vs. Labor, Vitagraph, Van Dyke
Brooke, 1r, Mar, Am(u), Drama

The daughter of a manufacturer is being
courted by a militia officer and by a clergyman
(played by Vitagraph's top two male stars,
Earle Williams and Maurice Costello). Meanwhile, a "committee" of dissatisfied workers at
her father's plant are denied their request for
recognition of their rights. A strike is declared
after the manager also spurns the young minister's intercession on the workers' behalf.
Labor agitators at a mass meeting stir up class
hatred and incense the men to march upon the
manufacturer's home. The militia officer, who
has been visiting the daughter, hastily exits her
house, promising to return with his regiment.
But when the angry mob of workers storm the
home, it is the clergyman who valiantly rushes
in, restores calm and secures a promise from
the capitalist to respect the rights of his employees. This film's text provides an interesting example of the concept of social salvation
through cross-class teamwork that was being
actively promoted at the time by practitioners
of the Social Gospel. Despite some reformist
clergy also dabbling in so-called "Christian Socialism," the Protestant religious denominations were viewed by the middle-class as a bulwark against radicalism. The "Comments"
section of *The Moving Picture World* observed:
"Perhaps the picture will have a salutary in-

fluence during this season when strikes per-
vade the air and from almost every section of
the country comes talk of industrial complaint."
[*MPW* 3/26/10:485: *MPW* 4/2/10:509]
Agit; Cap; Lab; Militia; Mtg; Mob; Reconcil; Strike; Viol
CAP-LAB COOP

The Egg Trust, Essanay, 1r, Mar, Am(u),
Drama

Although this film never portrays any radicals, it is an exceptionally mordant condemnation of monopoly capitalism. In the not so distant future the price of eggs reaches incredible
levels because a powerful trust has obtained
worldwide control of the previously humble
food staple. During a series of scenes the valuable commodity is shown being crated, transported and then stored in warehouses under the
constant guard of armed soldiers. Outside of
one storage facility a crowd (presumably working-class) has gathered and becomes greatly
agitated when the occasional egg is spotted.
Within the warehouse the crates are carefully
stacked and dated—some bear labels with
dates as far back as 1492. At a restaurant a startled German waiter must remove some eggs
from the safe when he receives his first order
for ham and eggs in two years. Meanwhile,
after a luxurious feast at the home of the Egg
Trust president, the guests are conducted to a
private sanctuary where everyone bows their
head in worship to a marble statue of a chicken
perched atop an enormous egg! Though primarily intended as satire, this film would appear to imitate the ironic juxtaposition between
the lives of the working-class and the exploitative rich that Griffith achieved the previous year in his famous *A Corner in Wheat*, q.v.
[*MPW* 3/5/10:351; *NYDM* 3/12/10:17]
Cap; Ger; Lab?; Militia; Mob
ANTI-CAP

From Tyranny to Liberty, Edison, J. Searle
Dawley, 1r, Aug, Russ/Am, Drama

The editor (Marc McDermott) of a revolutionary paper in Russia is betrayed in an anonymous letter sent to the authorities by his assistant. The secret police search the editor's house
and find his printing office. During the raid, the
man telephones his wife from a subterranean
nihilist meeting place. Discovering who is at
the other end of the line, the Russian officer in

charge whips the wife and threatens her child in order to force the woman to tell her husband to come home. But when the traitorous assistant enters, she contrives to have him mistaken as the editor. The nihilist and his family later flee to America.

[*MPW* 8/13/10:360; *NYDM* 9/10/10:27]
Atroc; Escape; Nih; Russ; Sec Pol; Viol
ANTI-RS

The Girl in the Barracks, Vitagraph, 1r, April, Russ, Drama

A young Russian peasant girl flees her cruel father after he discovers that she has been seeing a soldier. She goes to her lover's barracks and is explaining her predicament to him at headquarters when the General appears. The girl is quickly hidden in a closet and the commanding officer is left alone to sort through his correspondence. An anarchist who had been chosen at a meeting to assassinate the General sneaks into the room and is about to stab the officer when the girl comes out of the closet, grabs a revolver and shoots the anarchist. The grateful General visits her parents to secure their blessings upon their daughter's marriage to his new sergeant.

[*MPN* 4/9/10:15; *MPW* 4/16/10:615]
Anarch; Russ; Viol
ANTI-REV

The Girl Strike Leader, Thanhouser, 1r, July, Am(u), Drama

Lou leads her fellow workers in a walkout after their wages are arbitrarily lowered by management. When hunger forces them back to the job, only Lou refuses to return. The owner's son, who has come to admire her defiance, saves the strike leader from certain starvation by offering marriage. The progressive son then magnanimously restores the wages of his female laborers. Despite its suggestive title, this film avoided overt references to radical labor issues. Note: The film's plot was probably meant to portray the actual bitter strike of thousands of women shirtwaist makers (mostly immigrants) in New York City between November and December 1909 (sometimes referred to as "the rising of the 20,000"). Irrespective of the active support of both the suffragette and socialist movements, the strike was terminated without a settlement. A fictional autobiography centering around these events by labor activist Theresa Malkiel, "Diary of a Shirtwaist

Striker," was serialized in a socialist paper, the *New York Call*.

[*MPW* 7/9/10:107,114; *MPW* 7/23/10:193]
Cap; Fem Rad; Lab; Reconcil; Strike
CAP-LAB COOP

The Hero Engineer, Kalem, 1r, July, Am(r), Drama

The "hero" of this film is a railroad engineer named Thomas who defies striking compatriots in order to transport the superintendent to the bedside of his dying child. Encouraged by an agitator, a strike mob attempts to burn down the trestle over which the returning locomotive must pass. The superintendent's wife bravely resists the stone-throwing mob until the militia appears and puts the strikers to flight. The superintendent arrives in time to capture the agitator. In this Manichaean melodrama of the capital vs. labor problem the negative portrayal of militant labor is particularly insidious.

[*MPW* 7/9/10:99; *MPW* 7/16/10:143; *NYDM* 7/16/10:20]
Agit; Cap; Lab; Militia; Mob; Sab; Strike; Viol
ANTI-LAB

The Iconoclast, Biograph, D. W. Griffith, 1r, Oct, Am(u), Drama

A "discontented workman" (Henry B. Walthall) at a printing plant has become an indolent drunkard and, as stated in the *Biograph Bulletin*, alcohol is the "seed of irrational socialism." One day the owner (George O. Nicholls) shows some of his wealthy friends around the shop. The thick-mustached printer, incensed by the "inequality of their stations," rants at these guests and then lunges at his employer. Maddened by liquor after having been fired, the workman goes to the owner's house with a gun in order to wreak revenge. But when the printer sees the man at home with his crippled daughter the fallen employee breaks down and begs forgiveness. This was one of the earliest films to exploit the contemporary linkage of the workers' (particularly foreign-born) enhanced susceptibility to radical ideas while under the influence of alcohol. It may also be construed as a politicized reworking of Griffith's 1909 release, *The Drunkard's Reformation*. Note: It was not until 1908, following a series of strikes and determined resistance from the American Newspaper Publishers' Association, that the eight-hour day for unionized printers came into common practice throughout the industry.

[S (LC); *Biograph Bulletin*, p. 235; *NYDM* 10/12/10:30; *Var* 10/8/10:12]

Cap; Dom Rad; Lab; Liq Link; Reconcil; Unemployed; Viol
ANTI-LAB

Queen of the Nihilists, Yankee, 1r, Dec, Russ/Am, Drama

In the "Comments" section of *The Moving Picture World* this film is described as "a *typical* story of Imperial Russian persecution of progressive people." A leader of Russian revolutionists is arrested by Tsarist officials and later put to the knout before his young children, Sophia and Carl. They vow vengeance by their father's corpse. Eighteen years later the two are leaders of a band of nihilists. "Sworn to secrecy," they plot to assassinate the Governor-General who had ordered the execution of their father. But a Tsarist spy penetrates their hidden stronghold. All but Sophia, the "Queen of the Nihilists," are arrested. Later, disguised as a gypsy singer, Sophia gains access to the womanizing Governor-General. By drugging the Tsarist official's wine, Sophia is able to arrange for her tortured brother's release. A year later, having fled to America, the two are shown happily celebrating the Fourth of July. Note: Revolutionary violence in Russia was brutally repressed following the March 1880 assassination of Tsar Alexander II. But, in the early 1890s there arose a renewed period of terrorist activities among radical revolutionary circles in Russia.

[*MPW* 11/19/10:1174(ad),1182; *MPW* 12/3/10:1310]

Am Icons; Atroc; Decad; Escape; Fem Rad; Nih; Russ; Sec Pol; Siberia
ANTI-RS

Rachel, Kalem, 1r, Dec, Russ, Drama

Rachel (the name suggesting the character is meant to be a Jewess), the daughter of a shepherd on a large estate, meets and falls in love with a handsome young man. Unknown to her, he is the son of the prince who owns the estate. When her father offends Prince Fredovna, he is horsewhipped and expelled from the aristocrat's land. Sometime later, the displaced peasant and his daughter join a group of nihilists. Rachel is instructed to gain access to the

Fredovna household and to assassinate the hated aristocrat. Rachel is about to kill him when she is recognized by the prince's son. Allowed to leave the estate unmolested, Rachel shoots herself outside the nihilists' meeting place for having failed. George and Joyce Melford played the romantic leads. In 1911 George Melford would begin a long directorial career.

[*MPW* 12/10/10:1367; *NYDM* 12/14/10:30]

Jew?; Nih; Russ; Viol
ANTI-RS

The Right to Labor, Yankee, 1r, July, Am(s), Drama

The Caxton mills have been shut down for six months because a self-indulgent owner had allowed a greedy Irish manager to ignore the workers' urgent demands for higher wages. Schmidt, a secret anarchist, attempts to incite the starving men to riot. When the "wild-eyed" Schmidt accosts the capitalist's young daughter, mill mechanic John Strong comes to her rescue. After Strong introduces the child to his family at their "humble cottage," he escorts her back home. Schmidt sneaks up and tries to ignite a bomb beneath a window of Caxton's luxurious house, but the loyal Strong intervenes and tosses away the device. A grateful Caxton, after being told by John that all he wants is "a square deal for the men," agrees to grant a wage increase. The "Comments" section of *The Moving Picture World* noted: "Some of the horrible consequences of a strike are clearly shown, and the entire film is calculated to foster a better spirit between employers and employees [sic]."

[*MPW* 7/16/10:161; *MPW* 7/30/10:246; *NYDM* 8/6/10:28]

Agit; Anarch: Bomb; Cap; Ger; Irish; Lab; Pol; Reconcil; Strike; Viol
ANTI-REV; CAP-LAB COOP

Waiter No. 5, Biograph, D. W. Griffith, 1r, Oct, Russ/Am, Drama

The wife of a Russian Chief of Police visits the poor with an artist-socialist friend. Her sympathies aroused, she decides to join the revolutionary society that meets at the artist's studio. During a police raid, the chief, played by George O. Nicholls, is shocked to discover his wife among those arrested. Rather than see her exiled to Siberia or even executed, the Tsarist official arranges for their escape to America, disguised as peasants. Having exhausted their funds and living in poverty, the former member of the Russian elite takes a job as a waiter at a fancy restaurant. Years later, their son is in college and in love with the daughter, played by the teenaged "Little Mary" (Mary Pickford), of a wealthy family. Her parents come to the restaurant and try to discourage the girl from marrying the son of a waiter. But then an imperious foreigner wearing a diplomatic sash approaches the waiter and presents him with a pardon from the Tsar.

[S (LC); *MPW* 10/29/10:1004; *Var* 11/19/10:16]

Artist; Cap; Escape; Jew?; Lab; Russ; Sec Pol; Soc; Tsar
ANTI-RS

A Ward of Uncle Sam, Yankee, Dec, Russ/ Am/Cuba?, Drama

Michael, a Russian immigrant, joins the U.S. Army and fights heroically during the Spanish-American War. Following his recovery from battle wounds, the discharged serviceman returns to Russia to visit his mother and blind sister. On the day of his arrival, Michael discovers a Russian army officer accosting his sister, knocks the man down and drags him into the street. The cursing soldier vows revenge. Soon afterwards, Michael is arrested as a Russian citizen and is accused of plotting against the government. His desperate mother contacts the American diplomatic service. When the Tsarist authorities ignore official requests for Michael's release, a U.S. gunboat with Marines is dispatched. Aside from the implicit nihilist linkage, this film was probably the first to depict an armed confrontation between the United States and Russia (a U.S. Navy Lieutenant has an altercation in St. Petersburg with an evil Russian count in the 1912 Vitagraph release, *The Red Barrier*). Note: Continuing persecution of Jews and travel restrictions upon American citizens would lead to the U.S. government abrogating its commercial treaty with the Tsarist regime in 1911.

[*MPN* 12/10/10:12&16; *MPW* 12/17/10:1432]
Am Icons; Decad; Nih?; Russ; Sec Pol; Viol
ANTI-RS

1911

Beware of the Bomb, Eclair, Feb?, Am, Comedy

A cylindrical box thought to contain a bomb is found by a janitor. When the police refuse to touch it, the box is removed to the Municipal Laboratories. Tension is high and all in the room are silent as the box is opened to reveal a delicious, ripe pineapple! When another box appears the next day, precautions are thrown to the wind as the experts rush to get to the succulent fruit, only to be blown sky high by a concealed bomb. Note: An inside joke may have been intended with regard to the fruit, since among pre-Bolshevik Revolution terrorist circles a small bomb was commonly referred to as an "orange." Refer to Vitagraph's 1909 release, *The Infernal Machine*, q.v.

[*MPW* 2/18/11:378]
Bomb; Pol; Viol
CM/ANTI-REV

The Dynamiters, IMP, William Duncan, 1/2r, Feb, Am, Com-Drama

Jenkins is returning from a night on the town when he stumbles upon a crowd being addressed by an agitator. Full of distilled courage, Jenkins gets into the "free speech" spirit, waxing upon the subject of the downtrodden working-class. After the group breaks up, the agitator grabs Jenkins by the arm and leads the newly discovered orator to the basement meeting place of his anarchist co-conspirators—all of whom are drinking beer and have facial hair, making them appear to be foreign "types". Having donned masks, the anarchists blindfold Jenkins and persuade him to swear an oath to the cause. Lots are drawn from a human skull and Jenkins is selected to deliver a time bomb to a factory by 12 o'clock the next day. Jenkins awakens in the late morning and is thrown into a panic by the ticking box in his room. He repeatedly tries to dispose of the box, only to have it returned. Just before noon he gets an intelligent dog to deposit the bomb with the unsuspecting anarchists. Note: The basic concepts of Anarcho-Syndicalism played a major influence upon the leadership of the Industrial Workers of the World. The I.W.W., through its constant use of incendiary rhetoric, had become closely associated in the public's mind with industrial sabotage. Between 1908 and 1917 the I.W.W. also received a great deal of national attention as a result of its confrontational "Free Speech" campaigns.

[S (LC); *MPW* 2/25/11:437-438; *NYDM* 3/8/11:32]

Agit; Anarch; Bomb; Jew?; IWW?; Ital?; Lab; Liq Link; Mtg; Sab; Viol
ANTI-REV

Locked Out, Reliance, May, Am(s), Drama

When the employees of the plant call a strike, Johnson, the company president, hires "imported colored help," guarded by armed private detectives. During a demonstration by the striking workers, the detectives fire their weapons to quell the protesters. After a lock-out puts the strikers' families in desperate conditions, hungry women and children beg Johnson to give the strikers another chance. He turns a deaf ear. As a crowd of workers and their wives surrounds Johnson's house, he orders his guards to fire into it. Thoroughly revolted by the sight of the carnage, his wife leaves him. Haunted by visions of the martyred working-class, the old man dies. Note: The lock-out was one of the more notorious union busting tactics used by management. It was a common practice of the employers to then hire immigrant or black workers to replace native-born laborers. The purpose of this tactic was to play upon racial and/or ethnic animosities in an attempt to disrupt worker solidarity. Over seventy-five years later director John Sayles would address the issue in his 1987 release entitled *Matewan* (Cinecom).

[*MPW* 5/6/11:1029; *MPW* 5/13/11:1082; *MPW* 5/27/11:1185; *NYDM* 5/3/11:33]

Cap; Lab; Mob; Pvt Pol; Scabs; Strike; Unemployed; Viol
ANTI-CAP; PRO-LAB

The Long Strike, Essanay, Dec, Am(u), Drama

The son of the president of a large factory in Chicago is sent to the plant to investigate an ongoing strike. He meets and falls in love with the daughter of one of the workers. But his arrogant manner only serves to exacerbate the labor situation. The girl rescues him from the subsequent violence of the laborers. Exploiting their relationship, the girl is able to make a direct appeal to his father and thereby end the strike. Having helped to win the workers' demands, she then rejects her capitalist suitor and returns to her working-class lover. *The Long Strike* is rather unique in its ironic resolution of the romantic reconciliation of capital versus labor problems film formula. Reflecting on the portrayal of labor, the *New York Dramatic Mirror* reviewer commented: "[T]he working-man is treated more as a normal man than in most film stories dealing with this delicate subject ... yet ... The matter-of-course way in which the strike leaders ... are made to plot arson will not ... commend the picture to working people."

[*MPW* 12/23/11:989; *NYDM* 12/13/11:33]

Agit; Cap; Lab; Reconcil; Sab; Strike; Viol
ANTI-CAP; CAP-LAB COOP

A Martyr to His Cause, AFL/Essanay, Sept, Am(u), Drama

On October 11, 1910 the printing plant of the virulently anti-union *Los Angeles Times* was bombed, killing a score of employees. After months of investigation, private detectives arrested and illegally extradited the McNamara brothers, who were union activists. As a cause celeber of the American labor movement, the American Federation of Labor (AFL) mounted a vigorous defense campaign, that included the financing of the production of *A Martyr to His Cause: Incidents in the Life and Abduction of the Secretary-Treasurer of the International Association of Bridge and Structural Iron Workers*. The lead roles were "played by representative labor men with a national reputation...." The film portrays John J. McNamara as a loving family man who "through his industry and sobriety ... is promoted to the position of foreman" and is later elected secretary of his union. But on April 22, 1911, "Young Mac" is shown being arrested at union headquarters in Indianapolis—the authorities vainly searching the premises for dynamite. Business, the police and corrupt courts are portrayed conspiring to deny McNamara his legal rights. He is extradited to California. From his jail cell, the accused labor leader composes a message for his union brothers attacking the "enemies of labor," but also reasserts his faith that the public will allow him a fair defense. Essanay Film Manufacturing Company produced and commercially released two other strongly ANTI-CAP films in 1910 and 1911, respectively, *The Egg Trust* and *The Long Strike*, q.v. Note: The McNamara brothers received lengthy prison terms after pleading guilty on December 1, 1911.

[*New York Call* 9/25/11:4; Philip S. Foner, "*A Martyr to His Cause*: The Scenario of the First Labor Film in the United States," *Labor History*, 24 (Winter 1983), pp. 103–11]

Bomb; Cap; Lab; Pol; Pvt Pol
PRO-LAB

The Phoney Strike Breakers, Kalem, 1r, Oct, Am(r), Western Comedy

This motion picture is an early example of displacing class conflict through parody in a period of increasing numbers of strikes in western mining areas. Hugh, the foreman of a cattle ranch, is in love with the boss's daughter. To impress Molly, Hugh plots, with the acquiescence of her parents, to stage a strike. But the feisty girl discovers the scheme. So when the men go out on "strike," Molly and her girl-friends ride to the range dressed as cowboys and begin to do the men's work. Hugh and his now worried co-workers ride after the strike-breakers, only to discover the joke is on them.

[MPW 9/30/11:988; NYDM 10/11/11:29]
Lab; Scabs; Strike
NDB

The Rich and the Poor, American, 1r, Mar, Am(u), Drama

At the Stamford Iron Works, the men are discontented over poor pay, long hours (before 1918, the 10–12 hour day was the norm for laborers) and the "dictatorial manner" of proprietor Howard Armstrong. A foreign-born agitator, Fritz Schram, becomes their spokesman and spurs the workers into presenting management with an ultimatum: arbitration or strike. Superintendent John Craig, in love with Armstrong's daughter, discovers that the previous owner of the business had actually left it in trust to him, not Armstrong. Craig presses the man to confer with his employees. But at a subsequent meeting Armstrong is intransigent and even abusive to the workers' committee. A strike is declared. Over the weeks that follow, starvation and liquor create an explosive atmosphere. An angry mob sets forth with the intention of destroying the factory and killing Armstrong. The terrified owner seeks protection from Craig and relinquishes his false claims to the business. With Craig in command, the men return to work.

[MPW 3/25/11:667]
Agit; Cap; Ger; Lab; Liq Link; Mob; Reconcil; Sab?; Strike
ANTI-CAP; CAP-LAB COOP

A Strike in the "Make Young" Business, Eclair, 1r, Mar, Am(u), Com-Drama

Mr. Oldsport becomes enamored with a young lady, who advises him to have treatments to restore a semblance of his "lost youth." His first session at the "Make Young Agency" is so rejuvenating that the girl suggests he receive a second treatment. With visions of acquiring a new bride, Mr. Oldsport gleefully revisits the Agency. However, a strike has since taken place and some of the workmen have sabotaged the machinery. The terrifying results for Mr. Oldsport dash his romantic dreams. The message of this strike parody is extremely ambiguous, due to the unclear socio-economic status of Mr. Oldsport, as well as the means by which the Agency's management and workers were portrayed.

[MPW 4/1/11:725]
Cap?; Lab; Sab; Strike
NDB

The Strike at the "Little Jonny" Mine, Essanay, 1r, Sept, Am(r), Drama

Jim Logan (Gilbert M. Anderson; part owner of Essanay with George K. Spoor; better known as the popular cowboy star "Broncho Billy"), a young miner with an ill wife, is chosen by his fellow workers to present their demands for a higher wage scale to superintendent J. C. Phillips. But when Phillips tears up the miner's petition, they stage a walkout and head for the saloon to plan revenge. Jim refuses to endorse the violent course of action plotted by the strike committee and decides to warn his boss. After Jim leaves, his wife, who had received a check from Phillips to help out the family, struggles from her sickbed and rides off to notify the sheriff. A posse arrives just in time to save Jim and Phillips from a rampaging lynch mob. Sometime later, Logan again presents the superintendent with the men's demands and, this time, the reception is positive.

[MPW 9/23/11:904; NYDM 10/4/11:31]
Cap; Lab; Liq Link; Mob; Pol; Reconcil; Strike; Viol
CAP-LAB COOP

The Strike at the Mines, Edison, Edwin S. Porter, 1r, April, Am(r), Drama

Sanders, an orphaned young man played by Marc McDermott, becomes a hero when he warns some coal miners that one of the shafts is on fire. Later, the miners strike after their demands for higher wages are refused. When it becomes apparent that the manager has no intention of granting any concessions, the workers' mood grows ugly and they decide to flood the mine by blowing up its pump house. Sanders, learning of their sabotage plans, runs off to warn the manager. A mob of angry strikers attacks the manager, who had been guarding the pump house, but repents after discovering that their young friend was injured in the fracas. While visiting the manager's home a union committee is informed that the miners will be allowed to return to work at the old rates and that the recovering Sanders will be their new assistant manager. Note: This film may have been intended as a dramatization of a bitter ongoing coal strike taking place in Westmoreland County, Pennsylvania.

[*MPW* 4/15/11:847–848; *NYDM* 4/19/11:31]
Cap; Lab; Mob; Reconcil; Sab; Strike; Viol
ANTI-LAB

Tim Mahoney, The Scab, Vitagraph, May, Am(u), Drama

Following a spirited speech by Tim Mahoney, the labor union decides to send a delegation to present their demands to management. When no settlement is reached, a strike is declared. As weeks of idleness go by and his family begins to starve, the former loyal "union man" becomes the dirty Irish scab. The remaining workers are later also compelled by necessity to return to the factory, but Tim is shunned and ejected from the union. The other mens' youngsters even stone Tim's children. During a conflagration at the plant, Mahoney sacrifices himself while saving several of his fellow workers, including his most vicious detractor. At a special union meeting Tim is eulogized and his membership is posthumously restored. Note: The apparent lack of a "proper" wake, with alcohol, for the martyred Irish working man would suggest that this film was consciously directed at a dual class audience.

[*MPW* 5/27/11:1205; *MPW* 6/24/11:424; *NYDM* 5/31/11:31]
Cap; Irish; Lab; Mtg; Reconcil; Scabs; Strike
PRO-LAB

When Women Strike, Lubin, 1r, April, Am, Comedy

John Matthews' wife, a militant suffragette, walks out on strike from her home. John

remains unperturbed and proceeds to hire from an agency a pretty French maid as a scab. Satisfied with the new arrangement, he ignores a subsequent request for "arbitration" from suffragette headquarters. An alarmed Mrs. Matthews deserts the cause and hurries home.

[*MPW* 4/1/11:723; *NYDM* 4/5/11:31]
Fem Rad; Lab; Reconcil; Scabs; Strike
NDB

1912

The Agitator (The Cowboy Socialist), American, Allan Dwan, 1r, April, Am(r), Western

A ranch foreman visits the city and becomes inflamed by socialistic speeches made at gatherings by "hot-headed men." When he returns to the ranch and is spurned by the owner's daughter (a 15-year-old Mae Busch in one of her earliest film appearances), the foreman employs his newly learned political rhetoric and several bottles of whiskey to incite the cowboys (the perversion of an American western icon). The foreman then leads a drunken delegation that insists that the rancher divide his wealth equally among his workers. A shoot out erupts when the owner refuses to accede to their demand. A recently hired cowboy (J. Warren Kerrigan) comes to the aid of the besieged man and his family, subduing the rebellious ranch hands. Note: This western is an early example of the cinematic presentation of an American arcadia being threatened by the radical alien politics that were perceived to breed in evil urban environments. In fact, during the slack winter period, rural labor migrated to urban centers in search of casual work, gathering in so-called "slave market" sections of the cities. It was here that they were often targeted by I.W.W. propagandists (most particularly during the Wobblies' western "free speech" fights).

[*MPW* 4/6/12:70; *NYDM* 4/10/12:31]
Agit; Cap; IWW?; Lab; Liq Link; Mtg; Reconcil?; Rur Rad; Soc; Viol
ANTI-LAB; ANTI-REV

The Anarchist's Wife, Vitagraph, W. V. Ranous, 1r, Nov, Europe?, Drama

While walking in the park with her daughter, Gertrude Schmidt (Florence Turner) meets Princess Marie Louise (Mae Costello). Gertrude returns home with flowers given to her by the princess, only to discover her husband, Karl (Leo Delaney), plotting with some fellow anarchists to assassinate the royal lady. Learning of Gertrude's earlier encounter with Marie Louise, the anarchists give little Greta a bomb disguised in a floral bouquet to deliver to the princess. A desperate mother later escapes from confinement in her home, reaching Marie Louise in time to grab the bomb laden bouquet from the royal's hands and throw it in some water. Gertrude is injured by the explosion. Karl begs to be forgiven by his wife and the princess, before being taken away by a police officer. Note: This film was released in the U.S. on November 21, 1912, but then quickly withdrawn. *The Anarchist's Wife* was later distributed in Europe.

[S (NFM)]
Anarch; Bomb; Ger?; Pol; Viol
ANTI-REV

The Blood of the Poor, Champion, Ulysses Davis, 1r, Jan, Am(u), Drama

This is a Dickensian film on the exploitation of poor laborers by decadent capitalists. In exchange for the rent, the oldest daughter of a poor Jewish tailor becomes a maid in the landlord's home. While there, she falls victim to the wiles of the rich young fiancee of the landlord's daughter. The tailor's daughter is dismissed, while the man treats the affair as a joke and receives only mild admonitions from his intended and her mother. The old tailor "sweats his heart's blood" making a deadline to finish a coat for the rich man. He finishes the coat, then collapses and dies. When the young man arrives to retrieve the coat, he surveys the situation, and, not especially concerned, offers the tailor's daughter money, which she refuses to accept. With a "laugh on his lips" the unrepentant cad goes to his lavish engagement party. Edison released an upbeat variation on this theme in *The Triangle* [*MPW* 8/3/12:904], with a capitalist Mr. Goodfellow.

[*MPW* 12/30/11:1081; *NYDM* 1/10/12:34]
Cap; Decad; Jew; Lab; Unemployed
ANTI-CAP

The Bum and the Bomb (*The Bomb and the Bum*), Champion, Aug, Am, Comedy

A farmer named Si heads for New York City to learn about a, court case in which he is involved. While he is asleep in Central Park, a bum steals his carpet bag. Having read about recent bombings, the bum decides to pay a call upon Si's lawyer, whose address he found in the stolen bag. Using the bag as a prop and posing as a mad bomber, the bum extorts money from the frightened lawyer. The police remove the "bomb" and are about to dispose of it in Central Park when an angered Si appears and seizes his bag. Si later captures the bum in the park and hauls him off to police headquarters. The officers flee when they see his bag. This film was another in the bomb parody cycle (refer to Lubin's 1910 release, *The Anarchist's Grip*). What makes *The Bum and the Bomb* particularly significant is that its title highlights the popular linkage between the bum (itinerant worker; a primary target of I.W.W. organizing) and the bomb (the quintessential symbol of anarchy).

[*MPW* 8/24/12:804; *NYDM* 8/20/12:32]
Bomb; Dom Rad; Pol; Tramp
CM/ANTI-REV

A Case of Dynamite, IMP, June?, Am, Comedy

This was yet another bomb parody film. Although politically unspecific, it is included because it is not directly linked to the Black Hand nor to their tactics of threatening violence for purposes of revenge or extortion. Country store owner Jonathan Jay gives a lad a whipping for stealing apples. Later called to the city on business, while Jonathan is purchasing his train ticket the angered lad paints the word "Dynamite" across the side of his valise. The usual perils of the rube in the city are complicated by people's reactions to seeing the hayseed (bum linkage) carrying what they believe to be an explosive laden grip—especially since a notorious "gang of dynamiters" have been reported to be in town.

[*MPW* 6/1/12:862; *NYDM* 7/31/12:33]
Anarch?; Bomb; Pol
CM/ANTI-REV

The Cry of the Children, Thanhouser, George O. Nichols, 2r, April, Am(s), Drama

Taking its title (and many of its anachronistically captioned inter-titles) from a nineteenth century poem by Elizabeth Barrett Browning and a reformist tract from 1908 decrying child labor (*The Bitter Cry of the Children*, by socialist John Spargo), this film vividly portrayed the plight of children working in the mills. Although it never directly addresses labor radicalism, the film creates a Marxist dialectic by starkly contrasting the dire poverty of a working-class family, virtually enslaved by the system, with the excessive wealth of the young mill owner and his attractive wife. The mill working family leave their shabby cabin each morning to work together by the looms—"Little Alice, their one ray of sunshine, is to be kept free from the shadow of the factory." A delegation of workers that petitions their employer for a "living wage" is ejected from his office. Following a long strike, the mill workers are "vanquished" by "privation" and compelled to return to the job. As the owner is portrayed celebrating extravagantly with his satin-gowned and dinner-jacketed supporters, "The Victors," little curly-haired Alice (Marie Eline; the "Thanhouser Kidlet") is shown being forced to work in the weave rooms to help support her destitute family—"All day she drives the wheels of iron." In a number of shots that make her appear imprisoned by the tools of her trade, an increasingly sickly Alice eventually collapses by the loom she tends and dies. The mill owner's wife, the fatuous lady who had once offered to adopt the "joyous" little girl, watches the funeral at a snow-covered graveyard from her husband's car. The working father was played by James Cruze. At least four other films released during this period utilize the issue of child labor: *Suffer Little Children* (Edison; 1909); *Children Who Labour* (Edison; 1912); *Child Labor* (Majestic; 1913); *The Children of Eve* (Edison; 1915). The first three portray the little innocents suffering on the job and eventually winning the hearts of evil capitalists. But only *The Cry of the Children* shows labor militancy and an unrepentant factory owner. Director Nichols also used a real mill for the interior scenes. Note: By 1913 roughly 20 percent of all children in America were earning their own living.

[S (GEH;Vid); *MPW* 4/27/12:305–306, 368; *NYDM* 5/8/12:34]

Cap; Lab; Shp Flr Abu; Strike; Wrk Rel Dis/Inj

ANTI-CAP

From the Submerged, Essanay, Theodore K. Wharton, 1r, Nov, Am(u), Drama

John Wingfield, the only son of an eastern millionaire, is disinherited because of a dissolute lifestyle. He travels west to begin a new life, but soon discovers that the only work available is for temporary unskilled laborers.

Homeless and starving, John decides to end his life by jumping off a bridge. Just as he is about to take the plunge a ragged girl, played by Ruth Stonehouse, intervenes and persuades John to carry on. Barely able to walk, John swallows his pride and joins a breadline. Collapsing on a bench, a kindly member of the working-class brings John his food. While eating, John sees a newspaper notice that summons him home to his dying father. Two years later, as a restored member of the upper classes, the young Wingfield is considered prime husband material by an ambitious matron. But John is shocked by the callous attitude of her daughter and their well-dressed friends towards society's dispossessed during an evening of "slumming" in Chinatown. John abandons the debutante and revisits the west in search of the girl who had saved his life. They return to his home as man and wife. Although there is no indication of labor radicalism in this film (the scene of the breadline does not even portray a bearded man), its class consciousness is unusually strong. The protagonist's name is Charlie in the titles of the partial print surviving at the Library of Congress.

[S (LC,incomplete); *MPW* 11/9/12:588; *MPW* 11/16/12:639–40]

Breadline; Cap; Lab; Tramp; Unemployed

ANTI-CAP; PRO-LAB

The Girl At the Cupola, Selig, Oscar Eagle, 1r, Aug, Am(s), Drama

Silas, owner of the Wilson Foundries, is facing ruin as a result of competition from more efficient works. His daughter Jessie's (Kathlyn Williams; the popular "Selig Girl") fiancé, Jack Berry (Charles Clary), a self-proclaimed "Business Doctor," is called in to help. Jack's solution is to fire the oldest employees and to bring in new workers from out of town. The mostly foreign-looking foundrymen, including a hulky, leather cap-wearing stereotype, decide to petition management for the reinstatement of the men laid off. A delegation of three, led by the faithful old foreman named John, confront Jack at the small-town foundry's offices (after deferentially removing their hats). When they are told their request was denied, the workers demonstrate outside the offices and then walk off the job. As the train arrives with their replacements, the striking foundrymen, some of whom have just exited a bar, become a mob that assaults the scabs. Meanwhile, Jack has rolled-up his sleeves and refired the furnaces. The two groups of workers engage in a running battle of fisticuffs to the Wilson plant's barred doors. Breaking inside, the hotheaded leader of the strikers attacks Jack with a knife. The older John, one of the workers who had been dismissed, helps Jessie to save Jack's life. A timely pour of molten metal and the strong language of John quells the frenzied crowd of men. Capital-Labor reconciliation follows. A subtext of this film is that American capitalism needs its more mature native-born Anglo-Saxon workers to help impose restraints upon their unruly younger immigrant brothers (who comprised nearly two-thirds of the laborers in heavy industries by the end of 1910). The tragic consequences for a carpenter resulting from the weeding out of older employees by a ruthless new foreman was the theme of D.W. Griffith's *What Shall We Do with Our Old?* (Bio, 1911) [*MPW* 2/18/11:376].

[S (LC;Vid); *MPW* 8/3/12:472; *NYDM* 8/21/12:29]

Cap; Lab; Liq Link; Mob; Reconcil; Scabs; Strike; Unemployed; Viol
CAP-LAB COOP

The Girl Strikers, Kalem, 1r, June, Am(u), Drama

While Kotton, Sr., is on vacation, his son is left in charge of the factory. The female activists at the plant immediately begin making a series of demands, all of which the junior Kotton approves. When the old man returns, he reduces wages to the original scale. A strike is declared. Kotton, Jr., in sympathy with the strikers, leaves his home and marries one of their leaders. A year later, the senior Kotton learns he is a grandfather, makes up with his son and institutes at the factory the "progressive measures" (socialist?) recommended by junior. The *New York Dramatic Mirror* reviewer thought the scene that shows the evil foreman smoking a cigarette in the cotton mill to be unrealistic. Note: Between September 1910 and January 1911 nearly 40,000 Chicago garment workers, many of whom were female, went out on strike.

[*MPW* 6/8/12:950; *NYDM* 6/19/12:30]

Cap; Fem Rad; Lab; Reconcil; Shp Flr Abu; Soc?; Strike
CAP-LAB COOP

The High Cost of Living, Eclair, Etienne Arnaud, 2r, June, Am(u), Com-Drama

This is an "animated editorial" that uses allegorical figures to mock an "oligarchy of greed" that is responsible for the high cost of living. A struggling young couple attempt to fill their empty market basket with the necessities of life, only to be repeatedly thwarted by monopolistic "robber barons" who worship before the "Temple of Mammon" (the market place is symbolically encircled with dollar signs). The couple, along with other ordinary citizens, appeal to the figure of Justice. Together with Justice, the populace destroys the "golden idol" and arrests the plutocrats. Tried by Uncle Sam and found guilty by a jury of the people, the lords of commerce are led away to prison where they are forced to wear stripes and work on the rock pile. But the venal monopolists escape by tying greenbacks over their guards' eyes. Soon afterwards, the Temple of Mammon has been rebuilt and Justice kidnapped and imprisoned. *The Moving Picture World* reviewer made the following topical observation: "With election time close at hand and the air surcharged with politics, a picture of this kind is the kind managers are looking for."

[*MPW* 6/1/12:812]

Am Icons; Cap; Lab; Viol
ANTI-CAP

The High Cost of Living, Solax, Edward Warren, 1r, Oct, Am(s), Drama

White-haired "Old Joel," who has worked fifty years as an ironworker, is on trial for murder. Stating he would rather die than continue living in poverty, Joel *Smith* pleads his case in court. Joel's testimony is illustrated by a matching series of flashbacks (with a large number of dialogue inter-titles). After reluctantly agreeing to join his fellow ironworkers for a drink to discuss a possible strike, Joel is chosen to petition their employer for a raise. When the "Boss" denies their request Joel is forced to join the strike. Sometime later, with his family starving, Joel (wearing the suit jacket also worn in court) visits strike headquarters and finds the men in drunken revelry. Disgusted, he announces his intention of returning to work. One of the younger strikers accuses Joel of being a coward and picks up a sledgehammer. During the fight that follows, Joel kills the belligerent worker. The old man is acquitted by a tearful jury.

[S (UCLA); *MPW* 10/19/12:278 & 280]

Am Icons; Cap; Ital?; Lab; Liq Link; Strike; Viol

ANTI-LAB

The Home Strike-Breakers, IMP, 1/2r, Mar, Am(u), Comedy

Michael McCarthy and his fellow brick-layers form a "Local" and declare a strike. Mr. "Builder," whose business is suffering from the work stoppage, offers a $500 reward to anyone who can break the strike. Mrs. McCarthy learns of this and organizes the strikers' wives into a gang of scabs! The husbands, left at home with the domestic responsibilities, quickly return to the job site.

[*MPW* 3/9/12:896]

Cap; Irish; Lab; Scabs; Strike

CM/ANTI-LAB

How the Cause Was Won, Selig, 1r, Oct, Am(u), Drama

The owner of a large steel mill, Major Clarke, tells his fun-loving son Tom that he must make a living on his own. Tom dons workers' clothing and, under a false identity, becomes a steel worker at his father's mills. While thus earning his wages, Tom becomes engaged to Mabel Moody, the daughter of one of the plant's oldest employees, a Civil War veteran. When a wage cut is announced, Mabel, having learned of Tom's true identity, denounces him as a labor "spy." But at a contentious meeting of the workers, Tom casts the deciding vote for a strike. At this point, Major Clarke barges into the meeting and demands a hearing. The men start demonstrating against the "Big Boss" until "Old Man" Moody recognizes the Major as a fellow veteran. His appeal to "Americanism" is so strong that it leads to an equitable resolution of the labor dispute. Note: A subliminal message of Christian harmony may have intentionally been inserted by naming the "Old Man" Moody—thereby creating an associative linkage with the famous post-Civil War Evangelical revivalist, Dwight Lyman Moody (1837–1899). Ironically, several of the gospel songs that had been popularized by Moody were parodied in such Wobbly "hymns" as "There is Power in the Union" and "Hold the Fort."

[*MPW* 10/5/12:68; *NYDM* 10/16/12:29]

Am Icons; Cap; Lab; Mtg; Reconcil; Strike; Vet

CAP-LAB COOP

In Exile, Selig, 1r, June, Russ/Am, Drama

A Russian aristocrat, Count Romanoff, warns some nihilist friends that the Tsarist police are planning to raid their secret meeting. He then flees to California with his family, where they become fruit pickers in the orange groves owned by the wealthy Harrington family. Years later, the millionaire fruit growers threaten to disinherit their son after he falls in love with Olga, the beautiful daughter of the Romanoffs. When it is learned that a French relative has bequeathed his fortune to Olga, the parents approve the union. This film displays distinct plot similarities with *Waiter No. 5* (Bio; 1910), q.v.

[*MPW* 6/15/12:1060]

Cap; Escape; Lab; Nih; Russ; Sec Pol; Tsar?

ANTI-RS

Lazy Bill and the Strikers, Eclipse, 1/2r, Jan, Am(u), Comedy

Series character Lazy Bill incites his fellow male office, workers to stage a walkout. Following a number of encounters with the police, the battle-weary strikers retreat to their homes. After three days under the domestic iron heel of his wife, Lazy Bill returns to his old job.

[*MPW* 1/6/12:56]

Agit; Lab; Mtg; Pol; Strike; Viol

ANTI-LAB

The Long Strike, IMP, Herbert Brenon, 2r, Dec, Am(u), Drama

Jane's father and fiancé are factory workers on strike. The superintendent, played by William Dunn, is killed by Jane's father, who believes the man violated his daughter's honor. Her father suffers a mental breakdown and her sweetheart Jim is accused of the crime. Jane (Vivian Prescott) and a crusty old lawyer take a tug and intercept the ship carrying the man who can corroborate Jim's alibi. When the ship's captain refuses to let the sailor/witness return to shore, the sailor dives into the ocean and swims to the tug. They arrive just in time to save Jim from being convicted.

[*MPW* 12/14/12:1086; *MPW* 12/28/12:1293; *NYDM* 12/8/12:32]

Cap; Decad; Lab; Pol; Shp Flr Abu; Strike; Viol

ANTI-CAP

Los Anarquistas, Republic, 1r, April, Am, Drama

A poverty stricken foreigner joins the anarchist movement and, egged on by its leaders, becomes convinced the head of the Secret Service is in love with his wife. He accepts a commission to throw a bomb concealed in a bag at the president. The Secret Service man, having learned of the assassination plans and the whereabouts of the plotters' den, disarms the bomb. The anarchist subsequently tosses a harmless object at the president, but dies while attempting to escape apprehension. The Secret Service man marries his widow! *The Moving Picture World* review states the action takes place in "some European republic."

[*MPW* 4/27/12:330; *NYDM* 4/24/12:31]
Anarch; Bomb; Sec Ser; Viol
ANTI-REV

Lulu's Anarchist, Vitagraph, 1r, Mar, Am, Comedy

While on the job, Lulu Leach has been reading a dime novel about a dastardly anarchist named "Max Rosinsky, The Avenger" (twentieth century Reds substituting for nineteenth century red Indians as the heavies). So when a "foreign-looking" man and an associate rent the office next door to Lulu's employer, the impressionable girl becomes suspicious. Peeking over the transom, she observes the frightening alien showing the other man various disguises and removing what appears to be a bomb from his valise. Now thoroughly alarmed, Lulu calls Tom, her reporter boyfriend. Tom arrives with the police only to discover that the supposed anarchist is actually a "lightning-change impersonator" who was showing the act to his agent.

[*MPW* 3/2/12:797; *MPW* 3/16/12:962; *NYDM* 3/13/12:28]
Anarch; Bomb; Jew?; Pol
ANTI-REV

The Mayor's Crusade, Kalem, 1r, Dec, Am(s), Drama

A new mayor, Abraham Fendrick, is elected in a western town on the "reform" ticket (sometimes a euphemism for the Socialist Party, which had its greatest success in the United States at this time in the west). He is promptly challenged by the opposition press to investigate the local "sweatshop," owned by a man named Dale. Fendrick disguises himself as a laborer and attains employment at Dale's. He observes the poor working conditions and the collapse from overwork of a young girl at her sewing machine. Back at his office, as mayor, Fendrick summons Dale and presents the sweatshop proprietor with a reform document—sign or go to jail. Paradoxically, progressive reforms were viewed by many liberal Americans as an antidote to the more radical aspects of socialism. Note: At the end of 1911 there were over thirty American cities with Socialist mayors.

[*MPW* 12/14/12:1114; *NYDM* 1/1/13:35]
Cap; Lab; Soc?; Wrk Rel Dis/Inj
PRO-SOC

Mutt & Jeff and the Italian Strikers, Nestor, 1r, Jan, Am(r), Comedy

In 1911, Nestor signed an agreement with cartoonist Bud Fisher to use his popular comic strip characters in a weekly live action film series. Promoted as "Talking Pictures," these shorts simply featured superimposed captions around the actors playing the two "mirth-provokers." In *The Italian Strikers* the duo is "fatally forced to apply for work" at the C.O.D. Railroad—the "fatally" probably meant that they were portrayed as tramps who were caught "riding the rods" by railroad guards (known as "bulls") and then beaten into volunteering their labor. But when Mutt (the tall thin one) and Jeff (the short fat one) arrive at the job site it becomes clear that they have entered a labor "war" zone. A mob of striking Italians vow vengeance upon the scabs. A chase aboard handcars ensues. Jeff is able to make an escape, but Mutt is captured and given a rough bath in a watering tank. Note: From the fall of 1911 through the end of 1914 the Railway Employees Department of the AFL supported a bitter strike against the Illinois Central and Harriman Lines railroads. The two railway systems formed an empire that embraced most of the western half of the United States. During the strike, incidents of sabotage and the physical abuse of scabs commonly took place.

[*MPW* 1/13/12:152]
Ital; Lab; Mob; Scabs; Strike; Tramp?; Viol
ANTI-LAB

Petticoat Camp, Thanhouser, 1r, Nov, Am(r), Comedy

This is a classic example of a strike parody.

Several middle-class couples lease a lake island for a communal camping trip. But while the men go off hunting and fishing, their wives are expected to maintain the camp and do all of the cooking. Frustrated with being taken for granted, the women declare a "strike," informing their "Lords and Masters" in a note left at the camp that "your ex-slaves" have removed themselves to the next island. The husbands, after demonstrating their inability to prepare an edible meal, determine to be "strike breakers." The phony goons dress up in rough clothes and arm themselves with driftwood clubs. That night they row over to the adjoining island and raid their wives' camp, only to be chased off by the women with pistol fire! The chastened husbands return the following morning under a white flag. Florence LaBadie plays "The Strike Leader."

[S (GEH;Vid); *MPW* 10/19/12:276]
Lab; Reconcil; Strike
NDB

A Rough Ride with Nitroglycerin, Selig, William Duncan, 1r, Dec, Am(r), Advent-Drama

Hooves pound through this western adventure by the director of *The Dynamiters*, q.v. A gang of labor agitators decide to blow up an oil well. Riding horses stolen from in front of a saloon, the agitators pursue the hero, foreman of the oil well and fiancé of the owner's daughter. The suspense is heightened by the fact that the hero's wagon is carrying a load of nitroglycerin! A sheriff's posse follows right behind the agitators.

[*MPW* 12/28/12:1322; *MPW* 1/18/13:263; *NYDM* 1/8/13:28]
Agit; Cap; Lab; Liq Link?; Pol; Sab; Viol
ANTI-LAB

The Russian Peasant, Kalem, 1r, Jan, Russ, Drama

An impoverished peasant family on the Brokoff estate witnesses the luxury of the aristocrats and experience their disdain for the lower classes. Only Princess Olga shows any kindness to Dimitri and his sister Amuska. When a mob of rebellious peasants present Prince Brokoff with a petition demanding better living conditions, he dismisses it with scorn. Seized with "a spirit of anarchy," the peasants prepare to storm the estate. Dimitri, thinking of the princess, warns the aristocrats.

A priest is able to calm the rioting peasants and, with Olga's intercession, the Prince is persuaded to institute reforms. Note: Despite agrarian reforms, there were a number of localized peasant rebellions in Russia after the 1905 Revolution.

[*MPW* 1/13/12:140]
Anarch; Lab; Mob; Russ; Viol
ANTI-REV

The Strike, Solax, Alice Guy Blaché/Edward Warren?, 1r, Aug, Am(s), Drama

A southern European "Agitator" convinces the disgruntled laborers at a large factory to present the owner with a petition. When the "Boss" ignores their "unreasonable demands," the workers stone the windows as they storm out of the factory. At a mass meeting, the labor union orator induces the men to vote to blow up the plant (I.W.W. reference?—through its incendiary rhetoric, the radical union became associated with acts of sabotage, or, so-called "propaganda of the deed"—labor violence was specifically condemned at the American Socialist convention in May 1912). Jack Smith is selected by lot to deliver the bomb. The details of the sabotage mission are worked out at a meeting in his house. But, as the agitator exits the Smith home, he drops a lighted cigarette butt. Jack is at another mass meeting when he receives a phone call telling him that his house is on fire (a split screen is used). The boss, who is driving by, rushes Jack home and helps to rescue the Smith family. In the confusion, Jack tosses the bomb out the window. The following morning the little Smith daughter delivers a message from the workers to their employer: "We've had enough strike, boss, and are all ready for work ... [sic]."

[S (BFI); *MPW* 8/10/12:580]
Agit; Bomb; Cap; Ital?; IWW?; Lab; Mtg; Reconcil; Sab; Strike; Viol
ANTI-LAB; CAP-LAB COOP

The Strike at the Ranch, Pathé (Am), Jan, Am(r), Western

Colonel Milliken needs to round up his cattle for the semi-annual shipment to market. But the cowboys demand higher wages before they will agree to drive the herd to the railroad head. The crippled Milliken refuses and then turns to his neighbor, Colonel Jones, for help. The strikers kidnap Jones' daughter to dissuade him from assisting his friend. Her six year-old brother makes a dramatic rescue.

　　[*MPW* 1/6/12:60]
　　Cap; Lab; Rur Rad; Strike; Viol
　　ANTI-LAB

The Voice of the Millions, Rex, Stanner E.V. Taylor, June, Am(u), Drama

　　The downtrodden workers at a mill go out on strike, not for happiness, but for bread—"It was the ancient struggle of the weak many, against the mighty few, the inefficient millions against the invincible one." A working girl (actress Marion Leanord) organizes the meetings and gives repeated words of encouragement from the speaker's platform. The mill owner steadfastly ignores the entreaties of his workers though, even when they are passionately delivered by their beautiful young advocate. But the mill owner's son has listened to the girl and, dressed as a laborer, he begins to attend the mass meetings. One day the heartless capitalist dies, summoned before "a tribune greater than all the millions who had judged him." The capitalist's son pledges his love for the lady firebrand and donates his inherited "millions to the millions." The *New York Dramatic Mirror* reviewer was particularly impressed by the framing composition: "the film opens in darkness and closes in darkness, the lights gradually appearing at the beginning and gradually fading away at the end." Note: The battle cry of the workers participating in the well-known Lawrence Strike that had taken place during the winter of 1912 was: "Better to starve fighting than to starve working!"

　　[*MPW* 6/22/12:1164; *NYDM* 7/3/12:33]
　　Cap; Fem Rad; Lab; Mtg; Reconcil; Strike
　　ANTI-CAP; CAP-LAB COOP

The Wage Earners: A Story of Labor vs. Capital, Atlas, 3r, Oct?, Am(s), Drama

　　The workers at a railyard walk-out—apparently over dangerous conditions as well as low wages. The struggle with the agents of capitalism includes mob scenes and acts of sabotage.

　　[*MPW* 10/19/12:262(ad)]
　　Cap; Lab; Mob; Sab?; Strike; Viol; Wrk Rel Dis/Inj?
　　PRO-LAB

With the Mounted Police, Thanhouser, Dec, Am(r), Drama

　　The police at an aqueduct construction site have been alerted to the presence of a group of "dangerous aliens" among the laborers, who have threatened violence if certain job concessions are not made. A police detective, disguised as a worker, is sent to report on the activities of the conspirators. But the "spy" is discovered, captured and thrown into a newly finished reservoir that is slowly being filled. The officer's faithful dog leads a nearby country girl to the reservoir just in time. The dangerous conspirators are rounded-up.

　　[*MPW* 12/28/12:1336]
　　Agit; Lab; Pol; Viol
　　ANTI-REV

1913

All Hail to the King, Biograph, Dell Henderson, 1r, Mar, Am, Comedy

　　A tramp nods off on a park bench and dreams about a wealthy king who is told his life is threatened by assassins. The royal messenger is sent forth to secure a "king pro tem" so that his royal highness can "beat it." Our tramp is approached by the messenger and induced to accept the position by a promise of plenty to eat and drink. While he is enjoying his new station, particularly the pretty dancing girls in attendance, a bomb is tossed through the window. The unsuspecting tramp uses its fuse to light his stogie and then throws the bomb back outside. Learning that the would-be assassins were blown up by their own device, the ingrate king reclaims his throne and orders his substitute to be sent to the torture chamber. The tramp's dream is suddenly terminated by a policeman's club beating the soles of his feet. Note: This one-reel farce may not have been as innocuous at it seems today. By 1913 there was an association in the public's mind between migrant tramps and the Wobblies. There were numerous "anti-vag" (vagrant) campaigns at the time that were, at least partly, class motivated.

　　[LC,LU518; *MPW* 3/22/13:1248]
　　Bomb; Pol; Rev; Tramp; Viol
　　ANTI-REV

The Anarchist, IMP, Herbert Brenon, 1r, Oct, Am, Drama

　　A handsome anarchist, played by popular star King Baggot, is in love with a young woman (Leah Baird playing the role). Another suitor, whom she has rejected, informs the police as to the location of the anarchist's hideout. When the police raid his studio, the sound of a toy horn alerts the anarchist to the presence of a neighbor's child and prevents him from blowing up himself and his companions with a bomb. The anarchist and his lover hold hands as they surrender to the law. Reissued in November 1916 under the title *The Voice Upstairs*.

[*MPW* 10/18/13:302]
Anarch; Bomb; Pol
NDB

The Benefactor, Lubin, 1r, July, Am, Drama

Boris Kreshnef is a young socialist who advocates the redistribution of wealth. Most of his ire is directed toward the local millionaire, Jonathan Gedney. Gedney disowns his son, Donald, for marrying without his consent. The newlyweds are soon destitute and take lodgings at the building in the slums where Boris resides. Unaware of who Donald's father is, Boris secretly leaves food in the couple's room. Later, he finds a lost suit of clothes containing a wallet that just happens to belong to the elder Gedney. Again, the socialist plays benefactor. But this leads to Donald being accused of theft by his father. After an irate Boris sets the old man straight, the Gedney family is reconciled and the avid socialist is offered a job as the millionaire's secretary. This is an early cinematic portrayal of a socialist abandoning his principles, apparently without qualms, for capitalistic gain.

[*MPW* 7/19/13:338; *NYDM* 8/6/13:35]
Cap; Russ?; Soc; Unemployed
PRO-SOC; ANTI-CAP

Binks—The Strike Breaker, IMP, Feb, Am(u), Comedy

A "walking delegate" (organizer) for the waiters' union orders a strike when it is learned that one of the men working at the Astoria Hotel refuses to join the union. After beating up the man, the waiters walk out in the middle of the dinner hour. The desperate manager puts out a help wanted sign that attracts the unemployed Charley Binks (a series character played by Charles DeForrest). Having only recently been discharged from an insane asylum, Binks' job performance, climaxing with serving an order of "Lobster Salad Undressed" in his nightshirt, can only lead to chaos—a cinematic punchline borrowed from the well-known 1898 American Mutoscope production, *How Bridget Served the Salad Undressed*. Note: Radical unionism was highly organized in the New York culinary trades at this time. In fact, the I.W.W. had called strikes in 1905, 1908 and 1912. A waiters' strike in New York City about overtime pay, supported by the I.W.W., erupted after midnight on January 24, 1913. About two thousand waiters and trade sympathizers abandoned their diners, marched down Madison Avenue and broke the windows of numerous establishments, including Delmonico's and the Waldorf Astoria. It was nearly twenty-four hours before order was restored. The IMP (Independent Motion Picture Company; founded in 1909 by Carl Laemmle) studio just happened to be located on Manhattan at Eleventh Avenue and 53rd Street.

[*MPW* 2/15/13:714; *NYDM* 2/19/13:33]
Lab; Scabs; Strike; Unemployed; Viol
CM/ANTI-LAB

Boarders and Bombs, Biograph, Edward Dillon, ½r, Oct, Am, Comedy

A couple of unemployed actors sell part of their wardrobe, rent a $2 a week room and invite some fellow thespians to a party. The landlord's attention is aroused as the various guests arrive, the smuggled food bulging from beneath their eccentric garments appearing to him to be of a particularly suspicious nature. With his ear glued to the keyhole, the landlord listens in. As the beer begins to flow, a cacophony of dialogue from assorted stage melodramas reaches a crescendo. Suspecting his new boarders are anarchists plotting mayhem, the landlord summons his police buddy. The amiable law officer quickly sorts things out. Note: It was common in the teens for working-class households to supplement their incomes by renting rooms to boarders. In pre-Equity days performers were routinely expected to supply their own costumes, whose cost was often greater than the salaries they were paid.

[LC,LU1499; *MPW* 11/15/13:735; *NYDM* 10/26/13:41]
Anarch; Bomb; Pol; Unemployed
CM/ANTI-REV

Bobby's Bum Bomb, Punch, Mar, Am, Comedy

Juvenile series character Bobby steals his

father's new bowling ball. By inserting a piece of cord into the thumb hole to look like a fuse, the mischievous boy creates a "bomb" with which to have fun by frightening people. His father discovers these activities and is about to administer a spanking, when Bobby threatens to disclose to mother an indiscretion with a young lady.

[*MPW* 3/1/13:926]
Bomb
CM/ANTI-REV

By Man's Law, Biograph, William Christy Cabanne, 2r, Nov, Am(u), Drama

A greedy oil magnate buys a troubled independent refinery, thereby financially ruining the young brother and sister (played by Bobby Harron and Mae Marsh, respectively) who had recently inherited the business. Furthermore, in order to stifle competition and keep prices up, the capitalist closes the refinery. A mob of angry workers declares a strike against all of his concerns, but is quickly dispersed by the police whom the oil magnate had earlier summoned. The suffering of the strikers becomes so acute that the local paper publishes an editorial rebuking the wealthy capitalist: "One is forced to wonder if the days of desperation are over, when one hypocritical Money God can so sway the wheels of destiny that thousands of helpless men, women and children may be thrown defenseless upon the world." In a bizarre plot twist, the maligned capitalist, rather than resolve the labor dispute, is inspired to embrace philanthropy and support the Civic League and Society for Prevention of Vice. Meanwhile, the desperate young woman whose refinery he had closed has tragically succumbed to the entreaties of "white slavers" (a subject much in vogue and exploited in many films during this period). This Biograph film may have been an influence upon a better known 1916 release from the studio, *Intolerance* (the modern story), q.v. Note: The Clayton Anti-Trust Act of 1914 was passed in direct response to the abuses of the oil monopolies.

[PE (USC); LC, LU1644(s); *MPW* 11/15/13:766]
Cap; Decad; Lab; Mob; Pol; Strike; Unemployed; Viol
ANTI-CAP

The District Attorney's Conscience, Lubin, Arthur Johnson, 2r, May, Am(u), Drama

An Italian anarchist, Tony Gazeco, has been using lunch breaks to give speeches before his fellow factory workers (many of whom were apparently also portrayed as foreign stereotypes). As District Attorney Will Mason and his wife drive by, they observe Tony agitating the workmen to strike. The couple informs the owner, Fred Jackson, and the obstreperous Italian is fired. Later that evening, a drunken Tony confronts his former boss with a gun. After disarming Tony and confiscating his weapon, Jackson proceeds to a dinner engagement at the Mason's house. Will Mason arrives home after being called away on business to discover Jackson flirting with his wife. Unwilling to face them, Mason goes to his room, but returns to the parlor when he hears a shot. He discovers his wife standing over Jackson's body. However, Tony, observed running from the house, is apprehended and convicted for murder. The DA remains conscience stricken until a letter from the executed Italian confessing to the crime is delivered to his wife. The *New York Dramatic Mirror* reviewer commented that Charles Brandt, as Tony, provided "an impressive character sketch of a foreign laborer."

[*MPW* 5/17/13:726; *NYDM* 5/28/13:28]
Agit; Anarch; Cap; Ital; Lab; Liq Link; Pol; Strike; Unemployed; Viol
ANTI-REV

From Dusk to Dawn, Occidental, Frank E. Wolfe, 4r, Sept?, Am(u), Drama

This "story of the class struggle" is a proworker film directed by a socialist activist that mixed studio-produced scenes with actual footage of contemporary labor events—including scenes of workers peacefully picketing, speeches by prominent labor leaders and a Labor Day parade. Iron molder Daniel Grayson is fired from a large iron works for being a union agitator. Dan is later arrested during a strike riot with company guards that followed a lethal factory explosion. While being booked at the police station, Dan meets and falls in love with Carlena Wayne, a slumborn laundress who was arrested during a strike and charged with illegal picketing. Following the settlement of the strike, in which the iron workers won their demands, Dan is persuaded to run for governor on the Socialist ticket. His opponents bring conspiracy charges against Dan, but a famous lawyer, Clarence

Darrow (playing himself; in 1907 he had successfully defended "Big" Bill Haywood against a murder charge related to the December 1905 bombing death of Idaho's ex-governor), wins an acquittal for the workers' candidate. After his election Dan steadfastly overcomes great opposition to his signing of a "right to work" bill. Dan and Carlena then become "comrades for life." Note: Sometimes shown under the title, *Labor vs. Capital*, this film was exhibited on tour through the Ernest Shipman company rather than distributed by States Right. The film did particularly well in urban centers throughout the country, reportedly setting new attendance records in the Chicago and New York City areas.

[AFI, F1.1485; *Mot* 11/15/13:369; *MPW* 9/13/13:1185; *MPW* 9/20/13:1323(ad)]

Agit; Am Icons; Cap; Fem Rad; Lab; Mtg; Pol; Pvt Pol; Soc; Strike; Unemployed; Viol
PRO-LAB; PRO-SOC

Giovanni's Gratitude, Reliance, 2r, Dec, Am(u), Drama

Giovanni, an Italian newsboy, is rescued from a gang of toughs by George Rankin, the manager of a large factory. Following the death of his grandmother, the boy gets a job at the plant. When Giovanni overhears two Italians plotting to blow up Rankin's home, he reports it to the boss. A bystander is knifed when the discharged bombers attack Giovanni that evening. Giovanni flees to the hills. While hiding in the woods, he witnesses the same two troublemakers planning again to bomb Rankin's home. Giovanni follows them to the manager's house and blows them up with their own device. *The Moving Picture World* review never specifies whether the planned violence of the bombers is class and/or politically motivated, but near the film's end the two Italians are identified as "blackhands." At the time, Italians were associated in the popular mind both with labor militancy and with the organized criminal violence of the Black Hand. This film is therefore of interest for blurring the distinction between the two.

[*MPW* 12/27/13:1592; *NYDM* 1/14/14:72]
Bomb; Cap; Ital; Lab; Viol
ANTI-REV; PRO-CAP

Greater Wealth, Selig, Colin Campbell, 1r, Jan, Am(u), Drama

A wealthy steel manufacturer, John Sharon (Hobart Bosworth), has a dismal personal life. For example, his son, played by Wheeler Oakman, is a drunkard. Ed Young (Thomas Santschi), who has worked for Sharon many years, resents his employer's financial success. He is fired to reduce the payroll. Young falls under the sway of "professional agitators" after his daughter becomes critically ill. One agitator also insults the American flag. Attending an anarchists' meeting, Young is induced to kill the millionaire "enemy of mankind." He is about to carry out the deed when a chastened Sharon, whose own daughter has just died, calmly assures Young that the happiness of his family is the most important thing in the workers' life. Yet the *New York Dramatic Mirror* reviewer makes the astute observation that "the real cause of the discontent that breeds anarchists is not touched upon." The *MPW* probably most accurately assessed the film's intent: "to create a feeling of patriotism and love for the Stars and Stripes as the flag of equal opportunity." Note: In March 1904, Bill Haywood, as secretary of the Western Federation of Miners, distributed a handbill in Colorado that listed the miners' grievances on the 13 bars of the American flag; he was promptly arrested for Old Glory's defacement.

[*MPW* 12/28/12:1322; *MPW* 1/18/13:264; *NYDM* 1/8/13:29]

Agit; Am Icons; Anarch; Cap; IWW?; Lab; Unemployed
ANTI-REV

A Hero Among Men, Lubin, 2r, July, Am(u), Drama

This film was promoted in a *Motography* ad as part of a growing number of "labor movement stories." When the workers at the Imperial Arms Company are refused a 10 percent raise, they declare a strike. Militants attack the executive building and the company officials are forced to barricade themselves in president Menton's offices. A fire breaks out because a drunken watchmen fell asleep with a lit cigarette. The boyfriend of Menton's daughter affects a dramatic rescue of those trapped within as munitions begin to explode. His bravery is cheered by the workers. The following observation is made at the conclusion of *The Moving Picture World* review: The film is an "unusually successful presentation of a factory strike.... [But] it seems absurd that the president should grant the increase of wages after the factory had burned."

[*Mot* 7/12/13:7(ad); *MPW* 7/26/13:427 & 436]

Cap; Lab; Lig Link?; Reconcil; Strike; Viol
ANTI-LAB; CAP-LAB COOP

A Millinery Bomb, Vitagraph, Wilfred North, 1/2r, July, Am, Comedy

Wealthy Reggie Burrows is home with a toothache. Pressed by his nagging wife for shopping money, Reggie gives her a hundred dollars to get her out of the house. She goes off on a buying spree, including the purchase of a fashionable chapeau. Reggie meanwhile reads an article in the paper about bombs being sent to peoples' homes in hat boxes. When the wife's new hat is delivered, a frightened Reggie summons the police to investigate the round box. Two Irish cops arrive and immerse the package in a tub of water. Reggie is forced to dole out additional cash when his wife returns to their home.

[*MPW* 7/5/13:68; *NYDM* 6/16/13:29]
Bomb; Cap; Irish; Pol
CM/ANTI-REV

A Million Dollars, Solax, Jan, Am(u), Drama

Jim Fuller is a clerk at a broker's office. Dissatisfied with his pay, Jim expresses the socialistic concept that "every man should have a million dollars, and that the wealth of the world should be distributed equally." He goes home in a huff and then falls asleep in his easy chair. Jim dreams of a new "millennium" in which the riches have been redistributed. In this fantasy world he soon discovers that, because everyone is satisfied with their lot, no one is willing to do any work. Jim awakens and realizes that the world could not function without financial incentives. Or, as a pro-capitalism end title states: "Our employers are often far better than we give them credit for."

[*MPS* 1/24/13:5; *MPW* 1/4/13:92; *NYDM* 1/8/13:33]

Cap; Lab; Soc
ANTI-SOC; PRO-CAP

Nihilist Vengeance, Victor, Sidney M. Goldin, 2r, July, Russ, Drama

Jewish banker Zoleski is a nihilist. His daughter is in love with Prince Gortchakoff, a Christian. Count Zobanoff, a member of the Tsarist secret police, infiltrates the nihilist society. At a ball given by the prince, the drunken count insults the young Jewess. Publicly reproved by the prince, the count subsequently arranges for his fellow aristocrat to be arrested as a nihilist. Gortchakoff is disgraced and condemned to death. His Jewish girlfriend, remembering that her father had once saved the Tsar's life, gains a pardon from the Tsarina. In retaliation, the evil count arrests the girl's father and tortures him to obtain information about the other members of the nihilist movement. By a ruse, the prince is able to get the count to exonerate Zoleski and implicate himself in a nihilist plot. The count commits suicide. The prince, now a nihilist, joins the banker and his daughter. The female lead was played by the dark-haired Irene Wallace, formerly the vaudeville star known as the "Dresden Doll."

[*MPW* 7/12/13:236]
Atroc; Cap; Jew; Nih; Russ; Sec Pol; Viol
ANTI-RS

Rags to Riches, Rex, Jan?, Am(u), Drama

The striking steel workers at a plant are unwilling or unable to grasp that the business is failing. Without the cooperation of labor, the management is compelled to shut down the plant. Learning about the closure, the strike leader, with "ferret-like eyes," rouses the men into a mindless rabble. They attack the superintendent so violently that the man is left unconscious. When he awakens the superintendent has been rendered an amnesiac. After years of wandering about as a derelict, the former manager regains his memory and is reunited with his family.

[*MPS* 1/31/13:1]
Agit?; Cap; Lab; Mob; Strike; Unemployed; Viol
ANTI-LAB

The Riot, Nestor, Jan, Am(r), Drama

Mine owner John Brandon adamantly refuses to consider his workers' petition and locks them out of the mines. After weeks of deprivation, the desperate miners, carrying with them the sickly child of their leader, make a final appeal to the owner. Brandon's reply is to level a rifle at the men. The obstinate owner is overcome and tied up in a shack so that he can experience the hunger suffered by the mining families. The leader's daughter, opposing what the miners have done, leaves her sick bed and comes to Brandon's aid. When the owner takes her home, he sees the miners' suffering and agrees to grant their demands. The *New York Dramatic Mirror* review skeptically concluded: "An owner would not close a mine merely to starve his employes [sic]. The plot is overdrawn and improbable."

[*MPW* 1/18/13:298; *NYDM* 1/22/13:32]

Cap; Lab; Reconcil; Unemployed; Viol
ANTI-CAP; CAP-LAB COOP

The Sorrows of Israel, Victor, Sidney Goldin, 3r, June, Russ/Am, Drama

A Russian noblewoman (Irene Wallace) marries a Jewish student after he converts to the Russian Orthodox faith. The prince, to whom she was betrothed, swears vengeance. To that end, he incites the peasantry to commit brutal anti-Semitic acts. Unable to ease the suffering of the Jewish community with his new wife's money, the convert joins the nihilists. Through the machinations of the evil prince the young man is arrested for his political activities. With the help of his nihilist compatriots the former Jew and his wife are allowed to escape Russia and flee to America. Note: The Tsarist regime's policy of "Russification" included the promotion of conversion to the Orthodox church.

[*MPW* 6/14/13:1180]

Am Icons; Atroc; Escape; Jew; Nih; Russ; Sec Pol; Viol
ANTI-RS

The Strike, Kalem, 1r, Dec, Am(r), Drama

In this typical Capital vs. Labor film the pretty miner's daughter effects reconciliation through a romantic match with the mine owner's son. The evil foreman, who has incited the miners to strike, is both thwarted from insulting the heroine's honor and from igniting a bomb to destroy the hoist machinery. A wage increase is later granted by the owner. According to *The Moving Picture World* review, the film was shot on location at "a real mine and its buildings."

[*MPW* 12/20/13:1412; *NYDM* 12/10/13:41]

Bomb; Cap; Lab; Reconcil; Sab; Strike; Viol

CAP-LAB COOP

The Strike Breakers, Nestor, Feb, Am(r), Western

The title was apparently used to increase interest in the western by exploiting the topicality of labor unrest, because there are no strikes or strike breakers in this film. When the payroll is delayed, a group of miners is incited to riot by the foreman, Larsen, a jilted lover of the owner's daughter. The young lady and her boyfriend, the new sheriff, put down the workers' revolt.

[*MPW* 2/1/13:500; *NYDM* 2/5/13:32]

Cap; Lab; Pol; Strike?; Viol
ANTI-LAB

The Strike Leader, Reliance, Oscar Apfel, 2r, Feb, Am(u), Drama

Wingate, the boss, cuts wages at a large factory. The workers hold a mass meeting and appoint a committee, led by the popular Larry, to petition the capitalist. After Wingate refuses their request, his employees vote to go on strike. Larry has been seeing Wingate's ward, Margery, who is respected by the workers for her charitable deeds in the tenements. When the boss learns about the two from a jealous suitor, he invites Larry to visit his mansion, ostensibly to discuss the strike. But, when Larry arrives, he is made a captive in order to prevent his attendance at a crucial strike meeting. Though locked in her room, Margery is able to smuggle a message out to Larry's best friend. The workers are informed and head for Wingate's mansion to rescue their compatriot. After the police restore calm, Wingate is induced to reinstate the men's former hourly rates.

[*MPW* 2/8/13:614]

Cap; Lab; Mtg; Pol; Strike; Viol
PRO-LAB; ANTI-CAP

The Struggle, Kalem, George Melford, 2r, June, Am(u), Drama

A capitalist named Masterson leaves the day to day supervision of his iron rolling mills to Mooney, a brutal Irish foreman (Paul C. Hurst) who reduces wages and neglects safety procedures. Young Jimmie Blake is struck down by Mooney for being late and then is crushed by a falling iron beam. As they carry the seriously injured boy home, the outraged workers declare a strike. Under the leadership of the burly "Bat" Thomas (Carlyle Blackwell), the strikers return to the mills and beat up Mooney. Maggie (Marin Sais), who is Jimmie's older sister and Bat's sweetheart, sneaks

into the factory to steal money to help her injured brother. When Masterson arrives to investigate the situation, she alerts the strikers by phone. After Masterson finds her hiding in a closet, Maggie upbraids him for allowing working conditions to deteriorate, but later helps protect him from a mob of angry strikers. The factory offices are burned down, though, after a stove is knocked over during a struggle between Bat and Masterson. Masterson pledges to create a model iron works with Bat as the new foreman. Incorporating footage of actual factory scenes, this film contained an unusually strong argument for capital-labor cooperation. To quote *The Moving Picture World* review: "*The Struggle* is a picture that should go well in any community, and especially well in manufacturing centers. It is in the latter that the feelings of the men on screen will be thoroughly understood."
	[*MPW* 6/7/13:1009; *MPW* 6/21/13:1247; *NYDM* 6/2/13:28]
		Cap; Irish; Lab; Mtg; Mob; Reconcil; Shp Flr Abu; Strike; Viol; Wrk Rel Dis/Inj
		CAP-LAB COOP

Sweeney's Dream, Selig, Charles H. France, 1r, July, Am(u), Fantasy-Drama
	Sweeney, an Irish hod-carrier who has imbibed an excessive amount of "suds," dreams in his stupor of becoming president of a republic. He and an ill-mannered horde of compatriots infest the seat of government. Sweeney's first official act is to make his mark on a document that settles the hod-carriers' strike by granting the laborers a five dollar-an-hour wage scale (well over $50 today, in buying power). When the builders petition the president, they are reluctantly allowed to escape alive. Cold feet revive the drunken worker. This is a crude example of the widespread linkage (particularly among temperance advocates) of ethnic workers with alcohol abuse and a resulting predilection to radicalism. Sweeney was a series character played by actor John Lancaster. Note: This film is a good example of the persistence of a negative ethnic stereotype, since by the time of its release most hod-carriers were of either Italian or Polish descent.
	[*MPW* 7/12/13:226]
		Cap; Irish; Lab; Liq Link; Strike
		ANTI-LAB

Tempesta, Majestic, Aug, Italy/Am, Drama
	Tempesta (the name evokes associations with violence) is a reformist agitator in Italy (read Socialist), who is arrested and imprisoned for attacking the monarchy. A kindly American consul agrees to take care of the radical's family. Tempesta escapes and flees to the United States. Years later, he encounters his grown daughter in her artist fiancé's New York studio. The retired consul, who had adopted the girl after her mother's death, persuades the old agitator to conceal his true identity and return to the Italian ghetto. This work bears some resemblance to the Russian nihilist film genre. Note: An Italian anarchist had actually killed Austrian Empress Elizabeth in 1898.
	[*MPW* 8/2/13:570]
		Agit; Artist; Escape; Ital; Pol; Soc?
		ANTI-REV

The Volunteer Strike Breakers, Vitagraph, 1r, Jan, Am(u), Comedy
	Carefree college students Chester and Harris learn that, due to a strike, waiters are needed at all the major restaurants. They quickly secure employment, but run into trouble with the management when they become distracted by the arrival of Harris's fiancée and one of her girlfriends. Explaining to the girls that the jobs were taken as a lark, they decide to avoid further harassment from the management by quitting. Unfortunately for them, they are intercepted at the door by picketing strikers who are protesting the hiring of scabs. The college men and their lady friends are handled roughly by the angry mob before they reach the safety of a taxi. Note: Since college campuses were bastions of the middle-class and vehicles by which to satisfy their aspirations for business and/or professional careers, students were primary sources for the short term recruitment of non-industrial strike breakers.
	[*MPW* 1/18/13:284 & 286]
		Lab; Mob; Scabs; Strike; Viol
		ANTI-LAB

Why?, Eclair, 3r, June, Am(u), Drama
	The film posed such questions as: "Why does capital sit easily at dinner with church and justice and the army while labor is outside starving?" Roy, the wastrel son of a rich scientist who is attempting to discover a formula that will drastically reduce the cost of living, comes home drunk and has a nightmare. His

visions include that of a bloated cigar-smoking, whip-holding capitalist collecting wealth from the labor of barefooted children operating a treadmill and of traveling on a railroad whose cross ties are human skeletons. Roy's nightmare concludes with his attendance at a banquet with the leaders of society, at which labor's seat is conspicuously empty. As a workers' revolt spreads destruction throughout Manhattan, some workers, led by a wild-eyed immigrant type, burst into the banquet hall. Several of the powerful guests, who include a banker, a bishop and an admiral, pull out guns and begin firing upon the mob—when shot in turn by the outraged workers the capitalists are transmogrified into sacks of gold (hand-painted that color to highlight its dramatic effect)! Roy awakens and joins his startled father in the laboratory. This was one of the most radical pro-labor films to be released in America, because it questioned the necessity of the suffering of the working-class under capitalism. *The Moving Picture World* review stated: "Much of it is socialistic doctrine, strongly presented.... Many exhibitors will look upon this as too suggestive in certain parts." Note: Between 1905 and 1920 the I.W.W. published over a score of periodicals, including one entitled *Why?*

[LC, LU741; *MPW* 5/31/13:923; *MPW* 6/14/13:1138; *NYDM* 6/8/13:30]

Anti-Rel?; Cap; Lab; Mob; Rev; Soc?; Viol; Wrk Rel Dis/Inj

ANTI-CAP; PRO-LAB

The Wop, IMP, July, Am(u), Drama

Luigi, a widower who lives with his little daughter Rosie, is employed by a wealthy contractor named Cramp. A strike is declared. When Luigi attempts to cross the picket lines, he is roughly turned away. The prolonged strike reduces Luigi to poverty and adversely affects the fortunes of Cramp. The capitalist is arrested for attempting to abscond with stolen funds, but is treated with respect. Whereas the poor "Wop," when seized by the police for picking coal in the railroad yards, is hauled-off to jail. Cramp is subsequently released on an alibi, while the immigrant worker is sentenced to hard labor. Returning home after serving his time, Luigi is unable to find his daughter. While desperately searching for Rosie, he passes the sentencing judge's house and notices the man with a child. Luigi sneaks into

the judge's home that night intent upon murdering the child in revenge, but the little sleeper rolls over and reveals herself to be his Rosie. The judge, a symbol of the dominant ideology, is redeemed by his caring for Luigi's daughter, yet paradoxically, the ideology is also attacked by juxtaposing the unequal treatment of the laborer and the capitalist by the legal system.

[*MPW* 7/5/13:82 & 84]

Cap; Ital; Lab; Pol; Strike

ANTI-CAP

The Worker, Ramo, Will Davis, 3r, Sept, Am(s), Drama

The workers at the Bradford Mills protest "long hours and starvation wages." When the "autocratic" owner, James Bradford, refuses their demands, his desperate laborers declare a strike. The disruptions of the strike and the accidental shooting of one of the more militant workers, a fireman named Jameson (Stuart Holmes), causes Bradford to have a fatal heart attack. To the chagrin of his stepmother, Bradford's son, Jack, is left in control of the family business. Though having lived the good life in the city, Jack is responsive to the workers' needs. He reopens the mills and "endeavors to relieve the dire poverty" resulting from the strike. The stepmother conspires to discredit her stepson by implicating him in a relationship with the wife of the wounded Jameson. After an altercation with the liquor-crazed worker, all is happily resolved.

[*MPW* 9/13/13:1221; *NYDM* 9/3/13:28]

Cap; Lab; Liq Link; Pol; Reconcil; Strike; Viol

ANTI-CAP; CAP-LAB COOP

1914

After Her Dough, Komic/Mutual, Edward Dillon, 1r, Mar, Am, Comedy

Not long after a wealthy heiress named Fay Doughbags (Fay Tincher) moves to Quietville, news of her fabulous jewel collection becomes known to some "yeggs." The hobo burglars take over the police station and impersonate cops in a scheme intended to cover an associate's entrance into the rich woman's home. The "police" receive a tip from a concerned citizen who has observed mysterious activities in a nearby house. Although the mysterious activity is actually some anarchists, "haters of society" plotting, the "police" assume that their cohort has been detected. After "police" enter the anarchists' headquarters, the angry bomb throwers chase them to the station and blow up the building. Having nabbed the burglar in the heiress' home, the real police return to their now destroyed station and discover the thieves' bodies in the wreckage. Tod Browning played the "Leader of the Yeggs" and Baldy Belmont played the "Chief Bomb Thrower."

[*MPW* 3/28/14:1740; *MPS*]

Anarch; Bomb; Cap; Pol; Tramp; Viol
ANTI-REV

Beneath the Czar, Solax, Alice Guy Blaché, 4r, Feb, Russ/Am, Drama

When the evil chief of secret police, Petroff, lashes her nihilist father before her eyes, Anna Pavlova (Claire Whitney) is coerced into spying for the Russian government. It is arranged for Anna to meet Prince Cyril, a suspected sympathizer with the "reformers," i.e. the nihilists. But she proceeds to fall in love with him. Introduced to the inner circle of his radical associates at their secret subterranean meeting place, Anna hides away and then steals incriminating papers when they leave. The suspicious prince follows Anna to her home and persuades her to relinquish the purloined documents. Government agents, alerted by a spying servant, later arrive and arrest Anna. With the aid of a soldier, who is a member of the revolutionaries, the young woman is released from house arrest. Together, they eventually succeed in freeing the captured prince, blowing up the soldiers guarding nihilist headquarters, eluding pursuing Cossacks and escaping to America.

[*MPW* 2/14/14:880; *Var* 5/8/14:20]

Atroc; Escape; Nih; Russ; Sec Pol; Tsar; Viol
ANTI-RS

The Better Man, Famous Players, 4r, Aug, Am(u), Drama

Two Episcopal clergymen, Mark Stebbing (William Courtleigh) and Lionel Barmor (Arthur Hoops), love Margaret Wharton, the daughter of the rich owner of a traction (streetcar) company. Mark chooses a small slum parish near Wharton's work yards, while stodgy Lionel becomes rector of the fashionable St. Hildas—one can imagine him delivering a sermon, snippets of which may have mimicked the Rev. Russell Conwell's popular "Acres of Diamonds" sermon that assured the upper classes: "It is your duty to be rich." Mark is rebuffed by General Wharton when he attempts to secure a raise for the man's workers. The angered laborers go out on strike. Even after Mark succeeds in preventing the strikers from blowing up the yard buildings, the old general will not accede to his workers' demands. Strikebreakers are brought in and the militia called up to protect them. But when the scabs man the cars, they are violently repulsed by a mob of strikers. Some toughs among the scabs are so incensed that they decide to set fire to the oil house and blame it on the strikers. Margaret is found nearby and thrown into the burning building. Mark is able to save Margaret and prevent the militia from firing on the strikers. Margaret declares her badly burned reverend "the better man." The *New York Dramatic Mirror* review states that Stebbing's "muscular Christianity ... is tinged with socialism." Note: In 1911 an Episcopal linked organization was founded, the Church Socialist League, whose stated purpose was the abolition of the capitalist system.

[AFI,F1.0300; *MPN* 8/22/14:46; *MPW* 8/22/14:1150; *NYDM* 8/19/14:26; *Var* 8/14/14:21]

Bomb; Cap; Lab; Militia; Mob; Sab; Scabs; Soc?; Strike; Viol
ANTI-CAP

Bill Joins the W.W.W's, Komic/Mutual, Edward Dillon, 1r, Nov, Am(u), Comedy

This film was number nine in the seventeen episode Komic series featuring a mischievous office boy named Bill (Tammany Young). In the street, Bill joins a crowd of "W.W.W's" carrying signs and passing out leaflets proclaiming: "We Won't Work." Bill returns to the office, late, and regurgitates to the angry "Boss" (Tod Browning) some of the radical rhetoric he has imbibed. The boss, who is preparing to go on a motor outing with a young lady, impatiently dismisses the incipient activist. Left to attend the office on his own, Bill returns to the W.W.W. demonstration and begins addressing the crowd. But Bill is forced to flee back to the office after scuffling with club-swinging policemen who attacked the meeting. This is one of the earliest known unequivocal film allusions to the Industrial Workers of the World (I.W.W.), frequently pejoratively referred to as the "I Won't Works" and the "*We Won't Works.*" Note: Campaigning for the right to openly organize and agitate at street corner gatherings epitomized the I.W.W. "Free Speech" fights, reaching a climax during a series of actions over an eighteen month period beginning in 1912 that took place in San Diego. This was precipitated by the Fall 1911 passage of a city ordinance banning street meetings. Refer to *The Dynamiters* (IMP, 1911), q.v.

[S (LC); *MPW* 10/31/14:694; *MPW* 11/7/14:788]

Agit; Cap; IWW; Jew?; Lab; Mtg; Pol; Strike?; Viol
ANTI-LAB

Bill Organizes A Union, Komic, Edward Dillon, 1r, Aug, Am(u), Comedy

This was the fifth film release adapted from Paul West's humorous "Bill the Office Boy" series. When Mr. Hadley, "the Boss" (Tod Browning), imposes a new set of work rules, Bill and his office mates decide to form a union. Chipping in a nickel apiece, they purchase union badges. Bill's pal Izzy ("Fatty" Crane) is fired the next day and a strike is declared on his behalf. The unionized boys begin parading through the building. After the boss calls up the fire department, the demonstrators are abruptly hosed down and hauled back to work. This is an interesting example of the potential for political ambiguity in film comedies addressing topical issues, since the concluding images, though obviously intended to amuse by showing some feisty adolescents getting drenched, can also be interpreted as symbolizing the drowning of unionism's cause beneath a crushing torrent of water. In fact, pressurized water from fire hoses had become a commonly used weapon against strikers and radical protesters in the arsenal of the establishment. Ethel, the Stenographer, is played by Fay Tincher.

[*MPW* 9/5/14:1426]
Cap; Lab; Strike; Viol
ANTI-LAB

The Bomb, Lubin, Joseph Smiley, 2r, Dec, Russ, Drama

A Russian nobleman's invention of a bomb leads to the confiscation of his property by order of the Tsar. Killed by the shock, the old count's daughter Sonia vows vengeance upon the bearer of the decree, Duke Boris.

Sonia secures her jewels and flees to the poor part of the city with her father's bomb. While trying to find Sonia, whom he secretly admires, Boris discovers that she has joined a society of anarchists. In order to save Sonia, Boris disguises himself and joins the anarchists under the name of "Kamaroff." Michael, another member of the secret society, lusts for Sonia. After becoming a leader of the anarchists, Sonia orders the death of Duke Boris. She proceeds to his apartment with the bomb. In the darkness of his rooms, Sonia springs at Boris with a dagger. But her "thirst for revenge" is slaked when in the moonlight it is revealed that the Duke and Kamaroff are the same person. Michael, who has also learned the true identity of the man, arrives with the rest of the "brotherhood" to carry out the assassination decree. Instead, they are destroyed when Boris hurls the smoking bomb at the on-coming anarchists. This Russian–placed film is rather unusual in that it identifies the radicals as anarchists, rather than nihilists. Perhaps that is why its creators further went against the grain of the genre by portraying the anarchist Michael as sexually aggressive, rather than the typically decadent agent of the Tsarist regime.

[*MPW* 12/12/14:1572]
Anarch; Bomb; Fem Rad; Russ; Tsar; Viol
ANTI-RS; ANTI-REV

The Bomb Boy, Eclectic, George Fitzmaurice, 3r, Dec, Am, Com-Drama

Grand Duke Sergius, who is visiting the United States, is being followed by a nihilist named Anna Karensky. The Secret Service alert the local police to intercept her at the docks. Anna's colleagues warn the female radical before she disembarks from the boat. Anna gets her bomb past customs by hiding it in a hat box. She then dupes an unsuspecting messenger boy named Larry (Ernest Truex) into delivering the deadly package to her associates. Larry learns through eavesdropping about the true contents of the box and the plans of a nihilist waiter to blow up the Duke while serving him dinner. Larry is discovered, but escapes to the hotel where he bursts into the Duke's apartments. He finds the bomb under a covered dish and makes a mad dash outside to safely dispose of the device. The waiter is identified as an Italian named Ravelli, indicating that nihilism was no longer a term used exclusively to describe politically motivated Russian terrorism.

[LC,LU3740; *MPW* 12/26/14:1900; *NYDM* 12/14/14:42]

Bomb; Fem Rad; Ital; Nih; Pol; Russ; Sec Ser

ANTI-REV

Bombarded, Selig, Harry Jackson, 1r, June, Am, Comedy

Professor McSwat makes bombs for a hobby. Luke is in love with the professor's daughter, but has an aversion to explosives. When the father tests the young man's courage by introducing him to a bomb in the parlor, Luke decides to get even. Disguising himself, Luke enters the professor's home while lighting a cigarette with the burning fuse of a stick of dynamite! McSwat attempts to flee, only to have his exit blocked by a knife wielding "lady Nihilist." He is captured and bound to a tree with a "bomb" placed by his side. Luke then appears and coolly tosses the bomb away from the frightened man. A bum picks it up, examines it and then cracks open what is actually a coconut. Luke also captures the lady nihilist, who turns out to be Miss McSwat.

[LC,LP2755; *MPW* 6/6/14:1438]

Bomb; Fem Rad; Nih; Tramp

CM/ANTI-REV

Bombsky and the Bomb, Royal, May, Am?, Comedy

A brief review in *The Moving Picture World* ambiguously states: "A farce with eccentric characters that is lively and broad and a bit rough.... [The] unexpected happenings ... [in the] last half ... [are] truly exciting." The title would seem to indicate a parody of Russian bomb throwers.

[*MPW* 6/13/14:1541]

Bomb; Russ?

NDB

Called Back, Un/Gold Medal, Otis Turner, 4r, Dec, Brit/Ital/Russ, Drama

Two nihilist conspirators living in London, Dr. Manuel Ceneri and Signor Macari, are fighting for what they believe to be the freedom of Italy. They murder a man over an inheritance. Later, on a trip to Russia, Macari is sent to Siberia after being caught in a bomb throwing plot. Due to the efforts of a young man (Herbert Rawlinson) and woman who witnessed the crime, Ceneri is eventually tracked down and shot by British police. Note: Though the cited print sources refer to the protagonists as nihilists, politically motivated violence perpetrated by Italians was more apt to be associated in the contemporary public mind with the *Anarchist* movement—Italian born anarchist Gaetano Bresci (a thirty-year-old silk weaver from Paterson, New Jersey) killed King Humbert on July 29, 1900 and in March 1912 a crazed anarchist called Alba had attempted to shoot King Victor Emmanuel.

[LC,LP3817; *MPN* 12/5/14:44; *NYDM* 12/2/14:35; *Var* 1/23/15:26]

Bomb; Ital; Nih; Pol; Siberia; Viol

ANTI-REV

The Daughters of Men, Lubin, George Terwilliger, 5r, April, Am(u), Drama

The Crosby brothers manage an industrial conglomerate. But after marrying an actress, Reginald squanders a great deal of money on parties. One party is so lavish that it provokes an angry editorial in the labor paper. A strike is subsequently declared, whose leaders include an agitator fond of disparaging "the bosses," a German immigrant named Louis Stolbeck and his feisty daughter Louise (Ethel Clayton). Eventually, reconciliation is achieved when Grace, the Crosby's sister, arranges a meeting between her brothers and her boyfriend, a labor lawyer representing the striking union. The *Variety* reviewer dismissed the film as a "trite capital vs. labor story, carrying an incidental love theme."

[AFI,F1.0949; *NYDM* 4/22/14:34; *Var* 4/24/14:34]

Agit; Cap; Fem Lab; Ger; Lab; Reconcil; Strike

CAP-LAB COOP

Dough and Dynamite, Keystone, Charles Chaplin, 2r, Oct, Am(u), Comedy

Charlie Chaplin is an incompetent waiter in a combination French restaurant and bakery. The bakers (played by Slim Summerville, Edgar Kennedy and Charley Chase) declare they want "less work and more pay." After the owner rejects their demands, the bakers walk out on strike. Charlie is ordered to start baking. The strikers vow vengeance upon the scab. Outside, the fanatical head baker produces a box labeled "Dynamite." To carry out their "fiendish scheme" of revenge, the bakers conceal a stick of dynamite inside a loaf of bread. The strikers persuade a little girl to take the "fatal loaf" to the bakery and ask for a refund. Noticing that the loaf is too heavy, the owner has it sent back to the oven. The inevitable explosion destroys the premises. The strikers, who have been hiding in a nearby shed with their box of dynamite, are also blown up. In the 1923 rerelease of this film the dynamite is described in a literally illustrated art inter-title as: "A stick of Russian candy." Note: In 1917(?) a remake of *Dough and Dynamite*, starring Chaplin imitator Billy West, was produced and released by King Bee. But the baker, a stock character named Spaghetti *fired* for threatening the cashier, in the tradition of Black Hand films, is only seeking personal revenge when he and "His Pal" return to the bakery carrying bombs.

[S (LC); LC,LP3724; *MPW* 10/31/14:642] Bomb; Cap; Lab; Sab; Scabs; Strike; Viol ANTI-LAB

The Envoy Extraordinary, Santa Barbara, Mot Pict, Oct, Lorimer Johnston, 5r, Rur, Drama

The wife of the Prime Minister of a great power, the Countess Northstone, gives a large party at which she attempts to gain information by flirting with an ambassador whose government is suspected of plotting war. She sees a note he has received from Baron von Hatzfeldt, whom she knows to be the leader of an anarchist group called "The Brotherhood." The Brotherhood has bribed the ambassador in its attempts to incite a war. The Countess is able to disrupt these plans by publicly denouncing the Baron as a former soldier responsible for atrocities committed against unarmed peasants a decade earlier. Note: This film's release date would appear to have been delayed—probably a result of the outbreak of World War I on August 4th.

[AFI, F1.1176; *MPW* 7/25/14:558 & 560; *MPW* 8/8/14:843]

Anarch; Atroc; Cap; Ger?; Viol ANTI-REV

Escaped From Siberia, Great Players, Sidney Goldin, 3r, May?, Russ/Am, Drama

A couple of drunken Russian officers at a country inn insult the Jewish owner's daughter. Count Boris, the son of the Governor-General of Kiev, enters the inn and protects the girl. Her brother joins a secret order of nihilists. One of the officers seeks revenge by spreading a report that the innkeeper's family is suspected of being nihilists. Following a police raid of nihilist headquarters in Kiev, the innkeeper and his son are arrested. The father, who was not actually a member of the group, assumes responsibility and is sentenced to hard labor in Siberia. When he learns that Count Boris has fallen in love with the young Jewess, the Governor-General publicly degrades his son by ordering the insignia of his military rank torn off his uniform. Boris joins the "cause" and, after proving his loyalty, aides in the assassination of the Minister of Interior. Boris and the innkeeper's family then make a dramatic escape across the snow to a port where they embark on a ship that takes them to "God's Land of Liberty."

[LC, LU2687; *MPW* 5/2/14:734]

Bomb; Decad; Escape; Jew; Nih; Russ; Sec Pol; Siberia; Viol ANTI-RS

Facing the Gattling Guns, Mittenthal Film, 3–4r, April, Am(r), Drama

While on a business trip for Mr. Stacey, Gill Howe becomes acquainted with Kate Adams, the daughter of a contractor building a great dam. Because John Adams has trouble meeting the payroll, his laborers threaten to blow up the dam. Gill joins Adams and is able to secure a loan from the state governor. Meanwhile, his former boss and the project foreman conspire to incite the still unpaid workers to violence. The militia arrive with their Gatling guns, but are ordered by Gill to fire only blanks if the rioters threaten the dam. Stacey substitutes live ammunition for the blanks. A mob of workers attacking the project is fired upon, resulting in many casualties. Film footage shot by a news cameraman absolves Gill and helps convict Stacey. *Variety* reviewed the film as a three-reeler under the properly spelled *Facing the Gatling Guns*.

[AFI,F1.1243; *MPW* 5/16/14:1018; *Var* 7/3/14:21]

Agit; Cap; Lab; Militia; Mob; Sab; Viol ANTI-LAB; ANTI-CAP

A Fight for Freedom; or Exiled to Siberia (A Fight For Life), April, Solax, Alice Guy Blaché, 4r, Russ, Drama

An old man is sent into Siberian exile, "bringing the cruel vengeance of Russia down upon his head by daring to speak his mind in the interests of freedom." He is accompanied by members of his family, who later convince the authorities that he committed suicide. On the road returning to Moscow, they are aided by an ex-soldier named Ivan Romanoff, who was banished by his general father for refusing to participate in a massacre. Ivan falls in love with Viska, the beautiful daughter of the old man. Viska and Ivan join the nihilists and, unaware of Ivan's true identity, Viska is chosen to assassinate General Romanoff. At the last minute, Ivan prevents Viska from blowing up his father and, consequently, the two lovers are captured. The general is mortally wounded when a mob of revolutionaries storm the fortress in which Ivan and Viska are imprisoned. Having discovered the equality of man in his dying moments, the general's corpse is found in the embrace of a dead nihilist. Note: Use of the surname Romanoff creates a direct associative linkage with the ruling Russian dynasty (1613–1917).

[LC,LP2699; *MPW* 4/25/14:584; *MPW* 5/2/14(ad)]

Atroc; Bomb; Fem Rad; Mob; Nih; Russ; Siberia; Tsar; Viol

ANTI-RS

Firelight, Eclair, 2r, Aug, Am(u), Drama

John Marten, the owner of a large plant, becomes obsessed with money after the death of his child. In his mad quest for wealth the millionaire "slave driver" neglects the love of his wife. On their tenth wedding anniversary, which he has forgotten, the workers at his plant declare a strike. After Marten threatens to "import foreign labor" to break them, his wife receives a warning from the strikers that her husband will be killed if he leaves the house. Desperate to retrieve their love and save her husband's life, Mrs. Marten begins sorting through a chest of family memorabilia in front of the fireplace. John's love of life is reawakened and, remembering it is their anniversary, he decides to stay home with his wife. In a phone call to the office, Marten instructs his secretary to tell the strikers that all their demands will be met.

[LC,LU3112; *MPW* 7/25/14:615; *MPW* 8/1/14:738]

Cap; Lab; Reconcil; Scabs; Strike

CAP-LAB COOP

The Golden God: An Episode of 1950, Lubin, Romaine Fielding, Jan?, 5–6r, Am(s), Fantasy-Drama

Shot and completed in Las Vegas during the fall of 1913, this motion picture was judged too "inflammable" by censors and denied general distribution. An advance notice in *The Moving Picture World* comments: "Its theme is capital and labor…. One of the most picturesque scenes was a brilliant cavalry charge led by Mr. Fielding in a high-powered automobile equipped with a machine gun, operated by soldiers…. The period of the play is 1950, when, according to the screen portrayal, the giant Labor will strike its tyrant Gold." An airplane was also used to further emphasize the potential horrors of a future class war. Note: There appear to be similarities between the film's plot and that of Jack London's most politically radical novel, *The Iron Heel* (1907).

[*MPW* 12/13/13:1266; *MPW* 1/17/14:260 (ad); Linda Kovall Woal and Michael Woal. "Romaine Fielding's Real Westerns." *Journal of Film and Video*, Vol. 47, Nos. 1–3 (Spring-Fall 1995), pp. 21–22]

Cap; Lab; Militia; Mob; Viol

PRO-LAB

The Jungle, All Star Feature Corp, Augustus Thomas, Henry Irving & John H. Pratt, 5r, May, Lith/Am(u), Drama

An immigrant Lithuanian farming family struggles to survive in Chicago's notorious meat processing area, descriptively named Packingtown, in this film adaptation of the famous muckraking novel published by Upton Sinclair in 1906. One memorable scene shows the production of edible lard from a tank in which a worker had been scalded to death. A twenty percent wage reduction is ordered by Durham, the packing plant owner, due to the expenses incurred by his extravagant family. A violent and unsuccessful strike follows. The Lithuanian family is destroyed by the voracious industrial system. Jurgis (George Nash), the hero, is imprisoned for killing the foreman named Connor (identified in the source novel as a "red-faced Irishman" assaulted by Jurgis; played by the thickset, middle-aged Robert Cummings), who demanded sex with his wife (Gail Kane) in exchange for money to buy food for their starving child. When Jurgis is released, he is unable to locate any of his relatives. In despair, Jurgis attends a Socialist Party meeting where he listens to a speech delivered by Upton Sinclair (playing himself). Jurgis is inspired by the cause. He also rediscovers love with an old girlfriend, who had become a prostitute after being raped by Durham's son. The working-class couple start life anew, determined to create a "cooperative commonwealth." With the film's title in mind, the *Variety* reviewer made the following sarcastic observation: "This is not a feature picture of wild animals, just about wild socialists...." A special musical score for *The Jungle* was composed by Manuel Klein. Note: Hoboes and I.W.W.s congregated in improvised camps, called "jungles," located on the outskirts of towns. Packingtown, located on Chicago's South Side next to the stockyards and meat packing plants, was a tenement community primarily inhabited by immigrant Poles and Lithuanians. A major strike had taken place in Packingtown during the summer of 1904. Sinclair acquired the film's negative and in 1921–22 reissued an edited version through the Labor Film Service. Objections were raised by authorities, despite new inter-titles asserting that federal inspection regulations now insured that processed meats were sanitary.

[AFI, F1.2313; *MPW* 6/20/14:1675; *Var* 6/26/14:19; Brownlow, *Behind the Mask of Innocence*, pp. 472–78]

Cap; Decad; Irish?; Lab; Mtg; Mob; Pol; Shp Flr Abu; Soc; Strike; Viol; Wrk Rel Dis/Inj
PRO-LAB; ANTI-CAP; PRO-SOC

A Leech of Industry, Pathé, 3r, Mar, Russ?/Am(u), Drama

Because of his political beliefs, old Romanoff is forced to flee Russia with his family. In America, his two sons find jobs in a factory where many others of their nationality are employed. A plant explosion kills one son, who leaves behind a pregnant girlfriend. Ivan, his brother, reluctantly marries the girl. Years later, a self-employed Ivan risks his life's savings to win an important contract. His primary competitor and former employer arranges for both the theft of Ivan's bid and the discrediting of the Russian-American as an adulterer. In a dramatic race to the state capital to place their bids the evil capitalist is killed. Meanwhile, Ivan has also discovered a genuine affection for his wife.

[*MPW* 3/21/14:1576]

Cap; Escape; Lab; Nih?; Russ; Wrk Rel Dis/Inj
ANTI-CAP; CM/ANTI-RS

The Lily of the Valley, Selig, Colin Campbell, 3r, May, Am(s), Drama

In this film that was subtitled, "Evangel of the Toilers," Lily Vale (Olive Drake) is a dedicated young mission worker in the mill town of Commercial Valley. Her brother Philip (Wheeler Oakman), a lieutenant in the National Guard, is called-up when a strike breaks out in the mills. The strikers are led by foreman "Old" Bill Hanks and his fiery daughter Anna (Bessie Eyton). Following a riot in which a number of workers were wounded by the soldiers, Lily agrees to present the mill owner, Old Man Winter (a gray-whiskered, top-hatted caricature, played by Frank Clark), with a peace proposal. She has almost won over the capitalist when his window is shattered by a stone during renewed rioting. While the saddened "Lily of the Valley" is visiting her brother, she is killed by a stray bullet. In retaliation, the crazed lieutenant turns and fires the machine gun under his command into the demonstrating millhands. Among those killed are the father and brother of Anna. Waving a pistol over their bodies, Anna swears to avenge the martyred workmen. Coming to his senses after finding the contract in his dead sister's hands, Philip forces Winter to sign the labor pact so as to avoid further bloodshed. After being quietly exonerated by the authorities for the killings, Philip decides to dedicate his life to improving the conditions of the mill workers in Commercial Valley. He becomes a laborer in the factory where Anna works. Unaware that he was the man responsible for the deaths of her father and brother, Anna falls in love with and marries Philip. When she is later taken to his ornate home, Anna begins to suspect the true identity of her husband. During another outbreak of labor violence Anna, who has contemplated shooting Philip, sees him struck down by a striker's bullet. Anna returns to her people as an evangelist, administering to their needs and preaching the gospel of social peace.

[LC,LP2741; *MPW* 5/9/14:803; *NYDM* 6/10/14:44]

Am Icons; Cap; Fem Rad; Lab; Militia; Mob; Pvt Pol?; Reconcil; Strike; Viol
ANTI-CAP; CAP-LAB COOP

The Lost Paradise, Famous Players/Par, J. Searle Dawley, 5r, Sept, Am(u), Drama

The *Variety* review described this film as

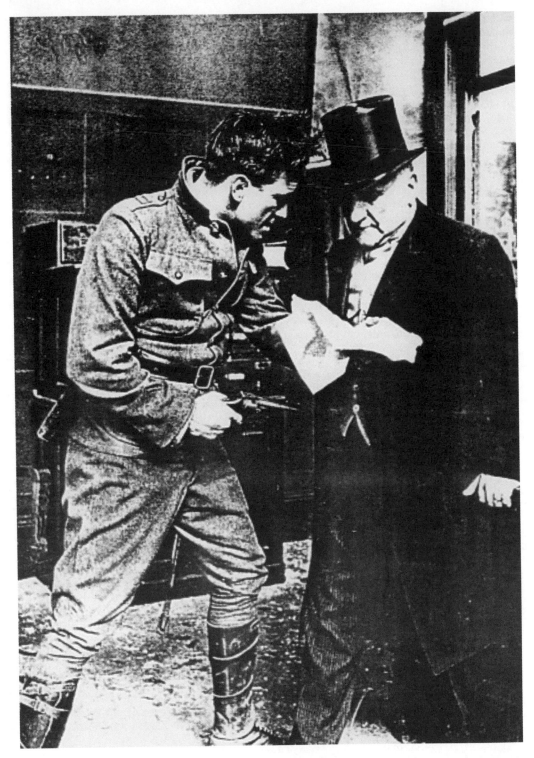

The Lily of the Valley (Selig, 1914): **With the labor contract soaked in his martyred sister's blood, a militia lieutenant demands that the mill owner sign, and thereby put an end to the senseless violence.**

"a capital and labor scenario with a socialistic frame." Reuben Warren (H. B. Warner), the foreman of an iron works, had his "volta-dynamo" invention secretly stolen from him years earlier by the iron works owner, Knowlton. Reuben is in love with Knowlton's daughter, Margaret (Catherine Carter), although the diamond bedecked young lady is engaged to another man. A strike is declared because of poor working conditions at the factory, just as Reuben receives proof of Knowlton's treachery. Reuben becomes the strikers' spokesman: "When you want me, send for my people." The usual mob and starvation scenes are counterbalanced by comic sequences with ethnic factory hands. Margaret breaks her previous engagement and marries Reuben. As the new half-owner of the mill, Reuben cheerfully accedes to the workers' just demands. This film included numerous exterior and interior scenes of an actual factory. Note: *The Lost Paradise* was the first Famous Players production distributed by Paramount.

[AFI, F1.2609; *MPW* 9/12/14:1495; *Var* 9/4/14:13]

Cap; Ger?; Lab; Mob; Reconcil; Soc?; Strike

PRO-LAB; CAP-LAB COOP

The Marked Woman, World, O. A. C., Lund, 5r, Dec, China/Russ, Drama

Following the accidental fatal running over of her little sister by mounted Cossacks, Olga Petcoff (Dorothy Tennant) is persuaded by her brother to join him in the "brotherhood" of nihilists. Olga is sent with an important message for her fellow revolutionaries in Port Arthur. During the voyage she meets and falls in love with Lieutenant Dare (played by the film's director) of the U.S. Navy. At the Pacific port she is captured by the Russian police who have occupied the nihilists' headquarters. After being branded, she is offered a choice of becoming the Russian ambassador's mistress or being sent to Siberia. Olga accepts the former. Shipwrecked on her way to Nanking, Olga is later abducted by and forced to marry The Empress Dowager's prime minister, Prince Ching (Walter Connolly). Several years later, during the Boxer Rebellion (1899–1901), the American lieutenant leads a military force that rescues Olga. But she is inconsolable since the prince unintentionally killed their son, and denounces all those who wage war.

[AFI, F1.2825; *MPW* 12/12/14:1596; *Var* 12/12/14:28]

Atroc; Decad; Fem Rad; Nih; Pac; Russ; Sec Pol; Siberia; Viol

ANTI-RS

Martin Eden, Bosworth/W.W. Hodkinson, Hobart Bosworth, 6r, Aug, Am, Drama

Martin Eden (Lawrence Peyton), a hard-bitten sailor, tires of working on tramp steamers and goes ashore in Oakland, California. During a ferry excursion he saves Arthur Morse (the handsome Herbert Rawlinson) from thugs. Introduced to Morse's intellectual circle and sister Ruth, Eden determines to win their respect by educating himself. But when his funds run out, Martin is forced to go back to the sea. Upon returning to Oakland, the autodidactic sailor attends a Socialist rally with Russ Brissenden, a poet anarchist he had met aboard ship. A cub reporter at the meeting hall is so impressed by Martin's impromptu speech that he portrays the man in the morning paper as Oakland's leading socialist. Appalled by the article, Arthur persuades Ruth to break off her incipient relationship with the sailor. Meanwhile, the alcoholic Russ has shot himself and Martin has become increasingly estranged from Lizzie, his working-class girlfriend. Martin begins to sell the stories he has been writing. But his artistic and financial success comes too late to bring him happiness. Despondent, he gives away his money to his Mexican landlady and a likable tramp. Returning to the sea, Martin jumps overboard on his final voyage. A prologue features author Jack London reading from his 1909 novel, upon which the film is based.

[S (LC, incomplete); AFI, F1.2852; LC, LU3029; *MPW* 5/16/14:920–921; *MPW* 10/10/14:253]

Anarch; Artist; Lab; Mtg; Pol; Soc; Tramp; Unemployed

PRO-SOC

The Master of the Mine, Vitagraph, W. J. Bauman, 2r, Feb, Am(r), Drama

Arthur Berkow (William D. Taylor), the son of a rich social climber, marries the daughter of an impecunious man of prominence. After later becoming "master of the mines," Arthur's harsh policies lead to a strike. When Arthur refuses to yield to their demands, the enraged strikers, led by Ulrich Hartmann (Otto

Lederer), plot to dynamite the mine. While attempting to carry out the deed, a cave-in entombs several of the miners. Arthur bravely descends into the shaft to effect a rescue, but is himself overcome just as the last miner is sent to the surface. Arthur's wife, who had planned to divorce him, is so moved by his sacrifice that she begs the men to help save her husband. After the other men refuse to come to her aid, Hartmann jumps into the lift bucket with the desperate woman. The trio escape immediately before the dynamite charge blows up the mine. *The Moving Picture World* review concludes by stating: "The mob scenes finely handled [sic]."

[LC, LP2026; *MPW* 2/28/14:1088; *NYDM* 2/18/14:36]

Bomb; Cap; Ger?; Lab; Mob; Reconcil; Sab; Strike; Wrk Rel Dis/Inj
CAP-LAB COOP

The Militant, IMP, William Robert Daly, 3r, Jan, Brit, Drama

With the continued real-life militancy of the suffrage movement in Britain and the joint membership of many well-known socialists, both in the U.S. and Britain, there evolved a linkage between radical feminism and women's suffrage. The ostensible purpose of *The Militant* was to condemn violence carried out by suffragettes. Thus, the film contains many scenes of "spectacularism," including the destruction of railroad tracks and the bombing of warehouses. A number of prominent American suffragettes allegedly had roles in this motion picture. The plot centers around the political rival of a member of Parliament secretly exploiting the devotion to the cause of the man's wife in order to bring down the government by crippling the country's system of food distribution.

[*MPW* 1/10/14:214; *MPW* 1/17/14:296]
Bomb; Fem Rad; Pol; Viol
ANTI-REV

My Official Wife, Vitagraph/Broadway Star, James Young, 5r, Aug, Am/Fr?/Russ, Drama

American Arthur Bainbridge Lennox (Harry T. Morey) is forced to visit Russia in order to settle the estate of his deceased daughter. Helene Marie (Clara Kimball Young; renowned for her pantomime skills), a beautiful young nihilist, ascertains that the married man will be traveling alone and persuades Lennox to let her cross the border with him as his wife. At their St. Petersburg hotel room Helene reveals her true identity to the American, but he does not betray her. Although Helene falls in love with Sacha Weletsky (Earle Williams), an officer of the Royal Guard, she continues conspiring with her revolutionary comrades to assassinate the Tsar at a ball. Lennox learns of this and prevents Helene from killing the Tsar by placing a sleeping potion in her punch. When the secret police become aware of the plot, Helene is able to escape aboard the yacht of the infatuated Sacha. A Russian submarine torpedoes the lovers' boat. This film was rereleased in December 1916. Note: Richard Henry Savage, responsible for a number of popular adventure stories set in Russia, wrote the source book: *My Official Wife: A Novel* (New York: Home Publishing, 1891). An extant photo still of a scene in which Helene Marie appears with a bearded man wearing a pince nez, who physically resembles Leon Trotsky, has led to specious speculations in several contemporary sources regarding the famous Bolshevik appearing in the film as an extra. In all likelihood the uncredited character was intended to represent a Jewish intellectual stereotype.

[AFI, F1.3107; LC, LP3182; *EH* 12/16/16: 21–22; *Var* 7/17/14:17]

Fem Rad; Jew?; Nih; Russ; Sec Pol; Tsar; Viol
ANTI-RS; CM/ANTI-REV

The Nihilists, Nestor, Oct, Am, Drama

Prosecuting attorney Thomas Madison is warned that the city is "infested with a desperate gang of Russians who teach Nihilism." Madison responds by instructing the local paper to publish that he intends to crush the movement. As a result, he is marked for death by the bomb throwers. Madison's brother, Frederick, has been receiving medical treatment from Dr. Petrosky, a leading member of the nihilists. Frederick has also fallen in love with the physician's stepdaughter, Zena. She is later selected to deliver the bomb that will kill the offending attorney. But when she discovers that he is the brother of her lover, Zena breaks with the nihilist gang and informs Thomas Madison of their plans. Detectives rush to Petrosky's home, only to find him and an associate dead from the poisonous fumes of their "infernal machine."

[*MPW* 10/17/14:398]
Bomb; Fem Rad; Nih; Pol; Russ; Viol
ANTI-REV

The Plot, Vitagraph, Maurice Costello & Robert Gaillord, 2r, Dec, Am, Drama

A band of Russians plot to assassinate Kasso, the new Russian ambassador to the United States. Reporter Roy Burton meets and falls in love with Vera, Kasso's daughter. When he overhears the lethal plans of the conspirators, Roy attempts to disrupt them. Instead, Roy is knocked-out and captured by the assassins. Alexis, their leader, places Roy under a hypnotic spell that will induce him to carry the bomb to the ambassador's house. Roy and Kasso are saved by the loving Vera, accompanied by two policemen.

[LC,LP3914; *MPW* 12/26/14:1872]
Bomb; Pol; Rev; Russ; Viol
ANTI-REV

Prosecution, Vitagraph, July, Am(r), Drama

The workers at a large western mining camp hold a raucous protest meeting after being informed of a general wage cut. The more militant among them, led by Cliff McClellan, blow up the mine hoist. When the company attorney later accuses McClellan of the deed, he is kidnapped and left to die in the desert. The love of McClellan's sister for the lawyer saves the latter's life. Her brother is sent to prison.

[*MPW* 7/4/14:106]
Bomb; Cap; Irish?; Lab; Mtg; Pol; Sab; Viol
ANTI-LAB

Rastus Knew It Wasn't, Lubin, Sept, Am, Comedy

Rastus (a dialect-speaking blackface series character), the janitor at the local police station, dodges a flying wash pail after the chief trips over it. Luigi, who is walking down the street with his sweetheart, is hit. When the angered Sicilian demonstratively complains, the cops beat him up. In order to regain the respect of his girl, Luigi swears revenge. In the meantime, Rastus has slipped into a movie theatre where he watches a "rather familiar" farce about an alarm clock being mistaken for a bomb. Upon his return to the station, Rastus finds the police terrified because they believe crazy Luigi has planted a bomb in the building.

But Rastus is sure the ticking mechanism is just another clock. The black porter is blown into the clouds when he takes an ax to the noisy object in the back yard. In this bomb parody the distinction between class motivated violence and personal revenge is blurred. This film bears some resemblance to the 1911 Eclair release, *Beware of the Bomb*, q.v.

[*MPW* 9/12/14:1544]
Bomb; Ital; Pol; Viol
CM/ANTI-REV

The Spirit of the Conqueror; or, The Napoleon of Labor, Nov?, Phoenix, 5r, Am(u), Fantasy Drama

The shades of great historical persons, including George Washington and Abraham Lincoln, gather at the border of Paradise to meet a messenger returning from earth to report on the suffering of humanity in the struggle between capital and labor. The "Master of Reincarnation" selects the spirit of Napoleon to enter the body of the newly born son of financier Peter Morgan. Years later, James Morgan (Frank Newburg) returns from college and, after meeting with an Irish labor leader, opposes his father's wage cuts. Having thus been disinherited, James forms an international labor association and calls a general strike (I.W.W.?). Three months later the country's economy is paralyzed. The militia is called out, but the soldiers refuse to fire upon the workers. The president sends a committee of senators to visit a dying James—his health destroyed by the strain of events. Following the meeting, they persuade capital to capitulate to labors' demands. The soul of Napoleon is allowed to return to Paradise. Note: Until the 1917 Bolshevik Revolution, Napoleon was considered (with mixed feelings in America) *the* symbol of a mass revolutionary movement; the lower class general of republican armies who defeated the forces representing many of Europe's more decadent aristocracies—and the "Marseillaise" was the most popular hymn of workers throughout the western world.

[AFI, F1.4207; *MPW* 11/21/14:1152]
Am Icons; Cap; IWW?; Irish; Lab; Mtg; Militia; Reconcil; Strike
PRO-LAB

The Strike, Thanhouser, Henry H. Lewis & Carl L. Gregory, 2r, April, Am(s), Drama

A professional labor agitator named Black

(anarchist color; the "Black Cat" sabotage symbol of the I.W.W.) invades the factory town of Peacedale and starts unionizing the employees of the Trask works. A factory worker who is discharged for incompetency provides Black with an excuse to incite a strike. With the owner refusing to make concessions, the workers and their families soon begin to suffer. A violent demonstration outside the owner's office leads to the wounding of Mary McLaren (the eighteen year old Muriel Ostriche; one of the most popular actresses of the mid teens; voted the "Moxie Girl" of 1914), the daughter of an older worker who had counseled against the men striking. Black later dynamites the factory, the resulting fire demolishing the building. One of the former strikers beats and kicks Black as the agitator flees town. Now realizing the folly of their strike, the workers attempt to reason with Trask, but the angry capitalist informs Peacedale that he has no intention of rebuilding in the community. Within a few months Peacedale has become a virtual ghost town. *The Moving Picture World* called "[T]his a strong picture and of much interest to labor organizations." But the *New York Dramatic Mirror* noted: "We are shown the worst elements of organized labor and none of the better; whereas capitalism is the virtuous, innocent party, save for a persistent obstinacy in refusing to compromise."

[*MPW* 5/2/14:674; *NYDM* 4/29/14:34; *Photoplay* 6/14:158–164]

Agit; Bomb; Cap; IWW?; Lab; Mtg; Mob; Pvt Pol; Sab; Strike; Unemployed; Viol
ANTI-LAB

The Strike of Coaldale, Eclair, Oct, Am(s), Drama

Joe Gregory (Stanley Walpole) is an engineer on the Coaldale Railroad and a leader of the union. When work conditions deteriorate, the men present Harland, the president, with demands. Disregarding entreaties from his daughter, Edith (Mildred Bright), the capitalist refuses to make concessions to the rail workers. During the strike that follows, there are many fights between the union men and the scabs hired by Harland. When Edith Harland suffers a concussion, Joe breaks ranks with the strikers and takes a train out to drive her to the hospital. Despite sabotage to a trestle, he is successful and Edith's life is saved. The bitter labor dispute continues, the frustrated strikers finally resorting to kidnapping President Harland. Joe, who has fallen in love with Edith, makes a successful appeal for Harland's life. Having seen the error of his ways, the president grants the men's demands. Joe is appointed the new superintendent. The train sequence bears resemblance to the one that takes place in the 1910 release, *The Hero Engineer*, q.v. Note: A prolonged strike by AFL members against the Illinois Central and Harriman Lines, that included numerous incidents of sabotage and attacks upon scabs, would formally conclude in December 1914.

[*MPW* 10/24/14:538; *MPW* 10/31/14:658]

Cap; Lab; Reconcil; Sab; Scabs; Strike; Viol
CAP-LAB COOP

Threads of Destiny, Lubin/General, Joseph W. Smiley, 5r, Oct, Russ/Am, Drama

A pogrom instigated by the Russian secret police results in death and exile for thousands of Jews. Isaac Gruenstein is sent to Siberia as a "political prisoner," but his infant daughter Miriam is made the ward of Ivan Russak, the chief of the secret police. Miriam (Evelyn Nesbit Thaw) is raised in a convent for eighteen years and then is summoned to Russak's chateau to become his mistress. Rachel Shapiro, an exile with Isaac, escapes Siberia with a note from the dying father warning his daughter about Russak. After reading the letter, Miriam summons the Jews of the city to rise up and rescue her. Miriam then escapes with Rachel and her new husband to America. Some years later, Miriam is happily married to an Arizona rancher and living in a Russian-American community. But then Russak appears on business for the Tsar. He threatens to reveal Miriam's past. Jewish nihilists in the community, fearing Russak may plan to continue his evil ways in America, end his life with a bomb.

[LC, LU3484; *MPW* 11/7/14:846; *NYDM* 10/28/14:33; *Var* 10/24/14:22]

Atroc; Bomb; Decad; Escape; Fem Rad?; Jew; Nih; Russ; Sec Pol; Siberia; Viol
ANTI-RS

The Unsigned Agreement, Gold Seal, Francis Ford, 2r, Jan, Am(s), Drama

A "labor agitator" sexually harasses an innocent factory girl named Nell (Grace Cunard). She is already in love with Harry, the wastrel son of the mill owner. During an altercation at a saloon, Harry believes he has killed the agitator. He flees town, joins the army and is sent to Cuba. Nell, who has been left in a "delicate condition," marries Harry's father. Recovering from his wounds, the vengeful agitator instigates a strike. He further manipulates the workers by misleading them to think that their demands have been rejected by the owner. The agitator then maliciously transforms the strikers into a frenzied mob that attempts to burn down the factory. Explosives inside the factory are ignited. The militia and "other citizens" (private police?) battle the strikers. In the midst of the struggle Harry returns and is killed. Despite the excesses of his workers, the owner had contemplated forgiving all, until he is informed of his son's death.

[*MPW* 1/17/14:338]

Agit; Bomb?; Cap; Decad; Lab; Liq Link; Militia; Mob; Pvt Pol?; Sab; Shp Flr Abu; Strike; Viol

ANTI-LAB

The Valley of the Moon, Bosworth/W.W. Hodkinson, Hobart Bosworth, June, Am(u), Drama, 7r

This was part of a series of Jack London stories filmed by Bosworth, including *Martin Eden*, q.v. Like *Martin Eden*, it is both semi-autobiographical and utopian socialistic. Billy Roberts (Jack Conway), a San Francisco area boxer and teamster, weds a pretty laundress named Saxon (Myrtle Stedman). But their happiness is soon disrupted by the teamsters voting to strike. A major riot occurs in Oakland (*The Moving Picture World* claims a 1000 extras were used) when imported scabs get off the train. The police ruthlessly intervene, their patrol wagons trampling some of the rebellious strikers. Billy's best pal is killed in the melee. When Saxon has a miscarriage, Billy turns to drink and winds up in jail. Upon Billy's release, the penniless couple leaves the city in search of an ideal community. After spending some time at an artists' commune, Billy is able to purchase a ranch (in Sonoma California's Valley of the Moon) with the prize money he earns in a boxing match. Note: Special showings of this motion picture were sponsored by socialist organizations. However, taking into account London's openly-expressed racism, it would appear that this film contained a nativist subtext—scabs, apparently foreign-born, are the catalyst of violence; the native-born hero and his blonde wife, *Saxon*, eventually achieving true happiness in the countryside by escaping the urban violence perpetuated by immigrant masses.

[LC, LU3030; *MPN* 8/22/14:55; *MPW* 8/29/14:1290; *NYDM* 8/12/14:28 & 29; *Var* 8/14/14:20]

Artist; Cap; Lab; Mtg; Mob; Pol; Scabs; Soc; Strike; Viol

PRO-SOC

What Is to Be Done?, Joseph Leon Weiss, 6r, Aug, Am(u), Drama

Borrowing the title of Nikolai Chernyshevki's (1828–1889) popular Russian novel of 1862, which espoused an altruistic urban-based communism, this motion picture was made in New York City by a socialist actor and union activist named Joseph Leon Weiss. It features a love story between the capitalist's son, Henry Dryer, and a radical young lady named Louise Lafayette, who works as a stenographer for the capitalist's company. Henry is made sensitive to the cause of the working-class through socialist books given him by Louise. When the older Dryer reduces wages by ten percent, declares his factory an "Open Shop" and refuses to seriously arbitrate with the labor committee, a strike is declared by the union. At the arbitration conference Louise had passionately invoked the memory of notorious abuses of labor, such as the Triangle Shirtwaist factory fire and the Ludlow massacre. In addition to using a labor spy, the hardened capitalist hires thousands of scabs and recruits strike breaking goons (sometimes suggestively referred to at the time as "sluggers") from a saloon. Appalled by what his father has done, Henry joins the strikers' cause. Many of the scabs declare solidarity with the strikers after witnessing brutal attacks upon picketers by the hired thugs. Chastened by the violence, Henry's father agrees to the workers' terms. But attacked by Wall Street for making the concessions, Dryer also announces a corresponding increase of the prices on "all the necessities of life." The workers who had gathered in a park to celebrate labor's victory, many proudly wearing union badges, raise up their hands in despair and cry: "What is to be done?" Although the AFI lists an August 1914 release date, this film's formal opening took place in November at Manhattan's Grand Street Theatre. Note:

Chernyshevki, whose book influenced the nihilist movement, was exiled to Siberia the year it was published. This film's stirring title was also the same as that of V. I. Lenin's major tract on Bolshevik organization and discipline, published in 1902.

[AFI, F1.4855; LC, LU3228(s); *New York Call* 11/22/14; 1/5/15:2]

Am Icons; Anarch; Cap; Fem Rad; Lab; Liq Link; Mtg; Nih; Pol; Pvt Pol; Scabs; Shp Flr Abu; Soc; Strike; Viol; Wrk Rel Dis/Inj
ANTI-CAP; PRO-LAB; PRO-SOC

Worms Will Turn, Lubin, Frank Griffin, 1/2r, July, Am, Comedy

In this amusing example of displaced class violence a sleeping bum named Bill Raggels (as in rags) is roughed-up by a policeman. Bill flees to the local hobo camp, where he plots revenge with his fellow itinerant indigents. A chase ensues after the tramps waylay their companion's "oppressor." This eventually results in a battle with the entire police force during which Bill and his fellow "roadsters" seize the station-house. The "nance cop" is played by Oliver "Babe" Hardy.

[*MPW* 7/18/14:472; *NYDM* 7/29/14:31]

Pol; Tramp; Viol
CM/ANTI-REV

1915

The Absentee, Majestic/Mutual, William Christy Cabanne, 5r, May, Am(u), Drama

In an allegorical prologue of this Capital versus Labor film, "Success," "the Absentee" (Robert Edeson), leaves "Might" in charge of his business while he pursues "Pleasure." In order to satisfy his wife and daughter, "Extravagance" and "Vanity," Might lowers the wages of the "Toilers" and pockets the difference. "Justice" informs "Success" of the situation and he returns to end the suffering of his workers. The primary story takes place at the National Hat works, owned by Nathaniel Crosby/"Success." Conditions rapidly deteriorate for the workers and their families after they go out on strike. Foreman David Lee/ "Contentment" goes crazy after his daughter is driven astray by starvation and he becomes "Evil," the man who leads the strikers to riot. When the office stenographer, Ruth Farwell/ "Justice" first attempts to alert Crosby, he tersely informs her that Sampson Rhodes/ "Might" is right. Crosby only takes things seriously upon learning that Rhodes has had the militia called out. Crosby orders the withdrawal of the militia and dismisses Rhodes. Crosby is saved by Ruth from being shot by Lee. A young worker named Tom/"Ambition" quells the angry strikers. Social harmony is restored by the marriage of "Success" and "Justice." Note: In some sources the allegorical capitalist played by Edeson was named "Power." A similar allegorical scenario was used to portray a man's struggle with his desire to succeed in business in *Man and His Soul* (Quality Picts/Metro, 1916).

[AFI, F1.0003; *MPN* 5/15/15:64; *MPW* 5/8/15:984; *Var* 5/14/15:19]

Cap; Decad; Lab; Militia; Mob; Reconcil; Strike; Viol
CAP-LAB COOP

The Bigger Man; or, The Bridge, Rolfe Photoplays/Metro, John W. Noble, 5r, Sept, Am(s), Drama

A prologue depicts the relationship between labor and capital throughout the ages. At a gigantic bridge construction site there arises trouble over low salaries and deplorable living conditions. John Stoddard (Henry Kolker), an engineer, has fallen in love with Janet Van Nest, the daughter of the contractor. When John fails to get the Board of Directors to grant concessions to the workers, the men, under the sway of a bearded agitator named Lavinsky (Jew?; Edwin Boring), go out on strike. Van Nest hires scabs and then calls up the militia to suppress the resulting labor violence. After John restrains Lavinsky from tossing a stick of dynamite at Van Nest, the capitalist agrees to settle the strike on condition that the engineer stop seeing his daughter. Janet leaves home to help the immigrant workers' families. His compassion reawakened by witnessing the reunion of one of these poor families, Van Nest consents to the marriage of John and Janet. An epilogue portrays the symbol of Justice admonishing caricatures of Capital and Labor: "Why quarrel? You are worthless without the other."

[AFI, F1.0325; LC, LP6784; *MPW* 9/25/15:2250 & 2252; *Var* 10/8/15:23]

Agit; Am Icons?; Bomb; Cap; Jew?; Lab; Militia; Mob; Reconcil; Scabs; Strike; Viol
CAP-LAB COOP

The Bomb Throwers, Pathé, Edwin August, 3r, Feb, Am, Drama

"Red Mike" Davis, a notorious bomb thrower, is in jail through the prosecutorial activities of District Attorney Lawrence. Following Davis' execution, his gang plots revenge. They unsuccessfully attempt to enlist the aid of Tony (Edwin August), an Italian organ grinder who plays for the Lawrence child. Then Tony's wife succumbs to a fatal illness and the "Reds" persuade him that the district attorney was responsible. The Italian swears a "cabalistic oath" with the revolutionary "gangsters," after which he is chosen to place a bomb in the Lawrence home. But after depositing a valise containing a bomb in the cellar of Lawrence's house, Tony is horrified to discover his little girl playing with the district attorney's wife. Tony retrieves the deadly device and tosses it away. The Reds, who had gathered nearby to witness the explosion, are blown up. Note: This film's internal history is particularly instructive regarding the not uncommon cinematic appropriation of topical events. *The Bomb Throwers* was originally released as a Black Hand film, described in the *New York Dramatic Mirror* as a "Drama of Italian Life on the Lower East Side of New York." But, in February, it was apparently retitled, reflecting the above plot description. In May the film was rereleased, the *Variety* review pointing out a fortuitous timeliness relating to a recent attempt by "Reds" to bomb St. Patrick's Cathedral in New York City. In fact, on March 2, 1915, two anarchists, Arbano and Carbone, were apprehended with a lighted bomb at the cathedral. During their April trial, the anarchists claimed to have been framed by the police—to whom they also made death threat gestures in court. The unrepentant pair of bombers were found guilty by the jury and sentenced by Judge Nott to 6–12 years.

[LC, LU4347; *MPW* 2/6/15:900 & 902; *NYDM* 1/20/15:31; *Var* 5/14/15:20]

Bomb; Dom Rad; Ital; Viol
ANTI-REV

The Boss, William A. Brady Pict., Plays/World, Emile Chautard, 5r, May, Am(u), Drama

Michael Regan (Holbrook Blinn) uses his fists to earn the money to purchase a saloon. With the profits earned from the sale of liquor he is able to rise out of the Irish slums and to start a more respectable business. By cajoling his men to work below the standard rate, Regan gains a monopoly of the grain-shipping contracts which had formerly been controlled by the old firm of Griswold and Son. While visiting the poor, Regan meets and falls in love with Emily Griswold—played by the producer's daughter, Alice Brady, in one of her earliest film roles. Soon afterwards, Regan offers an amalgamation with his rivals for permission to court Emily. But, following their marriage, Emily's embittered brother, James, rouses the men to strike. Regan refuses his workers' terms and abuses their delegate. While haranguing the strikers James is hit by a brick thrown by Regan's pal, Porkey McCoy. A riot ensues and Regan is arrested as an instigator. McCoy confesses and all is resolved.

[LC, LU5413; *MPW* 5/15/15:1168; *Var* 5/14/15:19]

Agit; Cap; Irish; Lab; Mob; Pol; Strike; Viol
ANTI-CAP

Coals of Fire, American/Flying "A," Jan, Am(u), Drama

The wealthy owner of a factory, John Vincent, neglects his invalid wife and his daughter for the love of his young son Ben. Years later, having devoted his life to Ben, Vincent achieves his dream of making his son a junior partner in the company. But the obsessed father has ignored the needs of his workers. Among the dissatisfied men at the plant is a fanatic whom they call "Mad John" (Jack Richardson). The crazed man attacks the capitalist oppressor and his son while they are touring the factory, fatally stabbing Ben. Vincent has a stroke and loses his memory, but his faithful daughter keeps the life-restoring coals of fire burning for her father by sending his grandson to him.

[LC, LU4374; *MPW* 2/6/15:892]

Cap; Dom Rad?; Lab; Viol
ANTI-CAP

Comrades Three, American, Henry W. Otto, Aug, Am(r), Drama

Ginger, a teenaged orphan who has fled a cruel woman who abused her, teams up with another homeless child on the road. Stanley Ward, a bored young man of wealth, decides to assume the role of a tramp for a couple of weeks. Stanley encounters the two hungry children and invites them to join the group of hoboes with whom he is sharing a meal. But trouble erupts when one of the "won't works," Higs, discovers that Ginger is a girl in boys' clothing. Stanley comes to her rescue and later takes the two waifs to his home. This film provides another example of the public's linkage between the I.W.W. ("I Won't Works") and tramps.

    [*MPW* 8/7/15:1072]
    Cap; Decad; IWW?; Tramp; Viol
    CM/ANTI-LAB

Cupid in A Hospital, L-KO, 1r, Jan, Am, Comedy

    Gin-swilling Billie (a series character played by a Charlie Chaplin imitator named Billy Ritchie) is in the hospital, where his flirtations with a pretty blonde nurse arouse the jealousy of a crippled anarchist. A couple of foreign-looking companions surreptitiously deliver a bomb on a visit to the anarchist so that he can carry out a "fiendish plan" of revenge. But after he places the bomb under Billie's bed, the nurse enters the ward and sits by Billie. Pandemonium erupts as the anarchist attempts to remove the device, culminating with both Billie and the anarchist being blown through the roof and splashing down in a nearby pond.

    [S (LC); *MPW* 1/2/15:130; *MPW* 1/9/15:222]
    Anarch; Bomb; Pol; Tramp; Viol
    ANTI-REV

The Dancer's Ruse, Biograph, 1r, Jan, Russ, Drama

    Lydia (Claire McDowell) is a famous Russian dancer admired by the military governor of the province. When Lydia learns that the governor has ordered the execution of her nihilist brother, she arranges an intimate meeting with the Tsarist official. With her sweetheart Dimitroff disguised as a butler, she secures the drunken lecher's autograph and then has him drugged. Lydia and Dimitroff, now dressed as the governor, drive to the prison and with a fake pardon save her brother from the firing squad. After crossing the border, the three board a ship for America.

    [LC, LP4291; *MPW* 1/30/15:713; *NYDM* 2/10/15:33]
    Artist; Decad; Escape; Nih; Russ
    ANTI-RS

A Daughter of the People, Dyreda Art Film/World, J. Searle Dawley, 5r, Feb, Am(s), Drama

    The two wealthy partners of a Massachusetts cotton manufacturing firm close the mills, declaring they have no other option due to an inability to acquire raw material. In reality, it represents a calculated attempt on the part of the greedy capitalists to corner the market. Sam Lloyd, an engineer in the mill, travels to a nearby town for work and discovers that senior partner Arthur Stillman is hoarding large quantities of raw cotton in a warehouse. Sam informs his fellow workers of this fact. The workers' leader, a burly stereotype named Bill Slinger (the surname connoting a warrior), incites them to set fire to the storage facility. During the resulting conflagration the leader's own son is killed. With vengeance in mind, a mob prepares to storm Stillman's mansion. Sam's girlfriend, Dell Hamilton, the popular daughter of a dyer, decides to prevent further violence by warning Stillman. But the callous man states he will only reopen the mills if Dell agrees to marry him. Dell consents to sacrifice herself for the good of her people. Later learning the marriage was illegal, Dell returns to the mills, where she is treated as an outcast. All is finally resolved when Stillman proclaims his true love for Dell and promises to right those wrongs for which he has been responsible.

    [LC, LU4340; *MPW* 2/20/15:1200; *NYDM* 2/17/15:28]
    Agit?; Cap; Lab; Mob; Reconcil; Sab; Unemployed; Viol
    ANTI-CAP; CAP-LAB COOP

Destruction, Fox, Will S. Davis, 5r, Dec, Am(u), Drama

    Jack Froment, the son of a wealthy manufacturer, returns from college to discover that his father has married a flirtatious younger woman named Ferdinande (played by the consummate vamp, Theda Bara). Following complaints about her extravagances, Ferdinande convinces her lover, plant manager Deleveau (a mustachioed Warner Oland), to reduce the workers' wages. She has learned her husband has a weak heart and hopes that labor unrest will speed him to his grave. The workers talk of striking, but the plant foreman insists that the union be consulted. Meanwhile, Jack has become sympathetic to the plight of the working-class after reading a political tract by John Stuart Mill (English; 1806–1873). At the union meeting hall, a brutish steel worker named Dave Walker (a wife-beating "cave man" type played by J. Herbert Frank) convinces the other men to teach the capitalists "a lesson they won't forget," by striking. The police arrest the "agitators" that attempt to storm the plant offices. Jack's father, his health weakened as a result of the incident, suffers a fatal heart attack after he observes Ferdinande embracing Deleveau. The situation becomes ugly as the strike continues and the idle men loiter at the saloon. When the militia is called up, an agitator named Lang (German?) leads the strikers in attacking the troops. The loyal foreman and Jack attempt to intervene. Following Lang's arrest for shooting the foreman, peace is restored. Ferdinande and Dave die together in the family mansion that he had set afire; Jack marries the deceased worker's pretty widow.

[LC, LP7296(s); *MPN* 1/8/16:98; *Var* 12/31/15:24]

Agit; Cap; Decad; Ger?; Lab; Liq Link; Militia; Mtg; Mob; Pol; Sab; Strike; Viol
ANTI-LAB; CAP-LAB COOP

The Disappearance of Harry Warrington, Kalem, 2r, ("The Girl Detective" series #2), Feb, Am, Drama

The series star girl detective, played by Ruth Roland, investigates the kidnapping of a young society man named Harry Warrington. With the address of an anarchists' rendezvous as her only clue, Ruth visits the dive in lower class attire. She befriends an habitué named Olga, the girlfriend of anarchist leader Michaels (Jew?; Paul C. Hurst). Michaels' associate goes by the alien-sounding name of Strundsky (William H. West). Because Michaels has been flirting with a "woman of the underworld," the jealous Olga leads Ruth to the anarchists' secret meeting room. It turns out that Harry, who had joined their organization in the belief that it was aiding poor slum dwellers, was kidnapped by the band when he failed to carry out an assigned bombing mission. Ruth's presence is detected and the "plucky heroine" is imprisoned along with Harry. The police arrive and, following a gun battle with the anarchists, the two are rescued. The *New York Dramatic Mirror* reviewer made the following observation: "Accustomed as screen patrons are to the kind of anarchists they have been given, this group of extreme citizens who meet in a coffee house and discuss their troubles rather openly, will appeal as having a deal of probability, much more, at any rate, than those in the usual offering."

[*MPW* 2/6/15:873; *MPW* 2/27/15:1288; *NYDM* 1/27/15:57]

Anarch; Bomb; Cap; Jew?; Pol; Russ?; Viol
ANTI-REV

The Eternal City, Famous Players/Select, Edwin S. Porter & Hugh Ford, 8r, April, Brit/Italy, Drama

David Rossi, an Italian orphan mistreated by a padrone in London, is rescued and schooled by an idealistic political refugee from his homeland, Dr. Roselli. Years later the doctor's daughter, Roma (Pauline Frederick), has become the mistress of the conniving prime minister of Italy, Baron Bonelli, while David is now the charismatic leader of Italian socialism. In the name of the people, David, played by the darkly handsome Thomas Holding, publicly denounces Roma and the Baron. But when David discovers that Roma was the girl with whom he had played at the doctor's home, class animosities dissolve. The Baron orders the police to attack a huge political meeting that David has announced to take place at the Coliseum and plots to have the socialist leader assassinated during the confusion. Roma discovers the Baron's plans, warns David and then hastily marries him after fleeing the country. David kills Bonelli when he believes that the Baron and Roma conspired to trick him into returning to Italy. Roma assumes responsibility for the murder and is about to be executed when David, having learned of her innocence and discovering that the pope is his father, persuades the Holy See to pardon his wife. This motion picture was based on a popular novel of the same name published in 1901 by Hall Caine. It was shot on location in Britain and Italy. Select Film Booking Agency was created by Famous Players to exploit and distribute *The Eternal City* and its other prestigious feature-length films. Reduced to five reels, this motion picture was rereleased in 1918. It was remade by First National in 1924, q.v. Note: Despite strong opposition from the Socialist Party, Italy entered the war on the side of the Entente in May 1915.

[AFI, F1.1183; *MPN* 1/9/15:45; *MPW* 2/13/15:1056]

Agit; Artist; Decad; Escape; Ital; Mtg; Mob; Pol; Soc; Viol
PRO-SOC

Fatty's New Role, Keystone, Roscoe Arbuckle & Eddie Dillon, 1r, Feb, Am, Comedy

The owner of Schnitz's Bar has been throwing out bums who have been partaking of his free lunch (a popular gimmick used to entice customers at the time) without buying any liquor. Some of the regular patrons, having already shown Schnitz a newspaper article about a bum blowing up inhospitable saloons, leave a phony threat note from the bomber on the bar. Chaos ensues when a bum, played by "Fatty" Arbuckle, carrying a large round cheese that looks like a bomb, enters Schnitz's establishment. Though played for laughs, this bomb parody reinforced the public's perception of the threat posed to society by the inherently anarchistic lifestyle (and potential violence) of the homeless itinerant who disdained labor.

[S (LC;Vid); LC, LP4385]
Bomb; Ger; Liq Link; Pol; Tramp; Viol
CM/ANTI-REV

The Funny Side of Jealousy, Big "U," C. Jay Williams, 2r, Mar, Am, Comedy

Jack is insanely jealous with regard to his beautiful wife. When he sees part of a letter from her long unseen brother, signed "Lovingly Ned," Jack draws all the wrong conclusions. The maddened spouse disguises himself as an anarchist, secures a time bomb and then later follows the two aboard a yacht. Posing now as the steward, Jack sets the bomb beneath the chair of his imagined rival. Comical complications result in an altercation that leads to Jack being formally introduced to his brother-in-law. Jack sits down in Ned's chair and is blown up. He must make a quick dive over the side to extinguish his ignited clothing.

[LC, LP4651; MPW 3/13/15:1658]
Anarch; Bomb; Viol
CM/ANTI-REV

Gus and the Anarchists, Lubin, 1/2r, Jan, Am, Comedy

Gus, a waiter at a cheap cafe played by Charles W. Ritchie, is fired for the unwanted attention he pays to a new cashier named Rosy. She promises the owner, Tom Dreck (Oliver "Babe" Hardy), that she will cure Gus of his lust if Tom will rehire him. With Tom's connivance, Rosy dresses up some of the other waiters as bearded anarchists and then invites Gus to join her "Suicide Club" at their secret

headquarters. A blindfolded Gus nervously agrees to be sworn in, but is ready to take flight when he is informed he must kill a man and then commit suicide. Gus runs home when additional waiters, disguised as "cops," burst into the room. The next day a cured Gus is shown diligently pursuing his waitering tasks.

[LC, LP4170; MPW 1/16/15:413; MPW 2/6/15:827]
Anarch; Fem Rad; Pol
CM/ANTI-REV

Hearts in Exile, World, James Young, 5r, April, Russ, Drama

Hope Ivanovna, played by the director's wife, Clara Kimball Young, has three suitors. She chooses wealthy Serge Palma, so that she can continue to afford to carry on her charity work with the poor. One of the rejected men, the stocky, bearded, middle-aged Count Nicholai (Montague Love), uses his position as head of the secret police to have her new husband and the other suitor, a poor medical student, arrested on false charges of being nihilists. Serge and the other man, Paul Pavloff, are sentenced to long terms in exile. Paul secretly switches places with Serge so that the husband can avoid the longer sentence in Siberia. After much suffering, Hope and her two men are reunited in Siberia. During a dramatic escape in a three-horse droshky, Serge is killed by Cossacks. Hope and Paul, who had become lovers, are free to live out their lives together. Re-released with new titles as *Hearts Afire* (1917), q.v.

[PE (GEH), LC, LU4992; MPW 4/17/15: 401; NYDM 4/14/15:28; Var 4/9/15:20]
Escape; Nih; Russ; Sec Pol; Siberia; Viol
ANTI-RS

Her Oath of Vengeance, Majestic, 2r, Sept, Am, Drama

Sergius is a political refugee from Russia (nihilist?) who works in a California fruit cannery. His daughter, Sophia, works in the orchards. Ivan, the overseer, uses his knowledge of Sergius' past to blackmail the man into allowing him to marry Sophia. When Ivan accosts the unwilling Sophia, the owner's wife discharges the overseer. Ivan forces Sergius to incite a strike for higher wages. He also secures a bomb for use in blowing up the cannery. Nicholas, Sophia's boyfriend, is able to prevent the cannery from being destroyed. However, Sophia swears vengeance against the

Grays for the injuries sustained by her father. But the pious Sophia is prevented from carrying out her revenge by the sight of Mrs. Gray, Madonna like, with her child. Note: This is a rare pre-Bolshevik Revolution example in film that makes a direct linkage between Russian revolutionaries and labor militancy in the United States.

[MPW 9/11/15:1910]

Bomb; Cap; Decad; Lab; Nih?; Russ; Sab; Shp Flr Abu; Strike: Viol

ANTI-REV

The High Road, Rolfe Photoplays/Metro, John W. Noble, 5r, April, Am(u), Drama

While traveling on the road to her home town, Mary Page (Valli Valli) reflects upon the events that led to her becoming the mistress of a New York writer and, later, a labor activist at a shirtwaist factory. Having abandoned her sinful life, Mary goes to work in a sweatshop. When owner Maddox mandates a wage cut, it is Mary who organizes a strike among her female compatriots. Maddox pays some goons to make trouble for the strikers. Due to the intercession of the politically powerful man who had once proposed to Mary, the women are allowed to return to work at their former pay rate. But one night, to force the girls to work overtime, the manager locks the door. When a fire breaks out, a number of the factory girls are killed. A reviewer for the *Motion Picture News* gruesomely noted: "The girls may be seen leaping from the windows to the street below. We don't see them land, but an effective touch is given by showing the bodies lain along the street covered with shrouds." Note: There was a well-known press photo showing just such a scene from the notorious Triangle Shirtwaist Company fire that occurred in New York City on March 25, 1911, claiming the lives of 146 workers. In November of 1915 Edison would release a film that was directly inspired by the incident, *The Children of Eve*.

[AFI, F1.1956; LC, LP6441; MPN 5/18/15:72]

Artist; Cap; Decad; Fem Rad; Lab; Strike; Viol; Wrk Rel Dis/Inj

ANTI-CAP

The Little Gypsy, Fox, Oscar C. Apfel, 5r, Oct, Scot, Drama

In early nineteenth century Scotland an abandoned gypsy infant, Babbie, is raised by Lord Rintoul of Thrums. Even though she has been brought up as an aristocrat, the teenaged Babbie (Dorothy Bernard) prefers to dress as a gypsy. She has also become enamored with the local minister, the priggish Gavin Desart (Thurlow Bergen). Meanwhile, the families in the nearby mill town barely survive, even as their menfolk work long hours as weavers in the factory. When the manufacturers' association arbitrarily lowers the "Schedule of Prices," the weavers protest. As this disturbance at the mill is shown being squashed, the film cuts to the sumptuous debut ball for Lord Rintoul's ward. A short while afterwards, with their "bairns" starving, the weavers meet secretly and vote to strike. Despite Gavin's attempts to stop them, an angry mob of weavers, led by the fiery Rob Dow, then torch the factory. Babbie, who identifies with the strikers, later eggs them on to violently resist when soldiers arrive to quell the rioters. Babbie is among those arrested. However, she escapes from jail and runs to the young minister for protection from the police. After many hardships labor peace is restored and the two lovers are allowed to wed.

[AFI, F1.2526; LC, LP6639(c); MPW 10/23/15:631]

Agit; Cap; Lab; Fem Rad; Mtg; Mob; Pol; Reconcil; Sab; Strike; Viol

PRO-LAB

The Magnet of Destruction, Thanhouser, 2r, Mar, Am(u), Drama

A wealthy college student, Arthur Grennell, is introduced at a lecture to an old scientist and his daughter Mignon. Lyell, the leader of a campus organization dedicated to the elimination of the rich, convinces Hilton, the scientist, that justice for the poor can only be achieved through violent class action. Thinking Lyell's group is a charitable organization, Arthur also joins. But he quickly abandons it after learning their true intentions. Lyell becomes manager of an out-of-town factory and induces the Hiltons to come along. At the factory Lyell has access to a magnetized crane used to lift scrap metal for the foundry out of river barges. Having been informed that a group of capitalists, including Arthur and his father, will be visiting the factory, Lyell plans to drop a load of iron upon them. Mignon, who is in love with Arthur, discovers Lyell's plot and in a dramatic encounter prevents him from carrying it out.

[*MPW* 3//27/15:1990]
Camp Rad; Cap; Dom Rad; Lab; Viol
ANTI-REV

The Man with the Iron Heart, Selig, George
Nicholls, 3r, Sept, Am(u), Drama
  James Boyd, the cashier for a large corporation run by "the man with the iron heart,"
arrives late to work one day after attending his
dying mother, and is fired. His grievance, as
well as others, such as the continued exploitation of child labor, lead the union to send a
strike committee to petition president I. M.
Mann. The mean capitalist defiantly responds:
"I'll close up the factories and let you starve."
Boyd visits the President's palatial home to
plead for the strikers with Mrs. Mann. Her husband then enters the house and physically
abuses the worker. Mann hires scabs to break
the strike. The police have to quell the riot that
occurs when the strikers confront the mob of
scabs. Mann is shot by a bearded rioter as he
enters his home. "Conscience" and "Death" (in
superimposed shots) appear before the deliri-
ous capitalist. Mann overcomes Death but,
after being forced by Conscience to observe
the results of his cruel actions, he summons
his estranged wife to his bedside and grants
the workers' demands. Note: A popular contemporary socialist catchphrase referred to the
plight of workers as being beneath the "iron
heel" of capitalism. Refer to Jack London's fu-
turistic 1905 novel, *The Iron Heel*, that concludes with the dedicated revolutionaries
crushed by the ruling oligarchy and the ignorant working masses running amok in the
streets.
  [LC, LP6206; *MPW* 9/4/15:1720–1721; *Var*
9/10/15:21]
  Cap; Lab; Mtg; Mob; Pol; Reconcil;
Scabs; Strike; Unemployed; Viol
  CAP-LAB COOP; ANTI-CAP

A Modern Magdalen, Life Photo, Will S.
Davis, 5r, Feb, Am(s), Drama
  Katinka, a plump factory girl, agrees to
become mill owner Lindsay's mistress in order
to escape her cruel parents and working-class
poverty. Katinka's excessive lifestyle soon
earns her the sobriquet of the "Madcap"
dancer. These activities also force Lindsay,
played by Lionel Barrymore, to borrow money
to meet his payroll and avert a strike. But Joe
Mercer, a laborer who loves Katinka, incites
the mill workers to riot when he learns of the
affair. After the workers attack Lindsay and burn
the factory, Joe prevents Katinka from committing suicide and persuades her to reform—
she becomes a nurse in the United States Army!
  [AFI, F1.3018; *MPN* 3/13/15:51; *MPW*
5/1/15:808]
  Cap; Decad; Lab; Sab; Strike; Viol
  ANTI-CAP

Money, United Keanograph/World, James
Keane, 5–6r, Feb, Am(u), Drama
  In 1921 a man known as "Croesus," John
D. Maximillian (Matt Snyder playing the surrogate John D. Rockefeller), has accumulated
control over the world financial exchanges.
One day his junior partner, Cyrus L. Livingston, escorts Maximillian's daughter Ruth
on a visit to their giant steel works, where Livingston antagonizes the plant superintendent,
George Crosby, by accosting his sweetheart,
office stenographer Hope Ross. Ruth intervenes when Livingston begins to fire Crosby
for his bare-fisted defense of Hope's honor.
With wages at only seventy-five cents a day,
Maximillian's workers are starving. When a
strike is declared by the union, the capitalist
shows his contempt for labor by throwing a
grand banquet (the "Million Dollar Dinner") at
his palatial home in New York City. The outraged workers, incited by an anarchist named
Antome Johanson, storm the estate. A drunken
Livingston, who was about to molest Ruth, is
thwarted by Crosby and then handed over to
the mob of strikers. Because of Livingston's
outrageous behavior, Maximillian strips him
of all his wealth. Livingston then plots with
the anarchist Johanson to kidnap Ruth and hold
her for ransom. After Hope is abducted by mistake, Crosby and Ruth pursue the villains and
effect a dramatic rescue. During a lightning
storm, the palace of "Croesus" is destroyed and
he is killed by a falling column. Ruth assumes
control of her father's financial empire, gener-
ously helping the poor and announcing to the
labor union: "My motto is and always shall be,
'A fair day's wage for a fair day's work.'" Information deposited for copyright in late 1917
suggests this film's titling was altered for a
planned rerelease in February 1918. This later
version specifically attacked the I.W.W.
  [LC, LU3762/1914, LU11618/1917(s); *MPN*
2/13/15:48; *MPW* 8/22/14:1110; *NYDM*
2/10/15:28]

Agit; Anarch; Cap; Decad; Lab; Mob; Pol;
Reconcil; Shp Flr Abu; Strike; Viol
     ANTI-CAP;   ANTI-REV;   CAP-LAB
COOP

The Money Master, Kleine-Edison, George
Fitzmaurice, 5r, Sept, Am(u), Drama
     In a prologue the viewer is introduced to
the sordid methods by which John J. Haggleton became the "uncrowned king of finance"
(negative surname associations with to haggle;
played by Frank Sheridan—an actor with the
"necessary physique for the popular conception of the capitalist"). When Haggleton's wife
learns that he hired an arsonist to burn down a
competitor's factory, she leaves with their infant son Philip. Twenty years later, Haggleton
discovers the whereabouts of his lost son.
Under the assumed name of Mr. Jackson, he
visits Philip, who lives in a New York City tenement. After a lecture by Philip on the social
conditions existing in the slums, "Jackson,"
moves into the East Side ghetto without money
to prove that any healthy individual can make
good. He then acquires a job at Moran's bakery, whose owner, unknown to Haggleton, was
years before ruined by the capitalist's machinations. Having studied the business' operations, Haggleton purchases an electric dough
mixer on the installment plan and quickly develops a successful bread trust. Although this
increases Moran's profits, he is stirred-up by
the socialistic rhetoric of some bakers who
have lost their jobs as a result of the new machinery. In an anarchistic rage against capitalists, Moran attempts to shoot Haggleton. But
Philip, who has come to love his father, jumps
between them and is wounded. Philip is taken
to the Haggleton home on Fifth Avenue, where
he is nursed back to health by his girlfriend.
     [AFI, F1.3039; LC, LP6472; *MPN* 9/18/15:
87; *NYDM* 9/8/15:35; *Var* 9/10/15:21]
     Anarch?; Cap; Jew?; Lab; Reconcil;
Russ?; Soc; Unemployed; Viol
     ANTI-CAP; CAP-LAB COOP

On the Breadline, Majestic, 4r, Oct, Am(u),
Drama
     Joe Benton, the leader of a bridge-build-
ing gang working in the country, marries a
pretty local girl named Bessie. They move to
the city where Joe is hired as a foreman on a
skyscraper project. Bessie becomes a clothes
model to support the couple after Joe is inca-

pacitated by a job injury. When Joe discovers
that Bessie has begun to do "indiscreet things"
with wealthy clients, he loses all ambition and
becomes a drunkard. As Bessie rises in society, Joe descends to the gutters. Then Joe joins
an agitator's "Army of the Unemployed" and
discovers he has oratorical talents as a representative of the oppressed. Arrested during a
demonstration, Joe's eloquence before the
magistrate so impresses a wealthy merchant
that the man arranges his bail. But due to the
ongoing treachery of a jealous admirer of
Bessie from the country, Joe is framed for a
petty crime, imprisoned and eventually winds
up as a derelict in the breadline. One day he is
accidentally struck and killed by the car of the
wealthy benefactor, now the new husband of
Bessie.
     [*MPW* 11/6/15:1202]
     Agit; Breadline; Cap; Lab; Liq Link; Pol;
Tramp; Unemployed; Wrk Rel Dis/Inj
     ANTI-CAP

Out of the Darkness, Lasky/Par, George
Melford, 5r, Sept, Am(s), Drama
     In this "more or less time worn story of
the struggle between capital and labor," to
quote the *Variety* review, Helen Scott (Char-
lotte Walker) neglects the Florida fish cannery
she inherited from her father. She even refuses
to see Harvey Brooks, the manager of the large
cannery that exploits hundreds of children and
female employees, when he attempts to petition the main office in New York to improve
working conditions. Helen is later rescued by
a cannery boat following a yachting accident
off the Florida coast. Having lost her memory
from a head injury, the destitute Helen accepts
a job as a thirty cents a day "wage slave" at
the fish processing factory managed by Harvey. Unaware of her true identity, Harvey falls
in love with Helen. A mob of disgruntled
workers declare a strike, tie up Harvey and set
fire to his office. Helen's memory is restored
while saving Harvey from certain death. Helen
reveals to Harvey who she really is and
promises her future husband to diligently
strive to improve the lives of the cannery
workers.
     [LC, LU6143; *MPW* 9/25/15:2199, 2252;
NYDM 9/22/15:33; *Var* 10/29/15:23]
     Cap; Lab; Mob; Reconcil; Strike; Viol
     CAP-LAB COOP

The Painted Anarchist, Kriterion, Feb, Am, Comedy

Artist Syd (the spelling of Sid and resulting change in pronunciation implying affectation) poses a live subject in a frame and passes the work off as a painting. While Syd is celebrating his masterpiece with some young lady friends, the tableau vivant steps out of the frame, lights his bomb and begins chasing everyone around the artist's studio. Syd and the "painted" anarchist become entangled in telephone wires after being blasted out of the building.

[LC, LU4542; *MPW* 2/13/15:1058]
Anarch; Artist; Bomb; Viol
ANTI-REV

Playing Dead, Vitagraph, Sidney Drew, 5r, Sept, Am, Drama

"Jimmie" Blagwin (played by the director, who closely resembles Woodrow Wilson), a prominent member of the Long Island social set, is confronted with a major domestic crisis when he realizes his beloved wife Jeanne (Mrs. Sidney Drew) has fallen under the spell of a socialist Svengali named Proctor Maddox. The foppish Maddox, introduced in an inter-title as both a socialist and a feminist, "airs his extraordinary views" to wealthy ladies over cocktails on the verandah of the country club. After Jeanne declares she wishes to marry Maddox in order to help him "uplift the world," Jimmie contrives a wild scheme involving a phony suicide to allow Jeanne to devote herself to the cause without creating a scandal. Jeanne's love for her husband is restored when she discovers his true devotion.

[S (LC); LC, LP6296; *MPW* 9/25/15:2197]
Cap; Decad; Fem Rad; Soc
ANTI-SOC

The Plunderer, Fox, Edgar Lewis, 5r, May-June, Am(r), Western

With their new degrees in mine engineering from Columbia, Bill (William Farnum) and Dick head west to take charge of the latter's inherited mine, the Croix D'Or. The two soon discover that the miners congregate at the local saloon and are under the influence of business competitors. Behind the scenes, mine owner Bully Presby (William Riley Hatch) tries to sabotage their operations in order to cover up his subterranean tapping of the Croix D'Or. When a staged dynamite "accident" fails to rid

him of his young rivals, Presby imports a wild-eyed labor agitator from Denver—probably intended as an allusion to the United Mine Workers, but in the script the man presents management with a card that reads: "Delegate of Consolidated Miners' Association"—a fictitious organization. After Bill and Dick reject the walking delegate's demands, the agitator gathers the miners at the saloon hall for a strike vote. But, meanwhile, Dick and Presby's daughter have fallen in love. She forces her father to confess all and make financial restitution. This film was rereleased in the summer of 1918.

[LC, LP6154(s); *MPN* 5/29/15:75; *MPW* 8/10/18:888]
Agit; Cap; Lab; Liq Link; Mtg; Reconcil; Strike
CAP-LAB COOP; ANTI-CAP

A Poor Relation, Biograph, 3r, Dec, Am(u), Drama

After being abandoned by an abusive husband, Alice Sterrett, a young mother played by Millicent Evans, is obliged to labor behind a sweatshop sewing machine. Years later, a cruel foreman rips the now sickly woman's inferior work from her machine and discharges her. Forced to go to the hospital, she leaves her children in the care of a kindly neighbor, an eccentric inventor named Noah Vale. Meanwhile, Mrs. Sterrett's estranged husband, who lusts for the owner's daughter, has become the junior partner at a manufacturing plant. "Inflated with power," Sterrett refuses to deal with a "labor union committee" that barges into the company offices. Gesticulating wildly, the workers swarm out of the plant. Reading about the strike in the paper, Noah sends a letter to capitalist Faye (Frank Norcross) concerning his new "labor saving machine." An armed strike mob that has attacked Sterrett's car outside his office is brutally subdued by mounted police. The heavy-set John Faye, who has agreed to see Noah at his home, is impressed by the inventor's plans. Faye later dismisses Sterrett after learning about the man's attempt to steal Noah's plans and of Sterrett's shameful neglect of his family. At the union meeting hall the men cheer when they are informed that their demands have been met. W. Cameron was cast as the "strike leader." This film was later picked up and distributed by Klaw & Erlanger.

[S (LC); LC, LP3430; *MPW* 12/4/15:1890; *NYDM* 11/27/15:32]

Cap; Decad; Lab; Mtg; Mob; Pol; Reconcil; Shp Flr Abu; Strike; Viol; Wrk Rel Dis/Inj
CAP-LAB COOP

Poor Schmaltz, Famous Players/Par, Hugh Ford, 4-5r, Aug, Am, Comedy

A successful German-American brewer insists that his daughter, Louise, marry a titled man. Herman Schmaltz (musical comedy stage star Sam Bernard), a poor barber, reads about this and determines to impersonate a count who has publicly renounced his title and declared himself an anarchist. Louise, who is in love with an American named Jack, presents the household cook as herself to the phony count. Later, the real count, who has been assigned to assassinate Louise's father, plants a bomb in a chair in the brewer's home. But, Anne, the notorious "Queen of the Reds," (Ruby Hoffman) who has fallen in love with Schmaltz, removes the bomb just as her man is about to sit down on the lethal device.

[AFI, F1.3496; LC, LU6144; *MPW* 9/4/15:1664–65]

Anarch; Bomb; Cap; Fem Rad; Ger; Pol
ANTI-REV

Princess Romanoff, Fox, Frank Powell, 6r, May, Russ/Fr/Am, Drama

Princess Fedora Romanoff (Nance O'Neil) is aided by army officer Vladimir Boroff (Stuart Holmes) when her sleigh becomes caught up in a riot of political prisoners being marched-off to Siberia. The couple later become engaged. But Vladimir is killed in a duel with Loris Ipanoff, the jealous husband of his former mistress (who committed suicide after the death of their love child). Vladimir's father, General Boroff, has encouraged an ongoing campaign bent upon obliterating the nihilist element in the country. Believing his son's death is "the work of the Nihilists," he swears vengeance. The fleeing Ipanoff is followed across Europe and then to America by a vengeful Fedora, as well as by Tsarist secret police agents. Fedora falls in love with Loris after learning the reason he shot young Boroff.

[AFI, F1.3566; LC, LP6038(s); *MPW* 7/24/15:734]

Bomb; Decad; Escape; Nih; Russ; Sec Pol; Siberia; Tsar; Viol
ANTI-RS

Regeneration, Fox, Raoul A. Walsh, 5r, Sept, Am, Drama

Owen Conway (Rockcliffe Fellowes), a tough young gang leader in New York City, saves a group of slumming socialites from trouble after they enter a notorious cafe. As they are fleeing the dive the group encounters a socialist speaker who points them out to his listeners as members of the oppressor class: "You wouldn't need reform if the rich would give less to foreign charity and more to the needy at their back doors." Moved by the suffering she has witnessed, Marie Deering (Swedish-born actress Anna Q. Nilsson) becomes a settlement worker. A relationship develops between Marie and Owen, whom she teaches to read and write. But Marie is later fatally wounded while Owen struggles with a gangster who had attempted to rape her. She dies peacefully in Owen's arms, having been assured by him that he will not seek revenge. The film, whose screenplay had been co-written by director Raoul Walsh, was rereleased in January 1919.

PE (MOMA); [LC, LP6444(s); *MPN* 10/2/15:83; *Var* 9/24/15:21; *MPW* 1/18/19:390]

Cap; Lab; Mtg; Pol; Soc; Viol
PRO-LAB; CM/ANTI-SOC

The Rights of Man: A Story of War's Red Blotch, Lubin/V-L-S-E, Oct, John H. Pratt, 5r, Rur/Am, War Drama

Prince Sigismund, influenced by Thomas Paine's defense of the French Revolution in the *Rights of Man* (1791–92), plots to overthrow the monarch of a Balkan kingdom. Fearing for his daughter's safety in war-torn Europe, the Prince encourages Princess Lorcha to marry Dr. Carew, an American Red Cross surgeon. Immediately following the wedding, a shell rips into the church, mortally wounding the Prince. Before he dies he informs Lorcha of a secret treasure earmarked for the revolution. Narrowly eluding royal cavalry, Lorcha rides through raging battlefields and succeeds in delivering the treasure to the Revolutionary Committee. After an encounter with troops loyal to His Royal Highness, Lorcha and the revolutionaries are successful in bringing down the authoritarian regime. Lorcha and her new husband then seek refuge from the war at the American embassy. The *Variety* reviewer testily commented that the film was "full of captions designed to further the cause of socialism [some of the so-called "socialistic" inter-titles were excerpted from *The Rights of Man*]. Caption after caption is full of such propaganda that would be cheered if shown at an Emma Goldman meeting...."

[LC, LP6770; *MPN* 10/30/15:92; *MPW* 10/30/15:1036; *Var* 10/29/15:22]

Am Icons; Escape; Pac?; Rev; Soc; Viol
PRO-SOC

The Silent Man, Lubin, Leon D. Kent, 2r, Dec, Brit/Russ, Drama

Olga Kosloff, a renowned Russian actress performing in Britain, visits a seaside sanitarium to observe varieties of madness. She is horrified when she recognizes "The Silent Man," rescued from a drifting boat five years earlier, as Prince Mikail (L. C. Shumway). In Russia she had helped to frame the prince at the bidding of a corrupt Minister of Police in a vain attempt to win the release of her nihilist sister. Falsely condemned as a traitor, Mikail was branded in the chest with the Romanoff double-headed eagle before being cast adrift in the sea. Olga secretly returns to the insane asylum at night to release Mikail. She then fatalistically boards a small boat with the maniac.

[LC, LP7022; *MPW* 11/27/15:1712]

Artist; Atroc; Fem Rad; Mad Russ; Nih; Russ; Sec Pol; Siberia; Tsar
ANTI-RS

The Song of the Wage Slave, Metro, Herbert Blaché, 5r, Oct, Am((s), Drama

Based on the eponymous poem by Robert W. Service, most of the film's title captions were excerpted from the then popular work. Ned Lane (Edmund Breese), a physically powerful and virtuous laborer at a large paper mill ("A brute with brute strength to labor..."), is in love with Mildred, the daughter of a co-worker. However, she has fallen in love with, and been compromised by, the owner's son, Frank Dawson. When the capitalist father breaks up the romance, the noble Ned marries the betrayed Mildred. Soon afterwards, the heartless millionaire dies in an accident. Ned, wishing for Mildred to be happily reunited with her child's real father, vanishes and makes it appear as if he was killed in a gambling brawl ("Whiskey and cards and women, they made me the devil's tool..."). After "roughing it" throughout the country, Ned becomes the leader of a mill hands' association at a great paper mill controlled by a trust secretly dominated by Frank Dawson. Egged on by Ned, a series of confrontations take place between capital and labor. But when Ned learns that a bearded "agitator" named Sims (Jew?) has placed a bomb in the Dawson home, he rushes to their house and sacrifices himself while carrying off the explosive device ("Master, I've done thy bidding, and the light is low in the west. And the long, long shift is over.... Master, I've earned it—Rest."). Dawson agrees to honor his workers' demands.

[LC, LP6541; *MPW* 10/2/15:93,152; *Var* 9/24/15:21]

Agit; Bomb; Cap; Jew?; Lab; Liq Link?; Reconcil; Strike?; Tramp?; Viol
CAP-LAB COOP; PRO-LAB

The Sons of Toil, Domino, Thomas H. Ince, 2r, April, Am(r), Drama

John Wesley, the owner of a coal mine, is confronted with an imminent strike when he rebuffs his workers' demand for a new wage scale. Wesley hires a labor spy, Guy Ford, to keep him apprised of what the miners' leader, Marsden, plans to do. Ford, who happens to be in competition with mine foreman Jim Denton for the affections of Marsden's sister, Delia, denounces Jim as Wesley's spy. Forced to leave the mine, Denton rejoins the U.S. Army as a sergeant. When the miners declare a strike, Denton returns with the soldiers to guard the collieries. During a confrontation with the striking miners Denton is unable to fire upon his former comrades and abandons the scene. The repulsed strikers regroup and determine to stop the arrival of a train load of "non-union" men. The mine proprietor and Ford, who were also on the train, escape the resulting melee and hide in a cabin. Denton and Marsden encounter one another and, with the assistance of the former's mother and the latter's sister, resolve their differences. Frightened by the approach of the angry strike mob, old man Wesley agrees to sign the higher wage scale. Denton appears at the cabin and, after helping restore calm, is accepted back by his troopers. Ford is driven out of town.

[*MPW* 4/17/15:393 & 464]

Cap; Lab; Mob; Reconcil; Scabs; Strike; Viol
CAP-LAB COOP; ANTI-CAP

The Strike at the Centipede Mine, Domino, 2r, June, Am(r), Drama

John Daly was a prospector who made his fortune by discovering the Centipede mine. Not a pretentious man, he spends his idle hours courting Hope, the daughter of his long-time friend and mine foreman, Bill Foster. A miner named Jim Foley, who also seeks Hope's hand, is fired for "highgrading" (stealing samples of the highest quality ore). In revenge, Foley "stirs up the slumbering class hatred of the rougher element" and incites a strike. Foster reluctantly joins his striking comrades. The status of the miners' families rapidly deteriorates, but Daly insures that none go starving by secretly funneling aid through Hope. As a result, the grateful wife of one of the strikers informs Hope of Foley's plans to seize the mine. The strikers accuse Hope's father of being a spy and hold him captive. The frustrated miners, led by Foley and an agitator named Bloom (Jew?), then invade the town saloon. Daly telegraphs the sheriff in the next town to bring men in order to prevent bloodshed. The strikers, now a drunken mob, kill the superintendent while attacking the men guarding the mine. The sheriff's posse arrives and breaks the strike.

[*MPW* 6/12/15:1850 & 1852]

Agit; Cap; Irish?; Jew?; Lab; Liq Link; Mob; Pol; Pvt Pol; Strike; Unemployed; Viol
ANTI-LAB

The Struggle, Rex, Joseph De Grasse, June, Am(s), Drama

A pay rate change for engineers and firemen leads to a nationwide railroad strike. The situation is so serious that managers from all over the country gather together on Decoration Day (the day designated to decorate the graves of the Civil War dead; now known as Memorial Day) to settle the dispute. Pauline, the granddaughter of a Confederate Army widow, is so inspired by the latter's story of her appeal to General Lee to end the Civil War that she makes an impassioned plea at the convention hall to the assembled railroad delegates to peacefully resolve "the present war between capital and labor." Meanwhile, "aroused to a point of frenzy," the strikers break into the hall intent upon doing violence to the railroad representatives. But calm is restored by Pauline, who continues delivering her conciliatory message from the speaker's platform. The two

sides agree to a compromise and celebrate the end of the strike with a mammoth barbecue! Note: In a 1912 novel written by Col. Edward House (future advisor to Woodrow Wilson), *Philip Dru—Administrator: A Story of Tomorrow*, it had been suggested that the growing financial disparity between the capitalists and the working-class could lead to the outbreak of a "second Civil War."

[LC, LP5453; *MPW* 6/5/15:1676]

Agit?; Am Icons; Cap; Lab; Mob; Reconcil; Strike; Vet
CAP-LAB COOP

Toil and Tyranny ("Who Pays?" series #12), Balboa Amusement/Pathé, Oct, Am(s), Drama, 3r

The lead characters are introduced by having them stand under a question mark—the symbol of the "Who Pays?" series. Karl Hurd (Henry King), a "toiler" at the mills owned by "lumber king" David Powers (Daniel Gilfether), is fired following an altercation with his abusive "chief foreman"—a "petty tyrant" who struts about in leather riding boots. Soon afterwards, the mill workers strike when this bullying foreman notifies the men they must work an additional hour a day and on Sundays, without an increase in wages. Powers responds by threatening to hire "others at lower wages." The formerly docile laborers (most of whom are wearing clean white shirts) are transformed into a bloodthirsty mob after listening to the violent exhortations of an agitator dressed in black. During an elaborate birthday party for Power's "spoiled" daughter Laura (Ruth Roland), a strike committee breaks in and protests about their starving families—an ironic contrast that is further accentuated by showing her being attended by male servants dressed in livery. Angry at the intrusion, Powers orders them off his property and then instructs his subordinates to oust the striking workers from company housing. A scene depicting a woman resisting these evictions from the "half-paid-for" homes concludes with a match dissolve to her informing the strikers of this latest capitalist outrage. Hurd, whose wife has died of consumption, steals a pistol from the agitator's back pocket in order to shoot Powers when the owner arrives at the mills in his limousine. But Laura, who has become sympathetic to the workers' cause, has borrowed her father's car to visit and help the strikers' families. She is killed by a crazed Hurd when he fires several shots into the "limousine with the drawn curtains." The final inter-title morally challenges the film audience: "Who pays for this tragedy of toil and tyranny?" This is a rare surviving film from the Balboa Amusement & Producing Company, a west coast studio located in Long Beach that was founded in 1913 by the Horkheimer brothers.

[S (UCLA); LC, LU6628; *Photoplay* 2/17/16:26]

Agit; Cap; Lab; Mtg; Mob; Pol; Scabs; Shp Flr Abu; Strike; Unemployed; Viol
ANTI-CAP

1916

Anton the Terrible, Lasky/Par, William C. De-Mille, 5r, Oct, Russ, Drama

Cossack Anton Kazoff (Theodore Roberts), known as "Anton the Terrible" for his delight in torturing people who come under his power, is chief of the Okrana (one of only a few American fictional films known to have used the official name of the Russian secret police). He has sworn to avenge the honor of his sister, who was defiled by Staff General Stanovitch (Horace B. Carpenter) fifteen years earlier. Shortly after the outbreak of the World War, the General Staff gives Anton full authority to discover a suspected high-placed spy working for the Germans. Anton is, in fact, that spy. Exploiting his enhanced position, Anton has Stanovitch's daughter Vera arrested as an anarchist when she attends a meeting of a radical society called the League. Anton later murders Stanovitch in order to procure important military papers for his German employers. While in prison, Vera discovers Anton's duplicity. After Vera is released from prison, she and her boyfriend, played by Harrison Ford, entrap Anton into incriminating himself. Note: A well publicized incident pertaining to corruption/collusion of the Tsarist regime with Germany had recently occurred. General Vladimir Sukhomlinov (1848–1926), Russian War Minister from 1908 to 1914, was married to a much younger woman whose lover was accused of being a German spy. This man, Colonel Myasoedev, was hanged for espionage in 1915.

[LC, LP9099; *MPN* 10/14/16:2395–96; *Var* 9/29/16:25]

Anarch; Atroc; Decad; Fem Rad?; Ger; Russ; Sec Pol; Spy-Sab; Viol
ANTI-RS

Arms and the Woman, Astra/Pathé, George Fitzmaurice, 5r, Nov, Am/Eur, Drama

A Hungarian peasant girl named Rozika (Mary Nash) and her brother Carl emigrate to the United States. While singing at a saloon on New York's lower East Side, Rozika attracts the ear and heart of David Trevor, president of a steel works. With the help of lessons paid for by Trevor, Rozika becomes an opera star. Meanwhile, Carl returns to Austria-Hungary after killing a man in a barroom brawl, and becomes an anarchist. Following the outbreak of the World War, Trevor is visited by an Englishman commissioned by his government to purchase war materials. Rozika, now married to Trevor, vainly implores him to refuse the order when she realizes the munitions will be used against her countrymen (Austria-Hungary was allied to Germany). Carl is sent back to America by the brotherhood to destroy Trevor's plant. Rozika learns of this and is able to intervene. Nevertheless, German spies successfully blow up the factory. In the glare of the burning plant a ruined Trevor tells his wife: "My dear, it is better so—it is better so." The film is supposed to have included documentary footage of New York slums and a munitions factory. This was one of several 1916 releases that developed a negative linkage of Germans (the militaristic state of Germany) with domestic radicalism in America. Note: Soon after the outbreak of hostilities, the American Socialist Party recommended an embargo against all belligerents. A wave of so-called "munitions strikes" against manufacturers working on Allied war orders took place during the summer of 1915.

[LC, LU8717; *MPN* 11/25/16:3329; *Var* 11/10/16:29]

Anarch; Bomb; Cap; Ger; Lab; Liq Link; Pac; Sab; Spy-Sab; Viol
ANTI-REV

As in a Dream, Rex, 3r, June, Am(u), Drama

A member of the "idle rich," Bronson Powers, is engaged to Elaine Cameron, the daughter of a wealthy manufacturer who is only interested in spending money to endow memorial libraries in his own name. While out riding her horse, Elaine is thrown and loses her memory. She wanders into the nearby tenement district, where she is rescued by Donald Robbins, a settlement worker. Sometime later the amnesia suffering Elaine secures a job in one of her father's sweatshops. Donald interprets it as a divine intervention when he discovers that Elaine is the child of the local "oppressor of the laboring classes." So after Cameron refuses to accede to a labor committees' petition to improve working conditions, an angered Donald forces the capitalist to observe the situation in the slums. Planning to present Elaine to her father, Donald breaks in upon a liquor-crazed Powers as he is about to accost his own fiancée! Elaine and Donald later marry and the Cameron fortune is pledged for use in easing the burdens of the "down-trodden laboring class." This film bears a strong resemblance to Paramount's 1915 release, *Out of the Darkness*, q.v. The negative linkage of a member of the upper class with alcohol abuse is unusual.

[*MPW* 6/10/16:1939]

Cap; Decad; Lab; Liq Link; Reconcil

PRO-LAB; ANTI-CAP

Behind the Screen, Lone Star/Mutual, Charles Chaplin, 2r, Nov, Am, Comedy

Chaplin's little David plays the overworked Assistant at a movie studio for a lazy stagehand, descriptively named Goliath (acted by the enormous Eric Campbell). During lunch break the Assistant suffers while sitting next to a mustache wearing, garlic eating (Italian?) stagehand. When several stagehands are awakened by a director from their post-lunch slumber, they protest: "How dare you wake us up, we strike!" Goliath refuses to join them. His Assistant, clutching the Tramp's trademark battered derby, is pressed into service operating a trapdoor on one of the sets. A healthy "Country Girl" who wants to get into movies, played by Edna Purviance, puts on coveralls abandoned by one of the strikers. In the meantime, the strikers return to the studio in order to wreak "Revenge." Two of them, including the garlic eater, are now wearing beards (for the anarchist look) and are carrying kegs of dynamite with long fuses. They sneak backstage. Between throwing pies for the Comedy Department, the Tramp Assistant helps out the young lady (mistaken for a man) in an altercation with the two bombers. Goliath is launched through the trapdoor when the explosives ignite.

[S (LC; Vid); LC, LP9557; *MPW* 11/25/16: 1222]

Anarch?; Bomb; Ital?; Lab; Scabs; Strike; Viol

CM/ANTI-REV

The Blacklist, Lasky/Par, William C. DeMille, 5r, Feb, Am(r), Drama

Colorado miners, many of whom are immigrants, work under slave-like conditions due to the restrictive hiring practices of the "Blacklist" imposed by the manager Norton and enforced by his armed mine guards. Vera Maroff (Blanche Sweet), who teaches the children at the company school, is defended by a miner named Big John after being insulted by the head guard. Big John is fired and later killed when he attempts to prevent his family's eviction from company housing—"They shot him like a dog." Vera takes in Big John's dispossessed wife and two children. Vera writes the mine owner, Warren Harcourt (Charles Clary; introduced in a scene portraying him attending a champagne dinner in white tie with other rich "Spenders"), while her Russian father (a bearded stereotype played by Horace B. Carpenter) contacts an anarchist society known as "The Red Brotherhood." Norton orders "the dangerous woman" to be dismissed from her teaching position. Harcourt arrives to investigate the situation, but refuses Vera's request to eliminate the Blacklist. The miners declare a strike and soon afterwards erect a tent city in a gully in the nearby hills so that they can prevent scabs from taking their jobs. Under the supervision of an anarchist representative named Frederick Holtz (Lucien Littlefield), lots are secretly drawn to determine who will end the "tyranny" by shooting Harcourt. Vera draws the fatal bean, but is unwilling to carry out the mission since she has fallen in love with the tall and handsome capitalist. When a mine guard is murdered by a sharpshooter, Norton orders his enraged men to open fire upon the tent city with rifles and a machine gun. Many of the wives and children of the strikers are mowed down. Vera joins the miners in resisting the guards' assault. When Vera's father dies in her arms cursing the "traitor" who had failed to carry out the Brotherhood's will, Vera decides to assassinate Harcourt and then commit suicide. She only wounds Harcourt, and after he prevents Vera from shooting herself, the mine owner gives her the Blacklist to tear up and asks her to teach him to understand the working-class. Note: The incidents dramatized in this film were based on the Colorado coal miners' strike of 1913–14 and the infamous Ludlow Massacre of April 1914. Although a few self-avowed anarchists and/or prominent Wobblies participated in this strike, *no organized* anarchist group was directly involved. But, at the time, alleged anarchist influences upon the strikers was attacked in the press and anarchist "terrorism" was specifically condemned in a popular book about the Colorado Coal Wars written by Robert Hunter, entitled *Violence and the Labor Movement* (New York: Macmillan, 1914). Material from Hunter's book was probably "borrowed" for *The Blacklist*'s screenplay, credited to Marion Fairfax and William C. DeMille.

[LC, LU7650; *MPN* 3/4/16:1319; *MPW* 3/4/16:1490; *Var* 2/18/16:21]

Anarch; Cap; Ger?; Lab; Pvt Pol; Reconcil; Russ; Scabs; Strike; Unemployed; Viol

PRO-LAB; CAP-LAB COOP; ANTI-REV

Brothers Equal, Thanhouser, 2r, June, Am/S Pac, Drama

The orphaned son of a rich trader grows up to become an ardent socialist. In order to be able to experiment with his ideal of "Brothers Equal in the Sight of God and Man," he travels with his family to a tropical island he owns. The proselytizing efforts of the Socialist and his fiancee are largely successful with the "native colored population." But a moral crisis arises when his fiancee's sister falls in love with a local fisherman. This is because it is learned that the Fisherman, played by Thomas A. Curran, is the Socialist's half-brother, the product of a union between their father and a native woman. The Socialist is quite willing to equally divide his property with the other son of the trader, but is horrified by the thought of a romance between "the dainty Northern girl" and a man of color. The Fisherman resolves the dilemma by sacrificing his life while saving his mother from a fire. This work is an early example of a politically oriented film attacking advocates of the radical left by implying that they are hypocrites.

[*MPW* 6/24/16:2297]

Cap; Lab; Soc
ANTI-SOC

The Bruiser, American/Mutual, Charles Bartlett, 5r, Mar, Am(u), Drama

"Big Bill" Brawley (as in brawler; played by William Russell) is a longshoreman who also boxes. Due to his popularity with the men, Bill is elected chairman of the employees' committee, which is seeking a wage increase from the Kenwick Shipping Company. When a threat to blacklist him fails to intimidate the hulking dock worker, Manson Kenwick, the unscrupulous owner, resorts to other tactics. In order to discredit Bill, Kenwick employs a spy among the longshoremen and even enlists his sister to vamp the worker. Kenwick actually succeeds in tricking the men into endorsing a pro-management agreement before Bill comes to his senses and forces the owner to sign a fair contract. The protagonist, "Big Bill," may have been so named in order to create an associative linkage with the well-known I.W.W. leader, William D. ("Big Bill") Haywood (1869–1928). The April *Moving Picture World* review deemed the film "especially fruitful as propaganda on the labor side."

[AFI, F1.0514; *MPN* 4/1/16:1912; *MPW* 3/25/16:2082; *MPW* 4/8/16:281 & 285]

Agit; Cap; IWW?; Lab
ANTI-CAP; PRO-LAB

The Circular Room, IMP, Ben Wilson, 2r, July, Am, Drama

Stuart Travers, played by the director, the son of an American steel manufacturer, becomes smitten with Maida. She is the ward of Count Orloff, the leader of a secret organization plotting to sabotage munitions factories in America. In the concealed circular room where they meet, the conspirators have produced a new bomb with which they plan to demolish the Travers steel works. When Von Tahn, one of the conspirators who has been romantically spurned by Maida, discovers that the girl has spied upon them, he binds her in the circular room and sets a timer on the explosive device. Maida is able to knock over a phone in the room and contact Stuart. The police and Stuart arrive in time to save Maida and arrest the returning saboteurs. This film is one of the earliest known fictional cinematic examples of a linkage being made between German espionage and radicals—refer to *Draft 258* (Metro, 1917), q.v. Coincidentally, *The Circular Room* was released the day before the infamous Black Tom munitions explosion that occurred on the night of July 29–30.

[*MPW* 7/29/16:834]

Bomb; Cap; Dom Rad; Ger; Pol; Sab; Spy-Sab; Viol

ANTI-REV

The Clarion, Equitable/World, James Durkin, 5r, Feb, Am, Drama

Dr. Surtaine is the wealthy producer of a patent medicine that contains morphine. *The Clarion*, the paper published in the city in which Surtaine manufactures his medicine, condemns his business. The doctor's son, Harrington (Carlyle Blackwell), buys the newspaper in order to suppress what he believes to be unjustified attacks upon his father. The idealistic son then launches an editorial campaign against the city's slumlord. Harrington also publishes the news of an epidemic in the tenement quarter known as the "Rookeries." Deprived of work by the quarantine, a "mob of foreigners" from the Rookeries, led by an anarchist named Max Veltman (German-Jew?), attacks the offices of *The Clarion*. But when Veltman hurls a bomb at an office building, several of the demonstrators are killed. The angry crowd turns against the anarchist. Harrington becomes engaged to the reformed slumlord's daughter and Dr. Surtaine agrees to stop producing his addictive cure-all.

[LC,LU7635; *MPW* 2/26/16:1374]

Anarch; Bomb; Cap; Ger?; Jew?; Lab; Mob; Unemployed; Viol

ANTI-REV

The Corner, Kay-Bee/Triangle, Walter Edwards, 5r, Jan, Am(u), Drama

A ruthless capitalist named David Waltham (George Fawcett) controls a syndicate that corners the food supply of a major metropolitan area. An unemployed railroad engineer, John Adams (Willard Mack), is caught stealing bread to feed his starving family and is sentenced to the workhouse. After serving his time Adams returns home to discover that his wife, played by Clara Williams, has sold her body to the rent collector. Waltham, meanwhile, remains indifferent to the growing number of breadline riots taking place in the poorer quarters of the city. An embittered Adams acquires a job at one of Waltham's giant storehouses. One night Adams induces the hated "monopolist" to visit the big warehouse by claiming that the police are there in response to rumors of plans by segments of the starving population to destroy his holdings. When Waltham arrives at the storehouse, Adams binds him and leaves the man to starve, hidden behind boxes of food. In his efforts to free himself, Waltham causes the towering pile of boxes to fall over and crush him. The comment was made in a *Moving Picture World* review that: "Such plays are silent contributors to social and political betterment, the more eloquent that they are not oratorical." This film was obviously influenced by Griffith's 1909 release, *A Corner in Wheat*, q.v.

[AFI, F1.0798; LC, LP10835; *MPW* 12/11/15:2028; *MPW* 1/1/16:142]

Breadline; Cap; Lab; Pol; Unemployed; Viol

ANTI-CAP

The Cossack Whip, Edison/K-E-S-E, John H. Collins, 5r, Nov, Russ/Brit/Am, Drama

Following an attack by revolutionaries upon Cossack guards escorting prisoners to Siberia, the Prefect of Imperial Police, Turov, orders a raid upon the whole district. A peasant girl named Darya (Viola Dana), hiding during a brutal assault by mounted Cossacks upon her village, witnesses her father and sister being carried off into captivity. The father is tortured for information, after which her sister Katerina is whipped and raped by Turov (his crimes made to appear even more horrendous to the contemporary audience by the presence of a mysterious oriental assistant). Darya swears revenge when she learns of this from her dying sister. With the help of a revolutionary named Sergius (Richard Tucker), a famous dancer whom she meets on the run in Petrograd, Darya flees to Britain. Under the tutelage of Madame Pojeska of the Russian Ballet (the Ballets Russes, under Diaghilev, evoked associations with modernist decadence), Darya is taught to dance. Having learned of her father's death in Siberia, Darya returns to Russia and with the help of Sergius becomes a prima ballerina. Turov, captivated by her performance on stage, invites Darya to his rooms. Pretending to flirt with him, Darya requests that she be taken to the infamous stone cell where he interrogates prisoners. Darya tricks Turov into manacling himself and then beats him with his own knout! A guard who has converted to the cause finishes off the police chief. Darya and Sergius escape across the border and sail for America.

[S (GEH; LC); LC, LP9158; *EH* 11/25/16: 21; *MPW* 11/18/16:1002; *Var* 11/17/16:26]

Am Icons; Artist; Atroc; Decad; Escape; Fem Rad; Rev; Russ; Sec Pol; Siberia; Viol
ANTI-RS

The Crucial Test (The Eternal Sacrifice), Paragon/World, July, Robert Thornby & Thomas Ince, 5r, Russ/Fr/Am, Drama

Countess Thanya (Kitty Gordon) falls in love with Vance Holden, a struggling American artist visiting Petrograd. But the "most hated man in Russia," the middle-aged Grand Duke Alexander Bagroff (J. Herbert Frank), is making unwanted advances upon Thanya. She promises to assist her brother Boris, the leader of a gang of social revolutionaries, when she learns he is plotting to assassinate Bagroff. Boris is captured while attempting to carry out the deed and is whipped in front of his sister to betray his associates. Thanya confesses and is imprisoned with Boris. After she refuses to become Bagroff's mistress, Thanya is sent into Siberian exile with her brother. During a storm, they escape and make their way to Paris. Thanya is reunited with and marries her beloved Vance. Bagroff comes to Paris and Thanya secretly agrees to give in to his sexual demands if he will commission a portrait from the still struggling Vance. Boris resolves the problem by killing the evil duke as he prepares to spend his first night with Thanya.

[LC, LU8631; *MPN* 7/15/16:273; *Var* 6/30/16:20]

Artist; Atroc; Decad; Escape; Fem Rad?; Rev; Russ; Siberia; Soc?; Viol
ANTI-RS

The Dawn of Freedom, Vitagraph, Paul Scardon & Theodore Marston, 5r, Aug, Am(r), Fantasy Drama

In this bizarre film presentation of American ideals (proclaimed by its producers to be a "stinging satire on the death of those ideals"), "The Patriot," Captain Richard Cartwright of Revolutionary War fame, is revived from a trance he was placed under over a hundred years earlier. The action begins when coal miners striking against his capitalist descendants blow up the Allegheny mine in which he is entombed. Dick, the son of the coal baron, discovers the dazed Patriot (Charles Richman) and takes him home. The social warfare resulting from the brutalization of the workers by the modern day Cartwright's refusal to pay a decent wage appalls the Patriot. When confronted by the strikers and the Patriot, Cartwright drops dead of a heart attack. Attempting to quell the rioting mob of strikers, the Patriot is mortally wounded. Nevertheless, "his courage and spirit—that of '76—is transformed to Dick … and everything ends happily for the workers." The "Strike Leader" was played by a regular early silent heavy, Edward Elkas. Note: The plot of this film may have been influenced by Edgar Rice Burroughs' 1912 novel, *A Princess of Mars*, that featured a messianic American hero named Captain John Carter.

[LC, LP8807; *MPW* 8/26/16:1450]

Agit?; Am Icons; Cap; Lab; Mob; Reconcil; Sab; Strike; Viol
CAP-LAB COOP

The Dollar Kings (#9 of "The Grip of Evil" series), Pathé, W. A. Douglas & Harry Harvey, Am(r), Drama

An idealistic young capitalist establishes a Utopian factory in the countryside that pays high wages. The bucolic workers' paradise is destroyed by labor agitators.

[Brownlow, *Behind the Mask of Innocence*, p. 489; *NYDM* 9/2/16]

Agit; Cap; Lab
ANTI-LAB

The Dragon, Equitable/World, Harry Pollard, 5r, Jan, Am, Drama

With long dark tresses and wearing a simple white dress, the innocent Messalla returns from a convent to live with her father in an old house in Washington Square (the address seemingly intended to imply he is a socialist sympathizer). The embittered man, who had lost his wealth and his wife to the allures of Fifth Avenue, warns his daughter about the "Dragon" that lurks in that street of greed. Determined to find her mother, Messalla naively heads up the avenue where she inadvertently causes death and calamity to those who had brought about her father's ruin. For instance, Messalla agrees to deliver a package, unaware that it contains a bomb, to the Wall Street millionaire with whom her mother lives. The mother leaves the man's home to rejoin her family just before it is destroyed by the explosion of the bomb.

[LC, LU7298; *MPN* 1/8/16:86; *Var* 1/14/16:19]

Bomb; Cap; G Vill; Soc?; Viol
ANTI-CAP

Dust, American/Mutual, Edward Sloman, 5r, July, Am(s), Drama

A symbolic prologue portrays laborers coining their lives into currency for their capitalist oppressors. Frank Kenyon (Franklyn Ritchie) is a reformist author (Socialist?) who wages a campaign against the unsafe conditions at the woolen mills (particularly the hazardous dust) owned by his fiancee's father. When the greedy capitalist's daughter, Marion Moore, refuses to try to persuade her father to improve the plight of his employees, Frank makes a dramatic gesture. At a benefit for Belgian War Victims in which Marion is portraying "Humanity," Frank jumps upon the stage to denounce John D. Moore by claiming the conditions at his factories are as destructive to human life as war. Frank also forces Marion to visit the home of a little girl whose hand was mangled while working in one of Moore's mills. Marion returns her engagement ring. Frank goes on to become a member of the legislature, where he successfully lobbies for a factory reform bill. But before its safety measures can be implemented, Moore and an employee are trapped in a blaze at one of his mills. When Frank organizes a rescue effort from an adjoining building, Moore cowardly shoves away the other man. The capitalist plunges to his death. A chastened Marion renews her engagement to Frank and pledges to help him fight for reform.

[AFI, F1.1124; *MPW* 7/22/16:653, 687; *NYDM* 7/1/16:32]

Cap; Lab; Reconcil; Soc?; Wrk Rel Dis/Inj
ANTI-CAP; CAP-LAB COOP

The Eternal Grind, Famous Players/Par, John B. O'Brien, 5r, April, Am(u), Drama

The *Variety* review contemptuously referred to this film as an "old style 'Capital vs. Labor' story." Mary Pickford stars as Mary Martin, one of three sisters working as seamstresses in a sweatshop owned by James Wharton. One of his sons, Owen (John Bowers), is a handsome settlement worker who labors in the dirty factory under an assumed name in order to better understand conditions. He falls in love with Mary. The other young Wharton, Ernest, is a woman "chaser" who makes her sister Amy his mistress. When Mary's sister Jane (Dorothy West) is diagnosed as consumptive, the owner denies financial aid for her treatment. Ernest offers to help, but only if Mary agrees to sleep with him. Instead, Mary confronts him with a revolver and forces the womanizer to marry Amy. Owen is seriously injured at the sweatshop when he falls through some rotten flooring. Mary refuses to go to Owen's bedside until the elder Wharton agrees to pay his employees "living wages" and make his factory a "fit place to work in." Note: *The Eternal Grind* would appear to be a filmic variation on the *Bertha, the Sewing Machine Girl* working-class melodramas that had been entertaining young women since the 1870s.

[LC, LU7797; *MPN* 4/22//16:2380; *Var* 4/14/16:24]

Cap; Decad; Lab; Reconcil; Shp Flr Abu; Wrk Rel Dis/Inj
ANTI-CAP; PRO-LAB

Flirting with Fate, Fine Arts/Triangle, W. Christy Cabanne, 5r, July, Am, Comedy

A poor artist, played by Douglas Fairbanks, has a rich girlfriend. When he thinks he has lost the lady's love, the artist hires "Automatic Joe" (an Italian gangster stereotype) to end his earthly suffering. But following a reversal of his fortunes, the artist no longer wishes to be killed. The artist has many real and imagined encounters with individuals whom he believes to be the killer in disguise. These include a mutually frightening run-in with a "fugitive Nihilist" (a bearded Russian stereotype wearing boots and a peasant blouse). Automatic Joe, meanwhile, has found God and joined the Salvation Army! *A Black Hand*, a short released by Royal in 1914, employed a similar plot.

[S (LC); *MPN* 7/8/16:105; *Var* 6/30/16:20]

Artist; Cap; Ital; Nih; Russ
CM/ANTI-REV

Graft (20 ep serial), Universal, Richard Stanton, 2r, No. 8, "Old King Coal," Feb, Am(r), Adventure

Fifteen men, who head various trusts, have engaged in a criminal conspiracy to fix prices by bribing public officials, sabotaging the organization of labor, and suppressing the peoples' dissent against their abuses. The first seven episodes of this socially conscious adventure serial included portrayals of the excesses of the grain, textile, munitions and railroad trusts. Bruce Larnigan (Hobart Henley), the son of the crusading District Attorney of New York who was murdered by the graft "Syndicate" (in the first episode: "Liquor and the Law"), has sworn to avenge his father. During the second episode ("The Tenement House Evil") Bruce is elected District Attorney and develops a relationship with Dorothy Maxwell (Jane Novak), the suffragette daughter of the head of the insurance trust. By the seventh episode, "America Saved From War," Bruce is working closely with his brother Tom. The Larnigans have tracked-down and seen killed several members of the dreaded trust while evading numerous attempts upon their own lives. Having narrowly escaped the explosion of an "infernal machine" placed in his home, Tom proceeds during Episode 8 to the Pennsylvania coal country to investigate conditions resulting from a strike. While striking miners, scabs and militia battle, Tom and the head of the coal trust, Weisner, engage in a scuffle and Weisner is accidentally killed. Tom discovers that the coal shortage and resulting higher prices are *not* due to the strike, but are a result of the manipulations of the graft Syndicate. Tom's report leads to government intervention.

[LC, LP7490; *MPW* 2/5/16:834]

Bomb; Cap; Ger?; Lab; Militia; Scabs; Strike; Viol

ANTI-CAP

Graft, Universal, Richard Stanton, 2r, No. 14 "The Iron Ring," Mar, Am(s), Adventure

Between Episodes 9 and 13 the insurance, gambling and milk trusts are engaged and their leaders destroyed, but at a terrible cost to the Larnigans. Tom Larnigan is killed and his brother Bruce goes insane. In Episode 12, "The Milk Battle," Bruce's cousin, Robert Harding (played by the director), a prominent lawyer from Youngstown, Ohio, takes up the cause. Although her father suffered a paralytic stroke while struggling with Tom, socially-conscious Dorothy Maxwell determines to help Harding, whom she loves, by presenting him with her father's diary, which contains incriminating information against the graft Syndicate. In order to prevent the merger of competing Ohio companies, in Episode 14, the steel industry of Pittsburg enlists the aid of the Syndicate leader Stanford Stone. He contacts Mark Gramble, head of the Labor Trust, "the man who creates

strikes and then furnishes strikebreakers to end it [sic]." After Harding learns what is going on, he travels to Youngstown, the center of the labor troubles. He is instrumental in helping to restore order and prevents a mob of local citizens from lynching two "paid labor agitators" who have been seized. Gramble is subsequently arrested and, with the confessions of his frightened agitators, is easily convicted. Having finally secured the diary from Dorothy containing the secrets of the criminal "fifteen," Harding is able to openly proceed against its two surviving members in the serial's concluding episodes. Stone is the last to die while attempting to escape from the police. Robert and Dorothy are then free to marry.

[LC, MP7771; *MPW* 3/25/16:2066]

Agit; Cap; Lab; Pol; Scabs; Strike; Viol

ANTI-CAP

Her Bitter Cup, Universal/Red Feather, Cleo Madison, 5r, April, Am(u), Drama

Rethna (played by the film's director), born into poverty, grows up to become a dedicated labor activist. She diligently strives to organize her fellow female factory employees against the unsafe, as well as unsanitary, conditions that exist due to the neglect of capitalist Henry Burke (William Mong)—"a factory owner, who oppresses his workers to a frightful degree." To achieve her goals, Rethna has an affair with Burke's disreputable son, Harry. After a year, Rethna breaks off with him and, to carry on her activities against the ruthless capitalists, agrees to marry his kindly brother Walter. Rethna uses her access to the Burke fortune to alleviate the workers' suffering. Walter, though he loves Rethna, leaves her when he discovers the actual reason for their marriage. Then, while she is at the textile mill petitioning the elder Burke to improve conditions, a fire erupts. Walter comes to the rescue, leading to a reconciliation with his estranged wife. A chastened Henry Burke commits himself to improving the lot of his employees.

[LC, LP7877; *MPN* 4/8/16:2062; *MPW* 4/29/16:855-56]

Cap; Fem Rad; Lab; Reconcil; Wrk Rel Dis/Inj

PRO-LAB; CAP-LAB COOP

Hesper of the Mountains, Vitagraph, Wilfrid North, 5r, July, Am(r), Drama

The vivacious Ann (Lillian "Dimples"

Walker) reluctantly leaves the comforts of New York society to accompany her sickly younger brother to the mountains of Colorado. While staying at the ranch of a friend, Ann also nurses the injured foreman, Raymond. Raymond later becomes part owner of a nearby mine. But the miners, under the leadership of the burly Jack Munro, declare a strike. Following the failure of arbitration, the sheriff organizes guards to protect the mine owners' interests. The strikers blow up Raymond's shaft house when he refuses to join their cause. Munro, a former West Point cadet, arms and drills the miners in anticipation of a confrontation with the sheriff's men. Raymond and his partner send a request for the militia to the governor. Just as the local authorities and the miners clash, the militia arrives and disperses the strikers. Disgusted with the miners' cowardice, a drunken Munro makes a suicidal attack upon the mine guards. Ann lends Raymond the money to buy new machinery on the condition that he call her Hesper (as in Hesperus, the evening star, especially Venus). Although the similarities appear to be rather tenuous, the *Variety* review links this film to the Colorado miners' strike of 1913–1914.

[LC, LP8790; *MPW* 8/5/16:1006; *Var* 8/4/16:28]

Agit; Bomb; Cap; Irish?; Lab; Liq Link; Militia; Pol; Sab; Strike; Viol
ANTI-LAB

Intolerance, Biograph, D. W. Griffith, 13–14r, Sept, Am (Modern Story)(s), Drama

In the modern story sequences of this interlapping multi-story film classic, the "autocratic industrial overlord" of the Jenkins Mills (Sam de Grasse) cuts wages by ten percent in order to finance the socially meddlesome activities of his spinster sister's "Uplifters" society (most likely an allusion to the Rockefellers and the Rockefeller supported American Social Hygiene Association, founded in 1913). These reformers are particularly incensed by the working-class drinking and sexual mingling that is observed taking place after hours at the employees' Annual Dance (the physical contact between unescorted women and men that occurred while performing such popular dances as the Turkey Trot were thought to promote prostitution). During the "great strike" that follows, the defiant workers, armed mainly with clubs and stones, are fired upon by the Gatling guns (declared obsolete by the U.S. Army in 1911, this weapon would continue to be used by some state militias until after WWI; due to the frequent use of militias to suppress labor demonstrations, the Gatling gun had become a symbol of labor repression; refer to *Facing the Gattling Guns*, 1914, q.v.) of the militia and brutally assaulted by rifle-firing factory guards. The jobless survivors (including the little "Dear One," played by Mae Marsh) and their families join an exodus to the "great city" nearby, where other hazards await the working poor. Note: John D. Rockefeller, who owned the Ludlow, Colorado, mines received a lot of negative attention during the extended hearings of a presidential Commission on Industrial Relations. Refer to the comments on the infamous 1914 Ludlow Massacre under *The Blacklist* (1916), q.v.

[S (LC; USC; Vid); LC, LP9934; *Var* 9/8/16:20]

Agit?; Cap; Lab; Liq Link; Militia; Mob; Pol; Pvt Pol; Scabs; Strike; Unemployed; Viol
PRO-LAB; ANTI-CAP

The Jester, Essanay, 3r, May, Am(u), Drama

Due to the bad press he receives from articles written by a girl reporter, Bob Blair, the wild son of a steel magnate, abandons his carefree lifestyle, dons overalls and becomes a laborer in his father's mills. The company is in financial trouble because of worker discontent, exacerbated by an agitator named Donovan who has been "planted in the shops" by a competing steel trust. Bob settles the labor unrest by beating-up the militant. The reporter resigns from her paper when she learns that it is secretly owned by the rival trust and goes to work for Bob, whom she has come to admire.

[*Mot* 5/20/16:1171; *MPW* 5/13/16:1212]

Agit; Cap; Irish; Lab; Viol
CAP-LAB COOP

The King's Game, Pathé, Ashley Miller, 5r, Jan, Russ/Am, Com-Drama

Count Sergius Dardinilis (Sheldon Lewis) flees Russia with his young daughter after killing the Grand Duke of Kiev for having an affair with his wife. While in American exile, Dardinilis becomes the leader of a nihilist band. Years later, Philip, the latest Grand Duke of Kiev, is visiting New York and is scheduled to participate in a military parade. Perciley, the nihilist who has been chosen by his vengeful leader to assassinate Philip, is apprehended by the American Secret Service. But since the partying Grand Duke has strayed-off, the government agents conceive the idea of substituting the look-alike "killer" for his intended victim (both men are played by the same actor, George Probert). They forcibly shackle him to the Grand Duke's carriage. Meanwhile, Dardinilis and his associates (one of the bearded stereotypes resembles the Kaiser) encounter Philip in the street and, mistaking him for the "killer," take the young Grand Duke to the house located along the parade route that they have rented. The nihilists hand Philip the bomb (disguised as a box of candy) to hurl at the Grand Duke's carriage. Philip, who has promptly fallen in love with the daughter of Dardinilis (played by serial queen Pearl White), plays along with the nihilists and then throws the candy (without the bomb) into the passing carriage. The sporting Philip exonerates Dardinilis, commissions him in the Imperial Army and marries his daughter!

[LC, LU7914; *MPW* 1/8/16:300; Pathé Press Sheet, private collection; *Var* 1/14/16:19]

Bomb; Decad; Escape; Nih; Russ; Sec Ser; Viol

ANTI-REV

The Lords of High Decision, Un/Red Feather, Jack Harvey, 5r, Feb, Am(u), Drama

After graduating from college, Wayne Craighill reluctantly agrees to join his father's Pittsburg-based steel business. Colonel Craighill (Joseph Gerard; also Joseph W. Girard) is currently engaged in an attempt to ruin an elderly independent coal operator named Gregory. Meanwhile, Wayne has become involved with Jean, Gregory's granddaughter. The Colonel is also conducting an active lecture campaign against the working-class. Not surprisingly, it becomes easy for an agitator to incite the steel workers at the Craighill owned mills to strike. Wayne rushes to the mills and is successful in getting the men to return to work. Later, when the Colonel's bank fails (a $100,000 shortfall that may be due to extravagances of his youthful new wife), some of his coal miners become a rampaging mob and attack the Craighill home. Wayne confronts the mob and restores calm by pledging to cover the bank's losses. But when no money arrives on payday, the workers begin to blow up the mines. As luck would have it, from one of the

wrecked mines a geyser of oil gushes forth, thus establishing a new source of income with which to pay the men's wages.

[LC, LP7547; *MPW* 3/11/16:1701–02]

Agit; Bomb; Cap; Lab; Mob; Reconcil; Sab; Strike; Viol

ANTI-CAP

Luke and the Bomb Throwers, Pathé/Phunphilms, Hal Roach, 1r, May, Am, Comedy

This film was one of 67 shorts released between 1915 and 1917 that starred Harold Lloyd as Lonesome Luke (another character patterned after Chaplin's baggy-trousered Tramp). Luke stumbles upon the secret meeting place of a band of anarchists. After the usual hilarious stunts, he is rescued from captivity by an armed citizen. The subdued bomb throwers are marched to the street and handed over to the police.

[*MPW* 5/27/16:1537]

Anarch; Bomb; Pol; Tramp?; Viol

ANTI-REV

The Manager of the B. and A., Signal/Mutual, J. P. McGowan, 5r, Sept, Am(s), Advent-Drama

Dan Oakley, the newly hired manager of the local branch of the Buckhorn and Antioch, imposes a tight new regimen on the formerly slack workers. This incurs the animosity of Griffith Ryder, the editor of the *Antioch Herald* and leader of the Labor Party (Socialist?). Under the constant agitation of Ryder, the workers declare a strike when they learn that Dan has given a job to his father, an ex-con. By force of personality, Dan enlists the help of a few loyal men to keep the yards operating. Some violence occurs, culminating in the destruction of the water lines. A resulting fire and the struggle to bring it under control creates a new atmosphere of mutual respect between Dan and his employees.

[AFI, F1.2796; *MPN* 10/7/16:229; *MPW* 10/7/16:132]

Agit; Cap; Ger?; Lab; Reconcil; Sab; Soc?; Strike; Viol

CAP-LAB COOP

My Official Wife, Vitagraph, Dec, (reissue—1914), Am/Fr?/Russ, Drama

[*MPW* 12/16/16:1654]

Fem Rad; Nih; Russ; Sec Pol; Tsar; Viol

ANTI-REV

Otto the Artist, Lubin, Edwin McKim, 2r?, May, Am(s), Comedy

Otto (a series character played by the diminutive Davy Don) is unsuccessful both in art and in his attempts to woo the wealthy Helena Dollarmark. Unable to pay his rent or even to feed himself, Otto willingly accepts a job as a house painter during a strike. But when the strikers spot the "scab" working on the Hotel Royal the chase is on. A cop, thinking Otto is a thief, collars the little man. The coat Otto had borrowed to disguise his escape from the angry strikers contains a painting stolen by his rival for the hand of Helena. Otto is absolved and wins the lady.

[LC, LP8247; *MPW* 5/20/16:1386]
Artist; Cap; Lab; Pol; Scabs; Strike
CM/ANTI-LAB

Pathé News No. 71 "The Black List" (Animated Cartoon), Pathé, Sept, Am, Comedy

This was a short animated cartoon by W. C. Morris inserted near the end of the September 2, 1916, release of Pathé's twice-weekly newsreel—subtitled: "Everything was peaceful and quiet—Until the International Katzenjammer Kid appeared on the horizon." This was one of several competing animated versions of the popular comic strip. Its title and subtitle strongly suggest a linkage to capital-labor disputes and to the I.W.W. Refer to *The Blacklist*, 1916, q.v.

[*MPW* 9/23/16:2035]
Ger; IWW?; Lab?; Viol?
NDB

Plotters and Papers, Beauty, Archer Mac-Mackin, Mar, Am, Drama

Johnny (John Sheehan) is a reporter covering a murder trial. While looking for Madam "Z," a mysterious witness who has been kidnapped, he inadvertently becomes entangled with a band of anarchists who call themselves the "Dastardly Dozen." After discovering a female member of the group who has been imprisoned by her compatriots for botching a job, Johnny is captured by the anarchists and tied to a cylindrical torture device. Following his rescue by a Secret Service agent who had been maintaining a hidden surveillance of the anarchists, Johnny locates Madam "Z" and receives a statement from her.

[*MPW* 3/18/16:1890]
Anarch; Atroc; Fem Rad; Pol; Russ?; Sec Ser; Viol
ANTI-REV

Pluck and Luck, Vim, 2r, Feb, Am, Comedy

Pokes, a plumber, is evicted from his small shop for nonpayment of rent. The local piano tuner invites him to share his store. Jabbs, Pokes' former landlord, has meanwhile incurred the wrath of two anarchist tenants of one of his homes. Mrs. Jabbs sends her pretty daughter, Ethel, to the piano tuner's. Only Pokes is in the store when she arrives. He is so smitten with Ethel that he impersonates the tuner so he can follow her home. But the anarchists arrive first at the Jabbs residence and place a time bomb in the piano. Pokes demolishes the piano, but discovers the bomb and saves the Jabbs family. Pokes and Jabbs were a comic duo played, respectively, by Robert ("Bobby") Burns and Walter Stull.

[*MPW* 2/26/16:1347]
Anarch; Bomb; Cap; Lab; Viol
ANTI-REV

The Price of Power, Fine Arts/Triangle, 5r, Jan, Am(s), Drama

A discontented cotton mill worker flees to another town, changes his name to John Roberts and rises to a management position. He eventually purchases the factory where he was originally employed and institutes a cold-hearted efficiency system (probably meant as a reference to the "scientific management" associated with Frederick W. Taylor—often referred to as Taylorism). Financial losses incurred by a strike of his desperate employees drive Roberts mad. He wanders away from the mill and joins a group of hoboes living nearby. When the scabs arrive that he had hired, John aids the strikers in resisting them. After the strike is broken, Roberts becomes a millworker again in his own factory, where he is slowly destroyed by the conditions that he had created.

[LC, LP8007; *MPN* 1/8/16:68]
Cap; Lab; Scabs; Strike; Tramp; Viol
ANTI-CAP

The Quality of Faith, Gaumont/Mutual, Richard Garrick, 5r, May, Am(s), Drama

Albert Richards, the young minister of a fashionable parish, is courting Louise Alford, the daughter of a wealthy cotton mill owner. Baker, the leader of the millhands, is rebuffed by Alford when he presents a petition to the owner requesting that the workers' hours of labor not be increased. During the resulting strike, Baker is arrested and sent to jail for inciting the workers to riot. Meanwhile, pastor Richards is dismissed from his position and his engagement with Louise broken after he publicly denounces the "inhuman conditions" at the mill. Richards takes to drink and falls under the influence of an atheist. The love of a former factory girl named Marna (a Slavic variation on Mary, as in Mary Magdalen?), whom he had aided after she was forced into a "shameful life" of prostitution, restores his faith. The evil capitalist drops dead of a heart attack. Note: The mill scenes were shot at a real cotton mill in Anniston, Alabama.

[*MPN* 5/20/16:3093; *Mot* 5/13/16:1112; *MPW* 5/6/16:1040]

Agit; Anti-Rel; Cap; Lab; Liq Link; Pol; Strike; Unemployed; Viol

PRO-LAB; ANTI-CAP

The Red Widow, Famous Players/Par, James Durkin, 5r, April, Am/Brit/Russ, Com-Drama

Cicero Hannibal Butts, an American corset salesman played by John Barrymore, is on his honeymoon in London when he becomes entangled with Russian danceuse Anna Varvara (Flora Zabelle), a notorious nihilist known as the "Red Widow." Mrs. Butts is recalled to New York due to illness in her family. Anna, who has learned that Cicero plans to continue on to Russia for business purposes, persuades the salesman to take her along as his wife, neglecting to mention that she is wanted by the Tsarist secret police. Once in Russia, Anna introduces Cicero to her nihilist associates as a dedicated bomb thrower. Lots are drawn for the privilege of blowing up the Tsar and Cicero receives the honor. A nervous Cicero quickly disposes of his bombs and then prevents Anna from hurling a similar explosive device at an official on the street. But at a subsequent nihilist meeting that is raided by the police, he is arrested. Cicero, who has been brought to the border to meet his supposed accomplice, is greatly relieved to discover Mrs. Butts. This film would appear to be a satiric version of the 1914 release, *My Official Wife*, q.v.

[LC, LU7049; *MPW* 5/6/16:982]

Artist; Bomb; Fem Rad; Nih; Russ; Sec Pol; Tsar

ANTI-REV

The Right Direction, Pallas/Par, E. Mason Hopper, 5r, Dec, Am(r), Com-Drama

Polly Eccles, a child of the slums whose father murdered her consumptive mother, decides to head for California on foot with her sickly baby brother. Along the way they are befriended by a tramp named Big Bill and a dog they call Rags. The completion of their trip is made easier after a collegian driving cross-country, Kirk Drummond, picks them up. When they reach the west coast, Kirk's father, the owner of a large mining complex, is appalled that his son has been traveling with a lower class woman. The vindictive capitalist, played by Herbert Standing, even arranges for Polly to be fired from her new job. But when his miners go out on strike and attempt to murder him, it is Polly who comes to his rescue. The old man then changes his direction, both in regards to Polly's budding romance with his son and on labor issues.

[AFI, F1.3721; *MPW* 12/30/16:1972, 2015]

Cap; Lab; Reconcil; Strike; Tramp; Viol

CAP-LAB COOP

A Sauerkraut Symphony, Kalem, 1r, Oct, Am, Comedy

This was one of nearly two hundred "Bud and Ham" one reel comedies released by Kalem between 1914 and 1916 that starred the team of Lloyd V. Hamilton (short and stout; mustache) and Bud Duncan (tall and thick-set; mustache). In this film the duo work at a sauerkraut factory whose employees strike for a "twenty-five hour day." A sauerkraut-hating anarchist named Krazy Killsky then threatens to destroy the factory. Note: Released at the time of the 1916 presidential election campaign, that featured attacks on German-Americans and so-called "hyphenism," and with a concomitant growing public concern over sabotage in the war manufacturing industries, this was a satire with a noticeable underlying topical edge.

[*MPW* 11/4/16:747]

Anarch; Ger?; Lab; Sab?; Strike

CM/ANTI-REV

The Scarlet Oath (The Other Sister), Peerless/World, Oct, Frank Powell & Travers Vale, 5r, Russ/Am/Eur, Drama

A Russian nihilist named Ivan Pavloff flees to America with his infant twin daughters, Nina and Olga, after the secret police kill his wife. Pavloff allows a wealthy childless couple that aids in establishing him in America to adopt Nina. Twenty years later Pavloff is a well-known revolutionary and writer on ni-hilism, assisted by his daughter Olga (Gail Kane, in a dual role as both adult twins). He is eventually prompted into returning to Russia to avenge the death of his wife by the offer to organize an assassination attempt upon Chief of Police Savaroff (Montagu Love). At a secret nihilist meeting in Warsaw (then located within that part of Poland controlled by the Russian empire), final details are being discussed for the killing of Savaroff when the police burst in. Savaroff suspends torture of Pavloff after Olga consents to spend the night with him. But when Olga learns that her father has died, she fatally stabs Savaroff. With the aid of Nina's fiancé, a diplomat in Warsaw who mistakes Olga for her twin sister, Olga is able to return to America. Sometime later Tsarist agents catch up with the lady nihilist kill her.

[LC, LU9394; *MPW* 10/28/16:_ _4; *MPW* 11/4/16:754; *Var* 10/13/16:25]

Atroc; Decad; Escape; Fem Rad; Nih; Russ; Sec Pol; Viol
ANTI-RS

The Secret of the Submarine, American/Mutual, May–Sept, George Sargent, 15/2r, Am, Adventure/serial

The American inventor of a submarine with a unique air intake device is plagued by assorted criminals, revolutionaries and spies. His daughter and a lieutenant in the U.S. Navy assist him through his various trials. Beginning in Chapter Four, they must deal with a Russian bomb thrower named Stephansky, the member of a "secret society" who has acquired the code books that contain the secret of the submarine.

[*MPW* 5/6/16:985; *Mot* 6/3/16:1278]
Anarch; Bomb; Russ; Spy-Sab; Viol
ANTI-REV

The Selfish Woman, Lasky/Par, E. Mason Hopper, 5r, July, Am(r), Drama

Alice Hale, whose family is financially strapped, reluctantly agrees to marry civil engineer Tom Morley (Wallace Reid). Morley's father, a wealthy banker who disapproves of Tom's work on a railroad construction project, offers Alice a million dollars to ruin Tom's railroad. Through the liberal use of money to purchase liquor, Alice and a crooked promoter named McKenzie create discord among the

workers. When the payroll is delayed a mob of workers, "crazed by drink," declare a strike and start burning down the construction camp. Alice, realizing her love for Tom, confesses her actions to the men and convinces them to return to the job.

[AFI, F1.3930; LC, LP8589; *MPN* 7/22/16: 455; *Var* 7/7/16:24]

Cap; Irish?; Lab; Liq Link; Mob; Reconcil; Sab; Strike
ANTI-CAP

The Sowers, Lasky/Par, William C. DeMille, 5r, Mar, Russ, Drama

Karin Dolokhof (Blanche Sweet) and her sweetheart, Prince Paul Alexis (Thomas Meighan), belong to the Russian League of Freedom, an underground organization bent upon freeing the peasants from the oppressive conditions existing under the Tsarist regime. When Paul, the League's leader, is ordered by the Tsar to marry Princess Tanya for "reasons of state," Karin insists that he go through with it for the good of the cause. Count Egor Strannik (Ernest Joy), a spy for the secret police and Tanya's ex-lover, convinces the lascivious princess to betray her new husband. This leads to a police raid upon a meeting of the League in which incriminating papers are seized. In a subsequent encounter between Paul and Egor, Tanya is killed, leaving Paul free to escape from Russia with Karin. The Peddler, a bearded stereotype who acts as a courier for the League, is played by Raymond Hatton. Realistic settings and costumes were used.

[S (LC, incomplete); LC, LP7853; *MPN* 4/8/16:2062–63; *MPW* 4/22/16:696]

Decad; Escape; Fem Rad; Jew?; Rev; Russ; Sec Pol; Tsar; Viol
ANTI-RS

The Suspect, Vitagraph/V-L-S-E, S. Rankin Drew, 5–6r, May, Russ/Brit/Fr, Drama

The *Variety* review stated: "[this] is the *old story* [my emphasis] of a girl whose family had been shattered by Duke Karatoff, nicknamed 'the butcher' for his cruelty to the populace, and who determines to be avenged." As a nihilist leader, a vengeful Sophie Karrinini (the popular Anita Stewart) organizes an assassination attempt in Russia upon the duke. After the bomb explodes harmlessly, the duke's son, Paul (played by the film's writer-director), chases the perpetrator to an apartment where he is knocked-out by another nihilist. Sophie decides to nurse Paul back to health rather than leave him to die. Unaware of her political affiliations, a recovered Paul proposes to Sophie and is accepted. When Paul learns his beautiful wife is a nihilist he leaves to expose her, but is ambushed and left for dead by one of her compatriots. The bomb thrower Mouroff (Edward Elkas), who had earlier attacked the duke, finds the unconscious man. Mouroff restores him to health and, discovering Paul has lost his memory, enlists him in the nihilist cause. Sophie flees Russia. Five years later, at a supposedly secret nihilist meeting in Paris, all the principals confront each other. Paul is killed, his son returns to Russia with the duke and Sophie departs for Britain with her English lover.

[LC, LP8303; *MPW* 5/20/16:1359; *Var* 5/19/16:18]

Atroc; Bomb; Decad; Escape; Fem Rad; Nih; Pol; Russ; Viol
ANTI-RS; ANTI-REV

The Thoroughbred, American/Mutual, Charles Bartlett, 5r, Jan, Am(r), Drama

Having failed in the stock market, Kelso Hamilton (dashing leading man William Russell) is prevented from marrying his sweetheart Angela Earle. Later framed for cheating in cards by the Earles' secretary, George Carewe, the now totally disgraced Hamilton heads out west to start over. Hamilton purchases a ranch and is able to make a go of it, despite some trouble with bandits. Meanwhile, the Earles have acquired a copper mine nearby, in the Santa Ynez mountains. But the unscrupulous Carewe, in league with the mine manager, has plotted to buy out the mine by stirring-up labor trouble among the Mexican miners. When the Earles visit their mine to investigate conditions, they are attacked by a frenzied mob of Mexicans. While the Earles are barricaded in the manager's home, a stray shot hits and blows up the powder house. The explosion is observed by Hamilton and some of his men, who proceed to the mine and effect a rescue. Note: During the teens, Mexican and Mexican-American workers were often mistreated and routinely disenfranchised. Ongoing tensions between the U.S. and Mexican governments following the 1910 revolution exacerbated nativist fears in the southwest. Throughout the fall of 1915 a major strike in the copper mining industry actually took place in Arizona, led

by Spanish-surnamed workers. Finally, in the month of this film's release, men under the infamous bandit leader Pancho Villa murdered sixteen Americans who had been forcibly removed from a train in Mexico.

[AFI, F1.4435; *MPN* 1/22/16:394; *MPW* 1/22/16:664]

Bomb; Cap; Lab; Mob; Sab; Strike?; Viol
ANTI-LAB

Those Who Toil, Lubin/V-L-S-E, Edgar Lewis, 5r, June, Am(r), Drama

Jane Brett (Nance O'Neil), "a daughter of the people," becomes a trained nurse. She returns to the Pennsylvania oil fields where her father works and begins to minister to the laborers' families, who live in "serf-like conditions." When her father is mortally injured on the job, an indignant Jane hastens to the city to awaken the millionaire owner of the oil fields, William Jameson (Herbert Fortier), to the injustices suffered by his workers. Jane is arrested for accosting him in the midst of a charity ball he is sponsoring to benefit The Society for the Prevention of Cruelty to Animals. After Jameson's son John secretly arranges for her release, Jane goes back to the oil fields. Along with the President of the Oil Workers' Union, Jim Morgan (John Sharkey), she agitates for a strike. Meanwhile, in order to investigate conditions, John incognito has become one of the oil workers. He and Jane fall in love. A strike is declared and the men attack the company guards in an attempt to fire the wells. Morgan, who is also in love with Jane, discovers John's true identity and leads a mob of workers to kill him. With Jane by his side, John confronts the angry strikers, convinces them he has their interests at heart and then leaves to force his father to give in to the workers' demands. *The Moving Picture World* reviewer noted: "The motives which actuate the characters in such a story are so vital to their welfare and so broad in their scope as to compel the spectator to take a firm stand upon one side or the other; the drab, unlovely lives of the humble toilers involved in the drama, demanding the sympathy of everyone who thinks and feels."

[LC, LP8792; *MPW* 7/1/16:103]

Agit; Cap; Fem Rad; Lab; Mob; Pol; Pvt Pol; Reconcil; Sab; Strike; Viol; Wrk Rel Dis/Inj
CAP-LAB COOP; PRO-LAB

Two News Items, Lubin, Edward Sloman, 1r, Jan, Am(u), Drama

The cub reporter of the *Daily Bugle* is chided by his editor for a lack of sense regarding news worthiness, pointing out that a story about a prominent person would naturally receive more lines than one about an "ordinary laborer." The reporter's first item the next day briefly notes that the body of Katie Fagan, 650 Barren alley, was found floating in the East River—"No reason was given for the suicide." Producer-director Sloman presents the rest of her story, which the reporter had "failed to write." Katie, played by Adda Gleason, had struggled to survive in the tenements with her husband Dan (Jay Morley), who worked at the factory complex of millionaire John Rockland (L.C. Shumway). But just as the couple have begun saving money for their expected first child, Rockland reduces the wages of his men by 25 percent. The resulting strike quickly impoverishes the Fagans. When Dan makes a desperate appeal to Rockland at his mansion, he is thrown out. Dan then secures a janitorial position at the Children's Outing Association, only to be callously dismissed by Rockland, its major sponsor. After Dan is arrested for sneaking into Rockland's home to secure the money owed to him, Katie is evicted from their room. Having lost the will to go on, Katie grabs the baby things she had saved and then throws herself into the river. The *Daily Bugle*'s front page headline reads: "JOHN ROCKLAND AGAIN CONTRIBUTES TO CHILDREN'S OUTING ASSN. Noted Philanthropist Gives Check for $50,000. Ten Thousand Children to be Made Happy by Week in Country." Note: The Rockland character was most likely intended to be yet another negative caricature of John D. Rockefeller.

[*MPW* 1/22/16:654]
Cap; Lab; Irish; Pol; Strike; Viol
ANTI-CAP

The Voice Upstairs, IMP, Herbert Brenon, 1r, Nov, Am, Drama

This so-called "Special Release" was a reissue of *The Anarchist* (IMP; 1913), q.v. The slightly different description which identifies the girlfriend (Leah Baird), rather than her jealous suitor, as the betrayer of her anarchist lover (King Baggot), suggests that the inter-titles were probably altered.

[LC, LP9404; *MPW* 11/11/16:909]
Anarch; Bomb; Pol
NDB

The Wages of Sin ("Beatrice Fairfax" series, #11), Theodore & Leo Wharton, Wharton/International Film Ser, Oct, Am, Drama, 2r

Beatrice Fairfax, played by Grace Darling, is an adventurous newspaper woman. She is assisted by her reporter boyfriend, the happy-go-lucky Jimmy (Harry Fox). Jane Hamlin, a young lady who lives on Madison Ave, finds a letter among the papers of her deceased inventor father instructing her to remove a certain box from his safe and to throw it in the ocean. Jane finds the rectangular box with three numbered buttons and a note attached: "Don't Touch! Loaded with Poison Gas." But then Clayton Boyd (Nigel Barrie), her slick-haired boyfriend, walks in. While the two lovers are on the couch in a now darkened room they spot a mysterious man on the balcony—Jane exits to phone the police, while Clayton hides. Sverdrup, a black bearded anarchist with a gun, stealthily enters and starts for the safe. Clayton grabs the gun and demands an explanation. The radical stereotype, who also wears a black hat, declares the box he seeks is "the only perfect infernal machine," and then offers the young man a $1000 to help him obtain it. Their various attempts to frighten Jane into relinquishing the box lead to her requesting the assistance of Beatrice. Yet after Beatrice and Jimmy successfully foil the two men, several of the anarchist's companions burst into Jane's home and seize the device. But Jimmy has secretly armed it by pressing button number three. The anarchists have just enough time to return to their hideout before the box explodes. Note: The introduction of poison gas with the traditional anarchist bomb was obviously influenced by the lethal use of such gases by the World War belligerents.

[S (LC, incomplete); LC, LP9465; *MPW* 11/11/16:915]
Anarch; Bomb; Pol; Russ?; Viol
ANTI-REV

War Brides, Herbert Brenon/Selznick, Herbert Brenon, 8r, Nov, Rur, War Drama

In an imaginary European kingdom, read Germany, Joan (Russian born stage actress Alla Nazimova in her film debut) has achieved stature in her community as a labor activist who successfully organized a strike for higher wages. At a victory picnic for the workers, Joan meets Franz, her future husband. When war is later declared, Franz and his three brothers are drafted. Following a great battle, the now pregnant Joan learns that she is a widow and that all her husband's brothers were also killed. With casualties continuing to mount, the King decrees that single young women should marry soldiers departing for the front. Joan's mourning is ended and her activist spirit is reawakened. After escaping the prison where she was incarcerated for her militant pacifism, Joan leads a demonstration of women who intercept the King's motorcade as it visits their village — vowing not to bear children if the war continues. When the king dismisses the women's entreaties, Joan shoots herself. The other women lift up their martyr and renew their vow. A tongue-in-cheek comment by *The Moving Picture World* reviewer is worth quoting: "The Joan of Nazimova, in her fierce resentment of the war brides decree and her out-spoken determination that she and her sex in general shall rear no more children to become food for cannon, belongs to the band of social firebrands [in film] that have been exiled, imprisoned or executed in the cause of Nihilism." Note: The film was released right after the 1916 election campaign, during which the debate between the advocates of pacifism and preparedness had reached a crescendo. The Joan character, as a symbol of the anti-war spirit, may thus have been partially based upon Kate Richards O'Hare (1877–1948). "Red Kate" was a nationally recognized spokesperson for the Socialist Party and leading figure in the peace movement, who had run for the U.S. Senate in Missouri. This financially successful film was withdrawn after America's April 1917 entrance into the war, but then quickly rereleased by producer Selznick after the insertion of new titles that placed the action in Germany.

[LC, LP9585; *MPN* 11/25/16:3331, 12/9/16:3654; *MPW* 12/2/16:1343–44; *Photoplay* 12/16:47–54 & 142–44]

Agit; Cap; Fem Rad; Ger?; Lab; Pac; Soc?; Strike; Viol

PAC; PRO-LAB

What Love Can Do, Universal/Red Feather, Jay Hunt, 5r, June, Am(s), Drama

Calvert Page (C. Norman Hammond) is the wealthy owner of a newspaper, as well as a number of western mines. His mistress, the independent Lil Magill, is a respected newspaper woman and the author of several books. Page's greed has led to discontent among his miners. They engage a lawyer, "Brad" Hamilton, to present their appeals. But Page refuses to listen to Brad and so the miners go out on strike. When a miner is killed in a subsequent riot, his embittered compatriots vow vengeance. Meanwhile, Lil has championed the miners' cause, contributing to a growing estrangement from Page. A mob of strikers, led by Tony (Italian?; played by Harry Mann), attacks Page's home. Tony breaks through the guards and is about to shoot Page when Lil throws herself in front of her lover, saving his life.

[LC, LP8321; *MPN* 6/10/16:3598; *MPW* 6/17/16:2099]

Cap; Ital?; Lab; Mob; Pvt Pol; Strike; Viol
ANTI-CAP; ANTI-LAB

The Yellow Passport, Shubert/World, Edwin August, 5r, Feb, Russ/Am, Drama

Sonia Sokoloff (Clara Kimball Young) is the beautiful opera-singing daughter of a Jewish family in Kiev. When Sonia repulses the sexual advances of their valet, Fedia, who actually is a Russian police spy, he swears allegiance to the anti-Semitic Black Hundred and incites a bloody nighttime pogrom. The entire Sokoloff family is killed, except for Sonia and her uncle. Sonia is ordered to leave Russia. In order to continue her voice lessons, she applies for a "yellow passport," which marks her as a fallen woman, but allows her to stay in the country. Sonia and her uncle finally decide to leave Russia and sail for America, after being harassed by Fedia, now a police inspector. In the United States, Sonia becomes a famous opera star and is engaged to be married. Her happiness is threatened by Fedia, who arrives in the United States and threatens to expose her alleged sordid past. All ends happily for Sonia when Fedia "meets a horrible death at the hands of the nihilists." This film was rereleased by World in March 1917 under the title, *The Badge of Shame*. [LC, LU10398] Note: A 1918 German version of this story, directed by Victor Janson and starring Pola Negri, was entitled *Der Gelbe Schein* (*The Yellow Ticket*).

[AFI, F1.5159; LC, LU7630; *MPN* 2/12/16: 878; *MPW* 3/25/16:2090; *Var* 2/14/16:28]

Artist; Atroc; Decad; Escape; Jew; Nih; Russ; Sec Pol; Viol
ANTI-RS

1917

The Barker, Selig/K-E-S-E, J. A. Richmond, 5r, Aug, Eur/Am, Drama

Leo Fielding, a language professor at King's University, reluctantly attends an anarchists meeting with his brother. Led by the Count DeGrasse, the black-robed members of the "secret society" draw for the black ball that will determine who will "remove" the prince of the country. A police raid leads to Leo's banishment. In America, a disillusioned Leo becomes a circus barker. Several years later he is reunited with his daughter, now an aerialist. Fielding was played by Lew Fields, best known as the partner of Joe Weber—the famous Broadway comedy team of Weber & Fields.

[LC, LP11228; *MPN* 9/1/17:1489; *MPW* 8/25/17:1230, 1265]

Anarch; Pol
ANTI-REV

Birth Control (The New World), B. S. Moss Motion Picture Corp, April, Am(u), Bio/Doc 5r

Outspoken birth control advocate Margaret Sanger (1879–1966), who had close links with the socialist and suffragette movements between 1910 and 1916 (including helping to organize the evacuation of workers' children during the Lawrence strike), played herself in this film in order to promote her cause and to neutralize her reputation as a political radical. With many real-life scenes of overcrowded slums inserted, Mrs. Sanger espouses her then revolutionary theories on family planning. The dramatic portion of the film centers around the tragic story of a poor woman named Helen Field who died from complications following a self-induced abortion. By relating this purportedly true story to her own struggle with the authorities to publicly discuss sexual issues and to operate birth control clinics in poor neighborhoods, Margaret Sanger makes a strong argument for the legal dissemination of birth control information. In an attempt to make the film "censorproof" it was provided with alternate advertising material under the title, *The New World*. It would appear that lit-

tle or no mention of Mrs. Sanger's former close associations with the Socialist movement, including her controversial column on sexual matters in *The Call*, "What Every Woman Should Know," was made in the film. Likewise, it can be assumed that the significant role played by radical socialist/anarchist Emma Goldman in advocating family planning was also ignored. In an apparent attempt to make *Birth Control* even more palatable to middle-class audiences, and in light of growing antagonism towards so-called "hyphenated" Americans as the United States entered the first World War, the name of the woman who died from septicemia was changed from Sadie Sachs (German-Jew) to the Anglicized Helen Field. Nevertheless, this film was attacked by the New York State License Commissioner, George Bell, for promoting class hatred. Note: Arrested on several occasions during the teens under New York's Comstock Act for operating a birth control facility in Brooklyn, Sanger was finally allowed to open her first legal clinic in 1923. Ironically, by the mid-twenties Sanger, had totally disassociated herself from the left, justifying birth control not only as a means of limiting unwanted pregnancies, but also as a method by which to purify the world's population.

[AFI, F1.0335; *MPW* 4/21/17:451; *Var* 4/13/17:27]

Cap; Fem Rad; Lab; Pol; Soc?
PRO-LAB

The Bottom of the Well, Vitagraph, John Robertson, 5r, Oct, Jamaica/Brit(r), Drama

A radical organization of mill workers called "The Well" has their headquarters situated behind the bar of a saloon. They plot to blow up the mansion of Amos Buckingham (Bigelow Cooper), their millionaire employer, after a workman's son is struck and killed by the chauffeur driven automobile of the heartless man. But, unknown to anyone, Buckingham has disguised himself in order to be able to join The Well and to study the working conditions of his employees. Following an explosion on the estate, the discovery of a charred body believed to be Buckingham's results in murder charges against all members of The Well. Upon the conviction of these men, Buckingham comes forward and discloses that the remains belonged to a cadaver disfigured by an accidental explosion that occurred while he

was conducting an experiment at his laboratory. With everyone acquitted, capital and
labor are reconciled. The Well's leader, who
has fallen in love with Buckingham's daughter (played by Agnes Ayres), is even welcomed
as a son-in-law by the humbled mill owner.

> [LC, LP11583; *MPW* 11/3/17:707]
> Cap; Lab; Liq Link; Reconcil; Rev; Viol
> CAP-LAB COOP

Breaking the Family Strike, Victor, Matt
Moore, 1r, May, Am(u), Comedy

Mrs. Carter joins the Wives' Union following an argument with her husband. When
Mr. Carter (Matt Moore) refuses to agree to
her typewritten "demands," she strikes and
goes home to mother. Mr. Carter calls a strikebreakers' agency that sends him Dolly Dimples, a little blonde from a burlesque troupe.
The wife returns, expecting her husband to capitulate. Instead, she discovers that Mr. Carter
is quite content with her young replacement.
Mr. Carter is forced to call in the local cop to
restore order in the house after his wife loses
her control and becomes embroiled in a vigorous hair-pulling bout with Dolly. The domestic analogy of capital vs. labor had been
done before on film, e.g., *When Women Strike*
(Lubin; 1911), q.v.

> [LC, LP10663; *MPW* 5/19/17:1173–74]
> Fem Rad; Lab; Pol; Scabs; Strike; Viol
> CM/ANTI-LAB

A Bundle of Trouble, Nestor, Louis Wm.
Chandet, 1r, Mar, Am, Comedy

The Russian ambassador is warned there
may be an attempt upon his life. Olga, his
daughter, prevails upon the ambassador to engage the celebrated Detective Potts. Potts and
Eddie, his assistant, proceed to the ambassador's residence. Along the way the two find
an abandoned bundle that they suspect is a
bomb. When they arrive, the detectives and
Olga are horrified to see the ambassador about
to drink from a bottle presented to him by three
mysterious men. After rushing up to the ambassador, they are informed the men are pro-
moters of a vodka substitute, and have re-
quested the diplomat's opinion of their
product. Eddie then opens the bundle, only to
discover that it contains a pair of silk stockings.
Potts and Eddie were played by the famous
comedy team of Lee Moran and Eddie Lyons.

> [*MPN* 3/10/17:1576; *MPW* 3/10/17:1662]

Bomb; Dom Rad?; Pvt Pol; Russ
ANTI-REV

By Right of Possession, Vitagraph, William
Wolbert, 5r, July, Am(r), Western

By the death of her father, Kate Saxon
(Mary Anderson) becomes the owner of the
Blue Goose mine in Colorado. She arrives at
the mine in the midst of a battle between rioting strikers, agitated by a "sleek delegate from
Denver" (United Mine Workers?) named Trimble, and a sheriff's posse. Kate resolves the dispute by granting the miners higher wages and
reducing the rent of their company owned
homes. A romance soon develops between Tom
Baxter (Antonio Moreno), a wealthy rancher
who is the sheriff, and the independent Kate.
They will later become estranged though, as a
result of a misunderstanding following *her*
winning of the local election for sheriff. But
Kate and Tom are literally returned to each others' arms during a cattle stampede started after
a disgruntled Trimble dynamites a nearby dam.

> [LC, LP11143; *MPN* 8/11/17:1021; *Var*
> 8/17/17:30]
> Agit; Bomb; Cap; Lab; Pol; Sab; Strike;
> Viol
> ANTI-LAB

The Car of Chance, Bluebird, William Worthington, 5r, July, Am(u), Com-Drama

Arnold Baird's (played by the 41-year-old
Franklyn Farnum) wealthy father dies, be-
queathing him only a seven passenger auto and
a hundred dollars. Arnold's romantic rival is
head of the Consolidated Trolley Company.
When an Irish union leader and a labor agitator named Israel Heimstone (German-Jew?) instigate a streetcar strike, Arnold steps into the
public transportation breech. With the aid of
some friends, he gathers a fleet of jitney buses
and organizes the Social Rapid Transit Company. Even after strikebreakers start the trol-
leys rolling again, the public prefers the jitneys. Arnold is made a general manager of
Consolidated and wins back his girl. Note:
During the first two decades of the century
there were hundreds of streetcar strikes. A prolonged and bitter strike occurred in Wilkes-
Barre, Pennsylvania, between April 1915 and the
spring of 1916. There was also a major streetcar strike in New York City during the latter
half of 1916 during which the transit executives
had publicly denounced the strikers for being

led by "alien" union organizers. Many so-called "tin lizzie" entrepreneurs took paying passengers in their converted cars, called jitneys.

[LC, LP10875; *MPN* 7/21/17:435; *MPW* 7/21/17:474, 538]

Agit; Cap; Irish; Jew?; Lab; Scabs; Strike
PRO-CAP; ANTI-LAB

Courage of the Commonplace, Edison, Ben Turbett, 5r, Nov, Am(r), Drama

A young college graduate, Johnny McLean (Leslie Austin), goes west to become the superintendent of a mine owned by his father. The local labor agitator and head foreman at the Oriel mine is a hard-drinking Irishman named Terence O'Hara (Ben La Mar). Despite Johnny's obvious goodwill, O'Hara presses the workers gathered at the saloon ("where all the trouble originated") to strike if their terms are not met. When Johnny temporizes during a meeting with the workers' committee at his office, O'Hara cautions the men to be wary of the "capitalist's word." On the day the strike is to begin, O'Hara and his work gang are trapped in the mine by a natural explosion. Johnny's determined rescue efforts both save the men and eliminate all support for the planned strike.

[S (LC); LC, LP11672; *MPN* 11/24/17:3663]

Agit; Cap; Irish; Lab; Liq Link; Reconcil; Strike
ANTI-LAB; CAP-LAB COOP

Darkest Russia, Peerless/World, Travers Vale, 5r, April, Russ, Drama

Thanya Lowenberg (Alice Brady) is a Jewish violin student in the Russian empire, who has grown to despise "all autocratic governments" following an incident during which several drunken Tsarist officers accosted her and then brutally murdered her father. Her brother Felix is a writer, "whose idealism is being slowly turned to revolutionism, through the oppression of his people." Felix, who after joining the nihilists begins writing articles in their pamphlet, *The Forward Cry*, falls in love with Olga Kalnoky, the daughter of the Minister of Police (played by J. Herbert Frank). They secretly marry. Meanwhile, Thanya and Ferdinand Mutkourf, the son of a high official, become sweethearts. The parents of Olga and Ferdinand arrange the betrothal of their children without consulting them. When Thanya refuses to lead the orchestra in playing "God

Save the Tsar" (Russia's anthem since 1833) at the reception announcing this engagement she is tied to a post and lashed before the assembled royalists. After a raid upon a nihilist meeting at her home, Thanya and Ferdinand are sent to Siberia. Six months later the two are about to be shot for attempting to escape when Ferdinand's father arrives with a pardon. Note: All *printed* sources list a different set of names for the cast, such as Ilda Barosky instead of Thanya Lowenberg.

[S (LC, incomplete); LC, LU10617; *EH* 4/28/17:25; *Var* 4/13/17:25]

Artist; Atroc; Decad; Fem Rad?; Jew; Nih; Russ; Sec Pol; Siberia; Tsar; Viol
ANTI-RS

A Daughter of the Poor, Fine Arts/Triangle, Edward Dillon, 5r, Mar, Am(u), Com-Drama

Rose Eastman (Jew?), a teenaged orphan played by the petite Bessie Love, lives in the slums with her uncle. Because of her poverty, she is easily influenced by the neighborhood socialist, Rudolph Creig (German?), who is writing a book attacking the evils of capitalism. Rose meets Jack Stevens, the son of the publisher for whom her uncle works as a janitor. Because she met him while he was fixing his car engine, she assumes Jack is a fellow proletariat and allows him to court her. The relationship having altered her class perspective, Rose is invited to the Stevens home. A jealous Rudolph storms into the house to protect Rose from capitalist manipulations. But Rudolph's attitude is abruptly changed when he is informed that the elder Stevens has decided to publish his book. Released about a month before the United States entered the war, this was one of the last American feature films until the early 1930s that would sympathetically portray a domestic radical. The plot of the 1913 release, *The Benefactor*, q.v., is somewhat similar.

[AFI, F1.0943; *MPW* 3/24/17:1949; *Var* 3/23/17:24]

Cap; Ger?; Jew?; Lab; Soc
PRO-CAP

Draft 258, Metro, William Christy Cabanne, 7r, Nov, Am, Drama

Mary Alden (Mabel Tallaferro, the "Sweetheart of American Movies") and her two brothers, George and Matthew, whose deceased father was a hero of the Battle of San Juan Hill, develop substantial differences on patriotism upon America's entry into World

War I. Elder brother Matthew is a socialist who denounces the impending draft at pacifist meetings. Observed addressing such a crowd by a German agent and his anarchist butler, Matthew is easily duped into aiding the cause of the enemy. On the day the draft is implemented (July 20, 1917) Matthew is again attacking it at a socialist meeting (the Socialist Party was the only national organization to formally condemn American participation in the war; the Espionage Act of June 1917 made it a crime to obstruct enlistment) when his sister jumps up on the speaker's platform and delivers a patriotic speech. Matthew, as well as most the rest of the crowd, is converted by his sister's eloquence. When she is later kidnapped by the angered German agents Matthew is moved to take action against their plans to sabotage an airplane factory. Brother George, now in uniform, and Mary's soldier sweetheart bring down the forces of good upon the agents of evil. Erich von Stroheim plays a non-credited role. The highly symbolic victory of TR's Rough Riders during the Spanish-American War had been featured earlier in a short film starring Tom Mix, *Up San Juan Hill* (Selig, 1910). For an alternate view of women's attitudes toward war, refer to *War Brides* (Herbert Brenon/Selznick, 1916), q.v. Note: *Number 258* was the first number drawn in the lottery to prioritize eligibility to be called-up by the army under the United States' new Selective Service Act—signed into law on May 18, 1917. During his June 1917 Flag Day speech, President Wilson condemned the anti-war movement as treasonous and stigmatized its members as conscious agents or unwitting tools of Germany. Initially, a significant number of draft age men failed to register or filed for exemptions after complying with the conscription law. There would be over a hundred instances of soldiers breaking up socialist meetings in the year following America's entrance into the war.

[LC, LU11272; *MPW* 12/15/17:1644, 1682; *Var* 2/8/18:39]

Am Icons; Anarch; Atroc; Bomb; Decad; Ger; Ital; Lab; Mtg; Pac; Sab; Sec Ser; Soc; Spy-Sab; Viol
ANTI-REV

Fanatics, Triangle, Raymond B. Wells, 5r, Dec, Am(u), Drama

Mary Lathrop (Adda Gleason), who mistakenly believes that wealthy steel mill owner Nicholas Eyre was responsible for her worthless husband's death, secretly plots revenge. Mary secures a position at the mills as Eyre's secretary, where she becomes entangled with a group of anarchists, led by the "wild-eyed" Professor Groesbeck (German linkage?; played by a regular teens heavy, William V. Mong). In league with the anarchists, a "sinuous" Mary helps to foment a strike among the steel workers. But when she is informed that the anarchists are preparing to destroy the plant, Mary hastens to the mill and convinces the men that they have been misled. The fleeing Groesbeck is killed when he falls into a cauldron of molten steel. Mary, having learned that she misjudged Eyre, willingly accepts his forgiveness and love.

[*MPN* 12/22/17:4403; *MPW* 12/15/17:1644]

Agit; Anarch; Cap; Fem Rad; Ger?; Lab; Reconcil; Sab; Strike; Viol
ANTI-REV; PRO-CAP

The Fires of Youth, Thanhouser/Pathé, Emile Chautard, 5r, June, Am(s), Drama

Called "Iron Hearted" by his workers because he refused to make safety improvements in his factories, steel magnate Peter Pemberton (Shakespearean tragedian Frederick Warde) suddenly decides to attempt to recapture the childhood joys that he had denied himself while relentlessly pursuing wealth. Under the assumed name of "Peter Brown" the old man returns to the mill town in which he grew up and becomes friendly with little Billy (the curly-haired Helen Badgley; a precocious child actress, also known as "The Thanhouser Kidlet"), the son of one of the factory employees. While living with Billy's family, Pemberton secures a position as a millhand in his own factory. His eyes opened to the unsafe conditions and dissatisfaction of the workers, Pemberton leaves to draw-up improvement plans. Billy, worried that his absent friend will be discharged, goes to the mill in his place and is badly burned by an explosion. The infuriated workers call a meeting and draw lots to determine who shall kill the owner. Pemberton draws the fatal card and is about to commit suicide in the woods when Billy's sister, played by the legendary Jeanne Eagles, intervenes. Pemberton is forgiven by his men after confessing his true identity and pledging to correct factory conditions.

[PE (BFI, incomplete); AFI, F1.1356; *MPN* 6/16/17:3794; *MPW* 6/23/17:1993]

Cap; Lab; Reconcil; Wrk Rel Dis/Inj
CAP-LAB COOP

The Flying Target, Cub, Milton H. Fahrney, 1r, Mar, Am, Com-Advent

Popular series character Jerry (played by the undersized George Ovey) is traveling out west when he is given five dollars by a couple of I.W.W.s to deliver a package to the local police station. When the building explodes immediately after he departs, Jerry decides to appropriate a motorcycle and flee the scene. But the real trouble begins for Jerry outside of town after he is waylaid by outlaw Bad Bill and forced to exchange the bandit's horse, known as the Flying Target, for his stolen motorcycle.

[*MPW* 3/10/17:1666]

Bomb; IWW; Pol; Viol
CM/ANTI-REV

The Girl and the Crisis, Un/Red Feather, William V. Mong, 5r, Feb, Am(s), Drama

Rioting workers attack the Wilmot plant, blowing up the powder house. Both capital and labor appeal to the governor to send the militia to restore order. When he fails to do this, he is assassinated by a radical named Poole. Oliver Barnitz, the Lieutenant Governor, accedes to the governorship. The remainder of the film centers around the moral and political dilemma Barnitz faces over whether or not to commute Poole's death sentence. His fiancée, Ellen Wilmot (Dorothy Davenport), convinces him to make the humane decision.

[LC, LP10231; *MPN* 3/3/17:1422; *MPW* 3/3/17:1372, 1405]

Bomb; Cap; Dom Rad; Lab; Militia; Sab; Viol
ANTI-REV

Hearts Afire, World, James Young, 4–5r, Jan, Russ, Drama

Re-release of *Hearts in Exile*, 1915, q.v.
[LC, LU9905; *MPN* 1/13/17:273]
Escape; Nih; Russ; Sec Pol; Siberia; Viol
ANTI-RS

The Hidden Spring, Yorke/Metro, E. Mason Hopper, 5r, July, Am(s), Drama

Copper City is a western mining town owned and ruled with an iron hand by Quartus Hembly. A friendly young lawyer named Donald Keith (Harold Lockwood) arrives in town and shelters the town drunk, Daniel

Kerston. After Hembly learns of this and brutally kicks Keith's dog, a hidden spring of resistance is awakened in the lawyer, who then declares war upon the heartless capitalist. Keith subsequently arouses the townspeople to take Hembly to court following his discovery that Kerston is the actual owner of the mining properties. Hembly's control over the court system leads to his acquittal, but so enrages the citizens of Copper City that a mob seizes him with the intention of beating him to death. Keith saves Hembly, allowing him to leave town after confessing his assorted misdeeds.

[AFI, F1.1949; LC, LP11104; *MPW* 8/11/17:956]

Cap; Lab; Mob; Viol
ANTI-CAP

The High Sign, Universal, Elmer Clifton, 5r, Dec, Am/Rur, Fantasy

Donald Bruce (Herbert Rawlinson), a college man, has learned little else at school other than some of the high signs of his fraternity. After being expelled, Donald has a dream in which he is impersonating his roommate, the self-styled socialist prince of Burgonia, who has been ordered back to his homeland. Upon his arrival in Burgonia, the "Prince" has a close encounter with anarchists. Fortunately for him, the leader of the anarchists recognizes Donald's high sign. The phone awakens Donald, with an urgent message from his girlfriend.

[LC, LP11869; *MPW* 1/5/18:92]

Anarch; Rev; Soc
ANTI-REV

The Iron Heart, Astra/Pathé, George Fitzmaurice, 5r, May, Am(u), Drama

Stephen Martin (Edwin Arden) lives lavishly in a mansion while treating his employees harshly, ruling his iron mills like a dictator. He is equally insensitive to his family. When Martin refuses the workers' demands for higher wages, a strike is called. His disinherited son, Tom, tries unsuccessfully to quell the men's anger. One night a mob of workers go on a rampage and burn the factory to the ground. Martin is ruined, but he is morally restored through the love of his family.

[LC, LU10645; *MPN* 5/26/17:3311; *MPW* 6/2/17:1499]

Cap; Lab; Mob; Sab; Strike; Viol
ANTI-CAP

The Lash of Power, Bluebird, Harry L. Salter, 5r, Nov, Am, Fantasy-Drama

John Rand (Kenneth Harlan), a small-town youth who admires Napoleon, falls asleep over a book about his hero and dreams of becoming a powerful capitalist. Having developed and sold a new explosive to a foreign country at war, he makes a fortune on the stock market. Using his financial power, the unsophisticated Rand dabbles in "society" and then attempts to ruin some members of the upper class who have snubbed him. After someone tries to kill him, Rand is awakened from his dream when an anarchist's bomb destroys his mansion.

[LC, LP11545; *MPW* 11/17/17:1034; *Var* 11/9/17:54]

Anarch; Bomb; Cap; Viol
ANTI-REV

One Kind of Wireless, Edison, Saul Harrison, 1r, Sept, Am(r), Drama

Tony, an Italian railroad worker discharged for drunkenness, loiters about the station. When the Irish track foreman chases him off, Tony decides to seek revenge. During the lunch break he sows "the seeds of discord among the other laborers" by telling them that the boss is planning to fire the entire track gang. The foreign-looking mob of workers goes out on strike and locks the foreman in a cabin. Tony then incites the men to sabotage the tracks in order to prevent "strike breakers" from taking their place. Jack, the teenaged son of the wireless operator, comes to the foreman's assistance. Note: Italian immigrants, often associated with radical syndicalism, dominated track gangs at this time. Any labor interruption of rail service during the war was looked upon by most Americans as tantamount to treason.

[S (LC); LC, LP11533]

Irish; Ital; Lab; Liq Link; Mob; Sab; Scabs; Strike; Viol
ANTI-LAB

One Law For Both, Ivan Film Prods, Ivan Abramson, 8r, May, Russ/Am, Drama

To secure the release of her revolutionary brother from a Tsarist prison, Elga Pulaski (Polish?) sacrifices her virtue to a Russian governor. Brother and sister sail to America, where Elga finds fulfillment as the wife of Norman Hutchison. Norman learns of Elga's "vile" past and orders her to leave their house. The intervention of Norman's sister, played by Leah Baird, saves the marriage—she reminds him of the wise counsel he had given her following the revelation that her husband had fathered an illegitimate child.

[LC, LU11038; *Var* 5/4/17:26; *Wid's* 5/10/17:296–97]

Decad; Escape; Rev; Russ
ANTI-RS

Panthea, Norma Talmadge Film/Selznick, Allan Dwan, 5r, Jan, Russ/Brit/Fr, Drama

Panthea Romoff (Norma Talmadge) escapes from the Russian secret police to Britain after being implicated in the nihilist activities of her brother. A brilliant concert pianist, she meets and marries an English composer, played by the handsome Earle Foxe. They travel to France, but the husband becomes increasingly melancholic when the opera he has composed is not produced. To preserve her husband's sanity, Panthea submits to the "full-blooded proposal" of an elderly Russian nobleman who is influential in music circles. When Panthea's husband learns of what she has done, he scorns her. In despair, she kills the decadent Russian baron. Panthea is arrested by the Tsarist secret police and sent into exile. After Panthea's husband discovers the true motive for her "sacrifice," he follows her to Siberia. With a presumably prewar setting, this was one of the last films in the Nihilist genre. A Russian police lieutenant is played by Erich von Stroheim. *Panthea* was rereleased in 1920.

[AFI, F1.3351; LC, LP9961; *MPW* 1/6/17:26, 139; *MPW* 7/31/20:622; *Var* 1/12/17:26]

Artist; Decad; Escape; Nih; Russ; Sec Pol; Siberia; Viol
ANTI-RS

Patria (No. 8, "Red Night"), Pathé, Leopold Wharton, Jan–April, 15 eps serial/2r, Am(u), Advent

As heiress to America's largest munitions-manufacturing plant and an ardent preparedness advocate, Patria Channing (Irene Castle) faces a series of challenges created by a nefarious alliance between Japanese and Mexican foreign agents. A strike among alien workers at her factories is fomented by the foreign agents and their hired agitators (begun during Episode #7). Baron Huroki (Warner Oland) furnishes the strikers with weapons, but the armed mob is quelled by loyal workers under the leadership of the Channing enterprises' management. After bravely conferring with strike representatives, Channing accedes to their demands on two conditions—that the workers undertake military training, at her expense, and that they renounce all associations with Huroki and his Mexican associate, De Lima. Later, Huroki leaks information related to the foreign agents' plans to blow up munitions stores awaiting shipment at the Black Tom docks in New York, hoping to kill Channing when she attempts to prevent the plot. In the final episode, "For the Flag," the heroine helps rout an invasion of the United States by the military forces of Japan and Mexico! Note: During the period of this serial's release a major "punitive expedition" by American military forces under General Pershing was in Mexico attempting to destroy the forces of Pancho Villa. *German* machinations in Mexico, as revealed in the Zimmermann telegram, led directly to the United States' entrance into World War I on April 2, 1917.

[PE (MOMA); LC, LU10442; *MPW* 3/10/17:1676]

Agit; Am Icons; Cap; Lab; Militia; Reconcil; Sab; Spy-Sab; Strike; Viol
CAP-LAB COOP

The Perils of the Secret Service (Adventure No. 3—"The Dreaded Tube"), IMP, 9 part series/2r, Mar (–Nov), Am, Advent

A member of an anarchist society called the "Red Brotherhood" has been sentenced to death for a "dynamiting outrage." The anarchist leader, who sells opium out of a curio shop in Chinatown, plans to release a vial (the "dreaded tube") containing the bubonic plague into the New York City reservoir if his compatriot is executed. Secret Service agents Yorke Norroy and Carson Huntley uncover the plan and, with the help of a drug-addicted secretary to the governor, are able to foil the anarchists. In several scenes, Norray is disguised as a Russian to combat the conspirators.

[*MPW* 3/24/17:1983]

Anarch; Bomb; Decad; Ital?; Russ; Sec Ser; Viol
ANTI-REV

The Raggedy Queen, Bluebird, Theodore Marston, 5r, Dec, Am(s), Drama

Raised by "crazy Anne" to believe she is the daughter of a queen, little Tatters regales the other children in the coal mining town of Oresville with her fantasies. Lem Braxton, a drunkard, has been stirring-up labor trouble in the mines. When a strike is declared, David Grant, secretary to the mine owner, is sent to negotiate with the workers. Braxton employs violent means in various attempts to prevent a settlement. Tatters comes to the rescue. It turns out that she is the daughter of the owner, whose late wife was an actress who appeared in royal roles.

[LC, LP11682; *MPN* 12/15/17:4222 & 4223; *MPW* 12/15/17:1641, 1678]

Agit; Cap; Lab; Liq Link; Strike; Viol
ANTI-LAB

Rasputin, The Black Monk, World, Arthur Ashley, 7–8r, Oct, Russ, Drama

The lascivious mystic Gregory Novik, later known as Rasputin (Montagu Love), is despised by his fellow villagers. After he accosts the local revolutionary leader's wife, he then betrays the cuckolded husband to the secret police. Assuming the guise of a monk, Rasputin travels to St. Petersburg. He acquires great power when the royal family is led to believe that his hypnotic talents helped save the life of the young Tsaravitch (a hemophiliac; Alexei was born in 1904). The corruption of the court by Rasputin is portrayed as the leading cause contributing to the peoples' discontent with the regime. When Rasputin attempts to arrange a "separate peace" with the Germans during the World War, he is murdered by the revolutionary whom he had earlier betrayed (actually assassinated in December 1916 by a group of conservative members of the Duma during a dinner party at Prince Felix Youssoupoff's home). Alexander Kerensky, the real-life Duma member who went on to lead the provisional government following the Tsar's abdication in March, is portrayed by actor Henry Hull. Yet, most of the members of the Romanoff family are given names in the film that are historically inaccurate. For instance, the Tsar is called Andre instead of Nicholas. *Rasputin* was a special film presentation produced by World's president, William A. Brady. Note: Born in 1871, the womanizing Rasputin had increasing influence over the Tsar's family (particularly the Tsarina) after 1906.

[LC, LU11502; *MPN* 9/29/17:2161; *Var* 9/14/17:35]

Decad; Ger; Rasputin; Rev; Russ; Sec Pol; Tsar; Viol; White Russ

ANTI-RS

The Rose of Blood, Fox, J. Gordon Edwards, 5r, Nov, Russ/Switz, Drama

Although she has filled his dead wife's place in "everything but name," Prince Arbassoff refuses to marry Lisza Tapenko (Theda Bara), his son's governess. Her former lover convinces her to go to Switzerland and join a revolutionary group. After the Prince is persuaded by his son to bring Lisza home and marry her, she continues to assassinate government officials for the cause—leaving a red rose on the body of each victim—which would also have created an associative linkage for the contemporary audience with Theda Bara's persona, her 1915 signature "vampire" performance in Fox's *A Fool There Was* concluding with the vamp crushing the petals from a giant rose over the corpse of her male victim. Ordered to kill the Prince for his collusion with the Germans, Lisza remains true both to Russia and her marriage vows by dying with the Prince when she dynamites their villa. Based upon a reading of the script, it would appear that this late November release was altered as a result of the Bolshevik revolution. For in the script, *Republican* troops arrive at the destroyed home and congratulate Lisza. That contemporaries were highly cognizant of the film's political bias is made clear by the following comment made in the *Motion Picture News* review: "Dealing with a section of Europe that is now more than ever in the public eye and favoring the masses as against the aristocracy of the Russia *that was* [my emphasis] *The Rose of Blood* seems certain of finding favor." The cast credits include a "Revolutionist" played by Hector V. Sarno, who would later appear in similar roles in such films as *A Little Sister of Everybody* (1918) and *The Right To Happiness* (1919), q.v. Note: Many Russian political émigrés resided in Geneva. Lenin and other Bolsheviks lived in Zurich, Switzerland during the 1914–17 period.

[AFI, F1.3780; LC, LP11670(s); *MPN* 11/24/17:36655; *MPW* 11/24/17:1232]

Bomb; Decad; Fem Rad; Ger; Rev; Russ; Sec Pol; Tsar; Viol

ANTI-RS

The Royal Pauper, Edison, Ben Turbett, 5r, Feb, Am(s), Drama

Irene, a pretty adolescent played by Francine Larrimore, lives in the poorhouse. She escapes its harsh realities by enacting fairy stories with her young friend William. One day "The Princess" is rescued from the poorhouse when her "Fairy Godmother," the wife of mill owner Chandler, adopts the girl. The Princess labels her reluctant capitalist benefactor "The Ogre." Although Mr. Chandler (Herbert Patti) eventually warms to his loving ward, becoming her "Fairy Godfather," he continues to rule his mills with an "iron hand." Meanwhile, William, "The Prince," played by Richard Tucker, has gone to work at Chandler's mills. Taken under wing by the mills' kindly superintendent, William has studied hard and invented a new loom that could "revolutionize the industry." But conditions at the mills, including Chandler's disrespect towards workers, has led to labor discontent. At a workers' meeting, all of whom are clean shaven and neatly dressed, it is agreed to send a delegation to Chandler to request a "square deal." However, after the delegation, led by a deferential William, is verbally abused and then fired by Chandler, his mill workers declare a strike. A miffed Chandler calls for 200 strike breakers to be sent to the mills. The following morning, these "scabs," escorted by shotgun armed guards, are attacked by a club-wielding, stone throwing mob of strikers. Dispersed by the gunfire of the guards, the now crazed mob of strikers storm Chandler's home. But just as the angered strikers are about to physically attack Chandler, Irene shields his body and declares: "I promise that you shall have all you ask." William and his mates are appeased, although some turn their anger upon an unscrupulous manager that Chandler had hired to help break the strike. Having been reunited with her "Prince Charming," the Princess finalizes capital-labor reconciliation by handing over William's plans for the new looms to a chastened Chandler. It should be noted that despite the absence of the usual troublemaking labor agitator in this film, the responsible William seemingly loses all control over his striking compatriots once the scabs are reported to have disembarked at the train station.

[S (LC); LC, LP10161; *Wid's* 2/15/17:107]

Cap; Lab; Mtg; Mob; Pvt Pol; Reconcil; Scabs; Shp Flr Abuse; Strike; Unemployed; Viol

ANTI-CAP; CAP-LAB COOP

The Secret Game, Lasky/Par, William C. De-Mille, 5r, Dec, Am, Spy Drama

This motion picture was released a little over a month after the Bolshevik revolution. Yet, it may be assumed that this event was not a factor that affected production. In fact, political conditions in Russia are never discussed in the film. Nevertheless, the plot concerning Japanese-American cooperation in foiling German spies and the transportation of American troops to Russia to help resist German incursions reflects upon a growing anxiety among the Western Allies with regard to the integrity of the Kerensky regime. This was a big-budget production starring Sessue Hayakawa, Jack Holt and Florence Vidor. Demonstrating the wartime suspicion about loyalties of the foreign-born in the United States, Miss Vidor's heroine receives the following introductory title: "Kitty Little, with a deeply concealed hyphen in her name." And the real German spy, played by Raymond Hatton, poses in drag as a housekeeper named Mrs. Harris!

[S (LC); LC, LP11743; *MPN* 12/15/17: 4223; *Var* 12/7/17:50]

Allied Interv; Am Icons; Ger; Russ; Sec Ser; Spy-Sab
NDB

Threads of Fate, Columbia/Metro, Eugene Nowland, 5r, Jan, Am(r), Drama

The wife of Pennsylvania coal miner Jim Gregory abandons him and their child for her Italian lover, Giovanni. Unable to care for his baby daughter, Dorothea, Jim leaves her on the doorstep of Sarah and Tom Wentworth. Dorothea (Viola Dana), now called "Dot," grows up with her foster parents, ignorant of her past. The Wentworths become wealthy after Tom inherits his father's coal mines. Meanwhile, the itinerant Jim (referred to as "the wanderer" in the credits) has become a labor activist who has connections with the Camorra (Black Hand). He rallies the discontented miners, many of whom are foreign born, and leads a delegation of strikers to the Wentworth mansion. Giovanni, posing as the Marquis del Carnacacchi, has returned from years in Italy and, failing to win the hand of Dot, attempts to abduct her. Jim comes to the rescue of his daughter, but is mortally wounded in the struggle with Giovanni. This was perhaps the last American film to make the linkage between the Black Hand and labor militancy.

Refer to *Giovanni's Gratitude* (Reliance, 1913), q.v.

[LC, LP10053; *MPN* 2/3/17:760; *MPW* 1/27/17:589]

Agit; Cap; Decad; Ital; Lab; Pol; Strike; Viol
ANTI-LAB

Under False Colors, Thanhouser/Pathé, Emile Chautard, 5r, Sept, Russ/Am, Drama

The beautiful Countess Olga (Jeanne Eagles), under the scrutiny of the secret police in revolutionary Petrograd, seeks refuge in the apartment of Jack Colton. Colton, who is in Russia to arrange a large American loan for the government, helps her escape from the country with a false passport. On the trans-Atlantic liner the countess shares a stateroom with a young American girl. When the ship is torpedoed and the girl dies of exposure, Olga assumes her companion's identity. Olga/Vera is adopted by Jack's father, played by Frederick Warde. All goes well until a secret group of revolutionaries enlists her aid to help the starving people of Russia. They plan to kill her rich guardian for the money and then keep it for themselves. Olga and the senior Colton, who is now aware of her true identity, foil the revolutionaries' avaricious scheme.

[AFI, F1.4637; *MPW* 10/6/17:132; *Var* 10/12/17:40]

Cap; Escape; Rev; Russ; Sec Pol; Viol
ANTI-REV

Wild and Woolly, Douglas Fairbanks Picts/Artcraft, Jun, John Emerson, 5r, Am, Western-Com

Jeff Hillington (Douglas Fairbanks), the son of the New York president of a western railroad, is an old west aficionado. One day Jeff, dressed in western garb, playfully stages a stick-up upon his unsuspecting father as the man enters his Wall Street offices. This leads to Hillington's decision to send his "anarchist" son west to investigate Bitter Creek, Arizona — representatives from that town have recently petitioned the elder Hillington to build a railroad line through their town. Jeff is played for a fool by the locals, but later wins their respect and the pretty girl when he helps them to overcome the machinations of a crooked Indian agent.

[S (LC; Vid); LC, LP10954; *MPN* 6/30/17:4110; *Var* 6/22/17:23]

Anarch; Cap
CM/ANTI-REV

1918

All Man, Vitagraph, Paul Scardon, Aug, Am, Drama

John Olsen (Harry Morey), a skilled mechanic at an iron foundry, is swayed by a socialist agitator named Sachs (German-Jew?) to participate in robbing the company safe. After serving five years in jail, he is saved by the prostitute with a heart of gold, played by Betty Blythe. John patriotically invests his stash of ill-gotten gains in Liberty Bonds and then donates them to the Red Cross. Since the other male criminal involved has an Italian surname, Peroni, this film provides yet another example of the linkage between the gangster stereotype and that of the radical left.

[LC, LP12696; *MPW* 8/17/18:1015; *Wid's* 8/4/18:25]

Agit; Am Icons?; Ger?; Ital; Jew?; Lab; Pol; Soc
CM/ANTI-REV

The Answer, Triangle, E. Mason Hopper, Mar, Am/Brit, Drama

John Warfield (Joe King), a young man brought up on socialism by an embittered class-conscious father, teams up with radical Guido Garcia (Francis McDonald), and together they establish a home for "down and outers" in San Francisco. After listening to John harangue a street crowd, a telephone operator named Goldie (Claire Anderson) joins the cause. Warfield's wealthy mother dies in Britain, leaving him a mansion. As soon as he settles the estate, Warfield sends for Goldie and they are married. The working-class girl quickly abandons the socialist movement and embraces a life of leisure. Guido, enraged by the situation, comes to England and shoots Goldie. Warfield returns to America and donates his estate as a children's home. The Goldie character is used to show a shallowness of commitment by many to socialism. Even Warfield rededicates his life to poor children while taking up with a progressive society lady. Nevertheless, this is one of the last films from the teens to take a relatively positive attitude toward socialism.

[AFI, F1.0120; *MPW* 3/21/18:4711; *Var* 3/22/18:19]

Agit; Cap; Dom Rad; Fem Rad; Ital; Mtg; Soc; Tramp; Viol
PRO-SOC

At the Mercy of Men, Select, Charles Miller, April, Russ, Drama

Vera Souroff (Alice Brady), a young music teacher in Petrograd, is seized by three officers of the Tsar's Imperial Guard and "outraged." The Tsar arbitrarily orders one of the men, Count Nicho, to marry her. Later, Vera's former fiancé, Boris Litofsky, now a crazed student revolutionary, persuades her retired military father to lead "the forces of the people." The threat of the Bolshevik hordes bring together our young heroine and her estranged aristocratic husband. The *MPW* reviewer was impressed by the "elaborate mob scenes."

[LC, LP12308; *MPW* 5/4/18:744; *NYDM* 5/4/18:632; *Var* 4/26/18:40]

Bol; Decad; Mob; Rev; Russ; Tsar; Viol; White Russ
ANTI-RS; ANTI-SOV

Cheating the Public, Fox, Richard Stanton, Jan, Am(u), Drama

Not only is this film pro-labor, but it is also a rare example of a wartime release that avoids presenting German and/or left-wing agitators as the agents of discord with capital. This is achieved by portraying the boss of Millvale, John Dowling (Ralph Lewis), as a greedy profiteer, who underpays his employees and takes advantage of war-generated shortages to overcharge his cannery workers for the basic necessities of life: "Until the war is over we have them in our hands." The factory workers' lives are made even more miserable by foreman "Bull" Thompson, known as the "slave driver." Chester, Dowling's college graduate son, who has begun dating a factory girl named Mary Gavin (Enid Markey), has meanwhile expressed a desire to introduce reforms. But after his father willfully cuts wages, the workers form a committee and threaten to strike. The elder Dowling damns his employees. When they go on strike and riot he has the "swine" dispersed by a truckload of armed guards. As one of these guards grabs Mary, she calls him a "slacker" and shouts: "Why aren't you fighting our [wartime] enemies instead of your own blood?" With their families starving, the strikers delegate Mary to plead their cause with the "monster." John Dowling accosts her and is shot during the struggle. Mary is condemned to die in the electric chair, but is saved at the last moment when it is learned Dowling's brutal foreman had committed the deed. Chester tells Mary: "I shall right every wrong done the people by my father and you shall be here in the office to guide me." Note: War profiteering was a major target of the American Socialist Party's animus.

[LC, LP11963(s); *MPW* 2/2/18:684, 717; *NYDM* 1/26/18:19; *Var* 1/25/18:43]

Cap; Decad; Irish?; Lab; Liq Link; Mtg; Mob; Pvt Pol; Reconcil; Shp Flr Abu; Strike; Viol

PRO-LAB;   ANTI-CAP;   CAP-LAB COOP

The City of Purple Dreams, Selig, Colin Campbell, Jan, Am, Drama

A filthy derelict (Thomas Santschi) is given a dollar for soap by a wealthy young lady he encounters to: "Keep clean and stay clean." But soon afterwards he falls under the influence of a fiery anarchist named Esther (Jew?), played with "Bolsheviki fervor" by actress Fritzi Brunette. At the command of Esther's band of "Reds" he blackmails a rich manufacturer "for the cause." For this effort he is committed to a mental institution (to be a Red is to be mad), from which Esther later helps him escape. The virile derelict, actually the son of a distinguished Virginia family, abandons the female revolutionary when he learns the pretty girl who gave him the money is the capitalist's daughter. Esther commits suicide. Released in the winter, the Esther character represents one of the earliest screen examples of the communist vamp. In the context of the times, interesting associations are created by the soap scene—"cleanliness is next to godliness" and, by extension, the closer one is to God, the further one is removed from potential contamination by the impure ideology of godless radicals.

[*MPW* 1/12/18:243; *MPW* 2/2/18:717; *Var* 2/15/18:51]

Anarch; Bol; Cap; Fem Rad; Jew?; Tramp; Viol

ANTI-REV

The Fall of the Romanoffs, Iliodor Picts/First Nat, Herbert Brenon, Jan-Mar, Russ, Drama

A hard-drinking illiterate peasant in Siberia, Rasputin (Edward Connelly), deceitfully acquires the reputation of being a seer. The ruffian then cynically begins to preach in the countryside. But this does not save him from the abuse of the mob when he is caught stealing in his village. Fortunately for Rasputin, he is rescued by a member of the royal family who, convinced of Rasputin's prophetic powers, determines to bring him to St. Petersburg. After Rasputin correctly predicts the Tsarina will give birth to a son, he is installed in the Winter Palace and becomes a trusted advisor to the royal family. When the 1905 Revolution erupts (a rare American film reference; refer to the 1905 Biograph release, *Mutiny on the Black Sea*), Rasputin enlists the aid of an eloquent monk named Iliodor (playing himself) to help quell the masses. But Iliodor, the "sinful angel," denounces the "sacred devil" when he becomes disgusted with the corrupt court under Rasputin's spell. For instance, a pogrom against the Jews follows the whipping of some Cossacks ordered by Rasputin. Illiodor must later flee to America when Rasputin implicates him in a fabricated assassination plot against the Tsar. During World War I Rasputin and the German-born Tsarina conspire to arrange a separate peace with Kaiser Wilhelm—the Tsarina even having a direct wireless line to the Kaiser installed in her dressing room!—from September 1915 to February 1917 the Tsarina was more or less in control of the government, following Nicholas assuming command of the army and physically removing himself to staff headquarters; the main telephone in the Winter Palace actually was located in Alexandra's drawing room. Rasputin is grievously wounded and then compelled to commit suicide by Russian patriots (in fact, he was murdered by a group of disaffected aristocrats in December 1916). Soon afterwards, the non-communist revolutionaries under Kerensky force the Tsar to abdicate and declare a republic (these two events actually took place in March of 1917). Footage is included of American "war socialist" Edward Russell (playing himself) addressing the Russian Duma (he was a member of the United States' "Root" Commission, that made a fact-finding visit to Russia in the summer of 1917—referred to in a title as "The treason-torn land of our ally."). Following an extensive ad campaign this lavish $30,000 Brenon production received a New York City premiere on September 7, 1917. Note: A plethora of anti-Tsarist pamphlets, stressing the Romanoff court's decadence and intimate connections with Germany, were distributed in Russia and abroad following the so-called "Glorious February Revolution."

[AFI, F1.1259; LC, LU11325; *EH* 11/10/17:7 (ad); *MPN* 7/21/17:325; *MPW* 6/30/17:2046; *Var* 9/4/17;35]

Atroc; Bomb; Decad; Escape; Ger; Jew; Liq Link; Mob; Rasputin; Rev; Russ; Siberia; Soc; Tsar; Viol; White Russ
ANTI-RS

The Firebrand, Fox, Edmund Lawrence, May, Russ, Drama

The title implies anarchism and, in fact, the leading anarchist journal in America at the turn of the century was so named. A Russian princess, Natalya (Virginia Pearson), reads the revolutionary book, *Song of Sorrow*, written by an American of Russian descent named Julian Ross (Jew?). She later meets him in Siberia, where as a prisoner Julian is routinely brutalized by Cossack guards. Meanwhile, Russia has become embroiled in the World War. Natalya's uncle secretly conspires with the Germans. Julian escapes and, together with a bearded radical "prophet" named Leonid, assassinates Natalya's uncle. She has Julian arrested. But the revolution allows for Julian's release and the discovery of documents incriminating Natalya's uncle lead to a romantic reconciliation. This spring release was one of the last films to refer to Tsarist collusion with the Germans (and one of the first post-Bolshevik revolution films to indirectly suggest a German-Bolshevik conspiracy). The *MPW*'s "Music for the Pictures" section suggested "The Dawn of Hope" by Casella as the musical theme for this film.

[LC, LP12487(s); *EH* 6/8/18:25; *MPN* 6/1/18:3307; *MPW* 6/29/18:1842]

Anarch; Atroc; Bol-Ger Link?; Ger; Jew?; Rev; Russ; Siberia; Viol
ANTI-RS

For the Freedom of the East, Betzwood Film/Goldwyn, Ira M. Lowry, Oct, China/Am, War Drama

Princess Tsu (Chinese vaudeville star Lady Tsen Mei), a convert to democracy, is the leader of a secret society organized to thwart German attempts to incorporate China into the Kaiser's ("The Spider of Berlin") world order. The princess discovers her uncle ("The Viceroy Who Loved German Gold") plotting with the head German spy in the Far East to raise a Chinese army to cooperate with the Germans and Bolsheviks in conquering Russia. She informs the local American diplomatic representative ("The American Anchor in China"). Tsu's martial arts skills are later needed to save an American Secret Service agent and the documents he possesses, revealing Germany's designs, from enemy spies. Copyright material indicates that this fall release included newsreel footage of American troops, sent to drive the "horde of Huns and Bolsheviki before them," entering "Vladivostok and being vociferously cheered by Count Otami and his Japanese army." Note: American and Japanese military personnel had actually begun landing in Vladivostok in August 1918. And, in fact, contemporaneous fears of German-manipulated Bolshevik domination of a then weak and factionalized China were repeatedly cited as a major justification for Allied intervention in the Siberian province of Russia. The film was rereleased a year later under the title *Eyes of Truth*.

[LC, LP12884; *MPW* 10/19/18:448; *MPW* 1/18/19:388]

Allied Interv; Am Icons?; Bol; Bol-Ger Link; Ger; Sec Ser; Spy-Sab; Viol
ANTI-SOV

The Girl from Bohemia, Astra/Pathé, Lawrence B. McGill, Aug, Am(s), Drama

In order to share in a legacy, a "temperamental soul" from bohemia pays farewell to her Washington Square studio apartment and returns to the homestead in Mayport. Although her "see-considerable" gown and cigarette smoking scandalizes the local sewing circle, Alice (Irene Castle) wins the heart of the owner of the Lehigh Shipyards. Meanwhile, the resident saloon keeper, socially shunned in town, uses his influence among the workers to promote a strike. When the strikers get out of control and plot to burn down the shipyards, Alice seizes an American flag and disperses the unruly mob with a patriotic speech. This film provides a good example of the neutralizing of dangerous radical impulses nurtured in the decadent city by the virtuous ambiance of small town America. It also reinforces the popular linkage of alcohol with uncontrolled immigrant workers. For instance, one of the pejorative appellations applied to the I.W.W. was "I Want Whiskey." Ironically, wartime prohibition, which was largely directed at foreign workers, contributed to labor discontent—"No Beer, No Work," was a common rallying cry at labor demonstrations.

[LC, LU12811; *MPN* 8/24/18:1211; *MPW* 8/24/18:1154; *Wid's* 8/18/18:9]

Am Icons; Cap; G Vill; Lab; Liq Link; Mob; Sab; Strike; Viol

CAP-LAB COOP

The Girl of Today, Vitagraph, John Robertson, Sept, Am, War Drama

A German spy-saboteur, Dr. Wolff, posing as a wealthy Danish scientist, infiltrates the 1776 Society. Wolff receives orders to destroy public transportation and munitions works in New York City in honor of the Kaiser's birthday (January 27). A saboteur ("bomb thrower") working for the doctor is followed from a scene of destruction to his home by the son of a war materials manufacturer. The foreign agents imprison the young man. A faithful patriotic girl named Leslie (the beautiful Corrine Griffith) and the son's family alert state authorities and eventually are able to vanquish the evil and lascivious Dr. Wolff. This film alludes to manipulation of domestic radicals by German agents in an attempt to hamper America's war efforts. The doctor's last name implies sexual decadence (he had propositioned the heroine) and connotes deceit. The following year the surname "Wolff" would also be applied to the German/Bolshevik agent in *Bolshevism on Trial*, q.v. Note: The screenplay was written by Robert W. Chambers (1865–1933), one of the most popular novelists of his time. He would later author one of 1919's more scurrilous Red Scare books, *The Crimson Tide*, which was promoted as a story about Bolshevism in New York City.

[AFI, F1.1594; LC, LP12879; *MPW* 9/21/18:1774; *MPW* 10/12/18:226 (cs)]

Am Icons; Bomb; Cap; Decad; Dom Rad?; Ger; Pol; Sab; Spy-Sab; Viol

CM/ANTI-REV

The Glorious Adventure, Goldwyn, Hobart Henley, July, Am(s), Drama

Pretty Carey Wethersbee (Mae Marsh) and her spinster aunt live with an aged black mammy in an old southern mansion. Following her aunt's death, Carey travels north, installing herself in the small-town home of Hiram Ward, a wealthy young mill owner. Vis-

iting the mills, Carey is appalled by conditions. She sells Hiram a valuable old silver dollar and distributes the money among the laborers. But instead of relieving the employees, her generosity incites a strike, the female workers actually attacking Carey. Nevertheless, when the mill is blown up, Carey defends the man whom she knows to be falsely accused. Through Carey's influence, Ward's callousness towards his workers is softened and he pledges to improve their conditions.

[LC, LP12640; *MPW* 7/20/18:463–64; *Var* 8/16/18:38]

Cap; Fem Rad; Lab; Reconcil; Sab; Strike; Viol

CAP-LAB COOP

The Golden Goal, Vitagraph, Paul Scardon, May, Am(u), Drama

John Doran (Harry T. Morey), a tough "man from the dregs," meets Beatrice Walton at "The Safe Harbor," a seaman's mission. The slumming Barbara, who is the daughter of a wealthy shipbuilder, finds the "cave man" type John amusing, and hires him to work on her father's estate. But after John confesses his love for the flirtatious lady, Beatrice has him fired. Determined to prove his worth, John secures a job at the Talbot shipyards, and quickly earns a series of promotions. John begins to educate himself with the help of the company stenographer, Laura Brooks (Jean Paige), and soon becomes president of the ship workers' union. Meanwhile, Walton (Arthur Donaldson) has failed at an attempt to merge Talbot's company with his trust. Recognizing Doran, Walton has Beatrice invite the young man to his house, where he offers him $15,000 "on account" to disrupt the Talbot shipyards. John accepts the bribe and organizes a strike for higher wages. In the series of labor fights that follow one of the striker's sons is injured. When he also learns from Laura about the suffering of the strikers' families, John agrees to urge a settlement with Talbot and returns the money to Walton. But Walton and his goons trick John into sending a message to the union meeting hall that advises the strikers to hold out for an exorbitant wage increase. When John learns that he has been duped by Walton, he fights his way out of the capitalist's home and confesses all to his fellow workers. The men are threatening John's life when Laura steps in and defends him. Labor peace is restored and John is reunited with his true love.

[AFI, F1.1647; LC, LP12376; *MPW* 6/1/18:1330; *Var* 5/31/18:29]

Cap; Irish?; Lab; Mtg; Reconcil; Strike; Viol

PRO-LAB; CAP-LAB COOP

The Great Love, Famous Players-Lasky/Artcraft, D.W. Griffith, Aug, Brit/Eur, War Drama

American Jim Young (Robert Harron), outraged by stories of German atrocities, enlists in the Canadian army. In London he falls in love with an Australian girl, Susie Broadplains (Lillian Gish). After Jim leaves for the front, Susie, who has recently inherited money, is ardently courted by the womanizing Sir Roger Brighton (Henry B. Walthall). The middle-aged Brighton and Susie marry, but his dissolute lifestyle leads to an entanglement with German agents, posing as pacifists, and their Bolshevik associates. Brighton is eventually coerced into helping the spies guide a Zeppelin bombing raid upon an important munitions plant. Jim, having returned from France, learns of these plans and foils them. Brighton commits suicide and Susie finds her "great love" in serving as a nurse in an English hospital. Mr. Seymour of Brazil, "formerly of Berlin," is played by one of Griffith's favorite heavies, George Siegmann.

[AFI, F1.1691; *MPW* 7/27/18:593; *MPW* 8/24/18:1155–56]

Atroc; Bol; Bol-Ger Link; Decad; Ger; Pac; Spy-Sab; Vet

CM/ANTI-SOV

The Hard Rock Breed, Triangle, Raymond Wells, Mar, Am(r), Drama

Don Naughton (Jack Livingston), the snobbish fun-loving son of a wealthy contractor, is sent as foreman to his father's rock quarries to take the place of the crooked Mike Carney (Louis Durham), an Irishman who also owns the Gem saloon. Carney uses the sale of rum to the workers to keep them under his "monarchical [sic] sway." Don decides to dismiss the unmanageable workers (to "strike on the job," or loaf, was an I.W.W. tactic) and hire a new gang of rock drillers. But Carney and his partner, Greek Louis, undermine the new foreman by importing anarchists and I.W.W.s to start a wildcat strike. Don has meanwhile won the respect of the men and the company engineer. Together, they defeat Carney's agitators in a brawl. After Don saves his predecessor from a lynch mob, the men return to work.

[AFI, F1.1762; *MPN* 3/16/18:1611; *MPW* 3/16/18:1556–57; *Var* 3/8/18:43]

Agit; Anarch; Cap; IWW; Irish; Lab; Liq Link; Mob; Strike; Viol

ANTI-REV; CAP-LAB COOP

Jack Spurlock, Prodigal, Fox, Carl Harbaugh, Feb, Am(u), Comedy

The campus activities of Jack Spurlock's pet bear, purchased while in a drunken stupor, lead to the young man's expulsion from Harvard. Spurlock senior makes Jack a purchasing agent in the family's wholesale grocery business. But after Jack (the muscular George Walsh; brother of Raoul) procures 200 carloads of onions he is exiled as a laborer to the onion sheds in Newark. When Jack arrives he witnesses a union organizer (a "corking" performance by New York Giants' baseball star Mike Domlin) addressing the workers: "We are squirming beneath his [Spurlock's] iron heel. We must stand up for our rights and strike for better conditions." Jack sides with labor and inspires their battle cry, "Smother Spurlock in Onions." Jack is delegated as the strike representative to negotiate with his father in New York. He is presented with a large legacy from his aunt by the elder Spurlock and shown the door. With the aid of an old school buddy, now in advertising, Jack uses the money on a "Live and Let Live" campaign for better capital-labor relations. His father agrees to rehire all the strikers, except Jack. While working in a cheap cafe on the East Side, Jack is introduced to Professor Jackson, inventor of an onion-based tonic called "Jackson's Exhilarator." The strike publicity has helped to create an increased demand for the tonic! The professor authorizes Jack to arrange for the purchase of his father's onion surplus, thus redeeming the prodigal son. Note: The film's working title, "In Onion There Is Strength," parodied the well-known union slogan.

[LC, LP12040(s); *MPN* 2/23/18: *MPW* 2/23/18:1137; *Var* 2/15/18:53]

Agit; Cap; Lab; Reconcil; Strike

CAP-LAB COOP

The Legion of Death, Metro, Tod Browning, Mar, Russ/Am, Drama

Following the death of Rasputin, an aristocratic brother and sister return to Russia from their studies of democracy in America. The Princess Marya (popular actress Edith Storey, renowned for her beauty and athletic prowess) organizes the "Legion of Death," a battalion of peasant women. They want to help save Russia from turmoil, due largely to dissatisfaction among many of the Russian soldiers created by German bribes (German gold). Upon the arrival of Kerensky and the Allied Commission at the front, the women are sent into the trenches. When a traitorous Grand Duke's troops are withdrawn, the unsupported legion is attacked and eventually defeated by the "licentious ... Huns." Marya's honor is saved by the timely arrival of American volunteers. Russia is also thereby freed from the "grip of autocracy." Note: 1. An anti-Bolshevik women's battalion was actually formed by a commoner in the Petrograd area in the spring of 1917—"to shame the men"—this "Women's Battalion of Death" suffered 80 percent casualties. Both the decadent Tsarist regime and the Bolsheviks were accused of being manipulated by the Germans. 2. This film was released soon after the Soviets signed the Treaty of Brest-Litovsk with Germany. At that time, British Royal Marines had been landed at Murmansk. Woodrow Wilson was under a lot of pressure to do likewise, but American troops would not arrive in northern Russia until September. Thus it is of some interest that in this *March* film release "American volunteers" are portrayed fighting in Russia.

[LC, LP12028; *EH* 3/30/18:23; *MPW* 1/26/18:572]

Allied Interv; Bol-Ger Link; Decad; Rasputin; Rev; Russ; Viol; White Russ
ANTI-RS

A Little Sister of Everybody, Anderson-Brunton/Pathé, June, Robert T. Thornby, Am(u), Com-Drama

Demure little Celeste (Bessie Love) lives in poverty on the East Side with her socialist grandfather, Nicholas Mannoff. Hugh Travers, a young playboy whose wealthy father suddenly dies, dons workers clothing and enters the factory he now owns under a false name in an attempt to understand why his employees have been threatening to strike. While working at his factory, Hugh meets and becomes smitten with Celeste. When she learns that Ivan Marask (Hector Sarno), a disgruntled anarchist who was fired, plans to shoot the owner, Celeste runs to warn her employer only to learn he is the co-worker she has come to love. Hugh

offers marriage and pledges to improve conditions at the factory.

[LC, LU12565; *MPN* 6/29/18:3874, 3950; *MPW* 6/29/18:1891]

Anarch; Cap; Lab; Reconcil; Russ?; Soc; Strike; Unemployed; Viol
CAP-LAB COOP; CM/ANTI-REV

Mr. Logan, U.S.A., Fox, Lynn F. Reynolds, Sept, Am(r), Western

Cowboy star Tom Mix plays a Secret Service agent named Jimmy Logan, posing as a drifter. He breezes into Sunrise, New Mexico, to clean up a strike at a government contracted tungsten mine that was instigated by a German propagandist, fronting as the owner of a local saloon. With German gold, Mr. Gage (the surname suggesting a challenge; played by Val Paul), whose real name is Meier, has bought the services of a drug-addicted agitator and his I.W.W. cohorts. At the film's end, the I.W.W.'s are literally herded onto freight cars by the patriotically aroused miners and shipped out. Jimmy's riding stunts have also helped save the mine owner's daughter from the lecherous German agent. Here, indigenous radicals are portrayed as decadents in league with America's enemies. Note: In July 1917 a notorious incident took place in Bisbee, Arizona, that was obviously the inspiration for the film. Nearly 1200 striking miners were forced into freight cars and later dumped in the middle of the desert in New Mexico. This so-called "deportation" operation was organized by Sheriff Harry Wheeler, a veteran Rough Rider and former gunfighter.

[LC, LP12852(s); *MPW* 10/19/18:448]

Agit; Am Icons; Atroc; Bomb; Cap; Decad; Ger; Irish?; IWW; Lab; Liq Link; Mtg; Pol; Sab; Sec Ser; Spy-Sab; Strike; Vig; Viol
ANTI-REV

My Four Years in Germany, First Nat, William Nigh, Mar-April, Ger/Bel/Fr/Am, War Drama

This film is the screen dramatization of American Ambassador to Germany (1913–1917) James W. Gerard's eponymous book. Newsreel footage is combined with staged action to help create an image of the Kaiser and his advisers as idiots and the Germans as ruthless savages. One early scene portrays a Socialist named Pierotes (as in pierrot?; played by William Nigh) among politicians protesting the notorious Zabern incident (in

1913 a military officer egged on his troops to abuse civilians in the small Alsatian town). Yet, when war is declared the following year, the Socialist becomes swept up in the tide of militarism and ardently declares: "Gott strafe Russland!... England!... There are no parties now. The Reichstag is united in defense of the Fatherland." Later, as a common soldier, Pierotes is forced to participate in the slaughter of Belgian women considered unfit for hard labor. When he rebels, the "misguided Socialist" is shot by his own men—his dying words: "Oh my Fatherland, if only my poor life were given—to—make you—a Republic!" Additional wartime atrocities illustrated include ill-treated interned foreign nationals and Allied soldiers at a prisoner of war camp being placed with Russians suffering from contagious typhus. Some Allied POWs not released through death from disease are portrayed being repatriated "the Hindenburg way"—by mass execution! It is reported to the Kaiser and his advisers, who are discussing unrestricted submarine warfare, that "50 million Dollars has been distributed for our cause in America"—compared in an inter-title to a gang of criminals distributing their "swag," a match dissolve to a group of foreign-looking men greedily taking the money is probably meant as an oblique reference to radicals being paid to commit acts of sabotage in the United States. A subtle linkage is also made to German support of the Bolsheviks when Hindenburg announces to the Kaiser at a staff meeting: "The revolution in Russia [the Bolsheviks seized power in Oct./Nov. 1917] has been launched successfully, I am bringing my forces back [the art title in the right corner of the inter-title is of a hand lighting the fuse of a bomb]." In an otherwise unrelenting example of crude anti-German propaganda, the attack upon socialism's support of the German war effort (and thereby indirectly, the patriotism of American Socialists who opposed U.S. participation in the war) is comparatively sophisticated. Note: Anti-German disturbances occurred in several cities following the screening of this film.

[S (LC; Vid); LC, LP12167; *MPN* 3/16/18: 1602; *MPW* 3/30/18:1863]

Am Icons; Atroc; Bol-Ger Link; Dom Rad?; Ger; Rev; Russ; Soc; Spy-Sab
CM/ANTI-SOV

On the Jump, Fox, Raoul A. Walsh, Oct, Am(s), Com-Drama

Jack Bartlett (George Walsh) of the *Express* interviews President Wilson during the Fourth Liberty Loan (September 1918). But the new owner of the paper, banker Otto Cromley, refuses to print the story. Jack resigns in protest and becomes an avid Liberty Bond salesman. When he learns that Cromley has fomented a strike at a hometown shell casing factory, Jack rides up to the workers' strike meeting dressed as Paul Revere, makes a patriotic speech and induces the laborers to return to the munitions plant. Now working for an opposition paper, Jack discovers that Cromley has stolen the formula of a gasoline substitute. He chases the banker to a schooner lying off the shore. Jack finds papers on Cromley that identify the man as the custodian of German funds to create a propaganda, spy and sabotage organization in the United States. The synopsis deposited with the Library of Congress indicates Jack has been working undercover as a Secret Service agent. This film's screenplay was based on a story that was also written by the multi-talented Raoul Walsh. Note: It would appear that Jack's speech was meant to emulate the famous Committee of Public Information (CPI) sponsored "4-Minute Men" patriotic speeches that were regularly given in wartime movie theaters by thousands of volunteer speakers.

[LC, LP12980; *MPW* 10/19/18:443; *Var* 11/8/18:41]

Am Icons; Ger; Lab; Sab; Sec Ser?; Spy-Sab; Strike; Viol
CM/ANTI-LAB

The One Woman, Mastercraft/Select, Reginald Barker, Oct, Am, Drama

A fiery preacher with a fashionable parish is cautioned by his deacon that he is alienating the "best people ... with your socialist rubbish." Forced to resign, a wealthy "free love" vamp provides him with the funds to build his "Temple of Man." He leaves his wife and children and enters into a common-law relationship with the woman, played by Clara Williams. But when war breaks out, the Reverend Gordon (Lawson Butt) cannot go along with the anti-conscription sentiments of his socialistic flock. He is defied by an anarchist named Stromoff who demands a vote against the draft. Gordon's patriotic opposition leads to his violent expulsion from the church. After other trials, he is reunited with his wife. Refer back to *Draft 258*; 1917—despite large socialist parties in both France and Germany, it was within the United States that the most vocal left-wing opposition to war participation developed. The notoriously reactionary Reverend Thomas Dixon was responsible for this film's screenplay. Note: A small Christian socialist movement evolved in the United States in the 1890s. But by the early 1900s some of its most ardent advocates had been discredited by accusations of promoting "free love" (referring to a sexual relationship without marriage; *not* to promiscuity). Christian socialists were not granted conscientious objector status by conscription authorities.

[PE (Pvt Coll); LC, LP12928; *Behind the Mask of Innocence*, pp. 461–62; *MPW* 12/7/18:1117; *Var* 9/20/18:45]

Am Icons; Anarch; Cap; Decad; Fem Rad; Pac; Russ?; Soc; Viol
ANTI-REV

The Prussian Cur, Fox, Raoul A. Walsh, Sept, Am(u), Drama

In the year before the United States declares war on Germany, the German ambassador, Count Bernstorff, sets up a spy network. Headed by the evil Otto Goltz, the group includes a labor agitator and a man who poses as a Roman Catholic priest. Meanwhile, a U.S. Congressman, who resembles real-life Senator Robert M. La Follette (who had actually voted against the U.S. declaring war), opposes a strong American response to German provocations, such as the sinking of the passenger liner *Lusitania* in May 1915. Once the United States enters the World War in 1917, the labor agitator incites defense workers to strike. Another German agent, Wolff von Eidel (a homonym of idle; negative wartime linkage with idler), is turned in to the authorities when he attempts to cajole a German-American to sabotage a western airplane factory. A group of pro-Germans attempt to rescue Wolff. In response, a posse of "loyal Americans" in cloaks and cowls attacks the disloyal rabble, kills the spy and rounds up the pro-Germans. The American vigilantes then compel the hyphenated Americans to kiss the American flag (a humiliation/submission tactic used earlier by vigilantes against I.W.W.s) before leading them to jail. Goltz's villainy had been further exaggerated by showing him brutalize the mother

of the dark-eyed Irish heroine, Rosie O'Grady (Miriam Cooper). Director Walsh also received credit for this film's script. Refer to *The Parlor Bolshevist*, a 1919 animated cartoon released by Fox, that portrays Mutt and Jeff forcing naughty radicals to sing the national anthem (Appendix 2). Note: Two members of the German embassy staff involved in the sabotage of the Black Tom munitions depot in 1916 were Horst von der Goltz and Wolf von Igel. In April 1918 a German-American named Robert Paul Prager was killed by a lynch mob for publicly discussing socialism.

[LC, LP12795(s); *MPN* 9/7/18:1592; *MPW* 9/7/18:1455]

Agit; Am Icons; Atroc; Ger; Irish; Lab; Pac; Sab; Spy-Sab; Strike; Vig; Viol
CM/ANTI-LAB; ANTI-SOC

Resurrection, Famous Players-Lasky/Par, Edward José, May, Russ, Drama

This film was based upon the 1899 novel by Leo Tolstoy. In pre-revolution Russia, Katusha (Pauline Frederick), a half-gypsy peasant girl, is betrayed by Nekludov, a young noble. Several years later, as a Moscow prostitute, she is unjustly convicted of complicity in the murder of a wealthy merchant. Nekludov, one of the jurors, is overcome by remorse and promises to obtain the Tsar's pardon. On her journey to Siberian exile, Katusha meets a Jewish humanitarian, Simonson (John Sainpolis), sent into political exile for his "radical teachings." He shows Katusha the way to her moral resurrection and defends her from one of the escorting officers. When Nekludov reaches Katusha with a pardon and offers marriage, she refuses, preferring to stay with Simonson. The "Music for the Pictures" section of the *MPW* suggested that the film close with the playing of Gretchinoff's "Hymn of New Russia."

[LC, LP12348; *MPN* 5/18/18:3002; *MPW* 5/18/18:1035; *MPW* 66/1/18:1290]

Decad; Jew; Rev; Russ; Siberia
ANTI-RS

The Road to France, World, Dell Henderson, Oct, Am(u), Rom Drama

Tom Whitney, a well-connected derelict played by he-man actor Carlyle Blackwell, is rejected for the draft—an old football injury. But he is persuaded by an Irish cop that he can still do his bit in the shipyards. Under an assumed name, Tom goes to work as a day laborer in the shipyard of his former fiancée's father, John Bemis. While on the job, he discovers several labor agitators attempting to foment a strike with "poison propaganda." They are led by Hector Winter (Richard Neil), who is in the pay of the German government. Tom successfully thwarts their efforts by reminding his fellow workers of the sacrifices of the men in the trenches—at least one worker is known to have a son fighting "over there." When a "ratlike criminal" employed by Winter murders Bemis, the German agent frames Tom for the deed. With the aid of some Secret Service men, Tom is able to defeat the "enemy within"—whose provocative theme music is "The Slimy Viper" by Borch. In the final scene, a reunited Tom and Helen Bemis watch the launching of *The Liberty*, another merchant ship delivered to sustain America's sea borne "Bridge to France." The film concluded with a sustained shot of the American flag, to be accompanied by the playing of the "Star Spangled Banner."

[LC, LU12960; *MPW* 10/5/18:86 (cs), 128; *Photoplay* 10/18:37–40 & 114–15]

Agit; Am Icons; Cap; Ger; Lab; Pol; Sec Ser; Spy-Sab; Strike; Tramp; Viol

CM/ANTI-LAB; CAP-LAB COOP

The Spirit of '17, Lasky/Par, William D. Taylor, Jan, Am(s), War Drama

Davy (a 22-year-old Jack Pickford playing an adolescent), the local Boy Scout leader in a western mining town, fills his head with romantic patriotism through listening to the war stories of the old soldiers at the Army veterans' home. Two German agents incite the miners to strike for higher wages. Davy overhears their plot to sabotage the mine by duping the powder man to plant a dynamite charge in the shaft. With the aid of an armed contingent of the old soldiers, Davy captures the alien plotters. Note: The para-military aspects of this film would have been further accentuated by the nearly identical appearance of the Boy Scout uniform to that worn by America's Doughboys.

[LC, LP11855; *MPW* 2/2/18:687; *Var* 1/25/18:41]

Am Icons; Bomb; Ger; Lab; Sab; Spy-Sab; Strike; Vet; Vig

CM/ANTI-LAB

The Transgressor, Catholic Art Assoc., Joseph Levering, Oct?, Am, Drama

Caleb Carson is the greedy owner of large steel mills in Crucible City. He ignores the pleas of his son, Charles, to install safety devices. By chance, young Charles is able to save mill worker Claire Daudet from death when she falls down an unprotected elevator shaft. Petroski, "a radical agitator of the I.W.W. type," comes to town and takes advantage of the workers' growing discontent. At a secret meeting, he delivers a fiery tirade. To further inflame the men, two of Petroski's associates steal Carson's car and deliberately run over a worker's daughter. A crazed mob starts wrecking the company offices and attempts to lynch Carson. Coming from the bedside of the dying child, Father Conway barely succeeds in pacifying the rioters. The radical's plot quickly unravels, though, after the deathbed revelation of the young girl that Caleb was not in the car that struck her. Caleb admits that his mill policies have been unfair and promises to make amends. The cast included Ben Lyon and Inez Marcel. Note: Because of the I.W.W.s' open scorn for organized religion, it became a target for attack by the Roman Catholic church. Refer to the opening comments under *The Burning Question*, 1919, q.v.

[PE (UCLA); AFI, F1.4544; LC, LP13001]

Agit; Atroc; Cap; IWW?; Lab; Mob; Reconcil; Russ?; Viol; Wrk Rel Dis/Inj

ANTI-LAB; ANTI-REV: CAP-LAB COOP

The Vamp, Thomas H. Ince/Famous Players-Lasky/Par, July, Jerome Storm, Am(s), Com-Drama

A new settlement worker, played by Douglas MacLean, and his bride Nancy (Enid Bennett) arrive in a Pennsylvania mining town. Phil Weil (Germanic surname; German pronunciation sounding like "vile") is a labor agitator who incites the miners at the local saloon to prepare to strike. Knowing hubby is away training Boy Scouts, Weil (Robert McKim) then attempts to seduce little Nancy with the aid of some whiskey. But golden-haired Nancy, suspecting Weil is involved in no good, vamps him into confessing that he was paid $1,000 to foment a strike. The mob of strikers is literally at her door when her husband arrives with a couple of Secret Service men and the captured German spy, who had hired Weil, in tow.

[LC, LP12645; *MPW* 8/3/18:716; *Var* 7/19/18:36]

Agit; Decad; Ger; Irish; Lab; Liq Link; Mob; Sec Ser; Spy-Sab; Strike
ANTI-LAB

The Wasp, World, Lionel Belmore, Mar, Am(s), Com-Drama

Grace Culver (English actress Kitty Gordon), a capitalist's daughter, is known by associates as "The Wasp" for her sarcastic remarks to men regarding the "slavery" of marriage. Angered by Mr. Culver's choice of a future son-in-law, Grace orders the chauffeur, Purcell (Rockcliffe Fellowes), to drive her and her maid to the country. Meanwhile, Brazos (played by the 50-year-old director), a secret German agent whose real name is Carl Wagner, has fomented a strike at one of the government-contracted factories owned by Grace's father. Passing by the plant on her trip, the car is attacked by an angry mob of strikers. After Purcell's attempts to resist are overcome, Grace and her servants are seized, the strikers planning to hold the beautiful lady for ransom. While the maid has escaped and gone for the militia, Grace and Purcell are entombed in the factory's cellar after a bomb Wagner had planted prematurely explodes. The militia arrive and all is resolved. During her trials Grace has fallen in love with Purcell, whom she has also learned is actually named Harry Courtland, the only son of a millionaire. This film's screenplay was written by Willard Mack.

[LC, LU12073; *MPN* 3/16/18:1610; *MPW* 3/16/18:1557; *Var* 3/1/18:19] Agit; Bomb; Cap; Ger; Lab; Militia; Mob; Sab; Spy-Sab; Strike; Viol

ANTI-LAB

Whims of Society, World, Travers Vale, Feb, Am, Drama

A young woman named Nora Carey (Ethel Clayton) struggles against poverty as an underpaid millhand at a New England ribbon factory. When she rebuffs the sexual advances of Marlinoff (Frank Beamish), the brutish foreman, he has her fired. But Hugh Travers, the son of the mill owner, has fallen in love with Nora and places her in an apartment. Marlinoff learns of this arrangement and informs the elder Travers. The heartless owner discharges Marlinoff and prepares to formally disinherit his son. Mr. Travers is about to sign a new will when he and his lawyers are blown up by a bomb that the vengeful Marlinoff had placed

beneath the factory office. The elder Travers was planning to remarry and bequeath his fortune to the daughter, played by Pinna Nesbit, of a manipulative penniless society matron, Mrs. Schulyer. Despite the apparent absence of overt political linkages, the mill owner is a negatively portrayed capitalist and the foreman with a Slavic surname conformed to the by now standard stereotype of a bomb thrower. By giving the other heavy in the film, Mrs. Schulyer, a Germanic last name, there is a subtle reinforcement of the perception of a Bolshevik-German connection.

[AFI, F1.4916; LC, LU12072; *MPW* 2/23/18:1136; *Var* 2/8/18:43]

Bol-Ger link?; Bomb; Cap; Decad; Dom Rad?; Ger; Lab; Russ; Sab?; Shp Flr Abu; Viol
ANTI-CAP; CM/ANTI-REV

The Winning of Beatrice, Metro, Harry L. Franklin, May, Am(u), Com-Drama

When her father is killed by a burglar in a scheme instigated by an unscrupulous business partner, Beatrice Buckley (May Allison) is forced to make a living on her own. She opens a candy factory whose "secret ingredient" of goat's milk leads to financial success. But this directly threatens the candy business of the same man, John Maddox, who had not only caused her father's death but also smeared his reputation by claiming he had committed suicide after failing in an alleged scheme to defraud the company. Maddox arranges for a labor agitator to go to Beatrice's candy factory in order to instigate a strike. During an ensuing fight at the plant, an agent of Maddox's is mortally wounded and confesses all to Beatrice.

[AFI, F1.5021; LC,LP12408; *MPW* 6/1/18:1330]

Agit; Cap; Lab; Strike; Viol
ANTI-CAP

The Yellow Dog, Universal-Jewel, Colin Campbell, Nov, Am, War Drama

A young lawyer becomes enraged by unpatriotic talk in a shipbuilding community. The defeatist comments include slanders upon the government and socialist remarks about the war being one engineered by the "capitalists." In response, the lawyer organizes the kids of the town into the "Boy Detectives of America" with a mandate to present such talkers with a "Yellow Dog" card (in addition to the shame

factor, this may have been intended as a sub-liminal visual assault upon the "Red Card" of I.W.W. membership). Nosey White (Antrim Short), the captain of the boys' club, helps expose a plot by a German spy/propagandist to destroy the shipyard. This film was based on a story that appeared in a May edition of *The Saturday Evening Post.* Note: It was also in May of 1918 that the notorious Sedition Act became law. Ostensibly directed at German propaganda and defeatism, it was used almost exclusively against labor radicals. Among the numerous patriotic and vigilante organizations formed during the war by the middle-class to combat enemies (largely imagined) on the home front were the Anti-Yellow Dog League and the Boy Spies of America. Both these organizations and the film were promoted by an extended ad campaign in the trade journals. One of the advertising "Catch Lines" provided to exhibitors exemplifies the xenophobic hysteria overtaking the nation: "Don't forget that the calamity howler within is every bit as harmful as the enemy without. Get rid of him." At least one Chicago area Yellow Dog Club actually demonstrated near a theater showing the film, carrying banners condemning Bolshevism.
[LC, LP12953; *MPW* 8/17/18:1015 (ad); *MPW* 10/15/18:120]
Am Icons; Cap; Ger; Lab; Sab; Soc; Spy-Sab; Vig
ANTI-SOC

The Yellow Ticket, Pathé, William Parke, May, Russ, Drama
Taking place in pre-war Russia, this Nihilist film features the struggles of a beautiful young Jewish girl named Anna (Fannie Ward) against the program-inciting Tsarist secret police. There is the usual bomb throwing incident. Eventually, she is forced to kill the head of the Okrana, played by Warner Oland, in order to save her honor. With the aid of a friendly American journalist (Milton Sills), who had been studying conditions in Russia, she is able to leave the country of her oppression. *The Yellow Ticket* can be viewed as either an anachronism or as an anti-Bolshevik film veiled in the Nihilist genre. Refer to *The Yellow Passport*, 1917, q.v.
[LC, LU12373; *EH* 5/25/18:25; *NYDM* 6/1/18:777; *Var* 5/24/18:35]
Atroc; Bomb; Decad; Escape; Fem Rad; Jew; Nih; Russ; Sec Pol; Viol
ANTI-RS

1919

The Adventure Shop, Vitagraph, Kenneth Webb, Jan, Am, Com-Drama
The alluring Phyllis Blake (Corrine Griffith) and some other bored socialites open the "Adventure Shop" to fabricate excitement for paying customers. Their first client is Mr. Potts, a wealthy pickle manufacturer who hopes to cure his jaded son. Phyllis intercepts Potts, Jr., in his cab upon his arrival in New York, pleading with him to help her find the "Green Gullabaloo." She then takes him to various locations in the underworld, including an alleged anarchists' meeting place. But Phyllis comes in for a surprise when they are both kidnapped by Black Hands and held for $50,000 ransom. It turns out that young Potts was wise to the scam and arranged for the unscheduled adventure.
[LC, LP13207; *MPW* 12/21/18:1387–88; *Var* 1/3/19:38]
Anarch; Cap; Ital
NDB

The Amazing Imposter, Am Film/Pathé, Lloyd Ingraham, Feb, Am, Comedy
Joan Hope (Mary Miles Minter), the teenaged daughter of a chewing gum manufacturer, meets a Russian countess on a train trip. Thrilled at being in the company of a noble woman and unaware that the "Countess of Crex" is actually a jewel thief, Joan readily agrees to exchange identities. As the countess, and now in possession of a stolen necklace, Joan finds herself pursued by a gang of jewel thieves, by two clownish "bad Bolshevikis" who demand "secret" papers and by an amateur sleuth. All is sorted out at her hotel.
[LC, LP13364; *MPN* 2/8/19:926; *MPW* 2/8/19:810]
Bol; Cap; Jewels; White Russ
CM/ANTI-SOV

The Belle of the Season, Metro, S. Rankin Drew, July, Am(u), Drama
This film was originally scheduled for release in early 1917. James Alden, the son of a newspaper owner, opens a settlement house. Geraldine Keen (Emmy Wehlen) the heiress to the Keen Mills, is horrified when she learns of the workers' poverty. Disguised in her maid's street clothes to observe conditions, "Jerry" is

accosted by a pug ugly tough named Johnson (Louis Wolheim), but James comes to the rescue. Meanwhile, the labor union shuts down the mills with a strike. Jerry sends a $10,000 check to Alden for the relief of the suffering families and begins to help out at the settlement house. Brophy, Jerry's executor, follows her there. Johnson, still lusting for Jerry, recognizes Brophy as the man who had blocked her efforts to improve conditions. Johnson rushes to the saloon where many of the strikers are gathered and incites a mob to go after Brophy. Alden steps forward and dissuades them from doing harm to the man. The next day Jerry turns twenty-one and accepts the strikers' demands.

[AFI, F1.0273; LC, LP14028; *Var* 8/1/19: 52]

Cap; Decad; Irish?; Lab; Liq Link; Mob; Reconcil; Shp Flr Abu; Strike; Viol
CAP-LAB COOP

Bolshevism On Trial (Shattered Dreams), Mayflower Photoplay/Select, April, Harley Knoles, Am(r), Drama

Captain Norman Worth (Robert Frazer), a wounded veteran of the fighting in France (?), is in love with Barbara Bozenta (Pinna Nesbit), a college-educated debutante whose experiences as a social worker have led her to embrace radicalism. Under the influence of a "professional agitator" named Herman Wolff (Leslie Stowe), they are duped into supporting the establishment of a utopian socialist island community. The nefarious Wolff almost immediately begins to undermine "Chief Comrade" Worth's authority in order to justify confiscating Paradise Island and ruling it with his "Red Guard." Wolff also wants to abandon his homely wife and make "comrade Barbara" his "consort." The young man's wealthy inventor father, Colonel Worth, sends his faithful Indian retainer to secretly keep an eye on developments. So when Wolff imprisons Worth's son the native-American reports back to the mainland. After U.S. Naval infantry retake the island, Norman hauls down the Red flag and proudly raises the Stars and Stripes. Brought before the commanding officer, a scowling Wolff is informed: "You have been under surveillance over a year, *Androvitch*." Promoted with an incendiary ad campaign in the trade journals, this April release was in the Red Scare vanguard—especially manifesting

the American fear of the Soviet proposition to spread a world revolution. It was probably influenced by the February-March Overman Senate subcommittee investigation of Bolshevism. Based upon a screening of a Library of Congress print and a comparison of the subtitles with information provided in contemporary reviews, it would appear that at some point there was an attempt to slightly alter the plot. For instance, the Worths are the Bradshaws, and there is no indication that Norman is a veteran. Also, during the first reel of the film, the heroine's surname is given as Alden. Note: the film was based on Thomas Dixon's 1909 novel *Comrades*, a satire of Upton Sinclair's social experiment in New Jersey.

[S (LC); LC, LP13580; *EH* 5/3/19:46; *MPW* 4/19/19:307–10 (ad), 424 (ad); *MPW* 4/26/19:549–50 (cs); *MPW* 5/3/19:717–18; *MPW* 5/17/19:966–67 (ad); *Var* 5/2/19:60]

Agit; Am Icons; Anti-Rel; Artist; Bol; Bol-Ger Link; Cap; Decad; Fem Rad; Jew?; Lab; Marx; Mtg; Pol; Rev; Russ; Soc; Strike; Trotsky?; Vet?; Viol
ANTI-SOV

Bonds of Honor, Howard Films/Mutual, William Worthington, Jan, Jap/Russ, War Drama

Due to gambling debts, a dissolute Japanese national named Yamashiro (Sessue Hayakawa), becomes entangled with Paul Berkowitz, a German agent. Yamashiro is induced to steal certain fortification plans, but is discovered by his father and twin brother. Refusing to redeem his family's honor by committing hara-kiri, Yamashiro flees to Vladivostok with Berkowitz and Olga (Marin Sais), a "traitor to Russia." Sent to bring his brother to justice, hero Sadao apprehends the spies, while his twin kills himself. Though Japan was an American ally during World War I, there may have been a racist subtext to this film—by reinforcing the concept of an Eastern/Asian Russia. Note: This motion picture also reflected upon a wartime concern of the U.S. government that pro-German elements in Japan might lead that country into an imperialist alliance with the Kaiser's empire.

[LC, LU13004; *ETR* 2/15/19:865 (cs); *MPN* 2/8/19:919 & 924; *Var* 1/31/19:53]

Bol-Ger Link; Ger; Jew?; Russ; Spy-Sab
CM/ANTI-SOV

Boots, New Art/Famous Players-Lasky/Par, Elmer Clifton, Mar, Brit, Com-Drama

"Boots" (Dorothy Gish), a slavey at a London inn near Parliament, reads romantic books and fantasizes over a handsome student boarder, played by Richard Barthelmess. But he only has eyes for an aggressive sculptress who keeps pet mice and whose room is full of "horrible statues" (abstracts; nudes?). This strange woman is actually one of the members of a Bolshevik council—"well-bred folk of the upper middle class...," according to the *NYT* reviewer. They have obtained an old map which shows the location of an underground passage between the inn and a nearby government building where President Wilson and King George are scheduled to discuss peace terms. Our heroine inadvertently crashes through the floor upon the Red lady as she is about to place a ticking bomb beneath the Allied leaders (Bolshevism as literally undermining the foundations of postwar Western solidarity and, therefore, future world stability). The man of Boots' dreams, Everett White, turns out to be a Scotland Yard operative. The Bolshevik woman, Mme. De Valdee (the French word *devaler* meaning to descend), is linked with vermin via her pet mice. Note: Woodrow Wilson had actually recently discussed the peace settlement and Allied intentions regarding Russia with Lloyd George in London. And, on February nineteenth an anarchist in Paris had shot French premier Georges Clemenceau. At the time of the film's release, the Versailles peace conference was in session, with the Bolshevik government unrecognized and not formally represented. Meanwhile, Allied troops continued a direct involvement in the Russian civil war on the side of the counter-revolutionary Whites.

[LC, LP13399; *MPW* 3/8/19:1390; *NYT* 3/10/19:9; *Var* 3/14/19:46]

Artist; Bol; Bomb; Decad?; Fem Rad; Pol; Sec Ser; Viol
ANTI-SOV

Bullin' the Bullsheviki, Eff & Eff, Frank L. Donovan, Nov, Russ/Am, Comedy

This is a burlesque of Bolshevism. It features an American girl named Lotta Nerve (Marguerite Clayton—Bronco Billy's regular leading lady) who goes to the Russian town of Killemoff to eliminate "Lean Itsky" (Lean as in Lenin; *It*sky as in Russian thing—played by the undersized Billy Ruge) and his drunken, bomb-throwing "*Bull*sheviki." Lean Itsky's assistants include one "Simonvich." Having been presented a forged letter of introduction by Lotta, the Red leader takes the blonde to a hotel room and attempts to remove her clothes. After ejecting the lecher, Lotta and her two aides purchase a Russian Army (most White forces were subsidized by the West) and confront the Red commander on the battlefield. Lotta sends a message to Lean Itsky—wash and work for a living, or else (purify oneself of radical filth or be exterminated; refer to *The City of Purple Dreams*, q.v.). Lean Itsky refuses and sends a rider to New York for reinforcements. The latter is promptly arrested for obstructing traffic when he crashes into a Bolshevik making a speech (possible allusion to journalist John Reed, who was arrested in September 1918 in New York City after completing a speech defending the Russian Revolution). Lotta and her soldiers vanquish the Reds, court martial the survivors and summarily execute them! As the Reds literally bury themselves, Lotta is cheered by her army for removing Bolshevism from the map. Although a crude cinematic exercise in slapstick, this film touched on several major themes. To begin with, it is one of the first fictional films to deal directly with the Bolshevik government. The Lean Itsky character was named "Trotzsky" in the copyright material, pointing out how Trotsky was initially better known and more closely associated in the contemporaneous public mind with the leadership of the new Soviet regime than Lenin. Moreover, Simonvich would appear to be a Jewish caricature and thus would reinforce the Jew-Bolshevik linkage, quite widespread at the time. Finally, the motion picture portrays a direct association between indigenous communists and Russian Bolsheviks. It was rereleased with extra scenes and new titles in February of 1920. The *MPN* reviewer found the latter version particularly confusing and disparaged the Keystone Kops style use of a "prop" Ford filled with police.

[LC, LU14020; *EH* 11/8/19:83 & 84; *MPN* 2/21/20:1971; *MPW* 1/17/20:472; *Var* 10/24/19: 61]

Atroc; Bol; Dom Rad; Jew; Lenin; Liq Link; Mtg; Pol; Russ; Spy-Sab; Trotsky; Viol; White Russ
ANTI-SOV

The Burning Question, Catholic Art Assoc., Oct?, Am, Drama

This was the second anti-radical film produced by the Catholic Art Association (papal encyclicals had specifically condemned communism as atheistic and socialism as a threat to private property rights). *The Transgressor*, q.v., had been made the year before. These films were apparently released for showing in Roman Catholic Churches and special screenings at cooperating movie houses. Trade reviews have not been located for either film. Nonetheless, despite some continuity problems, production qualities for *The Burning Question* are good. In *pre-war* America (and thus in the pre-Bolshevik revolution period) the firm of Thompson and Collins has come under attack from "Bolshevik" agitators after Collins fires a number of employees for supporting the "Red Cause." A series of consecutive titles directly links "Socialism," "Bolshevism" and "Anarchism." At a meeting of the radicals in a secret basement room, an exaggeratedly hook-nosed man (Jew?) exhorts his followers to "support the cause of our Brothers in Russia." Their attempts to blow up Collins aboard a ship owned by his company are thwarted with the help of a loyal secretary named Mary (Inez Marcel?). When war is declared by the United States, Mary's older brother and Collins both join the Army and go off to France. A paper announcing the Armistice also contains a story referring to German workers and soldiers seizing Berlin (the so-called Sparticist rebellion of January 1919). Soon after receiving coded orders from one "Rotsky" to "make [revolutionary] preparations" the Jew(?) Bolshevik leader, waving a Red flag, exhorts his followers to eliminate all individuals "suspected of treachery to that flag." War hero Collins, Mary's younger brother who is in the Secret Service, and a troop of soldiers storm Red headquarters just in time to save the virginal Mary (in addition to the Virgin Mary linkage, a cult surrounding Mary Washington, mother of George, existed at the time) from being defiled by the Jew(?) Bolshevik. The Reds are rounded-up and marched off (including a middle-aged woman who appears to be a lesbian stereotype). Note: In a well-publicized incident American soldiers had raided the Russian Peoples' House in New York City on May Day.

[S (LC; USC); AFI, F1.0543; LC, LP14270; *Var* 10/17/19:65]

Agit; Am Icons; Anarch; Bol; Bol-Ger Link; Bomb; Cap; Decad; Dom Rad; Fem Rad; Ger; Irish; Jew?; Lab; Rev; Russ; Sec Ser; Soc; Vet; Viol
ANTI-SOV

Common Property, Universal, Paul Powell, Oct, Russ, Drama

Married to a beautiful American, Paval Pavlovitch (Robert Anderson) seeks to prevent the Bolsheviks of Saratoff from carrying out a decree nationalizing all women between the ages of 17 and 35. The "local Lenine," Nikolai, lusts for Paval's dark-haired wife, Anna (Nell Craig). Lyof, the son of the village priest, is among the many who desire Tatyone (Colleen Moore), Paval's teenaged daughter. The U.S. cavalry arrives just in time to save the Pavlovitch family from the Red rabble. Note: This is an obvious allusion to Allied military intervention in Russia. The *MPN* review notes that Norma Talmadge had already played a similar role in *The New Moon*, q.v., and adds that although the purported Soviet decree "raised a lot of discussion earlier, it is generally discredited now." Yet, during the same month as this film's release, a story in *The New York Times* (10/26/19:5) appeared under the provocative headline: "Soviets Make Girls Property to State: Decrees Compel Them to Register at 'Free Love Bureau' on Attaining 18 Years." Although the Bolshevik regime never issued such a decree, during the highly volatile period of civil war (1918–20), a couple of provincial branches of the Commissariat for Social Welfare did initiate such actions. For instance, in Vladimir, a "Bureau of Free Love" was set up and a proclamation issued declaring all women over eighteen to be "state property."

[LC, LP14205; *MPN* 10/18/19:3046; *Var* 11/14/19:59]

Allied Interv; Anti-Rel?; Bol; Decad; Mob; Russ; Viol; White Russ
ANTI-SOV

Deliverance, Helen Keller Film, George Foster Platt, Aug, Am, Drama

The life of Helen Keller (1880–1967), famous for her triumph over the combined disabilities of blindness and lack of hearing, is dramatized in three episodes. In the final episode she plays herself. Along with showing Helen's interactions with some famous Americans, including Mark Twain, the film depicts Miss Keller developing a relationship with the daughter of an immigrant laborer named Nadja. After Helen enters college, Nadja becomes a worker slaving behind a sweatshop sewing machine. During the final episode the two women, reunited by Nadja's son losing his sight in World War combat, aid in the rehabilitation of wounded servicemen. Helen declares: "We are soldiers of the new Freedom that shall sweep all tyrannies from the earth!" In the concluding scene a Red Cross garbed Helen, blowing a trumpet, appears on a white charger leading a working-class multitude waving the flags of the Allied nations and marching toward "deliverance" in a new postwar world. The film was completed in December 1918 and was nine reels in length when released in August 1919. Helen Keller, an outspoken suffragette and well-known member of both the I.W.W. and the Socialist Party, had opposed the war. On November 10, 1919, she condemned the Allied blockade of Soviet Russia in the *New York Call*. Although the above plot description makes clear her pacifism and sympathies for the working-class, it would appear that direct references to her political leanings were not present in the film. Note: George Kleine subsequently acquired the rights to it and distributed a radically edited version of the motion picture in early 1920. It is presumed that in this version, released during the height of the Red Scare, the pro-labor theme originally present in the second and third episodes was significantly altered.

[S (LC, incomplete); AFI, F1.0986; LC, LU13725; *MPN* 8/30/19:1843 & 1873; *MPW* 8/23/19:1122; *Var* 8/22/19:76]

Am Icons; Cap; Lab; Pac?; Russ?
PRO-LAB

Everybody's Business, Charles Richman/W.H. Prods, Dec?, J. Searle Dawley, Am, Drama

There are no known reviews of this film and the copyright information is not available. The film was previewed in July of 1919, but does not appear to have been publicly exhibited prior to December 1919. It is highly likely that exhibition was restricted to special screenings for clubs and selected patriotic groups (it was recommended by the National Security League and the American Legion). Claiming the title was inspired by a comment made by President Wilson, the film's producers unashamedly promoted it as propaganda for the spirit of "100 percent Americanism" and against the danger of Bolshevism. One interview described *Everybody's Business* as "built around a simple human interest story of love and romance interspersed with thrilling melodramatic action and intensely dramatic incidents and situations."

[AFI, F1.1206; LC, LU13746; *EH* 9/27/19:32 (ad); *MPN* 8/9/19; 1254; *MPN* 8/16/19:1433; *MPN* 1/24/20:1067; *MPW* 8/9/19:871]

Am Icons; Bol
ANTI-SOV

Give and Take, Wyndham Gittens Prods, Wyndham Gittens, ?, Am, Drama

No reviews for this film have been found. News articles indicate it had a capital versus labor theme, with references to Bolshevism. Cast credits include Hector V. Sarno, who frequently played radical "types." *Give and Take* probably was never released.

[AFI, F1.1615; *MPW* 3/8/19:1329; *Var* 3/14/19:49]

Bol; Cap; Lab
NDB

The Great Romance, Yorke Film Corp/Metro, Henry Otto, Jan, Am/Rur, Adventure

Columbia University student Rupert Danza (the handsome Harold Lockwood) is summoned by a mysterious envoy to lead a *democratic* revolution in Rugaria. After the king is wounded by an anarchist, Rupert learns he is the legitimate heir to the throne. Following the death of the king, Rupert refuses the crown, but is elected president of the new republic.

[LC, LP13266; *MPW* 1/25/19:522, 546]

Anarch; Rev?; Viol
CM/ANTI-REV

Hawthorne of the U.S.A., Par-Artcraft, James Cruze, Nov, Rur, Rom Advent

A slang-spouting young American law clerk, Anthony Hamilton Hawthorne (Wallace Reid), who has recently broken the bank at Monte Carlo, quashes a violent revolution in the backward Slavic ruritania of "Bovinia." The symbol of the revolutionary party is a sinewy worker's arm holding a torch. Its leaders are a Colonel Radulski (as in radical; uses the "comrade" address) and an "ardent revolutionist" stereotype named Nitchi (as in nits;

played by Tully Marshall). There is an attempt to kill the king and the usual anarchistic mob storming the palace—the scene appositely tinted red. Significantly, it is American gold from our hero that not only buys off the revolution but creates a republican capitalist paradise within the year. The king abdicates, Hawthorne gets the princess (Lila Lee) and Radulski winds up as a waiter at the tourist trap hotel where a black jazz band plays.

[S (LC); *MPW* 11/29/19:536; *Var* 11/21/19: 55; *Wid's* 11/30/19:13]

Am Icons; Anarch; Bol?; Cap; Mob; Rev; Viol

ANTI-REV

The Heart of a Gypsy, Charles Miller Prods/ Hallmark Picts, Nov, Charles Miller, Brit, Drama

Rosalind Dane (Florence Billings), a wealthy Englishwoman who believes her Army officer husband was killed in 1917 while on a mission in Russia, lives with her young daughter in the country. She falls in love with a handsome member of a gypsy band that she has allowed to camp on the estate. During the midst of a lawn party her husband Ralph reappears unexpectedly. Ralph, accompanied by a mysterious man, has become "corrupted by the Soviet" regime. Rosalind threatens to kill him after she learns that Ralph works for the Bolsheviks and plans to take their daughter. But Ralph's unnamed companion, a Bolshevik secret agent, murders the Englishman for failing to carry out an unspecified mission for the Soviets. The copyright material indicates that the secret agent was originally intended to be a German.

[LC, LP14424; *MPW* 12/13/19:856; *Var* 12/5/19:61]

Bol; Cap; Spy-Sab; Viol

ANTI-SOV

Life's Greatest Problem (Safe For Democracy), Blackton Prods, J. Stuart Blackton, Jan, Am, War Drama

A shipbuilder's lazy "slacker" son, along with his butler and a couple of bums (one of whom is named "Big Steve" Reardon; played by Mitchell Lewis), are put to work in the shipyard following a raid inspired by Selective Service Director Enoch Crowder's famous "Work or Fight" order. The four become friends and are spiritually reborn through their new jobs.

Together, they are able to thwart the activities of a pro-German employee and an I.W.W. agitator (actor Sidney D'Albrook), as well as squelch a plot to sabotage the yards with a time bomb. Note: Crowder's May 1918 order was directed at draft age idlers, particularly those affiliated with the I.W.W. movement. And, in fact, a large number of so-called "Slacker Raids" were carried-out by the government (with Army participation) and patriotic organizations between April and September of 1918 (culminating in a massive drive to round-up slackers in New York City).

[S (LC); LC, LP13432; *ETR* 2/1/19:719 (cs); *MPN* 12/7/18:3387; *MPW* 1/18/19:389 (ad); *Var* 11/8/18:14]

Agit; Am Icons; Bol; Bomb; Cap; Ger; IWW; Lab; Liq Link; Pol; Sab; Spy-Sab; Tramp; Unemployed; Viol

CAP-LAB COOP; ANTI-REV

The Lone Wolf's Daughter, W.W. Hodkinson, J. Parker Read, Jr., Dec, Brit, Crime Drama

A former international jewel thief named Michael Lanyard, known as the Lone Wolf, marries Princess Sonia. The princess dies giving birth to a daughter. The child, Sonia, unaware of her true identity, is raised by a maid. An underworld group of Asian gangsters led by Prince Victor (exiled before the Bolshevik revolution; possibly for nihilist connections?), the first husband of Princess Sonia, has been working with Bolshevik agents to carry out a scheme to pump poison gas through the old gas pipes of London into Buckingham Palace and nearby well-to-do homes. In an effort to trap the Lone Wolf, who is now in league with the government, Victor tells Sonia he is her father and brings her to his home. The Lone Wolf exposes the plot. Poison gas may have been an indirect linkage to the Germans, due to their introduction and continued heavy use of it during the war. Louise Glaum starred in the title role (playing both the mother and the mature daughter). The Lone Wolf had dealt with German spies earlier in the year in the Paramount-Artcraft release, *The False Faces*.

[AFI, F1.2584; *MPN* 12/20/19:4531; *MPW* 12/20/19:1010; *Var* 1/23/20:59]

Bol; Russ; Sec Ser?; Spy-Sab

ANTI-SOV

A Man's Fight, United Picture Theatres of America, Aug, Thomas N. Heffron, Am(r), Drama

In the typically melodramatic prose of the day the *MPW* review stated that *A Man's Fight* "suggests the present labor unrest as well as visualizing the struggle of the individual against the odds of a tarnished name." Roger Carr (Dustin Farnum), the son of a rich old New York family, assumes the blame for the shooting death of a drunken cad who had accosted his sister. Ten years later a now middle-aged Roger, who has been spurned by his father, heads west and invests in a copper mine. As the leader of the independent owners, Roger attempts to institute reforms that will better the conditions of the hard rock miners. An opposing trust sends a representative back east to investigate Roger. Meanwhile, the trust has hired a couple of Irish labor agitators to instigate a strike at Roger's mine. A report disclosing that Roger is an ex-con arrives at the same time that his sister sends news of the deathbed confession by the family butler exonerating Roger of the murder. With the help of his faithful secretary, Roger is able to expose the agents of labor unrest.

[AFI, F1.2804; *MPN* 8/23/19:1689; *MPW* 8/23/19:1182–1183]

Agit; Cap; Irish; Lab; Strike?
CAP-LAB COOP

A Midnight Romance, First Nat, Lois Weber, Mar, Am, Drama

A princess seizes the opportunity to escape from her royal responsibilities after the liner on which she has been traveling is torpedoed off the American coastline. Having reached shore near a fashionable resort, Princess Marie (Anita Stewart) drops her title and takes a job as a maid at the seaside hotel. While enjoying a midnight ocean dip she has a romantic encounter with Roger Sloan (Jack Holt), the son of a wealthy capitalist. But, for the remainder of the season, Marie avoids the smitten young man. Following a brief reunion at the hotel's farewell ball, Marie helps Roger avoid being blackmailed and then disappears from his life again. Sometime later, Roger is invited to a reception for Princess Marie, and is amazed to discover that she is the mystery girl with whom he had fallen in love. Marie informs a delighted Roger that since the "Bolsheviki" have declared the downfall of the monarchy, she is free to marry a commoner.

[AFI, F1.2929; *MPW* 3/22/19:1696; *NYT* 3/10/19:9; *Var* 3/14/19:46 & 48]

Bol; Cap; Rev
CM/ANTI-SOV

The Mother and the Law, D.W. Griffith, D.W. Griffith, Aug, Am(s), Drama

This is a reedited and expanded version of the modern sequence from Griffith's 1916 film classic, *Intolerance*, q.v. A titled Prologue equates the capitalist Jenkins with the Kaiser and denounces intolerance as the primary "cause of the Russian Revolution." With the Red Scare heating up, Griffith added this misleading inter-title to the scene depicting the militia firing a lethal fusillade into the mob of strikers: "The militiamen having used *blank* cartridges, the workmen now fear only the company guards." In addition, a close-up shot of a striker firing his pistol, that suggests he initiated the labor violence, has been removed.

[S (UCLA); AFI, F1.3066; *MPW* 8/30/19: 1371; *Var* 10/3/19:56]

Cap; Ger; Lab; Liq Link; Militia; Mob; Pvt Pol; Rev; Russ; Strike; Unemployed; Viol
PRO-LAB; ANTI-CAP; CM/ANTI-SOV

The New Moon, Select, Chester Withey, May, Russ, Drama

Maria Pavlovna (Norma Talmadge), a Russian princess of democratic leanings, is having a ball to celebrate her betrothal to Prince Michail Koloyar (Pedro de Cordoba). Outside, a revolutionary mob is aroused in the ominous darkness of the New Moon by the "verbal lashes" of a "savage terrorist" named Orel Kosloff (Stuart Holmes). Kosloff is the tool of Theo Kameneff (Charles Gerard), the cunning leader of the "Anarchist Club," who is a Bolshevik opportunist in the pay of a foreign government (presumably Germany). A hand grenade is tossed onto the palace balcony, killing Maria's mother and a number of guests. The Reds break down the doors and begin to plunder the palace. Michail saves Maria's honor and sees her safely off in a carriage. Disguised as a peasant girl named "Sonia," Maria will use her jewels to purchase a small shop in the village of Vlosk. Michail takes the clothes of a drunken rioter and in that guise becomes a courier for the Red Army. He begins searching for his lost fiancee. As the provincial Bolshevik leader, Kameneff issues a Soviet decree nationalizing all women between the ages of 17 and 32. After recognizing Maria, whom he lusts for, Kameneff mandates a second "drastic order" that abolishes marriage and stipulates that the registered women are at the sexual disposal of men. The village women appeal to Maria to speak with Kameneff. But the Red tells Maria that he will rescind the order only if she agrees to become his mistress. Maria refuses and urges the other women not to comply. During the following orgy of violence, Kosloff rapes the daughter of the potter Lazoff (Marc McDermott) and lures Kameneff's sister Nadia (Marguerite Clayton) back into the province. A number of uncooperative women, including Nadia, are executed! After discovering Nadia among the dead, Kameneff orders Maria's arrest. The enraged Red is attacking Maria when her faithful fiancé and Lazoff burst into his headquarters. Lazoff strangles Kosloff, before shooting Kameneff. The reunited lovers cross the border together to begin a new life in freedom. Note: Leo Kamenev, a Jewish convert and brother-in-law of Trotsky's, was one of the actual leaders of the Bolshevik revolution. Between February and March of 1919 a widely publicized Senate subcommittee, chaired by Lee Overman, investigating Bolshevism, included lurid testimony about atrocities and the alleged "nationalization of women" in Russia. Refer to the notes for *Common Property*, q.v.

[LC, LP13708; *MPW* 5/24/19:1223; *MPW* 5/31/19:1359–60 (cs); *Var* 5/16/19:53]

Anarch; Atroc; Bol; Bol-Ger Link; Bomb; Decad; Escape; Jew; Liq Link; Mob; Rev; Russ; Viol; White Russ
ANTI-SOV

The Other Half, Brentwood Film/Robertson-Cole, Aug, King W. Vidor, Am(u), Drama

While a soldier on the battlefields of France, the son of the owner of the Trent Iron Works becomes a believer in the equality of all classes. Captain Donald Trent (Charles Meredith) returns home with the man who saved his life in the trenches, Corporal Jimmy. Despite the objections of his father, Donald joins Jimmy in working at the Trent factory. But the ruthless realities of the business world cause Donald's attitude to reverse when he takes over the iron works following his father's death. When Jimmy is made foreman and demands that repairs be made to protect the lives of the workmen, a hardened Donald refuses. Soon afterwards, Jimmy is temporarily blinded by the collapse of a factory wall. The workers declare a strike after Jimmy's attempts to re-

ceive restitution are ignored. Meanwhile, Donald's girlfriend Katherine (Florence Vidor), disgusted by his actions, refuses to marry him and joins the staff of a progressive (socialist?) newspaper called *The Beacon*. An article she writes for the paper reawakens Donald's social consciousness and leads him to institute humane business reforms.

[LC, LU14148; *MPN* 8/23/19:1687; *MPW* 9/6/19:1525]

Cap; Lab; Reconcil; Soc?; Strike; Vet; Wrk Rel Dis/Inj
CAP-LAB COOP

The Other Man's Wife, Carl Harbaugh Prod/Film Clearing House, Carl Harbaugh, June, Am(u), Drama

Mrs. Hartley, the wife of a wealthy shipyard owner who went to France with the AEF, comes under the spell of the suave draft-dodging J. Douglas Kerr (read cur; played by Stuart Holmes). Kerr is interested as much in the Hartley business as in Mrs. Hartley. To that end the "polished vulture" imports labor agitators to instigate a ruinous strike at the shipyards. Veteran Hartley returns after the Armistice and chases Kerr out of his home. The cast includes the Simons, a positive Jewish family from New York's East Side.

[LC, LP13733; *MPW* 6/21/19:1827; *Var* 6/13/19:50]

Agit; Am Icons?; Cap; Ger?; Jew; Lab; Strike; Vet
CM/ANTI-LAB

The Red Peril, Wharton Releasing Corp, C. V. Henkel, Oct, Am, Drama

At a private screening, Senator Clayton R. Lusk, head of the New York State Legislative Committee investigating Bolshevism, told the audience that this film would be "a highly effective weapon to combat the spread of the red menace." *The Red Peril* depicts how Bolshevik agents attempt to dupe loyal American workers into anarchy by using organized labor as their catspaw. The true blue workers rise up and defeat the radical agitators planted in their midst. The original print and negative of the film were destroyed by fire in June of 1919. *The Red Peril* thus had to be completely reshot.

[AFI, F1.3662; *MPN* 11/8/19:3473]

Agit; Bol; Lab; Spy-Sab; Viol
ANTI-SOV

The Red Viper, Tyrad Picts, Jacques Tyrol, Aug, Am, Drama

A newsboy on New York's east side, David Belkov (Jew?—played by Gareth Hughes), whose hero is Teddy Roosevelt, comes under the influence of a dark-haired anarchist named Yolanda Kosloff. After witnessing the eviction of an old woman, he joins the anarchist's band of fanatic agitators. They plan to instigate a street demonstration and kill a judge who has sentenced one of their number to death. David helps print incendiary leaflets composed by their leader, "Smith," while Yolanda practices tossing a bomb at the judge. However, David is shamed by the "Americanism" speeches of little Mary Hogan (a 26-year-old Ruth Stonehouse, who frequently played "little girl" roles, as the flag-waving adolescent), who declares her hatred for all traitors. After David reads about the anarchists killing Mary and, further, witnesses the negative impact of the leaflets on people in the streets, his patriotism is restored. In his crude phraseology David produces a pro-American flier condemning the anarchists: "They git paid for rilin' you up and you git killed. Be loyal to the country wot lets you in and gives you a chanst to live [sic]." After escaping from the infuriated Smith, David aborts Yolanda's attempt to blow up the judge. With the grateful judge's blessings, a chastened Yolanda and a wounded David are reunited. Note: An incipient Red Scare was kicked into high-gear by the infamous May Day letter bombs that were mailed to a number of prominent Americans, including Senator Lee Overman and Supreme Court Justice Oliver W. Holmes, Jr. An explicit reference to the incident appears in *The Volcano*, q.v.

[LC, LU14294; *EH* 9/13/19:65; *MPN* 9/6/19:2057; *MPW* 9/6/19:1531–32; *NYDM* 8/28/19:1378–79 (ad)]

Am Icons; Anarch; Bomb; Fem Rad; Irish; Jew?; Russ; Sec Ser; Viol
ANTI-REV

The Red Virgin, Rolfe/A. H. Fischer Feature, ?, B.A. Rolfe & Chester DeVonde, Am, Drama

It is debatable whether or not this "special feature" was ever released. No film under the title was copyrighted, nor have any reviews been found. The following comments were made in the November 29, 1919 issue of the *Motion Picture News*: "*The Red Virgin* treats current radicalism in Mystery Drama. The so-called Bohemian quarters of Art as breeding places for all forms of radicalism form the topic dealt with by Charles A. Logue in his story.... The subject is now being edited and titled.... A large cast, including Diana Allen, Eugene Strong, Marc McDermott...."

[*MPN* 11/8/19:3472; *MPN* 11/29/19:3939]
Artists; Dom Rad; G Vill?
ANTI-REV

The Right to Happiness, Universal-Jewel, Allen Holubar, Aug, Russ/Am(s), Drama

At the turn of the century, Mr. Hardcastle, an American millionaire in Russia, leaves his twin daughters (both adult roles played by Dorothy Phillips, known for her stylized acting) with a Jewish nurse while he goes on a business trip. During Hardcastle's absence a Cossack pogrom breaks out and the twins are separated. One is adopted by a Jewish family and reared in radicalism. The other is located by her father and together they return to America. Twenty years later the Russian twin, now known as Sonia, is sent by the Bolshevik regime to the United States to spread the revolution. Hardcastle has become an insensitive capitalist who has alienated his workers by refusing to increase wages or to hire veterans. In contrast, Vivian, his mission-working daughter, is shown distributing food to his employees' needy families. "Little Comrade" Sonia, unaware that Hardcastle is her father, incites the workers and leads a club-wielding mob that storms Hardcastle's Long Island mansion. When a fellow Russian agitator, called "The Fox," (Sergius Kerkoff; played by Hector Sarno) shoots at her twin sister, Sonia steps between them and is mortally wounded. Sonia's dying denunciation of mob violence causes Hardcastle to have a change of heart. The film concludes with Vivian's marriage to the factory foreman. Once again, having eliminated the radical aliens, the essential goodness of American workers is affirmed and reconciliation between labor and capital achieved. The Jew-Bolshevik linkage is also reaffirmed.

[PE (NFM); LC, LP14145; *EH* 9/20/19: 71–72; *NYDM* 9/25/19:1525; *Var* 9/5/19:61]

Agit; Am Icons; Atroc; Bol; Cap; Fem Rad; Jew; Lab; Lenin?; Mob; Reconcil; Rev; Russ; Strike?; Trotsky?; Vet; Viol
ANTI-SOV; CAP-LAB COOP

The Splendid Sin, Fox, Howard M. Mitchell, Sept, Brit/Russ, Drama

A childless couple, the Cathams, have a May Day party at their estate in England. Catham's sister Gertrude and her sweetheart Stephen Hartley (Wheeler Oakman), an American diplomat, make love in a deserted tower during a storm. Hartley proposes marriage, but is called away immediately to the Moscow consulate due to the dispatch of U.S. troops to Russia. Having finished his work there, Hartley is preparing to leave Moscow when he observes a Bolshevik mob attacking a group of starving women and children in front of the consulate. He dashes beyond the gates to assist them and is severely wounded. Months later, after recovering, Stephen returns to England. Gertrude has since died giving birth to their son. But it is agreed that the child should be adopted by the Cathams. Note: In the summer and fall of 1918, U.S. troops were sent to Russia and the last American diplomats withdrawn. An armed Soviet mob actually attacked the British embassy in Petrograd on August 31, 1918, and wounded their assistant naval attaché.

[LC, LP14163(s); *MPN* 9/6/19:2051; *MPW* 9/6/19:1528]

Allied Interv; Bol; Mob; Viol
CM/ANTI-SOV

The Stronger Vow, Goldwyn, Reginald Barker, April, Spain/Fr, Drama

The love of the sensuous Dolorous (Geraldine Farrar) for the tall, dark and handsome Juan (Milton Sills) is resented by her rugged cousin Pedro (Tom Santschi). Pedro kills her brother and leaves evidence implicating Juan. Later, while living in Paris, Dolorous is reunited with Juan. They marry soon afterwards. Pedro, also in Paris and working as an Apache dancer, is the leader of a band of Spanish anarchists. In a fit of jealousy, he kidnaps the two lovers. But another woman, whose sister Pedro had betrayed, informs the police. Note: During and after the first World War radical peasant groups and anarcho-syndicalist labor unions were very active in several provinces of Spain. Terrorist acts by anarchists in Catalonia swiftly rose between 1919 and 1923.

[LC, LP13613; *MPW* 5/10/19:938-39; *Var* 5/2/19:59]

Anarch; Decad; Pol; Viol
ANTI-REV

The Turn in the Road, Brentwood Film/Robertson-Cole, Mar, King W. Vidor, Am(s), Drama

Paul Perry (Lloyd Hughes), son of Perryville's leading capitalist, marries the daughter of the local fire-and-brimstone minister. When Paul's wife dies in childbirth, Paul denies God, leaves town and becomes a derelict. His wife's sister takes care of Paul's little son, Bob. Several years later, the "money-mad" Perry's refusal to grant a wage increase at his iron works results in his men welcoming a "crowd of Strike Agitators." Three employees are so enraged they seize Hamilton Perry (George Nichols) at his home, bind him in a chair and prepare to shoot the "iron master"— one of the suggested advertising Catch Lines provided by the *Motion Picture News*: "Labor tied Capital to a chair." At that moment, little Bob, with an armful of puppies, enters the room. The workers' anger is dissipated and grandfather's heart is softened. The strike is averted when Perry agrees to increase the men's wages. This well-received movie was the premiere production of the Brentwood Film Corporation, as well as the feature-length directorial debut of King Vidor. Vidor also wrote its screenplay.

[AFI, F1.4585; *MPN* 3/29/19:2020 & 2022; *MPW* 3/29/19:1841; *MPW* 4/5/19:96 (cs); *Var* 3/21/19:53]

Agit; Anti-Rel; Cap; Lab; Mob; Reconcil; Strike; Tramp; Viol
CAP-LAB COOP

The Undercurrent, Select, Wilfred North, Aug, Am(u), Drama

A veteran named Jack (played by the self-promoting super patriot, red-baiter and barrel-chested former AEF machine gunner, Sgt. Guy Empey) returns to his wife and child and takes up his old job at the steel mills. But after becoming unemployed, Jack begins mixing with disaffected "intellectuals" and alien agents at a German beer garden, who fill his head with an "undercurrent" of radical ideas. Meanwhile, the "Brotherhood" has made plans to start a general strike, blow up the mills, burn the homes of the owners and wreck the city. Jack is persuaded to make a speech endorsing their plans. However, before he leaves for the meeting hall Jack discovers that one of the "Reds" has invaded his home and attempted to violate his wife. Further inspired by a vision of his little boy holding the American flag, Jack goes to the Harmony Hall on the night of the uprising, denounces the radicals and destroys the Red flag (there were a number of Red flag incidents between so-called patriots and radical demonstrators on May Day, 1919). Jack escapes the resulting rioting and commandeers a train to the local Army barracks. The troops return with Jack to quell the disorder. The fanatic female radical, Mariska (played by the seductively dark-haired, twenty-six-year-old Betty Blythe), seeing the end is near, shoots her craven associates and then turns the gun on herself. The appreciative mill owner rehires Jack as a foreman. Note: Although this film's official release date is listed as August, it did not go into general distribution until November, during the middle of the Great Steel Strike (September 1919–January 1920).

[AFI, F1.4650; LC, LP14071; *EH* 9/6/19:63; *MPN* 11/29/19:3977; *NYDM* 12/4/19:1889; *Var* 11/21/19:55]

Am Icons; Bol; Decad; Dom Rad; Fem Rad; Ger; IWW?; Lab; Liq Link; Rev; Russ; Sab; Soc?; Strike; Unemployed; Vet; Viol
ANTI-SOV

The Uplifters, Metro, Herbert Blache, June, Am, Com-Drama

A pretty young stenographer named Hortense Troutt (May Allison) attends the local Button Makers' rally and hears Harriet Peebles Cull (People's Call?; to cull is to pick out something and put it aside as *inferior*; possible play on the name of the notorious socialist activist, "Rebel Girl" Elizabeth Gurley Flynn, 1890–1964; actress Kathleen Kerrigan) lecture on the subject of the "sweating serfs and suffering slaves of industry." As a newly awakened member of the "downtrodden," Hortense returns to work the next day and refuses any longer to put up with the "perfidy" and "baseness" of the rich. She also ignores the entreaties of Saul Shilpick, Jr. (Pell Trenton), her fiancé and the son of her now ex-employer. Hortense pays a visit to the female socialist. The latter calls our heroine "comrade" and invites the jobless girl to share her studio apartment in Greenwich Village. The new "sister" of the unkempt "short-haired women and long-haired men" of "Bohemia" soon discovers that she is merely a servant in disguise. But she is compensated by her love for the greasy poet Larry Hoden (as in coarse cloth; actor Howard Gaye)—known as the "Harvard Tramp." When Hortense lends him $40 to buy a new suit to wear at their wedding, he spends the money on liquor. While waiting for comrade Larry's return, she learns from one of his three existing wives that he is a practitioner as well as an advocate of free love—the randy Larry may have been a caricature of the well-known radical writer John Reed and this unnamed "Larry's Wife," played by Lois Wood, may have likewise been intended to represent Reed's real-life wife, Louise Bryant—material in the musical cue sheet would also suggest that the marriage certificate was to be signed in red ink. Our little blonde lady is saved by her former fiancé, "Sauljie," from the continued "freedom" of the "Bull-sheviki." The "bull," as in bullshit, routine had been used earlier that year in the star comedy one-reeler *The Bullsheviki*. All inter-titles in *The Uplifters* contained the hyphenated uncapitalized spelling, so as to place maximum emphasis on the "bull." This satire, part of Metro's "All Star" series, made use of most of the major non-violent, anti-communist film components, i.e. anti-intellectualism, debauchery and/or alcoholism and ideological hypocrisy.

[LC, LP13923; *MPW* 7/12/19:281–82; *MPW* 7/19/19:397 (cs); *Wid's* 6/29/19:3]

Artist; Bol; Cap; Decad; Dom Rad; Fem Rad; G Vill; Lab; Liq Link; Mtg; Soc; Tramp; Unemployed
ANTI-REV; ANTI-SOV

Virtuous Men, S-L Picts/Ralph Ince Film, Ralph Ince, April, Am(u), Drama

Young and virile Bob Stokes (the 200 pound-plus Elmo Lincoln), formerly a wealthy and popular New York clubman, goes on the bum after his fiancée jilts him. Bob wanders upstate (or, to the northwest; information is contradictory) to a camp of the National Lumber Company where he is given a job as a lumberjack by the sympathetic president, Willard. Bob's organizational abilities quickly improve productivity, to the chagrin of Robert Brummon (Robert W. Cummings), the stocky camp boss. Brummon is actually a Bolshevik agent who is there to sabotage the efforts of Willard to complete a government contract (in response to extensive I.W.W. activities in the northwest lumber industry, wartime Washington sponsored the Loyal Legion of Loggers and Lumbermen, which sent out patrols around camps to discourage AFL and I.W.W. organizers). One night Brummon (rum bum?) passes out liquor to the men and harangues them about being overworked and underpaid. But Bob handles the wildcat strike mob by physically beating the Bolshevik and then by appealing to the workers' patriotism. After Brummon is replaced as foreman by Bob, the bruised revolutionary starts a forest fire. Bob easily rallies the men to control the flaming woods. Brummon and his gang of "Red Radicals" later set out to obstruct work at the shipyards where Willard is now building a "mystery ship" for the government. Willard sends his new trouble shooter to the shipyards to counter the influence upon the workers of the "alien enemies." Bob's former fiancée, Marcia, who has become a pawn of Brummon, is ordered to lure him to her apartment to be killed. Once there, Bob learns from Marcia that the Reds have planted a time bomb to destroy the ship. Following a desperate fight with Brummon, young Stokes runs to the shipyards and saves the now completed vessel from destruction. Note: This film had an extended "Direct to the Public" exploitation campaign.

[AFI, F1.4750; *MPN* 4/26/19:2708; *MPW* 4/19/19:428–29; *MPW* 6/18/19:1973–74 (cs)]

Agit; Am Icons; Bol; Bomb; Cap; Dom Rad; IWW?; Lab; Liq Link; Mob; Sab; Spy-Sab; Strike; Tramp; Viol
ANTI-SOV; CAP-LAB COOP

The Volcano, Harry Raver/W.W. Hodkinson, George Irving, Aug, Am, Drama

A young school teacher on the East Side named Ruth (Jew?), played by Leah Baird, comes under the influence of a radical long-nosed Bolshevik writer named Alexis Minski (Russian Jew?—"a repulsively erratic sort" played by Jacob Kingsberry). Ruth loses her job when she allows the gesticulating Bolshevik to accompany her on a visit to the school superintendent to protest the under-nourishment of her children (during the Red Scare there was a great deal of public concern over the loyalty of teachers; a particularly avid witch hunt for Reds in New York City during 1919 led to numerous dismissals). Meanwhile, Ruth falls in love with Captain Nathan Levison, the man whose life was saved by her brother Davy during the Battle of the Argonne in France. But complications arise when Levison, who is an intelligence officer, is assigned

to keep a watch on Alexis (by the summer of 1918, U.S. military intelligence was regularly monitoring radical organizations). In revenge, Minski convinces Ruth that Levison plans her arrest. Following New York Governor Al Smith signing the state law banning the display of the Red flag (to demonstrate his anti-radicalism, news cameras were permitted to film this May 7th event) the Bolsheviks plot to assassinate him and other prominent Americans (topicality is made explicit here by showing a close-up of a list of names of those prominent individuals who were actual or intended victims of the notorious late April/May Day letter bomb scare—the thirty-odd names on the so-called "Bomb Honor List" included Attorney General A. Mitchell Palmer). Ruth's brother and other veterans burst in upon Alexis and his bomb-making gang and see to it that the Bolsheviks are arrested by the authorities. Ruth is reunited with Levison. The couple are wed at a double ceremony, attended by Governor Smith. Davy marries Olga, a former member of the Bolsheviks! By the end of the year, twenty-four states had passed bills making it illegal to show the Red flag in public. According to the *Variety* review, the original version of *The Volcano* was "strongly anti-Semitic." Explicit protests led to some awkward title changes—the hero acquiring a Semitic surname and the Bolshevik leader becoming "Minski(ovich)." Alexis ludicrously states in one inter-title, "I am not a Jew; I am a Bolshevik." The musical cue sheet makes a reference to a close up on the socialist paper, the *New York Call*—probably referring to the writing activities of Minski. Borch's "The Crafty Spy" was used as the "Bolsheviki Theme" music.

[AFI, F1.4767; *MPW* 8/9/19:857 (cs); *MPW* 8/16/19:1024; *Var* 8/15/19:71; *Wid's* 8/17/19:15]

Am Icons; Bol; Bomb; Dom Rad; Fem Rad; Jew?; Russ?; Sec Ser; Soc; Unemployed; Vet; Vig; Viol
ANTI-SOV

When Doctors Disagree, Goldwyn, Victor L. Schertzinger, May, Am, Comedy

Millie Martin (Mabel Normand) receives money from her tightwad father after amusing him with the story of how the daughter of the town's wealthiest man was pushed into a putrid pool by the "village Bolshevik." She later has adventures on a train trip.

[AFI, F1.4886; LC, LP13711]
Bol; Cap
CM/ANTI-SOV

When the Clouds Roll By, UA, Victor Fleming, Dec, Am, Com-Drama
    Daniel Boone Brown (Douglas Fairbanks) is a superstitious young man who toils at his uncle's Wall Street office. Bored with his life, Daniel visits the weird Dr. Metz. Daniel later experiences a series of strange nightmares, including one in which two men dressed and masked in black, called "Discord" and "Worry," topple a Lady Liberty, named "Reason," from her pedestal. Daniel's girlfriend, Lucette, is an art student living in Greenwich Village.
    [AFI, F1.4900; LC, LP14595; *MPG*, Vol. X, Silents, pp. 303–04; *MPW* 1/10/20:289]
    Am Icons; Anarch?; Artist; Cap; G Vill; Lab
    CM/ANTI-REV

The Woman on the Index, Goldwyn, Hobart Henley, Feb, Am, Drama
    Sylvia (Pauline Frederick), the widow of a gangster, goes to work as a secretary for a diplomat. After they marry, Sylvia discovers her name on the criminal index. Fearing exposure, she contacts the old police chief involved in the case, now a member of the federal Secret Service. He agrees to help on the condition that she play up to a foreigner named Hugo Declasse (Willard Mack; to be déclassé is to have lost class) who is suspected of "fomenting a Bolshevik uprising." When it appears Sylvia is paying too much attention to this man in the Washington social scene, her husband casts her out. All ends well after a Japanese agent, posing as a valet for Declasse, gains possession of documents revealing Hugo's crimson political colors.
    [LC, LP13374; *MPN* 4/5/19:2184; *Var* 3/28/19:39]
    Bol; Sec Ser; Spy-Sab
    CM/ANTI-SOV

Woman, Woman!, Fox, Kenean Buel, Jan, Am, Drama
    Alice Lindsay (the notorious Evelyn Nesbit), bored with her life in a small New England town, makes her way to New York City. In Greenwich Village she becomes part of the bohemian set. A radical young English writer named Gwenn Stevens (Gareth Hughes) proposes a "free love" union, but Alice refuses. Instead, she marries Samson Rathbone, a civil engineer. After Samson contracts malaria at a railroad project, Alice makes the "great surrender" to a wealthy jeweler to obtain the money needed to cure her husband. A parallel story is portrayed through a Japanese motion picture Alice watches in a theater. In the film within the film a young girl sells herself so that her family may survive while her brother joins the Army to fight the Russians during the Russo-Japanese War of 1904–05. Note: At the time of this film's release, Japanese and American troops were in Siberia fighting the Reds. And deadly disease was something else that was on virtually everyone's mind. Between the fall of 1918 and early 1919 a worldwide influenza epidemic claimed the lives of millions, including nearly 500,000 Americans.
    [LC, LP13323; *MPN* 2/8/19:917; *Var* 1/31/19:52]
    Artist; Cap; Decad; G Vill; Russ
    CM/ANTI-SOV

The World Aflame, Frank Keenan Prods/Pathé, Ernest C. Warde, Aug, Am(u), Drama
    Carson Burr (Frank Keenan; who also co-wrote the screenplay), a millionaire manufacturer, finds his domestic life disrupted as a result of his servants reading a Bolshevik paper called *The Red Messenger*. Sensing the potential for serious labor unrest, Burr runs for mayor and wins. Soon after the election, the bearded Red leader, Nicolai Poppoff (possible allusion to Nikolai or V.I. Lenin in given name; irate and/or indiscreet expressions related to the surname) incites the streetcar men to go on strike as the prelude to a general, city-wide strike (a general strike in Petrograd spearheaded the Bolshevik Revolution). Burr goes to the car barns with a squad of police, arms a strike-breaking streetcar (draped with an American flag?), gives orders to shoot and places thousands of vigilante police guards around industries. Some anarchists, including a dark-haired woman named Emma Reich (as in Goldman; German-Jew association?— played by Claire DuBrey), kidnap Burr's son Theodore (named in honor of Teddy Roosevelt) and threaten to kill him unless the mayor backs down. But Burr is not intimidated and he is able to win over the striking workmen by convincing them they were "misled by

alien propagandists." With the aid of armed veterans, the alien agitators are rounded-up and arrested. The mayor then gathers the local corporation heads and takes them with him to a mass meeting being held by the workers. Capital and labor agree to cooperate through a profit-sharing program. The Bolsheviks are deported. Note: Mayor Ole Hanson's nationally publicized/lionized stand against the January-February 1919 strike in Seattle (a general strike of 60,000 workers — Feb. 6–10), proclaimed as Red inspired by the press, was the inspiration for this film. Although federal troops were called in, the strike was peacefully terminated. The 1917 Bluebird release, *The Car of Chance*, q.v., also dealt with a streetcar strike.

[LC, LU14023; *EH* 8/23/19:56; *MPW* 8/9/19:876–77]

Agit; Am Icons; Anarch; Bol; Cap; Deport; Fem Rad; IWW?; Jew? Lab; Mtg; Mob; Pol; Reconcil; Russ?; Scabs; Strike; Vet; Vig; Viol

ANTI-REV; ANTI-SOV; CAP-LAB COOP

The World and Its Woman, Goldwyn, Frank Lloyd, Sept, Russ/Am, Drama

Marcia Warren, the daughter of an American mining engineer working in Tsarist Russia, becomes the ward of Prince Orbeliana following her father's death. She grows up loving the prince's son, Michael (Lou Tellegen), but he marries a Russian noblewoman. Marcia embarks on an opera career (Geraldine Farrar, the actress playing the part, was a diva of the Metropolitan Opera, who was also married to her film co-star). Prince Michael's wife and her lover are later killed by rioting peasants during the reign of terror that follows the Bolshevik revolution. These revolutionary scenes include one in which a Red pronounces that they will also rid Russia of her priests. The Prince returns from the front to Petrograd and declares his love for Marcia. But it is Marcia who must save Michael and herself by outwitting the lascivious Bolshevik commander named Peter Poreschine (as in porcine). A lady Red named Erina Rodina (as in rodent?) discovers the prince's identity and, together with Poreschine, unsuccessfully attempts to thwart the couple's escape plans during a dramatic confrontation. Disguised as peasants, the two lovers make their way to the American troops stationed in Archangel. The two lovers are wed

upon their arrival in the United States. Because *The World and Its Woman* was released at the height of the Red Scare, it is interesting to note a reviewer's comment appearing in *Harrison's Reports*: "the Bolsheviki stuff has been so done to death, that people are simply sick of it." On a lighter note, this film featured an operatic interlude at the Russian Royal Opera in which Miss Farrar performed the "Mirror Song" from Massenet's "Thais" — played on a phonograph — the commercial availability of the recording suggested as an exploitation "hook-up" for distributors. Note: U.S. military forces had landed there in September of 1918 and stayed in the Archangel area until June of 1919. Actual combat took place between the Doughboys and the Reds, but this was never portrayed in an American feature film (Harold Lloyd has a military encounter, of sorts, with the Bolsheviks in the 1919 Pathé comedy short, *A Sammy in Siberia* — refer to Appendix 2).

[LC, LP14079; *EH* 9/27/19:69; *Harrison's Reports* 9/6/19:44; *MPW* 9/20/19:1864–65; *NYDM* 9/18/19:1490; *Var* 9/12/19:52]

Allied Interv; Anti-Rel; Atroc; Bol; Decad; Escape; Fem Rad; Mob; Rev; Russ; Tsar?; Viol; White Russ

ANTI-SOV

1920

A Beggar in Purple, Edgar Lewis Prods/Pathé, Edgar Lewis, Nov, Am(s), Drama

As a young lad, John Hargrave (Leonard C. Shumway) unsuccessfully pleaded with rich paper mill owner Roger Winton for a job in order to save his invalid mother's life. Eighteen years later, Hargrave controls his own paper company. In an attempt to stymie his powerful new rival, Winton bribes Calvin Reed (as in John Reed?), editor of the I.W.W. sheet, *The Pillory*, to incite labor unrest at Hargrave's mill. With stolen company reorganization papers in his possession and expecting a strike against his competitor's company, Winton tries to manipulate a stock takeover. Hargrave's loyal stenographer, Margaret, helps preserve her employer's paper mill by exposing Winton's plot and authorizing a raise that averts the impending strike.

[LC, LU15688; *MPN* 11/13/20:3819; *MPW* 11/13/20:251]

Agit; Cap; IWW; Lab; Reconcil; Strike

ANTI-CAP; CAP-LAB COOP

Billions, Metro, Ray C. Smallwood, Dec, Am, Com-Drama

Before the revolution a Russian princess, played by Alla Nazimova, has taken up residence in New York City. Through an agent, she becomes the patron of several struggling young artists, including a mad Russian poet named Pushkin. She falls in love with an American poet who comes into great wealth by inheritance from his uncle Krakerfeller (as in Rockefeller). This leads to an attempted blackmail plot by a Jewish family to force him to marry their daughter. The real will of the writer's uncle then turns up leaving him penniless again. Meanwhile, the Soviet revolution has swept away the fortune of the princess. The two abandon the fast track of flappers and poseurs and start life anew in a garret in Washington Square.

[LC, LP15826; *MPN* 12/11/20:4503; *Var* 12/10/20:35]

Artist; Cap; G Vill; Jew; Mad Russ; Rev; White Russ

CM/ANTI-SOV

Dangerous Hours, Famous Players-Lasky/Par-Artcraft, Fred Niblo, Feb, Am(s)/Russ, Drama

A recent college graduate, John King (Lloyd Hughes), meets a female radical named Sophia Guerni (as in guerra—war; played by Claire DuBrey) when he is arrested during a labor demonstration. Falling under her sway, John is introduced to the decadent "intellectual" set at her Washington Square apartment. This group is enthralled by the blood-curdling revolutionary tales of a bearded Bolshevik fanatic from the "New Russia," Boris Blotchi (Jack Richardson). Inspired by the news of a National Strike, the group decides to exploit a sympathy strike in the small town of New Meadows at the shipyard owned by John's old sweetheart, the virginal Mary Weston. Working through a front organization of the Bolsheviks, John unsuccessfully attempts to enlist the cooperation of the local labor leaders. After John is rebuffed by the patriotic American workers, Blotchi assumes complete control over the radicals and wins the favors of a now-crazed Sophia. The Reds' incitement of east coast riffraff, including local drunks, results in a riotous mob destroying the business district and even to the burning down of a small white-painted church. John finally realizes he has been duped when his patriotism is mocked by the revolutionaries—Sophia literally damns America. Recovering consciousness after being black-jacked by a bearded radical, John rescues the besieged loyal union men defending the shipyard by blowing up the screaming Bolshevik-led mob with one of Blotchi's bombs. John is restored to the love of Mary and the respect of his white-haired father. Two labor agitators who had attempted to extort money from Mary, named Reagan and Fetton (described in an introductory title during an earlier scene as a "labor agitator and a blackmailer"), are tarred and feathered and carried out of town on rails! The inter-titles of this film were particularly effective in reinforcing basic images of the communist Other. For instance, John as the dupe, is juxtaposed in the painted art titles with a jester's fool's cap and Blotchi, the Red butcher, is juxtaposed with pictures of a knife dripping with blood. In an unusually graphic flashback, scenes of mass executions in revolutionary Russia (including the "little sons of Russian officers who fought in the Great War"—presumably White officers actively participating in the civil war) are shown and "nationalized" women are portrayed as being at the mercy of psychopathic Red Guards. The working title of this film was "Americanism (Versus Bolshevism)". Note: By referring to a general strike and featuring shipyard workers, there was an apparent attempt to create an associative linkage with the Seattle General Strike, which was initiated by a walk out of shipyard workers protesting a wage cut—refer to *The World Aflame* (Pathé, 1919), q.v.

[S (LC; Vid); LC, LP14488; *EH* 1/10/20:61–62; *MPW* 2/14/20:971, 1116; *MPW* 5/17/19:1054–55 (6 pg. ad between)]

Agit; Am Icons; Anti-Rel; Atroc; Bol; Bomb; Camp Rad; Cap; Decad; Fem Rad; G Vill; Irish; Jew?; Lab; Lenin?; Liq Link; Mob; Pol; Rev; Russ; Strike; Tramp; Trotsky?; Vet; Viol; White Russ

ANTI-SOV; CM/CAP-LAB COOP

Democracy—The Vision Restored, Democracy Photoplay, Sept, William Nigh, Am, Social Drama

This film was originally copyrighted in March and listed at 11 reels. *Democracy*, at seven reels, was recopyrighted in August. It would appear that its socialistic content was toned-down and release delayed until after the

Red Scare hysteria had abated. *Democracy* and *The Dwelling Place of Light*, q.v., both released in September, represent a major break with the paroxysm of anti-Bolshevism that had racked the country between April–May 1919 and July–August 1920. In fact, only one other virulently anti-communist film would be released after September in 1920, *The Face at Your Window* (Oct.) q.v. In its capital vs. labor format, *Democracy* is an anachronistic throwback to that genre that so frequently appeared on the screen between 1909 and 1917. A film that portrays labor positively would become a rare occurrence in movie theaters following the Red Scare. The paradoxical comment in the *Variety* review for *Democracy* is worth quoting to introduce the plot of the film: "...suffice it, it is propaganda worthy of approbation by 100 per cent Americans, although bordering too closely and unpleasantly on out-and-out socialism." Henry Fortune (as in Henry Ford?) is a selfish capitalistic autocrat. He has two grandsons, David and John. The latter easily advances up the corrupt ladder of capitalism while David (William Nigh) becomes a reporter and acquires a social consciousness. At a labor hall meeting "David Jones" responds to a "wild Russian" speaker and his anarchistic cohort when the anarchist suggests that munitions plants supplying the European war should be blown up. David is fired for his involvement in political activities. At a subsequent meeting, he learns that his brother, along with other capitalists, has plotted with "agitators" to create controlled disturbances in order to have an excuse to break labor. Soon afterwards, America enters the war and David joins the Army. In the shared adversity of life in the trenches he becomes comrades with the anarchist with whom he had quarreled, as well as with men from many other walks of life. After the war, David rescues his working-class wife (Mary, a blind girl) from John and then forces his brother to recognize the rights of humanity.

[LC, LU14813(s), LP15430; *MPW* 9/4/20:113–14; *Var* 9/3/20:45]

Am Icons; Anarch; Cap; Decad; Lab; Mad Russ; Mtg; Sab; Soc?; Vet

ANTI-CAP; CAP-LAB COOP

The Dwelling Place of Light, Hampton/W.W. Hodkinson, Sept, Jack Conway, Am(s), Drama

The villainous, womanizing general man-ager of the Hampton Mills, Claude Ditmar (Robert McKim), drives the men so hard at his New England factory that they strike. Janet Butler (Claire Adams), Ditmar's secretary, resigns following the discovery of his clandestine affair with her younger sister Elsie. Moved by the plight of the striking workers, including forced evictions from company housing, Janet attempts to help their families. While thus engaged, she meets and falls in love with Brooks Insall (King Baggot), a stockholder who is attempting to ameliorate the crisis. But due to their families' continued suffering, the workers (some of whom are Irish and Italian) resort to mob violence when strike breakers are brought into town. Eventually, labor peace is restored after the tyrannical manager is shot by the enraged mother of an impregnated Elsie. Benevolent capitalist Insall is installed in his place. Note: This film was loosely based upon a book written by American novelist Winston Churchill. The 1917 novel, apparently inspired by the Paterson strike of 1912, features an upper-class heroine who joins the I.W.W. to protest the tactics of the mill owners.

[LC, LP15686; *MPN* 9/25/20:2501; *MPW* 9/18/20:390]

Cap; Decad; Irish; Ital; Lab; Mob; Scabs; Strike; Viol

PRO-LAB

The Face at Your Window, Fox, Richard Stanton, Oct, Am(s), Drama

This Fox feature was a "special Americanization film made in conjunction with U.S. government propaganda against the spread of Bolshevism." One review commented that flag waving inter-titles made up over half the picture. Hiram Maxwell and Nicholas Harding are owners of factories in the industrial town of Hopewell, Virginia. The Maxwell Iron Works are run on a cooperative basis, but capitalist Harding prefers to force his wishes upon the workers under his control. Ivan Koyloff (Boris Rosenthal), an alien agitator at the Maxwell shops, stabs the owner's son in the back when the latter shows attention to Ruth, a pretty Russian working girl played by Gina Reilly. Revolted by Koyloff's attack upon Frank Maxwell (Earl Metcalfe), young Ruth becomes a Secret Service agent to counter "Bolshevik" activities among her people. This is needed, because a "stranger," Comrade Kelvin (Jew?; played by Edward Roseman), has just arrived in town from Soviet Russia. In a prefatory scene, the audience sees Lenin and his wife, along with Politburo member Zinoviev (Jew; leader of the Comintern), plotting out their strategy for revolution in America (Lenin's "Letter to American Workers" was widely distributed in the United States after March 1919). Fearing trouble, the employers meet and agree to cooperate with their workers. But Harding reneges, leading to a night shift revolt exploited by the Reds. With the alien dominated rabble destroying lives and property, the American Legion, accompanied by an old Civil War veteran, is summoned to restore order. Wearing Ku Klux Klan robes over their uniforms, the mounted Legionnaires rout the revolutionists! Following a patriotic speech by Frank Maxwell, capital and labor are reconciled and he and Ruth are reunited. The glorification of vigilantism in *The Face at Your Window* is reminiscent of the world war era anti-Hun excesses exemplified in such works as *The Prussian Cur* (Fox, 1918) q.v. Note: The American Legion was founded in February 1919 in order to, among other things, combat un-American Bolshevism. The animus of the "new Klan" of the 1920s was directed as much against aliens, Jews and Reds as against blacks. Nevertheless, by the time this film was released, in the fall of 1920, the public had had its fill of such fare. The fear of Red-inspired revolution *in the United States* would not again manifest itself on American movie screens until the mini-Red Scare of 1935.

[LC, LP15924 (c); *MPN* 11/13/20:3815; *MPW* 12/11/20:768–69]

Agit; Am Icons; Bol; Cap; Ital; Jew; Lab; Lenin; Mob; Reconcil; Russ; Sab?; Sec Ser; Vet; Vig; Viol

ANTI-SOV; CAP-LAB COOP

Help Yourself, Goldwyn, Hugo Ballin, Sept, Am, Comedy

Based on a *Saturday Evening Post* serial, "Trimmed in Red," this production was promoted under that title during the winter in the trade journals. Emily Ray (Madge Kennedy), an animal fancier who works at a department store, is taken in by her wealthy aunt. Rich cousin Rosamonde sponsors the Neo-Phytagoreans, a religious cult who believe in the transmigration of human souls into the bodies of animals. Professor Syle (as in silly) is invited to lecture the group on "parlor Bolshe-

vism" (so-called "parlor Bolsheviks" were loosely defined as influential individuals who were communist sympathizers—their alleged numbers were greatly exaggerated by reactionaries). Hoping to financially exploit the fatuous socialites, Syle converts to their religion and takes them to Greenwich Village to meet his comrades. These bohemian radicals include "a motley crew" of all the by now standard alien types: Epstein, the Jew; Tony, the Italian; Odoroskavitch, the odoriferous Russian. Emily's aunt invites these men, who plan to "paint society a bright red," to her home. Emily, socially put down as the "shop girl" by her cousin, suspects the intentions of the Reds. With the use of large amounts of vodka and the assistance of Rosamonde's brother, Oliver, "comrade" Emily exposes the radicals' true colors. Having "cured" Rosamonde, Emily marries Oliver. Professor Syle, also abandoning the cause, marries a society girl (middle-class responsibilities neutralizing the utopian intoxicants of Bolshevism). Among the few relevant Red Scare era comedies, this film is even more unique for its lack of overt class violence.

[AFI, F1.1860; LC, LP15627; *ETR* 10/9/20:2069 (cs); *MPN* 2/7/20:1488; *MPN* 4/3/20:3013 (ad); *Var* 9/24/20:43]

Bol; Dom Rad; G Vill; Ital; Jew; Liq Link; Russ

ANTI-REV

The Key to Power, Educational Films, William Parke, Jan, Am, Drama

A six-reel version of this film was originally scheduled for release in late 1918. But, primarily due to its heavy anti-German content, it was reedited (reducing its length to five reels) and not finally made available for exhibition until a year later. By placing greater emphasis on the problem of labor radicalism in the coalfields, it would appear that a deliberate attempt was made to exploit the ongoing Red Scare. Captain Bruce Wendell (Hugh Thompson) becomes the head of a coal mine company in West Virginia after his father is mortally injured in a car accident arranged by labor saboteurs. A German agent named Meyer and his socialist hireling Gross (a surname with inherent negative associations) bribe the railroad owner whose line hauls the coal to renege on his contract and create dissension among the miners, in order to disrupt deliveries of coal to the government. When Bruce struggles to keep the mine open, the radicals set off an explosion near its entrance in an attempt to destroy the central power house. The local Army garrison arrives in the nick of time to rescue Wendell and his girlfriend, played by Claire Adams, from the clutches of Meyer's gang. This was a rare film example portraying Federal troops, as opposed to militia, being used in a labor dispute.

[AFI, F1.2342; *MPN* 12/14/18:3604; *MPN* 1/4/20:310 (ad); *MPW* 12/21/18:1380; *MPW* 12/28/18:1562]

Cap; Ger; Lab; Sab; Soc; Spy-Sab; Vet?; Viol

ANTI-SOC

Lifting Shadows, Leonce Perret Prod/Pathé, Leonce Perret, April, Russ/Am, Drama

This film picks up the old Nihilist genre and awkwardly melds it to the anti-Bolshevik works of the Red Scare period. To quote the *Motion Picture News* review: "The strong dramatic moments, the killings, the bombs and Russians are all there, but the picture seems to revert back to the ones we used to see three and four years ago…. At the present time, there seems to be little demand for this type of picture." Yet, *Lifting Shadows* is significant, because the very crudeness of its political imagery highlights the linkages that were being made between the pre-Bolshevik revolution Reds and/or nihilists and the Reds of the new Soviet regime. In 1914, prior to the outbreak of World War I, Serge Ostrowski is a member of the executive committee of "The Circle of Death." Before making the ultimate sacrifice for the cause, he gives his daughter Vania (Emmy Wehlen) the secret plans for the campaign to spread their doctrines and create a social revolution in America. Five years later Vania is living in America and married to a wealthy drug addict, played by Stuart Holmes. At the Arts Club ball the shadow of her past falls upon Vania. Three members of the old radical committee approach Vania. The blood-crazed group, now representatives of the Bolshevik regime, want her father's plans in order to carry out the revolution in the United States. But Vania declares herself to be loyal to the Red, White and Blue. Vania's resistance leads to the convenient death of her dissolute husband and the exposure of a bomb plot to kill the governor at a dinner party. The Bolsheviks' headquarters are raided by the police.

[LC, LU14827; *MPN* 4/3/20:3171; *MPW* 4/3/20:139]

Bol; Bomb; Cap; Decad; Nih; Pol; Rev; Russ; Viol

ANTI-SOV

Little Miss Rebellion, New Art/Par, George Fawcett, Sept, Rur/Am, Com-Drama

The Grand Duchess Marie Louise (Dorothy Gish) of the mythical kingdom of Bulgravia is bored with the formalities of court life. One day she sneaks out of the palace and joins a company of American Doughboys stationed in the neighborhood who are playing baseball—"The game that follows the flag." That night she attends a "jazz ball" with a handsome young American soldier, Sergeant "Dick" Ellis (Ralph Graves), and falls in love. But shortly afterwards, the U.S. troops are withdrawn and a group of "Bolsheviki" plotters, led by Colonel Moro, start a revolution. The Grand Duchess and a faithful old guardsman flee to America with the crown jewels. On the East Side of New York City, the two take up residence in a tenement under assumed names. Bolshevik agents follow in hot pursuit, intent upon killing their former ruler and seizing the valuable royal crown. Returning home one day from her hash house job, she discovers the gang of Bolsheviks have bound and gagged the guardsman. They torture her to reveal the location of the jewels. Ellis, now a civilian, having recognized Marie Louise flipping pancakes in the restaurant window, has fortuitously followed her. The battered revolutionists are later led away in manacles by the police. And where were those royal baubles? In an American consumer icon, available even in humble furnished rooms, the ice box—hidden in the mashed potatoes! The film concludes with Dick handing his Americanized "princess" a stick of gum. George Siegmann played the "hissable villain" (*MPN*), whose surname would have created associative linkages in the contemporary audience with the Muslim Moro rebels defeated by American occupation troops during a vicious counter-insurgency campaign in the southern Philippine Islands (Fox's 1918 release, *Under the Yoke*, actually takes place during that insurrection). Note: Seigman, aka George A. Siegmann, was best known for his role as the evil mulatto in *The Birth of a Nation* (Epoch; 1915). This was the earliest example of the escaped royalty with crown jewels subgenre that would predominate among American made anti-Bolshevik films during most of the twenties, beginning in 1922 with another Paramount film, *The Face in the Fog*, q.v.

[LC, LP15421; *ETR* 9/11/20:1660 (cs); *MPN* 10/2/20:2709; *MPW* 9/25/20:528–29; *Var* 9/24/20:43]

Am Icons; Atroc; Bol; Jewels; Pol; Rev; Vet; Viol
ANTI-REV

Nurse Marjorie, Realart Picts, William Desmond Taylor, April, Brit, Drama

Lady Marjorie, played by Mary Miles Minter, shocks some of her family when she joins the nursing staff at a medical facility for the wealthy—the Duchess voices a concern that her daughter may even have to "wash the feet of stock brokers!" One of Marjorie's patients is a Labor Party member of parliament who is surgically treated to correct a squint. After his bandages are removed, John Danbury (Clyde Fillmore), known as "the People's John," becomes smitten with his comely nurse. Marjorie is likewise romantically attracted, but decides to test the MP's sincerity to his professed social principles by pretending to come from a humble Irish background. Meanwhile, John is being pressed by his colleagues and his father, the owner of a shipyard, to apply his political talents to a nationwide strike. After breaking up with Marjorie, John visits his father's shipyard and is addressing a crowd of strikers, when a disgruntled worker pulls out a gun and shoots the dedicated labor leader. Marjorie reads in the paper about the "cowardly attack by an … assailant … believed to be a Russian," and immediately travels to John's home to be by his side. A smiling Duke enters the room and contemplatively muses: "The tribune of the people marries an aristocrat who has labored for the people! The combination is irresistible!"

[S (LC); LC, LP14918; *Var* 5/28/20:42; *Wid's* 3/28/20:11]

Cap; Lab; Pol; Russ; Strike; Viol
CM/ANTI-REV

The Penalty, Goldwyn, Wallace Worsley, Aug, Am, Drama

Blizzard (Lon Chaney), whose legs were unnecessarily amputated when he was a youth, has grown up to become the "Lord and Master of the Underworld" in San Francisco. Blizzard's business enterprises include prostitution and a sweatshop fabricating straw hats. He is obsessed with wreaking revenge, both upon the doctor responsible for his condition and a society that has made him an outcast. Blizzard grotesquely hobbles about with short crutches upon leather-capped stumps. In order to punish the middle-class that has shunned him as a cripple, Blizzard has secretly stockpiled weapons in an underground chamber and masterminded an Irish associate's organization of "thousands of disgruntled foreign laborers." He discloses to the labor agitator, named O'Hagan, that on a designated day the thousands of "foreign malcontents," following a signal explosion, will be set lose to riot throughout the city. As he discloses this to O'Hagan, Blizzard madly envisions the armed rioters (wearing his straw hats; many with beards) shooting policemen, seizing the telephone exchange, burning buildings and battling the militia. Blizzard explains that as the police and military withdraw to protect the suburbs, the underworld will be free to loot the city. But, in the meantime, the Federal Secret Service, concerned about this criminal linkage with the "Reds," sends its top female agent to find out what the "cripple from Hell" is plotting. Agent Rose will eventually fall in love with Blizzard. The doctor, whom Blizzard wished to destroy, performs surgery on the tormented man, relieving the pressure on his brain which was responsible for his malevolent desires. Shot by a former criminal associate, Blizzard dies in Rose's arms declaiming: "Fate chained me to Evil—for that I must pay the Penalty."

[S (GEH; Vid); LC, LP15383; *MPW* 8/21/20:1069; *Var* 11/19/20:34]

Agit; Am Icons; Artist; Bomb; Cap; Decad; Dom Rad; Irish; Lab; Liq Link; Militia; Mob; Pol; Sec Ser; Viol
CM/ANTI-REV

The Perfect Woman, Joseph M. Schenck Prods/First Nat, July, David Kirkland, Am, Comedy

Mary Blake, a vamp played by Constance Talmadge, develops a crush on a misogynistic shipyard partner named James Stanhope when he addresses the "Working Girls Club Against Bolshevism." News of his speech reaches the shipyard and angers several radicals who work

The Penalty (Goldwyn, 1920): The "discontented" foreign workers of San Francisco, stirred-up to mass revolutionary action, as gleefully envisioned by a power-crazed gangster played by Lon Chaney.

there. Meanwhile, Mary decides to secure a secretarial job under the priggish Jim, but is turned down by the company character expert for being a flirt. After taking a course in character, dressing down and donning a pair of glasses, a new Mary passes muster and goes to work as personal secretary to Jim's mother. One night, the Reds, led by anarchist Grimes (Ned Sparks), enter the Stanhope home, gag and bind Jim and set a time bomb under his chair. While they are raiding the wine cellar, Mary comes downstairs in her kimono to get her comb, charms the Red standing guard, saves Jim and then assists in disarming the rest of the gang of radicals. *The Perfect Woman* provides a rare example in American film of the Reds being vamped.

[LC, LP16202; *MPW* 8/7/20:694–95, 779; *Var* 7/30/20:32–33]

Anarch; Bol; Bomb; Cap; Dom Rad; Lab; Liq Link

ANTI-SOV

Riders of the Dawn, Hampton/W.W. Hodkinson, Hugh Ryan Conway, May, Am(r), Western

Kurt Dorn (Roy Stewart) returns to the northwest wheat belt after heroic service in France in this adaptation of a Zane Grey novel (*The Desert of Wheat*, 1919). Kurt's homecoming brings out most of the town, including Civil War veterans and his sweetheart Lenore (Claire Adams). But before he can get down to farming again, Kurt is summoned to a secret meeting of the "Law and Order Committee" and made commander of a vigilante group called the "Riders of the Dawn." The purpose of its formation is to rid the community of a band of "radicals"/"hoboes" camping in the area who have been whipped-up by I.W.W. style rhetoric to undermine the laborers harvesting the wheat crop. Henry Neuman (Robert McKim), a German immigrant lawyer, has secretly organized the radicals. Sabotage activities of these radicals include torching the fields of some farmers. Neuman also lusts for Lenore. He arranges for a Russian vamp associate, Olga, to discredit the war hero by falsely claiming she is his abandoned French wife. Neuman's chief henchman, a "caveman" type tramp named Nash (Frederick Starr), brutally murders Lenore's sister when the teenaged girl discovers his nefarious activities. Neuman then kidnaps Lenore. Kurt rushes to the radicals' camp, dispatching Nash and rescuing Lenore from their villainous leader. The Riders arrive and round up the remaining Reds (in the source novel the placarded corpses of lynched Wobblies are left dangling from trees). This film would appear to have been influenced by Griffith's classic 1915 release, *The Birth of a Nation*. Rural radicalism had only briefly appeared in films before, during 1912, in such works as *The Agitator*, q.v. The topic would not be addressed again until the 1930s. Note: So-called "pick-handle brigades" of vigilantes in the Dakotas attacked the Wobblies during the latter's 1917 campaign to improve the working conditions of itinerant wheat bundlers. In addition, at the time of this film's release wheat prices were plummeting—between 1919 and the end of 1920 overall farm prices fell forty percent.

[LC, LP15879; *MPN* 5/15/20:4231; *MPW* 5/15/20:980]

Am Icons; Decad; Fem Rad; Ger; IWW; Lab; Rur Rad; Russ; Sab; Tramp; Vet; Vig; Viol

ANTI-LAB; ANTI-REV

The Skywayman, Fox, James P. Hogan, Sept, Am, Advent-Drama

A Lafayette Escadrille ace returns home after apparently recovering from combat injuries. However, it soon develops that his wounds have caused him to suffer amnesia. Though he can still fly a plane, Captain Locke remembers neither his parents nor his sweetheart. Accepting the advice of an unscrupulous doctor, girlfriend Virginia agrees to pretend she is the Tsar's niece who has had the crown jewels stolen from her by two Russians. Virginia tells the heroic captain that the foreign thieves are speeding away on a train and asks him to help her retrieve the valuable gems by overtaking the Russians in his plane. After catching up with the criminals, the captain discovers that the supposed princess' jewels had been given to the doctor (as part of an elaborate

scam to kidnap Virginia and acquire *her* jewels). When the doctor is finally tracked-down, a blow to Locke's head restores the veteran's memory. Note: Captain Locke was played by the real-life war hero, Lt. Ormer C. Locklear. Locklear was actually killed while performing the final night flying stunt of this film, on August 2, 1920.

[LC, LP15523 (c); *MPN* 9/11/20:2131; *MPW* 9/11/20:246–47]

Jewels; Tsar; Vet; White Russ

CM/ANTI-SOV

The Strongest, Fox, Raoul A. Walsh, Feb, Fr, Drama

This was loosely based on a turgid novel that had been published in 1898 by none other than France's "Old Tiger," Georges Clemenceau. Harle, a wealthy French paper manufacturer, worships money and neglects his wife. Twenty years later he has raised a daughter, Claudia, who, unknown to him, was the result of a liaison between his now deceased wife and a lover. Harle wants Claudia (Renee Adoree) to marry Henri, the ruined aristocratic lover of Claudia's mother. But Claudia has fallen in love with an American named Maurice. During a bitter labor dispute over wages, some of Harle's disgruntled workers abduct Claudia and hold her for ransom. Henri loses his life trying to rescue Claudia. Maurice eventually succeeds in liberating his sweetheart. Interestingly, there was no American lover or kidnapping in the novel.

[LC, LP14787(c); *MPN* 2/21/20:1973 & 1975; *MPW* 1/14/20:610]

Cap; Lab; Viol

ANTI-LAB

Uncharted Channels, Hampton/Robertson-Cole, Henry King, June, Am(u), Com-Drama

The "rascally Reds" are "burlesqued rather than moralized upon" in this motion picture. Timothy Webb, Jr. (H.B. Warner), an idle son of a millionaire, is disinherited and forced to become a plumber in his late father's factory. A mercenary/radical, Nicholas Schonn (German-Russian link; played by Sam de Grasse; to be shunned?) propagandizes the Webb workers. Schonn is aided in his machinations by Elsa Smolski (smolders?; Russian-Jew?), a so-called "intellectual." Together, they dupe a young heiress named Sylvia Kingston (Kathryn Adams) into donating $50,000 to the "cause" of the laboring classes. Timothy, along with other Webb employees, attends a meeting at the pretty parlor Bolshevik's fashionable home. The various worker stereotypes, including "garlic nuisances" (smelly southern Europeans) are stirred-up by the fiery speeches of Schonn and the revolutionary feminist— promising the "golden day when nobody shall do anything." Timothy is even ridiculed by the "red-eyed" (drunk) Bolsheviki for attending the reception in evening dress: "It is an insult!" Timothy senses a scam and convinces the impressionable Sylvia to get away from Schonn's influence and share the humble quarters of honest American workers. Sylvia falls for Timothy and provides him with the money with which he will eventually buy back his father's business. Meanwhile, striking Reds attack Timothy and a pal for doing some casual work. He is seriously injured, but is saved from death by loyal American union men coming to the rescue. After ridding the Webb factory of the Reds and winning the girl, our restored capitalist delivers a stirring dinner speech containing advice on the labor question. Once again, Americanism and the honest worker overcome the insidious effects of the poisonous propaganda of the evil Bolsheviki.

[AFI, F1.4627; *MPN* 6/26/20:147; *MPW* 7/24/20:506]

Agit; Am Icons; Bol-Ger Link; Cap; Fem Rad; Lab; Liq Link; Mtg; Reconcil; Russ: Strike; Viol

ANTI-REV; CAP-LAB COOP

West Is West, Universal, Val Paul, Nov, Am(r), Western

J.C. Armstrong owns the Great Torpedo gold mine in Texas. When his superintendent, Spencer, and manager, Mendenhall (German-Jew?), discover a rich vein they provide improper timbering and hire a crook named Black Beard to create an accident in order to precipitate a strike. It is their hope to generate sufficient trouble to prompt J.C. to cheaply sell-out his controlling interest to them. Spencer and Mendenhall meanwhile hire strike breakers, including Dick Rainboldt (Harry Carey), an unemployed cowboy. Dick needs the money, even though it queers him with his girl, the granddaughter of the strike leader. Later, Dick accepts $2,000 from Spencer and Mendenhall to blow up a mine tunnel to discredit the strikers. Dick carries out the job, but remains at the site of the explosion so as to expose the conspirators.

[LC, LP15800; *MPN* 11/27/20:4155; *MPW* 11/27/20:513]

Bomb; Cap; Ger?; Jew?; Lab; Scabs; Strike; Unemployed; Viol

NDB

Wolves of the Street, Art-O-Graf/Arrow Film, Otis B. Thayer, Feb, Am(r), Drama

When the elder Trevlyn, a financier, tries to break the corner in wheat by Wall Street profiteers, he is murdered. Son James (Edmund F. Cobb) leaves his western mine to continue the fight in New York City. While there, young Trevlyn's enemies get Bolshevik agitators to incite a strike at his mine. Aided by his sweetheart back home, who finds his double in a mission house, James returns to quell the labor unrest. The *MPW* review noted: "The Bolshevist, half hidden behind whiskers, is not convincing."

[AFI, F1.5056; *MPN* 6/5/20:4691]

Agit; Bol; Cap; Lab; Strike

ANTI-SOV

1921

The Ace of Hearts, Goldwyn, Wallace Worsley, Sept, Am, Rom Drama

At the meeting of a "Brotherhood" of anarchists, cards are drawn to determine who will blow up a capitalist they call the "man who has lived too long." The chosen assassin, a waiter named John Forrest (John Bowers), is given a time bomb to place beneath the table at his cafe where the intended victim comes for breakfast. But on the designated day Forrest refuses to go through with the plot when he realizes the explosion would also kill a young couple seated nearby. John's brothers in the "cause," distinctly bourgeois in appearance, gather to determine his fate. Henry Farralane (Lon Chaney), an artist and former rival for John's beautiful wife, blows himself up, along with his associates. John and his wife (Leatrice Joy) are thereby freed to live happily ever after. Raymond Hatton plays the evil stereotype known only as "the Menace," as in Red menace.

[S, (GEH;Vid); LC, LP16948; *EH* 1/28/22:68; *Var* 10/28/21:35; *Wid's* 10/30/21:12]

Anarch; Artist; Bomb; Cap; Viol

ANTI-REV

The Contrast, Labor Film Service, Guy Hedlund, Mar?, Am(r), Drama

Authored by Pittsburgh socialist John Slayton and produced with funds contributed by union miners, the *Wid's* review noted that the film's text deals "more with labor propaganda and social philosophies than it does with dramatic and screen values." The plot unfolds amidst the labor war that erupted during UMW unionization of the coal mining regions of southern West Virginia in late 1919. Under the onerous blacklisting system, the miners struggle against poverty while attempting to organize. In contrast, the mine owners are portrayed as living lavishly. In one scene, there is a cut from a starving girl stealing garbage to inside an owner's mansion where a maid feeds his dog a chicken dinner. After an accident occurs due to the neglect of proper safety devices by the owners, the coal miners strike. They also make an appeal to railroad workers to join them. Standing by the terms presented by the union, the miners and their families resist the violence unleashed by company guards, including the murder of union organizers and the destruction of their tent camp. The owners, fearing a national disaster, finally recognize the union and capitulate to the miners' demands. The director also stars as labor hero Jack Adams. Note: In May 1921 Governor Morgan had declared martial law in the state's Tug Valley mining region.

[*New York Call* 3/3/21:4; 6/2/21:4; 9/25/21: "Call Magazine:" 8 & 10; *Var* 2/24/22: 38; *Wid's* 6/5/21:9; Steven J. Ross, "Struggles for the Screen: Workers, Radicals, and the Political Uses of Silent Film," *The American Historical Review*, 96 (April 1991): 353–55]

Cap; Lab; Pvt Pol; Strike; Viol; Wrk Rel Dis/Inj
PRO-LAB

The Dangerous Moment, Universal, Marcel DeSano, April, Am, Drama

A young girl, played by Carmel Myers, who has come on hard times, works at a Greenwich Village cafe called the Black Beetle. Serving liquor in tea cups, the little restaurant is a bohemian haven. Among the varied clientele is an individual named Trotsky. She has trouble with the dissolute son of the Greek proprietor, but eventually finds love with an artist.

[AFI, F2.1185; LC, LP166346; *MPW* 4/16/21:756]

Artist; G Vill; Liq Link; Trotsky
NDB

Dawn of the East, Realart, Edward H. Griffith, Oct, China/Am, Rom Drama

Countess Natalya (Alice Brady) and Sonya (Betty Carpenter), her younger sister, reach Shanghai after fleeing the Soviet revolution. Natalya is just barely able to support herself and the sickly Sonya by singing and dancing at the Almond Blossom cafe. Disgusted with her situation, Natalya becomes involved with a villainous Chinese named Sotan (as in Satan?), who opposes his country's new Republic. Sotan arranges an allegedly non-legally-binding marriage between Natalya and a Chinese millionaire in order that the Russian refugees will have the funds needed to travel to the United States. Natalya later meets and marries an American diplomat, played by Kenneth Harlan, who is a China specialist. The evil oriental arrives soon afterwards and, claiming her earlier marriage is valid, attempts to blackmail Natalya into providing information from her husband concerning American intentions in China. The millionaire, *not* the diplomat, comes to the rescue. Although a so-called "royalist," Sotan's attempts to undermine the Chinese Republic may have been meant to imply collusion with the Bolshevik regime. Refer to the 1918 Goldwyn release, *For the Freedom of the East*, q.v. *Dawn of the East* is an interesting variation on the developing film formula of the aristocratic Russian finding refuge in the United States.

[AFI, F2.1236; LC, LP16972; *EH* 10/20/21: 67; *Var* 10/28/21:35]

Bol; Cap; Escape; Rev; White Russ
ANTI-SOV

The Dollar-a-Year Man, Famous Players-Lasky/Par, James Cruze, April, Am, Comedy

In one of his last starring film roles, Roscoe "Fatty" Arbuckle plays a successful laundryman named Franklin Pinney who is trying to break the social barriers at the Santa Vista Yacht Club. When a foreign prince visits the club, the other members conspire to keep Pinney from meeting the royal personage by arranging a fake kidnapping of the yokel. Meanwhile, Tipton Blair (as in Upton Sinclair?), a closet socialist, has been conspiring with a band of bewhiskered anarchists to kidnap "The Prince" (Edward Sutherland). A roughhouse climax occurs at the local "haunted house." Pinney and the prince become friends in the struggle. The *Variety* review repeatedly refers to the Blair character as a "parlor Bolshevik."

[LC, LP16383; *MPW* 4/2/21:515; *Var* 3/25/21:43]

Anarch; Cap; Sec Ser; Soc; Viol
ANTI-REV

The Four Horsemen of the Apocalypse, Metro, Rex Ingram, Mar, Argent/Fr, Drama

This film was adapted from the novel of the same name by Vicente Blasco Ibanez. After the death of its native-born patriarch, an Argentine family is divided between its German side and its French side. The French born son-in-law, Marcelo Desnoyers, fled to the New World from France in 1870—a newspaper clipping he keeps among his private papers, dated August 5, reveals that he was part of the "Socialistic Student Body…" that refused to oppose the German invaders during the Franco-Prussian War. The two halves of the family return to their respective homelands in the Old World. Marcelo's tango-dancing son Julio, played by Rudolph Valentino, will redeem the Desnoyers' honor through his ultimate sacrifice during the World War.

[S (*MOMA*, Vid); LC, LP16308; *Var* 2/18/21:40]

Pac; Soc
PAC

The Little Minister, Famous Players-Lasky/Par, Penrhyn Stanlaws, Dec, Scotland, Drama

In an early nineteenth century setting, the impoverished weavers of Thrums, enraged by the manufacturers' reduction of the prices paid for their product, burn a factory. Attacked while attempting to arrest the ringleaders, the constables are spared further violence by the intervention of Gavin (George Hackathorne), the local kirk's "little minister." "Babbie" (Betty Compson), an elfin gypsy girl, is suspected of being the spy who had informed the police of the names of the riot leaders. Babbie is actually the disguised Lady Barbara, daughter of Lord Rintoul. Rintoul has just recently returned after a number of years to assume his authority as magistrate of the district. When Babbie learns that her fiancé, the captain of the local army barracks, has been ordered to enforce the law, she sees to it that the weavers are warned of the soldiers arrival. An armed confrontation is averted and most of the weavers avoid arrest. Gavin, who has confessed to warning the weavers and helping the gypsy girl

escape, is about to be defrocked by the kirk elders when Babbie appears and reveals her true identity. The weavers' ringleaders, most forcefully represented by the "rebellious Tammas" (Thomas Whammond; played by Guy Oliver), are not positively portrayed. In 1915 Fox had released *The Little Gypsy*, q.v., which was also based on an 1891 James Matthew Barrie novel. In January 1922, Vitagraph would release yet a third motion picture version of *The Little Minister*. Since the Vitagraph film appears to have de-emphasized the labor angle, it is not included in the Filmography.

[AFI, F23122; LC, LP17404; *MPW* 1/7/22:112; *NYT* 12/26/21:13]

Agit; Cap; Lab; Mob; Pol; Sab; Viol
ANTI-LAB

Making the Grade, David Butler Prods/Western Picts, Sept, Fred J. Butler, Russ/Am, Com-Drama

Eddie Ramson (David Butler), the fun-loving drunken son of a wealthy family, is sent away by his father to join a private American relief expedition in Siberia. He falls in love with the local school teacher, Sophie Semenoff (Helen Ferguson). She is about to be executed for refusing to obey a Soviet edict ordering all women to marry when Eddie comes to the rescue. After some wild chases with the Bolsheviks, Eddie marries Sophie and returns with her to the United States. His marriage meets with the disapproval of his mother, so Eddie gets a job as a warehouse laborer and makes the grade. But then, local Reds find and kidnap Sophie. Mother Ramson overcomes the abductors. All ends well when Sophie confesses she is really a princess and that the Russian agents were after the family jewels. The reviewer for the *Exhibitor Herald* felt that the "many revolting scenes of Russian outrages" did not mix well with the comic aspects of the film. Both *Making the Grade* and *Help Yourself*, released in 1920, q.v., were based on short stories written by Wallace Irwin. Note: From shortly after the conclusion of hostilities, the American Relief Administration, under commissioner Herbert Hoover, had been coordinating efforts to feed the millions of starving people throughout war-devastated Europe—including Russia—"Better to fight Bolshevism with food than with bullets." In fact, a non-fiction film documenting these activities, entitled *Starvation*, was presented in early 1920 by

Frederick B. Warren (*MPW* 1/24/20:635). A considerable amount of its attention was devoted to Soviet atrocities in Russia, placing much of the blame for the horrible conditions in the rest of Europe upon the Bolsheviks—the *Variety* reviewer commenting: "A glance at the starving women and children and the endless breadlines should be a sufficient preventive against the reds in this country." (*Var* 1/16/20:61)

[AFI, F2.3353; *EH* 7/30/21:50; *Var* 2/10/22:35]

Atroc?; Bol; Cap; Decad; Dom Rad; Escape; Jewels; Lab; Russ; Siberia; Viol; Visit/Wrk SU; White Russ
ANTI-SOV

The Man from Medicine Hat, American Film Comp, Jan, Am(s), Advent-Drama

A reissue of Mutual's 1916 release, *The Manager of the B. & A.*, q.v.

[AFI, F2.3382; LC, LP16011]

Agit; Cap; Ger?; Lab; Reconcil; Strike; Viol
CAP-LAB COOP

Orphans of the Storm, UA, D.W. Griffith, Dec, Fr, Hist Drama

The blind Louise (Dorothy Gish) is taken to Paris for medical treatment by her adopted sister Henriette (Lillian Gish). Following Henriette's abduction by a licentious marquise, the two orphans from the countryside must struggle to survive amid the political injustices and social turmoil swirling about France immediately before and during the Revolution of 1789. Griffith's melodramatic excesses aside, he makes a direct linkage between the French and Russian revolutions in the opening titles: "The French Revolution rightly overthrew a BAD government, but we in America with a GOOD government should be careful lest we mistake fanatics for leaders and exchange our decent law and order for anarchy and Bolshevism." Danton (Monte Blue), noted as the "Abraham Lincoln of France," is portrayed largely sympathetically as a sincere revolutionary preaching the brotherhood of man. But Robespierre (Sidney Herbert) is depicted as a sneaky, misogynistic rabble rousing agitator spouting historical anachronisms. As one inter-title states: "The tyranny of kings and nobles is hard to bear ... but the tyranny of the mob under bloodthirsty rulers is intolerable."

[S (GEH; Vid); LC, LP18035; *Var* 1/6/22: 42]

Am Icons; Anarch; Atroc; Bol; Mob; Rev; Viol
ANTI-REV

Straight from the Shoulder, Fox, Bernard Durning, June, Am(r), Western

When a crooked superintendent at a western gold mine is fired, he incites the workers to strike. Cowboy hero Buck Jones, "the Mediator," arrives in Peaceful Valley and helps his buddy stop the strike and prevent the men from blowing up the mine. The heavy's name, Big Ben Williams (G. Raymond Nye), was probably meant to create an associative linkage with the notorious I.W.W. activist, William "Big Bill" Haywood.

[AFI, F2.5419; LC, LP16701 (c)]

IWW?; Lab; Sab; Strike
ANTI-LAB

You Find It Everywhere, Outlook Photoplays/Jans Film Service, Jul, Charles Horan, Am(u), Com-Drama

"[A] cross between a romance and a burlesque with a little propaganda thrown in," is how this picture was described in *Wid's Daily*. Andrew Gibson's father dies and leaves a small share of his piano manufacturing company to his workers. Taking their co-ownership seriously, the employees feel free to rush into Andrew's office at any time to voice their disapproval of his management of the company. Romantic complications arise when Jose Ferra (as in iron; hard as), one of the workmen, falls for Andrew's girl, Nora Gorodna (Catherine Calvert), and a society girl named Lila tricks Andrew (Herbert Rawlinson) into proposing to her. Andrew's answer to the problems caused by employee co-ownership at the factory is to turn the whole thing over to the workers. Out of a job, Andrew goes to Maine for a rest, but arrives home in time to rescue the factory from destruction at the hands of thugs hired by Jose and to win back Nora.

[AFI, F2.6577; *Wid's* 3/20/21:9]

Cap; Irish?; Jew?; Lab; Russ?; Sab
CAP-LAB COOP

1922

The Face in the Fog, Cosmopolitan/Par, Alan Crosland, Oct, Am/Russ, Mystery-Drama

The evil face that scowls out of the fog

during the credits belonged to the crooked-nosed actor Louis Wolheim. Frequently cast as a villain due to his ugly visage, he played the Red "terrorist" leader, Petrus, in this early film portrayal of the adventures of a reformed crook turned hero, Boston Blackie. The whole action of this five reel thriller, save a brief flashback to revolutionary Russia, takes place during one foggy evening in New York City. Having murdered the Grand Duchess Tatiana's father in Russia, Petrus and his Soviet thugs pursue her to America in an attempt to seize the Romanoff jewels she possesses. Tatiana (Seena Owen) swore to her dying father that she would dedicate her life to saving the jewelry until it could be used to help finance a restoration of the throne. Boston Blackie, played by Lionel Barrymore, and an American Secret Service agent come to the rescue of the beautiful political refugee. Note: Grand Duchess Tatiana Nickolaevna was the name of the second-born of Tsar Nicholas's four daughters.

[S (LC, incomplete); LC, LP18332; *MPW* 10/21/22:702; *Var* 10/13/22:42]

Bol; Decad; Escape; Jewels; Liq Link; Pol; Rev; Russ; Sec Ser; Tsar; Viol; White Russ

ANTI-SOV

Foolish Wives, Universal, Erich von Stroheim, Jan, Monte Carlo, Drama

A fake Russian count in Monte Carlo in 1919, played by "he-vamp" von Stroheim, preys on rich women. Among his lesser conquests is a bedraggled servant named Malishka, whom he has glibly promised to wed "as soon as the Bolsheviki are deposed." The dissolute "Count" Karamzin's attempt to seduce the fatuous wife of the American ambassador ultimately leads to his ignominious death. This was a "Super-Jewel" production whose screenplay was also written by the director.

[S (LC; Vid); LC, LP17550; *MPW* 1/21/22: 316; *Var* 1/20/22:35]

Bol; Cap; Decad; Viol; White Russ

CM/ANTI-SOV

The Hands of Nara, Samuel Zierler Photoplay/Metro, Harry Garson, Sept, Russ/Am, Drama

Nara Alexieff (Clara Kimball Young), the beautiful daughter of a wealthy landowner in Russia, is swept up in the Bolshevik catastrophe. Aided by a sympathetic revolutionist, she is released from prison and allowed to escape to America. Living in a dingy tenement on New York's East Side, Nara works for a faith healing charlatan to whom she had delivered a letter from the Bolshevik who had arranged for her freedom. It is thereby implied that this man, named Connor Lee, is/was a Bolshevik supporter. Interestingly, when he has reason to believe that his con game will be exposed, Lee flees the country. Eventually, Nara finds true love with a young American doctor.

[LC, LP18387; *Var* 9/22/22:41]

Artist; Bol; Dom Rad?; Escape; Rev; Russ; White Russ

ANTI-SOV

The Man Who Played God, UA, Harmon Wright, Oct, Eur/Am, Drama

While he is performing a command concert for a European monarch, a world renowned pianist (actor George Arliss) is made deaf when an anarchist attempts to assassinate the monarch with a bomb. Retreating into melancholy, he finds solace after studying lip reading and secretly using this new talent to learn about the problems of others. He plays God by anonymously arranging to help some of these people.

[LC, LP18468; *MPW* 10/7/22:504; *Var* 10/6/22:40]

Anarch; Bomb; Viol

CM/ANTI-REV

The New Disciple, Federation Film Corp, Ollie Sellers, April, Am(s), Drama

Although this pro-labor film was first screened in Seattle in May 1921 and premiered in New York City in December 1921, it was not formally released until April of 1922. The dismissive comments of the *Variety* reviewer are instructive: "[It] is a *lecture* picture ... [not] calculated to draw them [patrons] in." During World War I, industrialist Peter Fanning (a balding, as well as fat, capitalist stereotype played by Alfred Allen) was able to amass great wealth by exploiting his workers in the small town of Harmony. Following the war, he pushes labor too far and the union declares a strike. Evictions from company owned housing, the use of scabs and police raids are the tactics employed to cow the workers. Young and idealistic John McPherson (Pell Trenton), a veteran and the handsome son of a factory worker, is in love with Fanning's daughter

Mary (Norris Johnson). John thinks that both capital and labor are wrong. He tries to get the two sides to reduce their demands, quoting Woodrow Wilson's 1913 progressive reform and anti-trust book, *The New Freedom*. Meanwhile, Fanning's competitors, who have taken advantage of his problems, form a trust and try to take over his business by forcing Fanning into bankruptcy. The workers overcome the attempted imposition of the open shop "American Plan" and unite with farming interests to outbid the competing trust and run the mill as a cooperative. The American Plan was launched by industry in 1920–21 as a means of combating radicalism in labor by destroying unions—the so-called crusade would continue until 1923. Although *The New Disciple* received a Broadway opening, the *Variety* reviewer concluded this film had "little entertainment value and even less value as propaganda."

[AFI, F2.3809; *New York Call*: "Call Magazine:" 8 & 10; *Var* 12/23/21:35; *Wids* 12/25/21]

Am Icons; Cap; Lab; Pol; Scabs; Soc; Strike; Vet; Viol

PRO-LAB; ANTI-CAP

The Stranger's Banquet, Marshall Neilan Prods/Goldwyn, Marshall Neilan & Frank Urson, Dec, Am(s)/Spain?, Drama

Derith, "Derry," Keogh (Claire Windsor) inherits a west coast shipyard from her late father. But the laborers have been stirred-up by John, a red agitator embittered by a personal injustice. When a drunken worker loses his job and is kicked out of the union, he joins the agitator and his Russian companion. John, who has sworn to "tear up the whole damn fabric of society," harangues the working "slaves" to join the "red rebellion" by staging a walkout. When the militia is called up, Krischenko, an anarchist, wants to toss a bomb to make the streets "run red with blood." The faithful Scotch general manager, Angus (Rockcliffe Fellowes), joins Derry in appealing to John. But then John is shot by the drunken "fiend" (Jean Hersholt) who was attempting to kill the hardy Scotsman. A mortally wounded John eloquently addresses the massed workers and the strike is called off. Krischenko is deported. Derry proposes to Angus. Note: In October 1922 there had been a serious dock strike in Portland, Oregon.

[AFI, F2.5432; LC, LP18551(s); *Var* 1/5/23:44]

Agit; Am Icons?; Anarch; Bol; Bomb; Cap; Deport; Irish; Lab; Liq Link; Mtg; Militia; Russ; Strike; Viol

ANTI-LAB

A Tailor Made Man, Charles Ray Prods/UA, Joseph DeGrasse, Aug, Am(u), Com-Drama

John Paul Bart (Charles Ray) is a clothes presser in a Jewish-owned basement tailor shop. The young man reads a lot and has come up with some ideas on the labor-capital problem as well as a theory on the psychological impression created by expensive clothes. John is in love with Tanya, the owner's daughter, but she is engaged to the radical intellectual, Dr. Gustavus Sonntag (possible irony intended by surname, which means Sunday in German; played by Douglas Gerrard). "Borrowing" a customer's dress suit, John bluffs his way into a fancy reception. While there, John makes a favorable impression upon Abraham Nathan, president of the Oceanic Steamship Corporation. Later, on the shipping magnate's yacht, John successfully aborts an attack by labor agitators. The grateful Nathan appoints him as his head of labor relations. Meanwhile, Tanya, having grown disgusted with Sonntag, becomes smitten with the new John. The jealous doctor responds by attempting to sabotage John's efforts to prevent a strike at the shipyard. This film was remade by MGM in 1931.

[AFI, F2.5512; LC, LP18418; *Var* 10/20/22:44]

Agit; Am Icons; Cap; Dom Rad; Jew; Lab; Strike; Viol

ANTI-REV

1923

Bavu, Universal-Jewel, Stuart Paton, April-May, Russ, Drama

A brutish, bearded, illiterate peasant named Felix Bavu (Wallace Beery), egged on by the vampish Olga (Sylvia Breamer), takes personal advantage of the Bolshevik revolution. Appointed treasurer of the local Soviet, he deliberately incites the peasant mob to burn and loot the city, in order to enrich himself and his girl with the seized spoils (using such slogans as "Looting the Looters," these activities were actually encouraged by the Bolsheviks). Meanwhile, one of the Red leaders, a former servant and sweetheart of the beautiful Princess Annia (Estelle Taylor), arranges for her protection and plots to receive the passports needed for their joint escape from Russia. Alerted by the vindictive Olga of the lovers' plan, Bavu attempts to stop them. The film concludes with a chase and a dramatic crossing of the border upon a frozen river, with the pursuing Bavu sinking through the ice. One Bolshevik is known only as "The Shadow."

[AFI, F2.0297; LC, LP18860; *Var* 5/17/23: 23]

Bol; Escape; Fem Rad; Mob; Rev; Russ; Viol; White Russ
ANTI-SOV

Bell Boy 13, Thomas H. Ince Prods/First Nat, Jan, William Seiter, Am(u), Comedy

After attempting to elope with an actress, young college graduate Harry (Douglas MacLean) is disinherited by his rich uncle, a New York broker. Harry takes a $30 a month bellhop job at the Philadelphia Hotel where he has been stranded. Still trying to woo the pretty Kitty, who has come to agree with his uncle that Harry should become a responsible citizen, Harry neglects his new job. Then Uncle Elrod arrives and buys the hotel, just so he can have the irresponsible lothario fired. Harry shakes his uncle's hand and as an expository inter-title describes it, he takes up the cause of "Bolshevism." More precisely, in perversely humorous revenge, he incites the hotel staff to strike. When Uncle Elrod capitulates, Harry informs his "fellow agitators" that all their demands have been met. Only Harry and Kitty holding hands on the steps now impede the normal activities of the hotel.

[S (LC; UCLA); LC, LP18557; *Var* 3/29/23:36]

Agit; Bol; Cap; Lab; Mtg; Strike
CM/ANTI-SOV

Drums of Jeopardy, Truart, Roland G. Edwards, Nov, Russ/Am, Drama

Twin emeralds in Hindu statuettes are seized by the Bolsheviks from the Grand Duke after they have ruthlessly whipped him. Hawksley (Jack Mulhall), the Grand Duke's American secretary, and a faithful Russian servant retrieve the gems and flee to the United States. They are pursued by the bearded Soviet agent, Gregor Karlov, played by Wallace Beery. Karlov and his thugs make their American

headquarters in the "Little Russia" cafe. Hawksley meets and falls in love with his banker's daughter, Dorothy Barrows (Elaine Hammerstein). But Hawksley becomes a suspect when the banker is murdered. With the aid of Cutty, a Secret Service agent, the killer Karlov is slain and his Red "emissaries of violence" are rounded up to be deported.

[S (LC); LC, LP19983; *MPW* 3/15/24:214; *Var* 3/19/24:26]

Atroc; Bol; Cap; Deport; Escape; Fem Rad; Jewels; Liq Link; Rev; Russ; Sec Ser; Viol; White Russ
ANTI-SOV

The Enemies of Women, Cosmopolitan Prods/Goldwyn, Sept, Alan Crosland, Russ/Fr, Rom Drama

A year before World War I began, the middle-aged libertine Prince Lubimoff (Lionel Barrymore) kills a Cossack in a duel and is forced to flee Russia. Even after the war erupts, the Prince continues his wicked ways while in luxurious French exile. But after the outbreak of the Bolshevik revolution, Lubimoff returns to the motherland in an attempt to retrieve his wealth. In Russia, he winds up battling a red mob led by a bloodthirsty "terrorist," played by Ivan Linow. Lubinoff escapes to the West with only a small part of his fortune in jewels. Following further romantic complications in France, a chastened Prince decides to help the war effort by joining the French Foreign Legion.

[AFI, F2.1534; LC, LP19004; *EH* 4/21/23:53; *MPW* 4/14/23:756; *Var* 4/5/23:35]

Bol; Decad; Escape; Jewels; Mob; Rev; Russ; Viol; White Russ
ANTI-SOV

Fashion Row, Tiffany Prods/Metro, Robert Z. Leonard, Dec, Russ/Am, Drama

Olga Farinova (Mae Murray; "The Girl with the Bee-Stung Lips"), the mysterious new blonde sensation of Broadway, claiming to have escaped from Bolsheviks in the Winter Palace, masquerades as a princess. Actually, she is a peasant who abandoned her infant in the care of her younger sister in Russia. Despite the objections of the rich Mrs. Van Corland, Olga marries the lady's son. Meanwhile, Olga's child has died and her sister Zita (Murray playing a dual role) has emigrated to America, where she lives with a Jewish couple on the East Side. At a Russian Charity Ball, Olga is mortally wounded by the burly Kaminoff (Elmo Lincoln, "in another of his Russian 'heavies' of superior force"), a lover she had stabbed in Russia. Zita, whom Olga had repudiated, is adopted into the Van Corland family. Widower Eric Van Corland joins the relief expedition to Russia. Note: Between 1921 and 1923 the American Relief Administration operated independently, with the acquiescence of the Bolshevik government, in providing massive famine aid to the Russian people. Refer to the 1921 release, *Making the Grade*, q.v.

[AFI, F2.1648; LC, LP19732; *Var* 1/31/24:23]

Bol; Cap; Escape; Jew; Rev; Russ; Viol; Visit/Wrk SU; White Russ

ANTI-SOV

Gossip, Universal, King Baggot, Mar, Am(s), Drama

The third generation head of a large factory, Hiram Ward (Ramsey Wallace), refuses to meet the requests of his workmen for higher wages. A strike is called. After several weeks, the now-desperate workers march on Ward's home demanding food. In Ward's absence, a pretty southern belle who lives with the family invites the men in. When Ward finds out, he sends for the police, rushes home and fights with the men's leader, John Magoo. The humiliated worker prepares a bomb with which to blow up the plant. A fortuitous mistake saves the factory, but nearly leads to a fatal explosion at the Magoo home. With the intercession of the southern lady, the strike is settled. The plot of this film was very similar to such earlier capital versus labor/reconciliation films as *The Ringleader* (Pathé, 1909), *The Strike* (Solax, 1912) and most particularly, *The Glorious Adventure* (Goldwyn, 1918), q.v.

[AFI, F2.2202; LC, LP18710; *Var* 5/17/23:26]

Bomb; Cap; Irish?; Lab; Pol; Reconcil; Sab; Strike; Viol

CAP-LAB COOP

The Little Church Around the Corner, WB, William A. Seiter, Mar, Am(r), Drama

David Graham, an adolescent forced to work in the coal mines, receives aid for his education to become a minister from a mineowner named Morton (Hobart Bosworth). Having secretly nurtured a love for Morton's daughter (Claire Windsor), David (Kenneth Harlan) returns years later as pastor to the mining town. Morton defies a workers' committee threatening to walk out if unsafe conditions are not repaired. An angry David, referring to a party taking place at the Morton home, declares the miners' "toiling in darkness ... [supports] the very floor on which your guests are dancing"—accompanied by a shot that literally shows a group of bare-chested blackened miners straining to hold up the floor beneath Morton's well-dressed partying friends; an obvious cinematic representation of the widely reproduced William Balfour Kerr photogravure entitled "From the Depths," which originally appeared in a 1906 novel about the class struggle written by J. Ames Mitchell, *The Silent War*. An explosion and cave-in at the mine leads to an angry mob of miners and their families attacking the mine offices and accosting Morton. The frenzied mob is battling armed guards when David, who has just returned from a successful rescue operation, intercedes and (through a demonstration of his faith) effects capital-labor reconciliation. Much of this film was shot at a real mining complex and thus incorporated actual footage of working conditions in the mines, including scenes of the coal carts being hauled by mules through the narrow shafts.

[S (LC); LC, LP18673; *Wid's* 4/1/23:8]

Cap; Lab; Mob; Pol; Pvt Pol; Reconcil; Viol; Wrk Rel Dis/Inj

CAP-LAB COOP

Main Street, WB, Harry Beaumont, April, Am, Drama

Carol Kennicott (Florence Vidor), the new wife of Gopher Prairie's doctor, upsets the small town Minnesotians when she tries to introduce her arty Greenwich Village ways. Bored by the locals and misunderstood by her husband, Carol befriends Erik Volberg (Robert Gordon), a young idealist. But, when she refuses to elope with Erik, he leaves town. The elder Volberg, a socialistic-minded Swedish farmer played by Noah Beery, becomes infuriated with the situation and incites a mob that forces its way into the Kennicott home. The doctor comes to his wife's rescue and the couple is reconciled. This film version of the 1920 Sinclair Lewis novel negatively transferred the Socialist beliefs of the Miles Bjornstam character to Adolph Volberg.

[LC, LP19003; *MPW* 5/12/23:157; *Var* 5/3/23:22]

Artist; G Vill; Mob; Rur Rad; Soc
CM/ANTI-SOC

Potash and Perlmotter, Goldwyn/First Nat, Clarence Badger, Sept, Am(u), Comedy

Two old business rivals, Potash and Perlmotter (Alexander Carr), become partners in New York City's garment industry. Then Boris Andrieff (Ben Lyon), a destitute Russian violinist, is hired by them as a fitter. Boris promptly falls in love with Potash's daughter, much to the father's dismay, since he had hoped for an alliance with a rich lawyer. Among the other new employees are the fitters Rabec and Fishbein, labor agitators with anarchistic tendencies. At the height of the busy season these two instigate a walkout. That same night, when Boris and his lawyer rival are going over the firm's books, the strikers break in and begin destroying the machinery. In the scuffle that follows Rabec is shot. Boris is arrested, but is later vindicated when it is proven that Fishbein was responsible. A trailer for this film survives at the Library of Congress. What is particularly indicative of the depoliticized times is that this trailer features the romantic leads, assorted models in gorgeous gowns and scantily-clad showgirls from the "Ziegfeld Follies and Music Box Revue," but never alludes to the film's radical subplot.

[AFI, F2.4297; LC, LP19413; *Var* 9/13/23:28]

Agit; Anarch; Cap; Jew; Lab; Russ; Sab; Strike; Viol
ANTI-REV

The Rendezvous, Cosmopolitan/Goldwyn, Marshall Neilan, Nov, Russ, Drama

A Russian prince is banished to Siberia for marrying without the Tsar's consent. A daughter is born, orphaned and left in the care of a friend. During World War I the child, now a beautiful teenager named Vera (Lucille Ricksen), receives the unwelcome attention of the local Cossack leader (Elmo Lincoln). Following the revolution, Vera meets and falls in love with Lieutenant Walter Stanford (Conrad Nagel) of the American expeditionary forces. When Walter's company is ordered back to the United States, Vera's only protection is an English "Tommy" named Winkie (British intervention forces were in Russia between March 1918 and June 1920). The brutish Cossack, Godunoff, then returns as the new Red governor of the district. Beating Vera into deafness, he forces the girl to marry him. Vera is spared consummating this union by the arrival of two comic Jewish commissars who have Godunoff imprisoned for corruption. With the further assistance of these friendly Bolsheviks, Vera's Russian marriage is annulled, Walter's return to Siberia is arranged and her wedding to the American is performed. As the newlyweds arrive in the United States, the Stars and Stripes are inserted on the screen. Albeit as comic relief, *The Rendezvous* provides a rare positive cinematic portrayal of some Soviet officials.

[LC, LP19822; *EH* 1/19/24:42; *MPN* 1/12/24:134]

Allied Interv; Am Icons; Bol; Decad; Escape; Jew; Rev; Russ; Siberia; Tsar; Viol; White Russ
ANTI-RS; ANTI-SOV

1924

After a Million, Sunset Prods, Jack Nelson, April, Am, Com-Drama

In order to fulfill the requirements stipulated in the will of Count Orloff, a Russian exile, the beautiful young Countess Olga (Ruth Dwyer) must marry her American chauffeur within a given time. Coincidentally, the American, Gregory Maxim, must reach a specific bank by a certain time. In a thrilling chase sequence, a gang of Bolsheviks, led by one Ivan Senine (as in "Lenine"—played by Alphonse Martell), attempts to prevent Maxim from reaching his destination.

[AFI, F2.0050; *Var* 5/14/24:28]

Bol; Russ; White Russ
CM/ANTI-SOV

The Eternal City, First Nat, George Fitzmaurice, Jan, Italy, Drama

This was a modernized version of Hall Caine's popular novel, filmed in Italy. That is, the love story has been centered around events in Italy from the close of World War I to the triumph of Mussolini's blackshirted fascists in October 1922. Baron Bonelli (Lionel Barrymore), a wealthy art patron and influential politician, seeks to gain dictatorial power by secretly supporting a revolution led by a radical fanatic named Minghelli (Montagu Love).

His Reds, many of them wielding axes, instigate a number of strikes. While roaming the streets, the Reds often single out war veterans for special abuse. In the midst of this social turmoil rises a man dedicated to restoring order to Italy, Benito Mussolini! Following a mass rally of his blackshirts (fond of throwing stilettos bearing anti-strike warnings) in the Coliseum, the uniformed paramilitaries march out and defeat Minghelli's red mob. Actual footage of the Italian premier was incorporated into the film. *The Eternal City* had first been made as a motion picture in 1915 by Famous Players, q.v. Perhaps in deference to virulent attacks upon Roman Catholicism by the Klan, the heroine's linkage to the papacy in the 1915 version was eliminated. In the 1920 Fox production, *The Face at Your Window*, q.v., American Legion veterans in Klan robes swoop down on the evil Reds.

[LC, LP19782; *The Daily Worker* 1/18/24; *EH* 12/1/23:55; *Var* 1/24/24:26]

Bol; Cap; Decad; Fasc; Ital; Lab; Mob; Pol; Rev; Strike; Vet; Vig; Viol
ANTI-REV

The Fifth Horseman, E.M. McMahon, Sept, Am, Drama

A patriotic/religious "Young American" (John Franklin; played by Cornelius Keefe) works to help a dissolute Tom Mather and his troubled family find peace and happiness. The Mathers are also aided by Confederate veteran and KKK advocate, Colonel Woodson (Leslie Stowe). Tom associates with a local bootlegging political boss who operates out of a saloon and whose henchmen include a "shifty-eyed foreign type" named Orloff. When the city administration disappoints him, Boss Gorman (Jew?) tells Orloff to whip up his radical friends. Working with the police and "Federal Dry Agents," the Young American sees to the elimination of Gorman and his radical associates. The American flag, as icon, is heavily worked into this film. Note: A revitalized xenophobic, anti-communist Ku Klux Klan reached its zenith in America between 1923 and 1925 (D. W. Griffith's 1915 release, *The Birth of a Nation*, was frequently shown for recruiting purposes). Bootleggers (often immigrants) were a particular target of the "new" Klan ("Beer and Bolshevism" was a popular rhetorical catchphrase used by the organization).

[AFI, F2.1684; LC, LP21581(s)]

Am Icons; Dom Rad; Fasc; Jew?; Liq Link; Pol; Russ; Vet; Vig; Viol
ANTI-REV

The Fighting American, Universal-Jewel, Tom Forman, June, Am/China, Comedy-Advent

Bill Pendleton (Pat O'Malley), a veteran aviator of the first World War who has been enjoying the fast life on campus as an All-American fraternity man, goes too far when he bets he can marry any girl his Greek brothers name. After being expelled from Buckley College for "conduct unbecoming a student" and his disgusted father disowning him, Bill secretly secures a stevedoring job with the Pendleton Line. The object of the bet, Mary Brainard (Mary Astor), who has actually fallen in love with Bill, graduates and heads for China to join her missionary father. Bill recognizes Mary when she boards a China bound ship. In order to follow her, Bill becomes a stowaway. Other passengers include Fu Shing (Warner Oland), "a fanatical Chinese patriot … returning home to start another revolution," and his mysterious "half-caste" advisor and "expert aviator" named Quig (a large man with a thick black mustache, wearing a worker's cap, played by a regular Hollywood heavy of the 1920s and 1930s, Edwin J. Brady, aka Edward Brady and Ed Brady). When Quig accosts Mary on deck, Bill comes out of his hiding place in a lifeboat to defend her honor. Later, while Fu Shing and his army are "terrorizing the countryside," a destitute Bill is wandering about the Chinese interior. A rebel raid upon the American Mission where Mary teaches results in her being taken hostage by Fu Shing. Bill learns of this and teams up with a hard-drinking buddy and former American soldier named Danny (Raymond Hatton), now the "great General Po Hsing-Chien" of the Nationalist Army. Since Danny's troops are on "strike for last month's pay" the two are forced to attack the revolutionary forces' headquarters with the army's single antiquated airplane. After defeating the evil Quig and his Chinese gunner in aerial combat, the fighting Americans land and Bill is reunited with Mary. Fu Shing has been entertaining the young lady, having recognized the fraternity pin she is wearing—Fu Shing and Bill are fraternity brothers! Fu Shing becomes an ally of the Nationalists "for the good of China," Bill negotiates a shipping contract with the government for the good of the Pendleton Line and Mary wins a responsible husband. Despite a Forward that urges the audience to not take seriously this "masterpiece of nonsense," the racially mixed Quig character can be viewed as a representative of the oriental despot image associated with the Bolsheviks by many in America (reinforced by the knowledge of the ethnic heritage of Lenin). Note: Between 1923 and 1927 the Soviets were intimately involved with the ruling Kuomintang Party of China (the Chinese Communists maintained an uneasy coalition with the Nationalists). Coincidentally, Danny's "General" character may have been loosely based upon the real-life English-born adventurer Morris Abraham Cohen (1887–1970) who, under the name "General Cohen," served with the inner ranks of the Nationalist Chinese leadership.

[S (Vid); LC, LP20236; *Var* 6/4/24:26]

Cap; Chin Comm?; Decad; Lab; Strike; Vet; Viol

ANTI-REV

A Fool's Awakening, Metro, Harold Shaw, Jan, Russ/Brit, Drama

A young Englishman, John Briggs (Harrison Ford), has worked for many years as a Russian nobleman's chauffeur. When the Bolsheviks seize power, he is arrested for this association. Briggs escapes across the Polish border, where he finds a diary on the corpse of an Imperial Russian secret service officer identified as Alexis Triona. The diary describes the White Russian's adventures as an undercover operative among the revolutionists. After Briggs is discharged from British military service at war's end, he can only find a low paying job as a London cabbie. In desperation, Briggs poses as Triona and publishes the diary in autobiographical form. The resulting celebrity creates marital complications that take the rest of the film to resolve.

[AFI, F2.1867; LC, LP19941; *Var* 3/19/24:26]

Bol; Escape; Rev; Russ; White Russ

ANTI-SOV

Isn't Life Wonderful?, UA, D.W. Griffith, Dec, Ger, Drama

Griffith, in semi-documentary style, condemns the Kaiser's autocracy by portraying the deleterious effects of the war upon the common people of Germany. But in typical melodramatic fashion, the harshness of the images will be tempered by the "triumph of love over hardship." A refugee family from western Poland struggles to survive political unrest, riots and endless economic difficulties in the suburbs of post-Armistice Berlin. The son, Paul (Neil Hamilton), gas-wounded in the war, returns to rejoin his family and sweetheart Inga (Carol Dempster). The period of hyper-inflation (1922–1923) is graphically illustrated when Inga, anxiously waiting in a long queue outside a butcher shop, watches as repeated new price postings escalate the cost beyond the amount she can pay—reminiscent of the famous breadline scene in Griffith's *A Corner in Wheat* (Bio, 1909), q.v. Police, armed with rifles, stand guard at the entrance of the shop. Desperate unemployed workers, periodically shown roaming about, are increasingly hostile toward anyone they believe to be exploiting food shortages. Rudolph, an acrobatic musician who has joined the family, is forced to share a room with a menacing wild Russian. Paul secures a land allotment and secretly grows potatoes during his off hours from work in the shipyards. As Paul and Inga are taking home a handcart load of harvested potatoes, they are attacked by a group of starving laborers who seize all of the potatoes. Although Paul is a fellow worker, their leader, "The Giant," apologetically explains that they must feed their families; that the war has made "beasts [of] ... us." Note: Griffith had originally scripted the film to represent the hero as receiving his gas wounds while resisting the French-Belgian invasion of the Ruhr in 1923.

[S (LC;Vid); AFI, F2.2762; LC, LP21265; *Var* 12/3/24:27]

Breadline; Ger; Lab; Mad Russ; Pol; Unemployed; Vet; Viol

ANTI-REV

Manhandled, Famous Players-Lasky/Par, Allan Dwan, Aug, Am, Com-Drama

When her mechanic boyfriend forgets their date, Tessie McGuire (Gloria Swanson), a gum-chewing, bobbed-hair department store clerk from the sticks, accepts an invitation from an eccentric author to attend a party at a friend's Greenwich Village studio. Impressed by her imitations of celebrities (including one of Chaplin's Little Tramp and another of Beatrice Lillie impersonating a Russian aristocrat), the owner of a stylish emporium offers Tessie a job wearing his gowns while posing as an exiled Russian princess. A humorous scene shows Tessie responding with a look of total incomprehension when a voluble White Russian matron corners her (the inter-titles in Cyrillic). Her boyfriend has meanwhile been otherwise engaged, promoting an auto device he has designed. The newly made millionaire inventor later returns to Tessie's furnished rooms, finds her in finery, and assumes she has been "manhandled."

[S (MOMA;Vid); LC, LP20414; *Var* 7/30/24:24]

Artist; Cap; G Vill; Lab; White Russ
NDB

Torment, Maurice Tourneur Prods/First Nat, Maurice Tourneur, Feb, Russ/Jap/Am, Advent-Drama

Count Boris (Jean Hersholt) escapes the Bolshevik "massacre" of nobles with the crown jewels. He intends to use them to help the famine victims in Russia. Three international thieves have other plans in mind. But one of them, an American named Hansen (Owen Moore), meets the pretty Marie (Bessie Love) on the boat to Japan and decides to change his crooked ways. The 1923 earthquake overtakes all involved, trapping them together in a Yokohama bank vault. The count is killed. Hansen eventually winds up with the jewels, which he pledges to use for the benefit of the poor. The *Film Daily* reviewer noted that director Tourneur used many newsreel clips of the September First earthquake and fire to add action to the "overworked crown jewels plot."

[AFI, F2.5784; LC, LP19939; *EH* 3/8/24: 54; *FD* 4/27/24:6]

Bol; Escape; Jewels; Rev; Russ; Viol; Visit/Wrk SU; White Russ
ANTI-SOV

Triumph, Famous Players-Lasky/Par, Cecil B. DeMille, April, Am(u)/Brit, Drama

King Garnet, a wealthy young wastrel played by Rod La Rocque, fails to live up to the stipulations of his father's will, and thus is summarily notified by the executors that the Garnet Can Factory will henceforth be run by the manager, William Silver (Victor Varconi). Given only five dollars with which to live, King is further informed by the family lawyer that William is his half-brother by virtue of a secret European marriage. William, whose anar-

chistic preaching has just incited his fellow workers to begin smashing the machinery, promptly demands that they "cut out the rough stuff." As the factory's new overseer he assumes the posture of an insensitive capitalist. A romantic rivalry has also developed between the two male leads for Anna Land (Leatrice Joy), a forewoman at the plant. But King, the former dandy, has been reduced to sleeping on park benches. Anna chooses Silver's new wealth as a means to help with her operatic aspirations. The romantic dynamics change after the loss of her voice and the caddish Silver nearly ruins the business. King has meanwhile proven himself by working his way up from laborer to manager of the factory. Theodore Kosloff plays Varinoff, a radicalized Russian worker at the plant.

[PE (GEH); LC, LP20203; *NYT* 4/21/24:21]

Anarch; Cap; Lab; Ital; Russ; Sab; Tramp; Unemployed; Viol
ANTI-REV

When a Girl Loves, Halperin Prods/Associated Exhibs, April, Victor Hugo Halperin, Russ/Am, Rom Drama

Sasha Boroff's (Agnes Ayres) wealthy family is stripped of its fortune by the Bolsheviks (actual footage from the revolutionary period—"troublesome times"—is interjected for historical verisimilitude). Her lover, Count Michael (Percy Marmont), the former favorite singer of the Tsar's, is sentenced to death by the Boroff's ex-coachman. This wicked Rogojin (George Siegmann), now a despotic Red official, forces Sasha to agree to marriage. But Rogojin is mysteriously killed and the Boroff clan is able to make an escape to America. In New York City Sasha becomes a nurse and, to further help her family, consents to marry a successful surgeon. Domestic complications arise when Michael is discovered to be alive and celebrated as the world's greatest baritone.

[AFI, F2.6229; LC, LP20010; *EH* 5/17/24: 51; *Var* 5/21/24:24]

Bol; Decad; Escape; Rev; Russ; Tsar; White Russ
ANTI-SOV

1925

Abie's Imported Bride, Temple/Trio, Roy Calnek, June?, Am(u)/Russ, Comedy

In the thirty years since the Lavinsky family emigrated to the United States, they have risen from running a small shop to becoming the wealthy owners of woolen mills. So when Rabbi Levey makes a pitch for the starving Jews in Russia, old Isaac willingly writes a check for $5,000. His son Abie goes further and makes an impassioned plea to their employees for each to pledge a dollar of next week's wages. The response is so enthusiastic that the father, at first, mistakes the surging group of workers around his son for strike demonstrators! Abie is delegated to go to Russia with the money and participate in the relief work. He returns to America with a wife and her family. Isaac is pleased his son has been saved from gentile flappers. Note: An independent work produced in Philadelphia, this film was primarily exhibited in movie theaters whose patrons were predominantly Jewish.

[AFI, F2.0001; LC, LP21570]
Cap; Jew; Lab; Russ; Strike; Visit/Wrk SU
NDB

Beggar on Horseback, Famous Players-Lasky/ Par, James Cruze, Aug, Am, Com-Fantasy

An impoverished composer named Neil McRae (Edward Everett Horton) struggles to complete a symphony in his East Side studio apartment. In order to survive, he must write hack music for Tin Pan Alley. He is persuaded by his doctor to propose to music student Gladys Cady, the plump shimmying daughter of an obnoxious nouveau riche family. Cigar smoking Mr. Cady is constantly on the phone to his broker and his wife continuously chews gum. Neil is so upset by events that he takes a sleeping powder. In the surreal nightmare that follows, he finds himself in a grotesque cathedral where the ushers carry bouquets of banknotes. Later, at the reception at the Cady home, his new mother-in-law is physically attached to her chair and wears a gown made of coins, while Mr. Cady remains connected to a gigantic telephone. In despair, Neil slays the family with a magnified knife. A score of policemen arrest McRae and bring him before a golf-playing judge, Mr. Cady! Neil is sentenced to live in Cady's widget factory where he is made to perpetually write jazz songs in his cell. After a time, Neil joins with others in a violent revolt and is mercilessly being cut up by knives when he is awakened by his beautiful artist neighbor, Cynthia (Esther Ralston).

Neil has found his true soul mate. Though in no way a radical political tract, *Beggar on Horseback*, based on a 1924 play by George S. Kaufman and Marc Connelly, is a symbol-laden satiric assault upon the excesses of 1920s American capitalism. A more explicit political exploitation of such symbolism is contained in the 1913 Eclair release *Why?*, q.v.

[S (LC); LC, LP21822; *MPW* 6/20/25:859; *NYT* 6/6/25:9; *Var* 6/10/25:37]
Artist; Cap; Lab; Pol; Rev; Viol
ANTI-CAP

The Coming of Amos, Producers Distrib Corp, Paul Sloane, Sept, Australia/Fr, Rom Drama

An Australian sheep rancher, Amos Burden (Rod La Rocque), visits his haughty artistic uncle who lives on the Riviera. During a gathering at Uncle Davey's salon, Amos frightens many of the guests with a boomerang demonstration. However, he makes an impression upon the beautiful Princess Nadia Ramiroff of Russia (Jetta Goudal). Her older poet husband, Ramon Garcia (Noah Beery), had tricked her into marrying him. Ramon had gone to Petrograd during the "Terror," acquired power, and promised to save Nadia's family if she became his wife. Instead, Nadia was informed on her wedding day that her people had been executed. She fled to France and thus wound up at Uncle Davy's party. However, the mad poet catches up with Nadia, and with the help of some thugs, kidnaps her. On his island castle, Ramon puts her in a dungeon and proceeds to flood the chamber when she refuses to submit to him. Amos subdues Garcia's flunkies with his boomerang, rescues Nadia and then shears the heavies' clothes off with a pair of scissors!

[S (LC, incomplete); LC, LP21791; *Var* 9/16/25:41]
Artist; Atroc; Bol; Escape; Rev; Russ; Viol; White Russ
ANTI-REV

Coming Through, Famous Players-Lasky/Par, Edward Sutherland, Jan, Am(r), Drama

Tom Blackford (Thomas Meighan), chief clerk of Pittsburg Steel Corporation, dreams of becoming superintendent of mines. Denied the promotion, he courts Alice Rand (Lila Lee), the daughter of the corporation's president. After their marriage, Mr. Rand, who wants Tom to fail, puts him in charge of

Colton, the most unruly mining camp in the company's holdings. Tom quickly runs afoul of the hard drinking mine foreman, Joe Lawler (Wallace Beery), when he has "The Club" saloon destroyed. Lawler and the "boss" of the bar incite the workers to strike. Several attempts are also made on Tom's life. Tom later wins back the miners when he proves that Lawler was cheating them with faulty scales.

[AFI, F2.0985; LC, LP21172; *Var* 2/11/25:32]

Cap; Lab; Liq Link; Reconcil; Strike; Viol
ANTI-LAB

Daughters Who Pay, Banner Prods, George Terwilliger, May, Am, Drama

A little brunette named Mary Smith (Marguerite De La Motte) takes off her glasses during the weekdays and poses as "Sonia," a Russian cafe dancer. But every Sunday she returns to her suburban home, where she is known as Miss Smith. Dick Foster (John Bowers), the son of a millionaire, has fallen in love with the exotic dancer. Bob Smith, her brother, has meanwhile embezzled $10,000 from his employer, Foster, Sr. As Sonia, she makes a deal with Dick's father to let her brother go. Soon afterwards, it is revealed that Mary has been working with the Secret Service on a roundup of Soviet agents. Mary can speak fluent Russian because her father had been a Russian consul for eight years—and while in Russia she had also studied ballet.

[AFI, F2.1232; LC, LP21211; *Var* 5/13/25: 38]

Artist; Bol; Cap; Deport?; Russ; Sec Ser; White Russ?
ANTI-SOV

Eve's Lover, WB, Roy Del Ruth, July, Am(u), Drama

Eve Burnside (Irene Rich), a successful thirtyish business woman who owns a steel mill, declines the repeated offers made by Austin Starfield to buy her out. Fearful his business cannot survive another year without her plant, Austin persuades Leon (Bert Lytell), an impoverished Eastern European count who had embezzled money from him, to romantically pursue Miss Burnside. After the honeymoon, a flapper (Clara Bow) who was the former lover of Count Leon, informs Eve that Leon was paid by Austin. Meanwhile, Austin has hired agitators to disrupt operations at the steel works. Eve joins her manager and receives a workers' delegation—"[a] fanatic and two pugs." The unnamed radical leader (Lew Harvey) demands the right to control management and a 50 percent share in the profits! When Eve dismisses this as ridiculous, the agitator storms away and from atop an upturned crate incites the gathered workers to walk out. The mob literally brushes Eve aside when she begs them to reconsider. Leon, who really loves Eve, intercedes by punching out the leader of the agitators. The men are turned and head after Austin, who has been watching the mayhem he plotted with binoculars from inside a cab.

[AFI, F2.1568; LC, LP21321(s); *Var* 7/29/25:34]

Agit; Cap; Lab; Mob; Strike; Viol
ANTI-LAB

Fifty-Fifty, Encore Picts/Assoc Exhibs, Henri Diamant Berger, Nov, Fr/Am, Drama

A rich American businessman, Frederick Harmon (Lionel Barrymore), has become bored on his vacation in Paris. But then he meets the wily Grand Duke Popovitch, who makes his living as a tourist guide of the demimonde and philosopher on the human condition. At "La Chat Rouge," Frederick becomes enamored of the beautiful Ginette, a fashion model by day and an apache dancer by night. They marry and return to America, where he soon falls prey to the machinations of Mrs. Nina Olmstead, a divorcee. This Mrs. Olmstead is aided by the Grand Duke, who was invited to New York to lend atmosphere to the "Russian Bear" cafe. Ginette is able to reconcile her marriage by tricking the Russian scoundrel into exposing Mrs. Olmstead.

[AFI, F2.1689; LC, LU21509; *EH* 6/20/25: 49]

Artist; Cap; Decad; White Russ
NDB

The Only Thing, Elinor Glyn Prods/MGM, Jack Conway, Nov, Rur, Rom Drama

A royal wedding in the Mediterranean kingdom of Chekia is interrupted by a revolution led by a fiery fanatic named Gigberto (Arthur Edmund Carew). The old king is killed and the beautiful Princess Thyra of Svendbord (Eleanor Boardman) is carried off by the handsome Gigberto. "Drunk with power, the victorious rabble" establish a "Red Tribunal" to deal with the fate of the aristocrats. When they discover that Gigberto desires Thyra, the other "Reds" label him a "traitor" and condemn him to death along with the aristocrats. An English duke, Harry (Conrad Nagel), who has also fallen in love with Thyra, switches places with Gigberto in prison. The two are later tied together and, along with other prisoners, sent out to sea to drown aboard a leaking barge. As the barge is sinking Harry breaks their bonds. The swimming couple are rescued by the crew of Harry's yacht. As they declare their mutual love, Thyra and Harry observe a burning Chekia on the horizon. The *Variety* review described this film as "*The Tale of Two Cities* given a little modern Red touch."

[AFI, F2.4033; LC, LP22059(s); *Var* 11/25/25:39]

Atroc; Bol; Escape; Liq Link?; Rev; Viol
ANTI-REV

The Phantom of the Opera, Universal-Jewel, Rupert Julian, Nov, Fr, Horror

In turn of the century Paris the Opera House, which is built over long-forgotten medieval dungeons, is plagued by the mysterious "Phantom." But the real trouble begins when he falls in love with the beautiful understudy Christine (Mary Philbin) and threatens to disrupt performances if she is not allowed to sing the lead. A police official discloses that the horribly disfigured Phantom, played by Lon Chaney, is a madman named Erik, "born" (created) during the Boulevard Massacre (a slaughter of demonstrating Parisian workers by members of the National Guard, precipitating the June 1848 Revolution that was brutally suppressed). It is later added that the Phantom's hiding place is located "deep within the torture chambers where he himself was confined during the second Revolution." Therefore, it is implied that the Phantom was physically and mentally mutilated by the events surrounding the socialist inspired insurrection.

[S (LC;Vid); LC, LP21689; *Var* 9/9/25:35; 2/12/30:14]

Atroc: Decad; Rev; Viol
CM/ANTI-REV

A Regular Fellow, Famous Players-Lasky/Par, Edward Sutherland, Oct, Rur, Comedy

In an obvious satire on the publicity surrounding England's Prince of Wales, the prince of a mythical Balkan kingdom (Raymond Griffith) officiates at an endless series of public ceremonies. He falls in love with a pretty tourist, but the royal family insists he wed a princess from the adjoining country. Following his father's death, the prince's coronation receives some unwanted attention from a bomb-thrower (whose deadly sphere is repeatedly returned to him by a dog). Still wanting to marry the girl he loves, the prince secretly propositions the accommodating "revolutionary" (referred to as a "Bolshevist" in the press book; played by Nigel De Brulier) to overthrow him and establish a republic! The concluding plot twist has the grateful people electing the dethroned monarch as their president and presenting him with a long new itinerary of state functions to perform.

[AFI, F2.4529; LC, LP21881; *Var* 10/14/25: 42]

Anarch; Bomb; Rev
ANTI-REV

Satan in Sables, WB, James Flood, Nov, Fr, Drama

Michael Lyev Yervedoff (Lowell Sherman), a Russian Grand Duke living in Paris, spends his exile in the pursuit of women. After he falls in love with a feisty girl from the slums, an ex-flame makes trouble for him and his younger brother. Following his brother's suicide, the middle-aged prince decides to reform and *return* to his native land.

[AFI, F2.4803; LC, LP21847; *Var* 10/14/25:40]

Bol?; Decad; White Russ
NDB

1926

The Adorable Deceiver, R-C Picts/Film Booking Offices of Am (FBO), Oct, Phil Rosen, Rur/Am, Rom Com

With revolutionary soldiers in hot pursuit, King Nicholas and his daughter of the little Balkan state of Santa Maria, flee to the safety of America. In their haste to escape, Princess Sylvia (Alberta Vaughn) only managed to bring along a few of the crown jewels. After pawning the last of the gems, the family must abandon their expensive rooms and move into the East Side boarding house of Mrs. Schrapp. With her father forced to work a menial job to pay the rent, Sylvia is left alone in their squalid room. Agents of the new republic have meanwhile tracked-down the royal personages. When they come one evening to her door, Sylvia flees in terror. She spends the rest of the night in the showroom of her favorite automobile company. In the morning, the indignant sales manager sends Sylvia to promote the car to a nouveau riche family. No sale. But young Tom Pettibone is impressed by her imperious manner and decides to use Sylvia to help him climb the social ladder by introducing her to his country club set as the Princess of Albania. Problems arise when both some revolutionary assassins and two thieves masquerading as the king and princess of Santa Maria appear at the club.

[AFI, F2.0036; LC, LP23148]
Escape; Jewels; Lab; Rev
ANTI-REV

The Beautiful Cheat, Universal-Jewel, Edward Sloman, Feb, Eur/Am, Com-Drama

Al Goldringer (Alexander Carr), the stereotypical Jewish motion picture president of a financially troubled studio, has his press agent take their pretty shopgirl discovery, Mary Callahan (Laura La Plante; promoted as the "girl-next-door" type), on a European publicity tour. Mary returns to the United States as "Maritza Callahansky," a Russian actress who supposedly possesses the crown jewels. This deception results in the usual plot complications, climaxing during a party at a Long Island mansion owned by the absent parents of one of the studio extras.

[AFI, F2.0312; LC, LP22359; *Var* 4/21/26:34]
Irish; Jew; Jewels; White Russ
NDB

Broken Hearts, Jaffe Art Film, Maurice Schwartz, Feb, Russ/Am, Drama

This was a Yiddish theater film production of a stage play. Benjamin Rezanov (Maurice Schwartz), a writer with political ideas, is persuaded by the actions of the Tsar's Cossacks that it would be in his best interest to flee Russia. He leaves behind his mother and wife. Rezanov winds up on New York's East Side where, after being told his wife is deceased, he marries the daughter (Lila Lee) of a cantor. Some time later, a letter arrives stating that his Russian wife is still alive. Benjamin travels to the new Soviet Russia only to discover that his

first wife had died in hospital. Rezanov returns to his American wife and their new child.

[AFI, F2.0642; *Var* 3/10/26:40]
Atroc; Bol; Escape; Jew; Russ; Tsar; Visit/Wrk SU
ANTI-RS

Diplomacy, Famous Players-Lasky/Par, Marshall Neilan, Sept, Fr/Russ, Mystery-Drama

The opening title of *Diplomacy* dedicates the motion picture "...to the secret service of all nations." At Deauville, a "fashionable" French coastal resort on the English Channel, a number of diplomats come together for an informal conference. Baron Ivan Ballin (Gustav von Seyffertitz), who carries "credentials from the Bolshevik Government of Russia" is also in Deauville. He is not above employing torture and a beautiful vamp in order to find out the contents of a secret treaty between China and Britain (never specified). The "complex international matter" necessitates an incognito visit by Count Orloff (Edmund Carew), "an exile from old Russia," to the Soviet Union. But having been betrayed by the arch-villainous Baron, Count Orloff is immediately arrested by Red Guards as he gets off the plane in Moscow. Friends are able to arrange for the White Russian's escape. And with the help of an American Secret Service operative, played by Matt Moore, the Red agents in France are foiled.

[S (LC;Vid); LC, LP23132; *Var* 9/15/26:16]
Atroc; Bol; Escape; Sec Ser; Spy-Sab; White Russ
ANTI-SOV

The Grand Duchess and the Waiter, Famous Players-Lasky/Par, Feb, Malcolm St. Clair, Fr, Rom Com

A wealthy playboy named Albert becomes smitten with the Grand Duchess Zenia (Florence Vidor), whom he has observed through his opera glasses while attending the ballet in Paris. Albert, played by the debonair Adolphe Menjou, follows the beautiful Russian and her entourage to their hotel. The manager informs him that the Grand Duchess' "country is a republic now but she refuses to know it." In fact, the inhabitants of the royal suite are forced to sell a necklace that once belonged to Catherine the Great in order to pay the hotel bill. Albert poses as a waiter to get near Zenia. But when she discovers both her love for him and his true identity, Zenia Pavlovna flees Paris. Several weeks later, Albert and some friends stop at a country inn. Love is reawakened when he finds Zenia and the other royal Russians attempting to operate the inn. In 1934 Paramount released a musical remake starring Bing Crosby, entitled *Here Is My Heart*.

[S (LC); LC, LP22392; *Var* 2/10/26:40]
Cap; Jewels; Rev; Russ; White Russ
CM/ANTI-SOV

Into Her Kingdom, First Nat, Svend Gade, Aug, Russ/Am, Drama

Due to an alleged insult upon the Grand Duchess Tatiana (Corrine Griffith playing the Tsar's second daughter), the parents of a peasant family are sent to Siberia (and eventual death) and their son, Stephan Mammovitch (Einar Hanson), is thrown into a St. Petersburg jail. Seven years later, the revolution occurs and Stephan is released. Embittered, Stephan joins the Bolsheviks. In the darkness of the cell where the royal family has been gathered for execution, the Grand Duchess is saved by a faithful maid taking her place. When the unidentified Tatiana is later brought before a commissar for questioning, Stephan recognizes her. But a desire for personal revenge upon the girl whom he had once worshipped and the entreaties of Ivan, who had tutored the two as children, persuades Stephan to not denounce her. Instead, he arranges for their marriage and flight to America. They settle down in New Jersey where Stephen works in the mills and Tatiana clerks in a store, amusing herself by telling fairy tales about princesses to the neighborhood children. Having come to truly love Tatiana again, but sensing her unhappiness with her present life, Stephan travels back to Europe to contact the imperial agents who could proclaim her Empress of all the Russians. Yet when they arrive at her humble home, she comes down the stairs with her newborn child in her arms and denies her royal birth, proclaiming as she gazes upon the baby, "Here is my kingdom." Note: Rumors persisted throughout the twenties and beyond that some of the Tsarist family had escaped their execution by the Bolsheviks—reported by the Bolsheviks to have taken place at Ekaterinburg in July 1918.

[LC, LP22990; *EH* 7/24/26:55; *Var* 8/11/26:14]

Atroc; Bol; Escape; Lab; Rev; Russ; Siberia; Tsar; Viol; White Russ
ANTI-SOV

Meet the Prince, Metropolitan Picts Corp of Cal/PDC, Aug, Joseph Henabery, Am/Russ, Com-Drama

Prince Nicholas Alexev (Joseph Schildkraut) has fallen asleep on a frilly couch on the fire escape landing of an East Side tenement in New York. He dreams of being at his luxurious mansion in Russia and discussing with his friends the mounting labor unrest threatening the country's stability. A mortally wounded servant staggers into the room and gasps, "Revolution!" The palace is then invaded by a vicious mob that Nicholas and the other male royalists are forced to fight in order to allow the women to escape. At this point a milk bottle crashes from above, rudely awakening the Prince. He enters the dressing room he shares with his sister and the faithful friends who stood by him at the palace. When Nicholas goes to a pawn shop to raise money for the rent, he encounters a wealthy vixen named Annabelle Ford (Marguerite De La Motte). This will eventually lead to a wild car ride to the justice of the peace.

[AFI, F2.3544; LC, LP22819; *EH* 8/7/26:81]

Bol; Cap; Escape; Mob; Rev; Russ; Viol; White Russ
ANTI-SOV

Men of Steel, First Nat, George Archainbaud, July, Am(s), Drama

Jan Bokak (played by the film's screenwriter, Milton Sills) is a poorly educated immigrant laborer at the Minnesota ore mines who flees after taking the rap for a murder committed by his girlfriend's brother. He gets a job at the steel mills owned by "Cinder" Pitt (Frank Currier). Jan begins to study during his off hours and becomes a socialistic leader of the steel workers. But then "Red" agitators wreck part of the mill. Jan is seriously injured while saving the life of Pitt's daughter (May Allison) during the destruction. The grateful millionaire owner takes the worker into his home to recuperate. Romantic complications lead to the resurfacing of the murder accusation. Following a dramatic confrontation at the mills, Jan (now using the Anglicized name John Brook) proves his innocence by forcing a confession from the killer, played by Victor McLaglen. The film was made on location at the Ensley Mills of the United States Steel Corporation in Birmingham, Alabama. Note: Beginning with the Passaic, New Jersey textile strike in January, 1926 marked a year of resurgent Communist Party–supported labor militancy.

[AFI, F2.3556; LC, LP22868; *Var* 7/14/26:14]

Agit; Cap; Dom Rad; Lab; Mob; Sab; Soc; Viol

ANTI-REV

The Midnight Sun, Universal-Jewel, Dimitri Buchowztski, Nov, Russ, Rom Drama

In 1913 an American girl, using the name of Olga Balashova (Laura La Plante), has advanced to prima ballerina of the Imperial Russian Ballet. Olga falls in love with Alexi, an officer in the Grand Duke's personal guard. But complications arise when the younger brother of Alexi, the spokesman for a group of nihilists, insults the Grand Duke and is ordered exiled to Siberia.

[AFI, F2.3605; LC, LP22558; *Var* 4/28/26:48]

Artist; Nih; Russ; Siberia

ANTI-RS

My Official Wife, WB, Paul L. Stein, Oct, Russ/Aust, Rom Drama

Based on the copyrighted synopsis this may have been the opening title of the film: "Russia, before the World War, a land of despotism. In subterranean meeting places revolutionists plot the overthrow of the Romanoffs. The country is a volcano that promises at any moment to erupt and plunge everything into misery and chaos." Helene, the Countess Orloff (Irene Rich), is engaged to the licentious Ivan (Stuart Holmes). In the costume of a peasant girl, Helene is accosted by a group of Ivan's friends on her way to a masquerade. Sascha (Conway Tearle), the son of a Grand Duke, actually spends the night with her at an inn. When his father learns of Sascha's part in the orgy, he accuses Helene of conspiring with nihilists. Following a farcical hearing, Helene is exiled to Siberia. A remorseful Sascha arranges to have Helene rescued and provided with a passport. She becomes a cafe dancer in Vienna. Sascha, under the name of "Alexander," visits and falls in love with Helene. Since she does not recognize him, she agrees to be his "official wife" so she can go back to Russia and confront the man who raped her. War and revolution intervene. Sascha is forced to flee the Bolsheviks. Destitute, he becomes the head waiter in a popular Viennese cafe. Helene meets him there and, having discovered their mutual love, all is forgiven.

[AFI, F2.3751; LC, LP23142; *FD* 10/17/26:17]

Bol; Decad; Escape; Nih; Rev; Russ; Siberia; Tsar?; White Russ

ANTI-RS; ANTI-SOV

Rose of the Tenements, FBO, Phil Rosen, Dec, Am, Drama

Two orphans, of separate parentage, are raised by an elderly Jewish couple named Kaminsky, who own an artificial flower factory on New York's East Side. When the Kaminskys die, young Danny and Rose learn that the business has been left to them. Danny has meanwhile come under the influence of the socialist agitators, Willofsky and Emma Goldstein (read Alexander Berkman and Emma Goldman?). Having fallen in love with Emma, Danny enthusiastically supports the "cause" and refuses to enlist when America enters the war in 1917. He even hits a policeman when Emma and Willofsky are attacked by a crowd at an anti-war rally. However, when Emma tries to throw a bomb, Danny stops her. An Irish ward leader gets the charges dropped against Danny and he is allowed to join the U.S. Army. A joyous Rose will be waiting for him when he returns. To quote from *Hollywood's Image of the Jew*: "Aimed at immigrant Jewish audiences, its message is to reject the old world socialism for new American values of capitalism and democracy." Note: Joseph P. Kennedy had purchased Film Booking Offices of America (FBO) in February 1926.

[LC, LP23352; *EH* 12/4/26:61; Lester D. Friedman, *Hollywood's Image of the Jew*, p. 35; *Var* 4/13/27:22]

Agit; Bomb; Cap; Fem Rad; Irish; Jew; Pac; Pol; Soc; Viol

ANTI-REV

Siberia, Fox, Victor Schertzinger, Mar, Russ, Drama

Sonia Vronsky (Alma Rubens) is a school teacher who abandons Tolstoy's pacifism and begins talking of "anarchy" with the people. An officer in the Imperial Army, Petroff (Edmund Lowe), is in love with her. But an attack on an official leads to a wave of suppression in which Sonia and her brother are swept up. They are exiled to Siberia. Petroff is also sent there on official assignment and secretly renews his romance with the beautiful teacher. When the Bolshevik revolution occurs, the prisoners seize the officers and, after getting drunk, begin to shoot them. Sonia helps Petroff escape. Egor Kaplan (Lou Tellegen; Jewish-Bolshevik stereotype?) is the local leader who uses the position "as a cloak" to conceal his greed and lust for Sonia. Egor unsuccessfully pursues the lovers in a boat as they make their escape across the frozen wastes on a sleigh. There are distinct plot similarities with the 1923 Universal release *Bavu*, q.v.

[AFI, F2.5032; LC, LP2261l(s); *Var* 6/2/26:15]

Anarch; Bol; Decad; Escape; Fem Rad; Jew?; Liq Link; Pac; Rev; Russ; Siberia; Viol
ANTI-SOV

The Sorrows of Satan, Paramount, D.W. Griffith, Oct, Am, Drama

Geoffrey Tempest (Ricardo Cortez), a tormented intellectual, and Mavis Clare (Carol Dempster), a struggling writer, are fellow lodgers at a boarding house in a large city. Poverty brings them together, and they plan to marry after spending a night together. Mavis has faith, but Geoffrey damns God for his situation. A debonair devil in top hat and tails, played by Adolphe Menjou, appears at the door and introduces himself as the trustee of the estate of Geoffrey's uncle. Mavis is abandoned, and soon afterwards the "new millionaire" is enmeshed with the voluptuous Princess Olga Godovsky—"a Russian noblewoman flung by the Revolution into the household of her English uncle"—actress Lya De Putti, with bee-stung lips. Satan, calling himself Prince Lucio (as in Lucifer) maneuvers the two into an ill-conceived marriage. After Olga commits suicide, Geoffrey realizes his true love, overcomes the menacing shadowy presence of Satan revealed, and achieves salvation with the bedside embrace of a forgiving/true believing Mavis.

[S (MOMA; Vid); LC, LP23647; *Var* 10/20/26:60]

Decad; Rev; White Russ
CM/ANTI-SOV

Steel Preferred, Metropolitan Picts/PDC, James Hogan, Jan, Am(s), Com-Drama

Wally Gay (William Boyd) is an ambitious worker who has risen from the slums of Steelburg to the engineering department of the Creeth Mills. He invents a new type of Bessemer furnace, but due to the jealousy of Waldron (Nigel Barrie), his immediate superior, Wally is prevented from presenting his plans to the mill owner. After Wally is discovered trying to circumvent Waldron, the latter arranges for the young man's demotion. Wally later rescues the owner's daughter, played by Vera Reynolds, when an accident occurs at the plant. This leads to romance and a positive meeting with James Creeth (Hobart Bosworth) to discuss his furnace plans. In retaliation, chief engineer Waldron bribes a labor leader to spread the rumor that the new furnaces will be unsafe. A walk-out is called. Hearing of this, the young inventor engages the ringleader in a dramatic fight in the plant. After Wally defeats the man, the strikers agree to return to work. Comedy relief is provided by screen veterans Charlie Murray and William V. Mong, steel workers with a "fondness for hooch."

[AFI, F2.5381; LC, LP22132; *Var* 12/23/25:36]

Agit; Cap; Lab; Liq Link?; Strike; Viol
CAP-LAB COOP

The Volga Boatman, PDC, Cecil B. DeMille, April, Russ, Rom Drama

A handsome peasant boatman named Feodor (William Boyd) is humiliated by Prince Dimitri Orloff (Victor Varconi). Sometime later, the Bolsheviks seize power. The family palace of Princess Vera (Elinor Fair), Dimitri's fiancée, is stormed by the Reds. One of the attackers is slain and Feodor, the political commissar in charge of the revolutionary forces, demands a life for a life. Princess Vera is seized and condemned to death. But when Feodor is left alone with Vera, he realizes he cannot kill her. He tries to fake her death, but is betrayed. Barely escaping an angry mob, the two seek refuge at an inn. The White Army arrives, led by Dimitri, and both Vera and Feodor are captured. After Prince Orloff learns that the supposed bride of the "Red Leader" is actually Vera, he orders that Feodor be executed the next day during a ball at White Army headquarters. Tied to an iron gate before a newly-dug grave, Feodor is about to be shot by a firing squad when Red forces recapture the town. All the surviving nobles, still dressed in their evening finery (designed by the soon-to-be legendary Adrian), are forced to take up the harness of a Volga boat to the Reds' new seat of government, where the "Great Tribunal" will determine their fates. Before the drunken, jeering Bolsheviks, Vera and the other aristocrats begin towing the boat up river. Feodor, who has declared his love for her, picks up the harness beside Vera. The Tribunal listens to Feodor's petition for mercy, granting Vera and Dimitri the choice of either exile or "helping to build the new Russia." A chastened Dimitri chooses the former, while Vera embraces her revolutionary boatman. This earliest-known American film since the October Revolution to feature a "Red" hero was 120 minutes long and color tinted. Interestingly, while the term "Bolshevik" never appears in any title, Red characters are frequently addressed as "Comrade(s)" in the inter-titles. Note: *The Volga Boatman* was the flagship release of DeMille's new independent production company, Producers Distributing Corporation (PDC). Although the opening titles declare that the film's story "takes no sides" politically, the conservative DeMille was so fascinated by the Soviet regime that he had originally planned to shoot the film on location.

[S (GEH; Vid); LC, LP22696; *EH* 3/20/26:91–92; *Var* 4/21/26:34]

Atroc; Bol; Decad; Escape; Fem Rad; Liq Link; Mob; Rev; Russ; Tsar; Viol; White Russ
ANTI-RS

1927

High Hat, Robert Kane Prods/First Nat, James Ashmore Creelman, Mar, Am, Comedy

Von Strogoff, an irascible German directing a film on the Bolshevik revolution, fires a lazy extra named Jerry (Ben Lyon) for falling asleep on a prop bed. As the disheartened Jerry prepares to leave the Superba-Prettygood Pictures lot he observes his rival for a cute wardrobe mistress stealing the "Great Romanoff" jewels that had been entrusted to her. Jerry follows the thieving Tony to a meeting with crooks in Greenwich Village. Jerry is captured by them, escapes and then chases Tony back to the New York studio for a bang up finale that is filmed by mistake. The pearl neck-

lace turns out to be paste, but Jerry's "closeup" will be kept in the motion picture. This was not the first film to poke fun at the persona of Erich von Stroheim. *My Neighbor's Wife* (C.S. Elfelt Prods/Davis Dist. Div., 1925) featured a crazy film director named "Eric von Greed."

[AFI,F2.2485; LC, LP23738; *Var* 4/27/27: 17]

Bol; Ger; G Vill; Ital?; Jewels; Rev; Russ: Tsar?
CM/ANTI-SOV

Lost at the Front, First Nat, Del Lord, May, Am/Russ, Comedy

This film was obviously inspired by the success of Paramount's 1926 war burlesque *Behind the Front*, featuring the team of Raymond Hatton and Wallace Beery. First National's comedy duo was a Mutt and Jeff style match of the tall, Irish-playing Charlie Murray and the short, stocky, Jew-playing George Sidney. In *Lost at the Front* they are cast as an Irish cop named Mike and a German bartender named August. They both vie for the attentions of Olga, a Russian sculptress. A couple of years into the war, the middle-aged August is called up to the German reserves. He leaves with a wireless machine he bought from a tramp, which he believes can help end the war. When America enters the war, Mike tries to join the service so he can find August and prevent him from using the radio mechanism to destroy the Allies. He is rejected because he is too old. However, Olga is able to arrange the policeman's induction into the Russian Army! Mike captures August on the eastern front. They dress up in drag in an attempt to escape the battling armies, but wind up being shanghaied into the Russian women's "Battalion of Death." The two are saved from the revolution by the Armistice and are allowed to return to the United States. Meanwhile, Olga has married a third party. The women's battalion formed during the Kerensky regime had been featured in Metro's 1918 release *The Legion of Death*, q.v.

[AFI, F2.3190; LC, LP23955; *Var* 6/15/27:21]

Artist; Bol?; Ger; Irish; Pol; Rev; Russ; Tramp; White Russ
NDB

Mockery, MGM, Benjamin Christensen, Aug, Russ, Drama

In a Siberian battlefield during the post-revolution Russian civil war, Sergei, the Hare-lip (Lon Chaney), desperately searches for food among the corpses. The Countess Tatiana Alexandrova (Barbara Bedford), disguised as a peasant to spy on the Reds, comes upon the starving man. She gives the "slow-thinking" Sergei food and promises friendship in exchange for his services as a guide to No-vokursk. When the two, who claim to be married, are discovered by a Bolshevik de-tachment, Sergei is mercilessly whipped across the chest in an attempt to force him to reveal Tatiana's true identity. White soldiers chase the Reds off and take the Countess to their headquarters to deliver her report. She arranges for the loyal Sergei to work as a ser-vant at headquarters, the home of a "newly-rich war profiteer"—an overweight stereotype with an obnoxious wife. In Novokursk Tatiana resumes the frivolous life of the aristocracy while being courted by Captain Dimitri (Ri-cardo Cortez). Meanwhile, the ignorant disfigured peasant feels snubbed by the Count-ess' indifference and is jealous of her love for the handsome White officer. Sergei begins to listen to the revolutionary harangues of the fat, vodka-swilling cook, Ivan: "You fool! ... Do you think those upstairs pigs ever keep their promises to us downstairs? We are all equal [pours unequal amounts of vodka] ... But [conspiratorially] things will soon be different!" When the White soldiers leave town, many of the lower classes, incited by revolutionary agitators (both male and female) rise up as a mob and join the attacking Red Army. Dimitri's White troops return and fight the Reds for possession of Novokursk. Sergei, crazed with liquor, tries to rape Tatiana, but is distracted by the battling forces that have burst into the home. Forgiven by Tatiana, Sergei is later mortally wounded while saving her from sexual assault by Ivan and a bearded revolu-tionary. Although unattractive qualities are portrayed by the Whites, anti-Bolshevik de-monology predominates (largely achieved through visuals, such as smartly uniformed and clean-shaven White soldiers versus dirty, motley uniformed Reds—since there are *no* specific references in the film's titles to either Reds or Whites).

[S (GEH; Vid); LC, LP24747(s); *MPN* 9/27/27:713; *Var* 8/24/27:23]

Atroc: Bol; Cap; Decad; Fem Rad; Liq

Link; Mob; Rev; Russ; Sec Ser; Siberia; Viol; White Russ

ANTI-SOV

Mountains of Manhattan, Gotham Prods/ Lumas Film, James P. Hogan, June, Am(u), Drama

A former fighter named Jerry Nolan (Charles Delaney) turns in his boxing gloves for an iron "rigger" job on a skyscraper by day and study at an engineering school by night. Pretty Marion Wright (Dorothy Devore), daughter of the contractor, catches the eye of both Jerry and "Bull" Kerry (played by direc-tor James P. Hogan), the brutal foreman who is involved in graft on the job. Jerry saves Mar-ion from an accident at the construction site. In gratitude, "Big Bill" Wright fires Kerry and gives Jerry the job of foreman. "Bull" retali-ates by inciting the men to strike. The film's resolution comes about during a fight between Jerry and the agitator on the high beams of the unfinished building. Jerry emerges with both the job of superintendent of construction and Marion as his wife.

[AFI, F2.3723; LC, LP23935; *FD* 6/26/27:9; *Var* 5/11/27:20]

Agit; Cap; Irish; Jew; Lab; Shp Flr Abu; Strike; Viol

CAP-LAB COOP

The Princess from Hoboken, Tiffany, Allan Dale, Mar, Am, Comedy

Ma and Pa O'Toole, with the help of their daughter Sheila, run a small restaurant in Hoboken. It caters to a mixed ethnic crowd, including a Jew, an Italian and a Russian, known as "Whiskers." Inspired by press reports about a White Russian princess, who is a for-mer ballerina, staying in Chicago, they turn the place into a night club called the "Russian Inn." Sheila is persuaded to impersonate the princess for the opening. Prince Anton (Lou Tellegen), an unscrupulous Russian, ostensi-bly collects money for fellow refugees, but pockets it for himself. He importunes a rich patron, Mrs. O'Brien, to sponsor a bazaar for Russian relief. Anton also tries to get Sheila to go along with a scam involving jewels by threatening to expose her as an impostor. The arrival of the now-obese real princess and im-migration officials lead to Anton making a hasty departure (with his man, Pavel, played by Boris Karloff).

[AFI, F2.4349; LC, LP23870; *Var* 5/25/27:20]

Deport?; Irish; Ital; Jew; Jewels; Russ; White Russ

CM/ANTI-SOV

Seventh Heaven, Fox, Frank Borzage, May, Fr, Drama

Chico (Charles Farrell), a self-proclaimed "atheist," works in the sewers of the Paris district known as "The Sock." A kindly priest arranges for Chico to get a coveted job as a street cleaner. A proud Chico becomes fast friends with his fellow street cleaner, whom he addresses a couple of times as "comrade" (implying that the atheist is also at least a nominal socialist). One evening, Chico rescues Diana (Janet Gaynor), who is being mercilessly beaten in the street by her absinthe-crazed sister. He and Diana share his seventh story garret, become lovers and plan to wed. But then Chico is called-up into the army when France goes to war with Germany in 1914. The two lovers only have time to declare their spiritual marriage. Although having just been officially listed on Armistice Day as killed in action, Diana cannot believe Chico is dead. As she sadly gazes down upon Parisians celebrating the war's end a blinded Chico comes to her side. This film was remade by 20th Century–Fox in 1937.

[S (MOMA; Vid); LC, LP24098; *Var* 5/11/27:14]

Lab; Soc?

NDB

Shanghai Bound, Paramount, Luther Reed, Oct, China, Advent-Drama

The Paramount Press Sheet summarized the background for this motion picture in the following manner: "Modern China—mysterious with its age-old civilization, militant with its new Western ideas, dangerous with its Bolshevism, revengeful with its hate of Occidental interference, riotous with its famine." And, in fact, Soviet and Chinese Communist influence upon the new republic's coalition government, headed by the Kuomintang (KMT), had reached its peak in the 1926–27 period. This culminated in early 1927 with a series of strikes and anti-foreign riots, particularly in Hankow (on the Yangtse River east of Shanghai) and in Foochow. In the spring the right wing of the KMT would launch a full scale purge of the communists. It is amidst this chaos of revolution/civil war that Jim Bucklin (Richard Dix), the captain of an old river freighter, anchors at a small town east of Shanghai. He leaves the boat and makes his way through scenes of devastation to a little cafe. A group of fatuous westerners, including the ship's American owner, and an effeminate Englishman enter and demand to be fed. A mob of hunger rioters led by a revolutionary "bandit" named Scarface (Tetsu Komai) attack the occidentals, killing their chauffeur. Jim, fighting off the threatening Chinese, is able to rush the frightened party aboard his ship and head down the river toward Shanghai. A vengeful Scarface, wounded in the fray, leads his men on land toward some narrows where he plans to cut off the fleeing ship. Discovering that most of his crew has deserted, Jim orders his wealthy passengers to help operate the boat (including the owner Louden's pretty daughter, played by Mary Brian). During the dramatic encounter with the revolutionary bandits, Jim is knocked overboard and has an underwater fight with Scarface. A U.S. Navy destroyer arrives and takes aboard the freighter's survivors. Note: In late 1926 Metro released *Tell It to the Marines*, starring Lon Chaney. In the last quarter of this film American Marines battle uniformed Chinese "bandits."

[AFI, F2.4957; LC, LP24520; *Var* 11/9/27:21]

Chin Comm; Escape; Mob; Rev; Viol

ANTI-REV

Surrender, Universal-Jewel, Edward Sloman, Mar, Aust/Russ, Drama

In a small Galician town near the Russian border lives a Rabbi and his pretty daughter Lea (Mary Philbin). At the stream that divides the countries, she meets a gentile named Constantine (Ivan Mosjoukine; the most popular pre-revolution star in Russia, who fled the Bolsheviks and became a French screen idol), who is both an aristocrat and a colonel of the hated Cossacks. However, Lea is at first unaware of his status, since he had been dressed in a peasant blouse while hunting. The Rabbi, played by Nigel De Brulier, then insults the "Russian—persecutor of our people," for showing an interest in Lea. Following the outbreak of the World War, Constantine and his Cossacks occupy the border town. Later, wearing the distinctive fur cap of a Cossack officer, he announces that if Lea does not come to his rooms by a certain hour, his troops will burn the villagers in their homes—"like rats." She visits the prince, prepared to "surrender" herself to his will. But Constantine has succumbed to an overwhelming admiration of the proud Lea, pledges his eternal love and allows her to return home unmolested. The Austrian army retakes the town that same evening. Rabbi Mendel dies defending Lea, who was being stoned by the ungrateful villagers. A title advances the film to its concluding scene: "Years of darkness, bloodshed, revolution—then peace and sunshine." Constantine, now a member of a communal farm (presumably his former estate, where he had been hunting in the opening sequence), accepts a ladle of water from a "comrade" worker in the fields, and then crosses the stream and embraces Lea.

[S (LC; Vid); AFI, F2.5486; LC, LP24200; *Var* 11/9/27:25]

Bol; Jew; Rev; Russ
ANTI-RS

The Tender Hour, John McCormick Prods/ First Nat, May, George Fitzmaurice, Fr, Rom Drama

Marcia Kane (Billie Dove), the beautiful young daughter of an American capitalist living in Paris, is tricked by her father when he tells her that Wally, her true love, is dead. He then pressures her into marrying the middle-aged White Russian Grand Duke Sergei (Montagu Love). After the loveless ceremony, Marcia learns of the deception when Wally (Ben Lyon) bursts into her room. Furious, she repulses Sergei and vows that she will be his wife in name only. With a little help from some underworld friends of Wally's, the two lovers are eventually able to convince the Grand Duke to consent to a divorce.

[AFI, F2.5564; LC, LP23880; *Var* 6/8/27:15]

Cap; White Russ
NDB

1928

Adoration, First Nat, Frank Lloyd, Dec, Russ/Fr, Drama

At a ball in Petrograd on the eve of the revolution, Prince Serge Orloff (Antonio Moreno) mistakenly becomes convinced that his wife Elena ("American Beauty" Billie Dove) is having an affair with another man. The violent collapse of Imperial Russia forces the three to flee separately to Paris, arriving there as penniless refugees. The statuesque Elena becomes a clothes model while Serge works as a waiter—when he is sober. Elena finds Serge and is eventually able to convince him she was never the mistress of Vladimir. The couple is reconciled and Serge is able to obtain new employment as a chauffeur.

[AFI, F2.0037; LC, LP25848; *Var* 1/16/29:14]

Escape; Rev; Russ; White Russ
CM/ANTI-SOV

The Adventurer, MGM, Viachetslav Tourjansky, July, Caribbean, Advent Drama

Texas engineer Jim McClellan (Tim McCoy) manages the gold mines on the West Indies island of Santo Diego. He is in love with Dolores de Silva (Dorothy Sebastian), the daughter of the island's president. The wealth of the little country, though, has attracted the attention of an international cast of "lawless men." One inter-title states: "A Russian, posing as a bull-fighter and calling himself the Tornado is the principal disturber." But even he defers to the leadership of a "brave comrade from Russia," named Samaroff (Michael Visaroff). Together, they organize a revolution and seize the mines. The Tornado also insists on marrying Dolores. Although he promises Dolores that her father will be spared if she cooperates, The Tornado orders the deposed president to be executed immediately following the wedding. Jim and his pal Barney overcome the drunken revolutionaries and lead a counter revolution. The foreign "riffraff" are captured. Russian-born director Tourjansky had fled the Bolsheviks in 1919. Note: In 1927 the U.S. government became alarmed by the "Socialist" administration in Mexico that was supplying arms to radical rebels, including Sandino, in Nicaragua. A diplomatic and publicity campaign was mounted against an alleged Nicaraguan-Mexican-Soviet conspiracy to impose a "Mexican-fostered Bolshevist hegemony" in Central America that would threaten the Panama Canal. This is the only known feature film from the period to specifically refer to Soviet interference in Latin America (*not* to be confused with several films released during the 1920s that portrayed apolitical South American "revolutionists").

[AFI, F2.0039; LC, LP25461(s); *EH* I/14/28:43]

Bol; Cap; Decad; Lab; Liq Link; Mob; Rev; Russ; Viol

ANTI-REV; ANTI-SOV

Clothes Make the Woman, Tiffany Stahl Prods, Tim Terriss, May, Russ/Am, Rom Drama

Tiffany studios has created a new popular star named Victor Trent (Walter Pidgeon) out of a former Russian extra. At a lunch meeting, Hollywood executives desperately search for a follow-up film idea to headline their latest matinee idol. Victor suggests a story based upon his actual experiences during the Bolshevik Revolution. He recalls in flashback how he was among the Reds who captured the Tsar and his family. When in a dark cellar the "comrades" were ordered to rid Russia of the Romanoffs forever, he did not have the heart to shoot Princess Anastasia (Eve Southern). Instead, the young revolutionary, with a prominent red star shoulder patch, risked his life to arrange for her escape from Russia—beginning with a nighttime cart ride, the unconscious Anastasia hidden beneath a load of hay, and ending with her solo dash across the border in an open car. "Vic's … yarn" is approved by the executives and an order goes out to Central Casting for "Bolsheviks" to be used in Tiffany's new film, "A Daughter of the Czar." While searching for the female lead, Victor discovers Anastasia among the extras and arranges for her to play the part she once lived! In the course of reenacting the cellar murder scene, Victor accidentally wounds her. Tiffany's "Russian mystery girl" recovers and marries Victor. The similarities with Paramount's *The Last Command*, q.v., released earlier in the year, are inescapable. Note: Grand Duchess Anastasia Nikolaevna, the youngest daughter of Tsar Nicholas II, would be the member of the Romanoff family most often rumored to have escaped execution. The most persistent claimant would be the enigmatic Anna Anderson, who first showed up in Germany in 1919.

[S (BFI); AFI, F2.0930; LC, LP25203(s); *Var* 6/6/28:13]

Artist; Atroc; Bol; Escape; Rev; Russ; Tsar; Viol; White Russ

ANTI-SOV

Give and Take, Universal-Jewel, William Beaudine, Dec, Am(s), Com-Drama

In this "part-talkie" Jack Bauer (George Lewis) returns from college to be greeted by the hometown band at the train station. After giving his sweetheart Marion a ring, he immediately sets out to organize the workers in his father's fruit cannery into an Industrial Democracy. This results in a strike and an estrangement between Marion and Jack, since her father is the factory foreman. Jack's father (John; played by Jean Hersholt) seems near financial ruin when he receives a large order. The men go back to work, but then doubt is cast on the validity of the contract for canned goods. When Bauer is unable to meet his payroll, his workers go on a rampage. Later, peace is restored and Jack's courtship is resumed when the order is confirmed.

[AFI, F2.2118; LC, LP25524; *Var* 1/9/29:11]

Camp Rad; Cap; Lab; Reconcil; Strike; Viol

CAP-LAB COOP

The Last Command, Paramount, Josef von Sternberg, Jan, Russ/Am, Drama

Sergius, a palsied middle-aged man living in a seedy Hollywood boarding house, gets a call from casting to appear at the Eureka Studio to play a Russian general. While looking into his make-up mirror, Sergius (Emil Jannings) is transported to the last days of Imperial Russia in 1917, where he is the vain and proud General Dolgorucki, Grand Duke Sergius Alexander, at his headquarters near the front. Leo (William Powell) and Natascha (Evelyn Brent), two "revolutionists" posing as traveling troop entertainers, are brought before him. The man is the same person who is now directing the motion picture for Eureka. Later, over drinks in his rooms, the general gives Natascha a valuable pearl necklace and tells her that she is now "my prisoner of love"—it compliments the distinctly non-proletarian, twenties high couture, white gown worn by Miss Brent. Reds at a secret meeting, led by a Trotsky look-alike (Fritz Feld?), declare that the time for Russia to become a republic has arrived and send out orders for street demonstrations to begin. The troops sent to disperse them are overwhelmed. A bayonet and banner waving mob (including women) prepares a "reception" for the "masters of Russia" arriving in the General's train. Upon exiting his private railway car, the General is mocked and stripped of his insignia; his subordinates are shot. The captured general is then forced back onto the train, his fate to be determined in Petrograd. Natascha, shoving the necklace he had given her into his hands, later helps the stunned General to escape from the train. Back in the present on the movie set, the former Imperial Army officer, momentarily transformed into a Russian general again, grabs a prop Tsarist banner and exhorts the soldier extras to fight for the fatherland—as the cameras roll, the stage pianist is directed to play the Tsarist "National Anthem." The spent man collapses, dying in the arms of his old Bolshevik nemesis-cum-director.

[S (MOMA; Vid); LC, LP24895; *NYT* 1/23/28:18; *Var* 1/25/28:12]

Artist; Atroc; Bol; Escape; Fem Rad; Jewels; Liq Link; Mob; Rev; Russ; Trotsky?; Tsar; Viol; White Russ

ANTI-RS; ANTI-SOV

The Mating Call, Caddo/Paramount, James Cruze, July, Am, Drama

Leslie Hatton (Thomas Meighan) returns from service in France to his Florida farm to discover that Rose (Evelyn Brent), his war bride, has had their marriage annulled. The sultry Rose has married rich townsman Lon Henderson, the leader of the local chapter of the Klan, called "The Order" in the film titles. The now worldly Rose returns from a European vacation and, fed up with Henderson's infidelities, tries to renew her relationship with Leslie. Leslie is not receptive, but he is lonely. His solution is to travel north to Ellis Island where he induces Catherine (Renee Adoree), a Russian girl, to marry him in exchange for a home in the United States. Leslie later learns that Catherine was a member of the Tsarist aristocracy. After Leslie is subjected to a "tribunal" of the Order for his alleged responsibility for the death of a local girl, he and Catherine hear the mating call.

[LC, LP25596; *Var* 10/10/28:15]

Decad; Fasc; Vet; Vig; Viol; White Russ
ANTI-FASC

The Red Dance, Fox, Raoul Walsh, Dec, Russ, Rom Drama

The *Variety* review stated somewhat facetiously that this film "seeks ... to give justification ... for the Czar's overthrow." Rasputin and his court intriguers, who surround the Tsarina, believe Grand Duke Eugen (Charles Farrell) knows too much about their attempts to undermine the morale of the Imperial Army. Eugen is sent to a town where Cossack depredations have caused great discontent and is ordered to marry the blonde aristocratic vamp, Princess Varvara (Dorothy Revier). Tasia (Delores Del Rio), a dark peasant girl whose parents were lost in the terrorism, is sold into marriage by her relatives to a brawny, illiterate soldier named Ivan Petroff (Ivan Linow), but he is too drunk to remember the wedding. The local revolutionary agitator persuades Tasia to revenge her parents by shooting the bridegroom of Princess Varvara. Tasia, who has fallen in love with the Grand Duke, misses when she fires at him. She flees and later becomes the Red dancer of Moscow. A room beneath the stage serves as a secret Bolshevik meeting place. After the revolution, Ivan is made a general in the Red Army—frequently reminding his compatriots that he has "brains." It is decreed that Eugen be executed; Tasia rushes to his quarters to warn him. Ivan, who has come to love Tasia, discovers them together and, not willing to hurt Tasia, arranges for the faked shooting and burial of Eugen. A plane is made available for the lovers' escape from Soviet Russia. This was the first film since early 1919 to allude to the German-Bolshevik linkage, e.g., *The Legion of Death* (Metro 1918), q.v. Note: Secret accords to the 1922 Russo-German Treaty of Rappallo had led to close military cooperation between the two countries. Revelations concerning these German violations of the Versailles Treaty began to surface in late 1926, renewing fears in the West of German collusion with the Bolshevik regime.

[LC, LP25395(s); *EH* 9/22/28:54; *Var* 6/27/28:14]

Agit; Atroc; Bol; Bol-Ger Link; Decad; Liq Link; Rasputin; Rev; Russ; Tsar; Viol; White Russ

ANTI-SOV

The Scarlet Lady, Columbia, Alan Crosland, Aug, Russ, Drama

When a Red meeting is raided by the Cossacks, the beautiful black-haired peasant Lya (Lya de Putti) finds refuge on the estate of Prince Nicholas Korloff (Don Alvarado). Home from the battle front, the Prince is amused by the little revolutionist whom he finds hiding under his bed and allows her to

The Last Command (Paramount, 1928): Bolshevik agent Natascha (Evelyn Brent) is seated next to a brutal revolutionary leader in the private car of the captured tsarist general—now the scene of an orgy. The smiling Red is just about to shoot his drunken rival for the lady's affection. Note that the sullen Natascha wears the pearl necklace the smitten general had earlier bestowed upon her.

stay. They begin a short relationship that is abruptly ended when a loyal servant informs Nicholas that Lya had been the mistress of the notorious Red leader, Zaneriff (surname possibly meant to evoke linkages with the ongoing rebellion by the Rifs against colonial rule in Morocco; played by Warner Oland). With the outbreak of the revolution, the palace of the prince is seized by a Red mob and made the local Bolshevik headquarters. Nicholas, who is disguised as a servant, is recognized by Lya, but she does not betray him. Soon afterwards, Zaneriff discovers that Lya has sheltered the Prince and orders that Nicholas be executed with the rest of the Royalist prisoners. In the cellar of the palace, in a scene that was perhaps meant to evoke associations with the execution of the Tsar and his family, the Whites are lined up by the graves they were compelled to dig for themselves. They are shot one at a time by the gloating Zaneriff. Nicholas has been saved for last. Lya tells Zaneriff that she would like to give the Prince a final message, in lead. But when the obliging villain hands her his automatic, she turns the weapon on him, his corpse falling into the grave meant for the aristocrat. Lya disguises Nicholas in Zaneriff's greatcoat and the two drive off in the Red leader's car to the border. The *Variety* review wryly comments: "Scenario conforms to the American supposition that all revolutionists are bums, cutthroats and bloodthirsty with blue bloods able to teach 'em how to live and die, as a title explains."

[AFI, F2.4835; LC, LP25664; *Var* 8/22/28:16]

Atroc; Bol; Escape; Fem Rad; Mob; Rev; Russ; Viol; White Russ

ANTI-SOV

A Ship Comes In, Pathé, William K. Howard, June, Am, Drama

A Hungarian family arrives in New York City before the first World War. They settle

down on the East Side and Papa Pleznik (Rudolph Schildkraut) finds a job as a janitor in the Federal Building. Papa loves America and looks forward to becoming a citizen. However, a fellow countryman, an anarchist named Sokol (Fritz Feld; who resembles Lenin), sulks about, heaps abuse on America and disparages the old man's optimism: "Don't be a fool! You won't find happiness here! ... All governments are alike. They take everything—give you nothing." By 1917 Papa has become a good friend of Judge Gresham and is preparing to be made a "relation" of Uncle Sam. But the judge has been targeted for assassination by Sokol for sending one of his "bearded comrades" to jail for treason. On the day Papa is scheduled to be sworn in as a citizen, he comes to work with a cake Mama (Louise Dresser) baked for the judge. While he attends to his duties, Sokol sneaks in and places a time bomb in the bottom of the cake box. Amidst the atmosphere of "war-time hysteria," Papa is sent to jail for the explosion that injured the judge and killed a secretary. Sometime later, a now-crazed Sokol wanders into the street and is run over by a troop truck. A death bed confession results in Papa's release from jail. Note: This film epitomizes the 1920s nativist fixation upon the so-called theme of "100 percent Americanism."
[S (LC); LC, LP25281; *EH* 6/16/28:66; *Var* 9/5/28:28]
Am Icons; Anarch; Fem Rad; Bomb; Lab; Pol; Viol
ANTI-REV

Tempest, UA, Sam Taylor, Aug, Russ, Rom Drama
In 1914, "before the red tempest of terror," Sergeant Ivan Markov (John Barrymore) studies hard to become one of the few peasants to ever receive a commission in the Imperial Dragoons. A scraggly, wild-eyed peddler (Jew?; purveyor of cheap and/or fake articles; the *Variety* reviewer thought his appearance "suggested" Trotsky) addresses him as "comrade" and passes around leaflets to the troops: "Slaves of the Czar Awake. Our Day Is Coming. Join the Socialist Revolutionary Party...." Ivan is awarded a commission, but quickly loses it and is imprisoned when he is found drunk in the bedroom of the general's beautiful daughter, Princess Tamara (played by German actress Camilla Horn). In a superimposed shot that gives the peddler a devilish appear-

ance, the agitator gleefully sets fire to the officer's insignia that had been stripped off Ivan. Even after war is declared, the vindictive aristocratic fiancée of Tamara, sensing the growing love between her and the peasant soldier, arranges for Ivan to be left in solitary confinement. During the revolution, the barracks are stormed and the peddler, now the local commissar, assures "comrade" Ivan that the people of Russia need leaders like him. Ivan, now an honored member of the Red Tribunal, witnesses aristocrats, including the officers who had humiliated him, being themselves degraded and executed. As a savage mob cheers the pronouncement of each sentence, the commissar peddler is observed to take pleasure in wielding the stamp that officially seals the fate of the condemned. The obvious sadism of the commissar in demanding that Ivan sign Tamara's death warrant leads Ivan to shoot the bloodthirsty revolutionary and to flee with Tamara across a snow covered landscape to the Austrian border. What may possibly be a poster with Stalin's image and a portrait of Trotsky appear in two separate scenes during the latter part of the film. This big budget production was designed to feature the talents of matinee idol Barrymore. Note: Former NCO's in the Tsarist army would form the backbone of the Red Army.
[S (GEH; LC; Vid); LC, LP25492; *NYT* 5/18/28:28; *Var* 5/23/28:21]
Atroc; Bol; Escape; Jew?; Mob; Rev; Russ; Trotsky?; Tsar; Viol; White Russ
ANTI-SOV

The Woman from Moscow, Paramount, Ludwig Gerger, Nov, Russ/Fr, Drama
This was an anachronistic revival of the old Nihilist genre with Pola Negri in her last starring role in America. When Princess Fedora's fiancé is shot by a suspected nihilist in 1880's Russia, she follows the assassin to Paris. Love, betrayal and suicide follow. This film featured sound effects along with a musical score.
[LC, LP25791; *EH* 6/16/28:66; *Var* 11/7/28:15]
Nih; Russ; Viol
ANTI-REV

1929

China Bound, MGM, Charles F. Reisner, May, Am/China, Comedy

A sales clerk in an antique shop becomes romantically entangled with the daughter, played by Josephine Dunn, of the owner. This results in the shop owner taking his family to China. With the aid of a ship stoker on the ocean liner, the love smitten clerk is able to pursue the young lady. Further complications arise on the Asian continent when in Chew Chin Chew they are all imprisoned by the Rebel Army forces of General Hong Kow. Nationalist soldiers eventually arrive and chase away the revolutionaries. This film featured the Mutt and Jeff style comedy duo of George K. Arthur and Karl Dane, who had earlier starred together in the 1927 MGM release, *Rookies*. Note: At this time, the Nationalists were systematically suppressing communist forces that had attempted to establish themselves in the major urban centers of China.

[AFI, F2.0872; LC, LP881(s); *Var* 8/5/29:26]

Cap; Chin Comm; Lab; Rev; Viol
ANTI-REV

The Cocoanuts, Par, Robert Florey & Joseph Santley, Aug, Am, Comedy

An unscrupulous hotel manager named Mr. Hammer (Groucho Marx) tries to cash in on the twenties Florida land boom. At one point he stands on a stairwell and exhorts the bellboys, whom he addresses as "wage slaves," to provide their services *without* pay. Based on a 1925 George S. Kaufman play, the Marx Brothers' first feature film could be viewed as a satire on the excesses of capitalism. Groucho's loud-mouthed parody of an agitator could also be construed as an indicator of the weakness of militant labor throughout the decade.

[S (Vid); LC, LP5776; *Var* 5/29/29:14]

Agit?; Cap; Lab
NDB

The Cock-Eyed World, Fox, Raoul Walsh, Oct, Russ/ Am/ Nicaragua, Com-Drama/mus

Marine sergeants Flagg and Quirt (Victor McLaglen and Edmund Lowe) continue after World War I from where they left off in *What Price Glory?* (Fox; 1926). As members of the Allied intervention forces in Vladivostok, the two have a brawl over a female Bolshevik named Katinka. After similar problems with a wise-cracking flapper from Coney Island, the boys wind up fighting each other and revolu-

tionaries down in Nicaragua. The Central American sequence includes an aerial bombing of the rebels. According to the *Variety* review of this "All Dialog" [sic] motion picture, the "dialog frequently cracks 'big business' as being responsible for wars of aggrandizement, such as the Nicaragua campaign." This film was a box office money grosser.

[PE (USC); AFI, F2.0940; LC, LP586(s); *Var* 8/7/29:208]

Allied Interv; Bol; Cap; Fem Rad; Russ; Sandino; Viol
ANTI-REV; ANTI-CAP

Devil's Chaplain, Trem Carr Prods/Rayart, Duke Worne, Mar, Rur/Am, Rom Drama

In a mythical Balkan kingdom, Princess Therese (Virginia Brown Faire), betrothed to the heir to the throne, pretends to be a leader of the revolutionary mob that storms the palace in order to save the Prince. In Washington, the exiled heir is protected by an American Secret Service man, Yorke Norray. After numerous scrapes with international spies and revolutionary agents (including Boris, played by Boris Karloff), the Prince is restored to his throne. The Princess, though, decides to return to America with the dashing Yorke.

[AFI, F2.1322; *Var* 5/22/29:27]

Escape; Mob; Rev; Sec Ser; Spy-Sab; Viol
ANTI-REV

Flight, Columbia, Frank R. Capra, Sept, Am/Nicaragua, Advent-Drama

A Yale graduate whose wrong-way run lost the New Year's Day football game with Stanford, joins the Marine Corps. Fouling up in flight school as well, Lefty Phelps (Ralph Graves) winds up in Nicaragua as a mechanic. With a Marine outpost under attack by native rebels, Lefty is chosen as an observer/gunner on an aerial mission to give support to the beleaguered Marines. His plane is shot down in a swamp and the pilot mortally wounded. As the "bandits" close in on him, Lefty's pal, Panama (Jack Holt), flies in to the rescue. The leader of the rebel bandits is referred to in print materials as both Sandino and Lobo, or "wolf" in Spanish. In the film screened, a British print available at the Library of Congress, he is only called Lobo. However, the "bandit leader," who has been ambushing Marines and is the self-described general of a 3,000 man army, was obviously based upon Augusto Sandino. To accentuate his cruelty, Lobo is portrayed sending photos of the mutilated corpses of captured Marines to their commanding officer. During the battle scenes, Lobo leads his "outlaw" army under a black banner emblazoned with the skull and crossbones. This was Capra's first sound film. Note: Throughout 1928 and 1929, Sandino's forces battled U.S. Marines in Nicaragua.

[S (LC; Vid); AFI, F2.1819; LC, LP884; *Var* 9/18/29:15]

Am Icons; Rev; Sandino; Viol
ANTI-REV

The Godless Girl, Pathé, Cecil B. DeMille, Mar, Am, Drama

The opening title of this silent film, with synchronized score and sound effects, reads: "It is not generally known that there are atheist societies throughout this country attacking through the youth of the nation the beliefs that are sacred to most of the people." Judith Craig (Lina Basquette), the daughter of an avowed atheist, forms a high school club known as "The Godless Society." The vixen secretly prints circulars extolling "The Society" and has them placed in the students' lockers. This results in a threat of expulsion from the principal. It also brings her activities to the attention of Bob, a neighbor and a devout Christian—"No fanatics are so bitter as youthful fanatics," an intertitle notes of Judith and Bob. He organizes an attack upon a meeting of the group of atheists ("Where little rebels blow spitballs at the Rock of Ages") that results in the accidental death of a girl (identified only as the "victim"). Both Judith and Bob are sent to reform school. At first, Judith remains rebellious, abusing another girl who reads the *Bible*. But then Judith undergoes a religious transformation when attempting to touch hands with Bob, whom she has come to love, across an electrified barbed wire fence that separates the boys from the girls. The figure of the cross is burnt into their palms! After further trials, the two are pardoned. Note: In 1921 a "Union of the Militant Godless" was formed in the Soviet Union as part of what became a sustained anti-religious campaign. The son of an Episcopal minister, DeMille would make several films promoting religion and attacking promiscuity.

[S (UCLA); AFI, F2.2139; LC, LP25553(s); *Var* 4/3/29:11]

Anti-Rel; Fem Rad; Pol; Viol
ANTI-REV

The Leatherneck, Ralph Block Prods/Pathé, Howard Higgin, Feb, Fr/Russ/China, Advent-Drama

At U.S. Marine headquarters in Tien Tsiu, China, private William "Tex" Calhoun (William Boyd) is being court-martialed for murder and desertion. The story of Tex and his two Marine pals is then related in a series of flashbacks. After the three privates first met in France, they were posted with the Allied Intervention forces in Vladivostok. At a bar, they encounter a brawny "mysterious mug" who identifies himself as Captain Heckla (Fred Kohler) and who claims to be glad to hear "lingo" he can understand. Heckla introduces the Marines to a kindly old man named Petrovich who has "been hit pretty hard" by confiscations following the revolution. But he still owns a potash deposit in Manchuria. Tex falls in love with and marries Petrovich's daughter, Tanya. Soon afterwards, the Civil War grows hot again and Heckla now appears as a leader of the Red Guards. Tanya's father, brother and loyal servant are murdered and she is kidnapped. Posted to China, Tex's buddies read in the paper about a Heckla Potash Company that is offering stock. His Marine pals, Fuzzy (Alan Hale) and Buddy (Robert Armstrong) desert to seek revenge. Tex follows as soon as he learns what's going on. When Tex catches up with the others in Manchuria, he discovers the body of Heckla, a dying Buddy and a mute Fuzzy, driven insane through torture. Not convinced of the veracity of his story, the officers of the court-martial are about to sentence Tex to death when Tanya appears and corroborates the tale. It is implied that Heckla was a mercenary world revolutionary who had once lived in the United States. This film had a few "talking" sequences.

[S (LC, incomplete); LC, LP167; *Var* 4/24/29:22]

Allied Interv; Am Icons; Atroc; Bol; Cap; Rev; Russ; Viol; White Russ
ANTI-REV

Noah's Ark, WB, Michael Curtiz, June, Europe, Drama

The Oriental Express to Paris in 1914 carries the usual cosmopolitan mix of passengers. In one compartment the travelers include Mary (Dolores Costello), a beautiful blonde Alsatian actress, Nickoloff (Noah Beery), a lecherous middle-aged,   monocle-wearing   Russian officer, and two American youths. A discussion with a bearded mystic on religion is begun in which the Russian, a Frenchman and a German disparage Christianity. Nickoloff proclaims, "Military might is the only God!" He further asserts, "Faith is food for fools.... If there is a God why doesn't he show himself?" At this point, the train is wrecked. At a nearby inn where the survivors are gathered, Nickoloff attempts to accost Mary. An American, Travis, is forced to knock him out. Several years later, Travis is fighting in the trenches and Mary is dancing behind the lines in a troop canteen. Colonel Nickoloff, the former Tsarist Secret Service man who is now working for Allied Intelligence, appears. When Mary repulses his advances, he exacts revenge by placing incriminating documents in her luggage. As Mary is about to be executed as a German spy, a shell from a railway cannon lands in the courtyard. The scene is then transformed to an ancient town with an analogous Biblical theme. Nickoloff is now the pagan King Nephilim and Mary becomes Miriam. Noah saves Miriam as the floods drown the idol worshipers. Back in modern times, Mary and Travis are in a Red Cross hospital when a messenger arrives with news of the Armistice. After insinuating the German-Bolshevik link, Godless communism is symbolically destroyed by religious faith. The film contains a strong pacifist message, ending with the mystical minister declaring to the lovers that "war is now an outlaw...." This motion picture was a part-talkie, with sound effects and a musical score.

[S (LC; UCLA; Vid); LC, LP417; *NYT* 3/13/29:28; *Var* 11/7/28:15]

Anti-Rel; Bol-Ger Link?; Decad; Jew; Pac; Russ; Spy-Sab; Viol

PAC; CM/ANTI-SOV

The Shady Lady, Paul Block/Pathé, Edward H. Griffith, Jan, Cuba, Drama

This is the story of competing gun runners, played by Robert Armstrong and Louis Wolheim, and a tall blonde named Lola (Phyllis Haver), with a shady past, whose lives come together in Havana. The arms being shipped are going to Central American revolutionaries, read Nicaragua. Dialogue sequences were included in the final reel of this film.

[AFI, F2.4949; LC, LP8; *Var* 3/27/29:24]

Rev; Sandino?

NDB

They Had to See Paris, Fox, Frank Borzage, Sept, Am/Fr, Com-Drama

Pike Peters, an Oklahoma garage owner played by Will Rogers, strikes oil. His wife insists that the family leave rural Claremont (a play on Claremore, Rogers' real-life hometown) and visit Paris. Once there, the nagging Mrs. Peters (Irene Rich) attempts to break into society by arranging a marriage between their daughter and a mercenary aristocrat, the Marquise de Brissac. At a soiree at their rented chateau "His Imperial Highness, Grand Duke Makiall of Russia," is introduced. Despite the $1000 honorarium he was paid to attend, the petulant Russian with a goatee is bored by the social pretensions and is about to leave when the caviar is served. After gorging himself, the Grand Duke again prepares to make his exit when he encounters the folksy Pike seated alone on the staircase, clothed only in a dressing gown. A few drinks later, they are fast friends. Inebriated, the two return to the other guests, Pike now wearing a suit of armor. Pike and "Mike" awaken together in bed the next morning! Pike escorts the Grand Duke to his touring car, asking him to visit Claremont and give a speech to the Rotary Club. The Grand Duke sadly responds: "I wish I could invite you to my country, but I have none." That afternoon Pike adamantly refuses to pay a dowry for his daughter. After Pike discovers his son living with an artist's model on the Left Bank, he successfully endeavors to persuade his family to return home to Oklahoma. This was an all-sound motion picture.

[S (Vid); LC, LP675(s); *Var* 10/16/29:17]

Artists; Bol?; Cap; Decad; White Russ

CM/ANTI-SOV

The Bat, United Artists, Roland West, Mar. 1926, Am, Drama

A master thief, known as "The Bat" for his furry disguise, visits the estate leased by wealthy spinster Cornelia Van Gorder. When the nervous lady appears with a gun, her servant Lizzie (Louise Fazenda) responds: "I put up with you through rheumatism and socialism, but I'm not going to put up with you through spookism."

[S (UCLA; Vid); LC, LP22528; *Var* 3/17/26:38]

Cap; Soc

NDB

Appendix 1
Selected Relevant Foreign Films
Released in the U.S., 1909–1915

1909

The Babies' Strike, Italia

Tots, whose nurses have abandoned them to go out with their sweethearts, declare a strike. The babies make banners with specific demands and begin picketing. The strike is amicably settled. The Turin based Italia Film Company specialized in comedy.

[*MPW* 9/4/09:314]

Cops on a Strike, Pathé

The Paris police walk out on strike, ignoring the pleas of the mayor. In retaliation, he releases convicts from the local jail. The convicts promptly capture the police, who have been attending a strike meeting, and then place *them* in prison.

[*MPW* 11/20/09:722; *Var* 11/13/09:13]

Nat Pinkerton, Great Northern

This was part of a series featuring the famous detective. The film depicts Pinkerton foiling a band of anarchists who were attempting to blow up the governor. The police join in with an assist. The Great Northern Film Company was the American name for Nordisk, a Danish studio founded in 1906, which prior to World War I dominated the international film market.

[*MPW* 5/22/09:676]

The Ringleader, Pathé

An indolent fellow at a lumber yard is fired by its elderly president. After hours, the discharged man incites his fellow workers to strike. The foreman and his son, who had refused to sign the strike pledge, are attacked by an angry throng of strikers after the president refuses to honor their demands. The workers are cowed by the death of the foreman's son in the fracas. The ringleader is turned upon, and receives "his just punishment."

[*MPW* 4/10/09:452]

The Strikers, Urban-Eclipse

The workers at a French stone quarry are sown with the seeds of discontent by an indolent comrade. He is joined by a "walking delegate" from the labor organization who incites the men to strike. Their young foreman refuses to join them in a protest parade. When the quarry's owner rebuffs the strikers' demands, the agitator whips the men into a frenzy. They arm themselves and then viciously attack the quarry grounds. The foreman, enraged by the mob's actions and by the agitator's lust for his sweetheart, barges through the crowd and challenges the "bombastic soldier of fortune" to a duel with picks. The cowardly agitator slinks away, and the men return to work.

[*NYDM* 8/28/09:18; *MPW* 8/21/09:263; *MPW* 9/4/09:315]

1911

At the Gringo Mine, Méliès

When the mine owner refuses their demands for a higher wage scale, the miners (Mexican?) seize him and the foreman. The enraged men then bind the two to a post and place a wired keg of dynamite beside them. Having doubts, the man chosen to set the keg's charge delays. This gives the owner's daughter, who is in love with the foreman, just enough time to come to the rescue. Salaries are not raised, but all is forgiven.

[*MPW* 7/22/11:140]

1912

The Nihilists' Conspiracy, Great Northern, 2r

Count Leo Zachokin is in love with Sonja Adamovitch (Jewess?). When the Count later discovers her membership in a band of nihilists, he is captured by her compatriots and threatened with death. Sonja saves the Count's life by getting him to agree to help acquire a list of nihilists condemned by the secret police. After the Chief of Police discovers the list's theft, the nihilist's meeting place is raided. Leo and Sonja flee the scene in his car, but die together in a fiery crash.

[*MPW* 2/24/12:720]

Vengeance vs Love, Great Northern

A Russian "reformer" is arrested on a capital crime by order of Count Alexis, and later shot. Paul, the son of the executed man, joins his father's anarchist society and vows vengeance. But Paul's plans are ultimately thwarted by his love for the Count's daughter.

[*MPW* 2/3/12:428]

1914

Germinal, Pathé, 5r

This film was based upon an 1885 novel by Emile Zola. When a mine engineer discovers rotting timber shoring the shafts, the miners are informed their wages will be lowered to cover the cost of repairs. Urged on by an anarchist, the miners declare a strike. A "spy" among the men keeps management informed, while also helping to organize strikebreakers.

Sabotage of the elevator ropes results in an accident—and when the scabs escape up a ladder they are forced to run through a gauntlet of angry strikers. After a bloody confrontation with the militia, the strike is resolved. The miners, including a woman, return to work. The enraged anarchist floods the mines, with disastrous results. The French would remake this labor classic in 1963 and 1993. The latter film was produced by Cinema 2 and directed by Claude Berri.

[PE (FRA); LC,LU1488; *MPW* 1/24/14: 416]

The Red Club, Dansk Kinograf, 4r

A Russian count decides to marry another noble, thus casting aside his lover Sonja. Seeking revenge, Sonja joins the Red Club. "The red ones" duly inform the count of their intentions to kill him. Various attempts are made upon the count's life, Sonja perishing in the process.

[LC,LU2472; *Var* 5/22/14:23]

1915

The Black Spot, Cosmofotofilm-London Film, 4r

An old Moscow University professor is discussing his revolutionary ideas with some students at his home when the secret police break in. The professor's wife dies while watching the knout applied to her husband. Grand Duke Paul, having observed the situation, intercedes. The professor and his daughter, Olga, are allowed to go into exile in Britain. The expatriates join a nihilist group. When it is later learned that the Grand Duke Paul will be visiting England, Olga is chosen to assassinate him. All is happily resolved.

[LC,LU2977; *MPW* 1/2/15:87; *MPW* 1/ 23/15:586]

A Daughter of Russia, Swedish Biograph, 4r

Paul and Olga fall in love at the university. But when Paul's parents learn of his liaison with a revolutionist of the "fanatical type," they maneuver their son into a marriage with a more suitable lady. After learning of Paul's marriage, a depressed Olga goes out into the street and incites a mob with her revolutionary rhetoric. Olga is arrested and sent to Siberia. Paul, now under police suspicion, goes

to a small Siberian village with his wife to practice medicine. While attempting to escape her exile, Olga seeks refuge at Paul's home. A jealous wife betrays the revolutionary. In remorse, Paul's wife later secretly arranges for Olga to be allowed to escape again. Olga dies in the Siberian wastes.
[*Var* 4/9/15:20]

The Revolt, London Amusement Film, 5r

Andrius, the Prince of Navantia, marries a commoner named Vera. Her brother belongs to an anarchist gang led by the evil Michail Cacurat. When the Prince's father and brother are murdered by anarchists, he ascends the throne. Vera, whose brother was arrested for the deed and has died in prison, becomes estranged from her husband. The villain Michail is later killed by Andrius, after which he and Vera go into exile on a farm in Britain.
[LC,LU9131; *Var* 2/5/15:23]

The Strikers, Apex, 4r

Thomas Massell, the orphan of a laborer, is adopted by a mechanic. He grows up to become a skilled iron worker, who has also invented a new blasting machine. But when the owner of the Kingbridge Iron Works refuses to grant a wage increase, it is Massell whose "burning speech" arouses his fellow iron workers to vote for a strike. Several weeks later a starving worker steals Massell's invention and tries to use it to blow up the factory. Massell is able to contain the explosion, thereby saving both the factory and the life of Kingbridge's daughter. An injured Massell wins the pretty lady's hand and concessions from management.
[*MPW* 1/30/15:736]

Appendix 2

Topical American Shorts, with Coding, 1918–1920

1918

Bill Bolshevik, The Soap Boxer, Spuyten Duyvil Film, Feb?, L. Franklin Van Zelm, Am, Cartoon

A soap box orator named Bill leaves the park where he has been "uttering irresponsible sayings" before a crowd and goes to work in a grocery store. But his constant political agitation results in his losing that job, as well as several others. In the end, he is back at the park, selling soap!

    [LC,MP1149(c)]
    Agit; Bol

Bulling the Bolsheviki, Fox, Bud Fisher, Oct, Russ, Cartoon, 1/2r

Mutt and Jeff visit Russia, "the land of forty revolutions per minute," first encountering a crying bewhiskered Bolshevik seated upon a rapidly swelling bomb. Soon afterwards, the comic duo find themselves at Bolsheviki headquarters where plenty of vodka is being swilled during the "5 o'clock bomb party." In order to escape the "bomb inhalers" Mutt and Jeff disguise themselves with beards.

    [*MPW* 10/5/18:48(ad); *MPN* 10/26/18:529]
    Bol; Bomb; Liq Link; Russ

A Bum Bomb, Nestor, w/p John McDermott, Sept, Am, Comedy, 2r

Ezra, who belongs to the Black Brotherhood, has a "harmless hobby" of making bombs. After receiving orders from his brothers to kill a certain judge, Ezra places an explosive device in a melon. Comic situations ensue during a series of bomb switches made by his friends, Betty and Joe, and a shadower from the Black Brotherhood.

    [LC,LP12835; *MPW* 9/7/18:1435]
    Anarch; Bomb; Viol?

The Eagle's Eye, Foursquare, George A. Lessey; Jan–June. Am, Wellington Playter, Serial, 20eps, 2r

"The Strike Breeders," Episode 5; "The Plot Against Organized Labor," Episode 6; "The Menace of the IWW," Episode 19. This serial featured King Baggot as Harrison Grant, the leader of the patriotic Criminology Club, and Maguerite Snow as a Secret Service agent named Dixie Mason. They and members of their respective organizations collaborate to expose the espionage activities of the "Kaiser's secret army in America." To quote from a full-page ad for the serial: "This country [is]... menaced by furtive, non-uniformed armies whose weapons are spying, sabotage, bomb-planting, incendiarism, murder and a hundred forms of insidious and demoralizing propaganda." One episode includes an attempt by the German spy leader and some radical American colleagues to blow up a munitions wharf.

8　　　THE MOVING PICTURE WORLD　　　October 5, 1918

Bulling the Bosheviki (Fox, 1918): **The animated duo of Mutt and Jeff had routinely tangled with spike-helmeted Prussians and their Kaiser since 1917. But this ad clearly indicates that although the U.S. was still technically at war with Imperial Germany in October 1918, some in America had already entered a period of undeclared war with the new Bolshevik regime.**

[Lauritzen, Einar, and Gunnar Lundquist, *American Film Index, 1916–1920*, p. 119; *MPW* 2/9/18:836; *MPW* 2/23/18:1050 (ad); *Photoplay* 5/18; 6/18; 7/18; 8/18:47–53 & 100; 9/18:49–56 & 114]

Agit; Am Icons?; Bomb; Ger; IWW; Ital; Lab; Mob; Pol; Sab; Sec Ser; Spy-Sab; Strike; Vig; Viol

The Fall of the Hog-Hund Zollerns, Success-Bound Film, Nov?, Am?, Frank B. Coigne, Comedy, 1r?

In this "Burlesque on the Hohenzollerns," the "principal Hog-Hund" is a butcher shop owner named William Keyser. He wants his son to marry their neighbor, Mabelle Frances (France). The Keyser and his sister Austriana start a quarrel with Mrs. Serb in order to foment trouble with Madam Russo (Russia) and her friend Mabelle—giving the Hog-Hund an excuse to seize Mabelle and isolate the latter. A "Right Brigade," under the generalship of "America Right," is formed in the name of justice. Meanwhile, Madam Russo, following the murder of her husband (the killing of the Tsar), resolves her differences with the Keyser and is faked into marrying him (the March 1919 Treaty of Brest-Litovsk). When the family of butchers start their final wedding drive for Mabelle Frances, Uncle Samuel and his "Boy

Scouts" come to the rescue.

[LC,LU13122]

Am Icons; Bol-Ger Link?; Ger; Russ; Tsar; Viol

The Geezer of Berlin, Jewel, Arthur D. Hotaling, Oct, Bel/Ger, Comedy, 2r

The "supreme boob" of Germany and his "Boche butchers" wreak havoc upon an innocent baker's family in Louvain, Belgium. Kaiser Willie, the geezer, and his German "germs" eventually wind up in the hell of the baker's oven! As a promotional gimmick the film's producer, M. Kashin, allegedly sent a cablegram to the Kaiser, offering him a Broadway engagement, via his Bolshevik friend, Nikolai Lenin. The note and the Kaiser's supposed reply were then inserted at the beginning of the film.

[LC,LP12686; *MPN* 10/5/18:2189]

Ger; Lenin

The Woman in the Web, Vitagraph, David Smith, April, Am/Russ, Paul Hurst, Serial, 15eps-2r

This action-packed serial is built around the Russian Revolution and crown jewels—Episode 13: "The Hidden Menace." It opens with The Princess (Hedda Nova), a member of the Imperial Commission in Washington, D.C., being ordered back to Mother Russia. But two members of the staff are plotting the overthrow of the Tsar, Baron Borusk, a secret agent of the Kaiser, and Colonel Kovsky, a Cossack who also lusts for the beautiful princess. Jack Lawford (J. Frank Glendon), the son of an American businessman who represents Tsarist interests, is in love with the princess and follows her to Russia. After the Tsar's overthrow, Jack and The Princess, who has been entrusted with the imperial jewels, must escape Russia.

[LC,LP12548; *MPW* 4/13/18:282]

Bol?; Cap; Decad; Escape; Ger; Jewels; Rev; Russ; Spy-Sab

1919

American Institutions, Ford, Cartoon

Uncle Sam finds in his warehouse a large rat eating away at grain sacks marked "American Institutions." He takes a shovel to the "varmint," who, when flushed out of hiding, is

revealed to have written on his side: "Bolsheviki (I.W.W.)." After Uncle Sam kills the vermin he states: "Bolshevists are the rats of civilization." Note: This minute-long piece was probably included as a segment of one of the Ford-sponsored newsreel series entitled *Animated Weekly*—a topical weekly provided to movie theaters between 1914 and 1921.

[S (NA, 200 FC—26666 (b))]

Am Icons; Bol; IWW; Viol

Berth of a Nation, Fox, Bud Fisher, Dec, Am, Cartoon, 1/2r

Mutt and Jeff are working on a train. While attempting to avoid a carnival lady's escaped snake the two capture a Bolshevik. The $5000 reward virtually guarantees that Mutt and Jeff will retire from the railroad. Note: This film was most likely intended to allude to the so-called "Red Special" trains that during 1919 had brought several car loads of "undesirable aliens" under guard to New York City for deportation.

[*MPN* 12/13/19:4328]

Bol; Pol?

Betty's Bolsheviks, Strand/Exhibitors, Mutual, June, Cartoon, NI

[Campbell, *Reel America and World War I*, p.266}

Bol

The Bullshiviks, Star-Universal, Eddie Lyons & Lee Moran, April?, Am, Comedy, 2r

Eddie and Lee, reporters for the "Morning Guess," are assigned to interview Russian countess Onanoff. While waiting for the butler to present their cards to her, the two boys smoke some cigarettes they find. A series of wild incidents ensue when the beautiful countess mistakenly believes the reporters are Bolshevik assassins. But actually it was all an hallucination—the cigarettes were doped!

[LC,LP13658]

Bol; Bomb; White Russ

Her Nitro Knight, Bull's Eye, Charles Parrott, ?, Am, Comedy, 1r

The extant print at the Library of Congress is a confusing (probably spliced together from fragments at some point) Billy West comedy vehicle. The film includes an extended sequence in which the popular Chaplin imitator has an encounter with a group of bearded bomb makers. They are introduced in their makeshift factory having a bit of fun tossing about an oversized round bomb. Their leader, whose dark pointed beard was probably intended to be a Jewish caricature, is named "Bull Sheviki." Billy is forced to accept a bomb to blow up the rich guardian, N. O. Dough, of a girl he wishes to date.

[S (LC,incomplete)]
Bol; Bomb; Cap; Jew?; Pol; Viol

Impropaganda, Par, Famous Players, Saul Harrison, Jan?, Am, Comedy, 2r

This burlesque of spy films was written by James Montgomery Flagg, with all the captions/inter-titles in comic verses. Commercial artist Phil Gerry and his "soul" partner Violet have a business conference with a client, a sausage maker named Shilling. Violet falls asleep while the men discuss a two-page ad for the "Saturday Evening Buth." Violet dreams that Phil is a Secret Service agent who has been following Colonel Shilling, a German posing as the leader of the "Society for the Suppression of the Wienerwurst in America." Violet, meanwhile, has been watching the notorious Emma Skunkstein (as in Emma Goldman?; convicted on charges of obstructing the draft in 1917, during 1918 specious accusations that she was a German spy were widely publicized) at a crowded boarding house in Washington, D.C. Disguised as a German lieutenant with his dashund, Phil follows the Colonel and his band of spies to the same boarding house. The enemy agents unsuccessfully attempt to escape from the bathroom down a ladder made of sausages.

[LC,LU13228; *MPW* 1/18/19:]
Am Icons?; Fem Rad?; Ger; Jew?; Sec Ser; Spy-Sab; Viol

The Janitor, Arrow/Hank Mann Comedy series, Fall?, Morris R. Schlank?, 2r, Am, Comedy

Russian stereotypes, wearing black cloaks, create trouble with their explosive "Bolshevik love tokens." A janitor, played by the broom mustached comedy star Hank Mann, is duped into carrying one of their bombs to a crowded restaurant. The Secret Service chief's wife, posing as "Cuckoo Carrie," vamps Hank in order to avert disaster. The Bolshevik gang, including a fat woman, are then literally chased into jail.

[S (Vid)]
Am Icons; Bol; Bomb; Fem Rad; Russ; Sec Ser; Viol

Look Out For The Snake, American Defense Society, Sept?

As part of their anti-Bolshevism campaign the American Defense Society distributed this short to exhibitors, "warning against [the] acceptance of radical politics."

[*MPN* 9/6/19:2006]
Am Icons; Dom Rad

A Sammy in Siberia, Pathé/Rolin, Hal Roach, April, Russ, Comedy, 1r

Harold Lloyd plays an American Doughboy, or "Sammy" (as in Uncle Sam), who becomes lost from his unit in snowbound Siberia. Chased up a tree by a wolf, he is rescued by a pretty peasant girl (Bebe Daniels) who has just escaped from a gang of bearded Red soldiers (including one who is very short). Together, the couple overcome her pursuers and then return to the peasant's hut where her father and two other women are being held captive by the rest of the vodka-swilling "Bolsheviki." Harold's acrobatics and wicked wielding of a vodka jug put the Reds to flight. The heroic Sammy is just beginning to get intimately acquainted with the grateful damsel when a patrol of Americans arrive and march him back to base.

[S (LC); LC,LU12443; *MPW* 3/2/19:1842]
Allied Interv; Am Icons; Bol; Liq Link; Russ; Viol

The Strike Breakers, Star/Universal, Eddie Lyons?, Jan?, Am, Comedy, 2r

Mrs. Moran is converted to "suffragettitus." She starts a strike and declares social revolution. Eddie quickly breaks up the disorder with an improvised crowbar.

[LC,LP13241]
Fem Rad; Rev; Strike

1920

Biff! Bang!! Bomb!!!, Christie, June, Am, Comedy, 1r

A reporter is fired by his editor for lack of good stories. He and his girl then disguise themselves as Bolsheviks with "trick-whiskers" in order to create some "copy" about the I.W.W. They actually wind up capturing some bomb throwers.

[*MPN* 6/26/20:137]
Bol; Bomb; IWW

The Land of Opportunity, Americanization Committee/Selnick Picts, Feb, Ralph Ince, Am, Drama, 2r

Morton Walpole (Ralph Ince), "an idler with an inherited fortune—busy with 'pink' theories," disturbs the tranquility of the Civic Club by attacking capitalism. After the other members walk out on the "Bolshevist" in a collective huff, Morton talks with William, the elderly club steward. In a patronizing gesture he gives William a copy of "Classes Against Masses," a booklet that promotes the equalization of wealth. William then relates (in flashback) the story of a poor young man unjustly accused of murder in the pre-Civil War period who was defended in court by Abe Lincoln— "I ..., sir, ... was the boy ... And the same America that gave lawyer Lincoln his opportunities to rise from a rail splitter...gave me justice in the courts—freedom—work—the opportunity to save." A humbled Morton looks up at a portrait of Lincoln and then tosses the booklet into the fireplace. Note: The film was released in commemoration of the birth of the "Great Emancipator" and, according to the *MPN* reviewer, was inspired by Secretary of the Interior Franklin Lane's "suggestion that motion picture producers ... [use] the power of the camera ... [to promote] Americanization." It was actually shown at 157 first–run houses throughout the country on Lincoln's birthday.

[S (LC); LC,LP14694; *MPN* 2/21/20:1971; *MPW* 2/21/20:1199–1200, 1286]
Am Icons; Bol; Cap

One Law for All, Universal, Oct?, Am, Western, 2r

A bearded immigrant from the "Country of the oppressed" is observed by "Square" Wilson (Hoot Gibson) having a misunderstanding with immigration officials. Square invites the man and his daughter to learn about Americanism at his Arizona ranch.

[LC,LP15628]
Am Icons; Bol

The Parlor Bolshevist, Fox, Bud Fisher, Dec, Am, Cartoon, 1/2r

Mutt and Jeff attend a Bolshevik meeting. The lanky Mutt is particularly impressed by the "fifty-fifty" idea. But when the "unshorn radicals" learn that Jeff has received a large inheritance, they seize his money for the cause. Left with only fifty cents apiece, Jeff grabs a pistol and demands the return of his money. Waving the flag in his other hand, Jeff then forces the Bolsheviks to sing the "Star Spangled Banner." The *MPN* reviewer, after asserting that the producers appeared to be primarily interested in attacking the principles of socialism, states that the cartoon is "not funny."

[*MPN* 12/18/20:4673; *MPW* 12/18/20:910]
Am Icons; Bol

******, Unidentified cartoon; early 1920?

A group of bearded radicals, including one wearing a sombrero, are herded aboard the "Soviet Ark." As the ship passes the Statue of Liberty she bends over and scorns the passengers. Note: A large number of radicals were forcibly deported aboard the USS *Buford*, dubbed the "Soviet Ark" by the press, on December 21, 1919. Among the deportees was the notorious anarchist, Alexander Berkman, who was (in fact) wearing a sombrero on the day of departure.

[S (PVT COLL,incomplete)]
Am Icons; Dom Rad

Billie Bolsheviki, 1919–1920?

An ugly fat child with dark frazzled hair is seated at the dinner table with a large bowel of stew. While voraciously consuming the bowel's contents, he screams for "More!" Billie Bolsheviki later enters the parlor, where a Lady Liberty caricature is playing the piano beneath a portrait of George Washington. The out-of-control child promptly takes an ax to her piano! Billie next walks out onto the porch, encountering Uncle Sam seated in a rocking chair. But when Billie attempts to harass Sam, the ungrateful Bolshevik child is chased off with a gun.

[S (PVT COLL, incomplete)]
Am Icons; Bol; Viol

Appendix 3

Selected American
Fictional Shorts, 1921–1927

1921

Gum Shoe Work, Fox, Bud Fisher, Feb, Am, Cartoon

Mutt and Jeff, playing detectives on the trail of a group of "bomb plotters," find a ticking package.

[*FD* 2/27/21:23]

1922

Cops, Comique Film/First National, Buster Keaton & Eddie Cline, Feb, Am, Comedy, 2r

Buster Keaton is hauling a load of furniture in a horse drawn wagon. While stopped at an intersection as the annual police parade passes by, a bomb tossed by an anarchist from a rooftop lands in Buster's hand. He innocently uses the bomb's burning fuse to light a cigarette, and then throws it away. The explosion disrupts the parade and leads to a wild chase.

[S (LC;Vid); LC,LP17630; *EH* 4/29/22: 60]

Danger, Educational, May?, Comedy

A Jack White vehicle—he becomes comically entangled with some "Bolsheviks" after the "bewhiskered bomb throwers" kidnap a princess.

[*EH* 5/13/22:58]

The Lucky Dog, Metro, Jess Robbins, ?, Am, Comedy, 2r

Part of the Sun-Lite Comedy series. Stan Laurel befriends a stray dog, leading to him bumping into a robber played by Oliver Hardy. At one point the robber threatens to blow up Stan with a dynamite bomb, which he refers to as "Bolsheviki candy"—reflecting the topicality of a film that was originally produced in 1919.

[S (LC; Vid); Randy Skretredt, *Laurel & Hardy: The Magic Behind the Movies* (Beverly Hills, CA: Moonstone Press, 1987), pp. 31–33]

The Radio King, Universal, Robert F. Hill, Sept–Nov, Am, Serial (10 chpts; 2r)

In this Universal Special "Chapter-Play" radical "terrorists" plot to incite a revolution in America. The terrorists seize a radio station to communicate with their "friends" in Europe. When they learn about government experiments to recall messages from the ether, the terrorists resort to torture and sabotage. To aid them in their plans they have Marnee, a hunchback electrical wizard, "who uses the forces of nature to menace mankind." A daring government radio specialist, played by Roy Stewart, foils the terrorists. Note: In 1924 the Soviet Union would become the first nation to make regular shortwave propaganda broadcasts.

[LC,LP18215…18381]

1923

Colonel Heeza Liar, Strikebreaker, W. Hodkinson, Dec, Cartoon

No Information, other than the title.

Extra! Extra!, Educational, Feb, Am, Comedy, 2r

In this Lloyd Hamilton production, the veteran short comedy star plays a press photographer whose checkered cap resembles that of a suspected "dynamiter."

[*MPW* 2/17/23:706]

Felix Revolts, Pat Sullivan, May, Cartoon

When the mayor declares cats "useless" and it is agreed to starve them out of town, Felix organizes his fellow felines to strike. Under a white flag, Felix visits the local rats and informs them of the situation. After the town's children are chased out of school by the rampaging rats, Felix wins a "contract" for the cats.

[S (Vid)]

A Midnight Cabaret, Vitagraph, Larry Semon, June, Am, Comedy, 2r

Bomb throwers, alternately described as anarchists and Bolsheviks, live in a room above a fashionable cafe where Larry waits tables. When the hungry radicals are foiled in their attempts to steal some diners' food, they begin to use up their stock of bombs. Larry Semon was one of Hollywood's most popular and highly paid comedians in the early 1920s. His stupid, baggy pants wearing, screen persona relied heavily upon inventive sight gags.

[LC,LP18933; *MPW* 6/9/23:524]

1924

Going to Congress, Pathé/Hal Roach, Rob Wagner, May, Am, Comedy, 2r

Will Rogers plays the town idler, Alfalfa Doolittle, who is chosen by the "party caucus" as the ideal candidate to run for Congress. The audience is introduced to Alfalfa at the general store, seated upon a cracker barrel while dispensing typical "Rogers-isms" on the nation's politics. At one point he is asked: "… do you think we will ever recognize Russia?" Alfalfa responds: "We will never recognize them unless they shave." After being "swept" into office by promising to bring rain to his constituents, Alfalfa takes the train to Washington, D.C. While conversing with the boys in the smoking car he is questioned about his position on the "Bolsheviki." Following a moment's squirming, Alfalfa solemnly states: "I never did favor these Third Party movements." This film was the first in a three-part series—*Our Congressman*, released in July, and it followed *A Truthful Liar*, released in August. Note: *Going to Congress* was exhibited in Cleveland during the Republican National Convention and in New York during the Democratic National Convention.

[S (LC;Vid); LC,LU20187; *MPW* 5/24/24:412]

1925

Alice's Egg Plant, Disney/Winkler, April, Am, Cartoon

"Little Red Henski" rooster, wearing a fake pointed beard, wire-rimmed glasses and a leather cap, and carrying a grip with "…I.W.W." written on its side, visits Alice's Egg Plant to foment a strike among the hens. This film was part of Disney's "Alice in Cartoonland" series, that featured a live-action girl interacting with animated characters.

[S (Vid)]

Felix All Puzzled, Pat Sullivan, Jan, Cartoon

While trying to help his master solve a crossword puzzle, Felix is kicked through the ether into the Soviet Union. Bearded Russians chase the "spy" and Felix is eventually blown back home by the explosion of a bomb. Felix is queried as to whether he got the seven letter word found chiefly in Russia. Felix peevishly responds that all he found was "trouble." "That's it!"

[S (Vid)]

1926

Animated Hair Cartoon #4, Red Seal, Marcus, Feb, Cartoon

This 1924–1927 series, produced by Max Fleisher, featured the manipulation of hair by cartoonist Marcus to create likenesses of famous people. A caricature of "Nikolai Lenin" appears near the middle of this half-reeler. An earlier edition of this series, released in January 1925, included "The late Czar of Russia, Nicholas II," who then becomes Russian novelist and playwright Maxim Gorky (1868–1936). Note: Gorky, who had been an admirer of Lenin, became disgusted with Bolshevik excesses and went into self-imposed exile in 1921.

[*MPW* 2/20/26:705]

Bombs and Bums, Jan, Cartoon

Mutt and Jeff, again. No information, other than the title.

The Globe Trotters, Dec, Cartoon

While traveling around the world, Mutt and Jeff spend some time in Soviet Russia. They visit a mattress factory where bearded peasants are shown entering one door and exiting another, without their beards. An interior shot reveals the assembly line removal of the men's beards and the stuffing of mattresses with their shorn hair!

[S (PVT COLL)]

The Volga Boatman, Jr., John Tansey, Am, Comedy, 1r

Kids playing "vulgar" boatmen and women in the canals of Venice, California, parody the feature film, *The Volga Boatman* (PDC, 1926), q.v. Or, to quote the opening title, after seeing the movie, "'Dailey's Dozen' came Russian out with ideas." It was part of the "Novelty Comedy" series called "Ribticklers."

[S (LC)]

1927

Here Comes Precious, Educational, April, Am, Comedy, 2r

Dirby-wearing comedian Jimmie Adams is promised marriage by a young girl. His rival, played by Eddie Baker, tries to chase Jimmie out of town. Eddie dons a disguise, "pulling the Bolshevik stuff." A popped street lamp light is mistaken for the explosion of a bomb.

[LC, LP23796; *MPW* 4/9/27:575]

Soldier Man, Sennett, Harry Edwards, Nov, Am, Comedy, 3r

Harry Langdon plays a doughboy who escaped from German captivity on November 11, 1918, and then wanders the battlefields unaware of the Armistice. He comes upon a "Bomanian" peasant blowing up stumps with leftover munitions, who warns the American "dumbbell" to stay clear—the inter-title first appearing in Cyrillic. Meanwhile, the dissolute King of mythical Bomania, also played by Langdon, sits shakily on his throne in the capital, reeking "with Red Rebellion—and wine." A sycophantic aide informs the King that if he does not sign a Peace Treaty he will wind up chopping wood (in exile) with his "cousin Wilhelm." After the king is kidnapped by the leader of the Rebellion, look-alike Harry is drafted by the aide to impersonate the King. Just as Harry is about to make love to "Mrs. King" his wife awakens the dreaming veteran and hastily dresses him for his participation in a hometown victory parade.

[S (LC;Vid); LC, LU22654]

Notes

Introduction

1. Robert Sklar, "Moving Image Media in Culture and Society: Paradigms for Historical Interpretation," *Image as Artifact: The Historical Analysis of Film and Television*, edited by John E. O'Connor (Malabar, FL: Krieger Publishing, 1990), p. 119.

2. See Louis Althusser, "Ideology and the Ideological State Apparatuses," in *Lenin and Philosophy* (New York: Monthly Review Press, 1971. See also, Noel Carroll, *Mystifying Movies: Fads and Fallacies in Contemporary Film Theory* (New York: Columbia University Press, 1988), 53 passim; Robert Sklar, "Oh! Althusser: Historiography and the Rise of Cinema Studies," *Radical History Review*, Vol. 41 (1988), pp. 10–35. An entire issue of a prestigious film journal has been devoted to the "Philosophy of Film History;" *Film History*, Vol. 6, No. 1 (Spring, 1994).

3. Nearly forty studios were in California by 1913, including Lubin and Essanay. In 1911 Nestor had been the first film company to locate in Hollywood. A full-page article in the *New York Dramatic Mirror* is informative: "Pictures Made in the Land of Sunshine: Film Colony in Southern California Has Gone From Six to Thirty-Nine in One Year." *NYDM* 1/15/13:49.

4. The Lonesome Luke character, with his "two-dot" mustache, was loosely based upon Chaplin's Tramp. See Annette M. D'Agostino, *Harold Lloyd: A Bio-Bibliography* (Westport, CT: Greenwood Press, 1994).

5. Between 1909 and 1913 there were numerous references to plot ambiguities in the trade reviews, particularly those appearing in the *New York Dramatic Mirror*.

6. See David Bordwell, Janet Staiger and Kristin Thompson, *The Classical Hollywood Cinema: Film Style & Mode of Production to 1960* (New York: Columbia University Press, 1985).

7. As noted by Brownlow, an "unbalanced portrait" of an uncomplicated America has evolved regarding those works that almost totally ignores the "astonishing range of subjects" that were actually engaged within the texts of numerous releases. Kevin Brownlow, *Behind the Mask of Innocence—Sex, Violence, Prejudice, Crime: Films of Social Conscience in the Silent Era* (Berkeley: University of California Press, 1990), pp. xv–xvi. An extensive overview of these topical sub-genres appears in Larry Langman's *American Film Cycles: the Silent Era* (Westport, CT: Greenwood Press, 1998).

8. See Martin F. Norden, "Women's Suffrage Films As Genre: A Good Travesty Upon the Suffragette Movement," *The Journal of Popular Film and TV*, Vol. 13, No. 4 (Winter 1986), pp. 171–177. In Edison's 1911 comedy, *The Rival Candidates*, the Woman's Suffrage Party loses a mayoral race to the Labor Party [*MPS* 6/11:85–92; *MPW* 3/18/11:602]

9. Refer to the charts accompanying the Filmography. A few motion pictures that contain no scenes of radicalism or labor conflict have been included because of their strong portrayal of class-based inequalities, e.g., *The Egg Trust* (Essanay, 1910); *The Blood of the Poor*

(Champion, 1912); *From the Submerged* (Essanay, 1912). For a less "narrowly" defined discussion of such films, numbering in the scores, see Steven J. Ross, *Working-Class Hollywood: Silent Film and the Shaping of Class in America* (Princeton, NJ: Princeton University Press, 1998).

10. See Murray B. Levin, *Political Hysteria in America: The Democratic Capacity for Repression* (New York: Basic Books, 1971), 91 passim; Burl Noggle, *Into the Twenties* (Urbana: University of Illinois Press, 1974), pp. 90–91.

11. Robert K. Murray, *Red Scare* (New York: McGraw-Hill, 1955). 105 passim.

12. By 1914 nearly 18,000 theaters were receiving more than seven million daily admissions. See Daniel J. Czitron, *Media and the American Mind, from Morse to McLuhan*, (Chapel Hill: The University of North Carolina Press, 1982), 40 passim.

13. Siegfried Kracauer, *From Caligari to Hitler* (Princeton, NJ: Princeton University Press, 1947).

14. Annette Melville and Scott Simmon, "Film Preservation 1993: A Study of the Current State of American Film Preservation." (Washington, D.C.: The Library of Congress, 1993), p. 61. The situation regarding surviving Red Scare era prints is illustrative—just nine of the ninety-one motion pictures identified in the Filmography are known to still exist. And, one of the most significant of those nine, *The Right to Happiness* (Universal-Jewel, 1919) can only be screened at the Netherlands Film Museum, located in Amsterdam.

15. The innate combustibility of nitrate stock resulted in frequent mishaps at processing centers and storage facilities. For instance, an explosion at a Philadelphia film vault on June 13, 1914, destroyed all the master negative prints of the Lubin Company that had so far been produced.

Although the 35mm format dominated by the early teens, a number of non-standard formats were also used. For example, a 28mm film was introduced by Pathé in 1912. See Paolo Cherchi Usai, *Burning Passions: An Introduction to the Study of Silent Cinema* (London: British Film Institute, 1994), pp. 10–12.

16. Additional methods of coloring film included toning, mordanting, hand-coloring and stencil-coloring. Cherchi Usai, *Burning Passions*, pp. 12–14. *Why?* (Eclair, 1913) con-

cludes with rampaging workers setting Manhattan ablaze, the flames hand-painted red.

17. The average speed of projection was more or less established at 24 frames per second by the early teens. However, because the speed of projectors' motors was not fixed and could be varied by a rheostat, the individual operating the equipment could alter the speed according to his whim. Cherchi Usai, *Burning Passions*, pp. 1–2; 16–17.

18. See Martin Miller Marks, *Music and the Silent Film: Contexts and Case Studies* (New York: Oxford University Press, 1997). Occasionally, cues for sound effects were included as well. Beginning in September 1909, Edison was the first motion picture studio to provide exhibitors with generic musical themes cued to specific scenes in its releases. The "Kalem Kalendar," which began appearing two years later, also contained on-screen cues. A few additional studios and cooperating sheet music companies were distributing thematic cue sheets as early as 1910. Gillian B. Anderson, *Music For Silent Films, 1894–1929: A Guide* (Washington, D.C.: The Library of Congress, 1988), p. xxix.

19. A complete orchestra-scored version (123 minutes) of *My Four Years in Germany* does exist through private collection sources and is available on video tape.

20. The difficulty in tracing the "internal history" of specific copies of a particular silent film and nailing down its "original" version(s) is discussed in detail in the final chapter of Paolo Cherchi Usai's *Burning Passions*, pp. 80–92.

21. Refer to the photo essay in Michael S. Shull, "Silent Agitators: Militant Labor in the Movies, 1909–1919," *Labor's Heritage*, Vol. 9, No. 3 (Winter, 1998), pp. 58–77.

22. Ephraim Katz, *The Encyclopedia of Film* (New York: Crowell, 1979). Unfortunately, later editions of Katz's book contain even fewer silent entries. The most extensive source on silent era biographical data, with *Variety* obituary citations, is Eugene Vazzana's *Silent Film Necrology* (Jefferson, NC: McFarland, 1995). Due to the crossover from vaudeville of many early film actors, some useful additional information can be found in Anthony Slide's *The Encyclopedia of Vaudeville* (Westport, CT: Greenwood Press, 1994).

23. David Bordwell, *Making Meaning: Inference and Rhetoric in the Interpretation of*

Cinema, (Cambridge, MA: Harvard University Press, 1989), p. 266.

24. See Umberto Eco, *A Theory of Semiotics* (Bloomington: Indiana University Press, 1979).

25. For an interesting case study of the origins and evolution of teens film acting styles refer to Roberta E. Pearson's *Eloquent Gestures: The Transformation of Performance Style in the Griffith Biograph Films* (Berkeley: University of California Press, 1992).

26. Marc Bloch, *The Historian's Craft* (New York: Knopf, 1953), p. 64.

27. An excellent example of the potential for interpretive confusion appears in the copyright material and the nearly identical trade journal synopsis of a one-reel comedy entitled *Depot Romeo* (Essanay, 1917)—one of the "types" waiting at a railroad station is ambiguously described as "a group of whispering Russians." Does this simply poke fun at a conspiratorial nature attributed to many Russians, or does it have more sinister connotations, such as alluding to unspeakable revolutionary plottings? Because the author was unable to acquire additional information on these Russians, *Depot Romeo* was not included in the Filmography. [LC, LP11821; *MPW* 12/22/17:1840]

28. The filmographic charts list 54 motion pictures with an anti-capitalist bias between 1909 and 1917; only 9 between 1918 and 1929.

29. Seventy-one films from 1918 to 1929 display a distinct anti-Soviet bias, while, despite a growing tolerance in the late 1920s, none can be classified as having a dominant pro-Soviet bias.

30. The AFI catalogue for motion picture shorts released in the United States through 1910, including many foreign productions, is primarily useful as a source of citations, since only Paper Print Collection films from the Library of Congress (heavily biased toward the Biograph studio) are annotated. Thus, the subject indexes are almost exclusively based upon information gleaned from the films' titles and credits. *The American Film Institute Catalog of Motion Pictures Produced in the United States: Film Beginnings, 1893–1910* (Metuchen, NJ: Scarecrow Press, 1995).

Chapter 1

1. See George E. Mowry, *The Era of Theodore Roosevelt and the Birth of Modern America, 1900–1912* (New York: Harper, 1958), chapter 12.

2. The more extreme attacks by muckrakers only occasionally were transferred onto the screen, the best known example being Upton Sinclair's 1906 novel, *The Jungle*.

3. See Page Smith, *America Enters the World* (New York: McGraw-Hill, 1985) and Robert M. Crunden, *Ministers of Reform* (New York: Basic Books, 1982).

4. Brownlow, *Behind the Mask of Innocence*, p. XVI.

5. For instance, Ross embraces the many films in which working-class characters twit the "respectable" middle-class, such as takes place in Charlie Chaplin's *Work* (Essanay, 1915). See Steven J. Ross, *Working-Class Hollywood: Silent Film and the Shaping of Class in America* (Princeton, NJ: Princeton University Press, 1998).

6. Brownlow, *Behind the Mask of Innocence*, pp. 442–451; Ross, *Working-Class Hollywood*, pp. 135–141.

7. Several general film histories have asserted that the early movie audience was overwhelmingly working-class, yet many nickelodeons were clustered in middle-class sections of cities. Two of the better known standard works are Lewis Jacobs, *The Rise of American Film* (New York: Teachers College Press, 1939) and Robert Sklar, *Movie Made America* (New York: Random House, 1975). An interesting discussion concerning movies displacing saloons as a venue of working-class entertainment appears in Roy Rosenzweig, *Eight Hours for What We Will: Workers and Leisure in an Industrial City, 1870–1920* (New York: Cambridge University Press, 1983), 191 passim. For revisionist comments upon the socio-economic composition of film audiences see Robert C. Allen and Douglas Gomery, *Film History Theory and Practice* (New York: Knopf, 1985), pp. 202–207; Eileen Bowser, *The Transformation of Cinema, 1908–1915* (New York: Scribners, 1990); John S. Gilkeson, Jr., *Middle-Class Providence, 1820–1940* (Princeton, NJ: Princeton University Press, 1986), pp. 257–258. A more recent demographic survey of New York City audiences before 1910 suggests that further research is required.

See Ben Singer, "Manhattan Nickelodeons: New Data on Audience and Exhibitors," *Cinema Journal*, Vol. 34, No. 3 (Spring 1995), pp. 5–35.

8. See Ross, *Working-Class Hollywood*, pp. 19–20. Paradoxically, while making a convincing argument that the majority of early teens moviegoers were working-class, with a penchant for raucousness, Ross' own statistics confirm the considerable size as well as importance of the middle-class audience.

9. *NYDM*, January 4, 1911, p. 3.

10. Kay Sloan, *The Loud Silents: Origins of the Social Problem Film* (Urbana: University of Illinois Press, 1988), p. 20.

11. LC Paper Print Collection, FLA 4609, *Execution of Czolgosz, with Panorama of Auburn Prison*. For a reproduction of Czolgosz's police photos, taken a month before his execution, see Richard Drinnon, *Rebel in Paradise: A Biography of Emma Goldman* (Chicago: The University of Chicago Press, 1961), opposite page 176.

12. Kevin Brownlow, *Behind the Mask of Innocence*, p. xviii. A majority of the nickelodeons were operating outside the larger cities. See Fuller, *At the Picture Show*, p. 48.

13. The first luxury cinema house, the Vitagraph Theatre, was opened on Broadway, February 7, 1914. See David Robinson, *From Peep Show to Palace: The Birth of American Film* (New York: Columbia University Press, 1996), chapters 6 & 11.

14. By the turn of the century political cartoonists had also established the visual cliché of the haggard, dark-skinned, bearded radical bomb-thrower (waving the ubiquitous black orb with a burning fuse) relentlessly menacing cherished American institutions and values. See Paul Avrich's two books, *The Russian Anarchists* (Princeton, NJ: Princeton University Press, 1967) and *Sacco and Vanzetti: The Anarchist Background* (Princeton, NJ: Princeton University Press, 1991).

15. This subtle blending of genres could also be aurally reinforced. For instance, the major contemporary guide for film music included under its "Sinister" heading, Wolf-Ferrari's "Dance of the Camorrists" and "Meeting of the Camorrists." Erno Rapee, *Encyclopedia of Music for Pictures* (New York: Belwin, 1925), p. 444.

16. *A Black Hand Elopement* (Selig, 1913) is an apolitical example of the Black Hand genre that is not included in the Filmography.

17. For an analysis of the production history of a 1915 Black Hand film whose plot was converted by retitling into an anarchist theme, Pathé's *The Bomb Throwers*, refer to the Filmography.

18. See Graham Adams, Jr., *Age of Industrial Violence, 1910–1915: The Activities and Findings of the United States Commission on Industrial Relations* (New York: Columbia University Press, 1966).

19. Some strike films have been excluded from the Filmography because of an apparent lack of a militant orientation. Three examples are: *Bridget on Strike* (Vitagraph, 1909), a comedy in which a middle-class couple is rendered helpless when their Irish maid walks out [*MPW* 5/22/09:676; *NYDM* 5/29/09:15], a spoof on a studio strike, *How They Work in Cinema* (Eclair, 1911) [*MPN* 8/12/11;27], and *The Ragamuffin* (Lasky/Paramount, 1916), a feature-length yarn about a street urchin falling in love with a member of the upper class, that includes a subplot in which a strike takes place at the dress factory where she is briefly employed [LC, LU7487; *MPW* 2/12/16:975].

20. The word "Strike" is featured in the title of over twenty 1911–1914 releases.

21. The visually created language of the mob could also be viewed as the nativists' nightmare of immigration gone amok—further exaggerated if fueled by alcohol. Roughly half of all the strike films contain a mob scene.

Although it is difficult to quantify, it would appear that distinctions between skilled and unskilled workers were often also intended to be inferred. For instance, housing may be viewed as an indicator of status. This would seem to be suggested in several screened films. In both *The Girl at the Cupola* (Selig, 1912) and *The Strike* (Solax, 1912), the positively portrayed Anglo-named skilled workers live in detached small town homes. These houses, which are apparently owned by the workers, have a marked middle-class ambiance. This starkly contrasts with the sparsely furnished company-owned cabin inhabited by millhands in *The Cry of the Children* (Thanhouser, 1912).

22. A few motion pictures began appearing in the latter half of the teens that center upon capitalists and/or managerial types

overcoming some moral crisis, but do not portray labor strife and are therefore not included in the Filmography, e.g., *The Conqueror* (Kay-Bee/Triangle, 1916) [LC, LP10729; *Var* 12/31/15:25]; *Fruits of Desire* (William A. Brady Picture Plays/World, 1916) [LC, LU7559; *MPW* 2/5/16:792, 848]; *Man and His Soul* (Quality Picts/Metro, 1916) [LC, LP7555; *Var* 2/4/16:28]; *The Customary Two Weeks* (Conquest Picts/Edison, 1917 [S (LC); LC, LP11233; *MPW* 8/25/17:1268].

23. Non-specific union references appear in additional films: *Tim Mahoney, The Scab* (Vitagraph, 1911); *The Strike* (Solax, 1912); *Binks—The Strike Breaker* (IMP, 1913); *From Dusk to Dawn* (Occidental, 1913); *Bill Organizes a Union* (Komic, 1914); *What Is to Be Done?* (Joseph Leon Weiss, 1914); *Destruction* (Fox, 1915); *The Man with the Iron Heart* (Selig, 1915); *Money* (United Keanograph/World, 1915); *A Poor Relation* (Biograph, 1915); *The Sons of Toil* (Domino, 1915); *Those Who Toil* (Lubin/V-L-S-E, 1916); *Breaking the Family Strike* (Victor, 1917); *The Car of Chance* (Bluebird, 1917).

24. Anarcho-syndicalism was a leftist political ideology that envisioned the abolition of private property and the replacement of the state by a voluntary association of workers' co-operatives and labor unions. For its close linkage with the I.W.W. refer to Salvatore Salerno, *Red November Black November: Culture and Community in the Industrial Workers of the World* (Albany: State University of New York Press, 1989).

25. In essence, the many provocative anti-labor and anti-radical inter-titles flashed before American movie audiences became cruelly effective counter-parodies of the I.W.W.'s familiar stickerettes, called "silent agitators."

26. *A Martyr to His Cause*, released through Essanay in 1911, was sponsored by the AFL to support the McNamara brothers, accused of bombing the *Los Angeles Times* building. Refer to the Filmography. For a detailed discussion of union financed films see Ross, *Working-Class Hollywood.*

27. See Salerno, *Red November Black November*, pp. 33–34.

28. *No* Anti-Capital films are in the comedy genre, but ten Anti-Labor films are presented in that genre.

29. Coded seven times, 1914 represented the peak year for purely labor-oriented acts of sabotage.

30. *MPW* 5/31/13:923.

31. In at least two films a visual linkage to aristocratic trappings was established by showing members of capitalists' families being attended by male house servants dressed in fancy livery—the capricious wife in *The Cry of the Children* (Thanhouser, 1912) and the pampered daughter in *Toil and Tyranny* (Balboa, 1915).

An interesting examination of labor attitudes toward capitalists during this period, based upon a content analysis of a radical journal, is included in Part Three of Louis Galambos' *The Public Image of Big Business in America, 1880–1940* (Baltimore, MD: The Johns Hopkins University Press, 1975).

32. This was one of a number of films that featured sequences of a capitalist hosting an opulent dinner. Additional examples include the well known cross-cut from a banquet table of the rich to a breadline of the poor in *A Corner in Wheat* (Biograph, 1909) and a mine owner's intimate champagne party in *The Blacklist* (Lasky/Paramount, 1916). Such scenes may have been influenced by the sensationalized Hyde Ball at Sherry's in New York City that took place on January 31, 1905. See Lucius Beebe, *The Big Spenders* (New York: Garden City, 1966), 121 passim.

33. In the Filmography Militia is coded 17/7 percent—12/1914–1916.

34. Refer to the Filmography for more information about the "autocratic" mill owner in *The Worker* (Ramo, 1913) and the "oppressor" manufacturer in *As in a Dream* (Rex, 1916). In *The Iron Heart* (Astra, 1917), it is said that capitalist Martin "ruled the works as a Czar." This allusion could be considered a bridge to the negative presentation of Tsarist officials in Nihilist films.

35. A restored version of *Intolerance*, with its original tinting scheme, is available on laser disc.

36. At the time of the film's release a common expression used to describe a tightwad was "nickel nurser"—an individual alleged to be prone to trying to rub the buffalo off the Indian Head nickel's reverse side. See Thomas J. Schlereth, *Victorian America: Transformations in Everyday Life, 1876–1915* (New York: Harpers Collins, 1991), p. 85.

37. Griffith's fictional organization was

probably intended to mimic The National Association of Manufacturers (NAM), an anti-union group founded in 1895. See Sarah Lyons Watts, *Order Against Chaos: Business Culture and Labor Ideology in America, 1880–1915* (Westport, CT; Greenwood Press, 1991), chapter 4. In 1912 NAM produced two shorts, in cooperation with the Edison film company, that patronized their workforce, *The Crime of Carelessness* and *The Workman's Lesson*. [*MPW* 12/28/12:1328; *MPW* 6/29/12:1262] For an in-depth discussion of related films sponsored both by industry and the government see Ross, *Working-Class Hollywood*.

38. Reconciliation (Reconcile) is coded 60/24 percent.

39. These negative onscreen worksite scenes had appeared often enough to arouse the ire of the National Association of Garment Manufacturers, which at its 1916 convention adopted a resolution protesting "the untruthful presentation in factories." *Motography*, 6/17/16:1399, "Factory Girls Over-Abused in Films?"

40. *MPW* 6/20/14:1675.

41. By 1916 roughly a thousand business firms in the U.S. provided housing for over a half million workers and their families. See Stuart D. Brandes, *American Welfare Capitalism, 1880–1940* (Chicago: The University of Chicago Press, 1970), chapter 5.

42. In reality, most working women contributed to the family income by living with their parents—an arrangement that was usually terminated by marriage. See Eisenstein, *Give Us Bread but Give Us Roses*, chapter 5. Only *Why?* may allude to married women "out-workers," engaged in the common practice of home production. The more extreme, for its time, feminist issue of equal pay for women appears to have never been raised on film. Three female-initiated strike parodies should be noted: *The Phoney Strike Breakers* (Kalem, 1911); *When Women Strike* (Lubin, 1911); *Petticoat Camp* (Thanhouser, 1912).

43. A musical variation upon this theme was popularized by vaudeville headliner Marie Dressler, "Heaven Will Protect the Working Girl"—and, by implication, will save an unemployed young lady from the "social evil" of prostitution.

44. A liquor linkage (Liq Link), primarily related to Capital vs. Labor films between 1909 and 1917, is coded 30/12 percent for that period in the Filmography.

Omissions of scenes portraying the consumption of alcoholic beverages can also be informative regarding the presumed social composition of a film's audience. For instance, it would have been expected for the martyred working-class Irish hero of *Tim Mahoney, the Scab* (Vitagraph, 1911) to have been honored with a "wet" wake, but, instead, the film concludes with a eulogy at a "dry" union meeting.

45. *MPW* 3/25/11:667. In actuality, this type of situation was often exacerbated by the dispensing on credit ("tick") of drinks to strikers.

46. Paul Boyer, *Urban Masses and Moral Order in America, 1820–1920* (Cambridge, MA: Harvard University Press, 1978), p. 210.

47. Although unclear in a number of these non-extant films, real-life neighborhood drinking establishments often had large enough back rooms to earn the name "hall." Thus, some of these filmic "meeting" halls may have also been located in bars—which is suggested in *The Plunderer* (Fox, 1915). See Klaus Ensslen, "German-American Working-Class Saloons in Chicago," Hartmut Keil, ed., *German Workers' Culture in the United States, 1850–1920* (Washington, D.C.: Smithsonian Institution Press, 1988), pp. 157–180.

48. The pacific labor action of boycotting is never portrayed on the screen. Likewise, picketing receives attention in only two films: *The Right to Labor* (Lubin, 1909) and *From Dusk to Dawn* (Occidental, 1913).

49. The evil capitalist named John Rockland in the 1916 Lubin one-reeler, *Two News Items*, was probably also intended as a negative allusion to Rockefeller. Septuagenarian industrialist and philanthropist John D. Rockefeller (1839–1937), a cadaverous caricature of the old miser, was a regular target of radical animosity throughout the teens. There had actually been demonstrations at his Pocantico Hills estate in 1914. See Helen C. Camp, *Iron in Her Soul: Elizabeth Gurley Flynn and the American Left* (Pullman: Washington State University Press, 1995), p. 59.

50. A review for *The Bigger Man* (Metro, 1915); *Var* 10/8/15:23. Another 1915 fall release that would tend to substantiate the *Variety* reviewer's claim would be *Children of Eve* (Edison). Because it is a moralizing reformist tract that makes no reference to militant labor or radicalism, it is not included in the Filmography. Nevertheless, the film portrays a stereotyped

capitalist who owns a canning factory using
female child laborers as labelers. Many of the
girls are killed when they are trapped on the
upper floors during a fire. Only too late does
the capitalist discover that the mortally injured
young lady who was secretly investigating conditions, played by Viola Dana, was his love
child. He dedicates the remainder of his life to
abolishing child labor. The *Motion Picture
News* singled out the film for praise precisely
because there was no "forced happy ending."
[S (LC,VBL 5550); LP6884; *MPN* 11/27/15:94;
MPW 11/6/15:1560]

51. Members of the I.W.W. were sometimes referred to as "Irresponsible Wholesale
Wreckers"—"wrecker" being the euphemism
for an individual who carries out acts of industrial sabotage.

52. *MPW* 5/15/09:634.

53. In early 1914 a five-reel version of an
eight-reel French adaptation of Emile Zola's
Germinal was released in the U.S. by Pathé.
One of the most telling scenes in this epic of
19th century French miners battling the oppressive forces of capitalism shows scabs escaping from a sabotaged mine being forced to
stagger through a gauntlet of abusive strikers.
Some rioting miners are later slaughtered by
troops. [LC, LU1488; *MPW* 1/24/14:416]

54. *MPW* 8/29/14:1290.

55. Although usually still involving some
form of violence, at least seven films featuring
scab activities released through 1914 were presented in the comedy format, including *Mutt
and Jeff and the Italian Strikers* (Nestor, 1912)
and *The Volunteer Strike Breakers* (Vitagraph,
1913). Both films feature incompetent scabs
being chased from a work site by the strikers
whom they had attempted to replace.

56. *NYDM* 5/3/11:33. See Philip S. Foner,
*Organized Labor and the Black Worker,
1619–1973*, 2nd ed. (New York: Praeger, 1974).
A detailed discussion of this subject also appears in one of the more polemical sections of
Upton Sinclair's muckraking 1906 novel, *The
Jungle* (pp. 254–59 of the International Collector's Library ed.). But there is no indication
in surviving print sources that would lead one
to infer the topic was included in its 1914 film
adaptation. In this context, a Lubin short released in August 1914, *He Wanted Work*, should
be noted. It portrays the story of a black man
named John Jackson, who is chased-off from
his new construction job by racist Irish hod-

carriers. But the real trouble begins after he returns to the site disguised as a stereotypical
"mick." [*MPW* 8/8/14:860]

Race, in a pejorative sense, was undoubtedly also exploited in *The Thoroughbred*
(American/Mutual, 1916), whose climax features Mexican copper miners going on a rampage and assaulting their Anglo employers.
The negative "greaser" image of Mexicans appeared regularly on movie screens of the early
twentieth century. *The Miner's Peril* (Reliance,
1914) is a prime example of the use of such imagery—although the violence of its Mexican
miners is unassociated with labor militancy.
[*MPW* 11/7/14:834]

57. An observation in a trade review
upon the performance of the actor playing the
foreman is worth noting: "Without overacting
he strives successfully to gain the spectator's
hatred." *NYDM* 6/2/13:38. Abusive foremen
appear in another dozen films, including *The
Jungle* (All Star, 1914) and *A Poor Relation*
(Biograph, 1915). See Daniel Nelson, *Managers and Workers: Origins of the Factory System in the United States, 1880–1920* (Madison:
University of Wisconsin Press, 1975), pp. 43–44.

58. An alternative form of labor sabotage
is an obvious subject of parody in *Binks—The
Strike Breaker* (IMP, 1913), when a nutty scab
waiter serves lobster salad undressed clothed
only in his undergarments.

59. See Salerno, *Red November Black
November*, pp. 48–53.

60. Richard Hofstadter, *The Age of Reform*, p. 73.

61. See M. J. Heale, *American Anti-Communism: Combating the Enemy Within* (Baltimore: Johns Hopkins University Press, 1990),
pp. 12–14.

62. Only one film is known to specifically
invoke Ludlow, the Socialist sponsored *What
Is to Be Done?* (Joseph Leon Weiss, 1914).

63. *NYDM* 6/10/14:44.

64. On April 20, 1914, the tent colony of
striking miners at Ludlow, housing nearly 1200
people, was assaulted and destroyed by members of the Colorado National Guard. Over a
dozen people in the camp were killed, including children and wives of the strikers. See
George S. McGovern and Leonard F. Guttridge, *The Great Coalfield War* (Boston:
Houghton Mifflin, 1972) and H. M. Gitelman,
*Legacy of the Ludlow Massacre: A Chapter in
American Industrial Relations* (Baltimore,

MD: The Johns Hopkins University Press, 1988).

65. In addition to the labor spy portrayed in *The Sons of Toil*, spies or individuals falsely accused of engaging in "infiltration tactics" for management make appearances in at least five other films: *How the Cause Was Won* (Selig, 1912); *With the Mounted Police* (Thanhouser, 1912); *What Is to Be Done?* (Joseph Leon Weiss, 1914); *The Strike at the Centipede Mine* (Domino, 1915); *The Bruiser* (American, 1915). Management often euphemistically referred to individuals carrying out industrial surveillance as "spotters."

66. William C. DeMille, the elder brother of director Cecil B. DeMille, had been an established playwright before entering the film-making business in 1916. Unlike his politically conservative sibling, William had liberal leanings. This was probably due to the influence of his father-in-law, famed radical activist Henry George.

67. Troops of the Colorado National Guard were primarily responsible for the massacre. Based upon an extant photo still of the "striker's city," on copyright deposit at the Library of Congress, DeMille's depiction of scattered tents in a scrub-covered ravine captured the barrenness of Ludlow's tent colony—though it was actually largely comprised of canvas-covered wood structures. See LC, Box #93, Motion Picture Division. At least one photo of the snow-dusted colony on the eve of its destruction exists, and has been reproduced in a number of texts. See McGovern and Guttridge, *The Great Coalfield War*.

68. The actual heroine of the strike was the feisty octogenarian activist known as Mother Jones. Her participation during the "war," as well as the significant role played by other women, is discussed by Priscilla Long in "The Voice of the Gun: Colorado's Great Coalfield War of 1913–1914," *Labor's Heritage*, Vol. 1, No. 4 (October 1989), pp. 4–23.

69. The ethnic make-up of the I.W.W. receives extensive attention in Salerno, *Red November Black November*. See also, Steve Golin's, *The Fragile Bridge: Paterson Silk Strike, 1913* (Philadelphia: Temple University Press, 1988).

70. See William Uricchio and Roberta E. Pearson, *Reframing Culture: The Case of the Vitagraph Quality Films* (Princeton, NJ: Princeton University Press, 1993) for a discussion of the "Napoleon fad" in teens America.

71. *MPW* 11/21/14:1152.

72. After 1912 the implementation of president Wilson's "New Freedom" program absorbed many of the concepts that had been most ardently espoused by the socialists. For the best account of this subject, see James Weinstein, *The Decline of Socialism in America: 1912–1925* (New Brunswick, NJ: Rutgers University Press, 1984).

73. See Kevin Brownlow, *Behind the Mask of Innocence*, pp. 432–433.

74. Ross, *Working-Class Hollywood*, pp. 95–98.

75. *New York Call* 1/5/15:2.

76. See Patrick Renshaw, *The Wobblies* (New York: Doubleday, 1967), pp. 116–128; Salerno, *Red November Black November*, pp. 21–33.

77. See Ira Kipnis, *The American Socialist Movement, 1897–1912* (New York: Columbia University Press, 1952); James R. Green, "The 'Salesman-Soldier' of the 'Appeal Army': A Profile of the Rank-and-File Socialist Agitators," in *Socialism and the Cities* (Port Washington, NY: Kennikat Press, 1975), edited by Bruce M. Stave, pp. 13–40.

78. In 1912 nearly 2,000 socialists served in public offices in over thirty states. See Kipnis, Chapter XVI; Paul Buhle, *Marxism in the United States* (New York: Verso, 1987).

79. An anti-anarchism provision had been included in the Federal Immigration Act of 1903. See Kenneth C. Wenzer, *Anarchists Adrift: Emma Goldman and Alexander Berkman* (St. James, NY: Brandywine Press, 1996), p. 42.

80. John Higham, *Strangers in the Land*, pp. 177–178.

81. Refer to Chapter 2 for an analysis of anti–Semitic film images.

82. *Var* 10/8/15:23.

83. See John K. Mahon, *History of the Militia and the National Guard* (New York: Macmillan, 1983) and Philip S. Foner, *Militarism and Organized Labor: 1900–1914* (Minneapolis, MN: MEP Publications, 1987).

84. *MPW* 12/15/17:1644.

85. Over fifteen films released between 1910 and 1917 are classified as Bomb Parodies—five appeared on American movie screens in 1915 alone. This type of film could also appear in the Black Hand genre, e.g.,

Mustaches and Bombs (Essanay, 1915). [LC, LP6257; *MPW* 9/18/15:1046]

86. A photo still from *The Red Widow* is instructive regarding the essentially comedic nature of the film. It shows Flora Zabelle, the stout middle-aged lady who plays the widow, draped in furs, on a sidewalk, tossing a basketball-sized bomb.

87. *MPW* 5/6/16:982.

88. See Hugh Seton-Watson, *The Decline of Imperial Russia, 1855–1914* (New York: Praeger, 1952).

89. For analyses of this political violence in Russia see Adam B. Ulam, *In the Name of the People: Prophets and Conspirators in Prerevolutionary Russia* (New York: Viking Press, 1977) and Anna Geifman, *Thou Shalt Kill: Revolutionary Terrorism in Russia, 1894–1917*, (Princeton, NJ: Princeton University Press, 1993). American intellectuals appear to have been passionately aroused by Russian revolutionary heroes. See Henry F. May, *The End of American Innocence: A Study of the First Years of Our Own Time, 1912–1917* (New York: Alfred A. Knopf, 1959), pp. 243–44.

90. Five films with at least some reference to nihilism would be released between 1918 and 1929, including *Lifting Shadows* (Pathé, 1920) and *The Midnight Sun* (Universal-Jewel, 1926).

91. The unifying theme in most of these films was the presence of a *passive* Jewish victim of Tsarist anti-Semitism. See Russell Campbell, "Nihilists and Bolsheviks: Revolutionary Russia in American Silent Film," *The Silent Picture*, No. 19 (1974), pp. 4–36.

92. Ibid.

93. A wave of anti-Semitic pogroms in Russia following the March 1881 assassination of Tsar Alexander II sparked a large-scale exodus of the Jewish population, many of whom would eventually emigrate to America. In 1911 the U.S. government formally terminated its commercial treaty with Russia when the Tsarist regime began refusing admission to foreign Jews, including American citizens. See Ann E. Healy, "Tsarist Anti-Semitism and Russian-American Relations," *Slavic Review*, XLII (Fall, 1983), pp. 408–424.

94. Brownlow, *Behind the Mask of Innocence*, p. 354.

95. Ulam, *In the Name of the People*, p. 135.

96. An anomalous 1914 film related to the Nihilist genre, appositely entitled *The Nihilists* (Nestor), features a bloodthirsty band of male Russian bomb-throwers in a large American city. They destroy themselves with their own device while attempting to blow up an overinquisitive prosecuting attorney. In direct confrontations democratic law and order in the United States will almost always overcome the alien forces of disorder.

97. Bruce Lincoln, *The Conquest of a Continent*, p. 276.

98. *Biograph Bulletin* No. 43, Mar 27, 1905 promotes this film as "timely for the up-to-date moving picture exhibitor…"

99. The knout, a uniquely Russian form of torture, was a thick, hard, meter-length leather whip that tore the skin off a victim's back. Fifteen to 25 lashes was the standard punishment; any additional lashes usually led to death. Its cinematic use would also tend to evoke memories of the slave-like status of Russian peasants under serfdom, which was not formally abolished until 1861.

100. See Nicholas V. Riasanovsky, *The Image of Peter the Great in Russian History and Thought* (New York: Oxford University Press, 1985).

101. By the mid-teens in America "Cossack" had also become a term of derision in labor circles, used to designate the police.

Red Guards, as portrayed in American films, are merely crimson Cossacks. A direct linkage between a Cossack pogrom and the unnatural birth of a female Bolshevik is made in *The Right to Happiness* (Un-Jewel, 1919)—a gentile, lost from her capitalist father in a pogrom, is raised by radical Jews. Her future revolutionary activities in the U.S. will resemble those of lady Nihilists.

102. Although it is aborted, a subplot involving the throwing of a bomb at the Tsar by a female nihilist is featured in Vitagraph's 1914 release, *My Official Wife*.

103. At least one pacifistic 1916 motion picture, *War Brides* (Herbert Brenon/Selznick), also broached the radical concept of capitalist-imperialism financially benefiting from drafted workers of one nation killing drafted workers of another country in order to protect the interests of elites.

104. This film, along with the early 1918 Select release, *At the Mercy of Men*, create an intertextual precedent that can be later linked to the so-called Soviet nationalization of women portrayed in several Red Scare films.

Chapter 2

1. Not a single film released during the Red Scare is known to use the term communism or to refer directly to the Communist Party. In fact, American radicals founded two communist parties in 1919—The Communist Party of America and the rival Communist Labor Party, with a combined membership of over 30,000, barely four thousand of whom spoke English. Both parties went underground in response to government repression. See Irving Howe and Lewis Coser, *The American Communist Party: A Critical History, 1919–1957* (Boston: Beacon Press, 1957).

For a rare fictional American cinematic look at this period, that includes a portrayal of this schism integrated with interviews of some of the surviving participants, see Warren Beatty's epic on the life of John Reed, *Reds* (Paramount, 1981).

2. Robert K. Murray, *Red Scare: A Study of National Hysteria, 1919–1920* (New York: McGraw-Hill, 1964), p. 166.

3. In the caption beneath a picture of "The Soviet Ark" appearing in the Literary Digest the ship's passengers are mockingly referred to as "America's Christmas present for Lenine and Trotzky." LD 1/3/20:14–15. See also, Wenzer, *Anarchists Adrift: Emma Goldman and Alexander Berkman*, chapters 8 & 9.

4. *MPW* 5/18/18:1040.

5. In order to consolidate their newly acquired political power the Bolsheviks had unilaterally declared an armistice with the Central Powers in November 1917. Leon Trotsky led the Bolshevik delegation that negotiated the formal peace treaty. See John W. Wheeler-Bennett, Brest-Litovsk: The Forgotten Peace, March 1918 (New York: St. Martin's Press, 1938).

6. See Craig W. Campbell, *Reel America and World War I* (Jefferson, NC: McFarland, 1985).

7. LC, LP12920; *MPW* 10/26/18:546 & 548.

8. LC, LP12628; *MPW* 7/13/18: 249–250.

9. LC, LP12186; *MPW* 3/23/18:1704.

10. Sometimes these linkages between Germans and domestic radicals could be quite oblique. A good example appears in *The Birth of a Race* (*Birth of a Race* Photoplay/State

Rights), a December release directed by John W. Noble, which was not included in the Filmography. A motion picture that was originally conceived as a race-affirmative work for black Americans, it becomes mired in a story about mankind from Genesis that concludes with an extended sequence dealing with the family of an ethnic German steel magnate in pre-Lusitania America. An individual referred to as "Herr Von H.," who may be a relative, appears to be an agent of the Kaiser sent to the United States to promote labor turmoil in the armaments industry. [AFI, F1.0338; MPW 5/10/19: 938; NYDM 11/233/18:776; Var 12/6/18:38; partial LC viewing print, VBK 2105–06]

11. LC, LP12734; *MPN* 9/7/18:1599 and MPW 10/26/18:550–551.

12. AFI, F1.2103, background notes.

13. This film was probably intended as a veiled attack upon the I.W.W., as well. For, in fact, the militant union had conducted "a discursive campaign against World War I before and after the U.S. entry... [which] put the IWW into open conflict with dominant institutions in American society." Francis Shor, "The IWW and Oppositional Politics in World War I: Pushing the System Beyond its Limits." *Radical History Review*, Vol. 64 (Winter 1996), p. 80. In September 1917, just two months prior to the release of Draft 258, over 160 Wobblies were indicted by the federal government for conspiracy to impede the war effort by, among other things, obstructing the Selective Service Act. See William Preston, Jr., *Aliens and Dissenters: Federal Suppression of Radicals—1903–1933* (Cambridge, MA: Harvard University Press, 1963), pp. 118–122.

14. These cinematic historical flashbacks mimicked popular wartime pageants, in which the people's patriotism was aroused by presenting brief reenactments of historical incidents. These public events invariably highlighted iconographic symbols such as the flag, as well as brief extracts of speeches from the American pantheon and the performing of chauvinistic songs. See Chapter 6 of David Glassberg's *American Historical Pageantry: The Uses of Tradition in the Early Twentieth Century* (Chapel Hill: The University of North Carolina Press, 1990).

15. The triumph of Theodore Roosevelt's Rough Riders at San Juan Hill in 1898 must have been especially symbol-laden for the 1917 audience watching this draft-oriented film.

Roosevelt was the personification of the individual dedicated to the "manly arts" and his Rough Riders' Cuban victory represented a romantic vision of patriotically-inspired volunteers achieving nationalistic glory.

16. Frederick C. Luebke, *Bonds of Loyalty: German-Americans and World War I* (DeKalb: Northern Illinois University Press, 1974), pp. 68–69; 140 passim. John Higham, *Strangers in the Land: Patterns of American Nativism, 1860–1925* (New Brunswick, NJ: Rutgers University Press, 1955), 194 passim.

17. During 1917 "Red Emma" and Alexander Berkman had also organized the No-Conscription League and held several rallies protesting the draft. The two were arrested by Federal agents for their part in the League on June 15. See Drinnon, *Rebel in Paradise*, Chapter XX.

18. As early as August 17, 1917, Senator Henry Ashurst of Arizona formally declared this sentiment before his colleagues. Congressional Record, 68th Congress, 1st Session, 1917, p. 6104. A 1917 New York Globe cartoon, encaptioned "The I.W.W. and the Other Features That Go with It," depicted a vertical arrangement of the letters IWW as the prominent facial features of a spike-helmeted Kaiser Wilhelm II (an oversized first W replacing his well-known upswept waxed mustache). This print cartoon has been reproduced in several books. See John Milton Cooper, Jr., *Pivotal Decades: The United States, 1900–1920* (New York: W.W. Norton, 1990), p. 304.

19. See Robert J. Maddox, *The Unknown War with Russia: Wilson's Siberian Intervention* (Rafael, CA., 1977). At least one short, *A Sammy in Siberia*, a Harold Lloyd one-reeler produced in 1919 by Pathé/Rolin, deals with this topic in a lighter vein. Refer to Appendix 2 for a plot synopsis.

20. See M.J. Heale, *American Anti-Communism*, 51 passim; Luebke, *Bonds of Loyalty*, 273 passim. *The Slacker*, a 1917 Metro release not included in the Filmography, portrays a German who had insulted the American flag being physically compelled to salute it. [LC, LP11071; MPN 8/11/17:979, 1020, 1170]

21. All but eight of these motion pictures received mainstream distribution. Many would appear to have had relatively high budgets and good production qualities. Refer to the Filmography.

In Appendix 2 twenty-three Red Scare oriented shorts are listed. At least one anti-Bolshevik foreign-made feature film was also widely exhibited in the United States, a Canadian production entitled *The Great Shadow* (Adanac/Republic, 1920). Its male lead was played by American star Tyrone Power, Sr., and the director, British-born Harley Knoles, included among his credits the notorious *Bolshevism on Trial*. *The Great Shadow* was probably intended to portray the Winnepeg General Strike of May–June 1919, which was sensationalized in the American press and linked on both sides of the border with the Seattle General Strike. [LC, LU15067; MPW 3/6/20:1636]; Peter Morris, *Embattled Shadows: A History of Canadian Cinema, 1895–1939* (Montreal: McGill-Queen's University Press, 1979), pp. 67–70; see also Kenneth McNaught and David J. Bercuson, *The Winnipeg Strike: 1919*, (Ontario: Longman Canada, 1974).

22. 11/12 percent of the topically relevant films released between 1918 and 1920 are coded Bolshevik-German Linkage (Bol-Ger Link).

23. See Thomas Schatz, *The Genius of the System: Hollywood Filmmaking in the Studio Era* (New York: Pantheon Books, 1988), Chapter 1.

24. See Alexander M. Bing, *War-Time Strikes and Their Adjustment* (New York: E.P. Dutton, 1921).

25. For more information on the activities of the CPI see Harold Laswell, *Propaganda Techniques in the World War* (New York: Peter Smith, 1938). For a discussion of the impact of the Espionage and Sedition Acts see William Preston, Jr., *Aliens and Dissenters*, 88 passim.

26. Emerson Hough, *The Web* (Chicago: Reilly & Lee, 1919), p. 463. Organized in March 1917, by war's end the American Protective League was made up of roughly 12,000 local units numbering over 200,000 part-time spy-catchers. For a concise history of the APL see Joan M. Jensen, *The Price of Vigilance* (New York: Rand McNally, 1968). Also refer to Luebke, *Bonds of Loyalty*, pp. 211–212.

27. *The Yellow Dog* (Universal/Jewel, 1918) actually features such a fictional patriotic organization, the "Boy Detectives of America." Refer to the Filmography.

28. From a review of one of the last Red Scare era films, *The Face at Your Window* (Fox, 1920); *MPW* 12/11/20:768. Throughout the first full postwar year, 1919, about a dozen war-related anti-German feature films were produced

and shown in America. For example, *The Winning Girl* (Famous Players-Lasky/Paramount), released in February, deals with German agents attempting to destroy airplane cloth at a textile factory and *The Sawdust Doll* (Pathé), released in April, stars a little girl who uses her doll as a torch to signal a troop train that it is in danger of being blown up by German saboteurs. See Craig W. Campbell, *Reel America and World War I* (Jefferson, NC: McFarland, 1985), pp. 185–191 [LC, LP13288, *MPW* 3/15/19:1527; LC, LU3587, *MPN* 4/5/19:2193].

29. U. S. troops were in Russia from August 1918 to April 1920. See Richard Goldhurst, *The Midnight War: The American Intervention in Russia, 1918–1920* (New York: McGraw-Hill, 1978); David S. Foglesong, *America's Secret War Against Bolshevism: U.S. Intervention in the Russian Civil War, 1917–1920* Chapel Hill: The University of North Carolina Press, 1995).

30. *MPN* 12/7/18:3347.

31. *The Literary Digest*: 2/22/19:11–13. See also "Our Bolsheviki Show Their Colors," *LD*: 9/20/19:7.

32. Obviously intended to create viewer associations with Germany's infamous official rationale for its violation of Belgium neutrality in 1914. The reference can be found in a studio pressbook clipping included in the film's copyright deposit. See LC, LP12884.

33. The film went into general release in early 1919, during the infamous Seattle shipyard strike, under the more patriotically explicit title of *Safe for Democracy*.

34. Promulgated by its Director, General Enoch Crowder, the order declared that unemployed men should be prioritized on the draft lists. See John Whiteclay Chambers, II, *To Raise An Army*, 194 passim.

35. The use of the surname Crosby for the agitator suggests that he was intended to be recognized as ethnically Irish. In the context of the war this is significant since it had been well-publicized that the militant home rule advocates in Ireland had received support from the German government for their efforts to eliminate British dominion. See Malachy Francis Caulfield, *The Easter Rebellion* (New York: Holt, Reinhardt & Winston, 1963). Yet, the overall filmic characterization during the Red Scare of Irish-Americans was positive— more so for women and largely regardless of class—hence the "lace curtain Irish" heroine

of 1918's *The Vamp* and the "shanty Irish" heroine of 1919's *The Red Viper*.

36. Seventeen motion pictures released during the 1917–18 period are coded under Sabotage—mostly involving disruptive actions directed at war-related industries, e.g., Draft 258 (Metro, 1917); *The Girl of Today* (Vitagraph, 1918); *The Wasp* (World, 1918). Refer to the Filmography.

37. Wildcat strikers who practiced sabotage were sometimes referred to as "sabcats."

38. Many of these strikers actually were members or sympathizers of the I.W.W. See Patrick Renshaw, *The Wobblies: The Story of Syndicalism in the United States* (Garden City, NY: Doubleday, 1967), pp. 235–236. "Report on the Bisbee Deportations Made by the President's Mediation Commission, November 6, 1917." Department of Labor, Washington, D.C., 1918.

39. *EH* 4/12/19:17. Quigley, a devout Catholic layman, would later co-write the 1930 Motion Picture Production Code.

40. Major units of the French Army landed in Odessa in December 1919; they were withdrawn from the Crimea before the end of April 1920. Richard Luckett, *The White Generals*, pp. 252–57. For more information on the general political situation, see Arno J. Mayer, *Politics and Diplomacy of Peacemaking: Containment and Counterrevolution at Versailles, 1918–1919* (New York: Alfred A. Knopf, 1967).

41. Two other films from the period take place in Great Britain and include scenes with Bolshevik agents: *The Heart of a Gypsy* (Hallmark Picts, 1919) and *Nurse Marjorie* (Realart, 1920).

42. Under the Aliens Order of 1919 Britain's Home Secretary established a Home Intelligence Department with extra legal powers as a separate branch of Scotland Yard. See Morton Keller, *Regulating a New Society: Public Policy and Social Change in America, 1900–1930* (Cambridge, MA: Harvard University Press, 1994), p. 101.

43. A direct reference to the May Day letter bombs is made in *The Volcano* (W.W. Hodkinson, 1919).

44. The May 1 international labor holiday was first observed in the United States in 1886, when it was declared the date of a nationwide strike for the eight-hour day. But it was the Haymarket Square riot in Chicago on that first May Day, during which over 200

workers were killed or wounded by the police, that memorialized the date for the American left.

45. The anti-radical juggernaut peaked during a series of raids by federal and local authorities upon the offices of left-wing organizations which were conducted between November 1919 and January 1920. See Murray, *Red Scare*, particularly chapters 12 and 13.

46. See *Red Scare*, p. 114.

47. The cooperative nature of their wartime relationship was epitomized by collective bargaining, enforced by the War Labor Board, which had been established by presidential proclamation in April 1918. See John S. Smith, "Organized Labor and Government in the Wilson Era, 1913–1921: Some Conclusions," *Labor History*, Vol. 3, No. 3 (Fall, 1962), pp. 265–86.

48. A few motion pictures released during the Red Scare era included strike scenes, but managed to avoid any reference to radicalism or labor militancy, e.g. *Dolly's Vacation* (Diando Film/Pathé, 1918) [AFI, F1.1079; LC, LU13098; *MPN* 12/28/18:3959]; *False Gods* (Rothapfel Picts./Independent Sales Corp., 1919) [S (LC); LC, LP13735; *Var* 5/16/19:52].

49. The Filmography codings are the following: Agitator (Agit) 27/30 percent; German (Ger) 25/28 percent; Russian (Russ) 34/37 percent.

50. Much of the contemporary press treated the Seattle General Strike in terms similar to the films. The Sacramento *Bee* wrote "no Government ... can survive half Bolshevik and half democratic" and the Seattle *Star* called it a "Bolshevik-sired nightmare." See "Meaning of the Western Strikes," *The Literary Digest*, March 1, 1919, pp. 14–15.

51. Beginning in the shipyards and significantly influenced by the I.W.W., well over 40,000 workers eventually participated in the city-wide strike. See Murray, *Red Scare*, pp. 59–64; Robert Friedheim, *The Seattle General Strike* (Seattle: University of Washington Press, 1964); Rob Rosenthal, "Nothing Moved but the Tide: The Seattle General Strike of 1919," *Labor's Heritage*, Vol. 4, No. 3 (Fall 1992), pp. 34–53.

52. *MPN* 8/9/19:1283.

53. Actually, an unarmed "Labor Guard" patrolled the city. Roosevelt, who died suddenly in 1919, had increasingly been identified with ultra-nationalism in his latter years and,

following the October 1917 Russian Revolution, had made numerous bellicose statements condemning Bolshevism. See Nathan Miller, *Theodore Roosevelt: A Life* (New York: Morrow, 1992).

54. In reality, over fifty aliens were arrested and detained. They were later shipped East in a sealed train, the "Red Special," to Ellis Island for deportation. However, due to protests, only three of this group had actually been deported by May 1919. See Murray, *Red Scare*, pp. 194–196.

55. *Red Scare*, 105 passim. Extant newsreels from the period show the Massachusetts National Guard deploying in Boston.

56. The *Exhibitor's Herald* review shamelessly exploited these concerns: "The present strike wave sweeping the country, the Red Menace, the delicate circumstances surrounding municipal, state and national government, all are incorporated into Frank Keenan's splendid drama.... Not since the advent of the first big war special has the exhibitor found himself confronted with a picture with such boundless advertising possibilities." *EH* 8/23/19:56.

57. An interesting variation on this theme of the wartime cleansing of capitalist-bred class-based animosities appears in an early 1918 Edison release, *The Unbeliever*. This war-oriented motion picture, which does not appear in the Filmography, features a young man from the wealthy elite who disavows religion and openly disdains "the masses." His combat experiences as a Marine on the western front will later eliminate his class biases and restore his faith in God. But the price for this capitalist's epiphany is paid by the battlefield sacrifice of the working-class protagonist. [S (LC); LC, LP12062; *Var* 2/15/18:52]

58. *Photoplay*: October 1918, pp. 37–40;114–115.

59. *MPN* 9/6/19:2055.

60. The apolitical cinematic vamp, or parasitic female seductress, which had already evolved before America's entrance into World War I and was epitomized by Theda Bara's character in *A Fool There Was* (Fox, 1915), "was dangerous because she could destroy not only a man's discipline and will by feeding off him, she could deprive him of his home, financial security, and social status." Plot resolution usually involved the rescue of the fallen man, followed by his reintegration into the family. See

Janet Staiger, *Bad Women: Regulating Sexuality in Early American Cinema* (Minneapolis: University of Minnesota Press, 1995), pp. 150 passim. For a somewhat tendentious political take on this theme see Bram Dijkstra, *Evil Sisters: The Threat of Female Sexuality and the Cult of Manhood* (New York: Alfred A. Knopf, 1996), pp. 148 passim.

61. These exotic clichéd characters were frequently played by dark-haired actresses, including Betty Blythe, Fritzi Brunette, Mae Busch and Claire DuBrey.

62. For discussions of both the content and historical context of the White Slave films, see Sloan, *The Loud Silents*, pp. 80–86, and Brownlow, *Behind the Mask of Innocence*, pp. 70–89. A more introspective analysis of the genre, concentrating on form, is made in Chapter 5 of Janet Staiger's *Bad Women*.

63. *Variety* 2/15/18:51.

64. Luxemburg was probably better known than Lenin at the time of her murder by para-military Freikorps troops in January 1919 during the suppression of the communist-led Spartacist uprising in Germany. The New York Times of January 18, 1919, commented that the manner of her death was "regrettable" but justified since she was a fomenter of anarchy.

65. *NYDM* 8/28/19:1378–79.

Ironically, this use of the image of the viper may have also been intended as a symbolic linkage to the Biblical imagery of the I.W.W. as a curled serpent crushing capitalism that had appeared in a number of that union's print cartoons. See Donald Winters, "Covington Hall: The Utopian Vision of a 'Wobbly' Poet" *Labor's Heritage*, Vol. 4. No. 2 (Summer 1992), pp. 54–63.

66. From Metro's press book for *The Uplifters*, LC, LP13923.

67. "Are Bolsheviki Mainly Jewish?" *The Literary Digest*, December 14, 1918, p. 32. See also Leonard Dinnerstein, *Anti-Semitism in America*, pp. 79–80, and Zosa Szajkowski, *Jews, Wars, and Communism, Vol. II: The Impact of the 1919–20 Red Scare on American Jewish Life* (New York: Ktav Publishing, 1974), 148 passim.

68. See Murray, *Red Scare*, 91 passim; Michael N. Dobkowski, *The Tarnished Dream: The Basis of American Anti-Semitism* (Westport, CT: Greenwood Press, 1979), pp. 221–27.

69. Jews are coded 21/24 percent in the Filmography during the 1918–20 period, up from 20/9 percent, 1909–17, eleven of which appeared between 1915 and 1917. The author has found no conclusive evidence that any of these films employed derogatory Jew-baiting terms, such as "kike," "hebe," "sheeny" and "yid."

70. See Frederic Cople Jaher, *A Scapegoat in the New Wilderness: The Origins and Rise of Anti-Semitism in America* (Cambridge, MA: Harvard University Press, 1994).

71. Further suggesting the moral decay of Bolshevism is the descriptively pejorative name of "Rotsky," signed upon a note sent from Russia to this Jew-Bolshevik, ordering him to make preparations for a revolution in the United States.

72. *Variety* 8/15/19:71.

73. A New York based review states that "the crusade of a local Yiddish daily" was responsible. *Var* 8/15/19:71.

74. *MPN* 6/26/20:506. This tact mimics wartime devil linkages with the "Satanic Kaiser." See Frederick C. Luebke, *Bonds of Loyalty*, 243 passim.

To Hell with the Kaiser (Screen Classics/Metro, 1918) concludes with the Kaiser entering the underworld and Satan abdicating his throne to the fiendish former ruler of Germany. [LC, LP12628]

75. *Bullin' the Bullsheviki* (Eff & Eff, 1919), initially released in November, was a dark burlesque of Bolshevism featuring the diminutive comic Billy Ruge as the Bolshevik leader named "Trotzsky." In later versions of the film he became Lean Itsky (a name that innovatively suggests an amalgamation of Lenin and Trotsky). Ruge's short height would also tend to visually symbolize the Bolshevik regime's lack of stature in/recognition by the United States.

76. See Richard Hofstadter, *Anti-Intellectualism in American Life* (New York: Alfred A. Knopf, 1963).

77. The reader should be cautioned to not conceive of "Parlor Bolshevism" as merely a comically derisive term for fatuous Bolshevik sympathizers in the United States. For, by conceptually as well as literally situating them in the parlor in some films, a near sacred space in the cultural imagination of the middle-class, the Parlor Bolshevik's violation of this space implicitly poses a direct threat to the American family. A common prop in such scenes, the piano, would have further accentuated the

sense of threat, since this middle-class status object also symbolized social harmony and domestic bliss. See Grier, *Culture & Comfort*.

78. *My Four Years in Germany* promotional sheet; private collection. Full-page ad for *Bolshevism on Trial*; *MPW* 5/17/19:967.

79. This cinematic deification of the American flag is largely attributable to the war, during which such public activities as saluting the flag and pledging allegiance to it were mandated. See Robert Justin Goldstein, *Saving "Old Glory": The History of the American Flag Desecration Controversy* (Boulder, CO: Westview Press, 1995), Chapter 2. Two of the more blatant film examples of the trend would include *The Slacker* (Metro, 1917) and *Her Country's Call* (American-Mutual, 1917). [*MPN* 11/3/17:3130; *MPW* 10/6/17:43 (ad), 126] In the former film, the sight of a ruffian abusing the Stars and Stripes inspires a draft-dodger to enlist. The final scene of *The Slacker* portrays the protagonist kissing the flag before shipping off.

80. Coben, "A Study in Nativism," p. 71. The slogan is eerily reminiscent of the Nazi's "Ein volk, ein Reich, ein Fuhrer." At the conclusion of a Mutt and Jeff animated cartoon, entitled *The Parlor Bolshevist* (Fox, 1920), Jeff uses a pistol to force a group of hairy Bolsheviks to sing the "Star Spangled Banner." See Appendix 2.

81. The five-pointed star the Red Army adopted in 1918 as its emblem was associated with Freemasonry/Jews as Masonic practitioners. *Richard Pipes, Russia Under the Bolshevik Regime*, p. 102.

82. A New York state bill making it a misdemeanor to display the red flag at public gatherings was signed by Smith on May 7, 1919. See Julian F. Jaffe, *Crusade Against Radicalism: New York During the Red Scare, 1914–1924* (Port Washington, NY: Kennikat Press, 1972), pp. 80–82; *New York Tribune*, 1/8/19: 1.

83. This was one of the more scurrilous anti-Bolshevik canards that made the rounds in the western media, including other American films, during the Red Scare. See Murray, *Red Scare*, p. 97. A full page ad in a trade journal for *The New Moon*, featuring Norma Talmadge, promotes the film as "A Story of the Nationalization of Women in Russia." *Exhibitor's Herald* 6/14/19:7. One review of *The World and Its Woman* (Goldwyn, 1919), after

describing a scene in which nationalized girls are taken into the "next" room by Reds and then, following a fade out, shown against a wall with their clothing torn, urged that it should be censored. *Harrison's Reports*, 9/6/19:44.

84. Alan Dawley, *Struggles for Justice*, p. 245. "One hundred per cent Americanism," a term coined by TR in 1915, was virtually *the* national slogan during 1919–20. See Burl Noggle, *Into the Twenties: The United States from Armistice to Normalcy* (Urbana: University of Illinois Press, 1974), p. 118.

85. Vigilante activities, of a sort, are also known to have taken place inside movie theaters. During a September 1919 screening of Goldwyn's *The World and Its Woman*, at the Strand in New York City, a patron named Manuel Lopez was first hissed and then physically attacked for his repeated clapping during scenes portraying Bolshevik excesses in Russia. He was rescued from his assailants, who included women, by a state trooper. Lopez was later charged with "inciting a breach of the peace." A review of the film, based upon a screening at the Strand, can be found in the *NYDM* 9/18/19:1490. For a description of and comment upon the Lopez incident, see the *New York Times* 9/8/19:28, "Mauled in Theatre for Red Applause"; 9/10/19:10 (ed.), "The Mind of the Nation."

86. *MPW* 4/19/19:424.

87. Or, in the more recent memory of the contemporary audience, this American soldier may have represented a one-man Czech Legion. In the summer of 1918 Czech forces that had originally been organized by Imperial Russia from POWs to fight Germany revolted against the authority of the new Bolshevik regime, seized several trains, and engaged in a series of running battles with the Red Army through Siberia until they reached the safety of the Allied forces in Vladivostok. See Richard Luckett, *The White Generals: An Account of the White Movement and the Russian Civil War* (New York: Viking Press, 1971), pp. 160–169; John Bradley, *Allied Intervention in Russia* (Lanham, MD: University Presses of America, 1984), Chapter 4.

88. Noggle, *Into the Twenties*, p. 91.

89. Jaffe, *Crusade Against Radicalism*, p. 36.

90. Sinclair Lewis, *Babbitt* (New York: Harcourt Brace Jovanovich, 1922), p. 331.

91. A stark visual dichotomy with subtle undertones appears to have been intentionally created during this sequence—the chaos in the streets of the slum-bred mob juxtaposed with the environmental order of the public park. See Paul Boyer, *Urban Masses and Moral Order in America, 1820–1920* (Cambridge, MA: Harvard University Press, 1978), chapters 17 and 18.

92. *NYDM* 10/9/19:1594. One is reminded of the notorious rape scene in *The Heart of Humanity* (Un-Jewel, 1919), during which Miss Phillips prepares to plunge a knife into her breast rather than submit to the evil Prussian, played by Erich von Stroheim. The melodramatic excesses of *The Right to Happiness* evoked the following comment by the film's *Variety* reviewer: "It is anti-Bolshevik propaganda ... dripping with crude sentimentality." *Var* 9/12/19:52.

93. One contemporary review of *The Uplifters* stated: "The story is a satire on the Bolsheviki and the rest of the long-haired cranks that will do anything to avoid honest work." *MPW* 7/12/19:281. The satiric bite of this film regarding the political flightiness of its misguided radical characters was aurally reinforced by the studio's suggested musical theme, "Birds and Butterflies" (Capricious Allegretto), by Vely. *MPW* 7/19/19:397.

94. *NYDM* 7/15/19:1112.

95. John Reed (1887–1920) was a handsome, womanizing, hard-drinking, Harvard-educated radical journalist who had also dabbled with satirical verse in the 1912–13 period. He later traveled to Russia during the revolution, actually participating in some of its events. See his *Ten Days That Shook the World* (New York: Boni and Liveright, 1919).

96. Robert McKim, the actor who plays Neuman, was an "accomplished villain" who had appeared as an evil and licentious German agent in a number of releases: *The Dark Road* (Kay-Bee/Triangle, 1917); *The Claws of the Hun* (Ince/Famous Players-Lasky, 1918); The Marriage Ring (Paramount/Famous Players-Lasky, 1918); The Vamp (Paramount/Famous Players-Lasky, 1918).

97. *MPN* 6/26/20:147.

98. *MPW* 5/17/19:966–67.

99. These scenes were actually shot at the Royal Poinciana Hotel in Palm Beach. *The American Film Institute Catalogue, 1912–1920,* F1.0413, background notes.

100. *Common Property* is the single Red Scare era feature film that contains a scene in which American troops engage in combat with the Reds.

101. A reference to the nationwide series of raids, instigated by Attorney General A. Mitchell Palmer, that resulted in the arrest of over 4000 suspected radicals. See Murray, *Red Scare*, pp. 212–217; A. Mitchell Palmer, "The Case Against the Reds," *The Forum*, 63 (February 1920), pp. 174–185. Responding to criticism of these raids by the Department of Justice, Palmer later justified his actions before the House Rules Committee on June 1, 1920, by describing his Red prey as "moral rats" whose "sly and crafty eyes" revealed an inborn predilection to "cruelty, insanity and crime." *NYT* 6/2/20:4.

102. Murray, *Red Scare*, pp. 94–98. In May 1919 a letter of endorsement by Senator Lee S. Overman was printed in full as part of a six-page promotional ad for the forthcoming Thomas H. Ince film entitled *Americanism (Versus Bolshevism)*: "You cannot render your country a greater service than this. The best way to crush out Bolshevism, ... now a very serious menace to our Civilization [sic], is by publicity, and there is no better way than by the motion pictures." Ince's film was later released in January 1920 under the title *Dangerous Hours*. *MPW* 5/19/19:1054–55 (ad; between the pages).

103. The Legion's membership had climbed past a million by the end of the year. See William Pencak, *For God and Country: The American Legion, 1919–1941* (Boston: Northeastern University Press, 1989). The organization's reactionary stance was clearly demonstrated when city authorities deputized the Legion en masse to help squelch the Denver tramway strike of 1920. But the most notorious Red Scare incident involving the Legion took place on November 11, 1919, in the logging town of Centralia in Washington state. During an Armistice Day Legion parade four war veterans and one Wobbly were killed as a result of a confrontation outside the local I.W.W. Hall. Eight members of the radical union were subsequently convicted and sentenced to long prison terms. Although none of the veteran oriented films specifically recreated this notorious incident, contemporary audiences would most likely have made associative linkages. See John McClelland, *Wobbly*

War: The Centralia Story (Tacoma: Washington State Historical Society, 1987).

104. *MPN* 5/15/20:4231.

105. Labor trouble had been brewing in the steel industry throughout the summer of 1919. In early September, under extraordinary pressure from the local steel unions, the National Committee for Organizing Iron and Steel Workers voted for a strike to begin on September 22. In response to the walkout of several hundred thousand workers, the steel companies mobilized tens of thousands of armed guards and mounted a massive red smear campaign. The strike was not formally concluded until January 8, 1920. See Murray, *Red Scare*, Chapter 9.

106. Or, as referred to in the *Variety* review of November 21, 1919: "supposed agents of the Lenine-Trotsky regime[sic]."

107. This locus of illicit pleasures takes on added significance since, by early 1919, the required thirty-six states had ratified the Eighteenth Amendment, banning the manufacture, sale, or distribution of intoxicants throughout the United States. A year later, over president Wilson's veto, Congress passed what became known as the Volstead Act.

108. The insidious nature of the Bolshevik contagion is further highlighted in this film by its suggestive exploitation of the popular linkage between prostitution and the spread of venereal diseases, particularly syphilis, which in the days before the discovery of penicillin was associated with a slow and debilitating death, often accompanied by madness.

109. There were a number of Red flag incidents between so-called patriots and radical demonstrators on May Day 1919; over a score of states would pass bills before the end of the year banning the public display of the Red flag. See Murray, *Red Scare*, pp. 233–35.

110. Following riots in early October 1919 by steel workers in Gary, Indiana, Federal troops were called in and Gary was placed under martial law. In response to investigations by Military Intelligence, the headquarters of local radicals were raided on October 15, netting a cache of Bolshevik literature as well as scores of arrests. See Murray, *Red Scare*, pp. 146–148.

111. LC, LP14071. In fact, "The Crafty Spy" was probably the most commonly used theme music for Bolshevik heavies throughout the Red Scare. This familiar piece was so des-

ignated in a number of musical cue sheets, including those for three other 1919 releases: *The New Moon* (Select), *Virtuous Men* (S.L. Picts/Ralph Ince Film), and *The Volcano* (W.W. Hodkinson)—respectively appearing in *MPW* 5/17/19:1359; *MPW* 6/18/19:1973–74; *MPW* 8/9/19:857. During the late teens *The Moving Picture World* contained a "Music for the Pictures" section. Beginning in August 1918 this was augmented with "Cue Sheets for Current Films," which provided compiled scores of ready-made music and even "special [sound] effects" suggestions for selected feature-length films—keying on inter-titles or descriptive passages. Likewise, the *Exhibitor's Trade Review* had a musical section that printed cue sheets into the early 1920s.

112. At the New York City screening of *The World and Its Woman* (Goldwyn, 1919), accompanied by a symphony orchestra, the beginning of Sibelius' "Finlandia" was played when the title "Bolshevism" was introduced. *NYDM* 9/18/19:1490. Published in 1900, after several performances "Finlandia" made its composer world famous: "With its resemblance to a fiery piece of oratory—eloquent, inflammatory, delivered in a thundering voice—it would stir any audience;... The tense opening atmosphere, with barking, brassy chords, chills the listener with foreboding." Arnold Perris, *Music As Propaganda: Art to Persuade, Art to Control* (Westport, CT: Greenwood Press, 1985), pp. 36–37.

113. *Var* 11/21/19:55.

114. Noted Red Scare historian Robert K. Murray states that many Americans considered colleges to be "hotbeds of bolshevism." Murray, *Red Scare*, pp. 169–173.

115. The title of the work upon which *Dangerous Hours* was based is revealing—"A Prodigal in Utopia"—a short story written by Donn Byrne and originally published in The Saturday Evening Post. *Exhibitor's Herald* 1/10/20:61.

116. By specifying this labor action as part of a national strike of shipyard workers the filmmakers would appear to have deliberately attempted to associatively link the plot of *Dangerous Hours* to the Seattle General Strike that had taken place a year earlier. See above discussion of *The World Aflame*.

117. Refer to the discussion in Chapter 1 about the use of "grips" by cinematic anarchists to carry their bombs.

118. The federal Sedition Act of May 1918, which would remain in effect until 1921, specifically outlawed "disloyal, profane, scurrilous, or abusive language" against the U.S. See Goldstein, *Saving "Old Glory,"* p. 80.

119. Another form of retribution awaits a couple of professional labor agitators who had traitorously collaborated with the Reds. In the film's penultimate scene, sarcastically introduced by a title as a "Social Note," the two tarred and feathered men are shown astride rails being ritualistically carried out of town to "parts unknown."

120. The American Eagle appears repeatedly in print cartoons of the era. A typical example would be the reproduction of an editorial cartoon in the *Literary Digest* that shows the Eagle tossing Reds out of America's nest. LD 1/17/20:14.

121. A similar episode depicts German soldiers brutally seizing Belgian women in *My Four Years in Germany*. During this lengthy episode there is a nearly identical rape scene in which a soldier corners a young maiden inside a darkened house, followed by a shot of her defiled body sprawled across a bed.

122. See Robert Fyne, "From Hollywood to Moscow," *Literature /Film Quarterly*, Vol. 13, No. 3 (1985), pp. 194–99; Michael J. Strada and Harold R. Troper, *Friend or Foe? Russians in American Film and Foreign Policy, 1933–1991* (Metuchen, NJ: Scarecrow Press, 1997), chapters 1 & 2.

Chapter 3

1. The final Senate rejection of the League took place on March 19, 1920. For a political analysis of America in the early 1920s see Burl Noggle, *Into the Twenties*.

2. Just one film is known to contain a direct comment upon the United States refusing to recognize the Soviet Union, *Going to Congress*. A 1924 Pathé twin-reeler featuring the comic talents of Will Rogers, it is delivered as a one-liner by his trademark folksy character with political savvy. For more details about this film, refer to Appendix 3.

3. Amazingly, V. I. Lenin is not directly portrayed or even mentioned in a single American feature. In fact, Lenin is only known to appear in a single fictional film, the 1926 animated short entitled "Hair Cartoons," Number

Four, in a Red Seal novelty series created by cartoonist Marcus, in which the hair of famous personalities is manipulated to create the likenesses of others. About midway through the reel of this issue screen star Sessue Hayakawa, becomes a woman (unidentified) who, in turn, is transmogrified into "Nikolai Lenin." [*MPW* 2/20/26:705] Other than newsreels, just two non-fictional works produced in the United States have been identified that include references to the Soviet Union's first leader: *Red Russia Revealed* (Fox, 1923), a two-reeler with "views of all the prominent government officials," [*MPW* 7/21/23:236] and *The Russian Revolution* (Collwyn Picts, 1927), a six reel compilation documentary that includes scenes of Lenin and Trotsky. [AFI, F2.4742]

4. Probably the best known 1920s film to include an anarchist stereotype is Buster Keaton's farcical two-reeler entitled *Cops* (Comique Film, 1922).

5. Contrary to popular stereotypes, the average Russian refugee was not from the aristocracy, but a former member or camp follower of one of the defeated White Russian armies. See Claudena Skran, *Refugees in Inter-War Europe: The Emergence of a Regime* (New York: Oxford University Press, 1995), p. 33. A 1921 Jack Ford film, *Jackie* (Fox), features a young Russian refugee in London, played by Shirley Mason, who apires to become a famous dancer. But a linkage to the Bolshevik Revolution cannot be verified. [AFI, F2.2776; *Wid's* 11/27/21:11]

6. Refer to the Filmography.

7. For the World War and American cinema see Michael T. Isenberg, *War on Film: The American Cinema and World War I, 1914–1941* (East Brunswick, N.J.: Associated University Presses, 1981); Craig W. Campbell, *Reel America and World War I: A Comprehensive Filmography and History of Motion Pictures in the United States, 1914–1920* (Jefferson, N.C.: McFarland, 1985); Leslie Midkiff DeBauche, *Reel Patriotism: The Movies and World War I* (Madison: The University of Wisconsin Press, 1997).

8. *The Patriot* (Paramount, 1928) features the morally ambiguous 1801 assassination of the mentally unstable Tsar Paul, played by Emil Jannings. [S (Vid); AFI, F2.4172; LC, LP25593]

9. Refer to Chapter 3. See Zosa Szajkowski, *The Impact of the 1919–1920 Red Scare on American Jewish Life* (New York:

Ktav, 1974); Michael N. Dobkowski, *The Tarnished Dream: The Basis of American Anti-Semitism* (Westport, CT: Greenwood Press, 1979), pp. 209–233.

10. Peter G. Filene's *Americans and the Soviet Experiment, 1917–1933* (Cambridge, MA: Harvard University Press, 1967) is the best source for relations between the two states during the 1920s. In a written statement made in 1920 by Wilson's Secretary of State, Bainbridge Colby, he asserted that the U. S. government would refrain from official relations with the Soviet Union because it had repudiated Russia's pre-revolution international obligations, maintained power through "savage oppression" of its opponents and its diplomats were "agitators" promoting "revolutionary movements in other countries." Secretary of State to Italian Ambassador, August 10, 1920, Foreign Relations, 1920, Vol. III, pp. 463–68. The Comintern actually was selling confiscated jewelry on the international market to raise cash. Refer to Theodore Draper, *American Communism and Soviet Russia* (New York: Random House, 1960), pp. 202–209.

11. Michael R. Marrus, *The Unwanted: European Refugees in the Twentieth Century* (New York: Oxford University Press, 1985), pp. 56–61; Skran, Refugees in Inter-War Europe, pp. 16–17 & 36–37.

12. *EH* 19/21/22:63.

13. The popular Boston Blackie character was first introduced to the public in a 1919 novel. Paramount released one other film in 1922 featuring Boston Blackie, *Missing Millions*, starring actor David Powell.

14. LC, LP18332.

15. The primary justification for American intervention in Russia between 1918 and 1920 was to prevent the Soviets from using stockpiled western supplies delivered to the Tsarist government to fight the Germans. In the hope of destroying the incipient Bolshevik regime, elements of the American Army and other allied military forces, sometimes acting in collusion with White Russian units, actually engaged in combat with the Red Army during this period. See John Bradley, *Allied Intervention in Russia, 1919–1920* (New York: Basic Books, 1968).

16. The Russian revolutionary film subgenre was well enough established by the time that Hollywood could issue four motion pictures *about* producing motion pictures dealing

with White Russians and/or about the Bolshevik upheaval, two of which feature extras who were formerly members of the Russian aristocracy. *The Beautiful Cheat* (Universal, 1926) involves the comic adventures of an Irish shop girl promoted by a studio press agent as princess Maritia Callahansky. *High Hat* (First National, 1927) concerns making a film about fake Romanoff jewels and is also played for laughs. But the two 1928 films, *The Last Command* (Paramount) and *Clothes Make the Woman* (Tiffany), are serious romantic dramas about White Russians and the movies.

17. Joan H. Wilson, *Ideology and Economics: U.S. Relations with the Soviet Union, 1918–1933* (Columbia: University of Missouri Press, 1974), pp. 71–102; 161–163.

18. This is the first known American film to have designated in its musical cue sheets the use of "The Internationale" as the revolutionary theme piece.

19. The Feodor character could be viewed as a Red Sheik, just another variation on the exotic romantic outlaw hero established in 1921 by Rudolph Valentino in *The Sheik* (Paramount).

20. An independent comedy short, part of the "Ribticklers" series, entitled *The Volga Boatman, Jr.*, parodied the feature. A one-reeler directed by John Tansey, it was probably released soon after its namesake appeared in movie theaters, in order to help promote the feature. In the short, a group of kids known as "Daily's Dozen," exit a screening of the feature and proceed to imitate the "Cecil Dumbill" film by play acting "vulgar boatmen and women" along the Venice, California, canal. [S (LC, FEA 4799)]

21. Irving Bernstein, *The Lean Years: A History of the American Worker, 1920–1933* (Boston: Houghton Mifflin, 1960).

22. Disney's spring 1925 animated release, *Alice's Egg Plant*, features a fowl outside agitator disrupting egg production at series character Alice's farm. "Little Red Henski" wears a leather cap and false beard and carries a grip with "Moscow, Russia—I.W.W." written across it.

23. *Variety* 6/23/22:34.

Labor issues are non-existent in *First Love* (Realart/Par, 1921). In this romantic comedy the heroine is a young factory worker who must overcome her infatuation with a handsome cad before finding true love with her capitalist employer. [S (LC, incomplete); LC, LP17229; *Var* 1/6/22:42]

24. See Gregory D. Black, *Hollywood Censored: Morality Codes, Catholics and the Movies* (Cambridge, MA: Cambridge University Press, 1994), Chapters 1 & 2.

25. *Wids* 6/5/21:9.

A virtual civil war had been taking place in the West Virginia coalfields since the conclusion of World War I, necessitating the dispatch of Federal troops on several occasions. See Roger Fragge, *Power, Culture and Conflict in the Coalfields* (Manchester University Press, 1996), chapter 3. *The Contrast* was banned in Kansas, where striking coal miners had also been battling the owners and state authorities. See Steven J. Ross, "Cinema and Class Conflict: Labor, Capital, the State and American Silent Film," *Resisting Images: Essays on Cinema and History* (Philadelphia: Temple University Press, 1990), eds. Robert Sklar and Charles Musser, p. 95.

26. Thomas R. Brooks, *Toil and Trouble: A History of American Labor* (New York: Dial Press, 1964), pp. 145–149.

27. *New York Call* 9/25/21, "Call Magazine," p. 8.

28. Though *The Whistle's* theme is described as "labor versus capital" by a *Variety* (4/1/21:41) reviewer, a lack of any reference to or portrayal of militant radicalism precluded its inclusion in the Filmography. A print is available at the Library of Congress; FEA 5936–41. Ironically, Hart's film still ran into censorship difficulties. For example, Pennsylvania censors demanded numerous alterations. See the *New York Call*, 8/5/21.

29. Throughout the entire 1921–29 period only five films displayed a distinct anti-labor bias; two a pro-labor bias. An interesting film to note from these years would be the 1924 prestige production of *Babbitt*, released by Warners and directed by Harry Beaumont. The script on copyright deposit has eliminated from Sinclair Lewis's eponymous source novel the subplot that centered upon a strike taking place during the Red Scare. [LC, LP20275; *NYT* 7/15/24:9; *Var* 7/16/24:22]

30. AFI, F2.4922; LC, LP21830.

31. Although not included in the Filmography, John Ford's *The Iron Horse* (Fox, 1924) should also be noted here. In relating an epic story of the mid-nineteenth century construction of the Transcontinental Railroad,

Ford includes scenes of surly Italian track layers (led by a stereotype named Tony) refusing to work without receiving their overdue wages. The "furriners" ignore the fists of an exasperated Irish foreman and the entreaties of their employer, but positively respond to the patriotic appeal of the capitalist's pretty daughter.

32. A series of strikes in the Passaic, New Jersey, textile mills took place between October 1925 and February 1926. Communist Party organizers were significantly involved and a number of violent confrontations took place between the strikers and police. The Party's United Front Committee sponsored the production of a film to raise funds. Directed by Sam Russak, the seven-reel film, entitled *The Passaic Textile Strike*, was first shown in the fall of 1926. After a brief prologue of crudely acted scenes, the remainder of the film is comprised of newsreel footage of the strikes and filmed reenactments. MOMA possesses a five-reel version of the film. See Brownlow, *Behind the Mask of Innocence*, pp. 498–508.

33. Geoffrey Perrett, *America in the Twenties: A History* (New York: Simon and Schuster, 1982).

34. Arno J. Mayer, *Politics and Diplomacy of Peacemaking: Containment and Counterrevolution at Versailles, 1918–1919* (New York: Knopf, 1967).

35. Gaetano Salvemini, *The Origins of Fascism in Italy* (New York: Harper & Row, 1973).

36. Erich Eyck, *A History of the Weimar Republic: From the Collapse of the Empire to Hindenburg's Election* (Cambridge, MA: Harvard University Press, 1967).

37. James P. Harrison, *The Long March to Power: A History of the Chinese Communist Party, 1921–1972* (New York: Praeger, 1972), pp. 91–165; Selig Adler, *The Uncertain Giant: 1921–1941, American Foreign Policy Between the Wars* (London: Collier-Macmillan, 1965), p. 127.

38. Howard F. Cline, *The United States and Mexico*, revised ed. (New York: Atheneum, 1971), pp. 196–203; 210–213. See also the first six chapters of John A. Britton's *Revolution and Ideology: Images of the Mexican Revolution in the United States* (Lexington: The University Press of Kentucky, 1995).

39. Eyck, *A History of the Weimar Republic.*

40. The communists were repeatedly

accused in these immediate postwar years of showing disrespect to and even accosting war veterans. It should be noted here that veterans comprised a major component of the reactionary para-military and/or fascist units that arose and defeated the communists in both Germany and in Italy. Refer to Robert G. L. Waite, *Vanguard of Nazism: The Free Corps Movement in Postwar Germany, 1918–1923* (Cambridge, MA: Harvard University Press, 1952).

41. *Var* 1/24/24:26.

42. The radical socialists, who began calling themselves "Maximalists" (as in Bolsheviks) in 1918, did openly support a series of major strikes between 1919 and 1921. The extremists of the Socialist Party broke away in 1921 and formed the Communist Party of Italy. Militant workers, many of whom belonged to one of these radical leftist parties, had frequently disparaged Italian war veterans or even publicly abused them. Furthermore, Italy's diplomatic failure to gain advantage from her contribution to the Allied war effort was labeled by the right as a "mutilated victory," and blamed on the left. A major appeal of the right wing extremists, led by Mussolini's Fascisti, was a promise to vindicate Italy's former fighting men. And anti-Bolshevism comprised the most strident aspect of the fascists' rhetoric. Refer to Salvemini, *The Origins of Fascism in Italy*.

43. William Pencak, *For God & Country: The American Legion, 1919–1941* (Boston: Northeastern University Press, 1989), p. 21.

44. Today, the preferred transliteration of Kuomintang is Guomindang. For more information on the Soviet influence in 1920s China, refer to Conrad Brandt, *Stalin's Failure in China, 1924–1927* (Cambridge, MA: Harvard University Press, 1958).

45. LC, LP24520.

46. The images of the communist Other could take on even darker tones when combined with the racist attitudes/fears of the day. Several motion pictures released in the first half of the 1930s that directly attacked the Red Chinese, including Warner Brothers' 1935 release *Oil for the Lamps of China*, would become prototypes of the virulently racist anti-Japanese films released during World War II. Refer to Eugene F. Wong, *On Visual Media Racism: Asians in the American Motion Pictures* (New York: Arno Press, 1978); Michael

S. Shull and David Edward Wilt, *Hollywood War Films, 1937–1945* (Jefferson, NC: McFarland, 1996), pp. 53–56, 143–146, 177–179, 226–233.

47. George Black, *The Good Neighbor: How the United States Wrote the History of Central America and the Caribbean* (New York: Pantheon, 1988), pp. 41–57. See also, Britton, *Revolution and Ideology*.

48. AFI, F2.1359; LC, LP18045. Virtually all surviving Harold Lloyd films, including *Why Worry?*, are now available on video.

49. LC print FGE 8020–25; *Var* 9/18/29:15; LC, LP884 (studio pressbook).

Augusto Sandino's revolt against capitalist exploitation began in 1927 with an attack upon the mining facilities of the American-owned LaLuz company. Eventually 6,000 U.S. Marines would be sent to Nicaragua to crush the Sandinista movement. See Neill Macaulay, *The Sandino Affair* (Chicago: Quadrangle Books, 1967).

50. In 1925 MGM had produced a less interesting revolutionary yarn taking place in a Mediterranean kingdom, *The Only Thing*, which also played upon the fear of a worldwide communist conspiracy by pointedly identifying the revolutionaries as "Reds."

51. The nom de revolution connotes upheaval, making a subliminal connection with rising Soviet leaders of the time such as Stalin (the revolutionary moniker meaning steel in Russian, changed from the Georgian Djugashvili).

52. By the early 1930s Hollywood would be less coy about showing Americans engaging communism overseas. A series of films refer to or portray such encounters in Nicaragua, China and the Soviet Union, including: *Central Airport* (WB, 1932); *Clear All Wires* (MGM, 1932); *War Correspondent* (Columbia, 1932); *Shanghai Madness* (Fox, 1933).

53. An odd example of the displacement of Soviet revolutionary imagery takes place in MGM's late 1929 release, *The Mysterious Island*, a part-talkie fantasy based upon a Jules Verne novel. Although the story takes place in the mid-nineteenth century in the Kingdom of Hetvia and is primarily concerned with explorations of an undersea world in diving vessels, a subplot involves revolutionary disorder roused by "oppression" of the people. What is particularly interesting is that most of the characters have distinctive Slavic names and that

the people are portrayed as Russian peasant stereotypes and the soldiers as brutal Cossack types. [S (Vid); LC, LP799; *Var* 12/25/29:30]

54. During the three year period encompassing 1932–1934, alone, I have identified over a score of films that engage domestic radicalism and/or militant labor issues, including: *The Cabin in the Cotton* (1st Nat/WB, 1932); *Washington Merry-Go-Round* (Col, 1932); *Ann Vickers* (RKO, 1933); *Golden Harvest* (Par, 1933); *The Power and the Glory* (Fox, 1933); *Our Daily Bread* (UA, 1934); *Sons of Steel* (Chesterfield, 1934).

Bibliography

Documents

The American Film Institute Catalogue of Motion Pictures Produced in the United States: Film Beginnings, 1893–1910. Metuchen, NJ: Scarecrow Press, 1995.
_____. Feature Films, 1911–1920, Volume F1. Berkeley: University of California Press, 1988.
_____. Feature Films, 1921–1930, Volume F2. New York: Bowker, 1971.
Catalogue of Copyright Entries, Cumulative Series Motion Pictures, 1912–1939, Library of Congress. Washington, D.C., 1951.
D'Agostino, Annette M., compiled by. An Index to Short and Feature Film Reviews in the 'Moving Picture World': The Early Years, 1907–1915. Westport, CT: Greenwood Press, 1995.
Lauritzen, Einar and Gunnar Lundquist. American Film Index, 1908–1915. Stockholm, Sweden: University of Stockholm/ Akademibokhandeln, 1976.
_____. American Film Index, 1916–1920. Stockholm: University of Stockholm/ Akademibokhandeln, 1984.

Periodicals

Exhibitor's Herald: 1921–1928.
The Literary Digest: 1909–1920.
Motion Picture News: 1914–1922.
The Moving Picture World: 1908–1924.

New York Dramatic Mirror: 1909–1919.
The New York Times: 1908–1929.
Photoplay: 1909–1921.
Variety: 1908–1929.

Films

The texts of films actually screened are the ultimate source.

General (Film)

Bowser, Eileen. The Transformation of Cinema, 1908–1915. New York: Scribner's, Macmillan, 1990.
Brownlow, Kevin. Behind the Mask of Innocence: Sex, Violence, Crime: Films of Social Conscience in the Silent Era. Berkeley: University of California Press, 1990.
_____. The War, the West and the Wilderness. New York: Alfred A. Knopf, 1978.
Campbell, Craig. Reel America and World War I: A Comprehensive Filmography and History of Motion Pictures in the United States, 1914–1920. Jefferson, NC: McFarland, 1985.
Campbell, Russell. "Nihilists and Bolsheviks: Revolutionary Russia in American Silent Film." The Silent Picture, No. 19 (1974), pp. 4–36.
Czitron, Daniel J. Media and the American Mind, from Morse to McLuhan. Chapel Hill: University of North Carolina Press, 1982.

Doyle, Billy H. *The Ultimate Directory of Silent Screen Performers: A Necrology of Births and Deaths and Essays on 50 Lost Players*. Metuchen, NJ: Scarecrow Press, 1995.

Eames, John D. *The MGM Story: The Complete History of Over Fifty Roaring Years*. New York: Crown Publishers, 1975.

Erens, Patricia. *The Jew In American Cinema*. Bloomington: Indiana University Press, 1984.

Ewen, Elizabeth. "City Lights: Immigrant Women and the Rise of the Movies." *Signs*, Vol. 5, No. 3, (Spring 1980 Supplement), pp. S45–S65.

Fuller, Kathryn H. *At the Picture Show: Small-Town Audiences and the Creation of Movie Fan Culture*. Washington, D.C.: Smithsonian Institution Press, 1996.

Furhammer, Leif and Isakson, Fulke. *Politics and Film*. New York: Praeger, 1971.

Gomery, Douglas. *The Hollywood Studio System*. London: Macmillan Publishers, 1986.

Hansen, Miriam. *Babel and Babylon: Spectatorship in American Silent Film*. Cambridge, MA: Harvard University Press, 1991.

Higashi, Samiko. *Cecil B. DeMille and American Culture: The Silent Era* Berkeley: University of California Press, 1994.

Hirschorn, Clive. *The Columbia Story*. New York: Crown Publishers, 1989.

_____. *The Universal Story*. New York: Crown Publishers, 1983.

_____. *The Warner Brothers Story: The Complete History of Hollywood's Greatest Studio*. New York: Crown Publishers, 1979.

Isenberg, Michael T. *War on Film: The American Cinema and World War I, 1914–1941*. East Brunswick, NJ: Associated University Presses, 1981.

Jewell, Richard B. *The RKO Story*. Westport, CT: Arlington House Publishers, 1982.

Jones, Dorothy B. *The Portrayal of China and India on the American Screen, 1896–1955*. Cambridge, MA: Center for International Studies, MIT, 1955.

Karnick, Kristine Brunovska and Henry Jenkins, eds., *Classical Hollywood Comedy*. London: Routledge, 1995.

Katz, Ephraim. *The Film Encyclopedia*. New York: Perigee Books, 1979.

Koszarski, Richard. *An Evening's Entertainment: The Age of the Silent Feature Picture, 1915–1928*. Berkeley: University of California Press, 1993.

MacCann, Richard D., ed. *Silent Comedians*. Metuchen, NJ: The Scarecrow Press, 1993.

Magliozzi, Ronald S. *Treasures from the Film Archives: A Catalogue of Short Silent Fiction Films held by FIAF Archives*. Metuchen, NJ: The Scarecrow Press, 1988.

Maland, Charles J. *Chaplin and American Culture: The Evolution of a Star Image*. Princeton, NJ: Princeton University Press, 1989.

Margolies, Ken. "Silver Screen Tarnishes Unions." *Screen Actor*, Vol. 23 (Summer 1981), pp. 43–52.

Marks, Martin Miller. *Music and the Silent Film: Contexts and Case Studies, 1895–1924*. New York: Oxford University Press, 1997.

May, Larry. *Screening Out the Past: The Birth of Mass Culture and the Motion Picture Industry*. Chicago: The University of Chicago Press, 1983.

Parish, James Robert and Michael R. Pitts. *The Great Spy Pictures*. Metuchen, NJ: The Scarecrow Press, 1974.

Pratt, George C. *Spellbound in Darkness*. Greenwich CT: New York Graphic Society, 1973.

Rapee, Erno. *Motion Picture Moods for Pianists and Organists: A Rapid-Reference Collection of Selected Pieces*. New York: Arno Press, 1970. (G. Schirmer, 1924).

Robinson, David. *From Peep Show To Palace: The Birth of American Film*. New York: Columbia University Press, 1996.

Ross, Steven J. *Working-Class Hollywood: Silent Film and the Shaping of Class in America*. Princeton, NJ: Princeton University Press, 1998.

Shull, Michael S. "Silent Agitators: Militant Labor in the Movies, 1909–1919." *Labor's Heritage*, Vol. 9, No. 3 (Winter, 1998), pp. 58–77.

Sklar, Robert. *Movie-Made America: A Cultural History of American Movies*. New York: Random House, 1975.

Slide, Anthony. *The American Film Industry: A Historical Dictionary*. Westport, CT: Greenwood Press, 1986.

Sloan, Kay. *The Loud Silents: Origins of the*

Social Problem Film. Urbana: University of Illinois Press, 1988.

Staiger, Janet. *Bad Women: Regulating Sexuality in Early American Cinema.* Minneapolis: University of Minnesota Press, 1995.

Vazzana, Eugene Michael. *Silent Film Necrology: Births and Deaths of Over 5,000 Performers, Directors, Producers and Other Filmmakers of the Silent Era, through 1993.* Jefferson, NC: McFarland, 1995.

Wong, Eugene Franklin. *On Visual Media Racism: Asians in the American Motion Pictures.* New York: Arno Press, 1978.

General (History)

Adamic, Louis. *Dynamite: The Study of Class Violence in America.* Gloucester, MA; P. Smith, 1960 (c. 1930).

Adler, Selig. *The Uncertain Giant, 1921–1941: American Foreign Policy Between the Wars.* Toronto: Collier-MacMillan, 1965.

Allsop, Kenneth. *Hard Travelin': The Hobo and His History.* London: Hodder and Stoughton, 1967.

Baker, Roscoe. *The American Legion and American Foreign Policy.* New York: Bookman Associates, 1954.

Banta, Martha. *Taylored Lives: Narrative Productions in the Age of Taylor, Veblen, and Ford.* Chicago: The University of Chicago Press, 1993.

Beebe, Lucius. *The Big Spenders.* Garden City, NY: Doubleday, 1966.

Bennett, David H. *The Party of Fear: From Nativist Movements to the New Right in American History.* Chapel Hill: The University of North Carolina Press, 1988.

Boyer, Paul. *Urban Masses and Moral Order in America, 1820–1920.* Cambridge, MA: Harvard University Press, 1978.

Brandes, Stuart D. *American Welfare Capitalism, 1880–1940.* Chicago: The University of Chicago Press, 1970.

Brecher, Jeremy. *Strike!* San Francisco: Straight Arrow Books, 1972.

Brody, David. *Workers in Industrial America.* New York: Oxford University Press, 1980.

Brooks, Thomas R. *Toil and Trouble: A History of American Labor.* New York: Dial Press, 1964.

Brown, Richard M. *Strain of Violence: Historical Studies of American Violence and Vigilantism.* New York: Oxford University Press, 1975.

Buckingham, Peter H. *America Sees Red: Anti-Communism in America, 1820s to 1980s.* Clarement, CA: Regina Books, 1987.

Buhle, Mari Jo. *Women and American Socialism, 1870–1920.* Urbana: University of Illinois Press, 1981.

Buhle, Mari Jo, Paul Buhle and Dan Georgakais. *The Encyclopedia of the American Left.* New York: Garland, 1990.

Burnham, John C. *Bad Habits: Drinking, Smoking, Taking Drugs, Gambling, Sexual Misbehavior, and Swearing in America.* New York: New York University Press, 1993.

Camp, Helen C. *Iron in Her Soul: Elizabeth Gurley Flynn and the American Left.* Pullman: Washington State University Press, 1995.

Canovan, Margaret, *Populism.* New York: Harcourt, Brace Jovanovich, 1981.

Cashman, Sean Dennis. *America in the Age of the Titans: The Progressive Era and World War I.* New York: New York University Press, 1988.

Chamberlin, William Henry. *The Russian Revolution.* 2 vols., New York: The MacMillan Company, 1935.

Chambers, David M. *Hooded Americanism: The First Century of the Ku Klux Klan, 1865–1965.* Garden City, NY: Doubleday, 1965.

Chambers, II, John Whiteclay. *To Raise an Army: The Draft Comes to Modern America.* New York: The Free Press, 1987.

Chatfield, Charles. *For Peace and Justice: Pacifism in America, 1914–1941.* Knoxville: University of Tennessee Press, 1971.

Churchill, Allen. *The Improper Bohemians: A Recreation of Greenwich Village in Its Heyday.* New York: E.P. Dutton, 1959.

Clark, Norman. *Deliver Us from Evil: An Interpretation of American Prohibition.* New York: W.W. Norton, 1976.

Cochran, Bert. *Labor and Communism: The Conflict that Shaped American Unions.* Princeton, NJ: Princeton University Press, 1977.

Conlin, Joseph R., ed. *At the Point of Production: The Local History of the I.W.W..* Westport, CT: Greenwood Press, 1981.

Cooper, John Milton, Jr., *Pivotal Decades: The United States, 1900–1920*. New York: W.W. Norton, 1990.

Costigliola, Frank. *Awkward Dominion: American Political, Economic and Cultural Relations with Europe, 1919–1933*. Ithaca, NJ: Cornell University Press, 1984.

Covert, Catherine L. and John D. Stevens. *Mass Media Between the Wars: Perceptions of Cultural Tensions, 1918–1941*. Syracuse, NY: Syracuse University Press, 1984.

Crunden, Robert M. *Ministers of Reform: The Progressives' Achievement in American Civilization, 1889–1920*. New York: Basic Books, 1982.

Culberson, William C. *Vigilantism: Political History of Private Power in America*. Westport, CT: Greenwood Press, 1990.

Daniels, Jonathan. *The Time Between the Wars: Armistice to Pearl Harbor*. New York: Doubleday & Company, 1966.

Daniels, Robert V. *Russia: The Roots of Confrontation*. Cambridge, MA: Harvard University Press, 1985.

Davis, David B., ed., *The Fear of Conspiracy: Images of Un-American Subversion: From the Revolution to the Present*. Ithaca, NY: Cornell University Press, 1971.

Dawley, Alan. *Struggles for Justice: Social Responsibility and the Liberal State*. Cambridge MA: Harvard University Press, 1991.

Derthick, Martha. *The National Guard in Politics*. Cambridge, MA: Harvard University Press, 1965.

Dick, William M. *Labor and Socialism in America: The Gompers Era*. Port Washington, NY: Kennikat Press, 1972.

Diggins, John Patrick. *The Rise and Fall of the American Left*. New York: W.W. Norton, 1992.

Donner, Frank. *Protectors of Privilege: Red Squads and Police Repression in Urban America*. Berkeley: University of California Press, 1990.

Draper, Theodore. *The Roots of American Communism*. New York: The Viking Press, 1957.

Dubofsky, Melvyn. *We Shall Be All: A History of the Industrial Workers of the World*. Chicago: Quadrangle, 1969.

Dyson, Lowell R. *Red Harvest: The Communist Party and American Farmers*. Lincoln: University of Nebraska Press, 1982.

Ellis, Edward R. *Echoes of Distant Thunder: Life in the United States, 1914–1918*. New York: Coward, McCann & Geoghegan, 1975.

Epstein, Melech. *The Jew and Communism: The Story of Early Communist Victories and Ultimate Defeats in the Jewish Community, USA, 1919–1941*. New York: Trade Union Sponsoring Committee, 1959.

Ewen, Elizabeth. *Immigrant Women in the Land of Dollars: Life and Culture on the Lower East Side, 1880–1925*. New York: Monthly Review Press, 1985.

Ferro, Marc. *Nicholas II: The Last of the Tsars* New York: Oxford University Press, 1993.

Fever, Lewis S. "American Travelers to the Soviet Union, 1917–1932: The Formation of a Component of New Deal Ideology." *American Quarterly*, Vol. 14 (Summer 1962), pp. 119–49.

Figes, Orlando. *A People's Tragedy: A History of the Russian Revolution*. New York: Viking, 1996.

Filene, Peter G. *Americans and the Soviet Experiment, 1917–1933*. Cambridge, MA: Harvard University Press, 1967.

Filippelli, Ronald L., ed. *Labor Conflict in the United States: An Encyclopedia*. New York: Garland, 1990.

Fogelson, Robert M. *America's Armories: Architecture, Society, and Public Order*. Cambridge, MA: Harvard University Press, 1989.

Folsom, Franklin. *Impatient Armies of the Poor: The Story of Collective Action of the Unemployed, 1808–1942*. Niwot: University Press of Colorado, 1991.

Foner, Philip S. *Organized Labor and the Black Worker, 1619–1973*, 2nd ed. New York: Praeger, 1974.

Fragge, Roger. *Power, Culture and Conflict in the Coalfields: West Virginia and South Wales, 1900–1922*. Manchester: Manchester University Press, 1996.

Galambos, Louis. *The Public Image of Big Business in America, 1880–1940: A Quantitative Study in Social Change*. Baltimore, MD: The Johns Hopkins University Press, 1975.

Gardner, L.C. *Safe For Democracy: The Anglo-American Response to Revolution, 1913–1923*. New York: Oxford University Press, 1984.

Gerson, Louis L. *The Hyphenate in Recent American Politics and Diplomacy*. Lawrence: University of Kansas Press, 1964.

Geyer, Dietrich. *Russian Imperialism: The Interaction of Domestic and Foreign Policy, 1860–1914*. New York: Berg, 1987.

Gilkeson, John S., Jr. *Middle-Class Providence, 1820–1940*. Princeton, NJ: Princeton University Press, 1986.

Gitelman, Z. *A Century of Ambivalance: The Jews of Russia and the Soviet Union, 1881 to the Present*. New York: Schocken, 1988.

Glassberg, David. *American Historical Pageantry: The Uses of Tradition in the Early Twentieth Century*. Chapel Hill: The University of North Carolina Press, 1990.

Glazer, Nathan. *The Social Basis of American Communism*. New York: Harcourt, Brace & World, 1961.

Goldstein, Robert Justin. *Political Repression in Modern America: From 1870 to the Present*. Boston: G. K. Hall, 1978.

_____. *Saving "Old Glory": The History of the American Flag Desecration Controversy*. Boulder, CO: Westview Press, 1995.

Graham, Otis L. *The Great Campaigns: Reform and War in America, 1900–1928*. Englewood Cliffs, NJ, 1971.

Green, Archie. *Wobblies, Pile Butts, and Other Heroes: Laborlore Explorations*. Urbana: University of Illinois Press, 1993.

Green, James R. *Grass-Roots Socialism: Radical Movements in the Southwest, 1895–1943*. Baton Rouge: Louisiana State University Press, 1978.

_____. *The World of the Worker: Labor in Twentieth-Century America*. New York: Hill and Wang, 1980.

Gutman, Herbert G. *Work Culture and Society in Industrializing America*. New York: Random House, 1977.

Harring, Sidney L. *Policing a Class Society: The Experience of American Cities, 1865–1915*. New Brunswick, NJ: Rutgers University Press, 1983.

Hawley, Ellis W. *The Great War and the Search for a Modern Order, A History of the American People and Their Institutions, 1917–1933*. New York: St. Martin's Press, 1979.

Haynes, John E. *Communism and Anti-Communism in the U.S.: An Annotated Guide to Historical Writings*. New York: Garland, 1987.

Heale, M.J. *American Anticommunism: Combating the Enemy Within, 1830–1970*. Baltimore: The Johns Hopkins University Press, 1990.

Hennen, John C. *The Americanization of West Virginia: Creating a Modern Industrial State, 1916–1925*. Lexington: The University Press of Kentucky, 1996.

Higham, John. *Strangers in the Land: Patterns of American Nativism, 1860–1925*. New Brunswick, NJ: Rutgers University Press, 1955.

Hofstadter, Richard. *The Age of Reform: From Bryan to F.D.R.* New York: Alfred A. Knopf, 1955.

_____. *Anti-Intellectualism in American Life*. New York: Alfred A. Knopf, 1963.

Howe, Irving. *Socialism and America*. San Diego: Harcourt, Brace Jovanovich, 1985.

Jaffe, Julian F. *Crusade Against Radicalism: New York During the Red Scare, 1914–1924*. Port Washington, NY: Kennikat Press, 1972.

Johnson, Michael R. "The IWW and Wilsonian Democracy." *Science and Society*, Vol. 28 (Summer 1964), pp. 257–74.

Jones, Maldwyn A. *American Immigration*. Chicago: The University of Chicago Press, 1960.

Judd, Richard W. *Socialist Cities: Municipal Politics and the Grass Roots of American Socialism*. Albany: State University of New York Press, 1989.

Keller, Morton. *Regulating a New Society: Public Policy and Social Change in America, 1900–1933*. Cambridge, MA: Harvard University Press, 1994.

Kennan, George F. *Soviet-American Relations, 1917–1920*. 2 vols. Princeton, NJ: Princeton University Press, 1956–1958.

Kimeldorf, Howard. *Reds or Rackets? The Making of Radical and Conservative Unions on the Waterfront*. Berkeley: University of California Press, 1988.

Kovel, Joel. *Red Hunting in the Promised Land: Anti-Communism and the Making of America*. New York: Basic Books, 1994.

Kraditor, Aileen S. *The Ideas of the Woman Suffrage Movement, 1890–1920*. New York: W.W. Norton, 1981. (Columbia University Press, 1965)

Kraut, Alan M. *The Huddled Masses: The*

Immigrant in American Society, 1880–1921. Arlington Heights, IL: Harlan Davidson, 1982.

Laslett, John H.M. *Labor and the Left: A Study of Socialist and Radical Influences in the American Labor Movement, 1881–1924*. New York: Basic Books, 1970.

_____, ed. *The United Mine Workers of America: A Model of Industrial Solidarity?* University Park: The Pennsylvania State University Press, 1996.

_____. *The Labor Wars: From the Molly Maguires to the Sit-Downs*. Garden City, NY: Doubleday, 1973.

Lens, Sidney. *Radicalism in America*. New York: Thomas Y. Crowell Company, 1969.

Leuchtenburg, William E. *The Perils of Prosperity, 1914–1932*, 2nd Edition. Chicago: The University of Chicago Press, 1993.

Levin, Murray B. *Political Hysteria in America: The Democratic Capacity for Repression*. New York: Basic Books, 1971.

Lipset, Seymour Martin and Earl Raab. *The Politics of Unreason: Right-Wing Extremism in America, 1790–1970*. New York: Harper and Row, 1970.

Little, Douglas. "Anti-Bolshevism and American Foreign Policy, 1919–1939: The Diplomacy of Self-Delusion." *American Quarterly*, Vol. 35, No. 4 (Fall 1983), pp. 379–390.

Lovenstein, Meno. *American Opinion of Soviet Russia*. Washington: American Council on Public Affairs, 1941.

Lynd, Robert S. and Helen Merrell Lynd. *Middletown: A Study in American Culture*. New York: Harcourt Brace, 1929.

McCartin, Joseph A. *Labor's Great War: The Struggle for Industrial Democracy and the Origins of Modern American Labor Relations, 1912–1921*. Chapel Hill: The University of North Carolina Press, 1998.

Mahon, John K. *History of the Militia and the National Guard*. New York: Macmillan, 1983.

Marrus, Michael. *The Unwanted: European Refugees in the Twentieth Century*. New York: Oxford University Press, 1985.

Marsden, George M. *Fundamentalism and American Culture: The Shaping of Twentieth-Century Evangelicalism, 1870–1925*. New York: Oxford University Press, 1980.

Miller, Robert Moats. *American Protestantism and Social Issues, 1919–1939*. Chapel Hill: The University of North Carolina Press, 1958.

Milton, David. *The Politics of U. S. Labor: From the Great Depression to the New Deal*. New York: Monthly Review, 1982.

Montgomery, David. *The Fall of the House of Labor: The Workplace, the State, and American Labor Activism, 1865–1925*. New York: Cambridge University Press, 1987.

Morlan, Robert L. *Political Prairie Fire: The Non-Partisan League, 1915–1922*. Minneapolis: University of Minnesota Press, 1955.

Nash, Michael. *Conflict and Accommodation: Coal Miners, Steel Workers and Socialism, 1890–1920*. Westport, CT: Greenwood Press, 1982.

Nelson, Daniel. *Managers and Workers: Origins of the New Factory System in the United States, 1880–1920*. Madison: The University of Wisconsin Press, 1975.

Painter, Nell I. *Standing at Armageddon: The U.S., 1877–1919*. New York: W.W. Norton, 1987.

Parenti, Michael. *The Anti-Communist Impulse*. New York: Random House, 1969.

Pencak, William. *For God and Country: The American Legion, 1919–1941*. Boston: Northeastern University Press, 1989.

Pethybridge, Roger. *The Social Prelude to Stalinism*. New York: St. Martin's Press, 1974.

Pipes, Richard. *Russia Under The Bolshevik Regime*. New York: Alfred A. Knopf, 1993.

Preston, William, Jr. *Aliens and Dissenters: Federal Suppression of Radicals, 1903–1933*. Cambridge, MA: Harvard University Press, 1963.

Prickett, James Robert. "Communists and the Communist Issue in the American Labor Movement, 1920–1950." Unpublished Ph.D. dissertation, University of California, Los Angeles, 1973.

Rajala, Richard A. "A Dandy Bunch of Wobblies: Pacific Northwest Loggers and the Industrial Workers of the World, 1900–1930." *Labor History*, Vol. 57 (Spring, 1996), pp. 205–234

Ramirez, Bruno. *When Workers Fight: The Politics of Industrial Relations in the Progressive Era, 1898–1916*. Westport, CT: Greenwood Press, 1978.

Renshaw, Patrick. *The Wobblies: The Story of Syndicalism in the United States.* Garden City, NY: Doubleday and Company, Inc., 1967.

Revolutionary Radicalism: Its History, Purpose and Tactics. Report of the Joint Legislative Committee Investigating Seditious Activities, New York State Senate, 1920.

Ribuffo, Leo P. *The Old Christian Right: The Protestant Far Right from the Great Depression to the Cold War.* Philadelphia: Temple University Press, 1983.

Rigenbach, Paul T. *Tramps and Reformers, 1873–1916: The Discovery of Unemployment in New York.* Westport, CT: Greenwood Press, 1973.

Rosenzweig, Roy. *Eight Hours for What We Will: Workers and Leisure in an Industrial City, 1870-1920.* New York: Cambridge University Press, 1983.

Roy, Ralph L. *Communism and the Churches.* New York: Harcourt, Brace & Company, 1960.

Saposs, David J. "The American Labor Movement Since the War." *Quarterly Journal of Economics*, Vol. 49 (1935) pp. 236–54.

Shepherd, Naomi. *A Price Below Rubies: Jewish Women as Rebels and Radicals.* Cambridge, MA: Harvard University Press, 1993.

Shewmaker, Kenneth E. *Americans and Chinese Communists, 1927–1945: A Persuading Encounter.* Ithaca, NY: Cornell University Press, 1971.

Smith, Page. *America Enters the World: A Peoples' History of the Progressive Era and World War I.* New York: McGraw-Hill, 1985.

_____. *Redeeming the Time: A Peoples' History of the 1920s and The New Deal.* New York: McGraw-Hill, 1987.

Solberg, Winton U. "The Impact of Soviet Russia on American Life and Thought, 1917–1933." Unpublished Ph.D. dissertation, Harvard, 1952.

Stave, Bruce M., ed. *Socialism and the Cities.* Port Washington, NY: Kennikat Press, 1975.

Sullivan, Mark. *Our Times: The United States, 1900–1925.* Vol. 6, "The Twenties." New York: Charles Scribners Sons, 1930.

Summers, Mark W. "American Cartoonists and a World of Revolution, 1789–1936." ed.

Jeremy D. Popkin. *Media and Revolution.* Lexington: The University Press of Kentucky, 1995, pp. 136–155.

Szajkowski, Zosa. *Jews, Wars, and Communism*, Vol. 1, "The Attitude of American Jews to World War I, the Russian Revolutions of 1917, and Communism (1914–1945)." New York: Ktav Publishing House, 1972.

Talbert, Roy, Jr. *Negative Intelligence: The Army and the American Left, 1917–1941.* Jackson: University Press of Mississippi, 1991.

Timberlake, James H. *Prohibition and the Progressive Movement, 1900–1920.* Cambridge, MA: Harvard University Press, 1963.

Tyler, Robert L. *Rebels of the Woods: The IWW in the Pacific Northwest.* Eugene: University of Oregon Press, 1967.

Weinstein, James. *The Decline of Socialism in America, 1912–1925.* New York: Monthly Review Press, 1967.

Wiebe, Robert H. *The Search for Order, 1877–1920.* New York: Hill and Wang, 1967.

Wilson, Joan H. *Ideology and Economics: U.S. Relations with the Soviet Union, 1918–1933.* Columbia: University of Missouri Press, 1974.

Introduction

Allen, Robert C. and Douglas Gomery. *Film History: Theory and Practice.* New York: Alfred A. Knopf, 1985.

Appel, John J. "Jews in American Caricature, 1820–1914." *American Jewish History*, Vol. 71, No. 1 (September 1981), pp. 103–133.

Berkhofer, Robert F., Jr., *The White Man's Indian: Images of the American Indian from Columbus to the Present.* New York: Alfred A. Knopf, 1978.

Bloch, Marc. *The Historian's Craft.* New York: Alfred A. Knopf, 1953.

Bordwell, David. *Making Meaning: Inference and Rhetoric in the Interpretation of Cinema.* Cambridge, MA: Harvard University Press, 1989.

_____, Janet Staiger and Kristin Thompson. *The Classical Hollywood Cinema: Film Style & Mode of Production.* New York: Columbia University Press, 1985.

Carr, Edward Hallett. *What Is History?* New York: Alfred A. Knopf, 1962.

Carroll, Noel. *Mystifying Movies: Fads and Fallacies in Contemporary Film Theory.* New York: Columbia University Press, 1988.

Cherchi Usai, Paolo. *Burning Passions: An Introduction to the Study of Silent Film.* London: British Film Institute, 1994.

Dinnerstein, Leonard. *Anti-Semitism in America.* New York: Oxford University Press, 1994.

Dinnerstein, Leonard, Roger Nichols and David Reimes. *Natives and Strangers: Blacks, Indians, and Immigrants in America.* Second Edition. New York: Oxford University Press, 1989.

Dobkowski, Michael N. *The Tarnished Dream: The Basis of American Anti-Semitism.* Westport, CT: Greenwood Press, 1979.

Dudley, Edward and Maxmillian E. Novak, eds. *The Wild Man Within: An Image in Western Thought from the Renaissance to Romanticism.* Pittsburgh, PA: The University of Pittsburgh Press, 1972.

Ellul, Jacques. *Propaganda: The Formation of Men's Attitudes.* Translated by Konrad Kellen and Jean Lerner. New York: Alfred A. Knopf, 1965.

Elsaesser, Thomas and Adam Barker, eds. *Early Cinema: Space Frame Narrative.* London: BFI Publishing, 1990.

Friedman, Lester D., ed. *Unspeakable Images: Ethnicity and the American Cinema.* Urbana: University of Illinois Press, 1991.

Fuller, Robert. *Naming the Antichrist: The History of an American Obsession.* New York: Oxford University Press, 1995.

Gregor, A. James. *Contemporary Radical Ideologies: Totalitarian Thought in the Twentieth Century.* New York: Random House, 1968.

Jaher, Frederic Cople. *A Scapegoat in the New Wilderness: The Origins and Rise of Anti-Semitism in America.* Cambridge, MA: Harvard University Press, 1994.

Jarausch, Konrad H. and Kenneth A. Hardy. *Quantitative Methods for Historians: A Guide to Research, Data, and Statistics.* Chapel Hill: The University of North Carolina Press, 1991.

Keough, William. *Punchlines: The Violence of American Humor.* New York: Paragon House, 1989.

Klapp, Orrin E. *Heroes, Villains, and Fools: Reflections of the American Character.* San Diego, CA: Aegis, 1972.

Kohn, Hans. *American Nationalism: An Interpretive Essay.* New York: Macmillan, 1957.

Krippendorff, Klaus. *Content Analysis: An Introduction to Its Methodology.* London: Sage Publications, 1980.

Laswell, Harold. *Propaganda Technique in the World War.* New York: Peter Smith, 1938. (Alfred A. Knopf, 1927)

Lee, Yueh-Ting, Lee J. Jussim, and Clark R. McCauley, eds. *Stereotype Accuracy: Toward Appreciating Group Differences.* Washington, D.C.: American Psychological Association, 1995.

O'Connor, John E., ed. *Image As Artifact: The Historical Analysis of Film and Television.* Malabar, FL: Robert E. Krieger, 1990.

Pearson, Roberta E. *Eloquent Gestures: The Transformation of Performance Styles in the Griffith Biograph Films.* Berkeley: University of California Press, 1992.

Pettit, Arthur G. *Images of the Mexican-American in Fiction and Film.* College Station, TX: Texas A&M University Press, 1980.

Riesman, David. *The Lonely Crowd: A Study of the Changing American Character.* New Haven, CT: Yale University Press, 1960.

Rogin, Michael. *Ronald Reagan, The Movie: and Other Episodes in Political Demonology.* Berkeley: University of California Press, 1987.

Rollins, Peter C., ed. *Hollywood as Historian: American Film in Historical Context* Lexington: The University Press of Kentucky, 1983.

Schmitt, Peter J. *Back to Nature: The Arcadian Myth in Urban America.* New York: Oxford University Press, 1969.

Shain, Russell E. *An Analysis of Motion Pictures About War Released by the American Film Industry, 1930–1970.* New York: Arno Press, 1976.

Sklar, Robert and Charles Musser. *Resisting Images: Essays on Cinema and History.* Philadelphia: Temple University Press, 1990.

Slotkin, Richard. *Gunfighter Nation: The Myth of the Frontier in Twentieth-Century America.* New York: Antheneum, 1992.

Stedman, Raymond. *Shadows of the Indian: Stereotypes in American Culture*. Norman: University of Oklahoma Press, 1982.

Susman, Warren I. *Culture As History: The Transformation of American Society in the Twentieth Century*. New York: Pantheon Books, 1984.

Taylor, Philip M. *Munitions of the Mind: A History of Propaganda from the Ancient World to the Present Era*, 2nd edition. New York: St. Martin's Press, 1995.

Todorov, Tzvetan. *The Conquest of America: The Question of the Other*. New York: Harper & Row, 1984.

Tyrell, Ian. *The Absent Marx: Class Analysis and Liberal History in Twentieth-Century America*. Westport, CT: Greenwood Press, 1986.

Weston, Rubin F. *Racism in U. S. Imperialism: The Influence of Racial Assumptions on American Foreign Policy, 1893–1946*. Columbia: University of South Carolina Press, 1972.

Wilkinson, Rupert. *American Tough: The Tough-Guy Tradition and American Character*. Westport, CT: Greenwood Press, 1984.

Wise, Gene. *American Historical Explanations: A Strategy for Grounded Inquiry*, 2nd ed., Minneapolis: University of Minnesota Press, 1980.

Zelinsky, Wilbur. *Nation Into State: The Shifting Symbolic Foundations of American Nationalism*. Chapel Hill: The University of North Carolina Press, 1988.

Chapter 1

Adams, Graham, Jr. *Age of Industrial Violence, 1910–1915: The Activities and Findings of the United States Commission on Industrial Relations*. New York: Columbia University Press, 1966.

Avrich, Paul. *The Russian Anarchists*. Princeton, NJ: Princeton University Press, 1967.

Cameron, Ardis. *Radicals of the Worst Sort: Laboring Women in Lawrence, Massachusetts, 1860–1912*. Urbana: University of Illinois Press, 1993.

Carnegie, Andrew, ed. by Edward C. Kirkland. *The Gospel of Wealth, and Other Timely Essays*. Cambridge, MA: Belnap Press, 1962. (orig. pub. 1900)

Craigie, John. "The Professional Strike-Breaker." *Collier's*, Vol. 46 (December 3, 1910), p. 20.

_____. "The Violent Act of Strike-Breaking." *Collier's*, Vol. 46 (January 7, 1911), p. 22.

Denning, Michael. *Mechanic Accents: Dime Novels and Working-Class Culture in America*. New York: Verso, 1987.

Duis, Perry R. *The Saloon: Public Drinking in Chicago and Boston, 1880–1920*. Urbana: University of Illinois Press, 1983.

Eisenstein, Sarah. *Give Us Bread but Give Us Roses: Working Women's Consciousness in the United States, 1890 to the First World War*. London: Routledge & Kegan Paul, 1983.

Fink, Gary M. *The Fulton Bag and Cotton Mills Strike of 1914–1915*. Ithaca, NY: ILR Press, 1993.

Foner, Philip S. *History of the Labor Movement in the United States, Vol. 7: Labor and World War I, 1914–1918*. New York: International Publishers, 1987.

_____. *Militarism and Organized Labor: 1900–1914*. Minneapolis, MN: MEP Publications, 1987.

Geifman, Anna. *Thou Shalt Kill: Revolutionary Terrorism in Russia, 1894–1917*. Princeton, NJ: Princeton University Press, 1993.

Grayson, Benson Lee. *Russian-American Relations in World War I*. New York: Frederick Ungar, 1979.

Healy, Ann E. "Tsarist Anti-Semitism and Russian American Relations." *Slavic Review*, XLII (Fall 1983), pp. 408–424.

Johnson, Oakley C. *Marxism in United States History Before the Russian Revolution (1876–1917)*. New York: Humanities Press, 1974.

Joll, James. *The Anarchists*, 2nd ed. Cambridge, MA: Harvard University Press, 1980.

Kipnis, Ira. *The American Socialist Movement, 1897–1912*. New York: Columbia University Press, 1952.

Koerner, Mark. "The Menace of Labor: Anti-Union Thought in the Progressive Era, 1901–1917." Ph.D. dissertation, University of Wisconsin, Madison, 1995.

Lincoln, W. Bruce. *In War's Dark Shadow: The Russians Before the Great War*. New York: The Dial Press, 1983.

_____. *Passage Through Armageddon: The*

Russians in War & Revolution, 1914–1918. New York: Simon and Schuster, 1986.

Long, Priscilla. "The Voice of the Gun: Colorado's Great Coalfield War of 1913–1914." *Labor's Heritage,* Vol. 1, No. 4 (October 1989), pp. 4–23.

Lord, Walter. *The Good Years: From 1900 to the First World War.* New York: Harper & Brothers, 1960.

Lowe, Heinz-Dietrich. *The Tsars and the Jews: Reform, Reaction and Anti-Semitism in Imperial Russia, 1772–1917.* Chut, Switzerland: Harwood Academic Publishers, 1993.

McGovern, George S. and Leonard F. Guttridge. *The Great Coalfield War.* Boston: Houghton Mifflin, 1972.

McNeal, Robert H. *Tsar and Cossack, 1855–1914.* New York: St. Martin's, 1987.

Maxwell, H. Bloomfield. *Alarms and Diversions: The American Mind Through American Magazines, 1900–1914.* The Hague: Mouton, 1967.

May, Henry F. *The End of American Innocence: A Study of the First Years of Our Own Time, 1912–1917.* New York: Alfred A. Knopf, 1959.

Mellinger, Philip J. *Race and Labor in Western Copper: The Fight for Equality, 1896–1918.* Tucson: The University of Arizona Press, 1995.

Mowry, George E. *The Era of Theodore Roosevelt and the Birth of Modern America, 1900–1912.* New York: Harper & Row, 1958.

Norris, Frank. *The Octopus: A Story of California.* New York: Doubleday & Company, 1901.

Pegram, Thomas. *Battling Demon Rum: The Struggle for a Dry America, 1800–1933.* New York: Iran R. Dee, 1998.

Pollack, Norman. *The Populist Response to Industrial America.* New York: W.W. Norton, 1966.

Salerno, Salvatore. *Red November Black November: Culture and Community in the Industrial Workers of the World.* New York: State University of New York Press, 1988.

Saul, Norman E. *Concord and Conflict: The United States and Russia, 1867–1914.* Lawrence: University Press of Kansas, 1996.

Schlereth, Thomas J. *Victorian America:* *Transformations in Everyday Life, 1876–1915.* New York: HarperCollins, 1991.

Sinclair, Upton. *The Jungle.* Garden City, NY: International Collector's Library, nd. (orig. pub. 1906)

Stults, Taylor. "Roosevelt, Russian Persecution of Jews, and American Public Opinion." *Jewish Social Studies,* Vol. XXIII (January 1971), pp. 13–22.

Tax, Meredith. *The Rising of the Women: Feminist Solidarity and Class Conflict, 1880–1917.* New York: Monthly Review Press, 1980.

Thompson, Arthur W. and Robert A. Hart. *The Uncertain Crusade: America and the Russian Revolution of 1905.* Amherst: The University of Massachusetts Press, 1970.

Tyler, Bruce M. "Racist Art and Politics at the Turn of the Century." *The Journal of Ethnic Studies,* Vol. 15, No. 4 (Winter 1988), pp. 85–103.

Ulam, Adam B. *In the Name of the People: Prophets and Conspirators in Prerevolutionary Russia.* New York: The Viking Press, 1977.

Uricchio, William and Roberta E. Pearson. *Reframing Culture: The Case of the Vitagraph Quality Films.* Princeton, NJ: Princeton Universty Press, 1993.

Valentine, Alan. *1913: America Between Two Worlds.* New York: Macmillan, 1962.

Veblen, Thorstein. *The Theory of the Leisure Class.* Boston: Houghton Mifflin, 1973. (orig. pub. 1899).

Watts, Sarah Lyons. *Order Against Chaos: Business Culture and Labor Ideology in America, 1880–1915.* Westport, CT: Greenwood Press, 1991.

Winters, Donald E., Jr. *The Soul of the Wobblies: The I.W.W., Religion, and American Culture in the Progressive Era, 1905–1917.* Westport, CT: Greenwood Press, 1985.

Witcover, Jules. *Sabotage at Black Tom: Imperial Germany's Secret War in America, 1914–1917.* Chapel Hill, NC: Algonquin Books, 1989.

Chapter 2

Asinof, Eliot. *1919: America's Loss of Innocence.* New York: Donald I. Fine, 1990.

Bindler, Norman. "American Socialism and the First World War." Unpublished Ph.D. dissertation, New York University, 1970.

Bing, Alexander M. *Wartime Strikes and Their Adjustment*. New York: Arno, 1971. (E. P. Dutton, 1921)

Brody, David. *Labor in Crisis: The Steel Strike of 1919*. Philadelphia: Lippincott, 1965.

Browne, Luis Edgar. *New Russia in the Balance: How Germany's Designs May Be Defeated and Russian Democracy Preserved*. Chicago: Chicago Daily News, 1918.

Bryant, Louise. *Six Red Months in Russia: An Observer's Account of Russia Before and During the Proletarian Dictatorship*. New York: George H. Doran Company, 1918. (Arno, 1970)

Bullard, Arthur. *The Russian Pendulum. Autocracy—Democracy — Bolshevism*. New York: The Macmillan Company, 1919.

Carroll, E. Malcolm. *Soviet Communism and Western Opinion, 1919–1921*. Chapel Hill: The University of North Carolina Press, 1965.

Chambers, Robert W. *The Crimson Tide*. New York: Appleton, 1919.

Coben, Stanley. "A Study in Nativism: The American Red Scare of 1919–1920." *Political Science Quarterly*, Vol. 79 (1964), pp. 52–75.

"The Commission of Inquiry, The Inter-Church World Movement Report on the Steel Strike of 1919." New York: Da Capo Press, 1971. (orig. pub. 1920)

Damon, Allaan L. "The Great Red Scare." *American Heritage*, Vol. IX (February 1968), pp. 22–27.

Daniel, Cletus. "In Defense of the Wheatland Wobblies." *Labor History*, Vol. 19 (1978), pp. 485–509.

Dijkstra, Bram. *Evil Sisters: The Threat of Female Sexuality and the Cult of Manhood*. New York: Alfred A. Knopf, 1996.

Fogelsong, David S. *America's Secret War Against Bolshevism: U.S. Intervention in the Civil War, 1917–1920*. Chapel Hill: The University of North Carolina Press, 1996.

Foner, Philip S. *History of the Labor Movement in the United States, Vol. 8: Postwar Struggles, 1918–1920*. New York: International Publishers, 1988.

Friedheim, Robert. *The Seattle General Strike.* Seattle: University of Washington Press, 1964.

"The German-Bolshevik Conspiracy." War Information Series, No. 20. Washington, D.C., 1918.

Goldhurst, Richard. *The Midnight War: The American Intervention in Russia, 1918–1920*. New York: McGraw-Hill, 1978.

Hanson, Ole. *Americans Versus Bolshevism*. Garden City, NY: Doubleday, Page and Co., 1920.

Harries, Meirion & Susie. *The Last Days of Innocence: America at War, 1917–1918*. New York: Random House, 1997.

Hough, Emerson. *The Web*. Chicago: Reilly & Lee, 1919. (Arno, 1969)

Karson, Marc. *American Labor Unions and Politics 1910–1918*. Boston: Beacon Press, 1965.

Kennedy, David M. *Over Here: The First World War and American Society*. New York: Oxford University Press, 1980.

Klingaman, William. *1919: The Year Our World Began*. New York: St. Martin's, 1987.

Lasch, Christopher. *The American Liberals and the Russian Revolution*. New York: Columbia University Press, 1962.

Levin, N. Gordon, Jr. *Woodrow Wilson and World Politics: America's Response to War and Revolution*. New York: Oxford University Press, 1968.

Luebke, Frederick C. *Bonds of Loyalty: German-Americans and World War I*. DeKalb: Northern Illinois University Press, 1974.

McFadden, David W. *Alternative Paths: Soviets and Americans, 1917–1920*. New York: Oxford University Press, 1993.

Maddox, Robert J. *The Unknown War with Russia: Wilson's Siberian Intervention*. Rafael, CA, 1977.

Miller, William D. *Pretty Bubbles in the Air: America in 1919*. Urbana: University of Illinois Press, 1991.

Mitchel, John Bruce. "Reds in New York Slums: How Insidious Doctrines are Propagated in New York's East Side." *Forum*, April 1919.

Murray, Robert K. *Red Scare: A Study of National Hysteria, 1919–1920*. New York: McGraw-Hill, 1964. (University of Minnesota Press, 1955)

Noggle, Burl. *Into the Twenties: The United States from Armistice to Normalcy*. Urbana: University of Illinois Press, 1974.

Peterson, H.C. and Gilbert G. Fite. *Opponents of War, 1917–1918*. Seattle: University of Washington Press, 1957.

Preston, William, Jr. *Aliens and Dissenters*. Cambridge MA: Harvard University Press, 1963.

Reed, John. *Ten Days That Shook the World*. New York: Boni and Liveright, 1919. (International Publishers, 1967)

Renshaw, Patrick. "The I.W.W. and the Red Scare, 1917–1924." *Journal of Contemporary History*, Vol. 4 (1968), pp. 63–72.

Roberts, Beth Alene. "A Study of American Opinion Regarding Allied Intervention in Siberia." Unpublished M.A. Thesis, University of Hawaii, 1938.

Rosenthal, Rob. "Nothing Moved But the Tide: The Seattle Great Strike of 1919." *Labor's Heritage*, Vol. 4, No. 3 (Fall 1992), pp. 34–53.

Scaffer, Ronald. *America in the Great War: The Rise of the Welfare State*. New York: Oxford University Press, 1991.

Shor, Francis. "The IWW and Oppositional Politics in World War I: Pushing the System Beyond its Limits." *Radical History Review*, Vol. 64 (Winter 1996), pp. 74–94.

Somin, Ilya. *Stillborn Crusade: The Tragic Failure of Western Intervention in the Russian Civil War*. New Brunswick, NJ: Transactions, 1996.

Spargo, John. *Bolshevism: The Enemy of Political and Industrial Democracy*. New York: Harper & Brothers, 1919.

_____. *The Psychology of Bolshevism*. New York: Harper & Brothers, 1919.

_____. *Russia as an American Problem*. New York: Harper & Brothers, 1920.

Szajkowski, Zosa. *Jews, Wars, and Communism*, Vol. II, "The Impact of the 1919–20 Red Scare on American Jewish Life." New York: Ktav Publishing House, 1974.

Trachenberg, Alexander, ed. *American Socialists and the War*. New York: 1917.

Ulam, Adam B. *Bolsheviks: The Intellectual, Personal and Political History of the Triumph of Communism in Russia*. New York: Collier Books, 1965.

Unterberger, Betty Miller. *American's Siberian Expedition, 1918–1920: A Study of National Policy*. Durham, NC: Duke University Press, 1956.

Wynn, Neil A. *From Progressivism to Prosperity: World War I and American Society*. New York: Holmes & Meier, 1986.

Yezierska, Anzia. "Soap and Water and the Immigrant." *The New Republic*, Vol. XVIII (1919), p. 117.

Chapter 3

Allen, Frederick Lewis. *Only Yesterday: An Informal History of the Nineteen Twenties*. New York: Harper & Brothers Publishers, 1931.

Avrich, Paul. *Sacco and Vanzetti: The Anarchist Background*. Princeton, NJ: Princeton University Press, 1991.

Bernstein, Irving. *The Lean Years: A History of the American Workers, 1920–1933*. Boston: Houghton Mifflin Company, 1960.

Borg, Dorothy. *American Policy and the Chinese Revolution, 1925–1928*. New York: Octagon, 1968.

Braemen, John, Robert E. Bremner, David Brody, eds. *Change and Continuity in Twentieth-Century America: The 1920's*. Columbus: Ohio State University Press, 1968.

Dumenil, Lynn. *Modern Temper: American Culture and Society in the 1920s*. New York: Hill and Wang, 1995.

Lewis, Sinclair. *Babbitt*. New York: Harcourt Brace Jovanovich, 1950. (orig pub. 1922)

MacLean, Nancy. *Behind the Mask of Chivalry: The Making of the Second Ku Klux Klan*. New York: Oxford University Press, 1994.

Murphy, Paul L. "Sources and Nature of Intolerance in the 1920s." *Journal of American History*, Vol. 51 (1964), pp. 60–76.

Murray, Robert K. *The Politics of Normalcy: Government Theory and Practice in the Harding-Coolidge Era*. New York: W.W. Norton, 1973.

Nash, Roderick. *The Nervous Generation: American Thought, 1917–1930*. Chicago: Rand McNally, 1970.

Perrett, Geoffrey. *America in the Twenties: A History*. New York: Simon and Schuster, 1982.

Skran, Claudena. *Refugees in Inter-War Europe: The Emergence of a Regime*. New York: Oxford University Press, 1995.

Stevenson, Elizabeth. *Babbits and Bohemians: The American 1920's*. New York: Macmillan, 1967.

Weisman, Benjamin M. *Herbert Hoover and Famine Relief to Soviet Russia, 1921–1923*. Stanford, CA: Stanford University Press, 1974.

Index